COMPUTERS AND INFORMATION PROCESSING

CONCEPTS AND APPLICATIONS

SECOND EDITION

James F. Clark, Ph.D.
Clark Systems Corporation

Warren W. Allen, M.A.
Dale H. Klooster, Ed.D.
Educational Technical Systems

DC14BA
PUBLISHED BY
SOUTH-WESTERN PUBLISHING CO.
CINCINNATI, OH WEST CHICAGO, IL DALLAS, TX LIVERMORE, CA

ISBN: 0-538-60131-0

Library of Congress Catalog Card Number: 88-61566

2 3 4 5 6 7 8 9 Ki 7 6 5 4 3 2 1 0

Printed in the United States of America

On the cover is an enlarged portion of a SOFTSTRIP® data strip, an optically-encoded pattern that can store up to 600 bytes per inch of any computer-generated information, on ordinary paper.*

PREFACE

Rapid advances in computer technology have had a significant impact on our society. These advances indicate that the computer will continue to have an ever-increasing role in the future. Recently, there has been a tremendous increase in the number of computers being utilized in our homes, businesses, and industries. Several factors have contributed to this increase: (1) the cost of the equipment has decreased due to new and more efficient methods of manufacturing, (2) small-scale, yet very powerful, inexpensive microcomputers now make it financially possible for small (as well as very large) businesses to purchase them, (3) the growth in the home/personal computer area has been explosive, thus contributing to the general public's better understanding of computer capability and use, and (4) more and more uses of the computer continue to be developed which take advantage of the computer's potential and capabilities.

The goal of this text is to prepare students to function in an environment—educational, personal, and vocational—in which computer confidence has become the expected norm. It seeks to develop an understanding of the entire area of computers and information processing, while at the same time developing precise hands-on skills in using common software applications. These applications include word processing, spreadsheet and database programs, as well as applications related to payroll, inventory, communications, and graphing.

For the student who is college bound, preparing for post-secondary technical education, or planning to enter the work force upon leaving high school, this text is ideal for developing the needed knowledge and skills. For those continuing their education, it provides the foundation for further study. For those beginning employment, it develops the basic skills required for successful computer use in many jobs.

Few would disagree that we are living in a complex society with complex informational needs. Many businesses have turned to the computer as a means of staying competitive, helping control costs, and managing their resources. If students are to be effective employees in these businesses, it is essential that they have an understanding of the uses and functions of computers.

TEXT ORGANIZATION

The *COMPUTERS AND INFORMATION PROCESSING: Concepts and Applications* textbook is divided into the following six parts: Introduction to Computers and Information Systems, The Computer System, Microcomputers and Operating Systems, Application Software, System Design and Programming, and Careers. In addition, appendices covering the history of computing, the internal representation of data, and BASIC programming are included.

FEATURES THAT ENHANCE LEARNING

This text includes many special features designed to both stimulate and enhance learning. Among them are the following:

- *Learning Objectives.* Each chapter begins with learning objectives to help students focus on the topics that will be covered.
- *Vignettes.* A vignette that enhances the topics covered is included in each chapter. These vignettes present new or unique uses for technology or software discussed in the chapter and provide interesting starting points for additional classroom discussion or research.
- *Chapter Summary.* Detailed chapter summaries provide a convenient way for students to review the key concepts presented in each chapter.
- *Key Terms.* Key terms are presented in boldface type in the text material and are listed at the end of each chapter for easy review.
- *Review Questions and Challenge Activities.* These end-of-chapter activities are designed to reinforce important concepts, to encourage students to complete additional research, and to enable students to make practical use of their knowledge.

SUPPLEMENTARY MATERIALS

Several supplementary items have been developed to enhance student learning and to assist in lesson preparation, instruction, and testing.

- *Workbook.* The student workbook is divided into two sections. The first section contains various types of study guides and exercises designed to reinforce students' understanding of the material presented in each chapter of the text. The second section contains computer activities and step-by-step procedures designed to correlate with each chapter of the textbook.
- *Software.* Computer software that simulates many of the most popular computer applications used today, including payroll, inventory, desktop tools, graphing, and communications, is available to reinforce students' understanding of the materials presented in the text through hands-on experience. *MICROTOOLS™: Integrated Software for Word Processing, Spreadsheet, and Database* is also available to provide experience with word processing, spreadsheet, and database applications. Each of the software packages is available for the following microcomputer configurations:

  1. Apple® IIe, IIc, and IIGS[1] (5¼″ format only) with a minimum of 128K memory, an 80-column card, a monitor, and at least one disk drive. Access to an 80-column continuous-feed printer is optional but recommended.

2. IBM® Personal Computer, PC/XT, and Personal System/2™[2] with a minimum of 256K memory running under DOS 2.0 or higher, a monitor, and at least one disk drive. Access to an 80-column continuous-feed printer is optional but recommended.
3. Tandy® 1000[3] with a minimum of 256K memory running under DOS 2.11 or higher, a monitor, and at least one disk drive. Access to an 80-column continuous-feed printer is optional but recommended.

- *Instructor's Manual.* The instructor's manual is available to all instructors who adopt the textbook for classroom use. The manual includes detailed chapter outlines and teaching suggestions for each chapter, solutions for all textbook and workbook questions and activities, and transparency masters.
- *MicroExam Diskettes.* A computerized test bank is available for the following microcomputers: Apple IIe, IIc, and IIGS (5¼″ format only); IBM PC and Personal System 2; and Tandy 1000. (Two disk drives are required to run the MicroExam software.)
- *Transparencies.* Multicolor acetate transparencies are available to enhance classroom discussion of key concepts presented in the text.

CLOSING COMMENTS

Few people would argue that the information age has been brought upon us through technological advances. Perhaps the most significant contribution has come from the computer industry. Increased research and development, coupled with a growing need for more sophistication, have contributed to an accelerated pace of technological improvement and accumulation of human knowledge. One only needs to look around the environment to see the many changes brought about by technology over the past few years. Rapid advances in technology have also affected the way businesses and industries function, causing them to become more complex and dependent upon more information to be competitive.

It has become crucial that students learn about computers and the characteristics, procedures, and techniques that enable them to have such a profound impact upon our environment, businesses, and industries. Students need to learn how computer systems are developed and how these systems must also change in order to keep pace with their surroundings. Upon completion of this text, students will have a strong foundation upon which to build as they begin their journey into today's information age.

[1]Apple, IIGS, Applesoft, the Apple logo, and ProDOS are registered trademarks of Apple Computer, Inc.
[2]IBM and PC/XT are registered trademarks of International Business Machines Corporation. Personal System/2 is a trademark of International Business Machines Corporation.
[3]Tandy is a registered trademark of the Radio Shack Division of Tandy Corporation.

CONTENTS

PART ONE
INTRODUCTION TO COMPUTERS AND INFORMATION PROCESSING

PART TWO
THE COMPUTER SYSTEM

PART SIX CAREERS

PHOTO ACKNOWLEDGMENTS

For permission to reproduce the photographs in the pages indicated, acknowledgment is made to the following:

Fiber optics photo used on the cover, part openers, and chapter openers by Lawrence Manning/West Light.
Satellite dish photo used on the cover by Wm. James Warren/West Light.

Part 1 Steven Hunt/THE IMAGE BANK
2 Levy/PHOTOTAKE
3 Courtesy of International Business Machines Corporation
5 Courtesy of International Business Machines Corporation (top, bottom left)
5 Apple Computer, Inc. (bottom right)
8 Courtesy of International Business Machines Corporation
10 Courtesy of International Business Machines Corporation (bottom)
11 Courtesy of International Business Machines Corporation
12 Boeing Commercial Airplane Company
13 INDEX/STOCK INTERNATIONAL, INC. (top)
13 © Tom Raymond/Medichrome (bottom)
14 Levy/PHOTOTAKE
17 © THE STOCK MARKET/Brownie Harris 1987
22 Photo courtesy of Hewlett-Packard Company
26 © Chuck O'Rear/WEST LIGHT
27 Photo courtesy of Hewlett-Packard Company (left)
27 Gabe Palmer/THE STOCK MARKET (right)
28 Photo courtesy of Hewlett-Packard Company (left)
28 Courtesy of International Business Machines Corporation (right)
29 Courtesy of International Business Machines Corporation (top)
29 Photo courtesy of Hewlett-Packard Company (bottom)
31 Courtesy Cray Research, Inc.
32 Photo Courtesy of Hewlett-Packard Company (top)
32 Courtesy of the Customer Service Division of TRW, Inc. (bottom)
33 Courtesy of International Business Machines Corporation

Part 2 Steven Hunt/THE IMAGE BANK
42 Courtesy of International Business Machines Corporation
43 Photo courtesy of Hewlett-Packard Company
44 Courtesy of Radio Shack, a division of Tandy Corporation
47 Owen Franken/STOCK, BOSTON
48 Courtesy of International Business Machines Corporation
49 Courtesy of International Business Machines Corporation
51 Photo courtesy of 3M Company (top right)
51 Courtesy of International Business Machines Corporation (bottom)
52 Courtesy of International Business Machines Corporation
58 Courtesy of International Business Machines Corporation
61 INDEX/STOCK INTERNATIONAL, INC. (top)
62 Photo Courtesy of Abaton, 48431 Milmont Dr., Fremont, CA 94538 (right)

63	Courtesy of International Business Machines Corporation
64	Courtesy of the Customer Service Division of TRW, Inc. (top)
64	Courtesy of International Business Machines Corporation (bottom)
65	Photo courtesy of Hewlett-Packard Company
66	Courtesy of International Business Machines Corporation (top)
66	Recognition Equipment Incorporated (bottom)
68	Courtesy of CompuScan, Inc. (top)
68	Photo courtesy of CLEARVIEW PRINTING CO., INC. (bottom)
72	Photo courtesy of Johnson Controls, Inc.
73	Overseas/PHOTOTAKE (top)
73	Courtesy of Chevron Corporation (bottom)
74	Courtesy of International Business Machines Corporation
75	Courtesy of Radio Shack, a division of Tandy Corporation
77	Photo courtesy of CLUB MED
82	Courtesy of International Business Machines Corporation (right)
83	Courtesy of International Business Machines Corporation
85	Courtesy of International Business Machines Corporation (top)
85	NEC Home Electronics (U.S.A.) Inc. (bottom)
86	Courtesy of International Business Machines Corporation
87	Courtesy of International Business Machines Corporation
89	Photo courtesy of NCR Corporation (left)
90	Photo compliments of VERSATEC, a Xerox Company
91	Exxon Office Systems (top)
91	Photo courtesy of Hewlett-Packard Company (bottom)
93	Photo courtesy of Hewlett-Packard Company
94	3M Document Systems Division
95	© THE STOCK MARKET/Dahlgren 1987
96	Photo Courtesy of McDonnell Douglas Information Systems Company (top)
96	Courtesy of International Business Machines Corporation (bottom)
98	NEC Home Electronics (U.S.A.) Inc.
104	Courtesy of International Business Machines Corporation
106	Sperry Corporation
108	Courtesy of International Business Machines Corporation
110	Courtesy of Radio Shack, a division of Tandy Corporation (top right)
110	Photo courtesy of Hewlett-Packard Company (bottom)
111	Control Data Corporation
113	Photo courtesy of Amdek Corp.
114	Supplied courtesy of N/Hance Systems, Dedham, MA. 1988
117	Photo courtesy of TECMAR, INC. of Solon, Ohio
118	Courtesy of Radio Shack, a division of Tandy Corporation
119	Courtesy of International Business Machines Corporation
122	THE STOCK MARKET/Lightscapes 1987

Part 3	Steven Hunt/THE IMAGE BANK
131	Courtesy of Apple Computer, Inc.
133	Heath Company
134	Courtesy of Apple Computer, Inc.
136	Courtesy of Hayes Microcomputer Products, Inc.
141	Photo compliments of COMPUTERLAND CORPORATION
142	Courtesy of International Business Machines Corporation
143	Joe Ruh
144	Photo courtesy of Hewlett-Packard Company
150	Courtesy of Apple Computer, Inc.
154	© THE STOCK MARKET/David Pollack 1987
155	Courtesy of International Business Machines Corporation

159 TRW, Inc.
164 Photo courtesy of Hewlett-Packard Company
166 Louis Kruh Collection

Part 4 Steven Hunt/THE IMAGE BANK
175 Courtesy of International Business Machines Corporation
176 Federal Express Corporation/Photography by Dana Duke
178 Photo Courtesy of Sperry Corporation
179 Photo courtesy of Hewlett-Packard Company
181 THE STOCK MARKET/G. Contorakes 1984
182 Courtesy of Pacific Gas and Electric Company (top)
182 Courtesy of International Business Machines Corporation (bottom)
183 Courtesy of International Business Machines Corporation
185 Courtesy of International Business Machines Corporation
187 Courtesy of International Business Machines Corporation
189 Texas Department of Highways
194 Courtesy of International Business Machines Corporation
202 Photo courtesy of Hewlett-Packard Company
209 Grumman Data Systems, Woodbury
210 © THE STOCK MARKET/Roy Morsch
216 U.S. Department of Housing and Urban Development
218 Courtesy of Apple Computer, Inc.
229 Photo courtesy of Hewlett-Packard Company
233 Courtesy of Apple Computer, Inc.
235 © THE STOCK MARKET/Richard Dunoff
246 Photo courtesy of Hewlett-Packard Company
252 Courtesy of CalComp
253 © THE STOCK MARKET/Mug Shots 1987
256 © THE STOCK MARKET/Thomas Braise 1987
259 USDA Photo
264 A.T.& T. Bell Laboratories
265 Courtesy of Radio Shack, a division of Tandy Corporation (top)
265 The Ford Motor Company (bottom)
266 © THE STOCK MARKET/Gabe Palmer (top left)
266 Photograph from Hazeltine Corporation 1979 Annual Report (top right)
282 Courtesy of International Business Machines Corporation
287 Courtesy of International Business Machines Corporation
289 Control Data Corporation
291 © THE STOCK MARKET/J. Barry O'Rourke
292 Courtesy of Apple Computer, Inc.
293 Courtesy of International Business Machines Corporation
294 © Steve Chenn/WESTLIGHT
295 Photo courtesy Inmac computer supplies
298 Peter Menzel/STOCK, BOSTON
299 Hayes Microcomputer Products, Inc.
302 Courtesy of A.T.& T. Bell Laboratories
309 © Chuck O'Rear/WESTLIGHT
310 © THE STOCK MARKET/Disario (left)
310 © THE STOCK MARKET/Tom Tracy (right)
311 NASA
320 Photo courtesy of Hewlett-Packard Company
327 Sperry Corporation
329 © THE STOCK MARKET/Gabe Palmer (top)
329 First Interstate Bancorp (bottom)
330 Courtesy of Radio Shack, a division of Tandy Corporation

331 Photo courtesy of General Motors Corporation
332 Courtesy of International Business Machines Corporation (top)
332 Sperry Corporation (bottom)
333 Courtesy of National Datacomputer, Inc.

Part 5 Steven Hunt/THE IMAGE BANK
341 Courtesy of International Business Machines Corporation (right)
343 Photo courtesy of Hewlett-Packard Company
346 Walgreen Company
353 Honeywell, Inc.
354 Photo courtesy of Hewlett-Packard Company
355 Courtesy of International Business Machines Corporation (left)
356 Courtesy of International Business Machines Corporation
360 Courtesy of Apple Computer, Inc.
366 United Nations Photo
367 Courtesy of International Business Machines Corporation
369 Photo courtesy of ITT Corporation
371 Courtesy of International Business Machines Corporation
372 Photo courtesy of Hewlett-Packard Company
375 Reproduced by permission of Hayes Microcomputer Products, Inc., © 3-88, Hayes Microcomputer Products, Inc.

Part 6 Steven Hunt/THE IMAGE BANK
395 Courtesy of International Business Machines Corporation (left)
395 Amhoist (right)
396 Courtesy of International Business Machines Corporation
398 Courtesy of Apple Computer, Inc.
399 Photo courtesy of Hewlett-Packard Company
401 Courtesy of International Business Machines Corporation
402 Four By Five
403 Courtesy of Pacific Gas and Electric Company
404 Courtesy of International Business Machines Corporation
405 Four By Five (top)
405 Courtesy of Honeywell, Inc. (bottom)
407 Courtesy of International Business Machines Corporation
408 Courtesy of International Business Machines Corporation
412 General Motors Corporation
418 The Library of Congress (right)
419 The Library of Congress (bottom left)
421 Courtesy of Burroughs Corp. (bottom)
422 The Library of Congress (top)
422 Courtesy of International Business Machines Corporation (bottom)
423 Courtesy of International Business Machines Corporation
424 Courtesy of International Business Machines Corporation (top)
424 Courtesy of Honeywell, Inc. (bottom)
425 Courtesy of International Business Machines Corporation
426 Charles Babbage Institute, University of Minnesota (left)
427 Photo Courtesy of Sperry Corporation
428 THE BETTMANN ARCHIVE
429 Photo Courtesy of Sperry Corporation (top)
429 Courtesy of International Business Machines Corporation (bottom)
430 Courtesy of International Business Machines Corporation
431 Courtesy of International Business Machines Corporation
432 TRW, Inc. (top)
433 Courtesy Mohawk Data Sciences

INTRODUCTION TO COMPUTERS AND INFORMATION PROCESSING

CHAPTER 1

COMPUTERS AND INFORMATION PROCESSING

LEARNING OBJECTIVES

After studying this chapter, you will be able to:

1. **Identify several characteristics of computers that have made them such powerful and popular tools.**
2. **Describe the characteristics of information processing.**
3. **Recognize the impact of the computer on society.**

INTRODUCTION

Some people compare the advent of the computer to the discovery of the wheel or the invention of the printing press. Others say its effects on society are more important than those of the Industrial Revolution. Some say that the very survival of the human race depends on it. A totally different opinion is that this device ignores human values, that it does not recognize individual differences and rights, and that it threatens our way of life.

The **computer** can generally be defined as an electronic device that does computations and makes logical decisions according to instructions and data that have been given to it. If the instructions and data are accurate, the computations and logical decisions it makes will also be accurate. If, however, the instructions and/or the data it is given are not accurate, it can just as easily make incorrect computations and decisions. The computer is a tool and, like the wheel and the printing press, can be put to either positive or negative use by its users—the human race.

This chapter describes the characteristics of the computer, examines its information processing abilities, and identifies a few ways in which its use has impacted upon our society. This chapter will also preview the topics and the organization of each of the remaining chapters of this text.

CHARACTERISTICS OF COMPUTERS

Why are computers used? Why have they become so popular? These questions can be answered by examining the characteristics of a computer. These characteristics include the computer's tremendous speed, accuracy, durability and reliability, versatility, cost-effectiveness, and technical growth.

Speed

Computers are electronic devices and, like all electronic devices, are exceptionally fast. Even the smallest, slowest computers are fast compared to human standards. For example, the slowest computers typically operate at speeds recorded in **milliseconds** (one thousandth of a second—1/1000). That is, these devices can perform 1000 instructions in just one second. Most mainframe computers today operate at speeds recorded in **microseconds** (one millionth of a second—1/1,000,000). These devices can perform 1,000,000 instructions in just one second. Newer, high-speed mainframe computers can operate at speeds approaching the **nanosecond** range (one billionth of a second—1/1,000,000,000). Research laboratories are experimenting with superconductive material which could enable computers in the future to operate at speeds approaching **picoseconds** (one trillionth of a second—1/1,000,000,000,000), a speed which is almost incomprehensible to the human mind.

NANOSECOND
(One billionth of a second)

Within the fraction of a second it takes this drop of water to reach the ground, a mainframe computer could perform all of the following tasks and more:

- ♦ compute the grade point averages for 2,500 students in 100 high schools
- ♦ calculate the total value of all the books in a large university's library
- ♦ figure the electric utility bills for 1,500 customers
- ♦ compute the fare for 1,000 passengers on 50 different airline flights

Because computers are so fast, they can perform tasks in a matter of seconds that would take humans weeks, months, years, or even a lifetime to complete. In some instances, computers can perform within a matter of seconds or minutes tasks that would be impossible for a person to complete by hand in a lifetime. Also, unlike humans, computers operate at a steady, untiring pace. They do not need to take a coffee break or sleep eight hours a night. The ability of computers to carry out the instructions provided to them in such a short period of time is one of the main reasons computers are used today. It is also a contributing factor to their increased popularity.

Accuracy

As previously stated, computers are only as accurate as the instructions and data provided them by humans. All too often articles are printed in newspapers and other publications wrongfully blaming the computer for errors. More often than not, these errors are caused by humans, not by the circuitry and mechanical devices which make up the computer. Similar to other electronic devices, computers are remarkably accurate.

Compare the accuracy of the internal workings of a computer to a simple light switch. When the switch is turned on, electricity is permitted to flow through the electric wire and the light bulb glows. When the switch is turned off, the circuit is broken, prohibiting the flow of electric current to the light bulb, and the light goes out. Repeated switching of the light switch on and off yields the same expected, predictable, consistent results time after time. Since the computer also relies on electricity to activate its electronic circuit boards, it, too, will perform in the same expected, predictable manner each time it is used. When a computer fails to function correctly, it is often because a mechanical device (comparable to a light switch) becomes worn out or an electronic component becomes burned out (comparable to a burnt-out light bulb). Like a light switch, it will either work or not work. When a failure like this occurs, a computer engineer or technician must replace the faulty mechanism in the computer.

Computers have proven so accurate that they are trusted in virtually every application, even those that involve life-and-death situations. For example, jet pilots and flight crews rely on computer computations for guidance and navigation of their craft. Hospitals rely on patient monitoring systems in critical care units. Businesses and industries rely on the accuracy of the information provided by computers to keep track of their resources and to make decisions that often involve large sums of money.

Many businesses use computers to keep track of resources.

Durability and Reliability

Like the light switch, computers are durable and extremely reliable devices. They can operate error-free over long periods of time. Also, like the light switch, computers have become more reliable and more durable with technical enhancements. Today's computer has fewer mechanical parts that can physically wear out. Improved materials that are more resistant to wear, heat, and other elements of the external environment contribute to the computer's durability and reliability. The development of tiny circuit boards with mind-boggling capabilities has also enabled computers to be more durable and less sensitive to their environments. The technological developments built into today's computers enable them to be installed and used in many and varied environments. They can be used as stationary devices or jostled about and still retain their ability to perform error-free over prolonged periods of time.

Versatility

Early computers were designed and developed for specific purposes. Generally, early computers were used for one of two specific types of applications: (1) mathematical computation, or (2) business data processing. The computers designed to handle mathematical computations had high-speed computation abilities but minimum input and output capabilities. The computers designed for business data processing had high-speed input/output devices to handle high-volume input and output applications but minimum computation capabilities. Therefore, users who needed a computer to perform engineering or design tasks involving a lot of mathematical problem solving chose to use the type of computer designed to handle those types of applications. Conversely, those users who needed a computer for business applications chose the type of computer specifically designed for that type of processing.

Today, due to technological advancements in the computer industry, most computers are considered to be **general-purpose computers.** That is, both their computation and input/output processing capabilities are such that they can be used for almost any type of application. For example, the same computer that is used to handle an engineering company's mathematical and design computations can also be efficiently used by the company to keep track of inventory, process payroll, project earnings, and fulfill all reporting needs. Today's computers are very versatile in what they can do. In most cases, they are limited only by the instructions provided them and the speed and sophistication of the input/output devices attached to them.

Due to recent advances in computer technology and miniaturization of computer components, computers and their component parts are being used in applications never before envisioned. For example, computer components are being used in home appliances (washing machines, ovens, etc.), home entertainment centers, traffic lights, automobiles, banking, assembly plants, space probes, art, music, education, hospitals, sports, and agriculture, to name a few. The versatility of the computer and its use in a wide array of applications are limited only by the imagination of the human mind.

The food at this nursery school is being monitored by computers for nutritional content.

Digital image processing is being used to help restore this piece of art.

Cost-Effectiveness

Early computers were huge and very expensive. It was not uncommon for a computer to occupy the floor space of a regulation size basketball floor and cost several million dollars. Today, a computer that fits inside a suitcase, weighs 10-20 pounds, and costs around $1,500 has 100 times the processing power of its early predecessors.

IBM's first computer filled an entire room.

In contrast, the Apple IIc will fit in a carrying case and has many more times the processing power.

The development of computer technology has been truly phenomenal. Consider what has happened to the costs and capabilities of other electronic devices such as calculators and watches. Their costs have dramatically decreased over the years, but their capabilities have dramatically increased. Figure 1-1 illustrates how computer costs and sizes have decreased, while at the same time computer speed, accuracy, durability and reliability, versatility, and capability have increased.

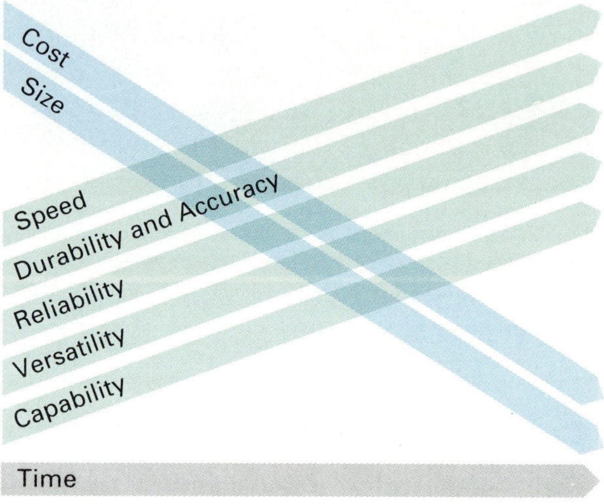

Figure 1-1
The speed and efficiency of computers have increased as their size and cost have decreased.

The cost of modern computers weighed against the varied tasks they can perform make them truly cost-effective devices. Based upon this industry's short history, one can expect that costs will continue to decline while capabilities will continue to rise.

Technical Growth

The computer is a unique device in that it actually fuels its own growth. In other words, its use in research for its computation and logic and decision-making capabilities allows it to participate in its own development. As computers become more sophisticated, other computers must be used to help design and build complex and intricate parts.

Another contributing factor in the popularity and growth of the computer is the never-ending thrust for new knowledge. Not only are computers being used in areas never before envisioned, but current users want their computers to do even more. This thrust is creating a demand for new, more powerful devices to meet an ever-growing need for more information and new knowledge. Again, the computer is actually fueling its own growth and proliferation.

CHARACTERISTICS OF INFORMATION PROCESSING

Information can be defined as knowledge that is given or received of some fact or circumstance. Humans share information with each other through spoken words, written communication, and a variety of other methods. Humans can also share information with and receive information from computers. This process of sharing information between humans and computers can be referred to as **information processing** (also called **data processing**).

Before information can be received from a computer, the computer must be given data and provided with instructions that tell it what to do to the data in order to produce the desired information. This textbook will describe how computers function and, in turn, how they are able to produce and communicate meaningful information. For now, the basic characteristics of information processing will be examined. These characteristics include inputting the data into the computer, processing the data after it has been entered into the computer, and outputting the processed data (information).

Input Data

Regardless of the form in which data exists (handwritten memos, invoices, payroll checks, etc.), it must be verified for accuracy before it enters the computer. This will help guard against errors in the output. Once the data has been verified and entered, the computer can make further checks for validity and completeness.

Process Data

After data has been entered into the computer and verified, it must be processed. Processing includes sorting, classifying, calculating, summarizing, and comparing. After this step is completed, meaningless data has been transformed into useful information.

Output Data

The processed data must be communicated to those who need the information. This can be done via a printed report, a graphic representation, a screen display, audio or spoken output, or transmission to a remote location. The output information must be in human-readable form, as well as an easy-to-read, easy-to-understand format.

SOCIETAL IMPACT OF COMPUTERS

The use of computers in society has affected everyone. Some ways in which computers affect daily living may be evident while others are more indirect. The following material takes a brief look at some of the common uses of computers in everyday living and their benefits to individuals and business.

Benefits to Business

Computers are needed to perform business operations requiring the handling of large amounts of data. Fortunately, there are several computer applications available to assist businesses in working with large volumes of data. For example, with the help of word processing software, business documents can be produced with speed and accuracy. Electronic spreadsheets allow businesses to make projections and forecasts that can be of value in making decisions concerning such activities as expansion and investment. Databases created on the computer allow companies to organize large collections of related data, such as customers' mailing addresses. Because these databases are stored on computers, files are easy to access and changes are easy to make. In almost every aspect, computers help businesses increase their efficiency and productivity.

Information Sources

Businesses known as **information utilities** have large computers that store huge amounts of information about many different subjects. These computer systems and their vast amounts of data are available for personal use. For example, information utilities can allow a computer user to read the daily news, research published works, send a letter to a friend, play games, make airline reservations, obtain the latest stock market quotations, or perform many other activities.

A small computer (with communication capabilities) attached to a phone line can be used to access an information utility's services. A fee is charged by the utility for the amount of time the individual's computer is hooked up to theirs. Some utilities may also require payment of additional fees depending upon the services used. The number of information utilities and the range of services they can provide are continually increasing.

Electronic Banking and Services

Computers and automation have made everyday tasks such as banking much more convenient.

Banks have used computers for years. Nearly every bank offers an electronic teller that is in service 24 hours a day. Many banks have issued their customers cards that permit them to use other banks' teller machines nationwide. A growing number of customers prefer the machine to a human teller, even during hours when the bank is open.

Another service becoming popular through the banking industry is the bill-payment-by-phone service. To use this service, a customer would tell the bank the name and address of each business to be paid on a regular basis, along with the account number at each business. Payments that are the same every month, such as rent or mortgage payments, can be scheduled for automatic payment. Items that vary in amount, such as the phone bill or electric bill, are paid when the customer instructs the computer to do so. In order to pay a bill, a customer would dial the computer's phone number and use the phone's keypad to enter the bank card number and secret password, the codes for the transfer of payment to the business from either the checking or savings account, the business code number (the bank provides this), the amount of money to be paid, and the date on which the payment should be made.

Another banking service involves the use of debit cards. A **debit card** is a small plastic card that looks just like a credit card, but it causes the amounts of purchases to be immediately deducted from the user's checking account rather than appearing on a bill days or weeks later. Since items must be paid for immediately, persons who use debit cards for purchases tend to be inclined to buy fewer items on impulse than those who use credit cards.

Shopping From Home

In addition to the use of debit cards, computers are changing the way in which people shop. Many stores have joined forces with the information utilities discussed earlier and cable TV stations to provide shopping services. After "browsing" through a list of items, and perhaps watching animated demonstrations of products on television, a person may immediately place an order. Consequently, individuals may now shop by computer in the comfort of their homes.

Shopping from home has been made much more efficient with computers.

Household Control

Surprisingly, a growing number of the newer household devices are computer-controlled. For example, refrigerators, ranges, microwave ovens, washers and dryers, stereos, televisions, videodisk players, and thermostats contain small computers. Some homes, however, have all aspects of their operation under the supervision of computers. The air-conditioning and heating system is under computer control to produce the most comfort at the lowest cost. Lawn sprinklers are turned on automatically whenever needed. Fire alarms and burglar alarms keep constant watch. Some control units can automatically call the fire department or police department if an emergency develops.

Many popular home appliances are now controlled by computers.

Learning Aids

Computerized learning aids come in many varieties, the most common of which are learning toys. There are also literally hundreds of computer-assisted learning programs in a vast array of subjects available for use on home computers. These programs range from simple arithmetic to calculus, from English grammar rules to creative writing and foreign languages, and from basic graphics to engineering design models, to name a few. There is widespread use of computers in schools as tools to make projects easier, to augment instruction, and to aid in research.

Computer-assisted learning has become very popular.

Weather and Environment

Probably every commercial television station in the country uses some form of computerized presentation equipment on its weather show. This equipment may show temperature ranges, precipitation levels, and wind flow. Computer-enhanced, animated weather satellite data can show the position and direction of storms and issue warnings for those in their paths. Computers are also used extensively for weather forecasting. Even though weather forecasting is still nowhere close to being 100 percent accurate, forecasts are closer to being accurate than ever before.

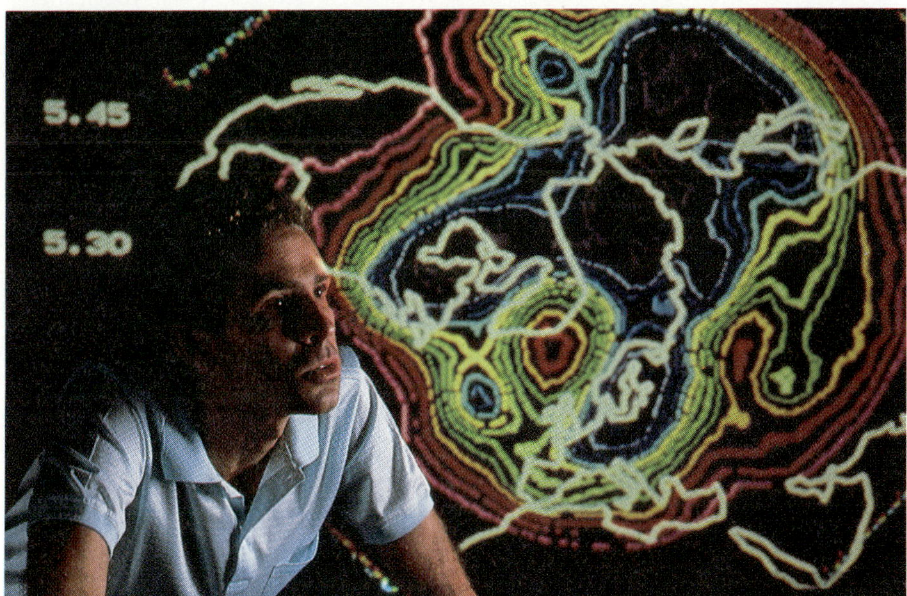

Computer displays are used to study world weather patterns.

In addition to weather forecasting, various other environmental successes are possible due to computers. Tracking the flow of oil spills and other pollutants in streams, for example, has helped overcome environmental hazards. This is because the path that water currents will take, changes in the wind, and changes in water temperature affect the direction in which pollutants will travel. When computers predict the direction of travel, action can be quickly taken to conduct clean-up operations and minimize damage.

Transportation

Almost every kind of transportation has been affected by computers. Rapid-transit trains operate with no crew members. Many aircraft can fly to their destinations and land under the control of the computer, making flight safer and more efficient. In this situation, the captain simply serves as a manager by telling the computer what to do. For a number of years, computers have provided functional controls such as spark control and fuel control in cars. Each new car introduced seems to add more computerization. Systems are already developed that keep cars from running into each other, as well as systems that always "know" where a particular car is and show its location on an instrument panel map. Another system reduces a car's wind resistance by changing its height and attitude toward the wind with the use of air bags that inflate or deflate at each corner of the car.

The computer in this jet improves flight safety.

Community Services

Fire fighting and the saving of lives are also aided by the computer. Computerized mapping systems can quickly point out the location of a problem and identify the emergency crew closest to the scene. Computers can help decide where to place equipment and personnel to ensure the shortest response time. In some communities, computers can keep fire fighters updated with floor plans of buildings in which they may need to fight a fire.

Crime Control

Crime control is another area in which computers help organize vast amounts of information. States have agreed, for example, to share drivers' license records for persons whose licenses have been taken away. This means that those individuals cannot go to a neighboring state to obtain a license. Other records of crimes committed are kept by the FBI's National Crime Information Center. This information has been used to find stolen cars driven across state lines. In other cases, computers have been used to analyze the details of a series of crimes that seemed to be committed by the same person, eventually leading to the arrest of the criminal. Law officers may have small computers in their cars for immediate access to information stored in these huge computer information sources.

An officer may use such a computer to check if a suspect car has been stolen. Society as a whole is better protected when the computer is used as a tool to help control crime.

Computers allow police officers to obtain instant information when and where it's needed.

Medical and Health Care

Computers have long been used by hospitals for routine record keeping. However, today many people owe their lives to the computer. A modern hospital is a showplace of computerized equipment. Sensors (devices that detect changes) can be attached to patients to tell when there are changes in temperature, heart rate, blood pressure, or other vital signs. If there is a negative change, the hospital staff is alerted immediately, in many cases saving lives. Medical tests that were once very time-consuming or impossible are now completed quickly by computer. A machine can scan the body and provide three-dimensional views never before thought possible. New technology is providing computers with the ability to replicate the workings of specific internal organs of a patient. This information can be enhanced, magnified, and animated in three-dimensions, thereby providing doctors with valuable information in diagnosing problems and/or preparing for surgery.

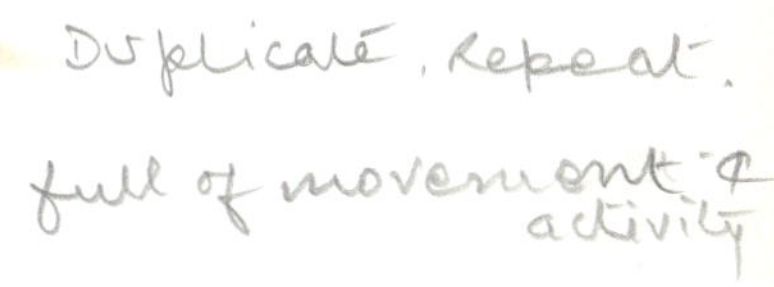

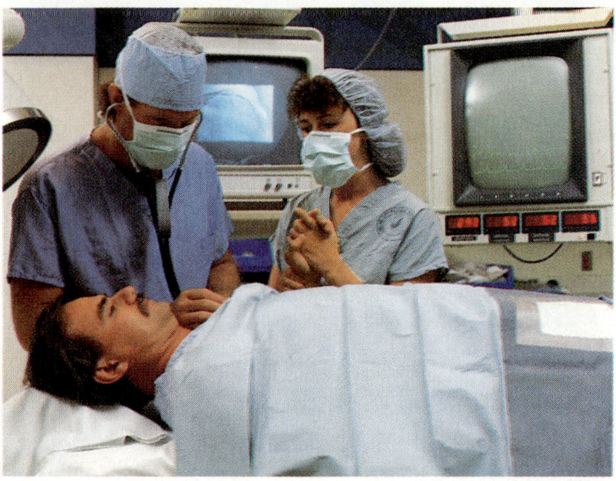

Computers help this physician provide more effective treatment.

An equally exciting area in the use of computers in the medical/health field is in patient treatment. Computer-controlled pumps can be used to inject drugs into the bloodstream. Technology is being developed so that the computer not only injects the drug but also performs the full-time measurement of chemicals within the body, with the computer making second-by-second decisions on how much of the drug is required. Such uses of the computer should provide much better treatment for illnesses such as diabetes.

Persons who have lost the use of their legs through spinal cord injuries are now walking with the aid of computer stimulation of their leg muscles. Important beginnings have been made toward artificial vision for the blind. Computer-controlled wheelchairs and robot arms that respond to the spoken word are proving to be of tremendous value to the disabled.

Routine and Dangerous Tasks

A major impact on employees has been the use of the computer to remove routine tasks. When the computer is put to use doing routine, boring tasks, the employees who previously performed these tasks can be freed to do more interesting work. Office jobs that require the same calculations to be repeated frequently and assembly line work that requires the same recurring tasks to be performed are examples of situations in which the computer can be put to good use. Computers are also used to handle hazardous materials and to perform tasks that are dangerous to humans.

This robot is transporting a case believed to contain a bomb.

AN OVERVIEW OF *COMPUTERS AND INFORMATION PROCESSING: Concepts and Applications*

The contents of this textbook are intended for those students who desire to learn why computers have become such an integral part of our society, how they work, and how they are used. The eighteen chapters of this text are divided into six logically related parts as described in the following paragraphs.

Part I—Introduction to Computers and Information Systems

Part I of this text is composed of Chapters 1 and 2. Chapter 1 (Computers and Information Processing) and Chapter 2 (Introduction to Computer Systems) preview the characteristics of computers and information systems. Hardware devices and software programs are discussed in relation to how they interact to complete the basic cycle of input, processing, and output. Finally, computers are categorized based on their size, shape, speed, capacity, and capability.

Part II—The Computer System

This part of the text is composed of four chapters: Chapter 3 (Computer Processing), Chapter 4 (Input—Putting Data into the Computer), Chapter 5 (Output—Getting Information from the Computer), and Chapter 6 (Auxiliary Storage—Retaining Data). These chapters identify and describe devices and components that enable a computer system to input, process, output, and retain data for future reference.

Part III—Microcomputers and Operating Systems

Part III is made up of two chapters: Chapter 7 (Microcomputers) and Chapter 8 (Operating Systems). The characteristics, architecture, capabilities, and utilization of the popular microcomputer are presented. The purpose of operating systems and how they function in a variety of environments from small computers to large mainframe systems are reviewed. Also, commonly used utility programs and compatibility issues are discussed to conclude this part of the text.

Part IV—Application Software

The next seven chapters compose Part IV of the text: Chapter 9 (Introduction to Application Software), Chapter 10 (Word Processing Software), Chapter 11 (Database Software), Chapter 12 (Spreadsheet Software), Chapter 13 (Computer Graphics), Chapter 14 (Communications), and Chapter 15 (Additional Application Software). The use of application software, where to obtain it, and the factors that must be considered when selecting it are provided in Chapter 9. In addition, word processing, database, spreadsheet, graphics, communications, desktop accessories, and expert systems are among several of the most commonly used application software packages that are discussed in detail in the following chapters.

Part V—System Design and Programming

Chapter 16 (System Development) and Chapter 17 (Programming Concepts) make up Part V of this text. The importance of designing new software and modifying existing software to keep pace with an ever-changing environment is stressed. An explanation of each of the specific tasks associated with analysis, design, programming, implementation, and review are discussed. In Chapter 17, examples of several of the most commonly used programming languages are presented and contrasted against one another in terms of the applications for which each is best suited.

Part VI—Careers

Part VI consists of Chapter 18 (Careers in the Computer Industry). Various job titles and the work environment for careers in the hardware, software, information processing, teaching, service, and supply areas are presented. Career advancement opportunities in the computer industry are also discussed, with emphasis on career paths and formal and informal educational requirements.

Appendices

Three appendices are included in this text. The first appendix (Appendix A—Computing History and Trends) traces the development of the computer from its infancy through four generations of technological advancements. Specialized computers, general-purpose computers, and the microprocessor era are discussed. Technical changes, trends, and challenges that lie ahead conclude this appendix.

The second appendix (Appendix B—Internal Representation of Data) explains through illustration and example how data is represented inside the computer and stored on auxiliary devices. This appendix is intended for those students who wish to obtain a more technical understanding of how the computer works internally.

The third and final appendix (Appendix C—BASIC Programming) is intended for those students who wish to learn how to write simple computer programs in the BASIC programming language. Programming concepts and instruction are provided in logic, input/output operations, arithmetic, decision-making, looping, and tables.

NEGATIVE ASPECTS OF COMPUTER USAGE

You would probably not want to return to a lifestyle in which computers were not used on an everyday basis. However, there are some very real problems that have resulted from computer use. Two of these problems are discussed below.

Computer Crime — No one really knows the extent of computer crime. However, you need only to examine the newspapers to read about the persons who get caught. Computer crime comes in many forms. It may involve changing computer records for personal gain, such as a student changing a course grade. Other criminals may use the computer to commit theft. For example, they may have merchandise shipped to a phony business at no charge, or they may enrich a bank account by transferring a few cents into it from each of thousands of other accounts. Then there are persons who purposely damage computer systems or data. For instance, a programmer who gets mad at an employer may cause the computer to erase vital records. There are cases of what might be called "spying" by computer, where a criminal will "listen in" on data being transmitted from one business location to another. Fortunately, computer users have become more aware of the dangers from computer-related crimes and are beginning to take more steps to protect their computer systems and data from misuse.

Computer crime can range from the theft of computer components to the illegal access of computer files.

Loss of Privacy — Many persons have a concern about the possible loss of privacy caused by computers. Information on millions of people is stored in thousands of computers across the country. Personal privacy begins to disappear when the first charge account or checking account is opened or with the first filing of an income tax return. Personal privacy is also lost when businesses collect too much information about a person or when that information is obtained by people who do not have the right or the need to have it. The problem of privacy is even greater when misinformation is passed on. Charge account billing errors, for example, can erroneously give persons poor credit ratings. Even after the billing errors have been corrected, the credit ratings may not be changed due to oversight.

Although negative aspects of computer usage do exist, there are precautions that can be taken to prevent such computer misfortunes. For example, computer crimes are less likely to occur when certain security measures are taken, such as the use of passwords and magnetic identification cards to help reduce unauthorized access to computer systems. Public awareness is another important factor in stopping computer misuse. The public must be informed of the seriousness and frequency of computer tampering. Finally, legislation that calls for harsher penalties to fall on those convicted of computer crime is becoming a key weapon against computer misuse. These safeguards, considered with the efficiency and overall benefits of computer usage, can greatly reduce the negative view many people have of the computer age.

CHAPTER SUMMARY

- A computer can generally be defined as an electronic device that does computations and makes logical decisions according to instructions and data that have been given to it. If the instructions and data are accurate, the computations and logical decisions the computer makes will also be accurate.
- Computers are electronic devices and, like all electronic devices, are exceptionally fast. Even the smallest, slowest computers are fast compared to human standards.
- Computers are remarkably accurate devices. More often than not, they are blamed for errors that are in reality caused by humans.
- Computers have become more reliable and more durable with technical enhancements. In addition, improved materials that are more resistant to wear, heat, and other elements of the external environment contribute to their durability and reliability.
- Today, due to technological advancements in the computer industry, most computers are considered to be general-purpose devices. That is, both their computation and input/output processing capabilities are such that they can be used for nearly any type of application.
- Computers are truly cost-effective devices. Their costs have dramatically decreased over the years, but their capabilities have dramatically increased.
- The computer is a unique device in that it actually fuels its own growth. That is, its use in research for its computation and logic decision-making capabilities allows it to participate in its own development.
- Information can be defined as knowledge that is given or received of some fact or circumstance. The process of sharing information between humans and computers can be referred to as information processing (also called data processing).
- The basic characteristics of information processing include inputting the data into the computer, processing the data after it has been entered into the computer, and outputting the processed data.
- Data that is input into the computer must be verified to insure it is accurate.
- Once data has been input into the computer and verified for accuracy, it must be processed. Processing of data includes sorting, classifying, calculating, summarizing, and comparing the data.
- After data has been processed, it must be communicated to those who need the information. The information must be in a human-readable form.
- The use of computers in society has affected individuals in their everyday living.
- Businesses known as information utilities have large computers that store huge amounts of information that can be accessed.

♦ Some common uses of computers in our everyday living include electronic banking and services, shopping from home, household control, learning aids, weather and environment, transportation, community service, crime control, medical and health care, and routine and dangerous tasks.

KEY TERMS

The following key terms were introduced in this chapter:

computer
debit card
general-purpose computers
information
information processing/data processing
information utilities
microseconds
milliseconds
nanoseconds
picoseconds

REVIEW QUESTIONS

1. What is the general definition of a computer? (Obj. 1)
2. What fractional part of a second is a: (Obj. 1)
   millisecond? ____________________
   microsecond? ____________________
   nanosecond? ____________________
   picosecond? ____________________
3. Why are computers considered to be extremely accurate devices? (Obj. 1)
4. What factors have contributed to the modern day computer's increased durability and reliability? (Obj. 1)
5. What is a general-purpose computer? (Obj. 1)
6. Why are modern day computers considered (for the most part) to be cost-effective devices? (Obj. 1)
7. How have computers participated in their own development? (Obj. 1)
8. Define the term *information*. (Obj. 2)
9. What is information processing (also referred to as data processing)? (Obj. 2)
10. Why should data be verified both before and after it has been entered into the computer? (Obj. 2)
11. Identify the functions included in processing data. (Obj. 2)
12. What are the most important characteristics of computer-generated output? (Obj. 2)
13. What is an information utility service? (Obj. 3)
14. Describe how computers can provide better service for bank customers. (Obj. 3)

15. How may computers be used in the home? (Obj. 3)
16. Name some ways the computer is used in dealing with the weather and environment. (Obj. 3)
17. How have computers affected transportation? (Obj. 3)
18. How have computers contributed to improved community services? (Obj. 3)
19. Describe ways in which computers improve medical and health care and the quality of life for those who are ill or disabled. (Obj. 3)
20. What are the advantages to humans of having computers perform routine and dangerous tasks? (Obj. 3)

CHALLENGE ACTIVITIES

1. Consult a computer magazine, your local newspaper, a computer store, your library, or other sources to obtain information about any of the computer characteristics discussed in this chapter. You may describe one or more of the characteristics of a particular computer or of computers in general. Prepare a report describing your findings regarding speed, accuracy, durability and reliability, versatility, cost-effectiveness, and/or popularity. (Obj. 1)
2. Visit a local business, industry, governmental agency, or other computer user. Find out how they are using their computer. Identify the kind of data input, what types of processing are performed on that data, and what information is output. Prepare a report summarizing what you learned. (Obj. 2)
3. Prepare a brief report about the use of computers in your school. The report may focus on either educational usage (i.e. math, science, English, or business subjects) or administration usage (i.e. computerized report cards, test scoring, school book inventory). (Objs. 1,2)
4. Consult a computer magazine, your local newspaper, a computer store, your library, or other sources to obtain information about ways computers are being utilized in our society. Prepare a brief report describing your findings. (Obj. 3)

CHAPTER 2

INTRODUCTION TO COMPUTER SYSTEMS

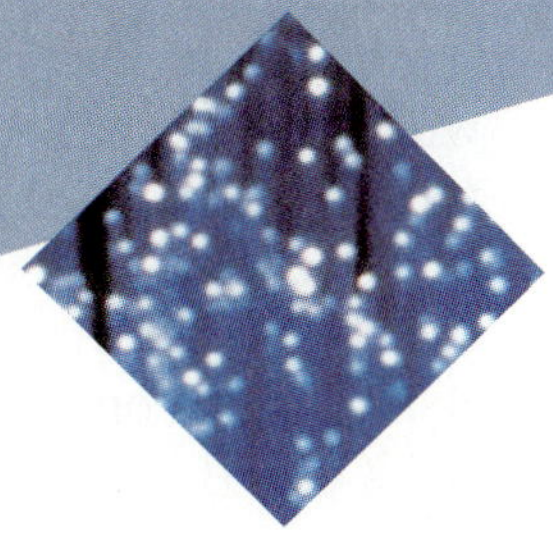

LEARNING OBJECTIVES

After studying this chapter, you will be able to:

1. **Describe a computer system.**
2. **Recognize and describe the difference between hardware and software.**
3. **Explain the basic information processing cycle of input, processing, and output.**
4. **Identify and explain the differences between microcomputers, minicomputers, mainframe computers, and special-purpose computers.**

INTRODUCTION

Computers are everywhere. They can be found in space vehicles, hospitals, law enforcement agencies, government, grocery stores, libraries, businesses, factories, schools, and even our homes. Their use and mere existence affect our society in general, as well as each of us individually in our everyday lives. The varied and widespread use of computers continues to be fueled by an ever-changing, expanding, technological growth. As technology finds more efficient ways of building more powerful computers, the users of these computers find more efficient ways to utilize technological innovations.

In general, a **computer** is an electronic device which accepts data and processes it into meaningful information in a form useful to humans. Computers are complex and powerful tools that enable us to perform tasks. Many of these tasks can be completed in a fraction of the time it would take a human being to perform them, and some of the tasks a human could not possibly perform at all. As with any tool, however, it is the user who determines the extent of a computer's usefulness. In other words, a computer's usefulness is limited only by the imagination and abilities of the humans who use it. It can do only what it is told to do.

This chapter will introduce you to the elements that comprise a computer system. Next, you will be shown how a computer system works. Finally, various types, sizes, and shapes of computers will be presented.

WHAT IS A COMPUTER SYSTEM?

A **computer system** can be defined as a combination of related elements working together as a whole to achieve a common goal. That is, a computer system is made up of elements (called hardware and software) that interact with each other. **Hardware** is the tangible, physical equipment that can be seen and touched. **Software** is the intangible instructions that tell the computer what to do. When both the hardware and software work together to accomplish a common goal they make up a **computer system**.

A computer is composed of several hardware devices of various sizes, shapes, and functions which must all work together as one system. These hardware devices enable the computer to accept data, process it into meaningful information, store it, and report it in a form humans can understand. A hardware device which enables the computer to accept data is called an **input device**. An example of an input device is a keyboard. A hardware device which processes the data into meaningful information is called the **processor**. A hardware device which permits storage of data is called a **storage device**. An example of a storage device is a disk drive. A hardware device which reports the information in a form we can understand is called an **output device**. An example of an output device is a monitor.

These pieces of hardware work together to form a computer system.

A computer system is also composed of several software programs that control the hardware devices, and in turn tell the computer what to do. A **program** can be defined as a series of detailed, step-by-step instructions that tell the computer precisely what actions to perform. Just as there are several hardware devices which must all work together, there are several software programs which must also work together as one system. For example, a program, called a **system program**, controls the computer's circuitry and hardware devices while another program, called an **application program**, instructs the computer to perform a specific, user-defined task as illustrated in Figure 2-1. You will learn much more about system and application programs in later chapters.

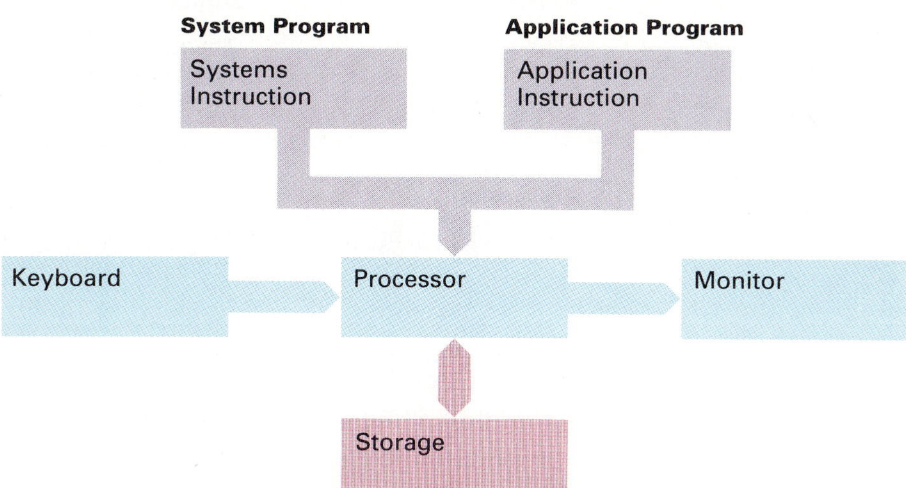

Figure 2-1
Hardware and software work together as a computer system.

When input, processing, storage, and output devices work together with system and application software programs as a whole toward the completion of a common goal or task, they comprise a computer system. You will soon learn that computer systems come in many different sizes and shapes. You will also learn that some computer systems are more powerful than others, and that some can perform specific tasks that others cannot.

HOW A COMPUTER SYSTEM WORKS

Data consists of facts in the form of numbers, alphabetic characters, special symbols, or words. The process of manipulating data into a form which humans can use, or learn new knowledge from, is called **information processing**. You have already learned that a computer system is composed of hardware and software working together toward a common goal. When a computer system is used to process data for the purpose of generating information from that data it is called an **information system**. In an information system, data is created or collected and fed into the system. Data that enters the system (via an input or storage device) is referred to as **input**. Useful information which leaves the system (via an output or storage device) is referred to as **output**; that is, processed information. In between the input and output stages, the data is processed. **Processing** takes place in the computer's processor where detailed instructions (called software programs) tell the computer what should be done to the data to produce the desired information. Refer to Figure 2-2 for an illustration of this basic cycle of input, processing, and output.

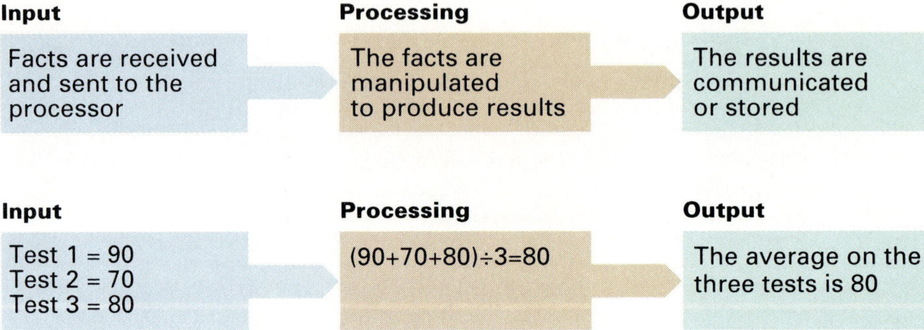

Figure 2-2
The basic information processing cycle consists of input, processing, and output.

In the example illustrated in Figure 2-2, the input consists of three test scores. The input is processed by summing the three test scores and dividing by three to obtain the average score. This average score is the output.

Input

The data that is input into an information system comes from many sources. Data about students in a school comes from registration information, grade reports, attendance rosters, and similar sources. Data regarding hours worked by an employee is taken from forms or time clock cards. Test score data is obtained from scored tests. Data that is fed into the computer for processing is commonly referred to as **raw data** or **original data**. If raw data is first written on forms, the forms are known as **source documents** because these forms become the source of the data that is entered into the computer's input device. Many applications do not use source documents. Instead, the data is fed directly into the computer as it is originated. Frequently, some of the input may be data that has already been collected and processed earlier. Figure 2-3 shows an example of an application of this type.

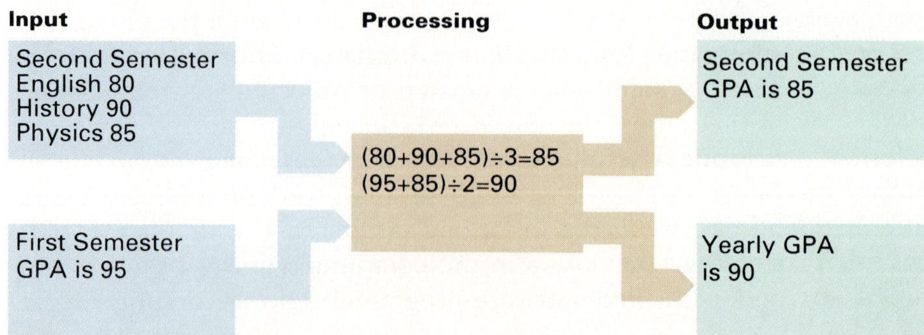

Figure 2-3
Both raw data and previously processed data may be used as input to a system.

Processing

Whether the data is raw data, previously processed data, or a combination of the two, it must go into the computer's processor to be processed. Processing includes such tasks as performing mathematical calculations, making comparisons, and arranging data into a desired order. Computers follow processing steps provided by software programs in much the same way that humans follow commands provided by the brain. For both, each step leading to the desired result must be included in the processing plan, and these steps must be in logical order. When steps are left out, when steps are out of order, or when logic is not followed in finding the solution to a problem, neither a human nor a computer will produce the desired result.

Output

When the processing of data is completed, output takes place. Output is the process of storing the processed information for later recall or communicating it to a user immediately. If stored, the information is available whenever needed by the user. In either case, the information will eventually reach the user. The user may be a human or the same or another computer system.

There is nothing new about the cycle of input, processing, and output. You have used it many times in making purchasing decisions or writing term papers. In making a purchasing decision, you collect information about a product and its prices in various stores. This is the input stage, which passes the data along to your brain. Your brain processes the data and decides at which store you should make your purchase. You then go to the store and purchase the item, thereby completing the output phase of the cycle. In writing a term paper, you first decide on the subject and consider an outline of what you wish to say about the subject. You collect many facts from reading, from interviews, and from expert opinions. These facts are the input. You then perform processing by arranging the facts in a logical order, checking for use of good English skills, and making corrections where necessary. Finally, the term paper is written, representing the output of your work.

The steps of input, processing, and output are essential in an information processing system. Regardless of the kind of information being produced, or whether the system is manual or computerized, the processing of data uses these same three functions. Data enters the processing system, various operations are performed on the data to convert it to useful information, and the useful information leaves the system. For example, names of students are data. Arranging the names in alphabetic order so a certain name can be found quickly is a form of information processing. Utilizing a computer system to record test scores made by students, to prepare electric utility bills for customers, to design a new automobile, or to control a steel mill are also examples of information processing.

TYPES, SIZES, AND SHAPES OF COMPUTERS

Computers come in a variety of types, sizes, and shapes with varying capabilities and speeds. Initially, all computers were large in size and were called **mainframes**. As computer technology grew, smaller, less powerful computers, called **minicomputers**, were developed. Later, technology developed the "computer on a chip," called a **microprocessor**. The microprocessor led to the creation of yet another category of computers, even smaller and less powerful than the minicomputer, called the **microcomputer**.

Technology has now caused the evolutionary scale of computers to move upward. That is, today's microcomputers have become more powerful than minicomputers used to be, today's minicomputers have become more powerful than many mainframes used to be, and today's mainframes are more powerful than ever before. This is primarily due to the micro-miniaturization of the computer processor. **Micro-miniaturization** is the technological process which enables an entire microprocessor to occupy the space of a tiny chip no larger than the size of your fingertip.

Microprocessors provide tremendous amounts of power and occupy a space comparable to the size of a ladybug.

Not only has this technology caused computers to become increasingly smaller in size, it has also caused them to become increasingly more powerful. Today, computer capabilities range all the way from very limited to very powerful, and, in size, from a hand-held unit to one that occupies a large room.

One method which can be used to categorize computers as micro-, mini-, and mainframe computers is to identify how they are used. Typically, a computer used in the home, on a person's lap, or in a small or large business, and which has less power and speed than a minicomputer or mainframe, can be classified as a microcomputer. A computer with less power and speed than a mainframe, but which is capable of storing and processing large volumes of data, can be classified as a minicomputer. A large computer with more power and speed than a minicomputer and capable of processing very large volumes of data quickly can be classified as a mainframe computer. In addition to these computer categories, many specially designed and equipped computers have exploded on the scene. These computers are used in many diverse functions, such as in automobiles, traffic lights, environmental control systems, space vehicles, and audiovisual equipment, to name a few. In the presentation which follows, each of these categories of computers will be discussed.

Microcomputers

A computer used in the home, on a person's lap, or in a small or large business, which has less power and speed than a minicomputer or mainframe, can be classified as a microcomputer. A microcomputer contains one or more microprocessors which can follow the instructions of a software program in a manner similar to its larger minicomputer and mainframe counterparts. Microcomputers have found their way into virtually every aspect of everyday living. For the purpose of this discussion, we will classify microcomputers into three sub-categories: (1) home computers, (2) personal computers, and (3) portable and lap-top computers.

Home Computers

A **home computer** can be defined as a microcomputer which is small enough to fit on a desk and powerful enough to satisfy the entertainment and informational processing needs of the household. Such needs include video games, word processing, financial planning, computerized shopping and banking, educational learning, and access to stock markets and electronic bulletin boards. Because of the ever-increasing power of the microcomputer, along with its reduction in price, it is quickly becoming a common household item. It is estimated that within a few years the number of home computers found in the American home will be comparable to the number of television sets.

Budgeting can be done using a home computer.

Video games are very popular among home computer users.

Personal Computers

A **personal computer** is a microcomputer designed for, and used primarily in, small and large businesses. In addition to businesses, personal computers have found their way into homes, schools, government, and industry. Many different input, storage, and output devices can be connected to these computers. This, coupled with its powerful processing capabilities, enables the personal computer to perform many and varied tasks, which has made it the most popular computer in use today. Small and large businesses and industries use these machines to perform individual processing tasks as well as to communicate with larger mini- and mainframe computers.

Businesses large and small use personal computers to keep track of inventory.

A personal computer typically has more capabilities and processing power than the home computer. It is considered the top of the microcomputer line. As a result of its popularity, many software programs are available from which the user may choose. Examples of these common software programs include programs in accounting, customer billing, communication, spreadsheets, word processing, and database applications.

Portable/Lap-top Computers

Portable and lap-top computers are very similar to their home computer or personal computer counterparts. The primary difference is that the **portable and lap-top computers** are lightweight, transportable microcomputers designed for easy carrying and/or use on a person's lap. One example of a portable computer is the programmable, hand-held calculator. These calculators contain sophisticated microprocessors and have limited input, output, and storage capabilities. They are commonly used for such applications as engineering and for those which require mathematical calculations. A second example of a portable computer is a compact, lightweight microcomputer (5 to 28 pounds) with the ability to connect several input, output, and storage devices. Because of its light weight, it can easily be moved from one location to another. Microcomputers which can be folded into a single carrying case for easy transportation are commonly referred to as lap-top computers. These computers are convenient tools for use in remote locations or when traveling. Also, many lap-top computers are battery powered and can be used when away from an electrical power source.

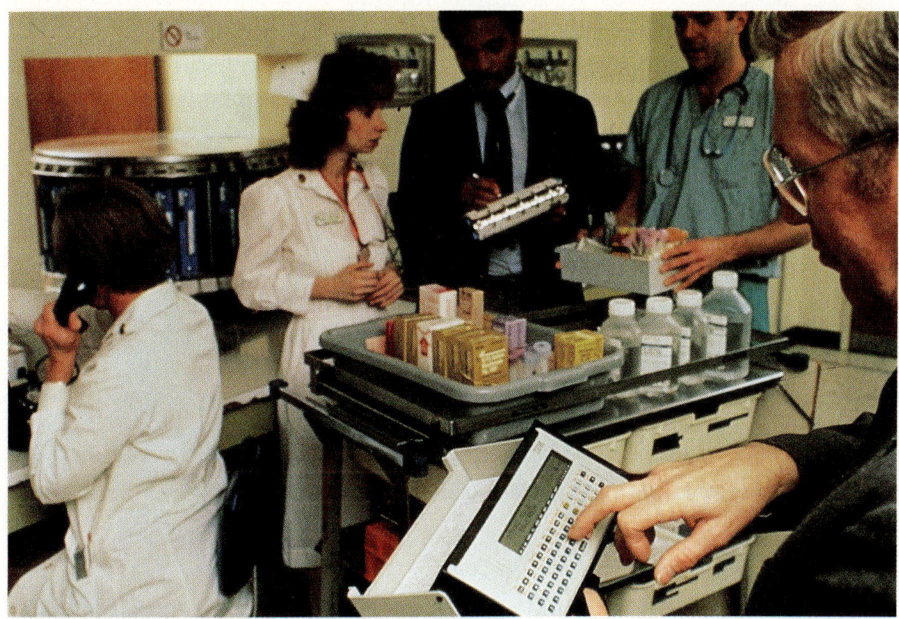

Portable and lap-top computers can be easily transported to different locations for a variety of uses.

Minicomputers

A minicomputer is defined as a computer with less power and speed than a mainframe but capable of storing and processing large volumes of data. Today's minicomputer is characterized by its ease of installation and operation. Because it is smaller than its minicomputer predecessors, it takes up less floor space and does not require special environmental control systems or power supplies. Its ability to handle a full line of input, storage, and output devices provides a great deal of flexibility. In addition, its processing power lends itself for use by multiple users in many different areas. For example, it can be used as a multi-station word processor linked to several other micros or minis all working together to support remote geographic locations.

Another feature of a minicomputer is its ability to expand and be tailored to the growing needs of the user. As an organization grows, its processing needs also grow. Additional input, storage, and output devices may be added to an existing minicomputer to accommodate growth. When the processing requirements of one minicomputer are exceeded, another can be installed and linked to the first one to meet the growing needs, as shown in Figure 2-4. It is also common to find one or more minicomputers located in remote offices and plants linked to a mainframe computer at an organization's main headquarters, as shown in Figure 2-5.

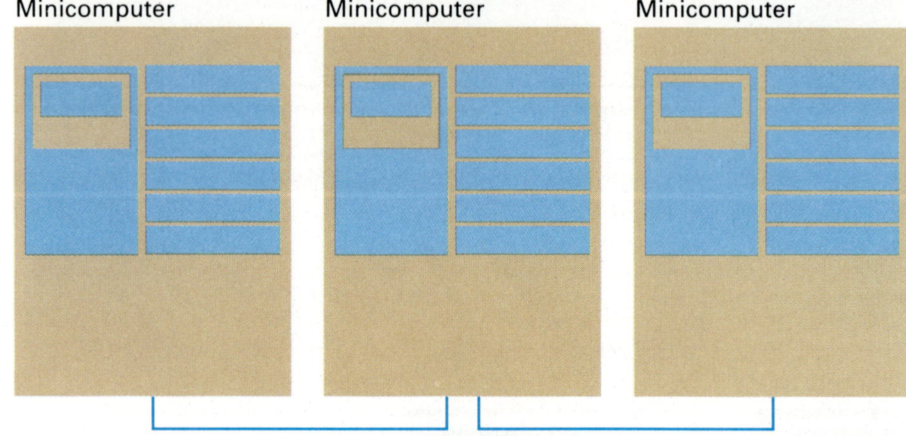

Figure 2-4
Minicomputers can be linked together to meet growing processing needs.

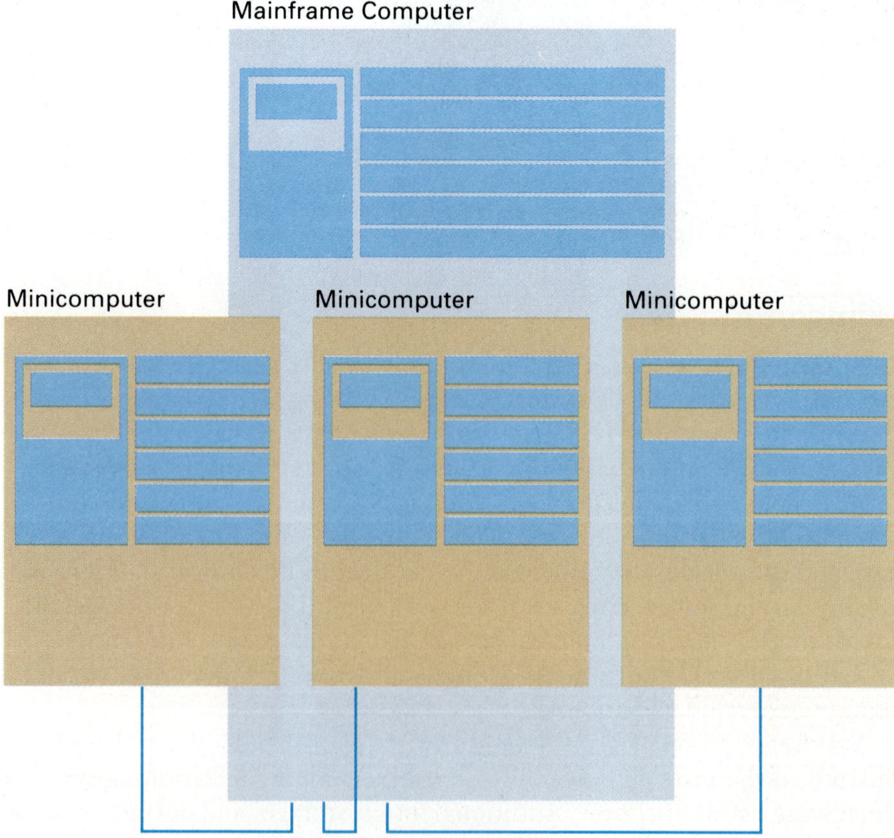

Figure 2-5
Minicomputers located in remote offices can be linked to a mainframe computer located at headquarters.

Mainframe Computers

A mainframe computer is a large computer with more processing power and speed than a minicomputer and capable of processing very large volumes of data quickly. The mainframe computer is the foundation of the computer industry from which much technological innovation stems.

A mainframe computer can store millions of characters and support many high-speed input, storage, and output devices. Organizations that require the processing capabilities of mainframe computers are usually very large, with a need for storing and accessing large amounts of data in a very short period of time. Examples of mainframe users include the federal government for processing of tax forms, state governments for driver vehicle registration, insurance corporations with huge policyholder databases, large banks and investment houses, large research and science industries, and other types of corporations.

Mainframe computers require special environmental controls, such as special power supplies and heating and cooling systems. Cables and wires which connect all its component parts together must be housed under a raised flooring platform on which the computer sits. Very sophisticated software programs control the operation of all the devices which comprise the system and often require the operator to have special training in order to effectively operate the system.

The largest, fastest, and most expensive computers in existence are special mainframe computers called **supercomputers.** Few supercomputers are built each year because the cost is so high and the applications for which they are used are so limited. Supercomputers represent the most advanced computer technology in the world today. They are used for advanced research and mathematical calculations in such areas as the space program, weather forecasting, and nuclear weapons research and development. Because of their lightning speed and tremendous power, they can perform complex tasks that cannot be accomplished by other computers.

This Cray supercomputer has tremendous processing power.

Specially Designed and Equipped Computers

The micro-, mini-, and mainframe computers discussed on the previous pages are referred to as general-purpose computers because they can perform many different tasks depending upon the software program they are using. **Special-purpose computers,** on the other hand, have been designed to perform specific, specialized tasks. These specially designed and equipped computers vary in size and power from a tiny microchip used in a microwave oven to a large automatic machine tooling system. Other examples and uses of special-purpose computers include the digital instrumentation and ignition systems in automobiles, the monitoring and control systems of space vehicles, the functioning of home appliances (washing machines, refrigerators, ovens), and the controls of traffic lights and assembly lines. Recent use of computers in robotics has also led to an increased use of robot machines. With the technological ability to develop these special-purpose machines, many of the mundane tasks which require monitoring and control will soon be done by computers.

Specially designed computers can be used to monitor aircraft flight, check equipment, and prescribe repairs.

AMAZING CHIPS

Scientists in the United States and Japan are trying to overcome the physical limits of chip design technology that began less than three decades ago. Each country is rushing to be the first to develop microcomputer chips that contain one billion transistors.

Transistor technology preceded chip technology. Transistors were smaller, more efficient, and more reliable than their predecessors the vacuum tubes. The major limitation of transistors was in their limited number of interconnections. In other words, because of the sophisticated circuitry of computers, an enormous number of connections between transistors was required. Unlike the number of transistor connections needed in a radio, the number of transistor connections in computers extends into the millions. Chip technology solved the interconnections problem by placing several transistors on a tiny silicon surface. Thus, computer power and storage capabilities expanded dramatically.

The number of transistors which can be placed on a chip has increased from fewer than ten in the early chips to thousands in the chips used today. Chip technology has enabled the chip's capacity to double every year since its creation until just a few years ago. However, today's chip designers have run into a problem concerning the physical limitations of a single chip; therefore, the interconnections problem of the transistor technology has resurfaced.

As additional components are packed together with ever increasing densities on a chip's surface, interconnections become so narrow that not enough electrons can pass through them in order to turn the chip's microscopic transistors on and off. It is estimated that with current techniques, a density of about 20 million devices per chip is the physical limit. Although this may appear to be more than adequate, researchers are already working on the billion-transistor chip they believe the future computer will need to run the applications that will be demanded.

Currently, there are two schools of thought on how to increase the number of components on a chip beyond the 20 million physical limit: (1) make each component that must be placed on the chip smaller (similar to what has been done for the last three decades), or (2) leave the components the same size, but make the physical size of the chip larger. Perhaps the most promising area of research involves mounting chips together on wafers (stacking them on top of each other), thereby making bigger chips. By using this technique, the processing power of the largest computer in the world (the Cray 2) would fit into a twelve-by-eight-inch box. Mounting chips on wafers would not only reduce the size of computers but would also enable more interconnections between chips. Since a wafer greatly reduces the distance an electronic signal must travel, this can yield tremendous increases in speed as well.

A chip no larger than the nib of a fountain pen can accommodate four million bits.

The extraordinary increase in computer power that we have observed during the past few years can be directly tied to the development of chip technology. The question yet to be answered is: Will the development of super-dense single chips, or the development of wafer technology, propel us into the next generation of supercomputers?

CHAPTER SUMMARY

- A computer is an electronic device which accepts raw data and processes it into meaningful information in a form useful to human beings. Computers are tools that enable us to perform many and varied tasks.
- Computer systems are composed of hardware devices and software programs working together as a whole toward a common goal.
- Hardware is the tangible, physical computer equipment that can be seen and touched.
- Software is the intangible instructions (software programs) that tell the computer what to do.
- A hardware device which enables a computer to accept data is called an input device.
- A hardware device which processes raw data into meaningful information is called the processor.
- A hardware device which permits storage of data is called a storage device.
- A hardware device which reports the information in a form humans can understand is called an output device.
- A program is a series of detailed, step-by-step instructions which tell the computer what to do.
- Information processing is the process of manipulating data into a form from which humans can use or learn new knowledge. When a computer system is used to process data for the purpose of generating information from raw data it is called an information system.
- The basic information processing cycle consists of input, processing, and output. All computer systems have this same basic processing cycle in common.
- Computers come in a wide variety of sizes, capabilities, and speeds. With the advent of the "computer on a chip" came a blurring of the categories in which various sizes and shapes of computers could be classified. Not only has this technology caused computers to become increasingly smaller in size but also increasingly more powerful.
- Microcomputers are a category of computers which can be used in the home, on a person's lap, or in a small or large business. Microcomputers have less power and speed than a minicomputer or mainframe.

- Minicomputers are a category of computers with less power and speed than a mainframe but which are capable of storing and processing large volumes of data.
- Mainframe computers are large computers with more processing power and speed than a minicomputer and are capable of processing very large volumes of data quickly.
- The largest, fastest, and most expensive computers in existence are special mainframe computers called supercomputers.
- Special-purpose computers have been designed and equipped to perform specific, specialized tasks. These specially designed and equipped computers vary in size and power from a tiny microchip used in a microwave oven to a large automatic machine tooling system.

KEY TERMS

The following key terms were introduced or redefined in this chapter:

application program
computer
computer system
data
hardware
home computer
information processing
information system
input
input device
mainframe
micro-miniaturization
microcomputer
microprocessor
minicomputer
output
output device
personal computer
portable/lap-top computer
processing
processor
program
raw data/original data
software
source documents
special-purpose computer
storage device
supercomputer
system program

REVIEW QUESTIONS

1. Identify at least six uses of computers (other than the ones given in the text) in our society and/or everyday living. (Obj. 1)
2. Define a computer system. (Obj. 1)
3. Explain the difference between computer hardware and computer software. (Obj. 2)
4. Explain the difference between an input device, a processor, a storage device, and an output device. (Obj. 2)
5. Explain the difference between a system program and an application program. (Obj. 2)
6. Describe an information system. (Obj. 3)
7. Explain how an information processing system works. (Obj. 3)

8. Describe the differences between a microcomputer, a minicomputer, a mainframe computer, and a special-purpose computer. (Obj. 4)
9. Describe the differences between a home computer, a personal computer, and a portable/lap-top computer. (Obj. 4)
10. Identify at least three uses of special-purpose computers (other than those given in this text). (Obj. 4)

CHALLENGE ACTIVITIES

1. Write a report describing how computers are used in the classrooms of your school, a school you are familiar with, or a school you have read about. (Obj. 1)
2. Write a report describing how a computer is used to perform an administrative function (i.e. grade reporting, attendance, accounting, inventory) in your school, a school you are familiar with, or a school you have read about. (Obj. 1)
3. Visit a local computer store, or write to a computer manufacturer, and ask for a brochure describing its most popular micro-, mini-, or mainframe computer. Give an oral report to your class based upon what you learn from the brochure. (Objs. 2,3,4)
4. Research and find a software package that operates on a micro-, mini-, or mainframe computer. Hint: Visit a local computer store, read a computer magazine, or check the software used in your school. Write a brief report describing the purpose of the software, what type of computer your selected software package runs on, how much it costs, and the minimum hardware and software requirements. (Objs. 2,4)

PART 2

THE COMPUTER SYSTEM

CHAPTER 3

COMPUTER PROCESSING

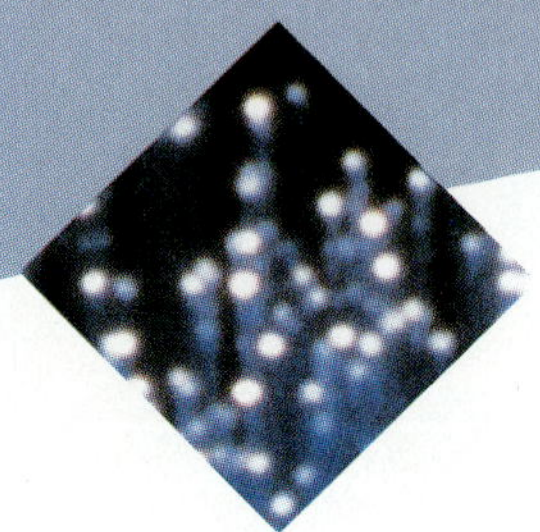

LEARNING OBJECTIVES

After studying this chapter, you will be able to:

1. **Define the four basic functions all computers can perform.**
2. **Define CPU (central processing unit) and identify several of its component parts.**
3. **Explain how a numeric address is used to identify memory locations.**
4. **Recognize and describe the difference between RAM and ROM memory.**
5. **Describe the functions a CPU's processor performs.**
6. **Describe how the processor directs the computer's actions.**
7. **Describe how arithmetic operations are performed by the processor.**
8. **Describe how logical comparisons are performed by the processor.**
9. **Explain how the computer performs the processing cycle.**
10. **Identify the processing functions associated with input, processing, and output.**
11. **Describe why hardware, software, data, and people are four essential components to all computer systems.**

INTRODUCTION

The basic steps of input, processing, and output are essential in any information system. Regardless of the kind of information being produced, or whether the system is manual or computerized, the processing of data consists of these same three steps. Data enters the processing system, various operations are performed on the data to convert it to useful information, and the useful information leaves the system. Computers follow processing steps in much the same way that the human mind does. For both, each step leading to the desired result must be included in the processing plan, and these steps must be in logical order. When steps are omitted, when steps are out of order, or when logic is not followed in laying out the solution to a problem, neither a human nor the computer will produce the correct, desired result. For example, when traveling from one location to another by automobile, several different roads must be traveled certain distances and in a predetermined order. If this plan is not followed and the roads are not traveled in the proper order and the right distances, it would be impossible to get to the desired destination.

Computers follow a logical processing plan just as a person follows a predetermined route when traveling from one location to another.

Many people believe that computers can do just about anything and that their level of sophistication requires a genius to program and run them. In reality, computers are very simple devices that can perform only four basic functions. A computer can (1) store data and programs, (2) function unattended due to its ability to interpret and follow instructions it is provided, (3) do arithmetic calculations, and (4) perform logical comparisons. What makes the computer such a powerful device, given only these four basic functions, is its tremendous speed, its accuracy, and its ability to store vast volumes of data.

In this chapter we will examine how the memory and processor components of the CPU (central processing unit) function. The **CPU** can be defined as the hardware device that stores data and programs, executes program instructions, and performs arithmetic and logic operations. It is often referred to as the brain of the computer system. In this chapter you will learn how the CPU's memory is utilized to store data and programs and how the CPU's processor controls the computer system's actions and performs arithmetic and logic operations.

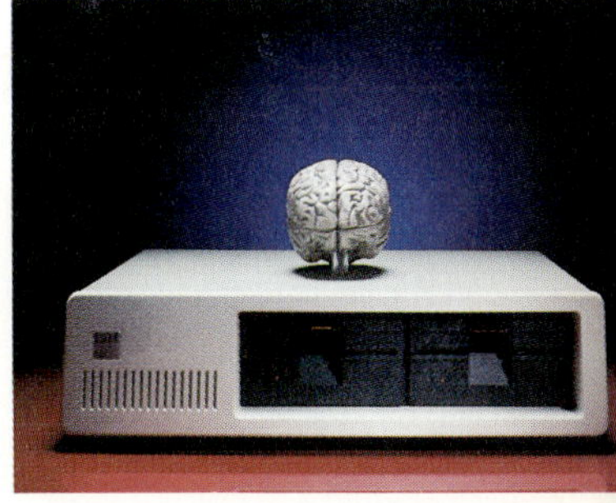

The CPU is often referred to as the brain of the computer system.

MEMORY

As you learned in Chapter 2, the computer must be given instructions, in the form of software, which tell it exactly what to do. The instructions that the computer follows are stored in locations known as **memory**. Memory may also be referred to as **main storage** or **primary storage**. From memory, each instruction is executed (carried out) by the processor. Likewise, the data which is to be processed is loaded into memory. It, too, spends most of its time in memory, being moved into the processor when necessary for processing. The processed data is then returned to memory for further use or output. Later in this chapter, you will learn how the computer's processor functions.

Memory chips can hold great amounts of data in a space as small as the eye of a needle.

The memory of a computer is made of electronic circuits that, like the processor, are contained in tiny chips. Memory can accept, hold, and release data, as well as the instructions for processing the data. Data and instructions are stored as electronic impulses in specified locations in memory. You can imagine memory as being like a large number of mailboxes with each box being labeled with an identifying number. This number is known as a **numeric address**. Any desired "mail" (data) may be placed in specified locations. Generally, the first storage location in memory is given an address of 0; the second, an address of 1. This process continues up to the number of memory locations available. The amount of data that can be stored in one memory location varies. However, with most computers, each location is generally capable of holding one byte. For now, think of a **byte** as the amount of space required to store one character or one value. (You may learn more about a byte and how alphabetic and numeric data is stored in a computer in Appendix B, Internal Representation of Data.) For example, the word "COMPUTER" requires eight locations, one for each letter, while the value 25 can be stored in one memory location. Figure 3-1 shows how the word "COMPUTER" might look if stored in memory beginning at location 101, and how the value 25 might look if stored in memory location 977. The processor can look at the data stored in a memory location without actually removing the data. Whenever a new item of data is placed in a memory location, however, it replaces the data that was previously there.

Figure 3-1
Data is stored in memory locations.

Numeric Addresses

The number of memory locations in a computer system is generally stated in terms such as 128K or 640K. The K is short for **kilo**, which means 1000. However, due to the different numbering system used inside the computer, one K (or kilobyte) of memory is really 1,024 memory locations or bytes of memory. Therefore, 128K of memory is really 131,072 (128 times 1,024) bytes (memory locations), and 640K of memory is really 655,360 (640 times 1,024) bytes. Many older, less powerful microcomputers can only address up to 64K of memory; that is, they cannot physically refer to a memory address larger than 65,536 bytes. Many modern microprocessors can address up to and including one **megabyte** (one million bytes). More powerful microprocessors and larger computers can address many megabytes of memory.

It requires only a fraction of a second for the processor to place data in memory or to reference data already there. The processor simply "addresses" the desired memory location. The concept is similar to placing a number of persons in a room and asking one of them a question. Only the person to whom the question is addressed answers. For example, you may ask, "Sue Jones, how much money do you have?" Sue, and only

Sue, will answer the question. Remember that in the computer, however, each memory location is identified by a numeric address rather than by a name. This concept is further developed in Appendix B—Internal Representation of Data.

There are many kinds of memory chips, and new ones are constantly being developed. However, memory chips can generally be classified as having either volatile memory or nonvolatile memory. Most computers contain both volatile and nonvolatile memory.

Volatile Memory

Volatile means prone to evaporate. Characters stored in **volatile memory** "evaporate" when the computer is powered down (turned off). That is, the memory locations lose their data when the power is turned off. Volatile memory is generally known as **RAM** (random-access memory). It is called random access because the processor can jump directly from one location to another in random order as data is stored and retrieved. This is where data is stored while it is being processed.

Nonvolatile Memory

Nonvolatile memory does not lose its data when the power is turned off. Therefore, it is frequently used to store instructions necessary for getting the computer started when it is powered up (turned on). Nonvolatile memory is frequently referred to as **ROM**, or read-only memory. This term is appropriate since the computer can only read data from a ROM chip; it cannot write or store data on the chip. Most special-purpose computers have ROM chips which contain the instructions that permit the computer to perform the specific tasks for which it was designed. For example, a ROM chip in a special-purpose computer may enable the computer to control a traffic light, do word processing, play an arcade game, or monitor instrumentation.

This computer is used to create special effects for Lucasfilm's "Star Tours" ride at Disneyland.

PROCESSOR

All computers do processing by following the detailed instructions of a software program. The chip that receives and carries out these instructions, located in the CPU, is called the **processor**. All computer systems, regardless of size or make, have processors. The processor is involved in all four of the computer's basic functions. It interacts with program instructions and data stored in memory. It controls and initiates the actions of the entire computer system by its ability to follow program instructions, such as reading data from an input device (keyboard) and transferring data to an output device (display screen). It performs arithmetic computations. It makes logical comparisons, such as determining if two numbers are equal. Therefore, the processor may be defined as that part of a CPU that interacts with instructions and data stored in memory, controls the actions of the entire computer system, and performs arithmetic calculations and logical comparisons. The processor chip performs the control, arithmetic, and logic functions of the computer, and separate memory chips are used to store programs and data. Other chips exist to perform specialized tasks, such as communications, video, graphics, sound, and keyboard control.

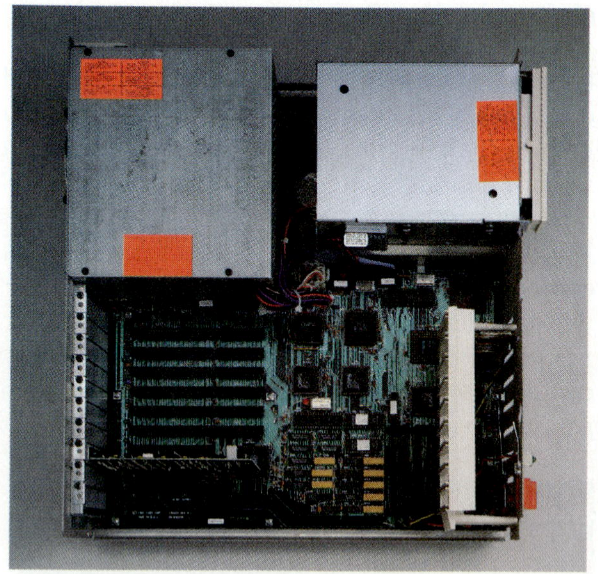

A computer can contain many different types of chips.

Control

The processor of a computer controls the computer's actions in a similar way that our brains control our actions. The processor chip, located in the CPU, receives instructions from a software program which is stored in memory. As each instruction enters the processor, it is interpreted. Once interpreted, the processor directs the computer's circuitry to perform the desired task. Only one instruction at a time is fed to the processor; however, thousands and even millions of instructions can be executed in just one second.

Because the processor can follow the instructions of a stored program, it can also direct and control all other computer components (i.e. the keyboard, display screen, printer). Therefore, in addition to processing activities, the processor controls all the input, output, and storage devices which are connected to the computer. It directs the transfer of data to and from these devices and maintains control over all activities of the entire computer system.

Arithmetic

A vast majority of computer applications requires arithmetic calculations. Numeric data, once read and stored in the computer's memory, often requires such arithmetic operations as addition, subtraction, multiplication, and division. Most computers can accurately perform thousands, and even millions, of these calculations in one second. Numeric data which requires arithmetic calculations is copied from memory into the processor chip where the actual calculations are performed. Once completed, the results of the calculations are stored back into memory for further calculations or future output.

Computers can perform arithmetic calculations very quickly and accurately.

To help you visualize how the computer performs arithmetic calculations, refer to Figure 3-2 and the following example. Suppose the computer must calculate a 6 percent sales tax on a $3.00 purchase and report the tax amount due. First, the processor would direct the computer circuitry to copy the contents of the memory locations containing the amount of the sale and the sales tax percentage to the arithmetic processor. Second, the processor would be directed to multiply the two numeric values to obtain the resultant product. Third, it would store the result in another memory location for future reference.

Memory (before arithmetic calculation)

Numeric Addresses

0	1	2	99	100	101	102	103	104	105	106	107	108	109	975	976	977	978
				T	A	X		=							3	.06	

Processor

Multiply what is in memory location 976 (3) times what is in memory location 977 (.06) and place the result (.18) in memory location 106

Memory (after arithmetic calculation)

Numeric Addresses

0	1	2	99	100	101	102	103	104	105	106	107	108	109	975	976	977	978
				T	A	X		=		.18					3	.06	

Placed here after calculation completed

Figure 3-2
Arithmetic calculations can be performed on data stored in memory.

After the tax amount has been calculated, the computer could be instructed to add the value in memory location 976 (3) to the value in memory location 106 (.18). The result of this calculation ($3.18) will be the total amount due from the customer for a $3.00 purchase with a 6 percent sales tax. Finally, the processor could direct the display and/or print devices to report all the information and calculations pertaining to this sales transaction.

Logical Comparisons

Like arithmetic operations, logical comparisons are performed on data located in memory. The computer's processor is given instructions from a program stored in its memory to compare the data stored in one memory location to the data stored in another memory location. Depending upon the result of the comparison, the processor will be directed to follow appropriate instructions. To help you visualize this concept, refer to Figure 3-3 and the following example. Suppose the software program had randomly chosen a number from 1 to 100 that you were to try to guess in as few attempts as possible. The processor would be programmed to compare the number you guessed (entered via the keyboard) to the number the program had randomly generated. If the number you guessed was less than the random number, a message telling you that your guess was too low would be generated and displayed on the display screen. If the number you guessed was greater than the random number, a message telling you that your guess was too high would be displayed. If the number you guessed was equal to the random number, a message telling you that you have guessed the correct number would be displayed.

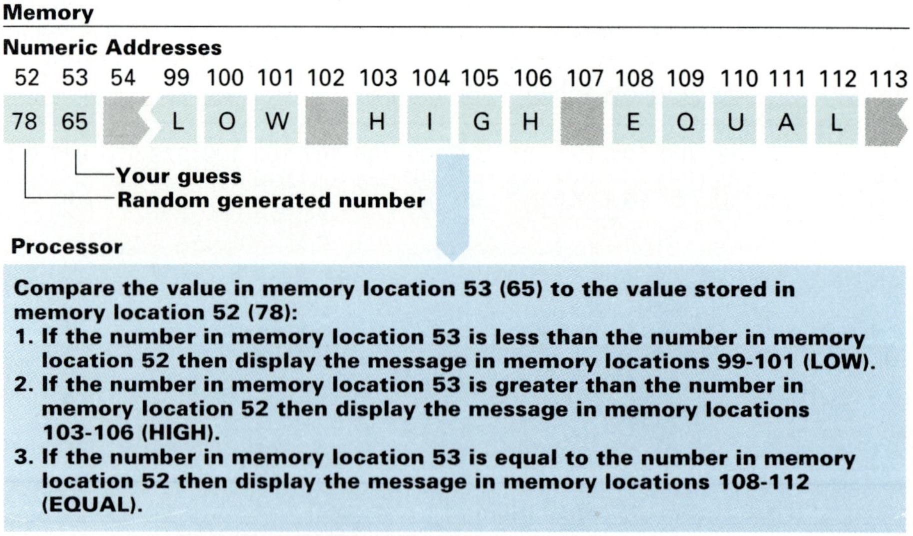

Figure 3-3
The processor can perform logical comparisons on data stored in memory.

Memory

Numeric Addresses

52	53	54	99	100	101	102	103	104	105	106	107	108	109	110	111	112	113
78	65		L	O	W		H	I	G	H		E	Q	U	A	L	

Your guess (53)
Random generated number (52)

Processor

Compare the value in memory location 53 (65) to the value stored in memory location 52 (78):
1. **If the number in memory location 53 is less than the number in memory location 52 then display the message in memory locations 99-101 (LOW).**
2. **If the number in memory location 53 is greater than the number in memory location 52 then display the message in memory locations 103-106 (HIGH).**
3. **If the number in memory location 53 is equal to the number in memory location 52 then display the message in memory locations 108-112 (EQUAL).**

Notice, in Figure 3-3, the number guessed (entered via the keyboard) was 65, and it was stored in memory location 53. The number randomly generated was 78, and it was stored in memory location 52. When the computer was instructed to compare the values found at these two memory locations, it found that the guess was too low. As a result, and based upon the result of the logical comparison, the computer was instructed to display the message LOW. It could then be instructed to permit another guess to be entered via the keyboard. This process could continue until the result of the logical comparison was equal (indicating the correct number was found) and the message EQUAL was displayed. Once the correct number was found, the computer could be instructed to stop or generate another random number to start a new series of guesses.

THE PROCESSING CYCLE

All processing functions of the processor are regulated by a clock that delivers regular impulses. The concept of how a computer clock works is somewhat similar to a bass drum in a band; the regular beat of the drum keeps the rest of the band following the proper tempo. Likewise, the computer's clock pulses keep the processor functioning in the proper tempo. Typical clock speeds for microprocessors are measured in megahertz. A **megahertz** is a million cycles, or pulses, per second. For example, a particular processor running at a clock speed of eight megahertz means that the computer can perform eight million tasks in a one second time span. However, since many processing operations require more than one clock cycle to be completed, fewer than eight million operations per second can be performed. Completing a simple arithmetic calculation, for example, may require several clock cycles. Generally speaking, the greater the computer's megahertz cycle time, the greater the number of tasks it can perform in any given time span. This also means that the faster the computer's cycle time, the faster it can complete the processing cycle of input, processing, and output.

Like the bass drum in a band, the computer clock keeps operations functioning at the proper speed.

As you have already learned, a computer's processing cycle is composed of input, processing, and output functions. Each of these functions is performed under the direction of the processor's control unit. To further visualize how the computer performs the processing cycle, refer to Figure 3-4 and the following processing steps:

Input:

1. Data and program instructions are read from an input device and stored in the CPU's memory, under the direction of the processor.

Processing:

2. The processor receives an instruction from the stored program and interprets it.
3. The processor directs the computer's circuitry to perform the desired, interpreted task(s).
4. Arithmetic and/or logical comparison operations are performed, and the results are stored in memory.

Output:

5. Steps 2, 3, and 4 are repeated until an output instruction is received by the processor directing it to transfer data from memory to an output device.

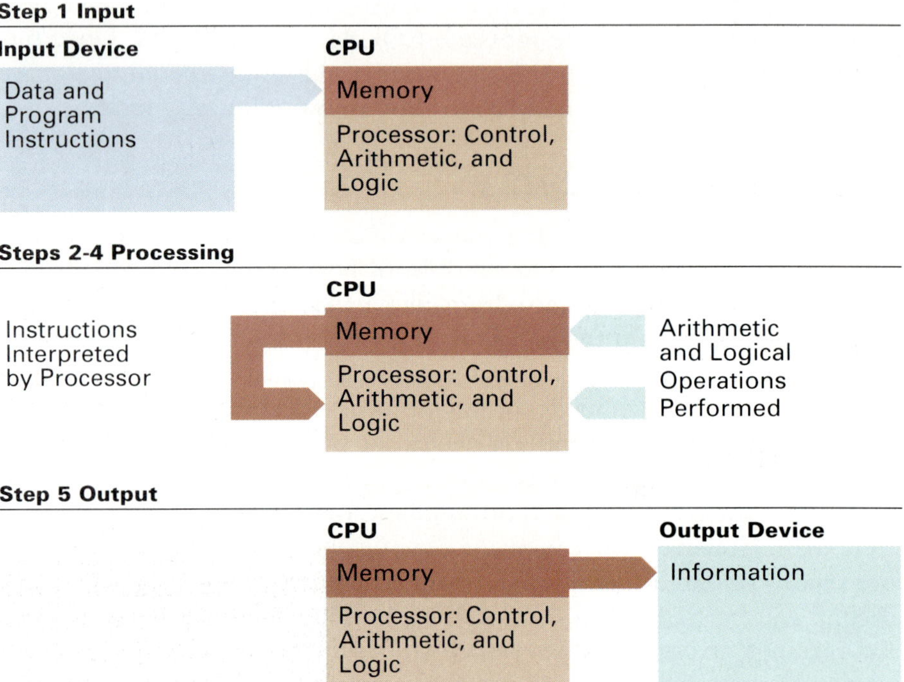

Figure 3-4
The processing cycle.

Additional instructions provided by the stored program could instruct the processor to repeat steps 1 through 5 until all data has been read from the input device, processed, and a report prepared. For example, if a computer were used to record the $3.00 sales transaction discussed earlier, each of the three basic processing steps of input, processing, and output would be performed. First, the input step would consist of inputting a description of the item purchased and the amount of the purchase into memory from an input device. Secondly, the processor would process the sales transaction data by calculating the sales tax and storing the results in memory as illustrated in Figure 3-2 on page 45. Thirdly, the information that was stored in memory, including the description of the item purchased, the cost of the item, the amount of sales tax, and the total due (cost plus sales tax), would be displayed and/or printed to an output device. Once the processing was completed for this $3.00 sales transaction, the processor could be instructed to accept another sales transaction. This processing cycle could be repeated for each item the customer purchased and for each customer who purchased goods throughout the sales day.

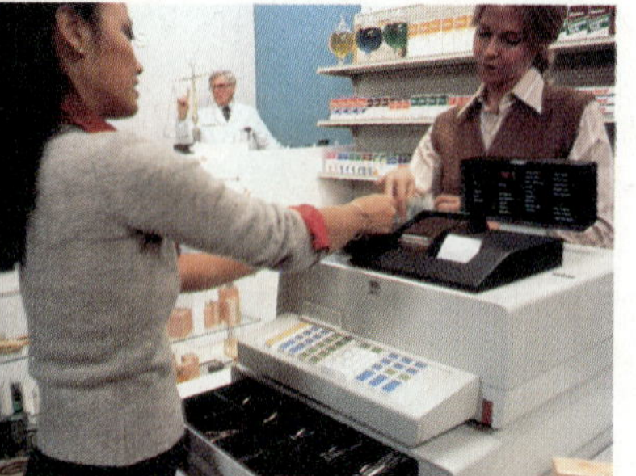

Computers can be used to calculate and record sales transactions.

PROCESSING FUNCTIONS

Each of the functions of input, processing, and output can be broken down into more specific tasks the computer is commonly asked to perform. These include collecting, coding/inputting, verifying, classifying, sorting, summarizing, decoding/reporting, and storing data and information.

Input Function

Input is the process of gathering data and entering it into the computer's memory. There are three specific tasks associated with the input process.

Collect Data

Raw data must be collected from appropriate sources. For example, if your report card were to be generated by a computer system, each course you completed along with the grade you earned would be collected. This data, collected from each teacher, would comprise the raw data required for the computer to generate your report card.

Brokers at this fish market use a computer system to process raw data as orders are received from supermarkets, restaurants, and fish stores.

Code/Input Data

Data which enters the computer system is coded into a language the computer can understand. After each alphabetic, numeric, and special character (i.e., A, B, 1, 2, *, $) is coded and stored in the computer's memory in a unit of measurement known as a byte, processing can be performed.

Verify Data

Data entering the computer's memory via an input device should be verified for accuracy prior to processing. For example, if your school uses an A, B, C, D, and F grading system, the computer can be programmed to check each grade entered to make sure it is equal to one of these valid grades. If not, the grade could be rejected and a message could be displayed indicating the detected error.

All raw data which pertains to a specific computer application must be collected from all originating sources; that is, from places and individuals who created the data. After it is collected, it must be entered into the computer system. When the input device reads the data, it codes each individual character and numeric value into a language the computer can understand as the data is transmitted to memory. Once the data is in the computer's memory, verification checks are performed to make sure it is as accurate as possible before processing takes place. There is an old saying in the computer industry, "Garbage in—Garbage out." This means that if inaccurate, unexpected data is entered into the computer system, unexpected results will be produced.

Processing Function

After the data has been collected, coded, and verified for accuracy, it is ready to be processed. Recall that the processor can control all actions of the computer, move data from one memory location to another, and perform logical and arithmetic operations. Because of these capabilities, the processor can perform three specific tasks.

Classify Data

The computer can group similar data items according to a pre-defined criterion. For example, each student may be classified by grade level: freshman, sophomore, junior, or senior. Or, as each student's report card is processed, the computer can calculate the student's average grade for all courses completed. All students with an "A" average can then be classified as belonging to the "A Honor Roll," and all students with a "B" average can be classified as belonging to the "B Honor Roll."

Sort Data

Data stored in the computer's memory can be rearranged into any pre-defined order. For example, all students who have been classified as "A" students can be arranged in alphabetical order by name within their appropriate grade level.

Summarize Data

Lengthy, detailed data can be summarized by the computer to produce more meaningful and useful information for the user. For example, the principal of a school might want to know the number of "A" and "B" students by each grade level. As the computer processes each report card, it can logically compare the calculated grade average to an "A" or "B." If equal, it would add a 1 to the "A" or "B" accumulator for the appropriate grade level. After repeating this processing cycle for each student, the desired, summarized information would be available for output.

Output Function

Output is the process of storing or reporting the processed information. There are two specific tasks associated with the output process.

Store Data

Data may be transferred from the computer's memory to various storage devices for future reference. These storage devices are commonly referred to as secondary storage. Therefore, any storage medium capable of storing computer data and information for future reference is known as a **secondary storage device.** Examples of secondary storage devices include diskettes, laser disks, and hard disk drives. Secondary storage devices will be discussed in detail in a later chapter.

Common storage devices include magnetic disks and laser disks.

Decode/Report Data

Recall, when data was input into the computer, it was coded into a language the computer could understand. Conversely, when data leaves the computer, it must be decoded from the computer's language back into the alphabetic, numeric, and special symbols you can understand. Once decoded, it can be displayed and/or printed into a meaningful report.

THE HUMAN ROLE

In this chapter you have seen how hardware and software work together to input data, process it, and output information. None of this, however, is possible without humans to build the hardware, program the computer, input the data, and use the information created.

In spite of advances in technology, humans are still the most important part of an information processing system.

A computer is nothing more than useless hardware without humans to program, operate, and use it. It is a harmless, non-threatening device that does only what humans tell (program) it to do. Humans make the choice to use its power to help or to harm themselves or others.

SUPERCONDUCTOR BREAKTHROUGHS

Superconductivity can be defined as the ability of some metals, such as lead or tin (or a combination of metals and other materials), to conduct electric current with no resistance. Superconductivity was discovered in 1911 by a Dutch physicist named Jeike Kamerlingh Onnes. He found that the common element mercury carried electricity with absolutely no resistance when cooled to approximately -460 degrees Fahrenheit (also known as absolute zero). Without resistance, electrons are not slowed down; thus, voltage is not decreased and harmful heat is not generated.

To keep a material capable of conducting electricity cooled to such an extremely low temperature required that it be immersed in liquid helium. For years this limitation rendered the application of superconductivity impractical. Recently, however, by combining ceramic materials with small amounts of elements known as *rare earths*, physicists have been able to create superconductors that function at much higher temperatures—as high as 9 degrees Fahrenheit. There is further evidence that superconductivity in a ceramic material may be possible at 90 degrees Fahrenheit. Such a breakthrough of allowing electric current to flow without resistance at higher temperatures opens up a vast array of new possibilities in the field of electronics. Superconductor technology possesses the potential of creating new products that could have a significant impact on our society and our lives.

As an example of the effect superconductivity can have, consider that today's electrical power plants must be located close to the customers who consume their electricity. With nonresistant superconductor transmission lines, these same power plants could send their electrical power over great distances without any loss of energy, thus minimizing the number of plants required and better utilizing the fuel and resources of existing plants.

Superconductivity makes objects appear to "fly."

Another potential use of superconductivity is in the area of *maglev* (magnetic levitation). Since superconducting material is capable of creating powerful magnetic fields with opposing polarity, it could lead to magnetically levitating transportation vehicles. Imagine a train capable of "flying" 6 to 12 inches above its tracks, being propelled by other magnetic fields. Without the friction caused by the contact of the wheel with the track, maglev trains could attain speeds in excess of 300 miles per hour.

Perhaps the most impressive application of superconductivity will be in the computer industry. With superconductor components to carry the electrical impulses, computers could operate literally hundreds of times faster than present day computers. Since superconductor materials do not generate heat, computers can be made much smaller. This is because it would no longer be necessary to provide space for ventilation or cooling fans, and electronic components could be packed more closely without fear of overheating or breaking down. Imagine a portable computer the size of a pocket calculator with more power than today's mainframe supercomputers! Computers could be made so small that even the most powerful devices would be small by today's standards.

Although superconductors are already being utilized in medical scanning devices and giant atom smashers, much work remains to be done before the new products can be realized. Major companies and universities in the United States and Japan are hard at work to create a more flexible superconductive material with a higher tolerance to warm temperatures and the ability to handle high voltages. Perhaps the next scientific breakthrough in superconductivity research will enable us to further benefit from this newly revisited technology.

CHAPTER SUMMARY

- Regardless of the kind of information being produced, or whether the system is manual or computerized, the same three processing steps of input, processing, and output are performed.
- Computers can perform only four basic functions. A computer can (1) store data and programs, (2) control its own actions by its ability to understand instructions it is provided, (3) do arithmetic calculations, and (4) perform logical comparisons.
- The CPU (central processing unit) can be defined as the hardware device that stores data and programs, executes program instructions, and performs arithmetic and logic operations. It is often referred to as the central brain of the computer system.
- Memory (also referred to as main storage or primary storage) is that part of the CPU where program instructions and data are stored.
- Memory is made up of electronic circuits that are contained on integrated circuit chips. Data and instructions are stored as electronic impulses in specified locations in memory and are identified by a numeric address.
- A byte is the amount of space required to store one character or one value.
- The number of memory locations (numeric addresses) in a computer system is generally stated in kilos, where one kilobyte is equal to 1,024 bytes of memory. Many microprocessors and most large computers can address one to many megabytes of memory (one megabyte equals one million bytes).
- Memory chips can be classified as being either volatile or nonvolatile.

- ♦ Volatile memory, generally known as RAM (random-access memory), is where data and programs are stored while they are being processed. Memory locations in RAM lose their data when the power is turned off.
- ♦ Nonvolatile memory is frequently referred to as ROM, or read-only memory. As the term implies, the computer can only read data from a ROM chip; it cannot write or store data on the chip. ROM memory does not lose its data when the power is turned off.
- ♦ A processor is that part of a CPU that interacts with instructions and data stored in memory, controls the actions of the entire computer system, and performs arithmetic calculations and logical comparisons.
- ♦ The processor, located inside the CPU, receives instructions from a software program which is stored in memory. As each instruction enters the processor, it is interpreted. Once interpreted, the processor directs the computer's circuitry to perform the desired task. In addition, the processor initiates and directs all the actions of the entire computer system.
- ♦ Numeric data which requires arithmetic calculation is copied from memory into the processor chip where the actual calculations are performed. Once completed, the results of the calculations are stored back into memory for further calculation or future output.
- ♦ Logical comparisons are performed on data located in memory. The computer's processor is given instructions from a program stored in its memory to compare the data stored in one memory location to data stored in another memory location. Depending upon the result of the comparison, the computer will be directed to perform appropriate instructions.
- ♦ All processing functions of the processor are regulated by a clock that delivers regular impulses. These impulses are measured in megahertz (one megahertz equals 1 million cycles).
- ♦ The processing cycle of a computer includes the following steps:

    1. Data and program instructions are read from an input device and stored in the computer's memory under the direction of the processor.
    2. The processor receives an instruction from the stored program and interprets it.
    3. The processor directs the computer's circuitry to perform the desired task.
    4. Arithmetic and/or logical comparison operations are performed, and the results are stored in memory.
    5. Steps 2, 3, and 4 are repeated until an output instruction is received by the processor directing it to transfer data from memory to an output device.

- ♦ Input processing functions are made up of three specific tasks: (1) collecting data, (2) coding/inputting data, and (3) verifying data.

- Processing functions are made up of three specific tasks: (1) classifying data, (2) sorting data, and (3) summarizing data.
- Output processing functions are made up of the two tasks of storing and decoding/reporting of data and information.
- A computer system is useless without humans to build its component parts, program it, input the data, and use the information created.

KEY TERMS

The following key terms were introduced or redefined in this chapter:

byte
CPU (central processing unit)
kilo
main storage
megabyte
megahertz
memory
nonvolatile memory
numeric address
primary storage
processor
RAM (random-access memory)
ROM (read-only memory)
secondary storage device
volatile memory

REVIEW QUESTIONS

1. Identify the four basic functions a computer can perform. (Obj. 1)
2. Define CPU and identify the tasks that it can perform. (Obj. 2)
3. What are two other common terms for memory? (Obj. 3)
4. How is a numeric address used by the computer to identify memory locations? (Obj. 3)
5. What is a byte? (Obj. 3)
6. How many bytes of memory does a 256K computer system contain? (Obj. 3)
7. How many bytes of memory does a 5 megabyte computer system contain? (Obj. 3)
8. Describe the difference between volatile (RAM) memory and nonvolatile (ROM) memory. (Obj. 4)
9. Define processor and identify the tasks that are performed by the processor chip. (Obj. 5)
10. Describe how the processor, located in the CPU, directs the computer's actions. (Obj. 6)
11. Describe how the processor performs arithmetic calculations. (Obj. 7)
12. Describe how the processor performs logical comparisons. (Obj. 8)
13. How many clock cycles per second are performed by a computer system running at 10 megahertz? (Obj. 9)
14. Identify the five steps associated with the processing cycle of input, processing, and output. (Obj. 9)
15. What are the three specific tasks associated with the input process of the processing cycle? (Obj. 10)

16. What are the three specific tasks associated with the processing process? (Obj. 10)
17. What are the two specific tasks associated with the output process of the processing cycle? (Obj. 10)
18. In your own words, explain why a computer is nothing more than useless hardware without humans to program and operate it. (Obj. 11)

CHALLENGE ACTIVITIES

1. Research information about a computer's processor, memory capacities, and internal clock cycle speeds. Write a brief report identifying your chosen computer and the information you found. Include any information you may have found regarding sample speeds (i.e. number of arithmetic calculations performed in one second). (Objs. 2,3,4,5,9)
2. Identify an application for which you or your school could use a computer. Describe how the data would be collected for input and verified for accuracy. (Obj. 10)
3. Using the same application chosen in Number 2 above, describe how the data would be classified, sorted, and/or summarized during processing to obtain the desired output. (Obj. 10)
4. Again, using the same application as Numbers 2 and 3 above, identify and describe what information is to be communicated (reported) to the user of your system. (Obj. 10)

CHAPTER 4

INPUT — PUTTING DATA INTO THE COMPUTER

LEARNING OBJECTIVES

After studying this chapter, you will be able to:

1. **Identify sources of raw data and explain how input devices are used to put data into the computer.**
2. **Identify and explain the usage of several of the more common input devices.**
3. **Identify several special-purpose input devices.**
4. **Define terminals and describe the difference between local and remote terminals.**

INTRODUCTION

Input devices are used to enter software instructions (programs) and data into a computer's memory. After a computer program has been entered into the computer's memory and it begins to execute, it can direct the processor to read data from any input device which is connected to the computer. The specific input device and the manner in which the data is entered into the computer's memory is controlled entirely by instructions provided by a computer program. In this chapter, you will learn more about data and the types of input devices used to enter it into the computer.

WHAT IS DATA?

You learned in Chapter 2 that data consists of facts in the form of numbers, alphabetic characters, special symbols, or words. Computers are used as tools to process or manipulate data into information which humans can use to obtain new knowledge. The data which is fed into a computer for processing is commonly referred to as raw data or original data. This is because this type of data is of no value by itself; however, when combined with other data, it creates useful information. Raw data that is input into a computer system comes from two sources: it is input directly into the computer as it is originated, or it is first recorded on a form and then fed into the computer at a later time.

Raw data that is input directly into the computer at the time it originates is often entered via the keyboard, read by a scanning device, or input by sound (i.e. human voice, telephone). For example, many law enforcement officers have keyboards and display screens in their cars for immediate access to information stored in a mainframe computer. When they need to check a car to see if it has been stolen, the license number can be keyed directly into the computer. Once the number has been keyed, the mainframe computer searches its files of vehicle license plate numbers until it finds a matching number. It then displays information regarding the known status of the vehicle in question on the officer's display screen.

Another example of raw data that is input directly into the computer is a sale of merchandise. Many retail stores use devices which can scan a sales tag and input the data regarding the type of merchandise sold, sales price, etc., directly into a computer at the time of the sale. The use of a push button telephone is another common example of directly inputting raw data into the computer. Many telephone carriers permit their customers to make long distance calls from anywhere in the country by keying-in their authorization codes using the telephone's push buttons. Each press of a key creates a pitched tone which the computer recognizes as the customer's authorization code. It then checks its file to make sure the code is valid before it permits the caller to place the call.

This waitress can input a credit card number to be checked by a central credit verification system.

A handwritten form containing raw data that is to be input into a computer is called a source document. It is called a source document because it is prepared by individuals who originate, or create, the raw data it contains. For example, many large companies have individuals who are employees in what is called a payroll department. It is their job to make sure that each of the company's employees receives his/her payroll check accurately and on time. They prepare a payroll input form containing the employee name and number, hours worked, overtime hours, etc., for each employee to be paid each pay period. The information contained on this form is keyed into the computer. The computer then prepares the necessary company payroll reports and employee paychecks for the payroll period. Source documents come from many different sources for many different computer applications.

Source documents contain raw data to be entered into the computer.

TYPES OF DATA INPUT DEVICES

Input devices come in many sizes and shapes, operate at different speeds, and have different capacities and capabilities. Many computers have more than one input device attached to facilitate various types of processing which must be performed. In many instances, the task that must be accomplished determines which input device is best to use. In other instances, input devices have been specially designed and developed to facilitate specific types of input and processing. In this section, we will discuss several of the more commonly used input devices.

Keyboard

The computer **keyboard** is the most popular and common way of inputting data into the computer. The keyboard of a computer is similar to that of a typewriter. When a key is pressed, the corresponding alphabetic, numeric, or special symbol is converted into a code and electronically sent to the computer's memory. Once the desired character is stored in memory, it becomes accessible for processing by the stored program.

There are a few keys which are unique to a computer and which, when pressed, direct the computer to perform specific tasks. Figure 4-1 shows a typical computer keyboard divided into four sections: (1) function keys, (2) typewriter keyboard, (3) numeric pad, and (4) directional keys. The arrangement of these keys and the tasks they perform vary from keyboard to keyboard.

Figure 4-1
Computer keyboards are often divided into four sections: numeric keys, typewriter keys, special function keys, and directional keys.

The keys labeled as **Function Keys** are designed to work in conjunction with the instructions in a stored program. A program can be written which will detect when a designated function key is pressed and will instruct the computer to then perform a specific task. For example, a program which instructs the computer to perform word processing activities could be written in such a way that when the F1 (Function 1) key is pressed, all text which is keyed from that point will be in bold print. When the F1 key is pressed again, the program will instruct the computer to return to normal print.

The **Typewriter Keyboard** section is very similar to the key arrangement of a typewriter. The ***Caps Lock*** key is used to lock the keyboard in either upper or lower case. When the Caps Lock key is on, upper case alphabetic characters and numbers may be keyed. When the Caps Lock key is off, lower case alphabetic characters and numbers can be keyed. The ***Shift*** key (there are two shift keys but only one needs to be pressed at any one time) must be pressed in conjunction with the special symbols denoted on the upper half of several keys regardless of the status of the Caps Lock key. The key labeled ***Enter*** (on some computers this key is labeled ***Return***) is commonly used to tell the computer to accept data as it appears on the display screen for processing or storage. Other keys, such as the ***Esc, Ctrl, PrtSc, Alt, Num Lock, Home, PgUp, End, PgDn, Del,*** etc., are active only if the program running in the computer at any given time is designed and written to utilize them. (Note that not all of these keys are available on all keyboards.)

The section of the keyboard labeled **Numeric Pad** is commonly used to key numeric data into the computer quickly. This is because the arrangement of the numeric keys is the same as that on a standard calculator keyboard. The section of the keyboard labeled **Directional Keys** enables the user to work with various areas on the display screen. Each arrow points in the direction which will be taken by the **cursor** each time the corresponding key is struck. The cursor serves as a marker and is often depicted as a flashing square (■) symbol.

One specialized type of keyboard is called a touch sensitive, keyless, or **membrane keyboard**. It is covered with a seamless material to protect it. The membrane keyboard is designed to withstand a hazardous environment. For example, it is most effective in locations where liquid may be splashed on it or where workers who operate it have grease on their hands.

When different areas (called buttons or blisters) representing keys of the membrane are pressed, the characters represented are transmitted to the computer in the same way as they are with a standard keyboard. Another difference between a membrane keyboard and a standard keyboard is that a membrane keyboard requires more pressure to execute each keystroke. Therefore, it is better suited for situations where simple, low-volume inputting is required.

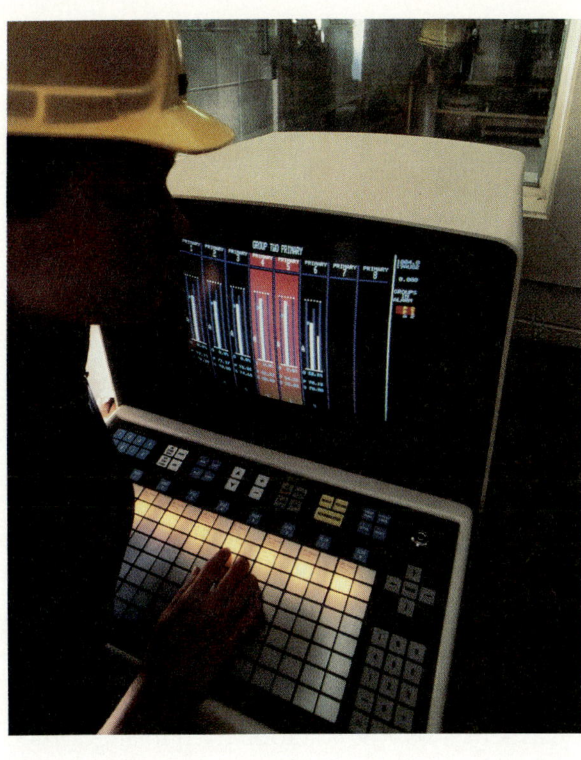

Membrane keyboards are often found in manufacturing environments.

Joystick

A **joystick** (also referred to as a controller) is an input device which sends coordinates of an x and y direction to the computer. That is, it sends the computer a set of numbers; one representing a horizontal location and the other a vertical location. The computer, in turn, uses these coordinates (sets of numbers) to determine a specific location.

The joystick consists of a plastic or metal rod mounted on a base. The rod (joystick) can be moved in any direction. As the rod is moved, an x (horizontal) direction and a y (vertical) direction can be input as data to a program that is stored and executed in memory. The result of this data may then be acted upon by the computer. For example, x and y directions may correspond to locations on the display screen. This location is denoted on the display screen by the cursor. As the joystick is used to move the cursor around the screen, a line can be drawn, enabling the computer to draw a graphic illustration or picture. Most joysticks also have one or more simple switches which can input data in a simple "on" or "off" response which the computer can be programmed to detect. For example, depressing a switch while the cursor is located within a box marked "clear screen" will direct the computer program to erase all the data which appears on the display screen.

A joystick can be used to move the cursor around the screen and is frequently used with games.

Joysticks are most commonly used for playing games. You may have already used a joystick to play some of the many popular arcade games.

Mouse

Like the joystick, the **mouse** is a pointing device used with a video display screen. Like its living counterpart, a computer mouse has a body and a tail. The tail is a wire connecting the body to the computer. The body of the mouse is palm-sized, has a ball for a stomach, and contains one or more push buttons. As the body of the mouse is moved over a hard, flat surface on its stomach, the ball rotates. The movement of this ball corresponds to the movement of the cursor on the display screen. When the mouse is moved forward, the cursor moves up; when the mouse is moved left, the cursor moves left; when it is moved right, the cursor moves right; and so on. Once the cursor has been positioned in the desired location, pressing a button on the mouse causes an action to be taken. The type of action depends on the computer program in use at the time. For example, suppose the computer is being used as an electronic-mail system. The cursor is moved to an image of an in-basket on the screen. When the button on the mouse is pressed, the waiting mail, such as letters for the day, is presented on the screen. The mouse is also frequently used to complement the keyboard and as a pointing device to make selections from several options available.

A device known as a **trackball** is designed to perform the same functions as a mouse. A trackball can be thought of as a stationary mouse (or a mouse on its back). It consists of a ball in a stationary housing. Some trackballs are designed as extensions of standard keyboards. Instead of moving the mouse around a desk, the user simply moves the trackball in the desired direction.

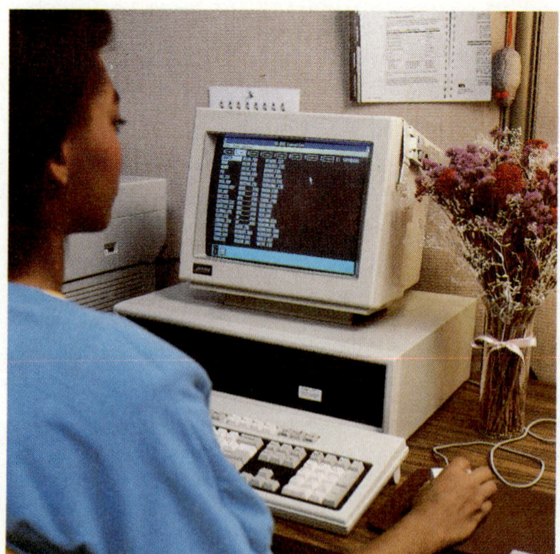

A mouse is often used as a pointing device. A trackball can be thought of as a stationary mouse.

Bar-Code Scanner

A **bar-code scanner** can read bars (lines) printed on a product. These bars, which represent data, are generally printed in a code known as the **Universal Product Code** (UPC). The code is printed on the product by the manufacturer and is made up of a series of vertical bars of varying widths that reflect a laser beam from a scanner. The bars are a coded form of numbers, as shown in Figure 4-2. The first five digits at the bottom represent the manufacturer or processor of the item. The second five digits identify that particular product. Note that the bar-code scanner does not read the actual digits; it reads the coded bar representation of the digits. The bars and scanners are designed in such a way that the codes can be read from almost any direction or angle.

Figure 4-2
The Universal Product Code that is printed on the labels of many retail items is read by a bar code scanner, a common input device.

Retail stores (especially grocery stores) use bar-code scanners to automate the check-out process. Bar-code scanners transmit the product identification characters directly to a computer. The computer then locates the correct price and description from data which it has previously stored. The customer gets a sales slip listing the names of the items purchased, and the items are automatically deducted from the store's inventory. Time is saved and errors are reduced because price tags do not have to be prepared and attached to each item, and cashiers do not need to key in prices.

Bar-code scanners are also used in industries other than the retail business. For example, the United States Postal Service places bar codes on certain letters for automatic routing of mail, and libraries use bar codes to identify publications.

Light Pen

A **light pen** is one of several types of input devices that may be used to point out locations on a display screen. For example, if a screen displays four options from which to choose, the user might be requested to press the light pen on the marker in front of the desired item. The tip of the light pen contains a phototransistor (a light sensing device) that sends the computer an x,y value of the pen location on the screen. The computer then calculates the position of the light pen and compares this location to where the items are displayed on the screen to determine which of the four items is chosen. Various actions can be performed with

Light pens can be used to point out locations on a display screen.

light pens, depending on the computer program with which they are used. For example, the operator may point to screen selections, draw shapes, move images from one part of the screen to another, and so on.

Graphics Tablet

A **graphics tablet** is a flat drawing surface, connected to the computer, upon which the user can draw graphic figures. A graphics tablet lets the user make new drawings, sketch freehand, or trace existing drawings while making corrections on the display screen with a light pen. The drawing or tracing is input into the computer's memory and can be programmed to appear on the display screen.

Depending on the model of graphics tablet used, drawing can be done with an ordinary pen, a special stylus pen, a cursor, or even a finger. A pen is often used so that the ink dispensed will show the graphics drawn on the tablet itself. A stylus pen is shaped like an ordinary pen but has a blunt tip. It is used to trace existing drawings or as a pointing device. A cursor is shaped like a mouse. Unlike a mouse, however, it contains a transmitting/pointing device (called a cross-hair pointing device). When the cursor is moved over an existing drawing, its position, as denoted by the intersection of two fine lines (cross hairs), is sent to the computer. Also, the cursor has several function keys (similar to the function keys on a keyboard) which may be utilized by the application software.

A graphics tablet makes it easy to input graphic figures.

Most graphics tablets are small enough to fit on a desktop, while some are as large as a drafting table. The capabilities of a graphics tablet and the accompanying computer software often determine how it will be utilized. For example, some graphics tablets are designed for educational use by young children, while others are more sophisticated and are used for engineering, architectural, and other professional applications.

Touch Display Screen

The **touch screen** is a display screen that allows users to use the most natural pointing devices of all—fingers. It is perhaps the simplest and easiest to operate of all input devices. When the screen is touched, it converts the area of the screen touched into an x,y coordinate and sends this data to the computer's memory. Once the x,y location is in memory, a software program can determine what action or task is to be performed. Thus, touching the screen has the same result as pressing a function key on the keyboard, making a selection with a light pen, or moving and clicking a joystick or mouse.

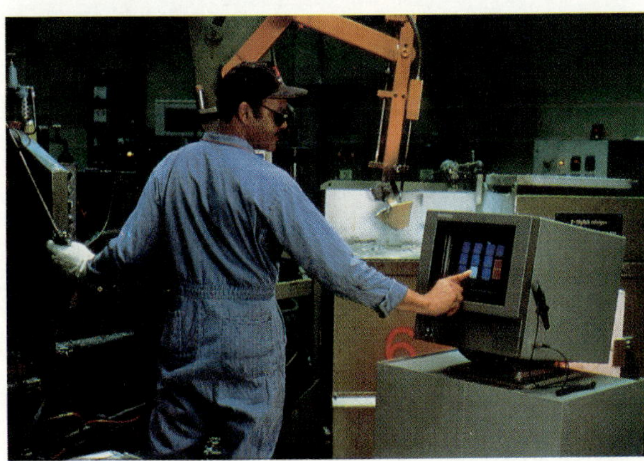

Touch screens are convenient input devices in factory settings.

Touch screens are used most often in shopping centers or similar display areas for providing information. They are also commonly used in bank teller machines, for placing orders in self-service discount stores, for business and industrial training, for educational applications, and for flight simulation.

Speech Recognition Device

For many applications, the ability to instruct a computer by voice command is valuable. This can be done through the use of a **speech recognition device** . For example, a laboratory technician may verbally give test results to the computer. By doing so, the technician bypasses the steps of writing the results on paper, converting them to computer codes, and then keying them into the computer. This enables the user to save time, and it reduces the number of errors made. In addition, both of the user's hands are left free to work.

A computer technician may speak over the phone to a computer in the parts warehouse to determine the availability of a part. You may command your voice-controlled telephone to make a call for you. Handicapped persons can command wheelchairs or robot arms through the spoken word.

Speech recognition devices can be used to provide visual feedback of sound. This can assist the hearing-impaired in learning speech.

As valuable as these applications are, the ideal speech recognition device would be one that could recognize free-form speech; that is, ordinary conversational speech. Most present systems, as impressive as some of their performances may be, can recognize only a few hundred words. They must be "trained" to recognize one or, at most, a few different voices. There is so much variation in speech from one person to another that it is very difficult for a computer to accurately recognize words. Humans use thousands of different words in everyday speech. Many words sound similar, and the meanings of many words vary depending on the sentences in which they are used. In order for the large-scale use of computer voice recognition to become possible, a system that can accurately recognize all those words in different situations must be developed. Research in advanced voice recognition is under way in many laboratories, but experts in the field think it will be a while before large-scale speech recognition becomes feasible.

Optical Character Reader

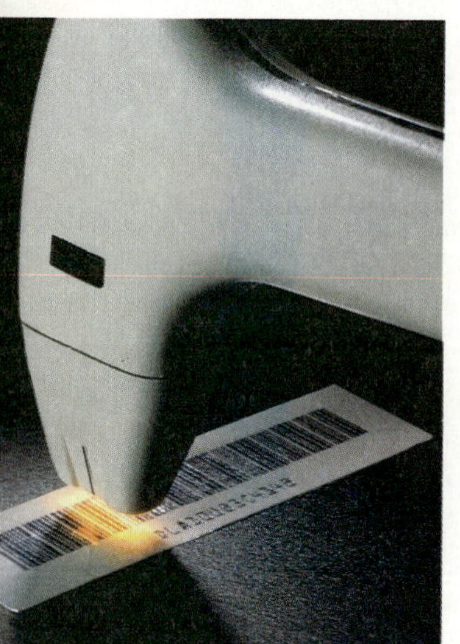

Optical scanners can be used to read bar codes and other print materials.

An **optical character reader** (OCR) is one type of scanner, or input device. It works like the reading method that humans use. When light is placed on a printed form, the human reader scans the form. Images of the letters, numbers, or marks are reflected to the eye. The images are transformed into nerve impulses and sent to the brain. The brain has been programmed through learning and experience to recognize the images. In a similar fashion, a character reader can read numbers, letters of the alphabet, and symbols directly from a typed, printed, or handwritten page.

Electronic elements placed in a matrix (row and column arrangement) inside the device react to light reflected from the page. The pattern of a letter falls on the matrix (as it would on a human retina), thereby generating electronic impulses. The impulses being received are mathematically compared to stored records of what the impulses from various characters should look like. When a character is identified, its code is transmitted to the processor.

An optical character reader reads only one character at a time from one location, or position, as it scans a document. Each of these positions may contain a digit, letter, or special symbol and is referred to as a marking position. It is therefore very suitable for handling large quantities of data or wide variations of responses. Figure 4-3 shows a piecework ticket for a payroll and also an invoice. These forms are used for recording optical characters in pencil.

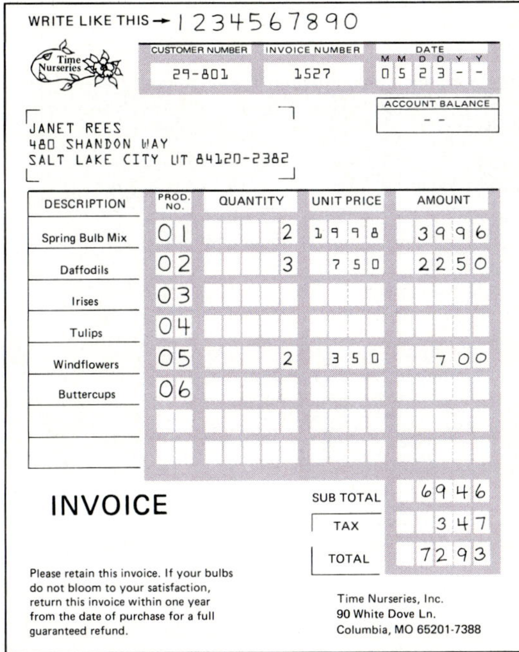

WRITE LIKE THIS → 1234567890

Time Nurseries

CUSTOMER NUMBER	INVOICE NUMBER	DATE MM DD YY
29-801	1527	05 23 - -

ACCOUNT BALANCE - -

JANET REES
480 SHANDON WAY
SALT LAKE CITY UT 84120-2382

DESCRIPTION	PROD. NO.	QUANTITY	UNIT PRICE	AMOUNT
Spring Bulb Mix	01	2	1998	3996
Daffodils	02	3	750	2250
Irises	03			
Tulips	04			
Windflowers	05	2	350	700
Buttercups	06			

INVOICE

SUB TOTAL	6946
TAX	347
TOTAL	7293

Please retain this invoice. If your bulbs do not bloom to your satisfaction, return this invoice within one year from the date of purchase for a full guaranteed refund.

Time Nurseries, Inc.
90 White Dove Ln.
Columbia, MO 65201-7388

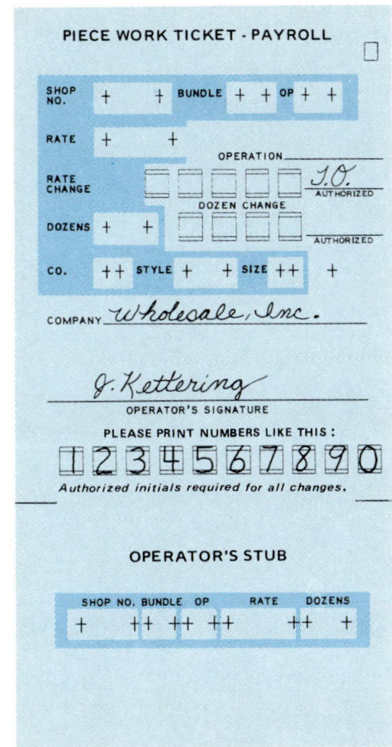

PIECE WORK TICKET - PAYROLL

SHOP NO. + + BUNDLE + + OP + +

RATE + +

OPERATION

RATE CHANGE J.O. AUTHORIZED

DOZEN CHANGE

DOZENS + + AUTHORIZED

CO. ++ STYLE + + SIZE ++ +

COMPANY Wholesale, Inc.

J. Kettering
OPERATOR'S SIGNATURE

PLEASE PRINT NUMBERS LIKE THIS:
1234567890

Authorized initials required for all changes.

OPERATOR'S STUB

SHOP NO. BUNDLE OP RATE DOZENS

Figure 4-3
Various forms are used for recording optical characters in pencil.

Note that the directions show the worker the proper way to print numbers so that the computer will accept them. The numbers scanned must be a close match to the model characters stored by the scanner, otherwise reading errors will occur. Note that only the specially printed characters on the ticket are intended for reading by a scanner. There is far too much variation in normal handwriting to allow present scanners to read it with an acceptable degree of accuracy.

The use of OCR forms makes it possible to have on-the-spot data recording at a low cost. For example, a worker can record the amount of time it takes to complete a job, a customer's purchases, and so on. The only equipment needed for this kind of recording is a pencil and an OCR form.

Some optical character readers read only data recorded in special styles of type and printing, such as those shown in Figure 4-4. However, many readers can accept almost any type style. Regardless of the needs of a business, there is probably a scanner on the market to meet those needs.

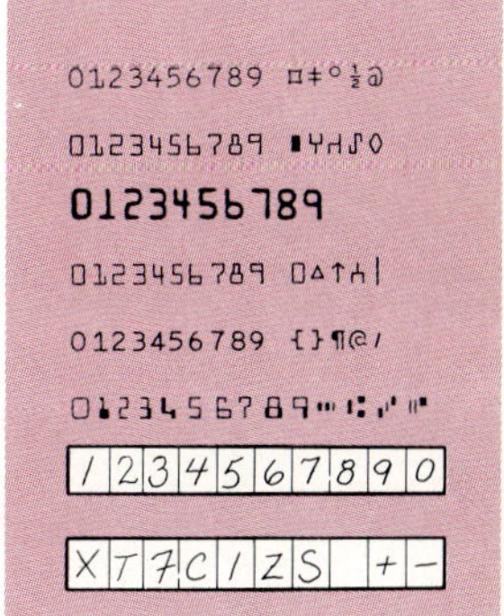

Figure 4-4
Special type styles are designed for optical character recognition.

OCR equipment is frequently used in department stores to read the price ticket on an item. Usually the scanner reads a stock number rather than the price; the computer to which the scanner is attached then looks up the stock number in a price table to determine the amount to charge for the item. This ensures that customers receive the sale prices on items that are specially priced. This type of system also makes it easy to change the prices when necessary.

The OCR has also become an important tool in the business office. Text that has been created on one typewriter or printer can very easily be input into another system through use of a character reader. This use of character readers will become less necessary, however, as more and more office equipment is linked together electronically.

Optical character readers can be used to input text directly from a printed page.

Optical Mark Reader

The **optical mark reader** is a scanner that senses the presence or absence of marks made by regular pencil or pen on specially designed forms. This is the simplest form of optical reader since it does not require the "intelligence" of a character reader.

Optical mark readers are often used to grade standardized tests.

The form is pre-defined into a matrix of marking positions. All the mark reader has to do is determine whether or not there is a mark (usually a rectangle or circle) at each of the positions. It is up to a computer program to determine what the presence or absence of a mark at a particular location means. Optical mark recognition is frequently used for test scoring, data collection, inventory control, and other applications where the number of different responses and volume of data are somewhat limited. The range of possible responses must be limited because each possible response must have a designated marking spot on the medium. Figure 4-5 shows one input medium that may be used. Note that the locations for recording each kind of data are pre-defined on the form.

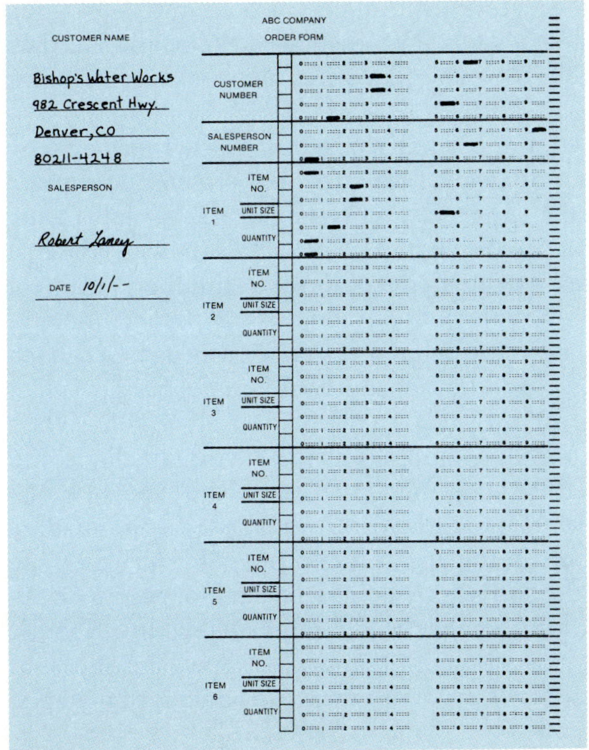

Figure 4-5
Optical mark readers use forms with pre-defined marking locations.

Magnetic Ink Character Recognition Reader

Banks in the United States use **magnetic ink character recognition** (MICR) for much of their data input. An MICR reader is an input device that is used to process data printed in magnetic ink with specially designed numbers and symbols. For example, a check may be written by one person to pay another for merchandise purchased. This check may be cashed in a bank other than the bank from which the check was written. Eventually the check must be returned to the bank of the person who originated the check so that the amount shown on the check can be deducted from the appropriate account. Then, at the end of the month, the check (along with all other checks written during the month) is returned to the customer along with a statement reflecting all checking activity during the period.

A bank must keep accurate records of deposits and withdrawals for each of its customers. It must also assist in keeping balances straight between banks. The extremely large volume of data required for this much record keeping requires a non-manual method of data input such as MICR. Without a data input system such as MICR, it would be extremely difficult for banks to process the many millions of checks written daily.

In MICR, checks and deposit slips have essential data printed on them in magnetic ink. The numbers and special symbols (there are no alphabet letters) appear in an unusual-looking style. This style gives each character a different magnetic area, creating differing electronic impulses when the documents go through a reader. The reader can transmit the data directly to a computer system for immediate processing or store it on disk or tape for later processing.

Note that the check in Figure 4-6 has characters printed in magnetic ink at the bottom in several different fields. (A field is a space or group of spaces needed to record a single fact.) Starting at the far left of the check is data to identify the bank on which the check is drawn. The first four numbers, 1232, represent the Federal Reserve number; the next four, 0523, are the unique identification numbers of the particular bank. The 2 in this field is known as a check digit; that is, it is used to check the accuracy of the reading of the other digits. The check digit is calculated from the preceding digits by using a mathematical formula. When the number is read, the formula is applied to the first eight digits and the result is compared to the check digit printed on the check. If the two digits are not the same, it means an error was made in the reading of the number. The numbers in the account number field, 6854509, are used by the bank to help it identify its individual customer accounts. All these numbers are printed on the checks and deposit slips in magnetic ink before they are issued to the account holder. The special symbols at the beginning and end of the two sets of numbers are punctuation marks.

Figure 4-6
Magnetic ink characters are used on checks.

Just as a capital letter is used at the beginning of a sentence and a period at the end, these symbols alert the MICR reader to the beginning and end of a group of numbers.

The figures in the amount field represent the amount for which the check is written, 200.00. These figures are imprinted in magnetic ink in the bottom right corner of the check. They are imprinted by the receiving bank after the check has been written, delivered to the person or business to whom it was written, and cashed or deposited in the bank. Deposit slips use magnetically encoded numbers in a similar fashion. In addition to entering data into the banks' computer systems, the MICR numbers are used to control machines that sort checks for return to the correct bank and depositor.

Magnetic Scanner

A **magnetic scanner** operates on the same principle as a tape recorder. The tape it reads, however, is usually only a few inches long. Some retail stores use price tags on which short strips of magnetic tape contain the stock numbers of the products. Strips of magnetic tape placed on security badges can contain information used to identify authorized individuals or codes used to unlock doors and vaults. The largest use of magnetic scanners, however, is to read encoded information on the back of credit cards and 24-hour teller machine cards used by banks. For the latter, a magnetic strip on the back of each depositor's identification card contains the person's account number and other information. When the card is inserted into the teller machine, the magnetic scanner reads the tape on the back of the card and transmits the depositor's account number to the processor.

The magnetic strip on the back of this bank card identifies the account number of the customer, who can then use the card in an automated teller machine to conduct financial transactions.

Real-Time Sensor

Real-time sensors are one of the most innovative and intriguing developments in computer input. Real time means "while it is happening." Therefore, a real-time sensor is like a sentry. It constantly monitors a process or event and transmits its findings to the processor without the need of human assistance. There are many applications for real-time sensors, but just a few will be discussed here. The computer that controls the ignition and fuel systems in your car uses several real-time sensors for input. Sensors are constantly measuring such things as engine speed, vehicle speed, and the level of carbon monoxide in the exhaust. This data is constantly input into the computer. After processing the information, the computer produces output in the form of commands to the ignition and fuel systems. These commands will keep efficiency as high as possible while, at the same time, keeping air pollution produced by the engine within an acceptable range.

Several of the major railway carriers have installed identification tags on each of their box cars. At strategic locations throughout the railway network, real-time sensors have been installed to read these identification tags on passing box cars. This information is transmitted to a mainframe computer that updates each box car's location as it passes the sensors. The resultant information helps account for the location of hundreds of box cars and has enabled the railway carriers to utilize them more efficiently.

In a control room in a large hotel, sensors are constantly measuring important variables such as temperatures. The computer checks to see if temperatures are within the normal ranges. If not, the computer can take corrective action by making adjustments to the equipment or by alerting a human operator to make adjustments.

A computer system is used to control the climate in this office building.

When a computer-controlled burglar alarm is activated, several real-time sensors will actively monitor the area and feed the computer information as to whether or not an intruder is present. Energy costs in large buildings can also be cut dramatically by computer systems equipped with real-time sensors. The sensors constantly transmit data to the computer telling it how much electricity is being used, which appliances are in operation, what the temperature is, and other information. The computer is then able to control the appliances to achieve the desired level of comfort and operation, while at the same time keeping peak usage of electricity as low as possible. Real-time sensors are also used in fire alarms and in the control of transport vehicles, such as airplanes and rapid-transit cars.

One of the most interesting developments in real-time sensors is the creation of robots with senses of vision and touch. A robot can input what it "sees" to the computer that is controlling its operation. This development makes it possible to use robots in applications not previously possible.

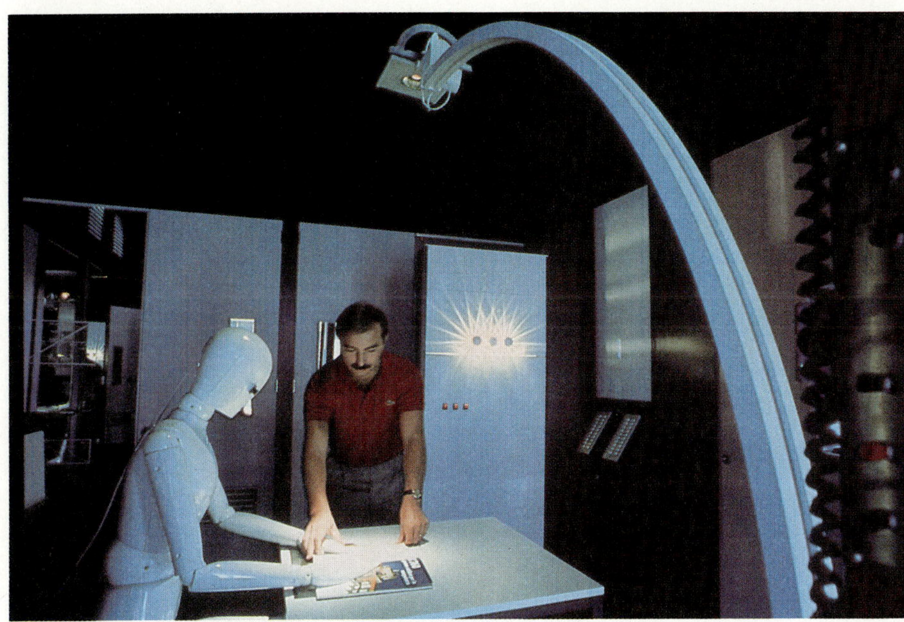

Robots equipped with touch and sight senses can input data into the computer.

Digitizer

A **digitizer** converts shapes into numbers for storage by computers. For example, if you have a favorite cartoon picture you would like to transfer to a computer for display, you can trace the picture with a digitizer. Many modern digitizers can scan a photograph or graphic illustration and transfer it directly into the computer without the need to retrace the picture. These digitizers are commonly used in desktop publishing and newspaper applications.

The digitizer transmits the proper numbers to reproduce the picture on the display screen. The picture you scan or trace is two-dimensional. That is, it is flat and has a length and a width. All digitizers can handle both one- and two-dimensional objects. Some can also handle three-dimensional objects. Three-dimensional objects have depth as well as length and width. A digitizer can be used by an engineer to trace an outline of an existing part. The size and shape of the part are thus input into the computer for analysis or further work on the design.

A digitizer can be used to scan a graphic illustration and input it into the computer.

Special-Purpose Data Input Devices

Several special-purpose devices have been built and/or interfaced into computers in order to permit the input of specific data. One such device is the electronic keyboard, which can be interfaced into the computer to mimic many different instruments. The capabilities of the electronic keyboard depend upon its sophistication and accompanying software programs. For example, one system may mimic only one type of instrument, while others enable the user to record different instruments on different tracks of tape and then combine the tracks. The entire tape can be played back and modified, and additional instruments can be added at the same time.

A musical keyboard is a unique input device.

Many fast food restaurants have specially designed keyboards with keys that identify each item on the menu. When a customer places an order, the appropriate keys are pressed, and the computer automatically totals the amount owed. Many large hotel chains also have specially designed keyboards which identify such items as room, phone, and food charges, to name a few. In addition, these devices can communicate with similar equipment at other locations to make future reservations.

Touch-tone devices are input media which translate audio tones into codes the computer can understand. This coded data is then sent to the computer for processing. For example, you may use a touch-tone telephone to key-in a bank account number in order for the computer to provide your current checking account balance. Most touch-tone devices use specially designed keyboards connected to the telephone to transfer data over the line.

TERMINALS

A **terminal** is any device which inputs or outputs data to or from a computer system. Each of the input devices discussed in this chapter may be referred to as a terminal. However, terminals are commonly thought of as equipment which consists of a display screen, a keyboard, and a communications channel (a cable or telephone line) connecting it to the computer.

Terminals are often described as being dumb or smart terminals. **Dumb terminals** do not have memory and are therefore totally dependent upon the stored program in the CPU to which it is connected. **Smart terminals**, on the other hand, do have memory. Depending on the model, amount of memory, and programming, these smart terminals can perform tasks ranging from simple text editing to sophisticated data processing. Smart terminals are often used to check the input data being keyed for accuracy before it is sent to the CPU for further processing.

All terminals are either directly cabled into the CPU or connected to it via a telephone line. They are called local terminals if they are directly cabled to the CPU, or remote terminals if connected via a telephone line.

Local Terminals

A **local terminal** is a device (usually a display screen and keyboard) located near the computer and directly cabled into the computer's CPU. Local terminals can be used to input the data a company needs for maintaining its records and conducting its day-to-day activities into a computer for processing. One example of local terminal users includes national insurance companies that need to input large volumes of their policyholders' data. The federal and state governments also use local terminals to input large volumes of data, such as tax data, vehicle registration, and license information.

Remote Terminals

A **remote terminal** is a device (usually a display screen and keyboard) located at some remote geographical site and connected to the computer by telephone line. A salesperson can use a remote terminal and telephone to transmit an order to the central computer over telephone lines. When the order is received by the central computer, an invoice will be prepared, and the merchandise will be shipped to the customer.

Telephone lines can be used to transmit data from one computer to another.

Additional use of remote terminals includes those used in state patrol cars for checking license plates for stolen cars. Many businesses with offices and warehouses scattered throughout the country use remote terminals to communicate customer orders and sales information to the central computer located at the home office.

INPUT TENDERFOOT: COMPUTER CAMPS

It wasn't too long ago when kids went to summer camp to swim, ride horses, paddle canoes, play softball, hike in the woods, and swat mosquitoes. Camps today still provide the same activities, but many camps have now added computers to their list of activities. Campers are now programming computers, investigating expert systems, directing robots, and conquering advanced application software.

The American Camping Association has identified approximately 150 camps in the United States that can be classified as either computer camps or camps that include some sort of computer instruction as part of their normal activities. The quality of computer instruction and activities in these camps varies a great deal. Therefore, if you're thinking about going to a camp that offers computer instruction, examine its curriculum before you sign up. Ascertain what needs you want fulfilled, then pick the camp that can best meet those needs. Keep in mind that camp offerings may range from a simple general computer literacy course to those that have the expertise to let students determine their own intensive course of study for several hours each day.

Before enrolling in a computer camp, be sure to find out what the ratio of campers to computers will be during the session. Several camps will not allow this ratio to exceed 1:1 (one camper per computer). If the ratio is greater than two campers per computer, be cautious. Also, find out what the camp has established as the camper-to-staff ratio and the qualifications and teaching experience of the computer personnel. Some of the computer personnel may be computer experts but may not have experience or training in teaching others. It is also important to find out what kind of computers are provided. Most camps have a variety of machines, but if you have a preference or want to learn about a specific computer, make sure the camp has what you want and permits access to it.

Many parents fear that their children (who want to attend a computer camp) already spend too much time alone at home working with their computers. At full-time computer camps, campers typically are provided a minimum of five hours a day to work with computers and are paired with another camper of the same age. This pairing of campers provides an opportunity to meet others, work together, and share common interests.

Camps that include computing as one of several of the more traditional activities may offer only one hour of computer time per day. It is up to the parents and camper to decide how much computing time is desired and to select a camp that fulfills that requirement.

Campers should also find out about medical care, living facilities, food services, and other activities. Because costs vary from one camp to another, it is important to find out if the costs cover all fees (i.e. computer time, software, books, diskettes, paper, and ribbons). Brochures should be obtained and read carefully well in advance of the time of enrollment. After narrowing the selection to one or two camps, it would be wise to visit and see first-hand what they have to offer. If you can't visit due to distance or schedule conflicts, prepare a list of questions and phone the camp director.

Computer camps provide computer instruction as well as more traditional activities.

CHAPTER SUMMARY

- Input devices are used to enter software instructions and data into a computer's memory.
- The specific input device and the manner in which the data is input into the computer's memory is controlled entirely by instructions provided by a computer program.
- Many computers have more than one input device attached to facilitate various types of processing which must be done.
- The computer keyboard is the most popular and common way of inputting data into the computer.
- A typical computer keyboard can be divided into four sections: (1) function keys, (2) typewriter keyboard, (3) numeric pad, and (4) directional keys.
- A cursor serves as a marker and is often depicted as a flashing square symbol.
- A joystick is an input device which sends coordinates of an x and y direction to the computer which then determines movement and a specific location on the display screen.
- A mouse is a pointing device used with a video display. As the body of the mouse is moved over a hard, flat surface, the cursor is moved a proportionate distance on the display screen.
- A device known as a trackball is designed to perform the same functions as a mouse. A trackball can be thought of as a stationary mouse.
- A bar-code scanner can read bars (lines) known as the Universal Product Code (UPC), that are printed on a product. Retail stores use bar-code scanners to automate the check-out process and help manage inventory.
- A light pen is one of several types of input devices that may be used to point out locations on a display screen. The end of the light pen

contains a phototransistor that sends the computer an x,y value of the pen location on the screen.

- A graphics tablet is a flat drawing surface connected to the computer upon which the user can draw or trace graphic figures.
- The touch screen is a display screen that lets the user point with a finger. It is perhaps the simplest and easiest to operate of all input devices.
- A speech recognition input device provides the ability to instruct a computer by voice command.
- An optical character reader (OCR) is one type of scanner, or input device, that can read numbers, letters of the alphabet, and symbols directly from a typed, printed, or handwritten page.
- The optical mark reader is a scanner that senses the presence or absence of marks made by regular pencil or pen on specially designed forms. This is the simplest form of optical reader since it does not require the "intelligence" of a character reader.
- A magnetic ink character recognition (MICR) reader is an input device that is used to process data printed in magnetic ink with specially designed numbers and symbols.
- A magnetic scanner operates on the same principle as a tape recorder. The tape it reads, however, is usually only a few inches long and contains specific information, such as a depositor's identification number or price of merchandise.
- Real-time sensors are one of the most innovative and intriguing developments in computer input. Real-time sensors constantly monitor a process or event and transmit the findings to the processor without the need of human assistance.
- The digitizer converts one-, two-, and three-dimensional shapes into numbers for storage by computers.
- Several special-purpose devices have been built and/or interfaced into the computer in order to input specific data into the computer.
- A terminal is any device which inputs or outputs data to/from a computer system. A terminal is commonly thought of as a device which consists of a display screen, a keyboard, and a communications channel connecting it to the computer.
- There are two types of terminals—dumb terminals (terminals with no memory) and smart terminals (terminals with memory).
- Terminals that are directly cabled to the CPU are called local terminals. Terminals that are connected to the computer via a telephone line are called remote terminals.

KEY TERMS

The following key terms were introduced in this chapter:

bar-code scanner
caps lock key
cursor
digitizer

directional keys
dumb terminal
enter key
function keys
graphics tablet
joystick
keyboard
light pen
local terminal
magnetic ink character recognition
magnetic scanner
membrane keyboard
mouse
numeric pad
optical character reader
optical mark reader
real-time sensor
remote terminal
smart terminal
speech recognition device
terminal
touch display screen
trackball
typewriter keyboard
Universal Product Code (UPC)

REVIEW QUESTIONS

1. What is the purpose of input devices? (Obj. 1)
2. Can input devices function without a computer program? Explain. (Obj. 1)
3. What are the four sections of a typical computer keyboard? (Obj.2)
4. Where are membrane keyboards primarily used? (Obj.2)
5. Explain how a joystick functions. (Obj. 2)
6. What is a mouse? How does it work? (Obj. 2)
7. Explain some specific uses of a bar-code scanner. (Obj. 2)
8. Explain how a light pen functions. (Obj. 2)
9. What is a graphics tablet? What can be used to draw on the graphics tablet? (Obj. 2)
10. What input device is the simplest and easiest of all the input devices to operate? Why? (Obj. 2)
11. Describe an application in which a speech recognition device would be valuable. (Obj. 2)
12. What types of input can an optical character reader send to a computer? (Obj. 2)
13. What type of input can an optical mark reader send to a computer? (Obj. 2)
14. What industry is the biggest user of magnetic ink character recognition (MICR) readers? (Obj. 2)
15. Identify two usages of magnetic scanners. (Obj. 2)
16. What is a real-time sensor input device? (Obj. 2)
17. What is the purpose of a digitizer? (Obj. 2)
18. Identify two special-purpose data input devices. (Obj. 3)
19. Define terminal. (Obj. 4)
20. What is the difference between a dumb terminal and a smart terminal? (Obj. 4)
21. What is the difference between local and remote terminals? (Obj. 4)

CHALLENGE ACTIVITIES

1. Observe the keyboard connected to your computer and write down the names of all the keys which differ from or are not included on a standard typewriter keyboard. Look up the purpose of each of these keys in the operations manual which accompanies the computer. If you do not have a computer keyboard available, refer to Figure 4-1 on page 59 to complete this exercise. (Obj. 2)
2. Describe an input device used with a software program and explain how it enables you to interact with the computer. As an alternative, research a computer application and describe the input device it uses. As another alternative, you may wish to describe how an input device enables you to interact with your favorite arcade game. (Objs. 1,2,3)
3. Research and find a computer application that utilizes a light pen, a graphics tablet, a touch display screen, a speech recognition device, a scanner, a real-time sensor, a digitizer, or a special-purpose input device and write a brief report describing how the device you selected is used. (Objs. 2,3)
4. Identify and describe two environments in which dumb, local terminals are used. Identify and describe two environments in which smart, remote terminals are used. (Obj. 4)

CHAPTER 5

OUTPUT — GETTING INFORMATION FROM THE COMPUTER

LEARNING OBJECTIVES

After studying this chapter, you will be able to:

1. **Describe the difference between monochrome and color display screens.**
2. **Identify and explain the difference between cathode-ray tube (CRT) and liquid crystal display (LCD) technology.**
3. **Identify and explain the difference between impact and nonimpact printers.**
4. **Identify and explain the usage of several of the more common impact printers.**
5. **Identify and explain the usage of several of the more common nonimpact printers.**
6. **Identify applications which use plotters.**
7. **Describe how computer output microfilm is created and used.**
8. **Describe how synthesizers function.**
9. **Identify applications which use real-time controllers.**
10. **Identify applications which use computer-controlled robots.**

INTRODUCTION

Like input devices, output devices come in many sizes and shapes, operate at different speeds, and have different capacities and capabilities. Output devices furnish the user with information which is generated by the computer. They are operated by the user and controlled by instructions contained in a software program stored in the computer's main memory. In this chapter you will learn about the most commonly used output devices. You will learn their characteristics and the kinds of applications for which they are best suited.

WHAT IS INFORMATION?

In Chapter 2 you learned that raw data is fed into a computer where it is processed and output in the form of information. **Information** is news or intelligence communicated by word or in writing and consists of facts, data, or knowledge derived from reading or instruction. Special output devices have been designed for computer systems which help facilitate the communication of the information they produce. This information may be communicated by devices which create such output mediums as printed reports, spoken words, music, pictures, graphics, charts, and microfilm, to name a few.

Output devices can be used to produce printed reports.

Graphics is one type of output medium.

In many instances the kind of information which must be communicated to a human determines which output device is best to use. In other instances, output equipment has been specifically designed and developed to facilitate the communication and processing of information.

DISPLAY SCREENS

Video display screens are the most commonly used output devices. They are called **video display screens** because the images they produce can be seen. These images consist of virtually all output the computer is capable of producing. Display screens are especially well suited for interactive applications requiring both input and output. When data is keyed into the computer it is displayed on the video display screen. After the computer has processed the input data, the resultant information is displayed back to the same screen for the user to review.

Display screens may be either monochromatic or color. A **monochromatic** or **monochrome** screen is a one color (green, amber, or white) display. Full-color displays are coming into much greater use. They do an excellent job of presenting information in an easy-to-understand form. A graphic (chart, drawing, or picture) looks much better in color. For applications involving detailed work with words and numbers, however, bright color displays may tire the eyes and be harder to read. For that reason, most color screens can easily be switched back and forth between monochrome and color modes.

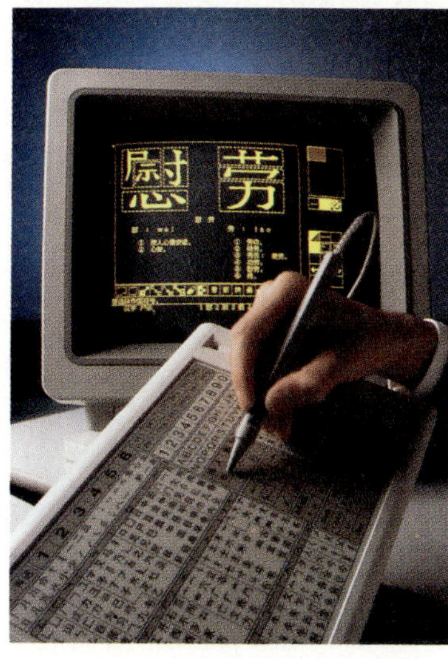

Monochrome screens are often more soothing to the eyes over extended periods of time, while color screens are usually better at presenting information in an easy-to-understand form.

Cathode-Ray Tube (CRT) Display Screens

Most display screens utilize the cathode-ray tube **(CRT)** technology. The CRT technology consists of (1) an electron gun which is a device that shoots a narrow electron beam containing the data received from the computer into a yoke (a device located at the base of the tube); and (2) a display screen which is coated with a phosphorescent material (a material which emits light). Wherever electrons hit the phosphorescent material on the screen, a small dot or light is lit. These tiny lights are called **pixels** (PIC-ture ELements). Each pixel can be lit (on) or not lit (off) as shown in Figure 5-1. The greater the number of pixels a given screen can display, the higher the resolution and the sharper the picture.

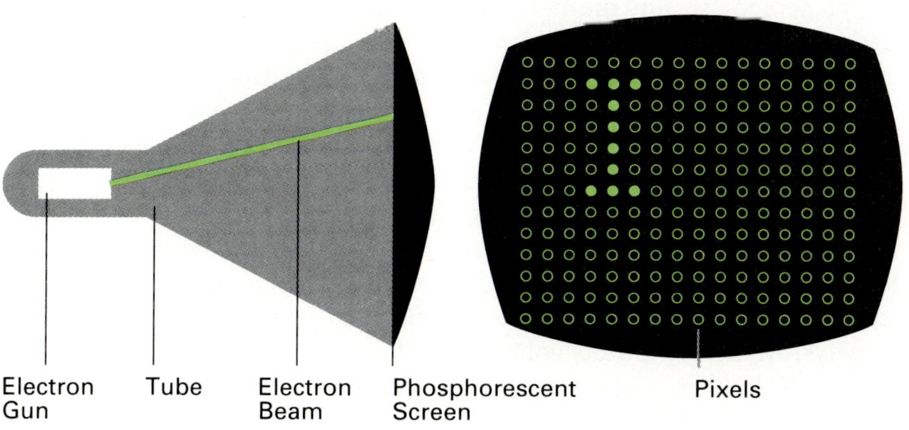

Figure 5-1
Pixels are lit to form images wherever electrons hit the phosphorescent material on the display screen.

Monitor is a term given to CRT screens that display information processed by the computer. Monitors are similar in appearance to television sets; however, monitors have many more pixels. Nearly every modern computer uses a monitor display screen. Many of the older home computers were designed to use television sets instead of monitors. The resolution of a typical television set is 256 x 192 pixels (256 pixels horizontally by 192 pixels vertically), or a total of 49,152 pixels. By contrast, a popular monochrome monitor has 640 x 240 pixels (640 pixels horizontally by 240 pixels vertically), or a total of 153,600 pixels. Comparable differences exist between color televisions and color monitors. As a rule, television sets can clearly display 40 characters per line, while monitors can display 80 or more characters per line.

There are basically two types of color monitors: RGB monitors and composite video monitors. An **RGB monitor** uses three different electronic signals to turn on the phosphorescent material within each pixel. One signal is the color red, another is the color blue, and the third is the color green. A **composite video monitor** uses a single electronic signal to turn on the phosphorescent material within each pixel. Because the RGB monitors use three signals for each pixel, they produce a sharper picture with better color than the composite video monitors. As a result, RGB monitors are more expensive.

Monitors can also be classified as either digital or analog. Unlike standard RGB and composite monitors which are digital, an analog monitor can display any color sent to it by the computer's video display.

Monitors usually contain either 24 or 25 lines of 80 characters each. Displays with 132 columns are becoming more common, as are those that can display up to 60 lines. A few can display the equivalent of several printed pages of text at the same time.

There are two primary methods of moving output from the computer to a monitor. In one method, called **character-oriented display,** the character codes are transmitted one after another from the processor to the display. The display stores the character codes in its own memory and performs the necessary electronic functions to display the characters on the screen. In this method, the processor sends the data directly to the monitor for display.

The second method is referred to as **memory-mapped** (or bit-mapped) **display.** In this case, the display actually serves as a "window" into the memory of the computer; that is, a group of locations in main memory is dedicated to holding information for the display. To change a character in a screen location, the computer just places the code of the character in the corresponding location in main memory. For displays that can show **high-resolution graphics** (very detailed graphics) and greater color selections, 64K or more of storage may be used just for memory-mapped displays. Many computers contain a Video Graphics Array (VGA) video adapter. A VGA is a separate hardware board or an integrated part of the main electronic circuit board inside the CPU which greatly increases the computer's graphic and color capabilities. VGA monitors are analog monitors. In general, the greater the number of individual pixels (points of color) that can be displayed on the screen and the greater the number of colors, the greater the memory and/or hardware required to hold the image.

Some monitors are capable of displaying high-resolution graphics.

Liquid Crystal Display (LCD) Screens

A liquid crystal display **(LCD)** screen is composed of an electrokinetic fluid (a fluid which changes color due to the effects of electricity in motion) positioned between two layers of glass. Each area of the display screen contains electrodes that, when activated with electrical charges, cause various light patterns (images) to appear on the screen. One problem with this technology is that when a group of electrodes is activated some of the charges may leak onto the surrounding areas of the fluid and distort the resolution.

The first LCDs were developed in the mid-1970s. They could display approximately 6 to 15 characters and were used primarily for watch and calculator displays. Today's technology has produced much larger LCD displays. Some of these larger LCD displays can display full-sized screens of 25 lines of 80 characters each. In addition, many of today's LCDs use low-power backlighting panels to produce a sharper image. Because LCD technology reflects or absorbs white light and uses a low-power supply, it is not conducive to color display. Therefore, LCD displays are monochrome displays used primarily with portable computers.

LCD screens are often used with portable computers.

Another display screen which physically appears similar to an LCD screen is the **gas-plasma display screen.** This display screen has a flat surface, is equivalent in size to a 12-inch CRT monitor, and is only about

1¼-inches thick. It usually contains 640 x 400 pixels which enable it to produce crisp, clear, orange-colored images. It, like the LCD screen, is monochrome and designed for use with portable computers.

PRINTERS

Printers are commonly used devices that place output on paper. Placing output on paper is generally called making a **hard copy** of the information. Printers are among the most common output devices. Nearly every computer application uses a printer in some way. Just a few uses of printers include printing bills, letters, and accounting records. There are tremendous differences in the types of printers available: differences in speed, print quality, price, and special features. Some printers can produce only alphanumeric characters; others can print detailed graphics. Some printers can use only one color, while others can print in several colors.

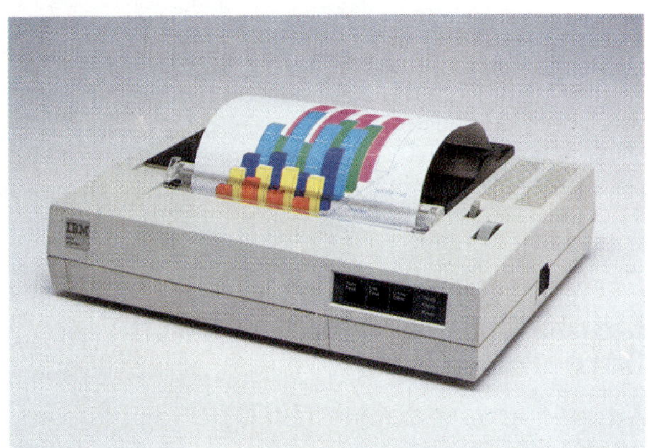

Some printers can print in a variety of colors for stronger visual impact.

Printers use several different methods to place characters on a sheet of paper. With some printers, the paper is physically struck to form the images; these printers are known as **impact printers.** Impact printers are best used when multiple copies of the same document are required. **Nonimpact printers,** on the other hand, form the characters without actually striking the paper. Regardless of the method of printing, a character code representing the character to be printed is sent to the printer from the processor. The printer then converts the code and produces the proper mechanical and/or electronic action to print the character.

The printers discussed in the following paragraphs are the types most commonly used. There are other types of printers, and manufacturers are constantly introducing new printer models, some of which utilize different technology.

Impact Printers

Impact printers are printers that produce images by physically striking a character against a ribbon and paper. Dot-matrix, daisy wheel, chain, and band printers are all examples of impact printer technology. Each of these different types of printers will be discussed in the material which follows. You will notice that print speeds and capabilities vary greatly among the impact printers. You will also notice that some printers print one character at a time while others are capable of printing an entire line at one time.

Dot-Matrix Printers

The dot-matrix printer is the largest and most popular of all printer categories. It creates an arrangement of dots, called a **dot matrix** (row and column arrangement of dots), to produce images. A **dot-matrix printer** can be defined as an impact printer that produces a character by forming it from rows and columns of dots. The mechanism of the printer that actually does the printing is known as the **printhead.** As it moves across the paper, tiny pins or wires in the printhead fire out to tap the paper through a ribbon to form the desired image made up of dots. There is a wide variation in the number and arrangement of the pins or wires used to produce the printed images. The most common arrangement is a simple vertical stack of nine pins, as shown in Figure 5-2.

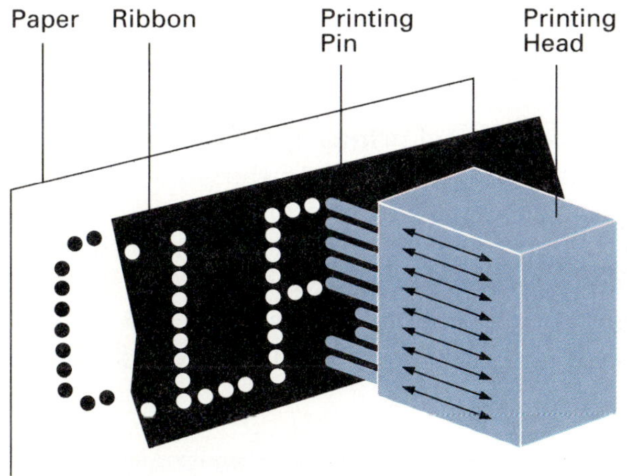

Figure 5-2
Tiny pins in the printhead tap the paper through a ribbon to form an image made up of dots.

Dot-matrix printers are very popular with microcomputer users.

The print quality of a dot-matrix printer varies depending on the number of dots (pins or wires) which form a character. The newer, 24-pin dot-matrix printer is becoming a very popular replacement of the 9-pin printers. If many dots are used, the character will look better than if it is made of only a few dots. For example, characters that are formed by a 5 x 9 (five columns, nine rows) matrix will not look as nice as ones formed in a 16 x 24 matrix. Many dot-matrix printers can produce hard copy output that is very near to letter-quality print; in other words, the characters appear as if they were made from unbroken lines and look as if they were produced by a high-quality typewriter. Some examples of dot-matrix output are shown in Figure 5-3.

Figure 5-3
Some dot-matrix printers can produce near-letter-quality output.

This output was produced on a dot-matrix printer. If you look closely, you can see the dots that form each letter.

This output was produced on a near-letter-quality dot-matrix printer. Compare this copy to the other copy, and notice the difference in quality.

The print speed of dot-matrix printers ranges from around forty characters per second to several hundred characters per second, which is quite adequate for most small computer systems. A few dot-matrix printers use more than one printhead to achieve even higher speeds. Compared with other types of printers, most dot-matrix printers are fairly inexpensive.

Daisy Wheel Printers

Like a dot-matrix printer, a **daisy wheel printer** is an impact printer. It gets its name from the fact that it uses a raised-character print wheel that resembles a flower. The daisy wheel mechanism rotates to position the character to be printed in its printing position. Once properly positioned, a hammer is then fired out to strike the desired character against the ribbon and paper causing it to be printed. The daisy wheel mechanism can be removed from the printer and replaced by other wheels containing different type styles.

Letter-quality printers use a daisy wheel mechanism to form their characters.

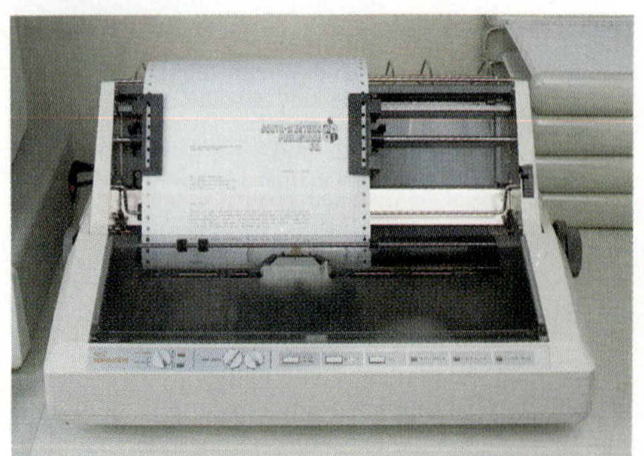

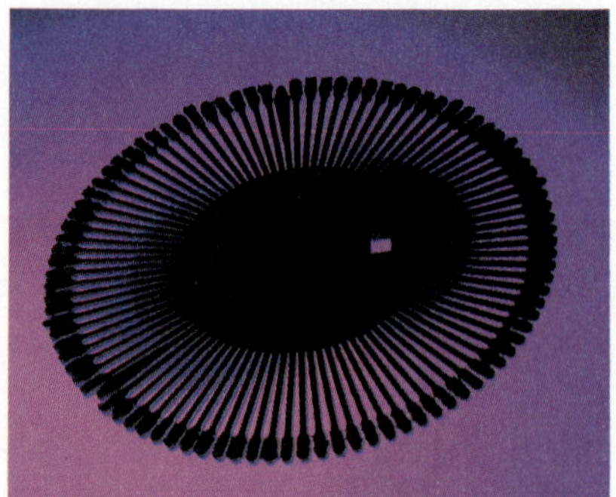

Daisy wheel printers are designed to produce letter-quality print. This is important when printing letters and other documents that must be of high quality. In exchange for such fine-quality output, however, the user pays a price in the form of low speed. Most daisy wheel printers are extremely slow because of the time it takes to rotate the daisy wheel in order to position each character for printing. Ten to 45 characters-per-second print speeds are common for daisy wheel printers. High-resolution dot-matrix and nonimpact printers are quickly making the daisy wheel printer obsolete.

Band and Chain Printers

Band and chain printers are impact printers that operate on the same general principle. A **band printer** uses a rotating band or belt containing all printable characters; a **chain printer** uses a rotating chain containing several sets of all the printable characters. Each of these printers contains hammers which fire out to strike the appropriate characters after they are properly positioned against the paper. A ribbon between the characters and paper produces the images. Different fonts (shapes of print characters) can be used on either printer simply by replacing the band or chain.

Band and chain printers are often used with mainframe computers. They produce high-quality output at very high speeds.

Band and chain printers have been used for many years on mainframe computers. Both produce high-quality, solid character images, and both have proven very reliable. They are much faster than the dot-matrix and daisy wheel printers described earlier and can print at speeds ranging from 150 to 3,000 lines per minute on continuous form paper. They are also much more expensive. Like the daisy wheel, chain and band printers are frequently being replaced by nonimpact printers.

Nonimpact Printers

Unlike impact printers which produce images by physically striking a character against a ribbon and paper, nonimpact printers use a variety of other techniques. Thermal, ink-jet, and laser printers are examples of nonimpact printers. Each of these three commonly used printers will be discussed in the material which follows. Like impact printers, you will notice that print speeds and capabilities vary greatly among the nonimpact printers. You will also notice that some printers print one character at a time while others are capable of printing an entire line or entire page at one time.

Thermal Printers

A **thermal printer** produces images on special heat-sensitive paper. It produces output via a matrix arrangement of heated rods. As individual rods representing the desired image are selected, they press against the heat-sensitive paper and burn the desired image onto the paper. The speed at which the rods move across the paper enables the printer to print at speeds between 30 and 150 characters per second. Thermal printers are some of the most inexpensive printers to purchase and are therefore frequently used with home computers. Although the printer itself is relatively inexpensive, the heat-sensitive paper is often very expensive. Also, the quality of the output produced by most thermal printers is less than that of a standard typewriter.

Thermal printing technology produces images on special heat-sensitive paper.

Another type of thermal printer uses a process called thermal transfer to produce its images. This type of printer's printhead contains electrodes (conductors of electric current) which heat a special sensitive film ribbon and melt the ink from the ribbon onto ordinary paper. Like the thermal printer described previously, the print quality of this type of printer is usually inferior to that of other printers.

Ink-Jet Printers

The **ink-jet printer** is a nonimpact printer which is growing in popularity. Most ink jet printers contain a mechanism, much like a miniature nozzle attached to a garden hose, which sprays liquid ink onto the paper. The spray pattern which is sprayed on the paper creates the desired characters. Ink-jet printers produce high-quality print, and many of them can produce different sizes and styles of characters on the same line. Some can print in several colors by over-spraying various colored inks to produce different color combinations. A typical ink-jet printer is capable of printing 150 characters per second.

Ink-jet printers spray ink on paper to produce printed characters.

Laser Printers

A **laser printer** is a nonimpact printer that works somewhat like a copying machine. Laser printers use an electrophotographic process (a process in which a beam of light creates an electrically charged figure on a metal drum receptive to photographic images) to create its images. Tiny ink particles (called toner) stick to the image, which the drum rolls onto the paper. This technology permits high-resolution text and graphics to appear on the same page. Laser printers can produce output much faster than impact printers. The most expensive and fastest ones connected to mainframes can print over 20,000 lines (300 pages) per minute. Smaller, less expensive laser printers which can be connected to personal computers commonly print over 500 lines (8 pages) per minute. A variation of laser technology uses an array of light-emitting diodes (LEDs) to accomplish the same output but at less cost and greater reliability.

Laser printers can produce very high-quality text and graphics.

Another advantage of the laser printer is that a business form (i.e. letterhead, invoice) can be printed in near-typeset-quality on blank paper at the same time the output data is being printed. The laser printer can also produce different sizes and styles of printing which exceed those of typewriters and approach typeset quality. An example of laser-produced output is shown in Figure 5-4.

Figure 5-4
Laser printers can produce high-quality output and have many different capabilities.

Adams and Barnham Associates

M E M O R A N D U M

To:
From:
Date:
Subject:

Today's laser printers are also capable of producing color output. As laser technology continues to develop, so will its ability to produce more precise color output. In addition, research is currently under way to produce laser-generated images called holograms. **Holograms** are images which appear to the human eye as three-dimensional images. Holograms may well usher in a new era of lifelike three-dimensional pictures. For example, an architect would be able to show precise images of a planned structure or a doctor would be able to study a three dimensional image of a living human organ prior to surgery. The development of laser-produced output is without question the fastest growing of all output technology.

WHICH PRINTER IS BEST?

You have seen that printers come in many sizes and have different capabilities and speeds. Impact printers have been around much longer than the newer, nonimpact technology printers, and users have been reluctant to change. One of the reasons is due to the durability of the impact printer. They pound away day after day and seldom need repair. Another reason is because many applications still require the use of multiple-part forms (i.e. W-2 forms, legal documents, invoices, reports, and government reporting), which are most easily produced by impact printers.

Choosing the best printer is not an easy task. The best guideline is to first determine what the printing needs are, and then shop around to find the printer which best meets those needs. Many shoppers will be shocked to discover that the price of a good printer may exceed the price of the computer to which it will be connected.

PLOTTERS

A **plotter** is most frequently used to print graphic output. It can draw maps, produce artwork, or draw any type of line. A plotter draws output using one or more pens that are controlled by instructions from the processor. Since the pens can contain various colors of ink, multicolored output can be produced. Depending on the design of the plotter, the images created by the plotters are produced by either moving the pens over the surface of a fixed sheet of paper (flat bed plotter) or by moving the paper under the pens (drum plotter). Therefore, most flat bed plotters are limited to printing on standard-sized sheets of paper while drum plotters can work on continuous form paper of almost unlimited size. Mapping, weather forecasting, drafting, and engineering are just some of the areas in which plotters are used. In addition to producing graphic output, the plotter can also perform many printing functions.

Plotters are very good at producing intricate graphic output.

COMPUTER OUTPUT MICROFILM

Computer output microfilm, commonly referred to as COM, is used when large amounts of data must be printed and stored for future use. Under such conditions, output printed on paper may require too much storage space. Also, too much time may be needed to search through the paper output to find a given item.

Computer output microfilm uses a photographic process similar to that of a camera. Computer output is reduced in size and recorded directly onto photographic film. As the unit reduces the size of the computer-generated text and/or graphics, it exposes the film in a manner similar to that in photography. Because the image of each character is reduced greatly in size, very dense storage (many characters in a small space) is possible. As a result, text and graphics can be recorded on microfilm much faster than they can be printed on high-speed printers and at a considerable savings. The microfilm may be developed in the unit itself or removed for development.

The microfilm produced may be in long rolls. It may also be in small rectangular sheets called **microfiche.** To read either type, a person must use a special reader. The reader is a machine that magnifies the stored images to a size that can be read by the human eye. Many of the readers can produce a hard copy of any required information. Most of the machines also have automated search mechanisms to help locate desired data.

Many companies are now storing data on microfilm or microfiche which can be read on a special reader, such as the one shown here.

COM provides a very fast way of recording output from a computer. The film itself is inexpensive and compact. However, complete COM systems can be very expensive. Government agencies, insurance companies, libraries, banks, utility companies, and other businesses that must store large volumes of computer-generated data are the most likely users of COM.

SOUND SYNTHESIZERS

One of the most fascinating areas of development in the computer area is the use of the computer to generate sound. The devices which are connected to the computer to make this possible are called synthesizers. A **synthesizer** is a device which can combine parts or elements of different sounds into a complex whole. Sound synthesizers can be categorized into two different areas: speech and music.

Speech synthesizers

Speech synthesizers are devices which project an imitation of the human voice. The process involves the analysis of words which are stored in the computer's memory by a computer program. As each word is analyzed, phonemes (basic units of speech which provide the small changes in sound that differentiate between word meanings) representing various letter combinations are generated. The phonemes are combined into recognizable sounds by applying rules of voice inflection (accent) and emphasis and are then projected over a speaker connected to the computer.

Another method of voice-generated output involves the storage of prerecorded spoken words and phrases. When an inquiry is made, the computer finds the appropriate recording and plays it back similar to the way in which a cassette player works.

The use of speech synthesizers and voice recordings is becoming more commonplace in our modern society. Talking machines are giving phone numbers to persons who dial directory assistance. They perform electronic banking by using the phone as a terminal. Talking typewriters, calculators, and reading machines are a tremendous aid for the blind. In addition, computer-assisted learning in such areas as foreign languages can be much more effective when the computer can speak.

Music Synthesizers

Music (or sound) **synthesizers** are devices which can blend sound waves to create music or brand-new sounds (sounds that are not commonly heard). With this technology, music (or other sounds) can be recorded on tape. With a computer connected to the tape and a synthesizer, the recording can be edited. For example, the tempo can be changed, several other recordings can be merged together, pitch can be altered, and voices and other instruments can be added. The music and recording industry uses specially designed computers connected to sound synthesizers extensively to produce quality sound.

Many musicians now use computers to help compose and record their music.

REAL-TIME CONTROLLERS

A **real-time controller** is an output device that converts computer output to some kind of action that controls a process. Often, the action consists of turning a valve on or off. In an automobile, the computer gives commands to controllers on the ignition and fuel systems. In an aircraft, computer commands constantly monitor and control cockpit instrumentation as well as engine operation. When commanded by a computer, a real-time controller performs the specific function for which it was designed.

Real-time controllers are constantly at work in an airplane cockpit.

ROBOTS

This computer-controlled robot is testing logic circuitry for use in another computer.

Robots can serve as output devices. Under the control of a computer, the robot produces output in the form of motion, which in turn performs work. If the instructions being given to the computer are changed, the robot's motions can change, and it can do a different kind of work. Computer-controlled robots are commonly used in industrial environments. Tasks that require repetition, situations which require very precise and finite work which humans could not perform on a consistent basis, and jobs that require the handling of materials which are dangerous or harmful to humans all lend themselves to this type of technology.

Research exploring additional utilization of robots (called **robotics**) is currently under way in many universities and research laboratories. Scientists are working to build a new generation of robots which have greater sensitivity to vision and touch, greater mobility, and an ability to follow and learn from human voice commands. Robots capable of seeing and recognizing obstacles, maneuvering around or over obstacles, handling a fragile egg, lifting a car, and learning from and responding to human commands would surely revolutionize our world.

WORKING AT HOME

Thanks to the personal computer, working at home is becoming more and more commonplace. The power of the computer and the numerous and varied applications for which it can be utilized have made it possible for hundreds of thousands of people to earn a living and pursue a vocation without even leaving their homes. Many individuals go into working at home because of the lifestyle it affords. Working at home gives these people a host of advantages that include increased efficiency, longer work days, reduced expenses, more flexibility, freedom to live where they want, and the comfort of their own workspace.

Some individuals find that when they have several projects going on at once, it is easier to concentrate on one at a time at home. At an office, co-workers may cause interruptions. There are social distractions and phone calls regarding other projects and a variety of other issues. Many workers find that an office in the home enables them to make optimum use of their time, thus permitting them to spend as much time on a given project as needed.

Individuals who work out of their homes avoid the time, expense, and physiological wear and tear on the nerves of commuting to and from their places of employment. By not having to commute, many home workers save one to two hours each day that can be used to get more work done or as personal leisure time.

People who run their own businesses and work at home save on office rent and utility expenses. One small office (depending upon the location) may rent for as much as $300 to $1200 per month. In addition, many office buildings also charge their renters for utilities (heat, electricity, phone service), insurance coverage, security protection, garbage pickup, and cleaning services. Because working at home has become so commonplace, customers of a home worker accept this type of business arrangement and do not consider meeting in a home office an inconvenience.

Individuals who work at home are masters of their own schedules. Scheduling their time provides a great deal of flexibility that is very important to their lifestyles and often enables them to fit things they want and like to do into their plans. Self-discipline, however, must be considered when the normal work schedule is altered to insure that the work gets done on time.

Working at home has given many people the luxury to live wherever they desire. Not having to commute to an office every day, coupled with the ability of the computer to communicate over long distances, has facilitated this flexibility. For example, an individual living and working on the east coast can use a computer to send his/her work to an employer's computer on the west coast in a matter of minutes.

When working in an employer's office, the employee must accept the workspace and environment provided. The workspace and environment may be small, inefficient, inadequate, or oppressive. In a worker's own home, he/she can create the environment and make the workspace more comfortable and efficient. Home workers can dress as they please, eat when they want, listen to their own tastes in music while working, or take relaxing breaks when desired.

There are two general categories of people who have offices in their homes—those who are self-employed, and those who are part-time home office workers. One type of part-time home office worker is a person who works with a personal computer in the evening and on weekends. For example, employees may borrow their company's personal computers (or use their own computers) to do work at home after normal business hours. Another type of part-time home office worker is an employee who works for a company and spends part of the normal work day at home on the computer. These employees use their home office to get away from the busyness of their employer's office when they need privacy or quiet working time.

Home workers have the advantage of working in a pleasant atmosphere that offers both privacy and convenience.

Many full-time, self-employed individuals have made the decision to work at home essentially because of the availability of the personal computer. Several have ventured out on their own, using the computer as their primary source of income. Working out of the home is efficient and convenient to small businesses for several reasons. First, it facilitates small businesses' demanding schedules. The self-employed frequently work irregular and long hours (not the typical 9 to 5 hours). The home office is always there and available for their use. Second, it is less expensive than renting office space in a large downtown office building.

For several years many large organizations have provided equipment and flexible schedules to enable their employees to do some of their work at home. Today, due to affordable personal computers and effective software, many large organizations as well as small businesses view the home worker as a new labor pool resource. For example, there are data-entry people working out of their homes that can be hired to key-in data for insurance companies, marketing groups, political organizations, hospitals, and other organizations. Such a labor resource permits companies to get work done during peak times without having to hire full-time employees who would be idle during slow times. Many of these workers are thus treated as subcontractors and paid on a piecework basis (paid based upon the work produced) by the employers.

In all of these cases, the quality of the output is what makes the home-office situation feasible. Whether a home worker is self-employed or hired by a company, the success of this type of work boils down to whether or not the material produced can be used by someone else. Because of this, it is extremely important that a home worker produce acceptable output through the use of good computer skills, a knowledge of the program being used, and superior and appropriate output devices.

CHAPTER SUMMARY

- Output devices receive and furnish to the user information which is generated by the computer. They are operated by the user and controlled by instructions contained in a software program stored in the computer's memory.
- Video display screens are the most commonly used output devices.
- A monochrome screen is a one-color green, amber, or white display.
- Most display screens utilize the cathode-ray tube (CRT) technology. Images are created on the CRT by patterns of tiny lit pixels. The greater the number of pixels, the higher the resolution and the sharper the picture.
- Monitor is a term given to video display screens used for displaying information processed by the computer. Monitors are similar to television sets; however, monitors have many more pixels.
- A memory-mapped display is a window which depicts a group of locations in main memory dedicated to holding information for the display.
- There are basically two types of color monitors: RGB monitors and composite video monitors. An RGB monitor uses three different electronic signals (one for each color) to turn on the phosphorescent material within each pixel. A composite video monitor uses a single electronic signal to turn on the phosphorescent material within each pixel.
- Liquid crystal display screens are monochrome displays used primarily with portable computers.

- Printers are commonly used devices that place output on paper. Placing output on paper is generally called making a hard copy of the information.
- Impact printers are printers in which the paper is physically struck to form the images.
- Nonimpact printers form characters without actually striking the paper.
- The dot-matrix printer is the largest and most popular of all printer categories. It is an impact printer that produces images by creating an arrangement of dots, called a dot matrix.
- The daisy wheel printer is an impact printer that contains each printable character on a wheel mechanism. The wheel mechanism is rotated to position the desired character to be printed in its printing position. Once properly positioned, a hammer strikes the character and forces it against the ribbon and paper thereby causing it to be printed.
- Band and chain printers are impact printers that operate on the same general principle. A band printer uses a rotating band or belt containing all printable characters; a chain printer uses a rotating chain containing several sets of all the printable characters.
- A thermal printer is a nonimpact printer that produces images on special heat-sensitive paper.
- The ink-jet printer is a nonimpact printer which uses a tiny nozzle to spray liquid ink onto the paper. The spray pattern which is sprayed on the paper creates the desired characters.
- A laser printer is a nonimpact printer in which a beam of light creates an electrically charged image on a metal drum receptive to photographic images. Tiny ink particles (called toner) stick to the image, which the drum rolls onto the paper.
- Holograms are images which appear to the human eye as three-dimensional pictures.
- A plotter is most frequently used to print graphic output (i.e. draw maps, produce artwork, etc.).
- Computer output microfilm (COM) is used when large amounts of data must be printed and stored for future use. It uses a photographic process similar to that of a camera.
- Speech synthesizers are devices which project an imitation of the human voice. The process involves an analysis of words and the application of language rules which are stored in the computer's memory by a computer program. Pre-recorded voice output is another form of computer output.
- Real-time controllers are specifically designed devices which produce some kind of action that controls a process. For example, the action may consist of turning a valve on or off to control a water level.
- Robots, under the control of a computer, produce output in the form of motion, which in turn performs work. Research in the area of robotics is currently under way to find additional uses of computer-controlled robots.

KEY TERMS

The following key terms were introduced or redefined in this chapter:

band printer
chain printer
character-oriented display
composite video monitor
computer output microfilm
CRT
daisy wheel printer
dot matrix
dot-matrix printer
gas plasma display screen
hard copy
high-resolution graphics
holograms
impact printer
information
ink-jet printer
laser printer
LCD
memory-mapped display
microfiche
monitor
monochromatic/monochrome
music synthesizer
nonimpact printer
pixels
plotter
printhead
real-time controller
RGB monitor
robotics
speech synthesizer
synthesizer
thermal printer
video display screen

REVIEW QUESTIONS

1. What is the difference between a monochromatic or monochrome display screen and a color display screen? (Obj. 1)
2. Briefly explain how a CRT screen functions. (Obj. 2)
3. What is a pixel? (Obj. 2)
4. What is the difference between a monitor and a television screen? (Obj. 2)
5. What is the difference between an RGB monitor and a composite video monitor? (Obj. 2)
6. There are two methods of moving output from the computer to a monitor. Identify and describe each method. (Obj. 2)
7. What is the term used to describe very detailed graphics? (Obj. 2)
8. Briefly explain how an LCD screen functions. (Obj. 2)
9. LCD and gas plasma displays are low-powered, monochrome displays used primarily with what kind of computers? (Obj. 2)
10. What is a hard copy? (Obj. 3)
11. What is the difference between an impact printer and a nonimpact printer? (Obj. 3)
12. Briefly describe how dot-matrix printers function. (Obj. 4)
13. Briefly describe how daisy wheel printers function. (Obj. 4)
14. Briefly describe how band and chain printers function. (Obj. 4)
15. Briefly describe how thermal printers function. (Obj. 5)
16. Briefly describe how ink-jet printers function. (Obj. 5)

17. Briefly describe how laser printers function. (Obj. 5)
18. What characteristics of a plotter make it an appropriate output device for drawing the plans of a large building? (Obj. 6)
19. Briefly describe how computer output microfilm is produced. (Obj. 7)
20. What is the term given to small rectangular sheets of microfilm? (Obj. 7)
21. Briefly describe how a speech synthesizer functions. (Obj. 8)
22. Name and describe two real-time controller devices or applications. (Obj. 9)
23. What is a computer-controlled robot? (Obj. 10)
24. What areas of robotics are research scientists currently working to improve? (Obj. 10)

CHALLENGE ACTIVITIES

1. Prepare a brief report about a CRT (monitor or TV) or an LCD screen connected to a computer. Describe the physical characteristics and features of the selected display screen, the need it serves, and how much it costs. Personal computer magazines, advertising literature, computer stores, local computer installers, and computer manufacturers are excellent sources for the information you will need to complete your report. As an alternative, prepare your report about the display screen connected to a computer in your school or home. (Objs. 1,2)
2. Prepare a brief report about an impact printer (i.e. dot-matrix, daisy wheel, band, or chain) connected to a computer. Describe the physical characteristics and features of the selected printer, the need it serves, and how much it costs. Consult personal computer magazines, advertising literature, computer stores, local computer installers, or a computer manufacturer for the information you will need to complete your report. (Objs. 3,4)
3. Prepare a brief report about a nonimpact printer (i.e. thermal, ink-jet, or laser) connected to a computer. Describe the physical characteristics and features of the selected printer, the need it serves, and how much it costs. Consult personal computer magazines, advertising literature, computer stores, local installers, or a computer manufacturer for the information you will need to complete your report. (Objs. 3,5)
4. Research and prepare a report about a recent or futuristic use of a speech or music synthesizer, a real-time controller, or a robot. Check personal computer magazines and your local newspaper for the information necessary to complete your report. As an alternative, make up your own futuristic use of one of these devices. (Objs. 8,9,10)

CHAPTER 6

AUXILIARY STORAGE—RETAINING DATA

LEARNING OBJECTIVES

After studying this chapter, you will be able to:

1. **Describe the need for auxiliary storage devices.**
2. **Identify the various types and characteristics of auxiliary storage devices.**
3. **Identify several of the most common magnetic disk devices, explain how they function, and describe how they are used.**
4. **Identify several optical storage devices, explain how they function, and describe how they are used.**
5. **Identify several magnetic tape devices, explain how they function, and describe how they are used.**
6. **Describe the usage and function of bubble memory, videodisk, and VCR tape as other types of auxiliary storage devices.**

INTRODUCTION

Auxiliary storage is storage that is not part of memory (main storage, primary memory) but is available to and under control of the processor. Thus, an auxiliary storage device can be used to record data whenever instructed to do so by the processor. When instructed, it will also access or read data back to the processor.

THE NEED FOR AUXILIARY STORAGE

In Chapter 3 you learned that primary memory, located in the CPU, is used to store both software programs and data. It would be ideal if every software program and all the data ever needed could be stored in primary memory at one time. This would enable the computer to perform programmed tasks and generate information from stored data almost instantaneously. This, however, is often not possible since the amount of primary memory in a computer is limited and relatively expensive. Typically, one (or a few) software program(s) can be stored and run in primary memory at one time. Only when data is needed is it retrieved, processed, and output. In this way, the limited amount of primary memory can be utilized economically and efficiently.

Many computer users have hundreds of software programs and huge volumes of data which cannot fit in the computer's primary memory at one time. They must be stored on an auxiliary storage device until they are needed. When required, the appropriate program can be loaded into primary memory, and it in turn can access the data it needs.

Because primary memory cannot accommodate the large amounts of data that need to be stored at one time, it is necessary to use auxiliary storage.

TYPES AND CHARACTERISTICS OF AUXILIARY STORAGE DEVICES

All auxiliary storage devices are either sequential-access or random-access devices. **Sequential access** is a term used to describe a device that records and reads back data only in a one-after-the-other sequence. **Random access** is a term used to describe a device that can go directly to the location of specific data without having to read through all the data preceding it.

A sequential-access storage device is somewhat like a cassette tape player. The tape player cannot get to the fourth selection, for example, without actually winding the tape through the first three. Even though you can set the tape player to function at fast forward speed, you still have to wait for it to move past the unwanted selections. A random-access storage device, on the other hand, is somewhat like a compact disk player; you can press the appropriate button, and the desired selection (fourth song) will be played immediately. It is not necessary to play through, or pass by, the unwanted selections.

The purpose of all auxiliary storage devices is to record data for future access. Individual items, or pieces of data, stored on auxiliary storage device media are called **data fields** or **data elements.** For example, the employee name, street address, city, state, and ZIP Code shown in Figure 6-1 are each referred to as a data field or data element. A collection of related data fields is known as a **record.** For example, the following data make up one record: Sara Cammery (employee name); 144 Brookfield Dr. (street address); Cincinnati (city); Ohio (state); and 45150 (ZIP Code). Since all the data in the data fields is related, that is, belongs to

Sara Cammery, it makes up a record. A collection of related records is known as a **file.** For example, all the company's employee records (including Sara Cammery's) that contain the same type of information (street address, city, state, and ZIP Code) make up a file. The file containing Sara Cammery's record could be called the Personnel File since it contains a record for each employee. You will learn in a later chapter that a file may also be referred to as a database. For now think of a **database** as an organized collection of related data.

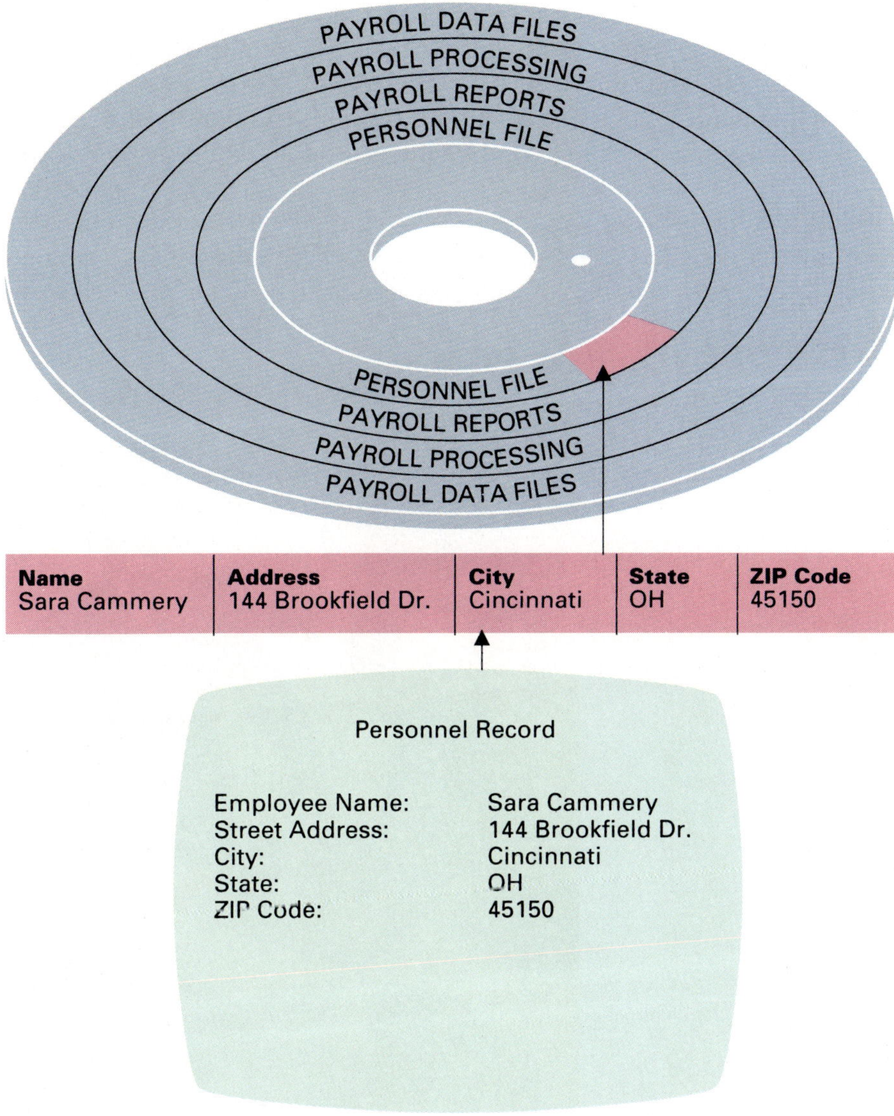

Figure 6-1
Auxiliary storage devices, such as disks, are often used to store such information as personnel and payroll files. Each file is made up of records, which consist of data fields or data elements.

When a software program needs data, it references the appropriate file and then accesses and loads a record from the file into memory. Once in memory, the individual data fields can be processed to produce the desired output. The time it takes the computer to actually load the desired record from the auxiliary storage device into its memory is called **access time.** The factors which affect the access time include (1) the amount of time it takes to position the access mechanism over the desired data (called **seek time** or **search time**), (2) the time it takes the record containing the desired data to pass under the reading mechanism while it is being read (called **latency**), and (3) the time required to transfer the data from the device into primary memory (called **data transfer rate**).

Access times vary greatly among auxiliary storage devices. For example, sequential-access devices may take several seconds, or even minutes, to access a given record of data. Random-access devices can access a given record of data within milliseconds (thousandths of a second). Transfer of data stored in primary-memory-like devices to another area of primary memory can range from microseconds (millionths of a second) in microcomputers to nanoseconds (billionths of a second) in supercomputers (mainframes).

Most auxiliary storage devices can be categorized as either disk (random access) or tape (sequential access). In the material which follows several different technologies and devices which make up these two categories will be examined.

Most auxiliary storage devices can be categorized as either disk (foreground) or tape (background).

Magnetic Disks

Data to be processed by a computer is often recorded on a **magnetic disk.** A magnetic disk is an input, output, and storage medium similar in appearance to a stereo record with a smooth surface. It is coated on both sides with microscopic bars made of a substance that can be magnetized. Recording is done magnetically by a method similar to that used by a tape recorder. The magnetic surface, however, is a rotating disk of grooveless tracks rather than a long strip. A **track** is a path on which data is recorded, usually on a magnetic medium. The tracks are arranged as shown in Figure 6-2.

Figure 6-2
The tracks of a disk are arranged one inside the other.

As the disk is rotated beneath a read/write head, the tiny bars are magnetized in the proper code pattern for each character. Figure 6-3 shows an imaginary section of one track on a disk.

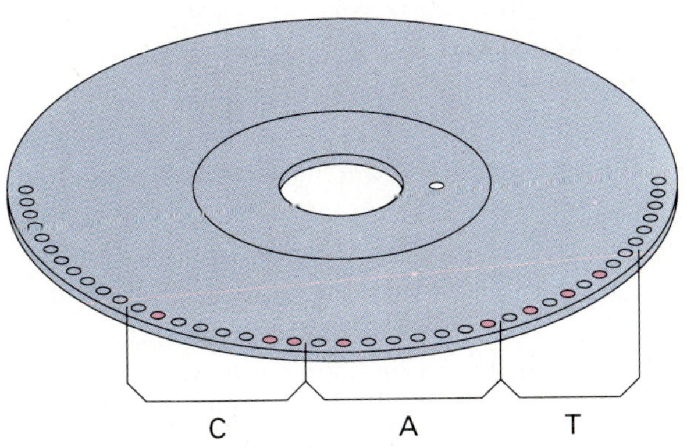

Figure 6-3
Coded magnetized spots represent characters on a disk.

Each side of a disk has a surface to which data may be written. Therefore, data on a disk may be recorded on either one or both of its surfaces. The disk drive uses a movable read/write head for each surface on which recording may be done. Thus, if recording is to be done on one side of a disk, there is one head. If recording is to be done on both sides of a disk, there are two heads. The heads travel in or out to position themselves over the disk track that is to be used. When new data is recorded to a specific area on a disk, any data previously recorded in the same area is erased. When data is read, on the other hand, there is no change; the data remains on the disk. This process is referred to as "destructive write/nondestructive read." It is similar to recording on a cassette; the new sounds will be recorded over any previous recording and, once recorded, can be played back many times.

A read/write head is used to store and retrieve data on a magnetic disk.

Disks are especially useful for applications in which data must be accessed in random order. A good example of such an application is an airline reservation system. In an airline reservation system, one caller may be interested in a flight to Los Angeles on February 4, and the next may want to fly to London on January 5. Once an inquiry is entered into the computer system, it must quickly access an auxiliary storage device, locate the desired information, retrieve it, and send it to the processor. The processor then must route the information to the appropriate caller. This entire process must occur within a few seconds time in order to provide the airline's customers with good service. The use of a disk is one of the most efficient and effective ways to provide such a service.

As mentioned earlier, data stored on a magnetic disk can be accessed randomly. Random access is sometimes referred to as **direct access.** That is, the head can move directly to the desired track rather than sequentially moving through all other tracks before it. If necessary, however, a disk drive can also access data sequentially. The ability to act as either a sequential-access or a random-access device has made the disk drive the most popular auxiliary storage device. It can be used for many and varied applications.

Magnetic disks can be divided into two categories: flexible disks and hard disks. Flexible disks and their drives (devices which house the disk and contain the mechanisms for reading and writing) cost much less than hard disks and their drives. However, flexible disks hold less data and are much slower.

Flexible Disks

A **flexible disk,** frequently referred to as a **diskette** or **floppy disk,** is a small, pliable magnetic disk. The first floppy disks were 8 inches in diameter and were used to load programs and data into mainframe computers. Today, disks 5 1/4 inches in diameter and 3 1/2 inches in diameter are commonly used. They represent the main medium for microcomputer auxiliary storage. The newer 3 1/2-inch disk's ability to store more than twice the data of the 5 1/4-inch disk, coupled with a more protective casing, has lead to its popularity. Most of today's micro- and personal computers come with disk drives which utilize the capabilities and capacities of the 3 1/2-inch disk.

Disks typically come in 8-inch, 5¼-inch, and 3½-inch sizes. The old 8-inch disks are no longer as popular as their 5¼-inch and 3½-inch counterparts.

Floppy disks are divided (formatted) into segments known as **sectors.** Imagine that a disk is divided into equal-sized segments as if it were a pie already cut into small pieces ready for serving. Each sector is further divided into a section for the sector address (used by the computer to locate the sector) and the data to be stored in the sector. A formatted disk with each of its tracks divided into sectors is shown in Figure 6-4.

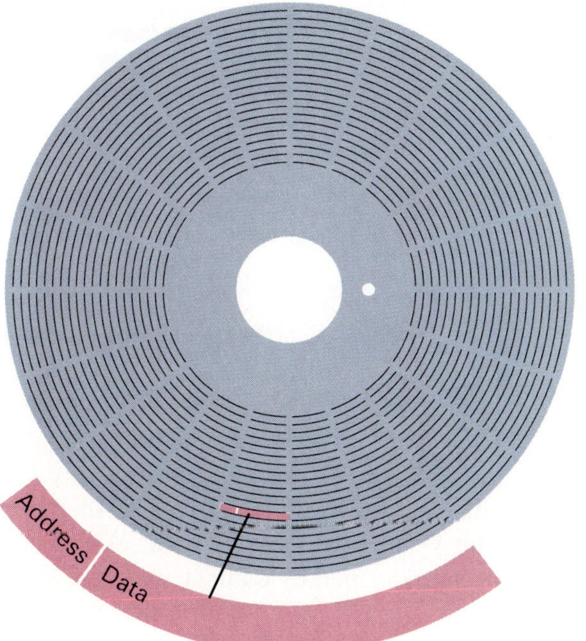

Figure 6-4
Each track on a disk is divided into sectors. Each sector is further divided into sections for the sector address and data to be stored.

One sector, filled with data, is the smallest amount of data that can be written or read at one time. The number of characters stored in one sector depends on the physical design made by the hardware manufacturer and on the computer's DOS (Disk Operating System). With many computer systems, a disk sector holds 512 characters. The amount of data that can be stored on one entire disk varies tremendously depending upon the way the particular drive and disk are made. Capacities from about 360KB (kilobytes) to 2MB (megabytes) are common, and 50MB of storage is possible.

Floppy disks are rotated inside their drives at about 300 revolutions per minute. The read/write head(s) actually make contact with the disk's surface as the drive operates. This friction causes wear, which in turn has limited the life of most floppy disks to an average of three years. Newer, high-quality diskettes are now burnished (highly polished) to assure smoothness and thereby eliminate tiny microscopic particles that could break off and scratch the surface. The read/write head(s) are made of hard ferrites (an almost pure metallic iron) embedded in hard ceramic sliders which reduce wear on the diskette to give it a longer useful life.

The popular 5 1/4-inch floppy disk drive comes in two basic sizes: full-height drives (about 4 inches high) or half-height drives (2 inches high). Figure 6-5 shows two personal computers, each of which uses the same 5 1/4-inch floppy disks but different size disk drives. The computer on the left side has two built-in, full-height disk drives. The computer on the right has two built-in, half-height disk drives.

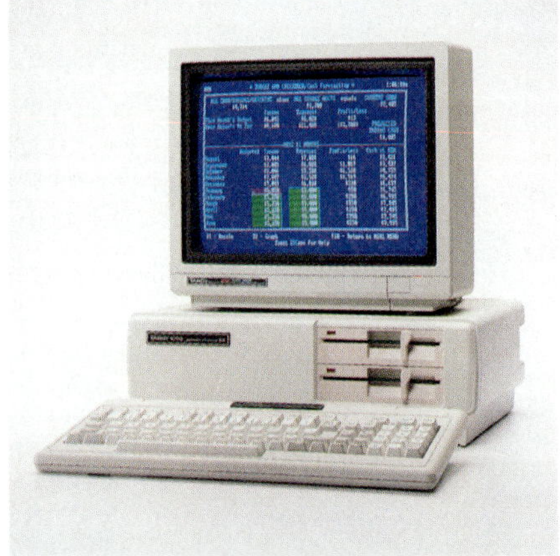

Figure 6-5
The computer on the left has full-height drives, while the computer on the right has half-height drives.

Hard Disks

A hard disk is so named because it is made of rigid material.

A **hard disk** is a magnetic disk that gets its name from the fact that it is made of rigid material; it does not bend like a floppy disk. While the read/write head on a floppy disk actually makes contact with the disk surface, the head of a hard disk floats on a cushion of air a tiny distance above the disk surface (often less than a millionth of an inch). Since there is no physical contact, there is no wear of the disk surface. The biggest danger of losing data on a hard disk occurs if the read/write head loses its cushion of air and touches the surface of the disk. This is called a "head crash" and often causes physical damage to the disk surface. Rotating at about 3600 revolutions per minute, hard disks can transfer data to and from the computer at a much faster rate than floppy disks.

Hard disks are available for personal computers as well as mainframe computers and are generally 5 inches, 8 inches, or 14 inches in diameter, although other sizes are available. Personal computers commonly use the 5-inch size while mainframe computers use the larger sizes. Also, hard disk drives for personal computers come in full-height as well as half-height sizes.

Winchester drives are sealed against dust and dirt.

In a hard disk drive, there may be one disk, or there may be several disks stacked on top of one another on a common vertical shaft called a **spindle**. When there are several disks, you may refer to the group of disks as a **disk pack**. There is just enough space between the disk surfaces to allow movement of the read/write heads (see Figure 6-6). Many hard disk drives use disks that are sealed against dust and dirt. These drives are called Winchester drives, which is a nickname for the technology used.

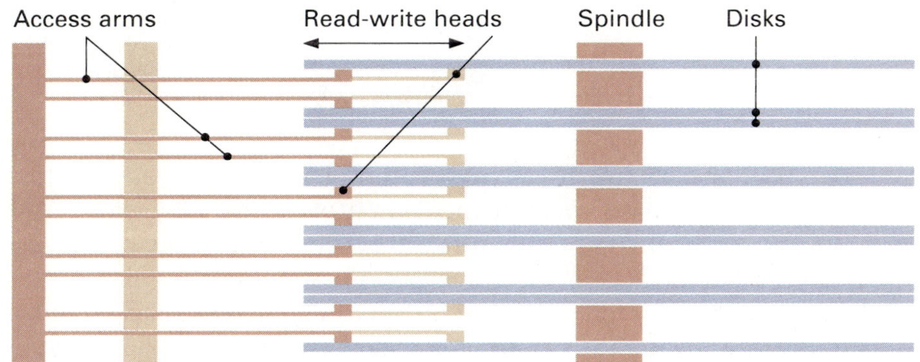

Figure 6-6
Read/write heads move between the disks in a disk pack, positioning themselves over the desired tracks.

The use of a disk pack can increase the speed of reading and writing by reducing the amount of head travel time. For example, suppose the words of a long document are to be recorded on disk. If the entire document is recorded on one disk surface, the write head moves into position over a track and uses all available space on that track. The head then moves to another track and uses all space available on that one, and so on. This may require several moves from one track to another. Suppose, however, that the data to be written is divided among several disk surfaces. In this case, all the write heads can move into position over the different surfaces, and the entire document can be written with no further head movement. This can greatly increase the speed of data reading and writing. You may refer to all the tracks of the same number on different disk surfaces as a **cylinder.** For example, all the third tracks put together make up a cylinder. See Figure 6-7 on the next page for an illustration.

A hard disk may be either fixed or removable. If a disk is removable, it may be taken out of the disk drive for storage and replaced by a different disk. This permits the same disk drive to be used by additional hard disks for more storage. A fixed disk cannot be removed from the disk drive; it is permanently mounted. Since the fixed disk cannot be removed, its capacity is limited to what the disk can hold. When a fixed disk is filled to its capacity, data files can be copied to other media for

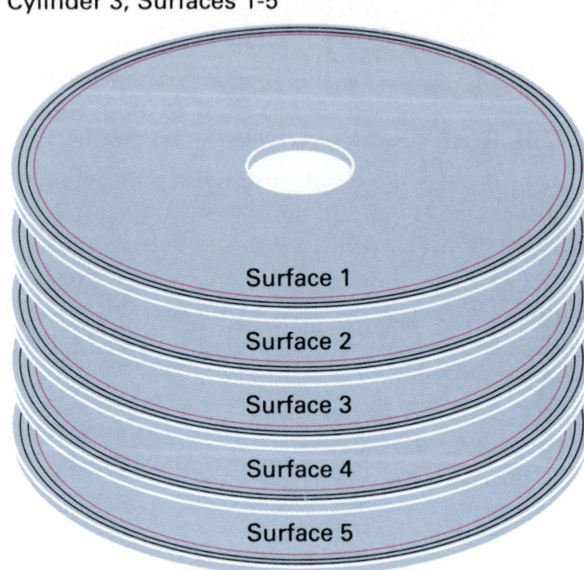

Figure 6-7
All the tracks of the same number on different disk surfaces make up a cylinder.

safekeeping, or data which has become obsolete can be erased to free up additional space. Most mainframe computers utilize removable disks while most personal computers utilize the fixed disk to meet their individual storage requirements.

Because a hard disk does not bend, data can be denser (packed much closer together) than it can be on a floppy disk. Historically, the densities of hard disks have doubled every 2.4 years—the result of an impressive evolution of development. Hard disk technology is commonly used with both personal and mainframe computer systems. Today's typical hard disks used with small personal computers have capacities of 20 to 40 megabytes. Since many disk drives are often attached to the same mainframe computer system, the total amount of storage that can be on-line at any one time is almost unlimited.

Bernoulli Disks

The **Bernoulli disk** is another type of magnetic disk technology which deserves mention. This concept uses a unique flexible disk drive in which the disk spins at a very high speed and is aerodynamically stabilized so that the head remains a fraction of an inch above the disk surface. The head literally flies above the surface of the disk.

The results of this technology yield a single disk storing as much as 20MB. This disk drive also has access times and transfer rates comparable to other high-quality hard disks and is well suited for removability and interchangeability with other computers.

Optical Storage Devices

Many computer experts believe that optical storage technology is the alternative to standard magnetic disk and tape storage. This technology uses finely focused laser beams to cram at least 50 times more data onto a given number of square inches. The high densities of optical storage devices have encouraged development of a technology that includes such devices as CD-ROMs, WORMs, and Erasable Optical Disks. They are as different from one another as the magnetic floppy diskette, hard disk, and Bernoulli disk are different from each other, yet they are based on a similar underlying technology.

CD-ROM

A **CD-ROM** (Compact Disk/Read-Only Medium) is one of the most exciting storage technologies that has been developed during the past one-and-a-half decades. The present day, 5-inch, silvery platter CD-ROM is a descendant of the 12-inch videodisks and, more recently, of the audio compact disks of the eighties. Storage capacities for CD-ROMs begin at about 200 megabytes and can store as much as 1GB (gigabyte—one billion bytes) per disk. On the average a CD-ROM can hold about 550 megabytes of usable data—the equivalent to over 1,500 of the popular 5 1/4-inch (360 kilobyte) floppy diskettes.

CD-ROMs (commonly referred to as laser disks) are also random-access devices. That is, the optical reading device can be instructed by the processor to position itself directly over the data which is to be read without first having to read all the data in front. This, plus the large storage capabilities, makes CD-ROMs very valuable for applications where huge quantities of data must be stored and later randomly accessed. For example, companies that must store large volumes of historical data, like the contents of an entire set of encyclopedias, could make good use of a CD-ROM.

CD-ROMs, which look like audio CDs, can store large amounts of data in a very small space.

CD-ROMs are produced in factories using exactly the same processes as audio CDs. Data is recorded by the presence or absence of holes burned onto the disk surface by a laser beam as shown in Figure 6-8. These microscopic holes are read back as digital data by a mechanism of lenses and mirrors and fed directly into the computer, where they can be handled just like any other data. This process is very similar to how an audio CD player can read the digital data recorded on a disk and convert it into sound (analog data).

Figure 6-8
Data is recorded on CD-ROMs by the presence or absence of holes burned onto the disk surface.

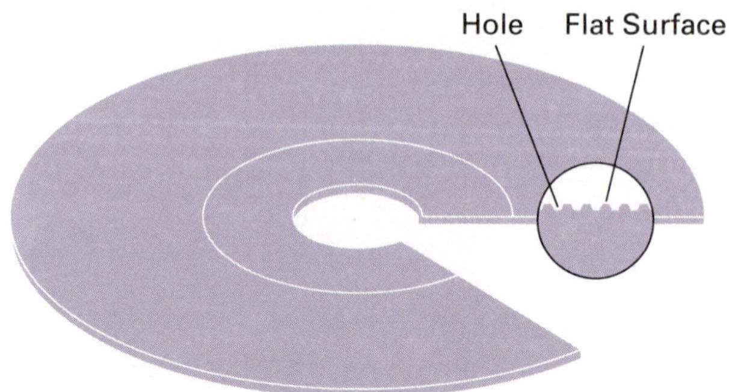

WORM Disks

WORM (Write Once/Read Many times) optical disk storage devices use laser beams and precision optics technology. Information is depicted by patterns of reflected light compressed onto a single disk. This is equivalent to storing the contents of several hundred books and/or thousands of graphic images into a unit no larger than a floppy disk drive. WORMs have been designed to serve as high-volume backup devices used to create a permanent archive of information. Because WORM disks can be written to only once, they are unalterable. Therefore, records on a WORM disk cannot be accidentally or intentionally changed. As a result, WORMs are excellent devices to use to create and then access huge files of data.

Because they can save vast amounts of data and are unalterable, WORMs make excellent backup devices.

All WORM disks store data as tiny holes in the recording surface made by a laser beam, similar to how a factory records data onto the surface of a CD-ROM. These depressions create physical changes on the disk's surface which cannot be changed or erased.

The WORM disk cartridge consists of a thin metallized-film material which covers a clear plastic disk. It is housed within a protected plastic case with a sliding metal door that allows the optical read/write head of the drive to access the disk. The disk cartridge is roughly 5 1/4 inches wide, 6 inches long, and 3/8 inch high. Data can be written to both sides of the disk simply by flipping it over and reinserting it into the disk drive. Capacities vary from 120MB to 500MB depending upon the manufacturer.

Erasable Optical Storage

Many hard disk manufacturers are scrambling to get into erasable optical storage technology. Such technology involves an optical storage medium in which previously recorded data can be altered or written over. A lot of money is being invested in this technology, and many manufacturers are hard at work to perfect such a product.

Erasable optical storage can be thought of as a simple extension of the current concept of magnetic disk storage. However, it is a technology very difficult to achieve. Recall that data recorded on optical disk media is physically burned into the surface. Erasing this previously recorded data so that new data can be written in the same space is no small task.

The THOR-CD (Tandy High-Intensity Optical Recording) was revealed as the first optical storage product that could be erased for repeated reading, editing, and recording. This media and its disk drives are multifunction, multipurpose drives. That is, the disks can be used as erasable optical media, and the disk drives can read prerecorded, factory-pressed CD-ROM disks. Although the THOR-CD may require some further refinement, the additional cost in electronics and drive mechanisms will not be significant. Most CD recorders should cost less than $500. Other erasable optical media and drives are being tested at numerous sites in the United States.

Many experts in the computer industry believe that the revolutionary optical disk technology (with its huge storage capacity of hundreds of megabytes per 5-inch disk) may someday have a significant impact on our current magnetic technology. Others believe that because this technology is moving so quickly, it will be vastly altered, or even replaced, before it becomes widely feasible. For example, research is exploring what is called **CD-I** (Compact Disk-Interactive) technology, which will enable optical disks to be utilized by flexible, general-purpose devices. This will allow a television, stereo system, and computer to be incorporated into a single unit home entertainment center.

There are those who believe the field of solid-state physics will produce a small, nonvolatile, integrated-circuit cartridge with the ability to store megabytes of data. Such a device would render spinning platters and optical storage technologies obsolete.

Magnetic Tape

A **tape** is a long strip of flexible plastic wound on a reel, like the tape used in an ordinary cassette tape recorder. Most tape is called **magnetic tape** because it is coated with microscopic bars of a material that can be magnetized. Magnetic tape may be on reels or contained in one of several kinds of cartridges.

Tape drives are devices which record data on the tape as magnetized spots in the proper pattern for each character. When the tape is read, the spots produce electronic impulses as they are moved past the read/write head of the tape drive. Figure 6-9 shows how the magnetic spots might appear if they were visible. Note that each character's code is recorded across the tape, with one bit in each **channel,** which is a recording path along the length of the tape. A read/write head is positioned over each channel on the tape. Tapes generally have nine channels. The heads either read the data that is already on the tape and transfer it to the computer for processing, or they write the processed data coming from the computer onto the tape.

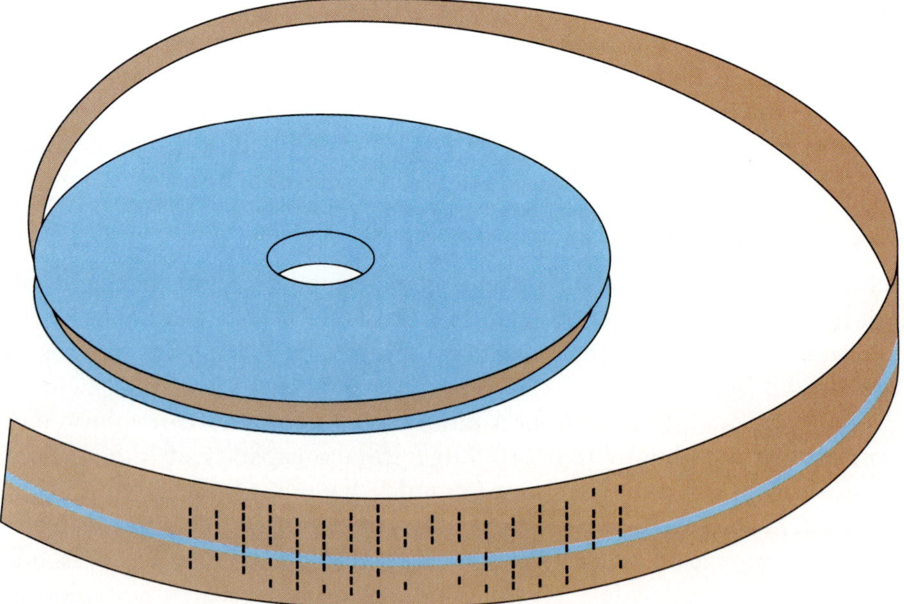

Figure 6-9
Data is recorded on tape as magnetized spots coded in the proper pattern for each character.

Writing on tape erases data previously recorded on it, just as it does with a disk. The new data erases the old as it is recorded. However, reading data on tape does not erase it. (You can erase a tape on a tape recorder by recording over it, but you can play a tape many times without erasing it. The concept is the same.)

A tape drive is a sequential-access device. In order for a certain item of data to be found on a tape, the computer must read all the items one after the other until it locates the desired one. The contents of the record can then be displayed on a monitor, printed, or otherwise processed. The use of tape is not practical for applications for which data must be stored or retrieved in random order. For some jobs, however, it is very appropriate. For example, suppose a historical log must be recorded each time an ambulance or police car is dispatched. All data relating to each call could be written onto tape. Tapes are also good for making a **backup,** which is simply a copy of all the data stored on an auxiliary storage device. The copy is made so that the data will still exist if the medium on which the data was originally stored is damaged or destroyed. Tapes come in a variety of sizes and shapes designed for specific purposes. In the material which follows, two of the most common tape media and the way each is utilized are discussed.

Tape Cartridges

A **tape cartridge** is a device used primarily on personal computers to provide backup for hard disks. The tape cartridge appears similar to the cassette tape (often called **digital audio tape**) used in the home or automobile. It differs, however, in that it is longer (ranging from 450 to 600 feet), may be of different sizes, and is of much higher quality—thereby enabling more storage of data in much higher densities. Today's machines move tape at speeds of 90 inches per second and can pack 60MB to 200MB into each cartridge. The storage of 200MB of data is equivalent to 550, 360KB floppy disks or 5, 40MB hard disks. The size of the tape drive itself is half the height of a standard floppy disk drive. Some particular models are designed to take up one of the floppy disk slots in a personal computer. Other similar devices are separate, standalone units which are connected to the computer via cable.

Tape cartridges are often used as backup devices for personal computers.

High-speed cartridge-tape drives move tape continuously, without starting or stopping (called **streaming** the tape). Even with this speed and high-recording density, it may take 20 to 30 minutes to back up the contents of a 40MB hard disk. This amount of time may seem long; however, it may be time well spent in light of the alternative—no backup at all. Lost data may take many hours, days, or even weeks to recreate. As these systems continue to evolve, they are likely to become more efficient and faster.

Tape Reels

Tape reels contain 1/2-inch-wide magnetic tape used primarily by mainframe computers for processing sequential applications and/or backup of data stored on disk. Tape reels are mounted on tape drives as shown in Figure 6-10. Data is recorded to the tape, or read from the tape, as it passes under a read/write head and is rewound onto a take-up reel. The area immediately below the tape reels contains two vacuum columns. The tape passes through the vacuum column on the left before it passes under the read/write head and through the vacuum column on the right before being rewound onto the take-up reel. These vacuum columns enable the tape to start and stop very quickly without breaking.

Figure 6-10
A tape reel is mounted on a tape drive. The tape passes through vacuum tubes and is then rewound on a take-up reel.

Large amounts of data can be stored on these tapes because of the length of the tape (2400 to 3200 feet) and high tape density. Common tape densities are 800, 1600, and 9600 bpi (bytes per inch). A 2400-foot-long reel of tape recorded at 1600 bpi can store approximately 46MB of data (2400 x 12 x 1600 = 46,080,000). Due to the speed the tape can be passed under the read/write head and its high recording density, data can be transferred to or from the tape at rates varying from 15,000 to over 1,000,000 bytes per second.

Tape reels are used to store data used for sequential applications. For example, a large company with hundreds of employees may use tape to process and store its employee payroll files. When reading the tape, each employee's record would be processed. Therefore, since all the records in the file are used each time the tape is read, it is a sequential application which efficiently lends itself to tape media. If, however, only a few of the employees were paid during various pay periods, or employees had to be processed in a random order, disk would be a better medium to use.

Since the majority of computer processing involves random access to data stored on disk, tape has been relegated to the role of backup. Data stored on disk is routinely copied (backed-up) to tape. If for any reason the data on the disk is destroyed, the data files can be recopied (restored) from the tape to another disk. Many companies regard the data stored on disk to be so valuable that they store the tape backups off-site (often in another building). That way, in case of a fire or similar disaster in which the entire computer system is destroyed, the backups (including the programs) can be copied to a similar computer, and the business can continue to operate.

Other Auxiliary Storage Devices

Bubble memory, videodisk, and VCR tape can be included in the broad categories of disk and tape auxiliary storage devices. Each of these devices are used for specific applications for which they are best suited.

Bubble Memory

Bubble memory is made up of small magnetic bubbles (called domains) arranged to represent data on a thin film of semiconductor material. These magnetic bubbles are magnetically charged particles which look like tiny spots on the surface of the semiconductor material. The spots are moved across the surface by electrical charges. Their presence or absence represents various on/off bit patterns which make up each of the alphabetic, numeric, and special characters.

Bubble memory is made of small magnetic bubbles arranged to represent data.

Unlike data stored in the computer's primary RAM memory, data stored in bubble memory is not lost when electrical power is turned off. As a result, it can be used for permanent data storage. Although this technology has been available for some time, it has not achieved the popularity of many of the auxiliary devices already discussed. Its production difficulties have led to high cost of manufacturing. Because it is small, lightweight, and can function on a very low power supply, it is starting to find greater usage in portable computers. As the portable computer market grows, so may the popularity of bubble memory as both a primary storage medium and an auxiliary storage device.

Videodisk

A **videodisk** is a magnetic disk device that records both the video impulses (pictures) and audio impulses (sound) of a TV signal and is available for instant replay. Videodisks can store huge quantities of data. For example, one videodisk can store up to 2GB on each side of the disk platter; that is equivalent to approximately 5500 double-density (360KB) floppy disks or 54,000 graphic images. This tremendous storage capability can be interfaced with a computer to become an effective educational training tool for both adults and children. A videodisk player can be connected to a TV monitor and a microcomputer for use in the classroom.

In one example of the use of a computer-videodisk system, a computer's software program controls the presentation of material on the videodisk. For example, once a lesson is started, the computer selects the appropriate textual material to be displayed to the TV monitor as well as movie segments (complete with commentary) from a particular part of the videodisk. After the lesson has been presented, the computer will test the student's understanding of the material by requesting him/her to key-in the answers. If, after grading the test, the computer detects a poor score, it again interfaces with the videodisk player to present a review segment of the lesson. Conversely, if the test score was good, the student's test results are recorded on the microcomputer's floppy disk, and the next lesson is presented.

The ability of stand-alone and computer-videodisk systems to combine graphics, motion, sound, and written text makes these media especially well suited for education at all levels. In schools, computer-videodisk systems can be used to bring new subject matter to remote areas, to augment textbooks and provide additional information, and to help special needs children with learning handicaps learn more quickly. Many industries use stand-alone videodisk technology to educate their employees. For example, videodisk training programs are distributed to car dealerships throughout the country by the manufacturers to teach auto mechanics about the engineering changes of new cars.

VCR Tape

The popular **VCR** (Video Cassette Recorder) **tape** (both VHS and Betamax) which is used in home video cassette recorders can also be used as computer auxiliary storage media. The storage capacity of video cassettes exceeds that of most auxiliary devices. A single tape may hold the equivalent of gigabytes (billions of characters) of data. The usage of this media is similar to the usage of cassette tape for backup as discussed earlier.

VCRs and computers were not designed to work together and are therefore incompatible devices. VCRs are designed to handle analog data (continuous or sound data), and computer data is in digital (numerical) form. In order to permit their connection, a data-to-video expansion card must be installed in the computer. This expansion card converts computer output into analog (video) signals, which can be stored on conventional VCR tape.

Two drawbacks to using VCR tape as backup exist. First, tape speed is relatively slow (about 13 megabytes every 10 minutes). Second, the quality of the tape is low, thereby causing recording problems. In order to solve the recording error problem, multiple copies of data are written to the tape. It is statistically unlikely that each of the copies will have the same recording errors. This multiple duplication of data reduces the capacity of a single 2-hour video tape to about 80 megabytes.

The primary advantages of using a standard VCR for data storage are cost and convenience. Both the VCR equipment and the VCR tape are mass produced and readily available at low prices. If the home or personal computer user already has a VCR, all that is needed to use it as an auxiliary storage device is a data-to-video expansion card.

HYPERTEXT SYSTEMS

It has been said that the accumulation of human knowledge is now doubling every ten years. Surely, the information age is upon us. We are becoming swamped in a virtual sea of information which is growing deeper with each passing day. How can we hope to sort through such vast amounts of data in order to find what meets our own individual needs?

The same computer hardware devices which have helped facilitate the information age are also superb devices to help us index data, and thus navigate us through the sea of information. The use of computer technology may well be the solution to the problems of indexing through the enormous amount of knowledge and information that has been brought about by the information age.

Indexing systems which we have learned to use are typically arranged in a numeric and/or alphabetic sequencing scheme. Humans, however, tend to visualize their thoughts in terms of association and pattern—not in terms of numeric or alphabetic sequences. Hypertext systems are being developed to permit their users to build channels of associations and patterns that will customize an index to their own particular needs.

Hypertext systems enable their users to view information nonsequentially. That is, with a hypertextual index, a user would be able to examine a large volume of information based upon his/her own interests instead of being forced to reference what may or may not be provided in a standard index. When using a hypertext system, the user can dictate the order of access and may access information in *any* order. The order may be by way of pattern and association, combinations of various viewpoints, or any other subjects desired. The larger the information base available, the more comprehensive the search. As a side benefit, items of information indirectly related to the search that might otherwise be missed may be found.

A true hypertext system is not yet available because the massive amounts of information accessible via computers do not currently exist. Efforts, however, are already underway to build hypertext systems and large bases of information. For example, *Grolier's Encyclopedia* is currently available on CD-ROM with indexing capabilities which enable its users to search for information based upon many associations never before possible via traditional indexes. Several professional and trade organizations (i.e. medical, engineering, and construction) are building large databases that will accommodate the hypertext concepts of access. Apple Computer, Inc. includes software entitled *HyperCard* with each of its Macintosh computers. This software enables Macintosh users to access information stored anywhere on their hard disk. Several word processing software packages have built-in database files that the user can access to check spelling, provide word association matches, and locate a great deal of other helpful information. Many relational database and filing systems now enable users to access information in a variety of patterns or associations.

In the future, technology is likely to equip us with hypertext systems and storage devices capable of storing massive amounts of data. Obviously, systems that deal with vast amounts of data will have to include vast amounts of storage. As the technology to produce and access hypertext grows, the technology to develop and expand storage devices will have to increase as well. With such systems we will be able to access information in ways which closely resemble our natural thought processes. Perhaps these technological tools will enable us to fully benefit from, and better utilize, the vast amounts of knowledge brought about by the information age.

Hypertext systems will allow us to access information through computers in ways never before imagined.

CHAPTER SUMMARY

- Auxiliary storage devices are not part of main memory but are on-line and available to the processor.
- Auxiliary storage is needed because not all programs and data can be stored in the CPU's primary memory at one time.
- Sequential access is a term used to describe a device (i.e. tape) that records and reads back data only in a one-after-the-other sequence.

- Random access is a term used to describe a device (i.e. disk) that can go directly to the location of particular data without having to read through all the data in front of it.
- Individual items, or pieces of data, stored on auxiliary storage device media are called data fields or data elements.
- A collection of related data fields or data elements is known as a record.
- A collection of related records is known as a file. A file may also be referred to as a database.
- Access time is the time it takes the computer to actually load the desired record from the auxiliary storage device into its memory. Factors which affect the access time include seek time, latency, and data transfer rate.
- A magnetic disk is an input, output, and storage medium in which data is magnetically recorded on the surface of a rotating disk.
- A track is a path on which data is recorded.
- Random access is sometimes referred to as direct access.
- A flexible disk, frequently referred to as a diskette or floppy disk, is a small, pliable, magnetic disk.
- Floppy disks are divided (formatted) into segments known as sectors.
- A hard disk is a rigid disk that is similar in size to a floppy disk but capable of faster access and much greater storage capacity.
- Hard disks may be composed of one to several disks stacked on top of one another on a common vertical shaft called a spindle. When there are several disks, they are commonly referred to as a disk pack.
- Since disk packs have more than one disk on a spindle, all tracks of the same number on different disk surfaces make up what is called a cylinder.
- A Bernoulli disk is another type of magnetic disk which is similar to a hard disk except the disk itself can be removed and interchanged with other computers.
- A CD-ROM (Compact Disk/Read-Only Medium) is a new technology with huge storage capacities. Data is recorded on CD-ROM disks by holes burned onto the disk surface by a laser beam.
- WORM (Write Once/Read Many times) optical disk storage devices have been designed to serve as high-volume backup devices. A WORM disk can only be written to once but can be read as many times as desired.
- Erasable Optical Storage devices can be thought of as a single extension of the current concept of magnetic disk storage. Optical storage devices, however, are capable of storing hundreds of megabytes on a single 5-inch disk.
- CD-I (Compact Disk/Interactive) is a concept currently under research which hopes to enable compact disks to store text, graphics, sound, and software. Future development of this technology could lead to a general-purpose machine that would incorporate a television, stereo system, and computer into a single home entertainment center.

- A tape is a long strip of flexible plastic wound on a reel. Most tape is called magnetic tape because it is coated with microscopic bars of material that can be magnetized.
- A channel is a recording path along the length of the tape. Most tapes have nine channels.
- A backup simply involves making a copy of all the data onto an auxiliary storage device. The copy is made so that the data will still exist if the medium on which the data was originally stored is damaged or destroyed.
- Cassettes (often called digital audio tape) can be used with a standard audio recorder as a low-volume and slow auxiliary storage device.
- A tape cartridge is a device used by personal computer users primarily to provide backup of large-volume hard disks. It appears similar to a cassette; however, it is of longer length, may differ in size, and is of much higher quality. This enables more storage of data in much higher densities.
- Tape reels contain 1/2-inch-wide magnetic tape used primarily by mainframe computers for processing sequential applications and/or backup of large volumes of data stored on disk.
- Bubble memory is composed of tiny, magnetically charged spots on the surface of semiconductor material. These tiny spots represent on/off bit patterns which make up each of the alphabetic, numeric, and special characters. Bubble memory can be used as both primary memory and auxiliary storage because the data it stores is not lost when the power is turned off.
- Videodisks are devices which can record video and audio TV signals and can store huge quantities of data. A videodisk can be connected to and controlled by a computer. The computer can be programmed to control the videotape and interact with the presentation to become an effective educational tool.
- The popular VCR tape which is used in Video Cassette Recorders can also be connected to a home or personal computer with the aid of a data-to-video expansion card and used as a high-volume auxiliary storage device.

KEY TERMS

The following key terms were introduced or redefined in this chapter:

access time
auxiliary storage
backup
Bernoulli disk
bubble memory
cassette tape/digital audio tape
CD-I
CD-ROM
channel
cylinder
data field/data element
data transfer rate
database
direct access
disk pack
diskette/floppy disk

file
flexible disk
hard disk
latency
magnetic disk
magnetic tape
random access
record
sectors
seek time/search time
sequential access
spindle
streaming
tape
tape cartridge
tape reel
track
VCR tape
videodisk
WORM

REVIEW QUESTIONS

1. What is the purpose of an auxiliary storage device? (Obj. 1)
2. Why are auxiliary storage devices needed? (Obj. 1)
3. What is the difference between a sequential-access device and a random-access device? (Obj. 2)
4. What is a data field (also called data element)? (Obj. 2)
5. What is a record? (Obj. 2)
6. What is a file? (Obj. 2)
7. What is a database? (Obj. 2)
8. Identify three factors which affect access time. (Obj. 2)
9. How is data recorded on a magnetic disk's surface? (Obj. 3)
10. What is a track? (Obj. 3)
11. For what purpose are disk storage devices especially useful? (Obj. 3)
12. Briefly describe a flexible disk (also called a diskette or floppy disk). (Obj. 3)
13. What is a sector? (Obj. 3)
14. Describe the difference between a one-hard-disk device and a multiple-hard-disk device. (Obj. 3)
15. Briefly describe a Bernoulli disk. (Obj. 3)
16. Why do so many computer experts believe that optical storage technology is the alternative to standard magnetic disk and tape storage? (Obj. 4)
17. What is a CD-ROM? (Obj. 4)
18. What is a WORM disk? (Obj. 4)
19. What is the biggest advantage of an erasable optical storage device over a magnetic disk? (Obj. 4)
20. Describe a magnetic tape. (Obj. 5)
21. What is a backup? Why are backups so important? (Obj. 5)
22. What is the primary use of tape cartridge auxiliary storage devices? (Obj. 5)
23. What is the primary use of tape reel auxiliary storage devices? (Obj. 5)
24. Identify at least two advantages of bubble memory used as either primary storage or as an auxiliary storage device. (Obj. 6)

25. For what type of applications are computer-videodisk systems best suited? (Obj. 6)
26. Why would a home or personal computer user use a standard VCR as an auxiliary storage device? (Obj. 6)

CHALLENGE ACTIVITIES

1. Consult personal computer magazines, a computer store, your school library, or other sources to obtain information about disk technology—either under development or recently available on the market. Prepare a report summarizing your research. Include information on the recording and reading of data, storage capacity, access times, cost, and the purpose it is intended to serve. As an alternative, prepare a similar report about a disk used on your school's computer. (Obj. 3)
2. Consult personal computer magazines, a computer store, your school library, or other sources to obtain information about optical storage devices—either under development or recently available on the market. Prepare a report explaining the recording and reading of data, storage capacity, access times, cost, and the purposes they are intended to serve. (Obj. 4)
3. Consult personal computer magazines, a computer store, your school library, or other sources to obtain information about magnetic tape and tape drive technology—either under development or recently available on the market. Prepare a report summarizing your research. Include information on the recording and reading of data, densities, length of tape, storage capacity, speed, cost, and the purpose it is intended to serve. As an alternative and if your school has a mainframe computer with tape devices, prepare a similar report about the tape device(s) used on your school's computer. (Obj. 5)
4. In this chapter you learned about several different auxiliary storage devices. Assume you have been asked to select the auxiliary storage device(s) that your school should purchase in order to automate its grade reporting system. All the grades for each student must be stored and used to prepare each student's report card each quarter or semester. Thereafter, all grades must be kept for five years after graduation. Select the auxiliary storage device(s), based upon what you have learned in this chapter, which you think will best do the job. Justify and support your selection(s). (Objs. 1,2,3,4,5,6)

PART 3

MICROCOMPUTERS AND OPERATING SYSTEMS

CHAPTER 7

MICROCOMPUTERS

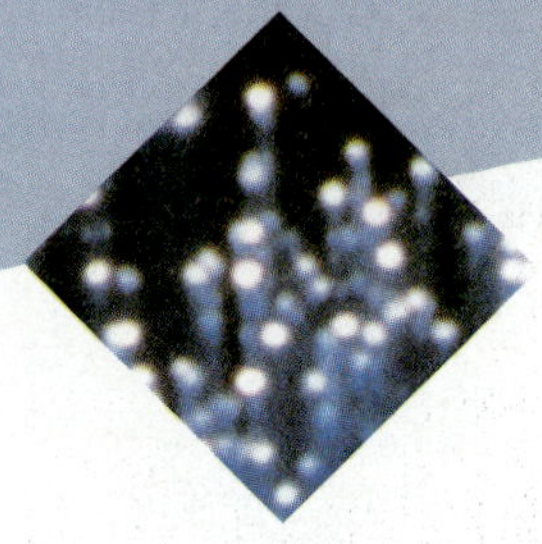

LEARNING OBJECTIVES

After studying this chapter, you will be able to:

1. **Describe the characteristics of microcomputers.**
2. **Explain why the designation of computers by size is becoming blurred.**
3. **Compare and contrast closed and open system architecture and relate them to system expansion.**
4. **Compare and contrast different methods of communicating with peripherals and make decisions on the preferred methodology under various circumstances.**
5. **Describe some of the issues of microcomputer compatibility.**
6. **Describe the function of microcomputer user groups.**

INTRODUCTION

Since their introduction in the late 1970s, microcomputers have revolutionized the way computers are used. In effect, they brought "computer power to the people" rather than allowing all computer operations to be dependent on large mainframes and their supporting cast of specialists. In this chapter you will learn the characteristics that make a computer a microcomputer. You will also learn some characteristics to consider in the selection and connection of microcomputers and their peripherals and about computer and software compatibility and user groups.

CHARACTERISTICS OF A MICROCOMPUTER

The name "microcomputer" was originally derived from the fact that the processing unit was contained on one microchip. The processor was referred to as a microprocessor, with the entire computer referred to as a microcomputer. Also, as perhaps implied by the name, microcomputers are at the bottom of the scale as far as computer performance is concerned; that is, larger computers can process data faster and can handle larger volumes of data.

While they have less processing power than larger computers, microcomputers provide more power per dollar of cost. On a unit-of-performance basis, the components of a microcomputer system, in general, cost less than do the components of a larger computer system. Also, the cost of software for microcomputers is usually substantially less than that of the same type of software for larger computers. While larger computers frequently require special environments in regard to temperature and humidity, microcomputers generally operate satisfactorily in any location that is comfortable to humans.

Microcomputers can be used almost anywhere humans can work comfortably.

At the time the term microcomputer was coined in the mid-seventies, only microcomputers used single-chip processors, and microcomputers were of relatively low computing power. Above them in the hierarchy were machines referred to as minicomputers. Minicomputers of the time did not use microprocessors. They had more power than microcomputers but less power than larger machines referred to as mainframes. Now, however, some microcomputers have more processing power than many minicomputers and some mainframes had at the time micros were introduced. Construction of larger computers has evolved to the point where some of the most powerful computers use multiple microprocessor chips working together to handle the processing load. This trend toward the use of microprocessor chips in all sizes of computers will probably continue.

Early microcomputers introduced in the late 1970s had 8-bit processors and typically 8 to 16 kilobytes of memory, though memory standards quickly increased to 32 or 64 kilobytes for some machines. They used very slow paper tape or magnetic tape cassettes (like a voice recorder) as auxiliary storage. The 8-bit processors could work internally with 8 binary digits at a time.

When the IBM PC was introduced in 1981 with a 16-bit processor, it quickly revolutionized the microcomputer industry. Many manufacturers standardized on the 16-bit chips, even as faster, more capable chips joined the original ones in the marketplace. After the introduction of the IBM PC, minimum memory standards increased quickly; first to 64K, then to 128K. Now 512K or 640K is required in order to use many of the more popular software programs.

Just as the first dramatic revolution in the microcomputer world was caused by the conversion from 8-bit to 16-bit chips, the second revolution is taking place in the conversion from 16-bit chips to 32-bit chips. The same advantages as before—the ability to process data faster and handle more memory—are firing this revolution. While most 16-bit processors cannot directly address more than 640K—requiring elaborate schemes to get around the limitation—32-bit chips can directly handle huge quantities of memory. Two megabytes has emerged as an accepted minimum standard amount of memory in 32-bit computers, with up to 16 megabytes being common. These "supermicros" are indeed putting some minicomputers and mainframes on the endangered species list, as many applications that previously required the more expensive computers now operate perfectly well on the much less expensive microcomputers.

SYSTEM ARCHITECTURE

System architecture refers to the methods by which the components of a computer are assembled. Architecture may be either open or closed.

Open Architecture

Open architecture refers to a method of assembling the components of a microcomputer (processor chip, memory, disk drives, etc.) in such a manner that expansion of the system is easily accomplished. A microcomputer using open architecture usually is based on a **system board,** sometimes called a **mother board.** The system board is the main electronic circuit board of the computer. A series of slots are mounted on the system board. These **slots** are connectors into which additional boards may be plugged. Each slot contains electrical contacts that make connection with other contacts on the edge of the cards that are plugged in.

Open-architecture microcomputers are generally assembled in one of two ways. Using the first method, many or most of the required components (including the processor chip, some quantity of memory chips, and chips to operate the disk drive) are mounted directly on the system board. Most or all slots are available for plugging in additional desired features, such as boards or cards to add additional memory above that which can be handled on the system board. With the second method of assembly, most components are placed on boards that plug into slots, while very few are placed on the system board. It is easier to update microcomputers that place the processor chip itself on a plug-in board because a new processor board that effectively upgrades the computer to operate faster can be plugged in.

With open-architecture systems, additional boards can be added into slots in the computer.

The more open slots a microcomputer has, the greater its expansion capability is. This is because more cards can be plugged in, each of which adds additional functions.

The primary advantage of open architecture, obviously, is that the computer can be easily expanded to add more memory, add extra disk drives, or provide for extra **peripherals** (equipment such as a printer that is connected to a computer to perform tasks which a computer cannot do itself). A disadvantage is that it costs more to produce a computer with open slots. To many users whose computer needs may expand after the initial purchase, the availability of slots with which to expand the system's capability is a top priority.

Even with the expansion capability an open-architecture computer has, there is one potential difficulty. Some expansion cards may be incompatible with one another, and some software may have difficulty running with some cards. This is a minor inconvenience, however, that can be avoided if the user studies the specifications of the various products before trying to combine them.

Closed Architecture

Closed architecture refers to a method of assembling the components of a microcomputer in such a manner that expansion of the system is not easily accomplished. This is done either by placing all components on the system board and having no slots or by using only the number of slots required for the standard configuration of the computer as it leaves the factory. In either of these cases, expansion of the computer system is difficult since no additional circuit boards can be plugged in.

Closed-architecture systems, such as this Macintosh, cannot be easily expanded.

The main advantage of a closed-architecture microcomputer is that it is economical to manufacture. Another advantage is that the possibility of software incompatibility with the hardware is reduced. This is true because the software developer can be sure that the software is written to work correctly with the standard configuration in the closed-architecture machine. For example, this avoids the kinds of problems experienced several years ago by software developers using a particular video board. Because of problems in the interaction of this board with other circuitry in the computer, the cursor would occasionally jump to random positions on the screen when the program tried to print on line 12. When this happened, the output that was intended for line 12 would be printed in the undesired random location. The only way around this dilemma was for the programmer to plan the program so that it never printed anything on line 12.

The lack of expansion slots represents a major disadvantage to many potential users. However, if a user is convinced that the capability built into the computer is all that will ever be needed, a closed-architecture system represents a more economical purchase.

SYSTEM EXPANSION

As indicated in the previous section, it is easy to expand microcomputers that are made with open architecture. This expansion is done by plugging additional circuit cards into open slots on the system board. In addition to the use of slots, many open-architecture computers have open sockets on the system board into which individual chips may be plugged to implement certain kinds of system expansion. The following paragraphs describe some of the more common capabilities that may be added. Frequently, several of these features may be combined on one plug-in card.

Additional Memory

As microcomputers have matured, it has become standard to include more and more memory with the systems. In the early years of microcomputers, four kilobytes of memory was standard. Now the standard amount of memory has grown so that it is common to find one megabyte of memory as standard. In spite of this growing standard, many users still find that they need additional memory. On some computers, there is a limited number of sockets on the system board available for plugging in additional memory chips without using an expansion slot. Beyond that limit, using one or more additional cards plugged into the slots of an open-architecture computer increases the memory.

Additional Ports

Peripherals to the microcomputer plug in through connections known as **ports**. For example, the printer plugs into a port. Other peripherals that may be plugged into ports include a mouse, a light pen, a plotter, or even a robot.

Peripherals, such as mice, can be plugged in through connections known as ports.

It is common for several ports to be included as standard equipment with a microcomputer. However, if the standard is inadequate, additional ports may be added through the use of plug-in cards.

Modem

A **modem** is a device that allows the computer to communicate over a telephone line with a computer at another location, which also must be equipped with a modem. In order to transmit data to the other computer, the modem translates the digital signals of the sending computer into the proper electrical impulses for transmission over the phone line. For signals coming from the other computer, the phone line's electrical impulses are converted back into the digital form required for processing by the computer. A modem may be either a plug-in card that is placed internally in the computer, or it may be an external modem, in which case it plugs into the computer through a serial port (see the following section on communicating with peripherals).

Modems allow computers to communicate over telephone lines. Modems can be located inside the computers, or can be external devices, as shown above.

Math Co-processor

A **math co-processor** is a chip that works in conjunction with the main processor chip of the computer. Its function is to speed up the computation of complex mathematical operations. Plugged into a socket on the system board, a math co-processor chip is extremely valuable for computation-intensive applications such as complex spreadsheets and computer-aided design or drafting.

Network Card

A **network card** provides the method for attaching a microcomputer to other microcomputers for the sharing of data and programs. The card plugs into a slot in the computer, and the cable connected to the other computers plugs into the card. A much more detailed description of connecting microcomputers in networks is provided in Chapter 14.

COMMUNICATING WITH PERIPHERALS

As you have learned, peripherals are connected to the microcomputer by means of ports. There are two main types of ports—parallel and serial. Each of them has peculiar characteristics that must be considered in connecting peripherals. For example, a printer designed only for connection to a parallel port cannot be connected to a serial port or vice versa. Many peripherals, such as most types of printers and plotters, are available for either serial or parallel connection. Others, such as modems which are always serially connected when used as external units, are available only for one type of interface.

Regardless of the type of port used, data is communicated between the microcomputer and the peripheral by using a code known as the American Standard Code for Information Interchange, commonly shortened to "ASCII." Under the ASCII code, each alphabet letter, numeric digit, and symbol is designated by a different numeric code expressed in binary form. For example, the letter *A* has a numeric code of 65. Converted to a binary number, the 65 is 1000001. You will note that a total of seven ones and zeros is used. Using seven binary digits (known as "bits" from BInary digiTS) in such a manner and going from number 0000000 to 1111111 can provide a total of 128 different combinations, therefore, making it possible to represent 128 different letters, digits, and symbols.

While the ASCII code in its pure form uses seven bits and represents 128 characters, most microcomputer manufacturers have added an eighth bit, which makes it possible to represent a total of 256 characters. This accommodates codes for foreign language symbols, line drawings, math symbols, and other special purposes. When an eight-bit code is used, characters that do not require the eighth bit have a zero in the first position. For example, the code for *A* discussed previously would have a leading zero added, making it 01000001. Another example of the use of an eight-bit code would be the representation of the radical sign (√) with the numeric code 251. In binary form in the computer, the 251 is 11111011. Appendix B addresses these coding schemes in detail.

Parallel Ports

Parallel ports derive their name from the fact that all eight bits representing a character are transmitted at the same time over eight different conductors. When a peripheral is connected through a parallel port, it is said to be using a parallel interface. Figure 7-1 shows how two different characters might be sent to a nearby printer (or other device) using a parallel interface. Parallel interfacing is usually not practical when the computer and peripheral are more than a few feet from each other.

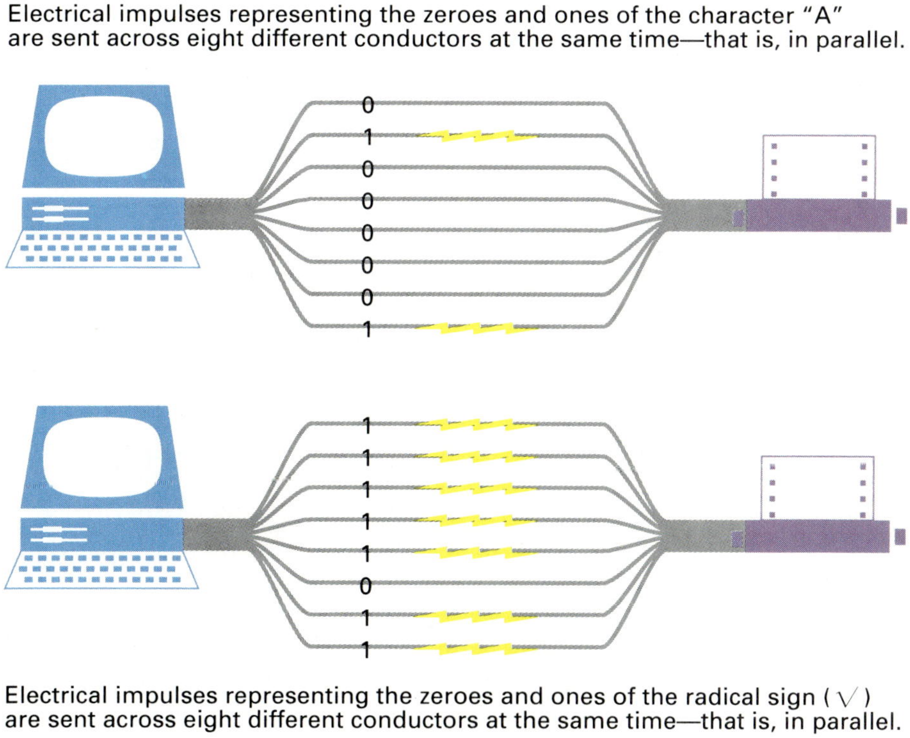

Electrical impulses representing the zeroes and ones of the character "A" are sent across eight different conductors at the same time—that is, in parallel.

0
1
0
0
0
0
0
1

1
1
1
1
1
0
1
1

Electrical impulses representing the zeroes and ones of the radical sign (√) are sent across eight different conductors at the same time—that is, in parallel.

Figure 7-1
When using parallel ports, all eight binary bits representing a character are transmitted at one time.

While the illustration shows eight conductors with electrical impulses traveling over them to the peripheral, a parallel port also contains other conductors. It is necessary to have conductors for grounds and control signals.

The two main advantages of using a parallel interface are its speed and its simplicity of use. Because all eight bits of a character travel to the peripheral at once, it works very quickly. Since a standard has developed for parallel interfacing, it is highly unlikely that a user will encounter difficulty making a peripheral operate properly when it is connected through a parallel interface. While there is a standard for what each of the conductors in a parallel interface does, there are different kinds of cable ends that are used. When connecting parallel printers, the two common cable ends are capable of handling a maximum of either 25 or 36 conductors and are generally referred to as the "DB25" and "Centronics" connectors, respectively. In addition, there are two versions of each of these: one with pins and one with receptacles into which pins are inserted for connections.

In hooking up a peripheral (most commonly a printer) with a parallel interface, the user must make sure that the cable ends match the hardware into which they will connect. It is very common to find that the parallel port on the computer is equipped with a DB25 connector with receptacles; therefore, a DB25 connector with pins is required to plug into the port. At the printer end, it is common to find a Centronics connector with receptacles on the printer, requiring a Centronics connector with pins on the end of the cable.

A parallel interface can also be used for connecting other devices, such as external disk drives. For this application, a configuration known as the small computer system interface (SCSI) is frequently used. Multiple SCSI connections can be "daisy-chained," that is, added one onto another, to connect several devices.

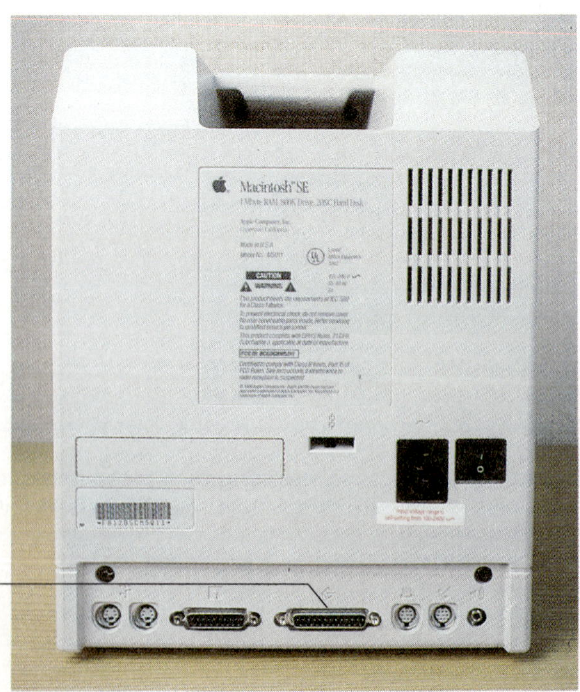

The Macintosh uses a SCSI configuration for connecting some peripheral devices.

Serial Ports

When using a **serial port,** the binary digits representing a character are sent over a conductor one after the other. This is in contrast to the parallel port, where all seven or eight of the bits are sent at the same time. Typical peripherals that might be connected through means of serial ports are printers, mice, and plotters. The method of transmission used by a serial port is illustrated in Figure 7-2, showing the transmission of the same two characters (A and $\surd$) that were used in illustrating the parallel port.

Electrical impulses representing the zeroes and ones of the character "A" are sent one after another across one conductor in the cable—that is, serially.

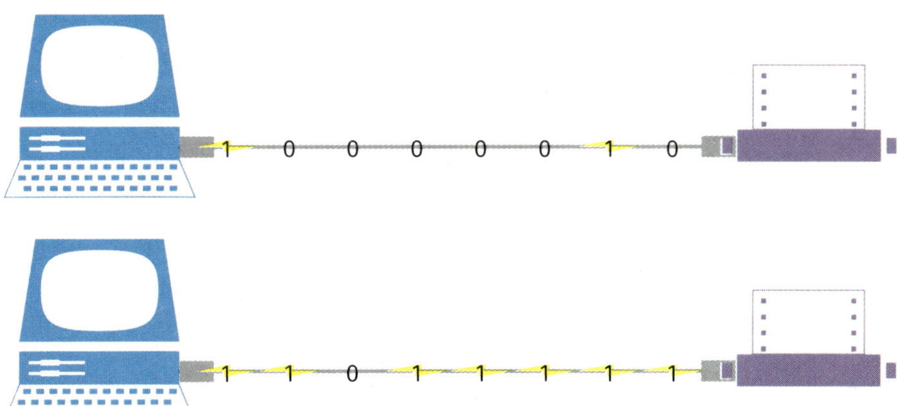

Electrical impulses representing the zeroes and ones of the radical sign ($\surd$) are sent one after another across one conductor in the cable—that is, serially.

Figure 7-2
When using serial ports, binary digits representing a character are transmitted one after the other.

While the illustration shows only one conductor, there are others actually used in making the connection. There is a conductor for data going from the peripheral back to the computer, as well as conductors for grounds and various control signals. However, the number of conductors used is still less than the number required for a parallel port, and serial cabling of longer lengths can be reliably used.

Although there are supposed to be standards for serial interfacing, various manufacturers have chosen to set up the conductors and the electronic impulses applied to them a little differently. Therefore, it is not unusual to hook up a peripheral using a serial interface and find that it will not work properly until various problems are resolved.

The probability of having difficulty setting up a serial connection is not caused by variations in the actual hardware conductor arrangement alone. Due to the nature of the serial interface, there are several variable settings related to how the data is sent over the conductors. It is necessary that the computer and the peripheral both be set the same way on all of these items. If they are different on even one item, the transfer of data will be incorrect, if it is transferred at all. These items are discussed in the following paragraphs.

Speed of Data Transmission

Since all the binary digits making up a character are transmitted over the same conductor, the frequency at which they are transmitted is variable. This rate of transmission (or speed) is known as **bits per second** (bps). You may also see the term baud rate used interchangeably with bits per second. Typically, serial ports can be set to transmit at some of the following speeds: 110, 150, 300, 600, 1200, 2400, 4800, 9600, 19200 bits per second. The effect of different speed settings at the microcomputer and peripherals is obvious. If the computer is transmitting at 9600 bps, while the peripheral is expecting to receive at 4800 bps, the peripheral will miss many of the bits.

Number of Data Bits

As you will recall, the ASCII code was developed as a seven-bit code, allowing a maximum of 128 different characters to be used. Manufacturers added an eighth bit, allowing up to 256 characters. Each of these bits is known as a **data bit.** Serial ports have to be configured to indicate whether each character coming through will be seven bits or eight bits. Again, it is obvious how garbage is produced if the computer and peripheral are not set the same. The computer might transmit eight data bits, for example, but a printer might take only the first seven of them to be the transmitted character.

Stop Bits

At the end of each character transmitted, either one or two bits (designated as **stop bits** and indicating the end of the character) are transmitted. Typically, at any speed higher than 110 baud only one stop bit is used. However, it is necessary that the computer and peripheral be set the same way. Serial transmission also includes a **start bit** indicating that a character immediately follows, but this parameter is not adjustable.

Parity Bits

As an error detection mechanism, it is possible to use something known as a **parity bit** with each character that is transmitted. (See Appendix B for a full discussion of parity bits.) When you choose to use parity bits, you may use a scheme known as even parity or one known as odd parity. The computer and peripheral must both be set the same as to the use of parity bits.

In connecting serial devices, you must be concerned about the cable ends and the internal connections of the conductors to cable ends. Connectors used with serial cables include the 25-pin DB25 type and the increasingly popular 9-pin. The safest way to ensure having a serial cable that will operate properly is to purchase one that is specified as being suitable for connecting your specific microcomputer and serial port model to your specific peripheral model.

In addition to being certain you have a correct cable, it is necessary to read the manuals carefully for the computer's serial port and the peripheral. It is also essential to set all necessary switches accordingly to ensure that the baud rate, stop bits, and parity match on both units.

COMPATIBILITY

With the explosive growth of microcomputers in the workplace and in homes, compatibility of computers becomes an important issue. Data can be converted and shared among stand-alone microcomputers of different types. However, it is much easier to share data and programs among computers that are already compatible, preventing the need to do any conversions. While there probably is no such thing as 100% compatibility between computers produced by different manufacturers, compatibility can be defined at several levels. These are the disk data format level, the operating system level, and the application program level.

Data generated by computers produced by different manufacturers can be converted and shared.

Disk Data Format Level

The lowest level of compatibility exists when data is stored on a disk in the same format by two different computers. This means that if one computer has been used to create a document or spreadsheet, for example, the other computer can read the data from the disk and further process it. However, the software used to create the data on the first computer and to process it on the second computer would be different. This is because computers compatible only at the disk data format level cannot run the same software. Of course, the same application program, for example, might be available in versions designed to operate on the different computers.

Operating System Compatibility

Different brands or models of computers may be able to use versions of the same operating system software (see the next chapter for more details on operating system software). This provides a higher degree of compatibility than only disk data format compatibility.

When different brands or models of computers can use versions of the same operating system software, a higher degree of compatibility is achieved.

Application Program Compatibility

The highest level of compatibility is reached when two different computers use the same disk data format, use versions of the same operating system software, and can run exactly the same version of applications software. This makes it much easier to run such applications as spreadsheet, word processing, and accounting software.

USER GROUPS

User groups are organizations of persons who use a particular kind of computer and/or software and are interested in mutual support in the use of that hardware and/or software. They provide a forum through which members can share knowledge, request assistance, and share public domain (uncopyrighted) software. Frequently, members of user groups are made aware of problems before the manufacturer is able to address them. Problems are frequently solved by members of the group.

In addition to their member support role, user groups also frequently act to try to influence vendors to take particular actions in the upgrading of hardware, software, or support. In this role, user groups provide a very important communications channel with the vendor.

The functions of user groups are carried out through meetings, newsletters, and electronic bulletin boards. User groups are not limited to users of microcomputers but exist for users of all sizes of computers as well as for various kinds of software.

User groups often meet in informal settings to discuss hardware and software issues.

TOP-FLIGHT PUBLISHING

It has been a productive flight for Chris Spears. As the computer at the controls of the 767 brings the huge aircraft into the San Francisco area, she snaps the screen of her lap-top computer shut. Having put the finishing touches on the last of four potential software manual layouts, she is confident that her meeting with a large software company will be successful.

Chris owns a small company that specializes in the writing and publishing of manuals for all kinds of products—from dishwashers to computer software to lawnmowers. Once research has been conducted on a product, Chris produces a draft of the operator's manual. The draft is proofed by the developers of the product and tested by several outside individuals to make sure that it is easy to follow.

As the draft of the manual is on its way to completion, Chris, herself, designs several proposed layouts. Among other things, these layouts show arrangement of the parts of the manual, the kinds of type fonts to be used for various headlines, the size of type to be used, the layout of the pages, and the illustrations intermixed with the print.

In previous years, Chris had hand-sketched layout proposals. This was very time consuming and gave the client only a rough idea of how the manual would look. More recently, she had used expensive photo-typesetting machines to actually typeset a few pages of the text. She would then manually cut and paste to arrange the text on the page. Both of these methods were slow and tedious.

Now, however, the layouts are produced using desktop publishing software and a microcomputer. By creating a simple style sheet, Chris can specify how large the headlines are to be and what font they are to use. The same is true of all other parts of a manual—the subheadings, the captions for figures and illustrations, and the text of the paragraphs (body text). In this way, the text of the manual can be displayed in the defined format.

All the software used for designing the pages as well as all the text and illustrations contained in the manual are stored on the computer. The same capabilities contained in Chris' lap-top computer required the size of a minicomputer a few years ago. Putting earlier lap-tops to shame, Chris' 32-bit microprocessor runs at a speed of 25 megahertz, has 4 megabytes of main memory, and has a hard disk that holds 80 megabytes. As an additional benefit, it can run on batteries so that Chris can work on the airplane where there are no electric outlets.

At the software company, the management is impressed with the quality of the manual and its proposed layouts. In addition to having the layouts on paper, management may also see the layouts in WYSIWYG (what you see is what you get) format on the computer's display. When the client proposes changing the format of the headlines, it takes just a few keystrokes to make the change automatically throughout the entire manual. The same is true when the client wants to change the font for the paragraph text from one typeface to another.

The convenience of the lap-top computer enables Chris Spears to show the proposed layout to her clients. Changes and revisions to the design can be incorporated immediately.

After the changes are made, the client requests a printout of the entire manual. Chris plugs one of the client's laser printers into her trusty lap-top, and in a matter of minutes the manual is on paper and in the client's hands in sharp looking 300x300 dot-per-inch resolution. Chris then begins processing the final product. She unplugs a normal phone line from the back of a phone in the client's office, inserts the plug into the jack on the back of her computer, and strikes a couple of keys instructing it to dial her office back in Atlanta. The computer then automatically transmits the finished manual to the typesetting machine. The manual emerges a few minutes later at almost 12 times the resolution (sharpness) of the laser print and is on the printing press that afternoon.

By using Chris' professional services, the client now has a manual that is easy for customers to understand, making it easier for them to use the software. Because of the advanced technology Chris used to reduce the turnaround time, the client's product was on the market before that of the main competitor.

CHAPTER SUMMARY

- The term microcomputer derives from the fact that the computer has a processor contained on one chip (microchip).
- Microcomputers have less processing power than contemporary minicomputers and mainframe computers.
- Microcomputers have more power than mainframes of a few years ago.
- The capabilities of a microcomputer with open architecture can be easily expanded, while one with closed architecture is difficult to expand.
- Slots on a system board are used to plug in additional circuit cards to expand a microcomputer's capabilities.
- Common items added when expanding a microcomputer are additional memory, additional ports, a modem, and a math co-processor.
- Communication with peripherals may be through either a parallel interface or a serial interface.
- The American Standard Code for Information Interchange (ASCII) is used when communicating with peripherals.
- Parallel ports (all bits of a character transmitted at once) operate faster and with less set-up difficulty than do serial ports. Serial ports (each character transmitted a bit at a time) can operate over longer distances but have enough variation in implementation and options to create difficulties in getting things working correctly.
- The cable used in connecting peripherals must have the proper ends to match the connectors on the microcomputer and the peripheral.
- While there is probably no such thing as 100 percent compatibility between different brands of computers, compatibility can exist at the disk data format level, the operating system level, or the applications software level.
- User groups serve the purpose of mutual support of users of a particular computer or program.

KEY TERMS

The following key terms were introduced or redefined in this chapter:

bits per second
closed architecture
data bit
math co-processor
modem
network card
open architecture
parallel port
parity bit
peripheral
port
serial port
slot
start bit
stop bits
system architecture
system board/mother board
user groups

REVIEW QUESTIONS

1. What are five characteristics of microcomputers that distinguish them from larger-sized computers? (Obj. 1)
2. What events have caused the distinctions between different sizes of computers to become blurred? (Obj. 2)
3. What is the difference between open architecture and closed architecture? (Obj. 3)
4. What are the advantages and disadvantages of open architecture? (Obj. 3)
5. What are the advantages and disadvantages of closed architecture? (Obj. 3)
6. Name several system capabilities that may be implemented when expanding a microcomputer. (Obj. 3)
7. What is the distinguishing feature of a parallel port? (Obj. 4)
8. What is the distinguishing feature of a serial port? (Obj. 4)
9. What are the advantages and disadvantages of using a parallel port? (Obj. 4)
10. What are the advantages and disadvantages of using a serial port? (Obj. 4)
11. Name and describe each of the three levels of microcomputer compatibility. (Obj. 5)
12. What is the function of a user group? (Obj. 6)

CHALLENGE ACTIVITIES

1. What factors would you consider and what process would you use in determining whether to purchase an open-architecture or closed-architecture computer, assuming that either type of machine is capable of providing the processing power needed? (Obj. 3)
2. What factors would you consider and what process would you use in determining whether to use a parallel port or a serial port for connecting a peripheral under consideration? (Obj. 4)

3. In the preceding challenge activities, you provided factors and processes you would consider in various situations. You now have an opportunity to apply those items to the following case study. Read the information given and then, for each question at the end, write your decision and the reasoning you used in reaching the decision. (Objs. 3,4,5)

   A writer has met with some degree of success in the past several years. Specializing in writing user's manuals for equipment produced by various manufacturers has provided all the work that the writer can handle. To this point, a simple word processor on a very small home computer has been used. Now, however, clients are beginning to demand that complex diagrams and drawings be included in high-quality, publication-ready copy of the manuals. Also, the writer is seriously considering adding a secretary and an assistant writer to help carry the work load.

   If the writer hires the new employees, additional office space will also be needed. Private work areas for the writer and the assistant will be needed, and the secretary will need work space. To provide the quality of printout now being demanded by clients, the writer will need a laser printer that will be shared by all three persons. The speed with which data can be sent to the printer can have a significant effect on the amount of time needed for printing each page, particularly when printing the necessary graphics. Looking to the future, the writer sees a real possibility that clients will want drafts of the manuals transmitted to them electronically for approval before the final print-ready versions are produced.

   In short, considering the entire situation, the writer has the immediate need to purchase a more powerful computer and a laser printer. There is also the probable need to provide additional office space when employees are added, as well as two additional microcomputers. Down the road, communication of manuals to clients over phone lines is a possibility.

   a. Keeping in mind that closed-architecture computers can do everything presently needed by the writer and that the writer needs to conserve money as much as possible, do you recommend an open-architecture computer or a closed-architecture computer. What reasons support your decision?
   b. Given that the model of laser printer wanted by the writer is available for connection by either parallel or serial port, which do you recommend and why?

CHAPTER 8

OPERATING SYSTEMS

LEARNING OBJECTIVES

After studying this chapter, you will be able to:

1. **Explain the purpose of an operating system.**
2. **Explain the functions of an operating system.**
3. **Compare and contrast the capabilities of single-user environments and multitasking environments.**
4. **Characterize common microcomputer operating systems.**
5. **Describe the functions of some commonly used utility programs.**
6. **Describe some of the issues of operating system compatibility.**

INTRODUCTION

A philosopher once said that a computer without software might as well be a boat anchor. This is very true, for without software the computer system will not work. In this chapter, you will learn about the operating system software that enables the various components of the computer system to communicate and function.

THE PURPOSE OF AN OPERATING SYSTEM

The software that controls the operation of the computer and enables communication between components to take place is called the **operating system.** It controls the operation of the processor, the auxiliary storage devices, and the input and output devices. The function of this software is in contrast to the function of applications software, which instructs the computer to perform a particular job, such as accounting or the control of factory equipment.

HOW OPERATING SYSTEMS FUNCTION

The functions of the operating system can be divided generally into three categories. These categories are (1) control of the system, (2) resource management, and (3) resource monitoring.

Control of the System

The first function of the operating system is to control the computer system. When the computer is started up (booted), the operating system software is loaded from disk into a designated portion of memory, and control of the computer is turned over to the operating system programs. There are enough instructions permanently stored in read-only memory in the computer to accomplish the loading of the first record of the operating system (the **boot record**) from disk into memory. The records on the disk drive are recorded in the format required by the particular operating system. Once the first record is in, it can control the loading of the remainder of the system. Figure 8-1 shows the process of booting the computer and turning it over to the operating system.

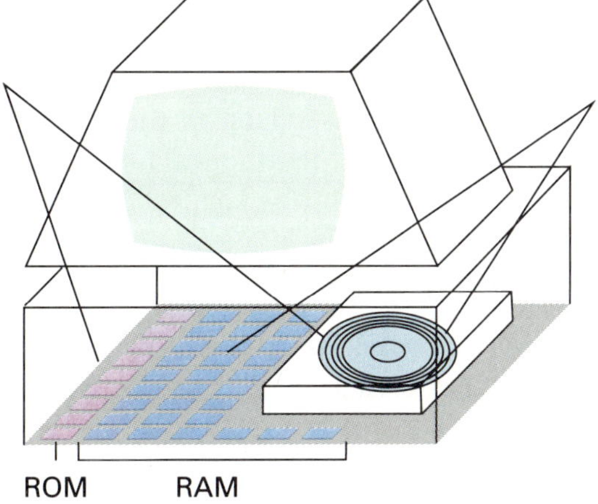

Figure 8-1
Instructions stored in read-only memory load the boot record into memory. The boot record then loads the remaining operating system instructions.

Once the operating system software is loaded, the computer is under its control. It can determine which programs to execute, how much processor time they get, and when they must cease operation. Depending on how the system is set up, the operating system may wait after boot-up for a command from the user, or it may immediately load and begin execution of a specified application program.

Resource Management

The resources of a computer system are its processor(s), memory, auxiliary storage, and input and output devices. The operating system controls all of these resources and determines when application programs may use them. The storing of data on disk drives, for example, is done under instructions from the operating system, as is the reading of data. The operating system is also in charge of communicating with and handling data from various input devices. Transmission of data to output devices in the proper format is also under control of the operating system. The services of the operating system in managing computer resources are available for use by application programs. For example, an application program that wants data stored on the disk informs the operating system, which actually handles the process of recording the data.

Resource Monitoring

The operating system can also monitor the performance of the resources. For example, the number of devices attempting to communicate with the computer and the amount of delay they encounter can be monitored. As another example, the operating system can monitor the number of attempts required before data is successfully read from a storage device. This monitoring allows for better analysis of problems as well as provides the data necessary for updating computer systems. By tracking the number of difficulties encountered by devices such as disk drives, the operating system can help users of the equipment know when maintenance is needed before a total system failure. The operating system can also check on problems created by such things as failure to close files after use, which may result in defective data on the disk. (Frequently, this defective data can be restored in its original form by the use of proper utilities. This is discussed later in this chapter.)

TYPES OF OPERATING SYSTEMS

There are many brands and versions of operating systems. Each operating system is designed to work with a particular processor. All of them, however, can be classified into one of two categories—operating systems that provide for single-program execution and those that provide for multiple-program execution, or multitasking environments.

Single-Program Execution

Operating systems that provide only for single-program execution can execute just one application program at a time. Under such a system, the operating system loads the application program into memory and

Operating systems that provide only for single-program execution can execute just one program application at a time.

starts execution of the application program's instructions. All the while, the operating system continues to make its resource management services available to the application program. Under such an arrangement, the main memory of the computer can be illustrated as shown in Figure 8-2.

Operating system software is loaded into part of memory and makes its management services available. It loads an application program into other memory locations and has the computer begin doing the steps of the application program.	Application program is loaded into another part of memory. As it executes, the program calls on the operating system for services.	Remaining memory is available for storing data used by the operating system and the application program.

Figure 8-2
While using a single-program operating system, the main memory of a computer may operate as shown here.

When a different application program is run, the new program takes the place of the first one in memory. The amount of memory space into which the application program is loaded is variable, depending on the size of the program. If an application program takes up a large amount of space for its instructions, less memory space will be available for the storage of data; if an application program takes up little space for its instructions, more memory will be available for the storage of data.

While single-application operating systems can handle only one application program at a time, it is possible to load several programs into memory, where they stay resident until needed. These programs may be loaded by a special user interface program that retains control of the computer and calls the loaded programs when they are needed. Alternatively, an additional program may be what is called a terminate-and-stay-resident (TSR) program, which is frequently used for such desktop accessory purposes as appointment calendars, phone directory/dialers, calculators, etc.

When a TSR program is used, it is loaded before any other application program. It puts itself into memory and sets up a watch over the flow of data coming (typically) from the keyboard. It then allows the user to load and execute any other application program desired. Since it is keeping watch over all keystrokes, however, it can recognize whenever a particular "hot key" combination is pressed. When the user strikes that combination, the TSR program takes control back to itself. When it is finished, it returns control to the other application program. When a TSR program is in use, the computer memory can be visualized as shown in Figure 8-3.

Figure 8-3
When a TSR program is used, the main memory of a computer operates as shown here.

Operating system software is loaded into part of memory and makes its management services available.	Terminate-and-stay-resident program is loaded. It then allows another application to be loaded and executed. The TSR program retains watch over all keystrokes so that it can become active again at a keystroke command.	Application program is loaded into another part of memory. As it executes, the program calls on the operating system for services.	Remaining memory is available for storing data needed by the TSR program, application program, and the operating system.

As an example of how a TSR program works, assume that you have loaded one that maintains a phone directory and dials the phone. Then you load and begin using a spreadsheet program. While using the spreadsheet program, you decide to make a phone call. You hit the hot key combination, and the phone directory program's menu appears on the screen. You select the number, the program dials it, and you carry on the phone conversation. Upon your exit from the phone dialer program, the spreadsheet program begins operating again.

Note that, even though there may be two or more application programs residing in the memory of the computer at once, only one of them is actually executing at a time. This is because a single-application operating system can handle execution of no more than one program at a time.

Under a single-program operating system, the application program that is executing generally has the freedom to use any portion of memory it desires. This means that a program that has not been written to be "well-behaved" can write over memory locations containing operating system instructions or reserved for other purposes. Some applications also take total control of the keyboard, preventing the use of TSR programs. It is not unusual for such difficulty to arise, especially when using several TSR programs at the same time. When a program destroys instructions or data that should not have been tampered with, disaster is sometimes the result. For example, it is possible that an ill-behaved TSR program might totally erase a large word processing document.

Multitasking Environments

In contrast to an operating system that can handle only one application program at a time, a **multitasking** operating system can juggle more than one action at a time. While the ability to handle more than one task at a time is valuable in many circumstances, it requires more complex instructions in the software, more computer memory, and additional cost.

The additional complexities can also make the multitasking operating system more difficult to use. Multitasking operating systems have one or a combination of the capabilities known as multiprogramming, multiprocessing, time sharing, or virtual memory.

Multiprogramming

Multiprogramming refers to the capability of running more than one application program at a time. The application programs may be executing for the same user or for different users. In a small business, for example, the user may want to do word processing at the same time the computer is printing out monthly statements for customers. If the computer has a multiprogramming operating system, both tasks can easily take place together.

Although multiple tasks appear to the user to be happening at once, this is not the case. In reality, the operating system is dividing the processor's time between the two tasks by a technique known as **time slicing**, which gives each program a small slice of time in turn. When two programs are running at the same time, one of them is frequently known as a **foreground task** and one as a **background task**. In this example, the word processing application would be the foreground task. Therefore, whenever the operator wants to key and process words, the computer will devote most of its time to that purpose. During pauses (even very short ones) in word processing activity, however, processor time is devoted to printing the statements, which would be the background task. Figure 8-4 shows how the computer's memory might be used in multiprogramming, with one foreground and one background task.

Operating system software is loaded into part of memory and makes its management services available. It loads application programs into other memory locations and begins giving slices of time to the application programs.	Foreground program is given as many time slices as it needs to function, having all of them available whenever needed.	Background program is loaded into another part of memory. When there are pauses in the system demands of the foreground program, the operating system gives time slices to the background program.	Remaining memory is available for storing data needed by the application programs and the operating system.

Figure 8-4
The main memory of a computer may operate as shown here when using multiprogramming.

Multiprocessing

Whereas multiprogramming refers to the ability to run more than one program at a time, **multiprocessing** refers to an operating system's ability to handle more than one user at a time, often with several operators using the same application software. As with multiprogramming, the operating

Through the use of multiprocessing, these members of the Hong Kong stock exchange can all use the same program at once.

system time-slices the processor's efforts in order to give processing time to all the users. In the case of several persons using the same application program at the same time, the operating system must maintain the status of each user as the time slicing is occurring. It must remember a user's exact place at the end of each allotted time slice so that processing may continue smoothly when the user's next processing turn is available. Figure 8-5 shows how memory might be used when multiprocessing is going on.

Figure 8-5
When multiprocessing occurs, the main memory of a computer might be used as shown here.

Operating system software is loaded into part of memory and makes its management services available. It loads application program into other memory locations and begins giving slices of time to the users of the program.	A portion of memory is allotted to the first user of the program, and the space is used for storage of data and control information for that user.	A portion of memory is allotted to the next user of the program, and the space is used for storage of data and control information for that user.	Remaining memory is available for storing data needed by the operating system.

Time sharing

Time sharing refers to the process of having multiple terminals attached to a single processor, which handles all operations for all the terminals. This is in contrast to having several microcomputers, each with its own processor, networked together to share resources. The use of time sharing can be less expensive than setting up networks. However, a time-sharing environment provides one processor that does all the computing for all the users, whereas a network provides each user with the services of a processor. For applications that require a lot of processor time, networking is preferred to time sharing.

With time sharing, like the other methods of multitasking, the operating system divides the time of the processor between the applications. Under time sharing (which is used to implement multiprocessing), as well as with multiprogramming, the time slicing performed by the operating system may be divided evenly between all users, or it may be divided according to priority. When it is divided by priority, certain programs or users are given higher priority than others and receive preferential treatment by the operating system. In the previous example of word processing and statement printing occurring at the same time, the word processing application has priority, and therefore the operating system gives time to the statement printing operation only when the word processing operator is pausing.

Time sharing allows these employees to be working on different programs at the same time.

Virtual Memory

While multiprogramming, multiprocessing, and time sharing refer to methods of multitasking, virtual memory refers to a management scheme designed to make the other methods more usable. Any computer system has a limit to the amount of physical memory installed. When multiple programs are loaded into memory under multitasking, it is easy to quickly exhaust all the memory. When memory is full, it would be necessary for some programs to be abandoned if it were not for virtual memory. **Virtual memory** is a method under which parts of large programs and some of the data that needs to be in main memory is temporarily stored on disk while its application is not executing.

To illustrate this concept, suppose that six different programs are being executed at the same time and there is not enough memory to hold all the programs and the necessary data at once. As you remember, time slicing divides processing time between applications. As you also remember, some tasks are designated as background and some as foreground tasks. Under virtual memory, as many of the six programs and/or their data as needed are stored temporarily on disk while they are not being processed and are reloaded into memory when it is their turn to be processed. In other words, a disk drive is acting as an extension of the available memory space with data and programs being swapped between the memory and the disk as needed. In a virtual operating system, these swaps are handled by the operating system and are totally transparent to the user of the programs.

Memory Protection

As you learned earlier in this chapter, an application program running on a computer is capable of directly storing data in various memory locations. While "well-behaved" programs will use the services of the operating system for handling all storage needs, "poorly behaved" programs may have been written to bypass the operating system and go straight to memory locations. It is easy to see the problems that can be created when several programs are in the computer's memory and are executing at once. One or more of them may begin writing to memory locations that are used by the others for data. Or, it is possible for one program to "kill" another program by storing data on top of the other program's instruction steps. It is quite easy for ill-behaved programs to cause an entire computer system to crash or quit operating.

To help prevent the kind of disasters that could result from programs wiping out each other and important data, some operating systems use a **memory protection** scheme. Under such a plan, the operating system assigns a section of memory to a program and then keeps close watch over the program to examine the address of every memory location it attempts to use. If a program attempts to use a memory location not assigned to it, the operating system can interrupt the program and cancel its attempted violation of memory space.

MICROCOMPUTER OPERATING SYSTEMS

The primary functions performed by a microcomputer operating system are essentially the same as the functions performed by the operating systems used with larger computers. However, the number of functions may be somewhat fewer.

Many of the functions or commands of operating systems are built-in or are resident. In other words, the instructions to make them function are included in the operating system software that is loaded into the computer's memory upon boot-up and stays there during operation. Other functions or commands take the form of **transients**; that is, the instructions to carry them out reside on disk until needed, at which time they are loaded into memory and executed. The instructions required for the resource management and control functions of DOS are among those that typically remain in memory while the computer is running. Less commonly used instructions (or ones that require lots of memory) are loaded from disk when needed.

The **user interface**—the way commands are given by the user to the operating system—may be by either of two methods. Traditionally, the user enters commands by typing them on the keyboard, a method known as command line entry. For example, to see a directory of all files stored on a disk, the user might key-in **DIR** or **CATALOG**. If the user does not know the needed command, the only thing to do would be to look it up in the reference manual. Operating systems developed more recently, however, may use a menu or graphic interface, making it easier to use the commands without having to memorize or look them up in a manual. Older operating systems sometimes have menu-type interfaces available from the original producer or other vendors. While menu-based operating systems are easier to use, they generally require more memory than do command-line based systems. Figure 8-6 illustrates a typical command to display a disk directory using a command-line interface and a menu interface.

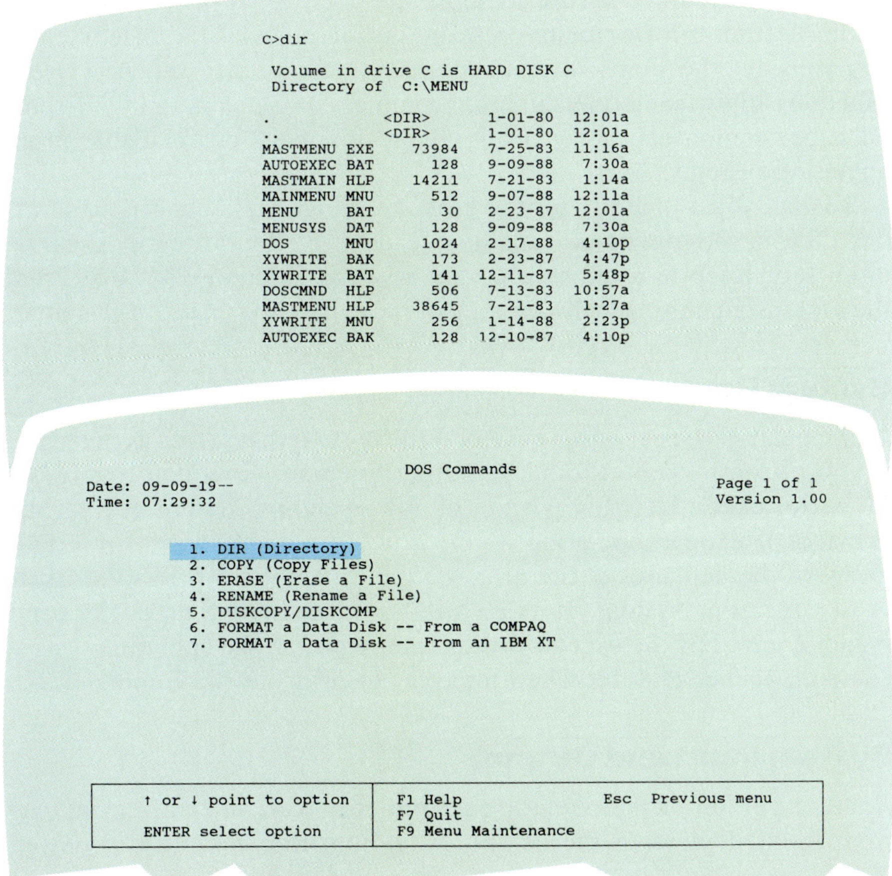

Figure 8-6
Operating systems may use either a command-line interface or a menu interface.

Microcomputer operating system functions can generally be divided into the following areas:

1. Functions related to system control
2. Functions related to system input and output
3. Functions related to file handling
4. Functions related to memory management
5. Functions related to multitasking

These functions can be represented graphically as shown in Figure 8-7.

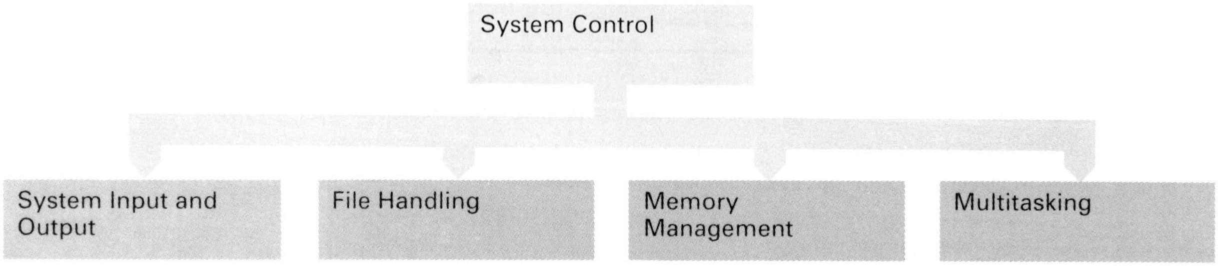

System Control

System Input and Output | File Handling | Memory Management | Multitasking

Figure 8-7
Operating system functions are generally divided into five areas.

Since microcomputers are much more readily available than minicomputers or mainframes for use by most students, the functions discussed in this section can frequently be tried out on an available machine. As you consider the items in this section, remember two things: (1) the functions apply (sometimes in more complex form) to operating systems on larger computers, and (2) not all the functions are available in all operating systems.

To give you a "flavor" for the kinds of things that operating systems do, a few of the functions available in each of the four categories will be discussed. Keep in mind as you look at these functions, however, that they represent only a small sampling of the capabilities that are available.

System Control

At the heart of the operating system is the portion that serves as the nerve center or control center for all the other functions. Frequently referred to as the **executive,** this portion of the operating system acts as the manager of all other operating system functions; it provides the interface between the demands of the user and the capabilities of the other parts of the operating system. In other words, the executive takes the commands entered by the user and determines which of the operating system components needs to be called into play to carry out the command.

System Input and Output

Another portion of the operating system takes care of transferring data from input devices to the computer or from the computer to output devices. The input and output portion of the operating system can handle almost any of the devices you learned about in Chapters 4, 5, and 6.

Since many of these devices use different codes to indicate what they are transmitting or react differently to different codes when receiving them, it is necessary that the operating system be able to tailor its responses or outputs to match the particular device. This is frequently accomplished by making a distinction between **logical devices** and **physical devices**. The physical device is the actual brand and model of printer, mouse, etc., while the logical device is generic in nature. For example, to the computer there may be a device known as PRN (for printer). The connection between the logical device and physical device is made by means of a small piece of software known as a **device driver**. The device driver is tailored to the specific input or output device, taking into account all the exact control codes being used.

Typically, input to the operating system comes from a device known as the default or standard input device. Output goes to a device referred to as the default or standard output device. These standard devices on a microcomputer are usually the keyboard and the display. The use of device drivers, however, makes it possible to use what is called **input/output redirection** (the capability of a device to accept input from or direct output to various sources). Input/output redirection is somewhat similar to using a stereo system with a receiver, a cassette deck, and a compact disk player as sources of sound. It makes no difference to the amplifier and speakers where the input of the sound is coming from; it is still accepted (from the source determined by the setting of a switch), amplified, and played. Likewise, output of the sound can be to either headphones or a speaker system; it makes no difference to the source of the sound and the amplifier as to where the output is going.

Typical microcomputer input and output devices are the keyboard and monitor.

In the same manner that a stereo system uses switch settings or headphones to specify the source and output devices for sound, a computer system uses software. This is possible because of the "independence" brought about by the device drivers. By using the drivers, the standard device may be temporarily redefined so that input to programs that usually comes from the keyboard, for example, may come instead from a file on disk. Conversely, output that would typically go to the screen may be directed to a disk drive or printer.

Other operating system functions related to input and output are the uses of filters and pipes. A **filter** is a DOS command (instruction) that reads data from the standard input device, manipulates it in some way, and writes it to the standard output device. Some of the things that filters can do are sort data into sequence, search the data for particular characters, or scramble data for security purposes. For example, data may be sorted as shown in Figure 8-8.

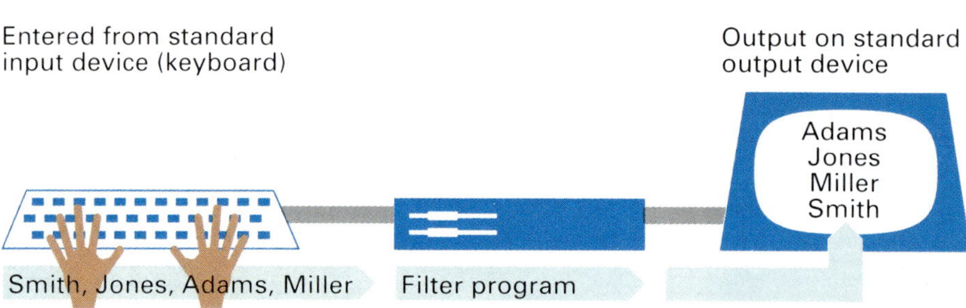

Figure 8-8
Data may be sorted in various ways with the use of a filter command.

Input/output redirection may be used with filters to obtain the data from any desired device and output it to any desired device. By using input redirection, for example, the sort filter could be used to sort the contents of a file stored on disk.

A **pipe** is a method of taking the output of one DOS command and using it as input for another one. For example, assume that a file on disk contains names of customers and their addresses, including two-letter state codes. You would like to create a new file containing only the names and addresses of those customers who live in California, stored in alphabetic order. By using input redirection, you obtain input from the existing disk file and subject it to the sort filter to get the names in order. The result of the sort is then piped to the find filter, which locates all the California residents. This data is then written through output redirection to a new file on disk. Figure 8-9 shows how the process would work.

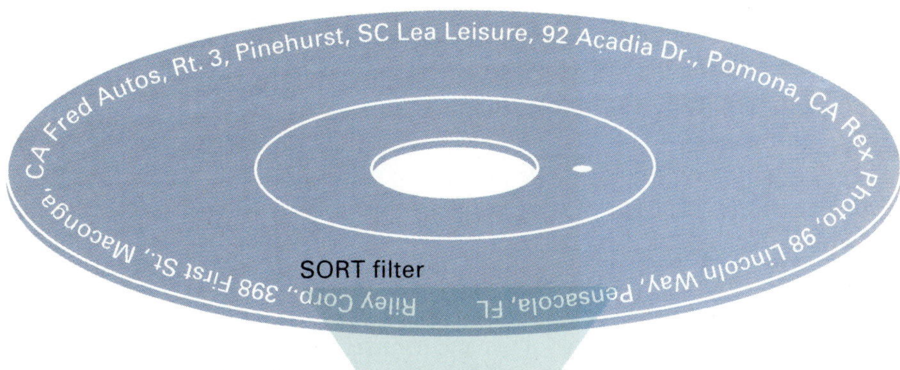

Fred Autos, Rt. 3, Pinehurst, SC
Lea Leisure, 92 Acadia Dr., Pomona, CA
Rex Photo, 98 Lincoln Way, Pensacola, FL
Riley Corp., 398 First St., Maconga, CA

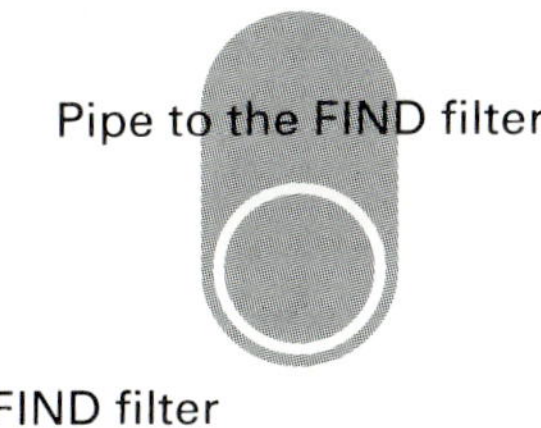

Figure 8-9
The output of one DOS command may be piped as input to another DOS command to produce a new file.

File Input and Output

The file input and output portion of the operating system performs functions related to the use of files. These include creating files, opening files, reading a record from a file, writing a record to a file, and maintaining the record of where individual files are located on disk.

In maintaining the record of where individual files are located on disk, most operating systems use something referred to as a **hierarchical directory structure**. Under a hierarchical directory structure, the storage space on a disk is divided into directories, which are further divided into subdirectories. The scheme is similar to a file cabinet which may have four drawers. Each drawer may then have several folders with individual documents placed in the folders. This type of directory structure is also known as a **tree structure directory.**

A hierarchical disk structure will contain a root directory. The root directory may then contain several directories, one for each of the kinds of applications performed, such as accounting and word processing. The accounting and word processing directories may then be divided into subdirectories for programs and data, with several different kinds of data being defined for word processing. Figure 8-10 shows this organization pictorially; note that the "shape" appears to be an inverted tree.

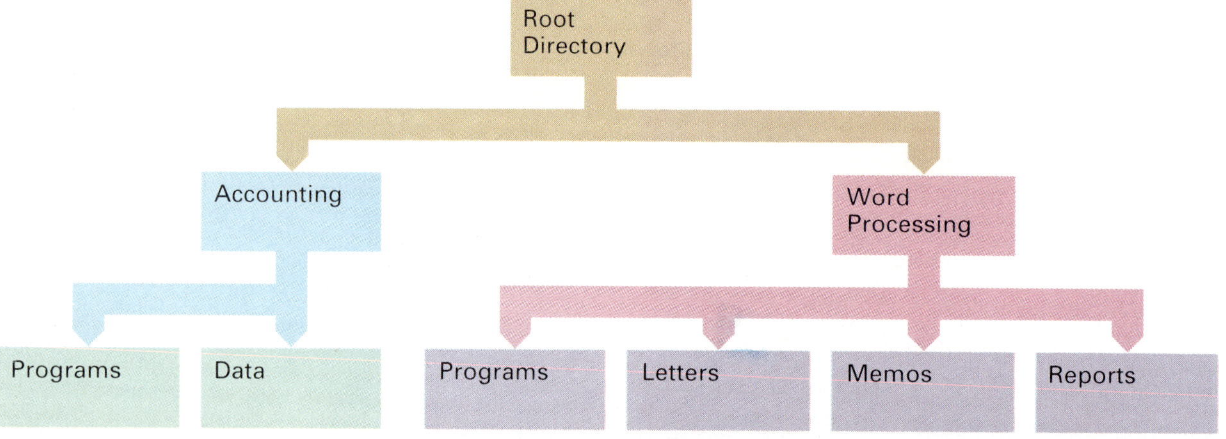

Figure 8-10
Most operating systems use a hierarchical directory structure to maintain files

Memory Management

The memory management portion of the operating system controls the assignment of memory to various uses. For example, the memory needed for loading an application program or storing data is allocated by the memory manager. In a protected-mode multitasking operating system, the memory manager "puts each application in a box" and makes sure it does not use memory outside that area. In addition to its memory assignment function, the memory manager also takes care of the actual movement of data into memory.

Multitasking

In a multitasking operating system, the processor's time must be divided among different applications that are executing, and memory must also be divided among the applications. In addition to these functions, the multitasking portion of the operating system ensures that a program's data and its current status are remembered when its time slice is over so that execution may continue from the correct point when the program again has processing time.

COMMONLY USED MICROCOMPUTER OPERATING SYSTEMS

There are several popular operating systems for microcomputers. As with all popular operating systems, these are constantly undergoing refinement and revision. In addition to the popular operating systems, there are numerous others available that have slightly different capabilities. The table below names some of the more popular operating systems and lists some of their characteristics.

Operating System	*Runs On*	*Type*	*User Interface*
DOS 3.3	Apple II	Single Program	Command
ProDOS	Apple II	Single Program	Menu
Finder	Apple Macintosh	Single Program	Menu
MultiFinder	Apple Macintosh	Multitasking	Menu
CP/M	Z80 processor machines	Single Program	Command
PC-DOS/MS-DOS	IBM PC and compatibles	Single Program	Command/Menu
OS-2	IBM PC and compatibles w/80286 or 80386 processors	Multitasking	Menu
Unix/Xenix	IBM PC and compatibles	Multitasking	Command/Menu

UTILITY PROGRAMS

The instructions loaded from disk when needed to carry out DOS functions are usually referred to as **utility programs**. In the following sections, several of the common functions performed by utility programs will be discussed. Depending on the operating system, these functions are accessible either by keying the appropriate command on a command line or by selecting a menu choice.

Formatting

Before a disk (or tape) can be used for data storage, it must be formatted. **Formatting** prepares the disk surface for storing data. Most formatting utilities perform two primary functions: (1) they check the disk surface for defects and lock out of use any sectors that are found to be defective, and (2) they set up directory space and file allocation tables. The directory space that is set up is used to record the name and status of each file that is stored on the disk. As files are stored on disk, the file allocation tables will be used to record exactly where on the disk the data is recorded.

The format of a disk generally varies from one operating system to another. Because of this, a disk formatted under one operating system is normally not usable by another operating system.

Configuring

A utility program is frequently used to configure the computer system. **Configuring** refers to the process of making the desired match between logical and physical computer devices. Remember that each of the actual peripherals attached to a computer is a physical device, while operating systems frequently are designed to use logical devices. An operating system, for example, might as a matter of course direct output designed for a printer to a logical device called PRN. In configuring the system, the user could direct all output designated for PRN to a particular printer attached to the system. Another logical device might be known as CON, which is short for console. Console is a term that originated in the days when all computers were physically very large mainframes, and the console was the separate desk-type station from which the operator controlled the machine. With present-day computers, configuration can tell the operating system exactly which peripheral is to be considered the console.

Backing Up and Restoring

All data of any value that is stored on a computer system should be backed up on a regular basis. **Backing up** is the process of copying the data to another medium so that a duplicate is available for use should the original copy be destroyed or become unusable. **Restoring** refers to the process of copying data from the backup media to a hard disk after a failure has been rectified. When dealing with floppy disk microcomputers, backups are generally done on another floppy disk so that the user has two or more disks containing the same data. With larger computers, including microcomputers with hard disks, it is common to use tape as the backup medium.

Sensitive data is often backed up to tape from which it can be restored if necessary.

Generally, there are two utility programs associated with backups. The first one makes a backup copy of designated or all data on a disk. The other restores data to the disk by copying it from the backup medium.

Sorting

Many computer applications, including some accounting programs, require that various data files be sorted in a specific order for processing. For example, it might be necessary for a file of customers to be listed in order by customer number before monthly bills can be sent to the customers. Operating systems frequently are supplied with utility programs to accomplish such sorting according to rules entered by the computer operator.

File Verification and Comparison

It is sometimes desirable, after a file has been created on disk or tape, to verify that it is in good condition and is readable. Sometimes, it is also desirable to ascertain whether two files contain the same data. For example, in order to verify whether or not updates were made on a file, a user would compare the file containing the old data with a file that should contain the updates. Utility programs that can perform both of these functions are readily available.

COMPATIBILITY AMONG OPERATING SYSTEMS

As you have learned, the data on disk drives is stored in the format required by the particular operating system, and this format varies from one system to another. Not only do different operating systems typically use different physical layouts for storing data on disk, the methods used for handling directories and file allocation tables also vary. This means that one operating system cannot automatically use data recorded by another one, even if both operating systems are designed for use with the same processor.

Generally, utility programs are available for converting data back and forth between the formats used by various operating systems, especially systems belonging to the same family. For example, it is quite easy to convert files between the formats used by Apple's DOS 3.3 operating system and its ProDOS system.

It is also common for operating systems to be upwardly compatible within the same family. For example, IBM's PC-DOS started out as Version 1.0. Later, Versions 2.0, 3.0 and 4.1 were released. Upward compatibility meant that files created under Version 1.0, for example, could still be used under Versions 2.0 and 3.0. This upward compatibility continued when OS-2 was introduced. Even though PC-DOS is a single-program operating system and OS-2 is a multitasking system, OS-2 can use data files created by PC-DOS. The reverse, however, is not usually true. Files created under newer releases of operating systems typically cannot be used by earlier versions.

THE CODE MODE: SENDING OUT SECRETS

One of the tasks that can be performed by some operating systems is the coding and decoding of data. The coding of data is known as **encryption**, while the decoding of data is known as **decryption**. The figure below shows the effects of these operations. Notice that in the encryption phase, readable data is turned into unreadable code, while in the decryption phase, unreadable code is turned back into readable data.

Sensitive data can be encrypted to protect it from unauthorized persons during transit or storage.

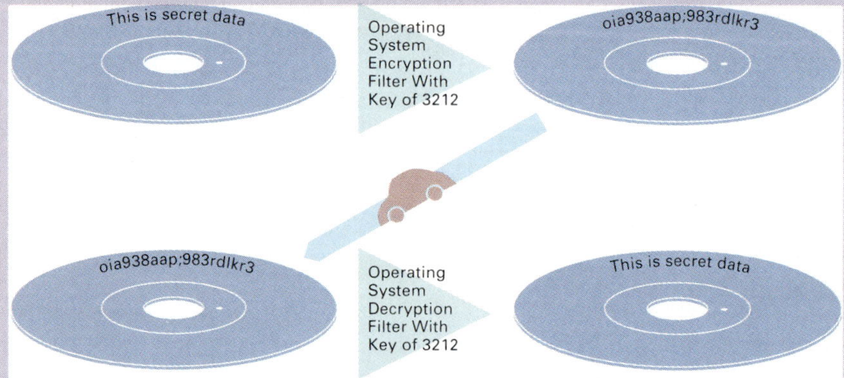

In the coding and decoding of data, an element known as a key is used. The key is an alphabetic or numeric value that is used by a mathematical formula in the encryption program to convert readable data into non-readable data. The same key must be used to decode the data. Obviously, the key value is not transported or stored with the encrypted data. Note that readable data means data that is readable to a computer—not necessarily to a human.

Coded data has played a large role in military combat over the years. The outcome of wars has been determined by success in breaking codes, and military advantage has been retained by the security of codes. In fact, much research that has contributed to the present sophistication of encryption techniques has come from the military.

While such cloak-and-dagger type applications of coding or encryption receive more publicity, encryption is also a technique used frequently by businesses. Much data, especially data in transit electronically from one location to another, is subject to piracy by electronic interception. Therefore, coding of such data can help a business retain its competitive edge.

"Enigma" was a famous World War II encryption device.

CHAPTER SUMMARY

- The operating system is the software that controls the operation of the computer and the communication between its components.
- The functions of operating systems can be divided into three categories: control of the system, resource management, and resource monitoring.
- Upon booting up the computer, the first record of the operating system, called the boot record, is loaded from disk into memory. It then initiates the loading and running of the remainder of the operating system software.
- The resources of the computer are its processor, memory, auxiliary storage, and input and output devices. All these are under control of the operating system.
- The operating system can monitor the use of system resources, as well as track problems in the system.
- Operating systems can be categorized as either single-program operating systems or multitasking operating systems.
- While a single-program operating system can execute only one application program at a time, it is possible for more than one program to be in memory at the same time.
- By using time slicing techniques, multitasking operating systems make the computer appear to do more than one task at a time.
- Multiprogramming means running more than one application program at a time, typically one in the foreground and others in the background.
- A foreground task is one that receives processor time priority; it is usually the one with which the user is interacting.
- A background task is one on which the computer works when the foreground task is not active.
- Multiprocessing is the ability of an operating system to handle more than one user at a time, often with several of them using the same application program.
- Time sharing refers to the use of several terminals attached to the same processor, with the one processor providing all the computing power.
- Virtual memory is used to enable multiple programs to run at once when there is insufficient memory to handle all their needs; it swaps data between memory and disk to give the appearance to the application programs that all the memory needed is available.
- Some operating systems provide protected-mode operation, under which each application program is restricted to the use of an assigned portion of memory and prevented from destroying other programs or data.
- User interface with an operating system may be either by command line or menu.

- The heart of an operating system is the portion that is in control of the other functions of the system; this part is frequently known as the executive.
- Other parts of the operating system control system input and output, file handling, and memory management.
- Device drivers are used to provide the connection between logical devices and physical devices.
- Input/output redirection enables input and output to be directed to any appropriate device desired.
- Filters and pipes are two functions provided by operating systems for the manipulation of data. Filters perform functions such as sorting, selection, and encryption; pipes provide the means of outputting the results of one function to the input of another function.
- In a hierarchical directory structure, used by most operating systems, the directory is arranged as an inverted tree with multiple branches.
- Microcomputer operating systems, in general, perform the same functions as do the operating systems on larger computers.
- Utility programs are loaded from disk whenever needed to perform the housekeeping functions of the operating system, such as formatting disks, configuring the system, verifying file contents, or backing up data.
- Different operating systems are designed for use with particular processors and use different disk formats. Therefore, there is generally no true compatibility between operating systems. However, there usually is upward compatibility between different releases in the same family. Also, utilities are available to convert data from the format of one operating system to that of another.

KEY TERMS

The following key terms were introduced or redefined in this chapter:

background task
boot record
configuring
decryption
device driver
encryption
executive
filter
foreground task
formatting
hierarchical directory structure
input/output redirection
logical device
memory protection
multiprocessing
multiprogramming
multitasking
operating system
physical device
pipe
restoring
time sharing
time slicing
transients
tree structure directory
user interface
utility programs
virtual memory

REVIEW QUESTIONS

1. What is the purpose of an operating system? (Obj. 1)
2. List the differences between the functions of operating systems and application software. (Obj. 2)
3. What is the first function performed by an operating system when a computer is turned on? (Obj. 2)
4. Name and differentiate the three primary functions performed by operating system software. (Obj 2)
5. Name the resources of a typical computer system. (Obj. 2)
6. List three areas in which monitoring of resources can be done. (Obj. 2)
7. Differentiate single-program operating systems and multitasking operating systems. (Obj. 3)
8. Support the fact that a single-program operating system can execute only one application program at a time, although it is possible for several programs to be in memory at once. (Obj. 3)
9. How does a terminate-and-stay-resident program function? (Obj. 3)
10. Multitasking operating systems perform multiprogramming and/or multiprocessing. What are the similarities and differences in these two processes? (Obj. 3)
11. What is the difference between a foreground task and a background task? (Obj. 3)
12. How does an operating system seem to perform several tasks at once? (Obj. 3)
13. When is virtual memory useful? How is it implemented? (Obj. 3)
14. What is the value of memory protection? (Obj. 3)
15. Describe the two methods of user interface with operating system commands. (Obj. 4)
16. What are logical devices and physical devices? What is the relationship between them? (Obj 4)
17. What is the primary advantage of input/output redirection? (Obj. 4)
18. How do filters and pipes help users process data? (Obj. 4)
19. Describe the structure of a hierarchical directory. (Obj. 4)
20. What is the purpose of utility programs? (Obj. 5)
21. Describe the process of formatting a disk. (Obj. 5)
22. What is the purpose of backup and restore utilities? (Obj. 5)
23. How compatible are different operating systems? (Obj. 6)

CHALLENGE ACTIVITIES

1. What factors would you consider in deciding whether to use a single-program operating system or a multitasking operating system? (Obj. 3)
2. What factors would you consider in deciding whether to use a command-line interface or a menu-driven interface? (Obj. 4)

3. For this exercise, you will continue to build on the case study you started in Chapter 7. Review the facts of the case: (Objs. 1, 2, 3)

   A writer has met with some degree of success in the past several years. Specializing in writing user's manuals for equipment produced by various manufacturers provides all the work that the writer can handle. To this point, a simple word processor on a very small home computer has been used. Now, however, clients are beginning to demand that complex diagrams and drawings be included in high-quality, publication-ready copy of the manuals. Also, the writer is seriously considering adding a secretary and an assistant writer to help carry the work load.

   If the writer hires the new employees, additional office space will also be needed. Private work areas for the writer and the assistant will be needed, and the secretary will need work space. To provide the quality of printout now being demanded by clients, the writer will need a laser printer that will be shared by all three persons. When printing the graphics which will be necessary, the speed with which data can be sent to the printer can have a significant effect on the amount of time needed for printing each page. Looking to the future, the writer sees a real possibility that clients will want drafts of the manuals transmitted to them electronically for approval before the final print-ready versions are produced.

   In short, considering the entire situation, the writer has the immediate need to purchase a more powerful computer and a laser printer. There is the probable need to provide additional office space when employees are added, as well as two additional microcomputers. Down the road, communication of manuals to clients over phone lines is a possibility.

   a. The software the writer wants to use is available in versions that run under single-program operating systems or multitasking operating systems. Which would you recommend to the writer? Support your decision.
   b. Now that you know more about operating systems, time sharing, and multiprocessing, would you recommend that the writer use a time-share system? Why or why not?

PART 4

APPLICATION SOFTWARE

CHAPTER 9

INTRODUCTION TO APPLICATION SOFTWARE

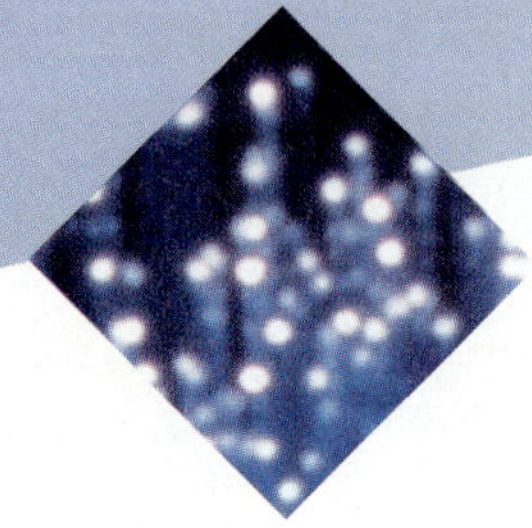

LEARNING OBJECTIVES

After studying this chapter, you will be able to:

1. **Explain why application software is needed.**
2. **Differentiate between custom application software and generic application software.**
3. **List advantages and disadvantages of custom application software.**
4. **List advantages and disadvantages of generic application software.**
5. **Describe different classifications of application software.**
6. **List sources of application software.**
7. **List and describe the guidelines for acquisition of application software.**

INTRODUCTION

In Chapter 8 you learned about operating systems and utility programs. These were the programs that control the different computer components, keep them communicating, and perform housekeeping chores for the operator. In this chapter you will learn about the other main category of software, known as application software. In contrast to the functions of operating software, application software is designed to perform the particular functions needed to solve problems for the user.

THE NEED FOR APPLICATION SOFTWARE

Software designed to meet a particular computing need of the user is known as **application software**. A computing need represents a problem to be solved for the benefit of the user, and the application software instructs the computer how to function to solve the problem. This is in contrast to the need for software to make the computer operate—a need that is met by operating system software. Software to handle word processing, software to do accounting, or software to control an aircraft's flight all represent application software. Without application software, a computer is useless.

Application software may be either custom or generic. **Custom application software** is written specially to meet the needs of an organization or individual. **Generic software**, on the other hand, is created by a developer for sale to various users. The following sections define these two categories and give the advantages and disadvantages of each.

Generic software is marketed to a variety of users.

CUSTOM APPLICATION SOFTWARE

In larger organizations, custom software is frequently written by an in-house staff of specialists. Smaller organizations sometimes employ independent consultants to write custom software. The fact that the software is written especially for the user leads to several advantages as well as several disadvantages.

Advantages of Custom Application Software

The advantages of custom application software are described in the following paragraphs. These are positive points to consider in making a decision as to whether custom or generic software is preferable.

Needs May Be Met More Exactly

The most obvious advantage that may be found in custom application software is that the needs of the organization or individual can be precisely met. The output desired from the software may be exactly defined, and the processing required to produce the output can be specified as needed. The method of inputting data to the programs may be designed to suit the particular wishes of the user. Even though generic software can frequently be installed with various options, true custom-written software is still usually better at matching needs exactly.

A Strategic Advantage May Be Gained

Traditionally, computers have been used to automate what was already being done manually. More and more, however, businesses are beginning to use computers to develop strategic advantage—that is, to give them a competitive edge over businesses that do not have similar software. For example, an overnight air express company that completely computerized the tracking of packages, including having computers in its delivery trucks, gained an advantage over its competitors. To accomplish the continuous tracking of packages, a new concept in computer applications was required—one that was custom written. Once other companies copied the idea, however, it was no longer a strategic advantage, even though it is still required in order to remain competitive.

Custom software is developed for a specific industry or company need.

The strategic use of the computer almost always requires custom written software. If software to do the function were already on the market, it could probably not be used as a strategic advantage. Also, the use of strategic software requires continual research and development of new ideas, since software to perform a particular function will remain unique for only a brief period of time after competitors find out about it.

System Resources May Be Used More Efficiently

Since it is written specifically to solve the problem at hand and no other, custom software is frequently more efficient in its use of system resources. It may require less memory and less disk space than generic software. This is because the requirements that the program must meet are known up front, and the program does not have to be written to handle contingencies that will not occur in the particular organization.

Programs May Execute Faster

The same factors that may result in the more efficient use of resources also may result in faster execution of custom programs. The program can be written to address the situations it will encounter and the solutions it must provide in its particular environment. Alternatives that will never occur need not be addressed. For example, if there is no possibility that a business will ever have branch offices, it is not necessary that its accounting programs be able to handle and consolidate financial figures from multiple locations.

Programs Can Be Changed to Meet Changing Conditions

When software has been custom written, it can be updated to meet changing needs of the user. Since it is custom written, the user has control over what will be done to the software and can order changes or upgrades as needed.

Disadvantages of Custom Application Software

While the advantages of custom software are important to consider, there are also disadvantages that must be weighed.

Development Time May Be Lengthy

Since custom software is written from scratch using a computer language chosen by the developer, it takes time to produce. The length of time depends on the language and development tools chosen, as well as on the complexity of the task and the skill of the developers. The time required for writing a custom application may be anywhere from several days to several years.

Resources Needed for Development May Not Be Available

Many businesses will not have the human resources needed to develop custom software. Development requires persons with excellent systems analysis and programming skills. Additionally, the financial resources necessary to do the job are considerable and may not be available in a company.

The development of custom software requires persons knowledgeable in systems analysis and programming.

Expense of Development May Be Much Greater

When custom software is written, the organization for which it is developed may well be the only user. When this is the case, it is necessary for all the costs of development to be paid by that organization. Development costs may range into the millions of dollars depending on the complexity of the application.

Cost May Be Unknown Up Front

Estimates for the cost of developing software are difficult to make with accuracy. Unknown or changing conditions, as well as problems that may be encountered during development, may make the costs of software much greater than originally anticipated.

Expense of Upgrades and Maintenance May Be Great

The same reasons that make original development of custom software expensive also tend to make upgrades and maintenance of the software very expensive. Maintenance refers to the resolution of problems that may occur during operation of the software and to refinement of the software. Upgrades refer to significant improvements in program function or performance. Upgrades and maintenance require much labor.

GENERIC APPLICATION SOFTWARE

Many applications are relatively standard for most users. In these cases, generic software is sufficient. Many programs related to word processing, accounting, and spreadsheets, for example, fall into this category. As with custom software, generic software has its advantages and disadvantages.

Advantages of Generic Application Software

The advantages of generic application software are discussed in the following paragraphs. In many respects, the advantages of generic software are the opposite of the advantages of custom software. This also applies to the disadvantages, which are discussed later.

Availability Is Immediate

Since generic software is "off the shelf," it can be purchased and put to work immediately. Only an installation process is necessary before it can start being productive for the organization. Depending on the complexity of the software, installation can take as little as a few minutes or as long as several months.

Cost Is Less

The cost of developing generic software can be spread among a number of users who purchase the product. This can reduce the cost dramatically in relation to the expense of developing custom software.

Reliability May Be Greater

Usually, generic software has been thoroughly tested before it is marketed. Additionally, many other users may have already used the software, adding their testing to that done by the developer. The testing to which generic software is thus submitted may be much tougher than the testing designed to ensure the quality of custom software written for one user.

Disadvantages of Generic Application Software

The disadvantages of generic software are related to its generic nature. These disadvantages are described in the following paragraphs.

May Not Be an Exact Match for Needs

The biggest disadvantage of generic software is that it may not be an exact match for the needs of the organization. The more specialized the need, the less likely it will be that generic software is capable of meeting the need.

May Require More System Resources

Generic software must be written to handle the many possible conditions that may be required by various users. The capability to meet these conditions often results in less efficient use of system resources. Programs are frequently longer, requiring more memory and disk space.

Generic software may not fully meet the needs of all users.

May Execute More Slowly

Being able to handle many different conditions may result in generic programs which will execute more slowly. This is caused by the necessity that the software continuously monitor the status of the various program options, many of which are never used by any one business.

May Not Be Adaptable to Changing Needs

If the conditions of the business change, it may not be possible to adapt generic software to the changing needs. This is because the program's code is under control of the developer, not the user. In such cases, it will be necessary either to select a different generic software package or develop a custom package. The table in Figure 9-1 shows the major considerations that distinguish custom and generic software.

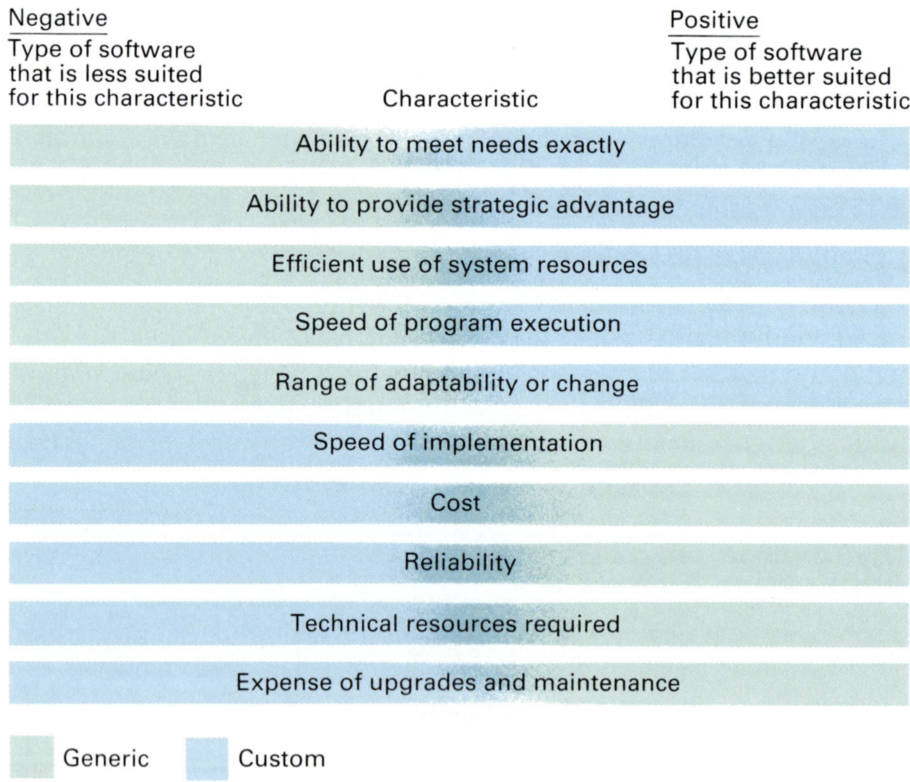

Figure 9-1
The choice of custom or generic software is based on the suitability of its characteristics for the application.

TYPES OF APPLICATION SOFTWARE

Application software can be categorized in different ways. One way to classify software is as business software, process control software, CAD/CAM, or expert systems software.

Business Software

Business software is used to facilitate the management or record keeping functions of a business. Business software, especially that used by small businesses, is frequently generic in nature. Larger businesses are more likely to use custom software. Commonly used types of programs are discussed in the following paragraphs. Remember that it is possible to obtain programs that do only a specific function or packages that can perform several of the functions.

Word Processing

Word processing programs allow the user to enter text, edit text, and print documents. They make it easy to send the same or similar letters to various persons by using pre-saved paragraphs that can be adapted to each person to whom a letter is to be addressed.

Word processing programs make it easy to create and edit text.

Graphics

Graphics software can produce either presentation graphics or graphs. Presentation graphics include illustrations or diagrams of virtually anything. Graphs represent data in pictorial form. Figure 9-2 shows samples of both types of graphics.

Figure 9-2
Both presentation graphics and graphs can be produced with graphics software.

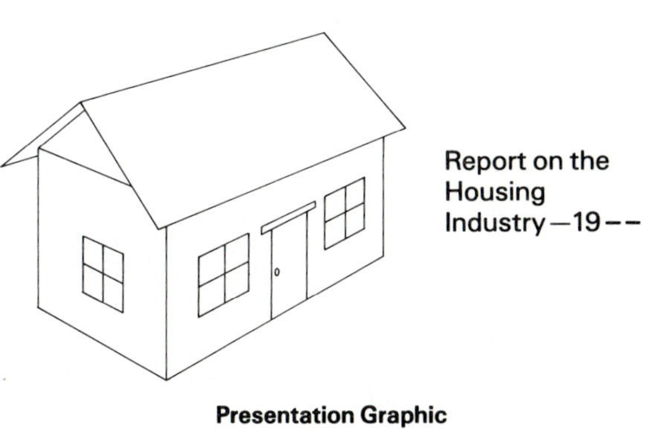

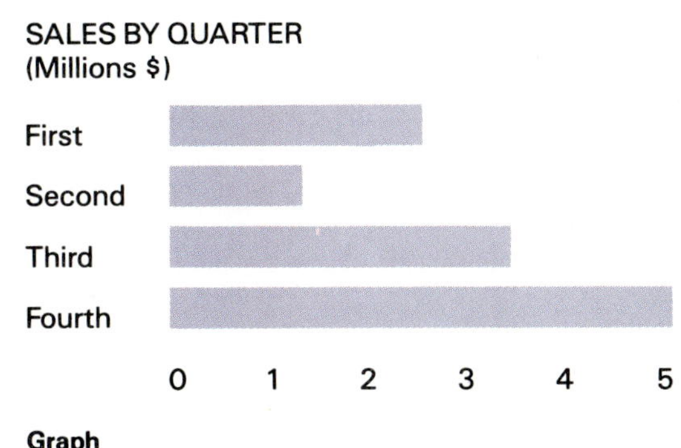

Desktop Publishing

Desktop publishing refers to the use of the computer to produce newsletters, catalogs, brochures, books, and other materials that are to contain different types of print. This makes these publications, which usually have diagrams or illustrations, appear superior to those produced by inexpensive printers. More sophisticated desktop publishing software can insert photographs, diagrams, and drawings directly into typeset text.

Desktop publishing systems make it easy to produce publications that include diagrams and illustrations.

Spreadsheets

Spreadsheets are row and column arrangements of data. Values in designated locations on the spreadsheet may be automatically calculated by the software based on formulas entered into those locations by the user. Spreadsheets are very useful for making "what if" projections as well as for record keeping functions. Data is usually entered via the keyboard. Output is displayed on the screen and can be printed out when the user desires. Spreadsheet programs frequently contain graphing ability, with the data for the graphs coming from the spreadsheet.

Spreadsheet programs gained in popularity because of their ability to perform "what if" analyses.

Databases

A database is a collection of data items that are related to one another in some way. Database programs provide an excellent means for entering, editing, and reporting the records of a business, such as customer lists and accounting records. Various reports can be produced by database software.

Project Management

Project management software helps a business complete a project on time and within budget. For example, in constructing a building, certain actions have to be taken in sequence. Project management software helps schedule those actions in the most efficient manner.

Process Control Software

Software designed to control a sequence of events is known as **process control software.** This software is part of a working process whereby the software takes action, receives feedback as to the result of its actions, then makes whatever corrections may be necessary. Examples of process control software, which is frequently custom written, can be found in various areas. Some of these uses are discussed in the following paragraphs.

Transportation

Process control programs can be found in many types of transportation. In automobiles, process control software controls ignition and fuel systems, as well as anti-lock brake systems and recently developed anti-collision systems. In aircraft, the software can control the flight pattern. The movement of subway systems can be controlled by software, with the computer ensuring that no trains ever get close enough to collide.

Manufacturing Plants

Manufacturing plants as diverse as those producing crude oil or computers may be controlled by computers. The software that does this controls valves, positions robots, and otherwise operates the process. A growing number of manufacturing plants are using computers that are networked together to control operations in the plant. Plants with such networked systems are using what may be referred to as **computer-integrated manufacturing,** or CIM. The primary advantage of networking the computers in a factory is that the overall process, rather than just individual machines, can be coordinated by the computer software.

Computers make it easier to control and coordinate plant operations.

Traffic Control

Traffic control systems can sense the number of vehicles traveling in particular directions and adjust the timing of traffic signals for the most efficient traffic flow. While such systems only turn lights on and off, they represent a very effective use of process control software.

Climate Control and Other Home Applications

In the home, process control applications for climate control, burglar alarms, and fire alarms are becoming much more common. Such systems not only make a home more comfortable, but safer as well.

CAD/CAM

CAD/CAM stands for **computer-aided (or assisted) design (drafting)/ computer-aided manufacturing.** CAD refers to the process of using graphic computer programs to assist in the design of a product. The sophistication of CAD software can range from simple drafting programs to complex programs that make multitudes of computations related to product performance. CAM refers to the use of computer data to operate tools, such as drilling machines, to manufacture a product. Although CAD and CAM may be used independently of one another, they are frequently integrated so that the result of the design phase is used automatically to produce a part. For example, human hip replacements can be custom-designed for a particular individual by using CAD technology. The output of the CAD program is then used to operate the machines that manufacture the custom hip joint.

Expert Systems

Software designed to assist in the application of a known body of knowledge is known as an **expert system.** For example, software exists that can help a doctor diagnose illnesses. Another program helps oil drillers determine where to drill to have the greatest likelihood of finding oil. Still another program helps determine the likely source of problems in computer systems. All expert systems operate in a similar fashion in that they quantify the knowledge of experts and make that knowledge available to help other persons solve problems. Great amounts of time are consumed in the development of expert systems amassing the knowledge various persons have accumulated over a period of years in the practice of their professions.

SOURCES OF APPLICATION SOFTWARE

Application software can be obtained from various sources. The number of sources will vary depending on the nature of the software, as well as whether it is custom or generic.

Custom-Designed

Custom-designed software is typically available only through two sources. The organization may develop it in-house, using its own employees. Or, the organization may determine the desired software capabilities and then contract with an outside vendor to actually produce the programs.

Generic

Software that is generic in nature can be obtained from several sources. Some of these are discussed in the following paragraphs.

Computer Store

For users of microcomputers, the local computer store or computer software store is an excellent source for ready-to-run software if the job to be done is a rather common one. These stores, however, generally stock only a limited variety of programs in each of the application areas. For example, a store might stock three or four brands of word processing programs or a couple of brands of database programs. An advantage of dealing with a good computer store is that advice, training, and assistance may be available through the store's staff. Organizations using larger computers will typically find little if any software available through computer stores.

Training is often available for hardware and software purchased through a computer store.

Mail Order

Much application software can be obtained through mail order. Larger distributors carry many popular titles, while more specialized vendors carry programs for particular computers or particular kinds of businesses. A big disadvantage of mail order is that support is often not available. However, mail order vendors may have lower prices than computer stores.

Manufacturers

Software manufacturers sometimes have direct sales forces that call on customers. This is most frequently the case with more complex, expensive software packages that run on more powerful computers. The larger the computer on which the package runs and the more expensive the software, the greater the likelihood the manufacturer will have a sales force working with customers. In-depth training in the use of the software is also usually available from such vendors.

Vertical Market Sources

Software products can be created to be sold across the board to a very wide range of users. Programs such as word processing and spreadsheets fall into this category. On the other hand, software may be constructed to meet the particular needs of one specific business or industry. In marketing lingo, a particular business or industry is known as a vertical market. For example, the insurance industry is a vertical market, and the banking industry is a vertical market. In many industries, consulting firms exist that assist the members of the industry in utilizing computer software to help operate their businesses. In many vertical markets, there may also be trade associations that make software available. For example, an association of financial advisers might make programs available to help its members meet the needs of operating their businesses—needs that in some respects are rather unique. The primary value of software from vertical market sources is that the software is frequently tailored to meet the particular needs of the market being served.

GUIDELINES FOR ACQUISITION OF APPLICATION SOFTWARE

Many computer users purchase application software by the "seat of the pants" method or on the recommendation of someone else who is using a particular program. However, there are several guidelines that can help make the selection and purchase more satisfactory.

Establishing Needs

The first step in the selection of any software should be to establish the need to computerize the anticipated application. For example, scheduling the meeting room in a small restaurant can be done through the use of a paper calendar or the use of computer software. In all likelihood, the scheduling will be easier (as well as much less expensive) if the paper calendar is used. Thus, before looking for a computer program to perform a function, it is wise to examine the procedure to be used to carry it out. Then, if it appears that computerization is wise, the search for the ideal software should begin.

Once it is determined that computerization will improve the completion of a particular operating function of a business, the exact requirements to be met by the software can be planned. Typically, this planning will take the form of deciding what output the software has to produce, then determining the input and processing necessary to generate that output. When the capabilities required of the software have been determined, the search for the most suitable software can begin.

If the functions to be performed by the software are intended to lead to a strategic advantage for the business, it may be possible to develop the software around a commercially available piece of software, such as a database program or a project manager program. Frequently, however, there is no choice with strategic programs but to have them custom written.

Performance

Software performance primarily means two things. First, the software must be capable of doing all the things expected of it. If the necessary functions cannot be handled, a software package should be avoided regardless of its price. Once it is verified that the desired functions are available in a piece of software, performance then refers to the speed and finesse with which functions are performed. One package may perform functions slowly and clumsily, while another performs them with speed and grace. It is important to remember, however, that there can be many possible combinations of speed and finesse (or the lack thereof). A program that performs some functions very nicely may perform others very poorly.

Documentation

If the user cannot figure out how to use a particular application program, it is of no value. Therefore, it is important that the chosen software be well documented. The software industry has come a long way from the days when users' manuals were vague, jargon-filled books written hurriedly by programmers. Most software now has readable, easily understood manuals. However, there are still wide variations in quality. In addition to well-written manuals, help screens that can be called up from disk while the software is in use are of great value.

Most software available today includes a readable, easily-understood manual.

When evaluating the documentation of a program, several criteria can be examined. For example, the following items can help determine the quality of documentation:

1. Does the manual have a complete table of contents?
2. Does the manual have a complete index, or are topics missing? (For example, in word processing, moving a block of text is a common operation and should certainly be included in the index.)
3. Does the manual proceed from simple to complex?
4. Are installation instructions included? Are they easy to follow?
5. Is the manual easy to read and understand by the person who will be using the software?

Ease of Learning

Time spent by employees in learning to use a new piece of software is unproductive time. The faster they learn the program and return to active work, the more productive they will be. Therefore, the ease with which a new software package can be learned should be considered.

Training

If a software package is at all complex, training will be required. It is important, therefore, to determine before the purchase of a package what training is available. Are classes available from the vendor of the software? Does a local technical school or college conduct classes?

Availability When Needed

Many software packages are announced and even advertised before they are ready for delivery to customers. These software packages are sometimes referred to as vapor ware. At times, demonstration packages may be available before the product is finished. Though it seems an obvious point, it should be verified that the product will be available when needed.

Value

After the items discussed in the previous paragraphs have been considered, there may be several software packages still under consideration. At this point, price can become the determining factor. Simply put, which of the qualified programs offers the needed capabilities at the lowest cost?

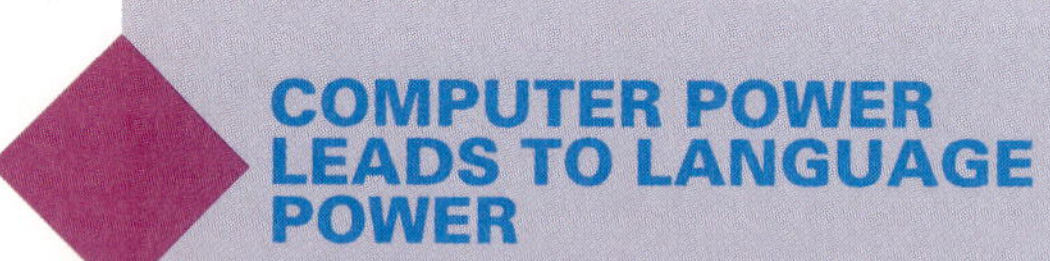

It has been a longtime dream on the part of many to use the power of computers to translate from one language to another. A story—truthful or not—has long been circulated concerning an early attempt on the part of the military to construct a program to translate back and forth between English and Russian. At the grand unveiling of the software, with all the generals gathered around, the developer keyed in the old phrase "Out of sight, out of mind." The computer communed with itself for a lengthy interval and then, one character at a time, typed out the Russian equivalent. To prove the ability to translate Russian back into English, the developer then keyed in the Russian version that had been produced by the computer. Again the computer communed with itself for a period and then proceeded to print out the translation—"Invisible Imbecile."

Language translation has come a long way since then. Application of the principles of artificial intelligence has led to software that, while still primitive, can certainly do much better than the early example. Some of the software that is now becoming usable utilizes printed input and output, while other software utilizes spoken input and output.

Imagine some of the applications of such software. Tourists would no longer feel insecure in planning independent ventures through foreign countries whose language they did not speak. No longer would they rush to buy translation dictionaries or to complete a crash course in the native language of the destination land. Instead, they would rush to the store to purchase or rent a hand-held translation computer. Then, while in the foreign land, they would speak their language into the translator, and it would in turn speak the other language to the listener. The foreign national would then reply in his or her own language, and the translator would produce the reply in the traveler's native language. Changing the language when changing countries will probably be as simple as plugging in a different memory cartridge.

Doctors could use computerized translators to converse with patients who speak other languages. Students could study books and periodicals written in other languages, with the software translating directly from the documents printed in Latin, German, French, Spanish, etc. Once perfected to the point of understanding nuances, such software could automate the translation process in international forums such as the United Nations.

The uses described above are still in the future, however. While present software is useful for some purposes, it is still too slow to work in real time. That is, it cannot keep up with normal speaking speed, with one of the programs typically requiring 10-15 seconds to respond with its translation. Too, the vocabularies that can be handled by existing systems are still very small, being limited to only several hundred words in most cases. However, progress should be rapid, leading soon to systems that can take their place as still another tool for human improvement provided by computer technology.

Translation software may someday eliminate language barriers for those traveling to foreign countries.

CHAPTER SUMMARY

- Application software is software designed to meet a particular computing need of the user.
- Application software specially written for the use of a designated organization or individual is known as custom application software.
- Custom application software may meet user needs exactly, may provide a strategic advantage, may use system resources more efficiently, may execute faster, and may be changed to meet changing conditions.
- Custom application software may require lengthy development time, may require developmental resources that are not available, may be

expensive to develop, may have cost overruns, and may be expensive to upgrade and maintain.

- Generic application software is application software that is created by a developer for sale to various users.
- Generic application software is immediately available, costs less, and may be more reliable.
- Generic application software may not be an exact match for needs, may require more system resources, may execute more slowly, and may not be adaptable to changing needs.
- Commonly used application software can be categorized as business software, process control software, CAD/CAM software, and expert system software.
- Business software is used to aid the management or record keeping functions of a business.
- Commonly used business application software includes word processing, graphics, desktop publishing, spreadsheet, database, and project management applications.
- Process control software is designed to control a sequence of events.
- Process control software is frequently used in transportation, manufacturing, traffic control, and home control applications.
- Computer-aided design/computer-aided manufacturing (CAD/CAM) software is used first to assist engineers in designing products and then to control machinery that manufactures the designed products.
- Expert systems assist in the application of a known body of knowledge to the solution of problems.
- Custom application software is developed in-house or under contract with an outside vendor.
- Generic application software can be obtained from computer stores, mail order distributors, manufacturers, or vertical market sources.
- The need to computerize an application should be established before beginning a software selection process.
- The most important criterion in selecting application software is performance—whether the product can do the job and how well it can do it.
- Documentation, ease of learning, and availability of training should be considered when evaluating software.
- When choosing among several software packages that are satisfactory in all other respects, price becomes the determining factor.

KEY TERMS

The following key terms were introduced or redefined in this chapter:

application software
business software
CAD/CAM
computer-integrated manufacturing
custom application software

database
desktop publishing
expert system
generic software
graphics
process control software
project management
spreadsheet
word processing

REVIEW QUESTIONS

1. Why is application software needed? (Obj. 1)
2. What is the primary difference between custom software and generic software? (Obj. 2)
3. What are the advantages of custom application software? (Obj. 3)
4. What are the disadvantages of custom application software? (Obj. 3)
5. What are the advantages of generic application software? (Obj 4)
6. What are the disadvantages of generic application software? (Obj. 4)
7. What are some types of application software that are generally known as business software? (Obj. 5)
8. What is process control software? (Obj. 5)
9. Name three uses of process control software. (Obj. 5)
10. What is CAD/CAM software? (Obj. 5)
11. What is expert system software? (Obj. 5)
12. What is an advantage of purchasing software from a computer store? (Obj. 6)
13. What is an advantage of purchasing software by mail order? What is a disadvantage? (Obj. 6)
14. What type of software is more likely to be sold by representatives employed by the manufacturer? (Obj. 6)
15. What is the primary advantage of software obtained through vertical market sources? (Obj. 6)
16. What is the first evaluation that should be made when selecting computer software for an application? (Obj. 7)

CHALLENGE ACTIVITIES

1. Describe the process you would use to determine whether to obtain custom software or generic software for a non-strategic application. (Objs. 2,3,4)
2. How would your process change for strategic software? Why? (Objs. 2,3,4)
3. Discuss the relative importance of the various criteria to be considered when selecting generic software. (Obj. 4)
4. Assume that you are going to convert the accounting system of your business so that the records will be kept on a computer. Your business is a small retail store that uses a standard accounting method recommended by your certified public accountant. It is the same one

she recommends to all her small retail business clients and is not tailored specifically for your type of business. You have no desire to change the general accounting methods, but you want to make them faster and more efficient by computerization. Keeping these facts in mind, answer the following questions. (Objs. 2,3,4,6,7)

a. Would you choose custom or generic software for use by your bookkeeper? Why?

b. Using sources that are available to you, such as magazine advertisements, software packages, and computer store personnel, identify a brand and model of software that would be suitable for purchase. In answering this question, you may assume any brand of hardware that you desire is available. Explain how you applied the criteria given in the chapter to the selection of the software.

c. Considering that your bookkeeper has never used a computer before, from which of the possible types of sources might you purchase the software? Why?

CHAPTER 10

WORD PROCESSING SOFTWARE

LEARNING OBJECTIVES

After studying this chapter, you will be able to:

1. **Describe the need for word processing software.**
2. **List the advantages of using word processing software.**
3. **Describe the roles of input, processing, output, and storage used by word processing software.**
4. **Name and describe the functions of enhancements to word processing software.**
5. **Describe how word processing software is used for correspondence.**
6. **Describe how word processing software is used for document construction.**
7. **Describe how word processing software is used by writers.**
8. **Describe how word processing software is used for desktop publishing.**
9. **Explain how to determine hardware needs in relation to the word processing capabilities being anticipated.**

INTRODUCTION

Word processing software is software specially designed to assist in the document preparation needs of an individual or business. It allows the user to enter text, revise text, and print text. It makes no difference whether the text is in the form of a memo, a letter, a report, or a legal document; word processing can make its preparation faster and more accurate. While businesses operated successfully for years with only handwriting and typewriters for the creation of text, the advent of word processing software has made working with text much more efficient.

ADVANTAGES OF WORD PROCESSING

A business or individual obtains many advantages by using word processing. Some of them are as follows:

1. Keying errors are easily corrected during the text entry process by simply backspacing and rekeying.
2. Errors discovered after the initial keying can be easily corrected by moving the cursor back to the point of error and keying the correction.

3. Revisions in the entered document may be made at will. Words can be changed, or blocks of text (phrases, sentences, paragraphs) can be copied or moved to new positions in the document. In making such changes, no text needs to be rekeyed.
4. Similar documents can be easily prepared for various recipients by using the power of the computer to make the changes that are necessary to customize the output to each person without rekeying the entire document.
5. Documents can be stored for reuse at a later time. For example, a business may need to send a very similar letter to various persons from time to time. The letter can simply be stored, then modified slightly and reprinted for each person.
6. Documents can be more accurate for two reasons. First, since entire documents do not have to be rekeyed in order to implement even major revisions, the likelihood of introducing new errors after the initial proofreading is reduced. Secondly, portions of text that are used repeatedly can be thoroughly proofread, stored on disk, and recalled when needed, thus eliminating the possibility of any errors being introduced during keying of the text into a new document.
7. Documents can be stored and retrieved electronically rather than filed in paper form.
8. Documents can be transmitted electronically from one location to another.

Word processing software offers many advantages to individuals who work with large amounts of text.

HOW A WORD PROCESSING SYSTEM FUNCTIONS

The normal computer system functions you have learned—input, processing, storage, and output—apply to word processing programs just as they do to other software. When execution of a word processing program is begun, a menu or command line is used to select the function to be performed. An opening screen with a command line and an opening screen with a typical beginning menu, known as an opening menu, are shown in Figure 10-1.

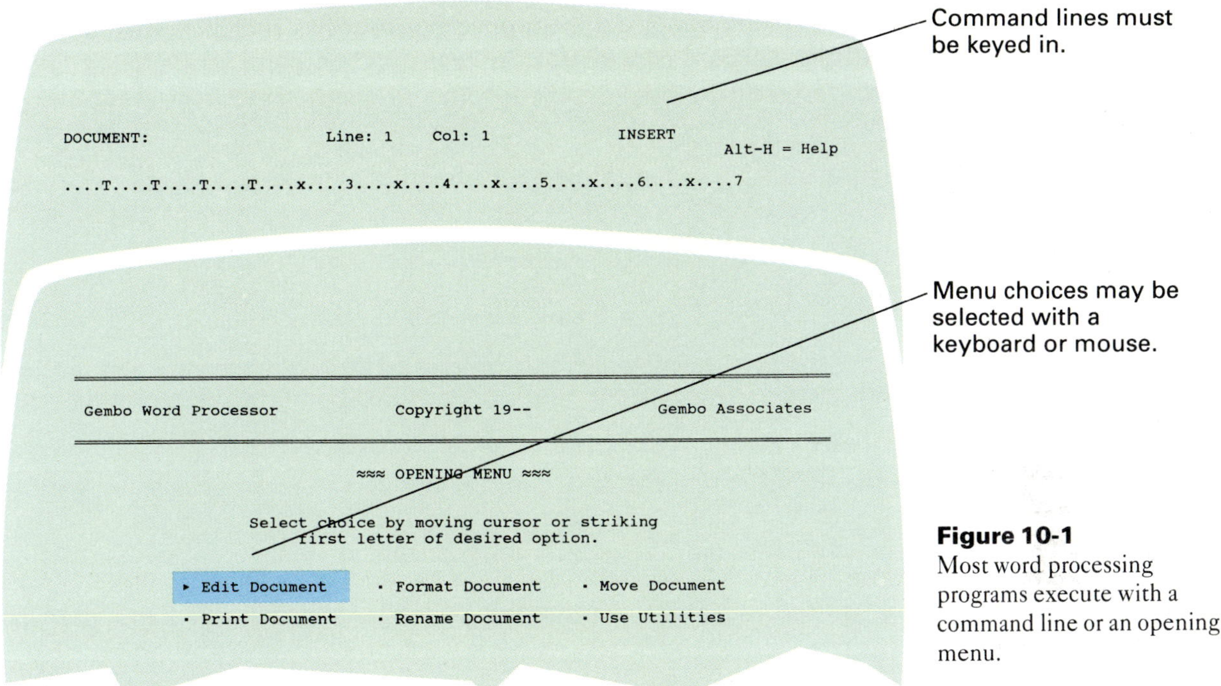

Figure 10-1
Most word processing programs execute with a command line or an opening menu.

The ways in which the word processing functions are normally used are discussed in the following sections.

Input

Input refers to the method used to get text into the computer. Typically, the text is entered through use of the keyboard, even though scanners are increasingly used for entering previously keyed text from other sources. For example, a business might have put together a procedures manual before obtaining word processing. To enter the contents of the manual into the computer so that revisions can be made without rekeying everything, a scanner can read the existing pages and store the text in the computer.

With most word processing software, settings such as line spacing and margins can be made either before or after the text is entered. Many programs allow the use of **formats, style sheets,** or **templates** for controlling these settings. These are simply pre-stored settings that may be called upon when starting a new document to "automatically" make the settings. For example, different formats are used for memorandums and letters; therefore, files designating these two formats could already be stored. When the user is ready to enter text, the word processing software can be told which of the formats to use. With some word processing programs, format files can also include standard wording. For example, a format might include the company name and the word "Memorandum" along with the headings: To, From, Date, and Subject. Figure 10-2 shows how the screen might appear once the user has specified such a format and the software is ready for the text to be entered.

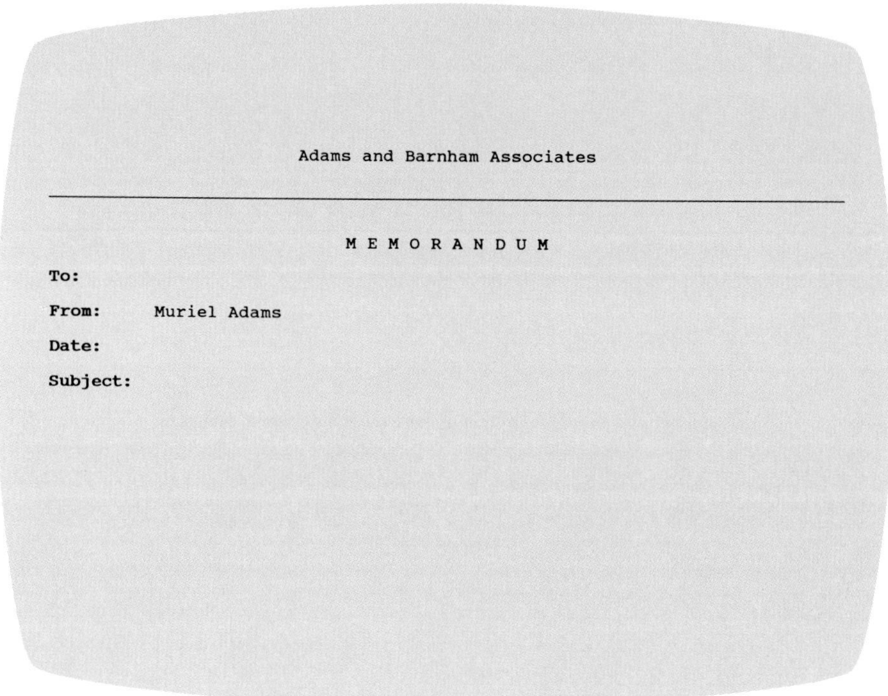

Figure 10-2
With most word processing software, format files that include standard wording or settings can be produced.

Text appears on the screen as it is entered by the operator. If desired, such special effects as boldface, underline, or italics may be attached to text as it is entered. Figure 10-3 on the facing page shows a document as it might look on the screen after having been entered.

Note that the headers are shown in boldfaced type and that the format looks correct for a memo, with each line ending the same place it will end when the memo is printed. When word processing software is capable of showing the document on the screen the same way it will look when it is printed, it is said to have **WYSIWYG** capability. WYSIWYG stands for "What You See Is What You Get." Obviously, it is preferable that what you see on the screen will resemble as closely as possible what is going to come out on paper when a document is printed.

The degree to which WYSIWYG is implemented with word processing software depends not only on the software but on the hardware as well. The best systems are capable of showing not just simple enhancements, such as boldface print, but various type fonts and sizes as well as proportionally spaced print.

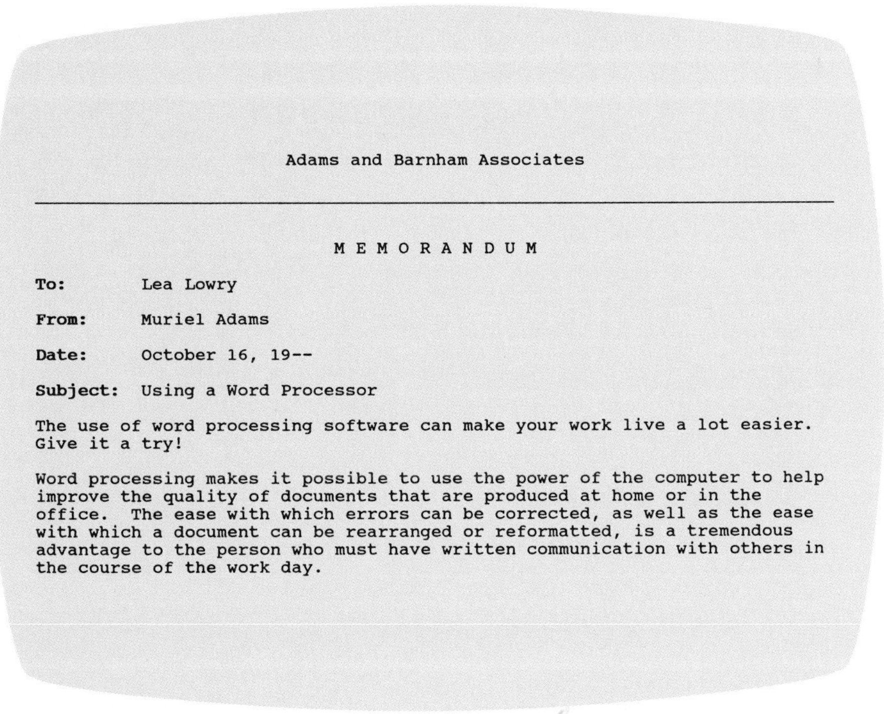

Adams and Barnham Associates

M E M O R A N D U M

To: Lea Lowry

From: Muriel Adams

Date: October 16, 19--

Subject: Using a Word Processor

The use of word processing software can make your work live a lot easier. Give it a try!

Word processing makes it possible to use the power of the computer to help improve the quality of documents that are produced at home or in the office. The ease with which errors can be corrected, as well as the ease with which a document can be rearranged or reformatted, is a tremendous advantage to the person who must have written communication with others in the course of the work day.

Figure 10-3
Text appears on the screen as it is entered.

Processing

Processing done by word processing software can occur either during the text entry process or during the editing or revision process. When editing and revising text, the user is changing the text. Changes may be made either to correct errors or to improve the technical quality of the writing. In the first line of the memo in Figure 10-3, for example, the word "live" is used when it should be "life." Even after the entire memo has been entered, the cursor can be moved back to the point of the error, and the correct letter can be keyed in, as shown in Figure 10-4 on the next page. The cursor can be moved either by the cursor control keys or a mouse. The use of a mouse is increasingly popular with word processing software and is especially appropriate for making menu choices, for moving the cursor to a distant point in the document, and for marking portions of text.

Entire words, phrases, or sentences can be inserted easily during the editing or revision process. All that is necessary is to move the cursor to the desired point of insertion, make sure the word processing software's insert function is turned on (usually by using the key labeled Insert), and key the desired text. Text following the insertion point will simply move out of the way to allow for the insertion. Figure 10-5 shows how this is done; the added word is highlighted. Note that some words automatically moved to the next line as existing text moved over to make space for the inserted word.

Figure 10-4
Corrections are easy to make with word processing software.

Adams and Barnham Associates

M E M O R A N D U M

To: Lea Lowry

From: Muriel Adams

Date: October 16, 19--

Subject: Using a Word Processor

The use of word processing software can make your work live a lot easier. Give it a try!

Word processing makes it possible to use the power of the computer to help improve the quality of documents that are produced at home or in the office. The ease with which errors can be corrected, as well as the ease with which a document can be rearranged or reformatted, is a tremendous advantage to the person who must have written communication with others in the course of the work day.

Use cursor control arrow keys or mouse to get to this point, then key in correction (f).

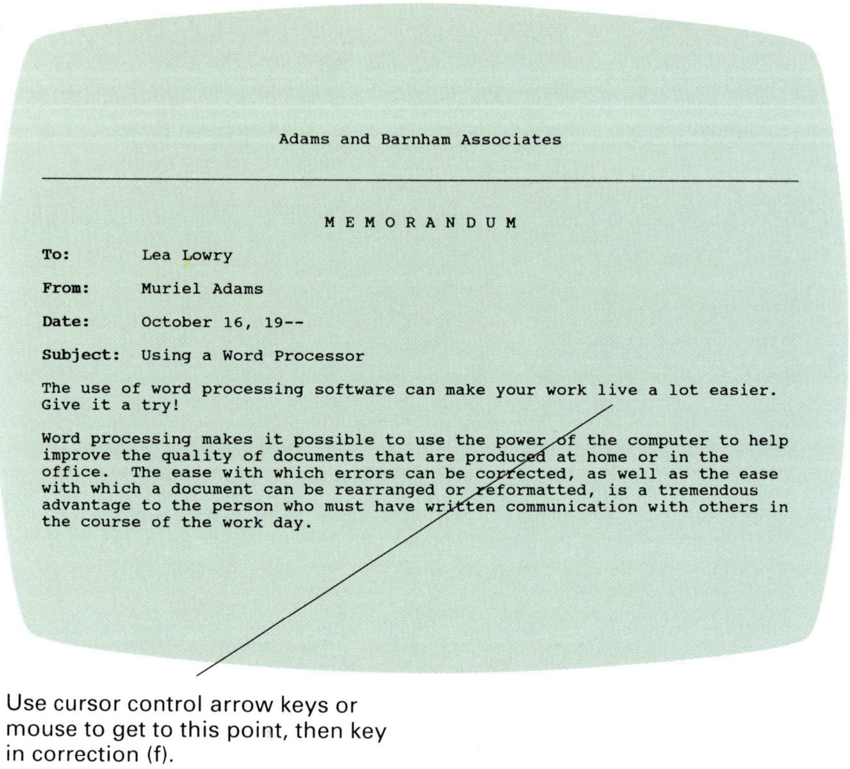

Figure 10-5
Words, phrases, or entire sentences may be inserted by using the insert function in the word processing program.

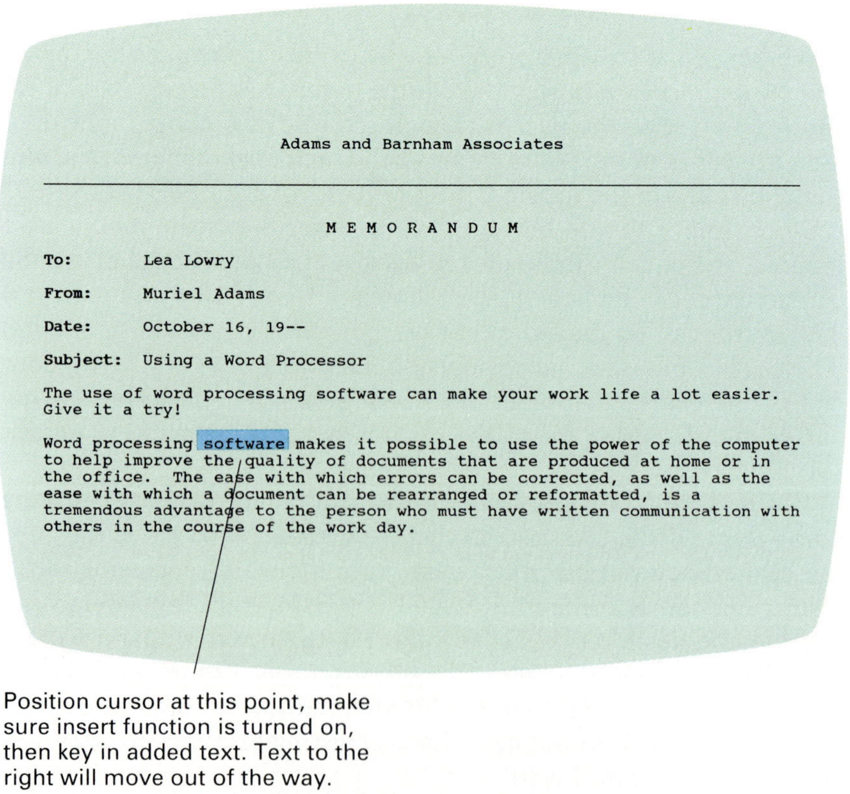

Adams and Barnham Associates

M E M O R A N D U M

To: Lea Lowry

From: Muriel Adams

Date: October 16, 19--

Subject: Using a Word Processor

The use of word processing software can make your work life a lot easier. Give it a try!

Word processing software makes it possible to use the power of the computer to help improve the quality of documents that are produced at home or in the office. The ease with which errors can be corrected, as well as the ease with which a document can be rearranged or reformatted, is a tremendous advantage to the person who must have written communication with others in the course of the work day.

Position cursor at this point, make sure insert function is turned on, then key in added text. Text to the right will move out of the way.

Another type of revision is to move or rearrange text. The amount of text to be moved may be anywhere from one character to many pages. The typical process is that the text to be moved is marked, as shown in Figure 10-6, and then moved by use of the appropriate command to its new location. This process is sometimes known as **cut and paste.** The "cut" part is when the text is marked and removed from its old location; the "paste" part is when the text is put down in or moved to its new location.

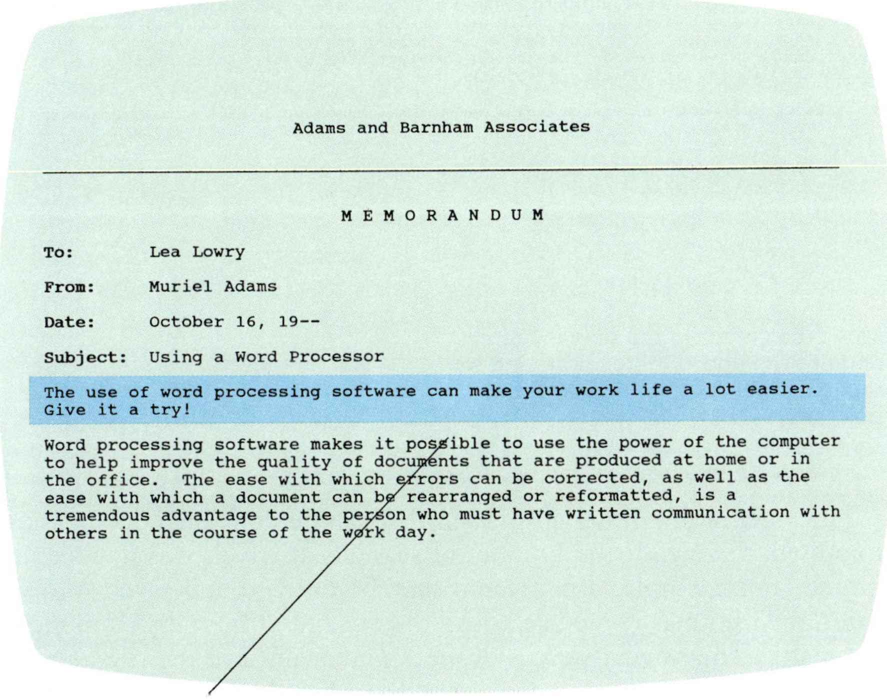

Adams and Barnham Associates

M E M O R A N D U M

To: Lea Lowry

From: Muriel Adams

Date: October 16, 19--

Subject: Using a Word Processor

The use of word processing software can make your work life a lot easier. Give it a try!

Word processing software makes it possible to use the power of the computer to help improve the quality of documents that are produced at home or in the office. The ease with which errors can be corrected, as well as the ease with which a document can be rearranged or reformatted, is a tremendous advantage to the person who must have written communication with others in the course of the work day.

Mark the text to be moved by giving the appropriate command; the text will usually be highlighted as you mark it.

Figure 10-6
To rearrange text, the text to be moved must first be marked.

Note in Figure 10-7 that the original first paragraph of the memo is being moved to the end, making it the second paragraph. Copying may be done in a similar fashion. When copying, the marked text remains in its old position and is duplicated in its new position.

Figure 10-7
Text that is marked can be moved to any new location.

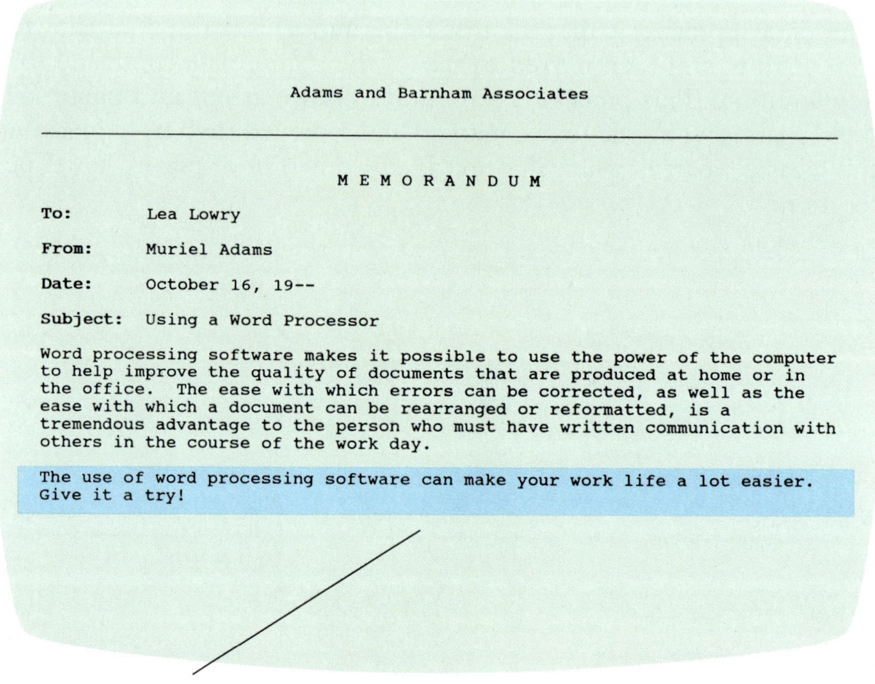

The amount of editing or revision that can be done on a document is unlimited. Likewise, the number of sessions at which it is done is unlimited. For example, a document may be entered and saved to disk. Later, the user may come back, load the document from disk into memory, make as many revisions as desired, and again save the text to disk.

In addition to the kinds of changes discussed thus far in this chapter, most word processing software will also allow the operator to change the type or style of print at any point in the document. Changes in these settings can be made during the initial text entry process or during editing.

Output

Once a document is entered and is in the form desired, it may be printed or transmitted to another location. While most documents are printed in hard copy form, the number of electronically transmitted documents is growing. If a computer is equipped with a laser printer, the quality of printouts can be higher than those from other types of printers.

Printing of output is accomplished by giving the appropriate command or making the appropriate menu choice. Figure 10-8 shows the memorandum as printed on a dot-matrix printer. Figure 10-9 shows the memorandum as it might look printed on a laser printer. Note the higher quality printout produced by the laser printer, as well as the various fonts. (Various fonts can also be produced by a dot-matrix printer, but they would not look nearly as nice.) If the word processor being used to produce the document has full WYSIWYG capability, the screen display would show the different fonts just as the printout does.

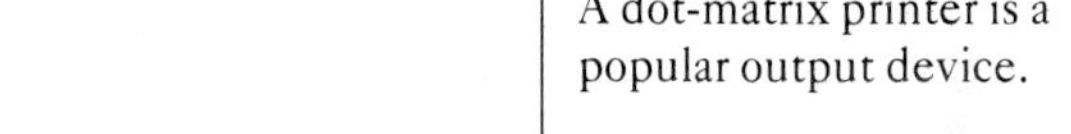

Adams and Barnham Associates

M E M O R A N D U M

To: Lea Lowry

From: Muriel Adams

Date: October 16, 19--

Subject: Using a Word Processor

Word processing software makes it possible to use the power of the computer to help improve the quality of documents that are produced at home or in the office. The ease with which errors can be corrected, as well as the ease with which a document can be rearranged or reformatted, is a tremendous advantage to the person who must have written communication with others in the course of the work day.

The use of word processing software can make your work life a lot easier. Give it a try!

Figure 10-8
A dot-matrix printer is a popular output device.

Figure 10-9
A laser printer produces high-quality output.

Adams and Barnham Associates

M E M O R A N D U M

To: Lea Lowry

From: Muriel Adams

Date: October 16, 19--

Subject: Using a Word Processor

Word processing software makes it possible to use the power of the computer to help improve the quality of documents that are produced at home or in the office. The ease with which errors can be corrected, as well as the ease with which a document can be rearranged or reformatted, is a tremendous advantage to the person who must have written communication with others in the course of the work day.

The use of word processing software can make your work life a lot easier. Give it a try!

Storage

As indicated earlier, any text entered into the computer with word processing software can be stored for later use. Word processing documents are usually stored on disks. Some word processing software requires that a document be stored before it can be printed. Others allow it to be printed before it is stored, if desired. It is a good idea, however, to store the document first. Then, if the printer has problems and hangs up the computer, the document will not be lost.

Storage of a document is done by giving the appropriate command or making the appropriate menu choice. Once a document is stored it may be recalled whenever desired for further revision or printing. Some word processors require the user to know the name of the document in order to recall it. Others allow users to search for documents by using key words contained in them or by browsing through a list of filenames.

WORD PROCESSING ENHANCEMENTS

In addition to the basic functions of word processors discussed in the previous sections, various enhancements are available. While the exact features depend on the particular software, the enhancements can be grouped into several categories as explained in the following paragraphs. Spelling checkers, grammar and style programs, and thesaurus programs assist in the creation of higher quality composition, while mail merge capability assists in the output of documents for various persons.

Spelling Checkers

Spell checking capability is built into some word processing software, while it is optional as a separate program for use with others. When the capability is built in, a simple command or menu choice invokes execution of the spelling checker.

Essentially, a **spelling checker** looks up words of text in its dictionaries and calls attention to not-found words. Usually there is a general dictionary consisting of many thousands of words stored on disk. In addition to the general dictionary, there may be special dictionaries for particular disciplines, such as law or medicine, plus individual dictionaries made up of words added by the operator over a period of time. Typically, spelling checkers can be asked to look up varying amounts of text—anywhere from one word to the entire document.

Less capable spelling checkers insert "flags" into the document for each word not found in the dictionaries, requiring the user to go back after the spelling check is finished and manually take care of the problem words. Better spelling checkers operate while in edit mode and stop at each word that is not found in the dictionary to allow for correction. More capable spelling checkers not only stop at each suspect word but also display suggested words that may have been intended and allow the chosen replacement word to be entered into the document by a simple keystroke or mouse click.

Figure 10-10 shows a screen during typical spell checking operation. Note that the program has highlighted a word that it did not find in the dictionaries and is suggesting dictionary words that are phonetically close to the misspelled word. Also, note that the operator can choose a word from the list by using the cursor control keys or the mouse and then indicate the action to take by striking one key or clicking the mouse on the choice. If the choice is made to correct the highlighted word, the erroneous spelling is immediately replaced by the correct one.

The user may choose a word from the list of recommendations using the cursor keys or a mouse.

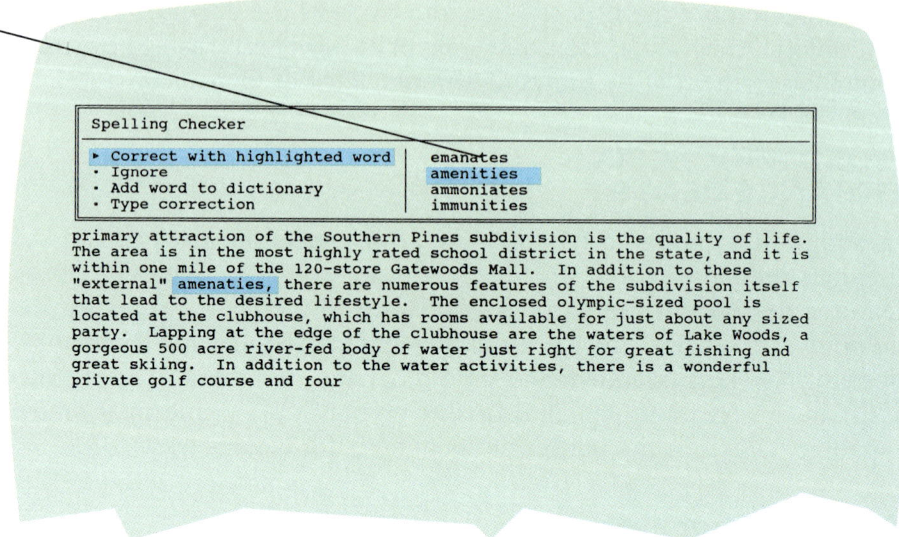

Figure 10-10
A spelling checker can look up words in its dictionary and call attention to those misspelled.

Thesaurus Programs

A thesaurus is a book or list of synonyms and is useful for finding alternative words to express ideas. **Thesaurus programs** function very similarly to spelling checkers except that the operator marks the word for which a synonym is desired. The program then looks up the word in a thesaurus stored on disk and suggests alternative words (and their definitions in many cases). For example, if the operator entering the memo from Figure 10-10 wished to use a word other than "great" to describe the skiing, the screen might look like Figure 10-11.

A replacement word may be chosen from the list of recommendations using the cursor keys or a mouse.

```
Thesaurus

▸ Replace with highlighted word
• Leave thesaurus with no change

creditable ... worthy of belief or praise
glorious   ... illustrious, magnificent
splendid   ... grand, excellent
worthy     ... honorable, meritorious

within one mile of the 120-store Gatewoods Mall.  In addition to these
"external" amenaties, there are numerous features of the subdivision itself
that lead to the desired lifestyle.  The enclosed olympic-sized pool is
located at the clubhouse, which has rooms available for just about any sized
party.  Lapping at the edge of the clubhouse are the waters of Lake Woods, a
gorgeous 500 acre river-fed body of water just right for great fishing and
great skiing.  In addition to the water activities, there is a wonderful
private golf course and four
```

Figure 10-11
A thesaurus program allows the operator to choose a replacement word from a list of alternative words.

At this point, the thesaurus is invoked and the word "great" is marked in the text. The operator would then use the cursor control keys or mouse to mark the chosen replacement word ("splendid" in the illustration). As soon as replacement of the word is chosen, the new word will automatically take the place of the old one.

Grammar and Style Programs

Grammar and style programs can do various types of technical checking of a document once it has been entered into the computer. It is common for grammar and style software to be separate programs rather than a built-in part of the word processing software. While the capabilities vary depending on the brand of software, some of the checks commonly made are:

1. Checking for sentence fragments
2. Checking the length of sentences
3. Checking for trite, overused expressions
4. Checking subject/verb agreement
5. Checking for some types of punctuation problems

Depending on the software, corrective action may be suggested. For example, if a program detects the phrase "consensus of opinion," it might suggest that simply saying "consensus" is more appropriate, or as another example, it might suggest replacing "point in time" with "time."

Mail Merge

Mail merge functions are found in almost all commercial word processing programs. Adding tremendous power to the basic word processing functions, mail merge allows the software to insert varying values into documents as they are being printed. While there are many applications of such power, several of them are as follows:

1. The same letter can be sent to different persons, with the name and address on the letter customized for each person.
2. Varying values can be placed in documents to customize them as required. A lease, for example, could have the street address of the property and the amount of monthly rent entered as appropriate at the time of printing.
3. Address labels can be printed for the mailing of various materials.

Mail merge typically uses data obtained from a separate file. For example, the separate file might contain names and addresses for a letter. When the letters are to be printed, the word processor will read the names and addresses from the file and print them on the letters. Figure 10-12 illustrates this process. Notice that markers in the letter body indicate where the name and address should be printed.

Figure 10-12

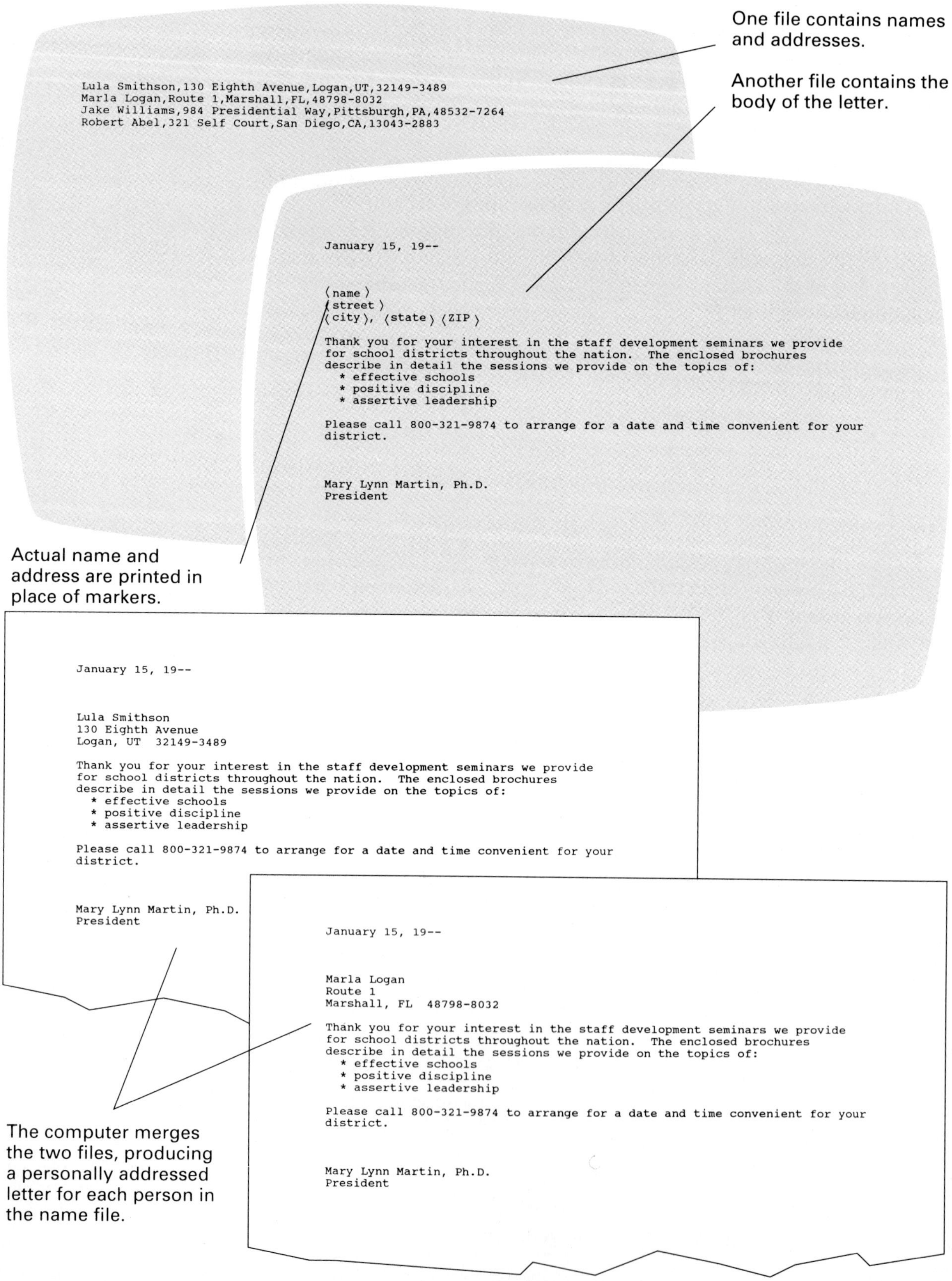

One file contains names and addresses.

Lula Smithson,130 Eighth Avenue,Logan,UT,32149-3489
Marla Logan,Route 1,Marshall,FL,48798-8032
Jake Williams,984 Presidential Way,Pittsburgh,PA,48532-7264
Robert Abel,321 Self Court,San Diego,CA,13043-2883

Another file contains the body of the letter.

January 15, 19--

⟨name⟩
⟨street⟩
⟨city⟩, ⟨state⟩ ⟨ZIP⟩

Thank you for your interest in the staff development seminars we provide for school districts throughout the nation. The enclosed brochures describe in detail the sessions we provide on the topics of:
* effective schools
* positive discipline
* assertive leadership

Please call 800-321-9874 to arrange for a date and time convenient for your district.

Mary Lynn Martin, Ph.D.
President

Actual name and address are printed in place of markers.

January 15, 19--

Lula Smithson
130 Eighth Avenue
Logan, UT 32149-3489

Thank you for your interest in the staff development seminars we provide for school districts throughout the nation. The enclosed brochures describe in detail the sessions we provide on the topics of:
* effective schools
* positive discipline
* assertive leadership

Please call 800-321-9874 to arrange for a date and time convenient for your district.

Mary Lynn Martin, Ph.D.
President

January 15, 19--

Marla Logan
Route 1
Marshall, FL 48798-8032

Thank you for your interest in the staff development seminars we provide for school districts throughout the nation. The enclosed brochures describe in detail the sessions we provide on the topics of:
* effective schools
* positive discipline
* assertive leadership

Please call 800-321-9874 to arrange for a date and time convenient for your district.

Mary Lynn Martin, Ph.D.
President

The computer merges the two files, producing a personally addressed letter for each person in the name file.

Most word processors can use data from a separate file to perform mail merge functions. In addition, many of them can ask for the data from the keyboard at print time. In using one of these programs, the operator would tell the program to print the letter that is stored in a particular file. Based on prompts stored in that file, the word processor program would ask the operator to key-in the name, address, and any other variable data. The letter—containing the variable data entered from the keyboard—would then be printed. Note that the variable data, whether from a file or from the keyboard at print time, is not limited to names and addresses. It can consist of any data located at any point in the document.

USES OF WORD PROCESSORS

In previous sections of this chapter, the capabilities of word processing software were discussed. Now, some of the common applications for which the software may be utilized will be explored in the following paragraphs.

Correspondence

In many companies, virtually all correspondence is performed with word processing software. This applies for internal memorandums as well as for letters going to customers, vendors, and other contacts outside the company. Mail merge capability is extremely important in using word processors for correspondence, since the time required for keying documents can be reduced drastically when the same or similar letters are used for several persons.

Document Construction

The term **document construction** refers to the act of combining various pre-saved paragraphs or sentences to produce a finished document. One area where such capability is frequently used is in the legal profession. In the practice of law, attorneys frequently prepare leases for their clients. For this purpose, standard paragraphs have existed for years, each for a particular application. For example, if it is prohibited for a person who rents property to in turn rent it to another individual, paragraphs will be needed in the lease to indicate this. If it is acceptable for the renter to rent to someone else, there will be a need for different paragraphs.

These various standard paragraphs, which may number into the thousands in some word processing applications, are known as **boilerplate text** and are pre-stored on an auxiliary storage device and combined with custom text as needed to produce the desired document. Figure 10-13 illustrates this concept.

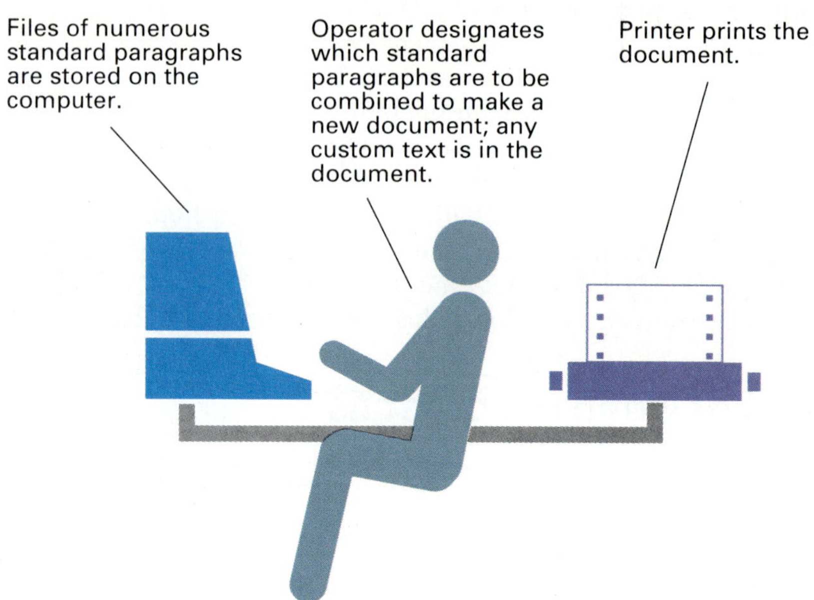

Figure 10-13
Boilerplate text is stored on the computer and can be combined with other text to produce a new document.

Note that the assembly of pre-saved paragraphs into new documents is typically done in memory as text entry and revision, not at print time. Once the paragraphs are assembled and any desired changes are made in the pre-saved wording, the document may be saved and printed just like any other document that has been created.

Preparation of Manuscripts

Word processing software can provide many functions of value to writers when producing manuscripts. In addition to the normal text entry and revision functions previously detailed, many word processors can also automatically produce tables of contents and indexes for manuscripts, format and place footnotes, and prepare bibliographies.

Desktop Publishing

One of the most exciting developments related to word processing is that of desktop publishing. **Desktop publishing** refers to the process of using the computer to produce an original layout for material to be printed. The software that does desktop publishing can produce a wide variety of print fonts on a laser printer (dot matrix can be used, but the quality is much lower) and can combine graphics with the text. The graphics can be prepared with a drawing program or by scanning them in with a scanner. Additionally, many "clip art" type graphics are available from various publishers which are ready to be included to enhance documents such as newsletters.

In the early days of desktop publishing, it was necessary to enter the text using a word processing program. Then a separate publishing program would combine the text with any desired graphics and put them in the format for printing. While the use of two programs—word processing and publishing—is still common, the two are now merging. It is increasingly common to find desktop publishing capabilities in word processing programs and to find more powerful text editing features in publishing programs.

Desktop publishing software allows the user to produce an original layout from material to be printed.

HARDWARE REQUIREMENTS

The kind of hardware required for word processing depends on the level of sophistication of the software. Word processing with some programs can be done on the most minimal microcomputer systems. Although there is word processing software available for virtually all computers, there are several points to keep in mind when selecting software and hardware.

1. Many of today's more sophisticated word processing programs require the use of a hard disk for satisfactory performance. If you do not have a hard disk computer, you can still obtain very workable, but less powerful, word processing software that does not need a hard disk.
2. The more sophisticated a word processing program is, the more memory it will require. It is common for programs to require 512K or more of memory for best operation.
3. Word processing software with true WYSIWYG capability (showing on screen the different fonts and sizes as they will actually appear) requires a high-resolution display as well as a fast processor for satisfactory operation. It is necessary to use as a minimum a 16-bit processor computer to get satisfactory performance with these programs.

A NOVEL TALE

In the olden days of book and magazine publishing, an author laboriously typed manuscript for the chapters or articles, frequently retyping pages as necessary. Scissors and paste were also frequently used to help rearrange the sequence of material. Once the author was finished, an editor would take over, making many editorial changes with pencil and again rearranging some segments with scissors and paste. Large volumes of paper manuscript made their way from author to editor and back again as changes were made.

When the editor and author finally agreed that the work was completed, the frequently almost-marked-beyond-recognition manuscript went to a typesetter. The typesetter would then decipher the many corrections and editing marks and key the data into a machine that produced simple, straightforward, typeset copy. Once off of the machine, segments of paragraphs, headlines, etc. were pasted into position on boards to get the desired layout effect. After much proofreading and correcting, the layout was photographed, and a plate was prepared for printing.

Word processing software has changed all that, however. Indeed, word processing software could accurately be called the "Writers' and Publishers' Relief Software."

Under the modern process, a writer creates manuscript using a word processor. Any changes desired—rearrangements, new words, spelling corrections, etc.—can be implemented quickly and almost effortlessly. When the author is satisfied with the manuscript, it can be sent quickly by means of a modem and phone line to the editor's computer. The editor then makes whatever changes are desired and sends the manuscript back to the author over phone lines for approval or negotiation.

Word processing software could be called the "Writers' and Publishers' Relief Software."

Once the editor and author are happy with the text, the computer is used to add codes to the manuscript to identify how the page layout should look. The resulting text is then fed to a laser printer or typesetting machine where the finished text is quickly produced. The pages come out in final format, with little if any pasteup of the final document required, and are ready for printing.

The bottom line of using word processing and publishing software is that books and magazines can be produced faster, more efficiently, and with less likelihood of errors. Thus, everyone benefits—writer, publisher, and reader.

CHAPTER SUMMARY

- Word processing software assists in the document preparation needs of a business or individual.
- Word processing software allows for easy correction of keying errors, either at the time they are made or later, and for easy revision of documents.
- Preparing similar documents for various recipients is easy with word processing's ability to modify standard text, either in memory or during the mail-merge function.
- Documents prepared with word processing can be stored for reuse.
- Word-processed documents can be more accurate due to the lessened amount of rekeying.
- Documents can be stored, retrieved, and transmitted electronically rather than on paper.
- Input to a word processing program is usually through use of a keyboard, even though scanners are used to convert existing documents for computer storage and revision.
- Style sheets, formats, or templates may be used to set margins, print sizes, etc., and to bring standard wording into a document.
- WYSIWYG means "What You See Is What You Get" and refers to the ability of a word processor to display the material on the screen as it will appear on the printed page.
- During processing of a document, errors may be corrected, and text may be moved or copied through a process known as cut and paste.
- Output may be directed to almost any printer; alternately, the document may be transmitted electronically to another computer(s).
- Storage of documents is done on disk, with the storage taking place before or after printing, depending on the brand of software and/or user preference; however, storage before printing is a good safeguard to use in case of printer problems.

- Word processing enhancements include spelling checkers, thesaurus programs, grammar and style programs, and mail merge functions.
- Spell checkers locate document words that do not appear in their dictionaries and call attention to them, frequently giving the operator a list of potentially correct words to choose from.
- Thesaurus programs present synonyms for desired words on the screen for operator choice.
- Grammar and style checkers can help the operator produce more technically correct compositions.
- Mail merge functions make it easy to produce the same or similar documents customized for various recipients.
- Word processors are frequently used for correspondence, for document construction, for the preparation of manuscripts, and for desktop publishing.
- While word processing programs are available for even the most minimal microcomputer, sophisticated programs used in business require computers with more speed and memory, as well as hard disks.

KEY TERMS

The following key terms were introduced or redefined in this chapter:

boilerplate text
cut and paste
desktop publishing
document construction
formats/style sheets/templates
grammar and style program
mail merge
spelling checker
thesaurus program
word processing software
WYSIWYG

REVIEW QUESTIONS

1. Define word processing software. (Obj. 1)
2. What does word processing software do that makes it a necessary part of today's business world? (Obj. 1)
3. List eight advantages of using word processing software. (Obj. 2)
4. How is the input function usually performed with word processing software? (Obj. 3)
5. What kinds of processing are typically performed with word processing software? (Obj. 3)
6. What kinds of output are possible with word processing software? (Obj. 3)
7. What kind of storage is usually used with word processing software? (Obj. 3)
8. What are formats, style sheets, and templates, and why are they used? (Obj. 3)
9. What is the advantage of WYSIWYG? (Obj. 3)

10. What is meant by "cut and paste"? (Obj. 3)
11. Describe the operation of a typical spelling checker. (Obj. 4)
12. Describe the operation of a typical thesaurus program. (Obj. 4)
13. Describe the operation of a typical grammar and style checker. (Obj. 4)
14. What is the purpose of the mail merge function? (Obj. 4)
15. Describe four applications of word processing. (Objs. 5,6,7,8)
16. What is boilerplate text? (Obj. 6)
17. What is the relationship between word processing software capability and hardware requirements? (Obj. 9)

CHALLENGE ACTIVITIES

1. What factors might you consider in deciding whether to purchase word processing software? Why would you consider them? (Objs. 1, 2,5,6,7,8)
2. Do all persons who need word processing software need sophisticated software with many capabilities? Justify your answer. (Objs. 5,6,7,8)
3. Which of the word processing functions and enhancements discussed in this chapter would be of value to almost all users of word processing software? Which would be of value only to selected users? Why? (Objs. 2,4)
4. In this chapter you have learned about many functions of word processing software. Each particular program on the market has its own unique combination of features. The purpose of this activity is to make you more familiar with a word processing package that is available for your use. If you have more than one package available, make the selection of one with the aid of your instructor. Then carry out the following activities, using the word processor's reference manual as necessary. (Objs. 3,4)
   a. List the capabilities discussed in this chapter that the word processing program implements.
   b. List the capabilities discussed in this chapter that the word processing program does not implement.
   c. List capabilities of the word processor that are in addition to those discussed in this chapter.
5. Use word processing software to complete the following steps. Print a copy of the memorandum after each step. (Obj. 5)
   a. Enter the memorandum as shown in Figure 10-3.
   b. Make the correction shown in Figure 10-4.
   c. Insert a word as shown in Figure 10-5.
   d. Move the first paragraph to the last as shown in Figures 10-6 and 10-7.

6. Use the mail merge function of word processing software to produce four letters using the addresses shown in Figure 10-12. (Obj. 4)
7. Use word processing software to enter the names and addresses of several of your friends. Then enter a letter inviting the recipient to a party. Be sure to tell what kind of party it is (graduation, birthday, etc.), when it is to be held, where it is to be held, and give a phone number for responding. Use mail merge to print a copy of the invitation letter for each of your friends whose name and address you entered.

CHAPTER 11

DATABASE SOFTWARE

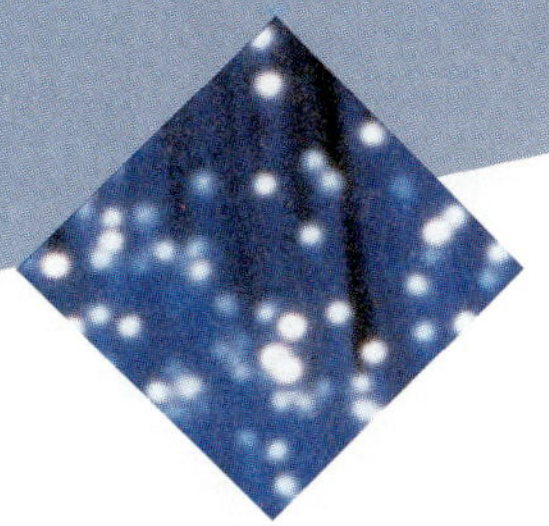

LEARNING OBJECTIVES

After studying this chapter, you will be able to:

1. **Define and state the purposes of a database.**
2. **Describe the functions performed by database software.**
3. **List and describe the main features of five types of database software.**
4. **Describe how to plan for a database.**
5. **Explain how database files may be used and shared.**
6. **Describe the purposes and characteristics of physical and logical views.**
7. **Explain the functions of database administration.**
8. **Describe the relationship between database capability and hardware requirements.**

INTRODUCTION

In this chapter you will learn about using the computer to maintain the data of a business or individual. This is done by using software frequently referred to as a **database management system** (DBMS). The name is derived from the fact that the software manages (processes) a database (an organized collection of facts).

PURPOSES OF A DATABASE

A **database** is a collection of organized data whose elements are in some way related to one another. Thus, all the data maintained by a club about its members is a database. Also, the records of accounts and sales of a business make up a database. In any event, the purpose of a database is to maintain all relevant data in such form as to be useful to its owner for record keeping and decision making. For a club, the database can be used for the preparation of directories, for mailing form letters to members, or for analyzing the characteristics of the membership. For businesses, the database can also aid in making and recording sales and in the analysis of data to provide information for management decision making.

As an example of a database, look at Figure 11-1 showing the membership records of the Adel Civic Club. Note that there is a row in the table for each member and that the columns indicate specific information about each member. As indicated by the terminology about files discussed in Chapter 6, each of the columns in the database can be thought of as a field, and each of the rows can be thought of as a record. The entire database makes up a file.

Figure 11-1
A database is commonly used to maintain records.

LAST NAME	FIRST NAME	PHONE	STREET	CITY	STATE	ZIP	MEMBERSHIP DATE	DUES PAID DATE
Miller	Samuel	433-9873	983 Caper Drive	Adel	GA	31673-6210	12/3/84	1/6/--
Bryars	Martha	433-2193	32 Main Street	Adel	GA	31673-1981	12/3/84	1/7/--
Sampson	Celia	412-5987	139 Fifth Avenue	Hahira	GA	31632-4643	12/3/84	2/8/--
Bryars	Larry	433-9146	349 Oakdale Drive	Adel	GA	31673-6594	12/6/85	5/6/--
Barnes	Gregory	433-0813	768 Main Street	Adel	GA	31673-9214	12/6/86	3/6/--
Xantho	Harriett	412-1089	Route 1	Hahira	GA	31632-8778	10/4/87	2/4/--
Marcus	Sanford	412-4444	769 Larry Drive	Hahira	GA	31632-3698	11/5/87	4/8/--
Saunders	Mae	433-1928	879 Bark Avenue	Adel	GA	31673-7011	4/8/88	1/8/--

Many things can be done with the data in the Adel Civic Club's database, including the following:

1. Information about new members can easily be added to the file.
2. Membership data may be easily changed when a member pays dues, moves, gets a new phone number, or drops out.
3. Mailing labels can be printed for sending the monthly newsletter and other club announcements to the members. Assuming that there are enough members to make it worthwhile, these labels can be printed in ZIP code order to qualify for reduced postage rates.
4. Directories showing members' names, addresses, and phone numbers can be printed for distribution. These directories will probably be printed in alphabetic order by member name.
5. A membership list in order by original membership date can be printed for honoring those with the longest service.

A database can be used to keep membership lists of organizations such as the Adel Civic Club.

6. Reminder letters can be printed to those members who have not yet paid yearly membership dues.
7. Data can easily be updated whenever an item changes.

All the functions that can be performed using the Adel Civic Club's database can be programmed by using a computer language code such as BASIC, Pascal, or C. However, the same functions can be obtained without programming by using readily available database software. The following section will discuss the functions of such software.

FUNCTIONS OF DATABASE MANAGEMENT SYSTEMS (DBMS)

By using commercial database software, the functions needed for entering data, manipulating data, and reporting information from the data are available without programming. One way of categorizing these functions is as follows: (1) creating the structure of the database, (2) adding data to the database, (3) editing data already in the database, (4) selecting and retrieving data, (5) designing reports, and (6) modifying the structure of the database. Depending on the computer and the brand of software being used, these functions are accessed by commands, by menu choices selected with the keyboard, or by making selections with a mouse. Figure 11-2 shows an example of how a main menu might appear for the selection of these functions.

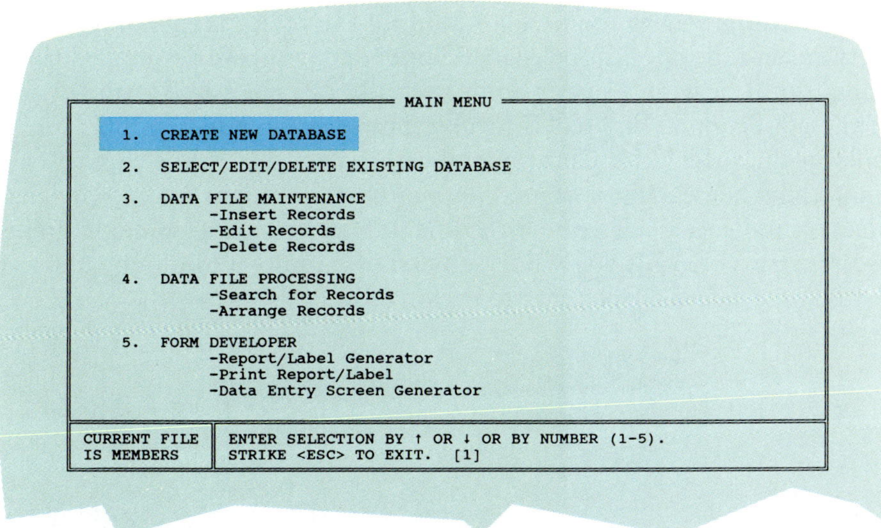

Figure 11-2
The main menu of a database program displays options available to the user.

Creating the Structure of a Database

A database is created by first determining the pieces of data that are to be stored and then by telling the database software what to do. In the case of the Adel Civic Club, the items to be stored are last name, first name, phone number, street address, city, state, ZIP, date of original membership, and date of dues payment.

Specifying to database software that a new data table, or file, is to be created is usually as simple as making a menu choice and providing a name for the table. The name should generally be descriptive of the kind of data to be stored, such as MEMBERS in the case of a civic club.

Once the table has been named, the names of the fields or columns of data to be stored must be entered. The maximum length allowed for the names varies depending on the software package, but generally some abbreviation is needed. For example, the names LAST, FIRST, PHONE, STREET, CITY, STATE, ZIP, MEMBDATE, and DUES-PAID might be used.

For each field or column named, the kind of data (alphanumeric or numeric) and the maximum width of the field or column in the table must be specified. With many software packages, the fields or columns to be indexed in order to make retrieval faster can also be indicated. For example, if it is important to quickly retrieve information by persons' names, the user can specify that the name should be indexed. Usually indexing can be specified at any time—during initial creation of the database or at some later point.

Entering data into the database is often referred to as appending data.

Adding Data to the Database

Entering data into a table of a database is commonly known as inserting or **appending** data to the table or **loading** the table. Depending on the software and the application, data is appended with a very simple default screen form or with a screen form specially designed by the developer of the application. Figure 11-3 shows how a default screen form might look for the Adel Civic Club's membership database, while Figure 11-4 shows how a specially designed data entry form might look. Note that brackets indicate places where the operator keys in data (some programs use reverse video blocks, while some show simply a blinking cursor at the point where a character is to be keyed).

Figure 11-3
A default screen form, such as the one shown here, is often used to append data to a table or file.

```
DATABASE: MEMBERS          Record   1 of   1                INSERT
                                                                  Alt-H = Help
..................................................................................
 1: LAST        [                         ]
 2: FIRST       [                    ]
 3: PHONE       [               ]
 4: STREET      [                         ]
 5: CITY        [                         ]
 6: STATE       [  ]
 7: ZIP         [          ]
 8: MEMBDATE    [         ]
 9: DUESPAID    [         ]
```

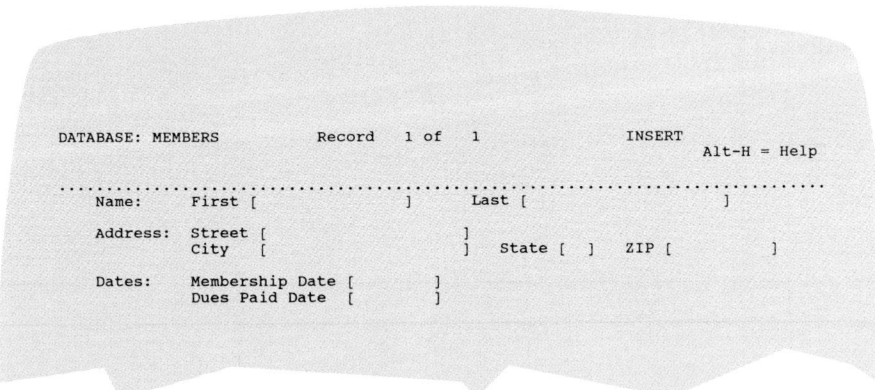
```
DATABASE: MEMBERS          Record   1 of   1              INSERT
                                                                  Alt-H = Help
.................................................................................
     Name:      First [                  ]    Last [                  ]

     Address:   Street [                 ]
                City   [                 ]   State [  ]   ZIP [          ]

     Dates:     Membership Date [        ]
                Dues Paid Date  [        ]
```

Figure 11-4
A specially designed data entry form may be developed and used for appending data.

In the custom data entry screen, note that the labeling that appears on the screen was determined by the developer of the screen and does not match the names of the columns in the database table. However, the software makes the connection between the locations on the screen and the columns into which the data should be entered.

Editing Data Already in the Database

Data stored in the computer changes from time to time, such as when someone moves, gets a new phone number, or pays dues. Also, an error may have been made in entering the data which requires a correction. In all such cases, the already-entered data may be edited. This is done by selecting the appropriate choice by command, keyboard menu, or mouse to display the existing data on the screen and then keying the corrections. Most database software allows editing to be done in either a row by row display, which looks like a table on the screen, or by using a screen form such as the one used for data entry.

Selecting and Retrieving Data

Data from a database may be displayed whenever desired by using either a menu or a command, depending on the software. For example, suppose the user wants to look up the phone number of Harriett Xantho. After the command to search for data is entered, the user would be asked for the field from which data should be retrieved. After responding to that query, the operator might see a screen such as the last one shown in Figure 11-5. Note that the sections in this example appear one after another as the user interacts with the program.

First, the command to search for the data is entered.

```
DATABASE: MEMBERS            Record    1 of    8              INSERT
Contains, Equal to, Less than, or Greater than                        Alt-H = Help
Select type of search by keying first letter: E
.................................................................................
  1: LAST          [Miller                   ]
  2: FIRST         [Samuel           ]
  3: PHONE         [433-9873    ]
  4: STREET        [983 Caper Drive          ]
  5: CITY          [Adel                     ]
  6: STATE         [GA]
  7: ZIP           [31673-6210]
  8: MEMBDATE      [12/03/84]
  9: DUESPAID      [01/06/--]
```

Next, the user must specify the field or column to be searched.

```
DATABASE: MEMBERS            Record    1 of    8              INSERT
                                                                      Alt-H = Help
Enter field number to be searched (1-9): 1
.................................................................................
  1: LAST          [Miller                   ]
  2: FIRST         [Samuel           ]
  3: PHONE         [433-9873    ]
  4: STREET        [983 Caper Drive          ]
  5: CITY          [Adel                     ]
  6: STATE         [GA]
  7: ZIP           [31673-6210]
  8: MEMBDATE      [12/03/84]
  9: DUESPAID      [01/06/--]
```

Finally, the user must specify the value to be searched for in Field 1.

```
DATABASE: MEMBERS            Record    1 of    8              INSERT
Enter the value to be searched for in field LAST:                     Alt-H = Help
Xantho
.................................................................................
  1: LAST          [Miller                   ]
  2: FIRST         [Samuel           ]
  3: PHONE         [433-9873    ]
  4: STREET        [983 Caper Drive          ]
  5: CITY          [Adel                     ]
  6: STATE         [GA]
  7: ZIP           [31673-6210]
  8: MEMBDATE      [12/03/84]
  9: DUESPAID      [01/06/--]
```

Harriett Xantho's record is retrieved, enabling the user to access her telephone number.

```
DATABASE: MEMBERS            Record    6 of    8              INSERT
                                                                      Alt-H = Help

.................................................................................
  1: LAST          [Xantho                   ]
  2: FIRST         [Harriett         ]
  3: PHONE         [412-1089    ]
  4: STREET        [Route 1                  ]
  5: CITY          [Hahira                   ]
  6: STATE         [GA]
  7: ZIP           [31632-8778]
  8: MEMBDATE      [10/4/87 ]
  9: DUESPAID      [02/04/--]
```

Figure 11-5
The procedure for selecting and retrieving data usually follows a series of organized steps.

While the use of prompts as shown in Figure 11-5 is easy for persons who do not use a program often, the use of commands is sometimes easier for those who use a program frequently. The same query might be performed as a command simply by keying in a line such as:

SELECT PHONE FROM MEMBERS WHERE LAST='Xantho' AND FIRST='Harriett'

Some software packages make it easier to retrieve or search for specific data through the use of special commands that are built into the software. For example, rather than keying in the full command to search for Harriett Xantho's data, the user may simply enter the special search command (control-s, for example) and enter the data to be retrieved.

With most software, virtually any field or combination of fields can be searched to display various data items. For example, if you were the club treasurer, you might want to know how many members have not yet paid their membership dues in a specific year. You could make this query through the use of menus, or you might key-in a command such as:

COUNT FOR DUESPAID<'1/1/–'

You can ask questions of the database because the database uses a **query language.** This language specifies the required syntax of statements that may be keyed in for the database to provide a response. While most queries resemble ordinary English, certain rules must still be followed. These rules vary according to the software package being used.

Designing Reports

Reports can be designed from stored data by using the database software's provision for creating reports. By an interactive process using a **report writer** portion of the software, the headings to be placed on the report and the data to be printed in each column of the report are defined. The data to be included may be sorted and selected in much the same way that data is sorted and selected with the query language. Also, control breaks may be specified. A **control break** means that a new page or report is to be started when a named data item changes. For example, in a merchandising situation, if the data is sorted or indexed by store number, the control break allows data for each store to be on a different report. An example of a report created by means of a report writer is shown in Figure 11-6. It is a listing showing the members of the Adel

ADEL CIVIC CLUB
ALPHABETIC MEMBERSHIP LIST--MARCH 1, 19--

LAST NAME	FIRST NAME	PHONE	MEMBERSHIP DATE
Barnes	Gregory	433-0813	12/6/86
Bryars	Larry	433-9146	12/6/85
Bryars	Martha	433-2193	12/3/84
Marcus	Sanford	412-4444	11/5/87
Miller	Samuel	433-9873	12/3/84
Sampson	Celia	412-5987	12/3/84
Saunders	Mae	433-1928	04/8/88
Xantho	Harriet	412-1089	10/4/87

Figure 11-6
Reports can be designed from data stored in a database by using a report writer.

Civic Club in alphabetic order. Note that the report is arranged differently from the order of data in the database in Figure 11-1 and does not include all columns of data, even though it could.

Modifying the Structure of a Database

Even with the best of planning, a column (field) may be omitted from a database, or a column may be narrower than it needs to be. With many database programs, the user can go back at any time, regardless of how much data is in the database, and make modifications. Unless a column is made narrower or removed, data will not be lost when a database structure is modified. If, for example, the LAST NAME column is modified to make it wider than originally defined, no data is lost. The exact method of modifying the structure depends on the software, but it is typically done by a menu choice or command, such as:
CHANGE WIDTH OF LAST NAME TO 15.

TYPES OF DATABASE ORGANIZATION AND ACCESS

There are several types of database organization structures available, each of which has its own method of access. The most useful type of database depends on the function for which it is needed. Some of the more common types of databases are listed in the following paragraphs.

Flat File Database

The simplest form of a database is known as a **flat file database.** Under this organization, the data can be visualized as being contained in one table. Each row in the table is a record, while each column is a field. Computer data stored in tables is very easy for humans to understand because the use of tables is familiar from other experiences. The example shown in Figure 11-7 makes use of a flat file database.

Figure 11-7
A flat file database is the simplest kind of database.

ADDRESS FILE

LAST NAME	FIRST NAME	ADDRESS	CITY	STATE	ZIP
Behrens	Donald	4325 Foley Road	Pensacola	FL	32503-8545
Canter	Felicia	321 Auburn Avenue	Cleveland	OH	44112-5921
Gordon	Adam	4831 Lakeshore Drive	Denver	CO	80214-4778
Parsons	Mary	3523 Vine Street	Seattle	WA	98114-3351
Secrest	Chris	117 East Third Street	Dayton	OH	45402-5417
Shelton	Betty	237 Euclid Boulevard	Atlanta	GA	30312-3483
Williams	John	598 Michigan Avenue	Chicago	IL	60603-1921

When using flat file database software, many different tables containing many different kinds of information can be created. However, there is no connection between the various tables; each of them is a stand-alone collection of data. The programs supplied as part of the flat file database package are used to set up the structure of the data to be stored, provide for the addition and editing of data, and provide facilities for locating and retrieving the data. Frequently, the user is limited to the capabilities provided in the purchased package of software. If other processing functions are needed, they must be written in a programming language that creates its own data files separately from those of the database package.

The manuals that are included with flat file database packages provide instructions for setting up the structure of the data, editing data, and locating and retrieving data.

With this review in mind, consider an example of a company using a flat file database—the case of Omega Burger ("The Last Word in Hamburgers"). The developers of Omega realized some time ago that the use of computers was a necessity. Omega's first computer application was with employee records. To keep employee records, the company used a flat file database with one table containing the necessary columns. The application worked very satisfactorily.

After employee records were underway, Omega decided to start computer processing of its payroll and general financial records (general ledger). To accomplish this, a separate software package was purchased that created its own individual financial data files.

Currently, the company has started an employee profit sharing program. The managers whose stores meet or exceed sales quotas receive stock in the corporation. Each manager is also eligible for free vacation trips if the store's performance is above the goal for two years in a row. This application is set up as another table in the flat file database. The hand-entered data is stored in a table containing the appropriate fields. Much of the data that goes into this table is also contained in the payroll table.

Because of the growing number of stores, Omega decides next to install a computerized inventory system. This system, which is custom written, will keep up with all equipment on hand in the stores. It will also update the quantity of each food item in each store. Store managers will report the use of food items to headquarters each week, and the amount will be subtracted from inventory. When headquarters ships food from the central warehouse, the computer system will add quantities back to the inventory.

Listed below are some of the characteristics and analyses of the system Omega has set up:

1. Each of the applications is totally separate; each has its own data files. Each of the data files is designed to meet the requirements of the particular application. Even though two of the applications use the same flat file database software, there is no communication between the different tables.
2. The same data may be contained in more than one file or table. For example, both the payroll file and the profit sharing file contain employees' names. Many figures from the payroll, profit sharing, and inventory files are reproduced in the general ledger files. Data that exists in more than one place is **redundant data** and should be avoided whenever possible.
3. The data is probably not as accurate as it could be. With the same data in more than one file, it is possible that one file is updated while the other is not. When data must be manually transferred from one computer application to another, as with Omega, there is an increased possibility of error.
4. When a new application is put on the computer, much effort must go into getting the original data into files. Much of this data may already exist in other files.
5. If the data needed for a particular application changes, it may take a lot of effort to modify data files and programs. For example, suppose records contain only enough space for a five-digit ZIP code. It takes substantial effort to locate and modify all files or database tables containing ZIP codes to allow space for nine-digit codes. As the data files are changed, all the specially written programs that use ZIP codes must also be changed to reflect the different file design.
6. The redundant data may cause the company to have to buy more auxiliary storage. While the price of auxiliary storage is much less than it once was, it can still be a significant expense.

For database applications that require different processing capability than that provided as part of the database software package, database management systems are available with an interface to a programming language. Thus, when customized capability is needed, a programmer can write a program that uses the data that has been stored in the database system.

To get a better idea of what database systems do, consider the example of a file cabinet with humans handling the storage and retrieval functions. Now imagine that you own a hamburger business and you have just hired a new employee. You tell the files operator to file the information about the employee. If you want to know how many hamburgers were sold by the store in Boston, you ask the files operator to find the information and give it to you. In similar fashion, application programs request the database programs to save or retrieve data.

Now return to the human example. Suppose your business grows. You buy more file cabinets and hire more files operators. Any files operator can use the data in any file. Likewise, many different application programs can use a database. The application programs store data by giving it to the database software. They retrieve data by asking the database software for it. The database program serves the function of the files operator searching the files.

With a computerized database system, as with a manual filing system, each record may be individually stored and retrieved.

There are several types of database organizations that provide more capability than that of a flat file database. They vary in complexity, capability, ease of use, speed, and computer power required. The differences are discussed in the following sections.

Relational Database

In the view of the user, a **relational database** also presents its data in the form of tables. As opposed to the flat file database, however, the different tables created may be "connected" or "related." In Omega Burger's case, therefore, one table might contain data regarding employees' names and addresses as shown in Figure 11-8 (just as it did in the flat file database). Another table might contain data on who has received profit sharing awards. Still another might contain payroll data. A common field connects the data in two or more tables. For example, the employee number appears in the Employee Data Table, the Profit Sharing Awards Table, and the Payroll Data Table. Note in Figure 11-8 how this field appears in all three tables.

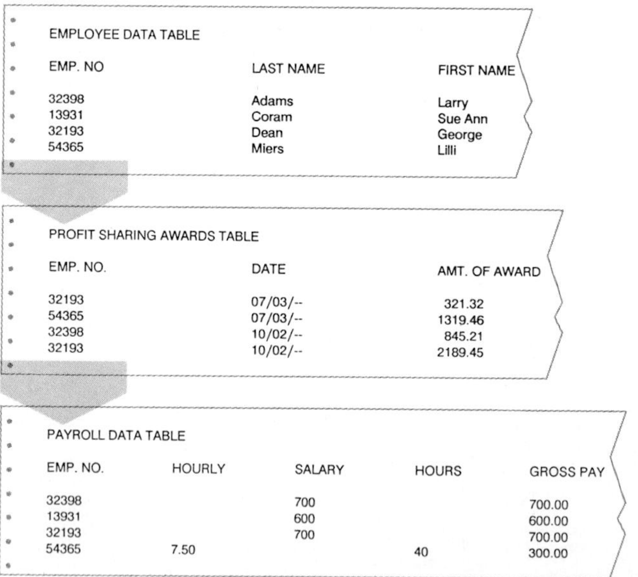

EMPLOYEE DATA TABLE

EMP. NO	LAST NAME	FIRST NAME
32398	Adams	Larry
13931	Coram	Sue Ann
32193	Dean	George
54365	Miers	Lilli

PROFIT SHARING AWARDS TABLE

EMP. NO.	DATE	AMT. OF AWARD
32193	07/03/--	321.32
54365	07/03/--	1319.46
32398	10/02/--	845.21
32193	10/02/--	2189.45

PAYROLL DATA TABLE

EMP. NO.	HOURLY	SALARY	HOURS	GROSS PAY
32398		700		700.00
13931		600		600.00
32193		700		700.00
54365	7.50		40	300.00

Figure 11-8
In a relational database, a common field connects one table to another.

By using several tables together, the user can extract various kinds of information. From Figure 11-8, for example, the total amount of profit sharing awards earned by George Dean can be determined by looking up his employee number in the Employee Data Table. The user can then look at the Profit Sharing Awards Table and find all the amounts earned by that employee number (321.32 and 2189.45). The two amounts total 2510.77. Note that there were no physical "links" of any kind between the items to show the connections between them; logic was used to find the proper values. In the same way, the software that operates a relational database makes the kind of comparisons or computations a human looking at the tables would make.

Relational database software makes the same kind of comparisons that a human looking at data could make.

With a relational database, it is possible to easily add tables, delete tables, or change tables. Also, since relationships between data may be established whenever needed, previously unthought-of computations or queries are easily handled. Because of its ease of use and flexibility, the relational database is very desirable. This flexibility, however, yields a slower operating speed and requires much more complex software than some other types of database software. However, much progress is being made in improving the speed, thus helping the relational database become a standard.

Hierarchical Database

Unlike a database that presents its data in the form of tables, a **hierarchical database** assumes data exists in some pre-defined rational order. For example, part of Omega Burger's database, if designed hierarchically, is shown in Figure 11-9. Note that only one store is shown, though any number could be used. In studying this diagram of a hierarchical database, consider that its organization is somewhat like a family tree, with "children" belonging to "parents."

Figure 11-9
A hierarchical database is organized somewhat like a family tree with every element of data belonging to a "parent" element.

Store 1

- 323-98-2893
  - Adams
  - Larry
  - 845.21
- 139-31-2143
  - Coram
  - SueAnn
  - 0
- 321-93-8982
  - Dean
  - George
  - 2510.77
- 543-65-8952
  - Miers
  - Lilli
  - 1319.46

In a hierarchical database, each element of data "belongs" to its "parent" element. For example, employee data "belongs to" or is a subdivision of the store. Profit sharing data "belongs to" or is a subdivision of employee data. In accessing the data, it is necessary to follow the tree structure. For example, to access the profit sharing data about an employee in this example, it is necessary to know the store in which the employee works and the employee's number. In other words, the program cannot go directly to the profit sharing data for sorting or selection and bypass the step of looking at the store location and employee data.

Hierarchical databases have been in use for a long time and are often used with minicomputers and mainframes. They are very fast and are often used in transaction processing such as point-of-sale systems in retail stores. However, since the definition of relationships must be defined up front, changes to the data relationships are difficult and time consuming. Accessing data only through the pre-defined structure is sometimes a disadvantage, though it is this feature that accounts for much of the speed of the system.

Network Database

A **network database** is an adaptation of a hierarchical database. It is much more complex in terms of the programs involved, but it sets up alternative paths through the data to make access more flexible. For example, in Figure 11-10 note that links have been added that go directly to the employee's last name without first going through the employee's number. As with hierarchical databases, network databases are used mostly with minicomputers and mainframe computers. Also like hierarchical databases, network databases have the disadvantage that the relationships are defined when the database is established, and changes to the structure are difficult.

Figure 11-10
A network database, which is structured similarly to the hierarchical database, sets up alternative paths to the data.

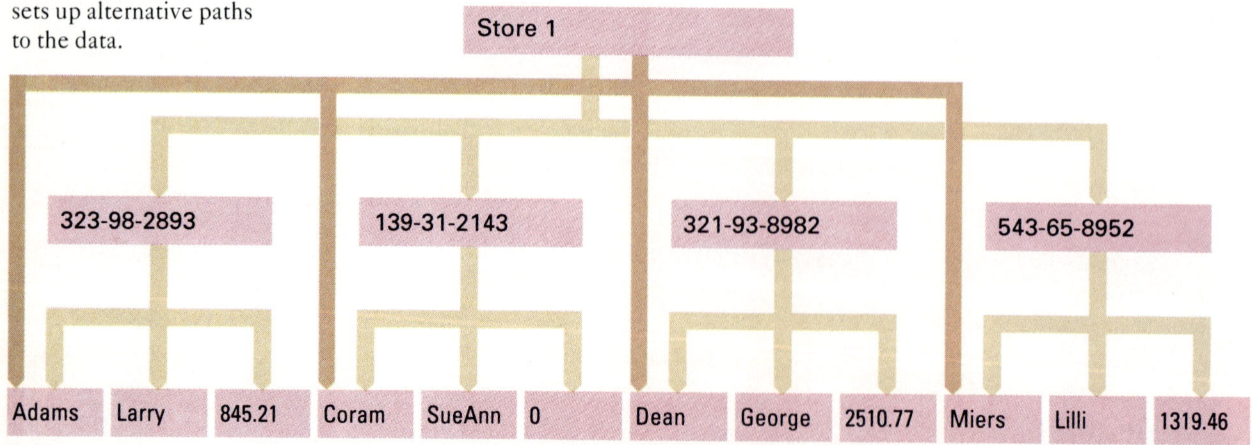

Post-Relational or Semantic Database

A semantic database can include information regarding the location (specific building, different city, etc.) of each employee within a company.

Some database developers have moved beyond the relational database, attempting to combine the advantages of the relational database and the hierarchical or network databases. While several approaches exist, the most promising one seems to be what is called the **semantic database.** The semantic database preserves the flexibility and capabilities of the relational database but builds in some pre-defined relationships when the database is created. For example, all the employees of a company work at some location of the company. That fact can be built into the structure of the database so that each time the database is asked for information, the user does not have to tell it that employees work in some location of the company.

PLANNING A DATABASE

Planning an efficient database involves setting up the structure of the actual database as well as designing the applications which will use it to the greatest advantage. The following paragraphs discuss how to plan for the tables needed, and how to design appropriate applications.

Planning for Tables

This section describes how to plan for tables. Many of the steps reviewed here apply to flat file database software. Others, however, apply only to the use of relational database software. In the planning phase of a database, the user decides what table or tables is/are needed and the types (columns) of data to be placed in each table. If an application previously done by hand is being converted to computer, the beginning point will often be the paper forms already in use. Consider the employee information and payroll for Omega Burger. Figure 11-11 shows an employee assignment sheet. This sheet documents the name, address, phone number, and assignment of an employee. Figure 11-12 shows a weekly payroll form that documents the weekly wage and deductions for each employee.

EMPLOYEE ASSIGNMENT SHEET—OMEGA BURGER INTERNATIONAL

Name__________ Emp. # __________
(Last, First, MI)

Assigned to Store No.__________ Position__________

Pay Rate: $______ Hourly $______ Salary

Street Address__________

City__________ State______ ZIP______ Home Phone__________

Figure 11-11
Paper forms are often the beginning point for planning a database.

Figure 11-12
Payroll forms contain important data that helps in planning a database.

WEEKLY PAYROLL SHEET—OMEGA BURGER INTERNATIONAL

Week Ending ____________

Name ____________ Emp. # ____________
(Last, First, MI)

Store Number ____________ Position ____________

Salaried ____________ Hourly for ____________ hours at $ ____________

Gross Pay ____________
Less:
Federal Income Tax ____________
Social Security Tax ____________
State Income Tax ____________
Health Insurance ____________
Other ____________ ____________

Net Pay $ ____________

Note in this example that many items from the employee data sheet are also on the payroll form. Since the payroll form for each employee will be prepared for each week of the year, much of the same data will be written over 52 times. This type of replication is common in many record keeping systems.

In planning the tables needed for a database, it is easy to see how data from the two forms can be combined. If you list all the data elements (or fields, or columns) from the two forms in Figures 11-11 and 11-12, you get the table shown in Figure 11-13. Sample data is included in the table to make it more realistic. As you examine these figures, keep in mind that these are examples only; the columns do not represent everything that might be necessary in a real application.

Figure 11-13
After combining all the data acquired from the forms, the table at the right is developed.

LASTNAME	FIRSTNAME	MI	EMPNUM	STORE	POSITION	HOURLY	SALARY	STREET	CITY	STATE	ZIP
Adams	Larry	M	32398	1	Manager		700	48 Rex Road	Morrow	GA	30321-2360
Coram	Sue	A	13931	2	Asst. Mgr.		600	892 Fifth Ave.	Macon	GA	31391-8545
Dean	George	C	32193	2	Manager		700	331 Royal Rd.	Macon	GA	31390-4871
Miers	Lilli	R	54365	1	Shift Mgr.	7.50		97 Lex Lane	Morrow	GA	30312-3591

LASTNAME	FIRSTNAME	MI	HOMEPHONE	WKENDING	HOURS	GROSSPAY	FEDTAX	FICATAX	STATETAX	TOTDED	NETPAY
Adams	Larry	M	404-382-8983	01/07/--		700.00	70.00	49.00	31.16	158.73	541.27
Coram	Sue	A	912-488-8892	01/07/--		600.00	54.00	42.00	23.15	127.72	472.28
Dean	George	C	912-231-9842	01/07/--		620.00	47.31	43.40	27.15	146.82	473.18
Miers	Lilli	R	404-338-4321	01/07/--	40	300.00	14.18	21.00	7.89	51.64	248.36

At first glance, the table in Figure 11-13 seems to be a reasonable table to use and indeed can be used in a flat file database. However, each row of the table contains data for one weekly pay period. As the pay periods are recorded, the number of rows increases. Look at Figure 11-14 to see how the table looks after four weeks of operation.

LASTNAME	FIRSTNAME	MI	EMPNUM	STORE	POSITION	HOURLY	SALARY	STREET	CITY	STATE	ZIP
Adams	Larry	M	32398	1	Manager		700	48 Rex Road	Morrow	GA	30321-2360
Adams	Larry	M	32398	1	Manager		700	48 Rex Road	Morrow	GA	30321-2360
Adams	Larry	M	32398	1	Manager		700	48 Rex Road	Morrow	GA	30321-2360
Adams	Larry	M	32398	1	Manager		700	48 Rex Road	Morrow	GA	30321-2360
Coram	Sue	A	13931	2	Asst. Mgr.		600	892 Fifth Ave.	Macon	GA	31391-8545
Coram	Sue	A	13931	2	Asst. Mgr.		600	892 Fifth Ave.	Macon	GA	31391-8545
Coram	Sue	A	13931	2	Asst. Mgr.		600	892 Fifth Ave.	Macon	GA	31391-8545
Coram	Sue	A	13931	2	Asst. Mgr.		600	892 Fifth Ave.	Macon	GA	31391-8545
Dean	George	C	32193	2	Manager		700	331 Royal Rd.	Macon	GA	31390-4871
Dean	George	C	32193	2	Manager		700	331 Royal Rd.	Macon	GA	31390-4871
Dean	George	C	32193	2	Manager		700	331 Royal Rd.	Macon	GA	31390-4871
Dean	George	C	32193	2	Manager		700	331 Royal Rd.	Macon	GA	31390-4871
Miers	Lilli	R	54365	1	Shift Mgr.	7.50		97 Lex Lane	Morrow	GA	30312-3591
Miers	Lilli	R	54365	1	Shift Mgr.	7.50		97 Lex Lane	Morrow	GA	30312-3591
Miers	Lilli	R	54365	1	Shift Mgr.	7.50		97 Lex Lane	Morrow	GA	30312-3591
Miers	Lilli	R	54365	1	Shift Mgr.	7.50		97 Lex Lane	Morrow	GA	30312-3591

LASTNAME	FIRSTNAME	MI	HOMEPHONE	WKENDING	HOURS	GROSSPAY	FEDTAX	FICATAX	STATETAX	TOTDED	NETPAY
Adams	Larry	M	404-382-8983	01/07/--		700.00	70.00	49.00	31.16	158.73	541.27
Adams	Larry	M	404-382-8983	01/14/--		700.00	70.00	49.00	31.16	158.73	541.27
Adams	Larry	M	404-382-8983	01/21/--		700.00	70.00	49.00	31.16	158.73	541.27
Adams	Larry	M	404-382-8983	01/28/--		700.00	70.00	49.00	31.16	158.73	541.27
Coram	Sue	A	912-488-8892	01/07/--		600.00	54.00	42.00	23.15	127.72	472.28
Coram	Sue	A	912-488-8892	01/14/--		600.00	54.00	42.00	23.15	127.72	472.28
Coram	Sue	A	912-488-8892	01/21/--		600.00	54.00	42.00	23.15	127.72	472.28
Coram	Sue	A	912-488-8892	01/28/--		600.00	54.00	42.00	23.15	127.72	472.28
Dean	George	C	912-231-9842	01/07/--		620.00	47.31	43.40	27.15	146.82	473.18
Dean	George	C	912-231-9842	01/14/--		620.00	47.31	43.40	27.15	146.82	473.18
Dean	George	C	912-231-9842	01/21/--		620.00	47.31	43.40	27.15	146.82	473.18
Dean	George	C	912-231-9842	01/28/--		640.00	49.18	44.80	29.20	152.14	487.86
Miers	Lilli	R	404-338-4321	01/07/--	40	300.00	14.18	21.00	7.89	51.64	248.36
Miers	Lilli	R	404-338-4321	01/14/--	40	300.00	14.18	21.00	7.89	51.64	248.36
Miers	Lilli	R	404-338-4321	01/21/--	40	300.00	14.18	21.00	7.89	51.64	248.36
Miers	Lilli	R	404-338-4321	01/28/--	40	300.00	14.18	21.00	7.89	51.64	248.36

Figure 11-14
With extensive use, some databases can become cumbersome and redundant.

As you noted from Figure 11-14, the table grows tremendously as payroll weeks go by, and many rows contain identical data in many of the columns. In reality, many of the columns cannot vary from week to week. For example, the employee's address may change, but if it does, he or she lives only at the new address. The pay figures, on the other hand, may change from week to week (such as George Dean's did in the week ending 01/28/—), and tax regulations require that a detailed record of earnings be maintained.

To keep from replicating so much identical data, a relational database can be used to divide the columns of the table into two tables—one with the constant or static data, and one with the variable or changing data that can have new values each week. Study Figure 11-15 to see how this can be done. Note that the table of constant data contains only one row for each employee, while the Payroll Data Table contains a row for each employee for each week. The employee number column is in both tables, thus connecting the two. In other words, this type of database allows the user to look at data in the Payroll Data Table and determine whose data it is. Conversely, it allows the user to look up a particular employee number in the Employee Data Table and then use the number to locate his or her payroll data in the Payroll Data Table.

Figure 11-15
A relational database is often more efficient than a flat file database.

EMPLOYEE DATA TABLE

LASTNAME	FIRSTNAME	MI	EMPNUM	STORE	POSITION	STREET	CITY	STATE	ZIP	HOMEPHONE
Adams	Larry	M	32398	1	Manager	48 Rex Road	Morrow	GA	30321-2360	404-382-8983
Coram	Sue	A	13931	2	Asst. Mgr.	892 Fifth Ave.	Macon	GA	31391-8545	912-488-8892
Dean	George	C	32193	2	Manager	331 Royal Rd.	Macon	GA	31390-4871	912-231-9842
Miers	Lilli	R	54365	1	Shift Mgr.	97 Lex Lane	Morrow	GA	30312-3591	404-338-4321

WEEKLY PAYROLL DATA TABLE

EMPNUM	HOURLY	SALARY	WKENDING	HOURS	GROSSPAY	FEDTAX	FICATAX	STATETAX	TOTDED	NETPAY
32398		700	01/07/--		700.00	70.00	49.00	31.16	158.73	541.27
32398		700	01/14/--		700.00	70.00	49.00	31.16	158.73	541.27
32398		700	01/21/--		700.00	70.00	49.00	31.16	158.73	541.27
32398		700	01/28/--		700.00	70.00	49.00	31.16	158.73	541.27
13931		600	01/07/--		600.00	54.00	42.00	23.15	127.72	472.28
13931		600	01/14/--		600.00	54.00	42.00	23.15	127.72	472.28
13931		600	01/21/--		600.00	54.00	42.00	23.15	127.72	472.28
13931		600	01/28/--		600.00	54.00	42.00	23.15	127.72	472.28
32193		700	01/07/--		620.00	47.31	43.40	27.15	146.82	473.18
32193		700	01/14/--		620.00	47.31	43.40	27.15	146.82	473.18
32193		700	01/21/--		620.00	47.31	43.40	27.15	146.82	473.18
32193		700	01/28/--		640.00	49.18	44.80	29.20	152.14	487.86
54365	7.50		01/07/--	40	300.00	14.18	21.00	7.89	51.64	248.36
54365	7.50		01/14/--	40	300.00	14.18	21.00	7.89	51.64	248.36
54365	7.50		01/21/--	40	300.00	14.18	21.00	7.89	51.64	248.36
54365	7.50		01/28/--	40	300.00	14.18	21.00	7.89	51.64	248.36

While the tables as designed in Figure 11-15 are quite workable, some additional improvements can be made to them. In this application, note that the employees of any given store live geographically close to the store. This means that the number of cities and states is small (with several employees in each) regardless of the number of employees. Therefore, storage space can be saved by removing the city and state columns from the Employee Data Table and adding a ZIP Code Table. Figure 11-16 shows such a table.

Figure 11-16
Modifications can be made to databases to make them more efficient.

ZIP CODE TABLE

ZIP CODE	CITY	STATE
30312-3591	Morrow	GA
30321-2360	Morrow	GA
31390-4871	Macon	GA
31391-8545	Macon	GA

When the database is in use, the software can get the ZIP code from the Employee Data Table and then look it up in the ZIP Code Table to display the city and state. Additional storage space can be saved by removing the columns in the Weekly Payroll Data Table for total deductions and net pay. This is possible because both of these values are computed from other values in the row of the table. Anytime either of them needs to be displayed or printed, it can be quickly computed by the database software.

The reduced redundancy makes the records more accurate. Any time an item of data needs to be changed, only one action is necessary to change it wherever it is recorded in the database. For example, if the user discovers that an erroneous employee number has been recorded for an employee, making the correction on one data entry screen corrects the entry throughout all tables that use the employee number. This feature also reduces the amount of labor necessary to maintain the data. The reduced redundancy may also reduce the amount of storage space required on disk.

Designing an Application (Application Generators)

A database package can be used just as it comes out of the box. However, its usefulness can be increased by the development of applications. The applications can use several different tables accessible from the same menu, making the system easier to operate. Instead of having to enter the proper commands or make the correct general menu responses, the user can choose from the custom menus the application provides. A custom menu looks similar to that shown in Figure 11-17. Selection of the desired choice tells the database software which of its functions to perform.

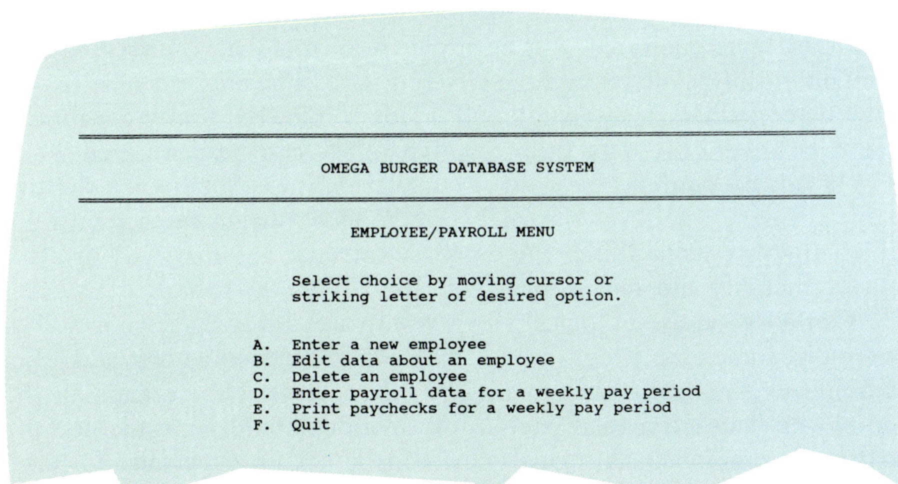

Figure 11-17
To increase the database's usefulness, applications can be selected from custom menus.

Many database software packages come with programs that generate the menus and underlying commands by simply having the operator answer a series of questions. These programs are known as **application generators.** Their use helps the user enjoy the advantages of a custom-written application without having to do programming.

Data in a database may sometimes be stored on one microcomputer and accessed only by the user of that computer.

USING AND SHARING DATABASE FILES

The data stored in a database is used and shared in several ways. First, the data may be on one microcomputer, and only the user of that computer can access the data. Or, the data may be stored on a minicomputer or mainframe computer and can be accessed by a number of people who use terminals or microcomputers. In the most advanced form, various tables of the database are stored on different computers networked together, with all the data available to all authorized users on the network. In such a case, a user need not know which computer the data is stored on. If the desired data exists, it is accessed (regardless of physical location) automatically by the system. Such a database with data stored in different locations and visible to all users is known as a **distributed relational database.**

Database software that can be used by more than one person at a time typically uses passwords and levels of access. This helps protect the data from unauthorized viewing or change. A user is assigned a password and access levels by the system operator. Levels of access may include no access, the ability to view but not change, the ability to change, and the ability to create and delete.

LOGICAL AND PHYSICAL VIEWS

The tables you have seen in this chapter have been physical in nature. That is, in the database, the tables physically exist as defined. In many cases, however, it is desirable to view the data from two or more tables as if they were one table. For example, the Employee Data Table may contain the ZIP code but not the city and state. The city and state names may be contained in a separate ZIP Code Table. By defining a **logical view,** however, the data from the two tables can be combined when displayed. By defining the view, a connection is made between the two tables. Then, whenever the ZIP code is displayed on the screen from the Employee Data Table, the database software automatically displays the correct city and state names from the ZIP Code Table.

Another good use of logical views is in maintaining data security. For example, some employees should be able to update some items and other employees should be able to update other items. Or, perhaps all the employee data other than payroll information should be available for a particular employee. A logical view can be set up especially for each employee or type of employee to make available only those fields that each should have access to. In other words, the use of logical views is a method of making available to employees only those fields with which they should be concerned.

DATABASE ADMINISTRATION

When one individual is using a database on a microcomputer, that individual can do whatever is desired. When multiple users share a database, however, each of them cannot be allowed freedom to modify the structure and contents of the database at will. It is necessary that someone be charged with the job of administering the database. The database administrator decides what tables are in the database, what columns of data are in each table, and what access is permitted for each user. In discharging these duties, however, the database administrator works closely with other administrators. Other administrators, such as persons in accounting, personnel, and sales, know more about their data needs than does the database administrator. In this respect, the database administrator is more like a traffic officer or an arbiter than a dictator.

HARDWARE REQUIREMENTS

The power of the hardware required for databases is related to the power of the database software and the number of users. Very simple database software, with only one user, can be operated on microcomputers with as little as 128K of memory and two floppy disk drives. More capable microcomputer database software requires as much as several million bytes of memory and a very fast processor, as well as a hard disk drive. The amount of disk storage required depends on the amount of data to be stored and on the size of the actual database software programs. The more powerful programs are rather large in terms of disk space required.

MUSIC MADE EASY

Since the earlier days of microcomputers, music and computers have been great friends. Synthesizer cards were developed that plugged into the early computers, and music could be keyed into the computer and then played automatically by the synthesizer. Also, if desired, the musician could plug a piano-type keyboard into the computer and play the music, with the synthesizer card producing the sound. The earliest cards had only one voice—that is, they could produce only one note at a time. It was not long, however, until cards with multiple voices, capable of playing full chords and using different sounds for each voice, were available.

It was not long until digital music technology became embedded in many musical devices themselves. Musical synthesizers, which had been large, extremely expensive devices capable of making only one sound at a time, became compact, inexpensive keyboard devices capable of making almost any sound desired and producing many effects at once. Even such traditional instruments as organs and pianos became part of the musical revolution as digitally created sounds replaced the traditional sources of sound in many of these instruments. In fact, virtually any traditional instrument can now be mimicked by its computerized counterpart. A special computer-type interface has even been developed for connecting different digital musical devices and computers to each other—the MIDI (musical instrument digital interface).

The lives of composers have been made much easier with the advancement of digital music technology.

While many sounds are created from scratch in electronic instruments through synthesizer techniques, many sounds (especially "reproductions" of the sounds of other instruments) may be produced by digitally sampling a traditional instrument or other sound and recording the mathematical pattern of the sound in the instrument's memory. Then this digitally recorded sound can be reproduced at will at any desired frequency. By using this technique, it is possible to make electronic pianos, for example, sound exactly like a fine acoustical instrument, including whatever unique characteristics gave that acoustic instrument its personality.

It has been possible for years for composers to enter their music on a regular computer keyboard. This process is similar to the one used to enter records in a database: the name of each note, along with its duration, must be painstakingly entered into the music "database" where it is stored in the computer's memory for playback by the computer or even for printing in musical notation form on paper. New software packages, however, have now made the interface between the composer and the computer much easier. The composer can simply sit at a regular piano-type keyboard and play the music as he or she makes it up. Each note played, complete with its duration, volume, and phrasing, is interpreted by computer software and stored in the computer. If the composer wants to listen to the piece as recorded, the computer can play it back. Any desired changes can be made by the composer, with the computer again accepting its input directly from the piano-type keyboard or from the computer's keyboard. Once the composer is satisfied with the work, the computer will automatically print out a piece of sheet music, perfectly reflecting the composition. With such a work saver for composers, hits will never have been easier!

CHAPTER SUMMARY

- A database is a collection of organized data whose elements are in some way related to one another.
- The functions of database management systems include creating the structure of the database, adding data to the database, editing data already in the database, selecting and retrieving data, designing reports, and modifying the structure of the database.
- In creating the structure of a database, the user names the table and describes the columns (names, type of data, width) the table is to contain.
- Adding data to an existing database is known as appending or loading and may be done with default or custom-designed screen forms.
- The ability to edit existing data makes it easy to update items, using either a default or custom-designed screen form.

- Querying and reporting of data may be done using criteria entered by the user.
- Selecting and retrieving data from a relational database is done by using a query language.
- A report writer function is included with many database systems to make the design of reports easier.
- A database that consists of only one table is known as a flat file database.
- The use of a database may make data more accurate because redundancy is reduced, the amount of labor necessary to maintain the data is reduced, and the amount of storage space needed on disk is reduced.
- A set of computer programs known as a database system or database management system (DBMS) provides the functions necessary to operate a database.
- A relational database presents its data in the form of tables. The relationships between different data elements and different tables are not defined in the structure of the database.
- Common fields provide the connection between different tables of a relational database.
- Querying and reporting of data in a relational database are very flexible because the relationships are defined at the time of need rather than when the database is created.
- It is easy to modify the structure of a relational database.
- A semantic database is built around the concepts of a relational database. However, a semantic database has some of the obvious relationships between data built into its structure, thus increasing its speed of operation and simplifying some queries.
- Database software handles the storage and retrieval of data, relieving application programs of that burden.
- A hierarchical database is arranged in tree fashion, with each level of data "belonging to" the level above. The arrangement is decided at the time the database is created. Data may be accessed only by following the hierarchical path to it.
- A network database is an adaptation of a hierarchical database, but it has multiple paths for accessing the data. Its design is decided at the time of its creation.
- In designing a computerized database, it is common to start with the paperwork forms previously used for the application.
- When designing the tables of a relational database, replication of data should be limited to the number of fields required to connect a table with other tables.
- A relational database is created by specifying its name and defining its tables.
- Reports printed from a relational database are custom-designed by means of report writer software.
- The structure of the tables and columns of a relational database can be modified without destroying already-entered data.

- Custom applications can be designed around relational databases without programming by using application generator software that comes with or is available for many database management systems.
- Databases can be used by one person or one microcomputer, shared by multiple users or by a computer system, or distributed.
- A distributed relational database stores various parts of its data on various computers, with data visible to the user whenever needed.
- Passwords are used to control access to data stored in a database.
- Logical views may be defined to present data from several tables as if it were stored in one table or to present only some of a table's columns to the user.
- A database administrator serves as arbiter of what is stored in a database and who has access to the data.
- The more powerful database software is, the more powerful the hardware must be in order to use it.

KEY TERMS

The following key terms were introduced or redefined in this chapter:

appending
application generator
control break
database
database management system
distributed relational database
flat file database
hierarchical database
loading
logical view
network database
query language
redundant data
relational database
report writer
semantic database

REVIEW QUESTIONS

1. What is a database? (Obj. 1)
2. What are some of the advantages of using a database system? (Obj. 1)
3. What functions are performed by a database management system? (Obj. 2)
4. What is the purpose of a query language? (Obj. 2)
5. What is the purpose of a report writer? (Obj. 2)
6. What are the characteristics of a flat file database? (Obj. 3)
7. Why is redundant data a problem? (Obj. 3)
8. What are the primary characteristics of a relational database? (Obj. 3)
9. What are the primary characteristics of a hierarchical database? (Obj. 3)
10. What feature is added to a hierarchical database to create a network database? (Obj. 3)

11. What feature is added to a relational database to create a semantic database? (Obj. 3)
12. What is meant by a distributed database? (Objs. 3, 5)
13. What role do paper forms play in the planning of a database? (Obj. 4)
14. In planning the tables of a relational database, why should data be replicated as little as possible? (Obj. 4)
15. What information does database software need in order to define a table? (Obj. 4)
16. What is the purpose of an application generator? (Obj. 4)
17. How do physical and logical views differ? (Obj. 6)
18. What does a database administrator do? (Obj. 7)
19. What is the relationship between database power and computer hardware requirements? (Obj. 8)

CHALLENGE ACTIVITIES

1. Under what circumstances is a flat file database appropriate for use? (Obj. 3)
2. It was stated in the chapter that the relational database is the emerging standard for database software. What are the most likely reasons it is becoming the standard? (Obj. 3)
3. Under what circumstances would the use of a hierarchical or network database system be most preferable? (Obj. 3)
4. Plan a simple one-table database (using flat file or relational software) that will store the numbers, positions, and names of members of a football team. Name the fields needed in that table, give the type of each field (alphanumeric or numeric), and give the length for each field. If you have a computer with database software, create the database on the computer. Then enter data for several team members with whom you are acquainted. Display the data on players arranged alphabetically, then arranged by position. (Obj. 4)
5. Assume that you are the secretary/treasurer of a civic club. You need to keep records on members' names, addresses, phone numbers, original membership dates, and dates of dues payment for the current membership year. This data can be kept in a database of only one table, using either flat file or relational software. Name the fields needed in that table, give the type of each field (alphanumeric or numeric), and give the length for each field. If you have a computer with database software available, create the database and perform the following functions: (Obj. 4)

   a. Add member Sam Jones, 3987 Eighth St., Merrillville, IN 39873-6122, 320-9875, membership date 8/3/89, dues not yet paid.

   b. Add member Marilyn Abel, 32 Gayle Drive, Merrillville, IN 39873-4380, 442-9873, membership date 2/6/78, dues paid 8/3/—.

c. Add member Jacki Sharon, 7643 Gulliver Trail, Valparaiso, IN 39874-1050, 234-9386, membership date 2/6/49, dues paid 1/2/—.

d. Display an alphabetic list of all members.

e. Display a list of all members who have not paid dues this year (only Sam Jones should appear).

f. Enter dues payment for Sam Jones on 8/7/—.

g. Display a list of all members who have not paid dues this year (no names should appear).

h. Delete member Jacki Sharon.

i. Display a list of all members to confirm that Jacki Sharon has been deleted.

CHAPTER 12

SPREADSHEET SOFTWARE

LEARNING OBJECTIVES

After studying this chapter, you will be able to:

1. **Define and give the origin of the spreadsheet.**
2. **Explain the purpose of spreadsheet software.**
3. **Describe how a spreadsheet is organized.**
4. **Explain how data and formulas are entered into a spreadsheet.**
5. **Describe how reports are printed using a spreadsheet.**
6. **Name and define some of the spreadsheet operations that can simplify use of the software.**
7. **List and describe some common uses of spreadsheets.**
8. **Describe how data is stored with a spreadsheet.**
9. **Describe the hardware requirements for spreadsheets.**

INTRODUCTION

In this chapter you will learn about the type of application software that has contributed to the sale of more microcomputers than any other type of software. With the introduction of the first capable spreadsheet software, many persons were able to justify for the first time the purchase of a personal computer.

THE ORIGIN OF THE SPREADSHEET

While this chapter addresses the spreadsheet as it is implemented by computer software, a manual form of the spreadsheet has been used for years. A **spreadsheet** is simply a row and column arrangement of data—a grid of labels, values, and numbers computed through the use of formulas. The example in Figure 12-1 shows a spreadsheet manually completed by a market analysis company. Businesses and individuals have been using such manually prepared spreadsheets for years by writing in the figures and performing the computations. The computations were originally done by hand, then by mechanical adding machines, mechanical calculators, and electronic calculators. In recent years, computerization of the spreadsheet has made its use much easier and has enabled much more complex computations to be completed.

Figure 12-1
Spreadsheets are often manually prepared by both businesses and individuals.

Lyle Marketing Research
FRUIT FLAVOR PREFERENCES
Westland Mall, July 18, 19--

FLAVOR	NO. YOUTH	% YOUTH	NO. ADULTS	% ADULT
Apple	24	32	31	29
Banana	13	17	23	21
Peach	17	23	22	20
Strawberry	7	9	4	4
Other	14	19	28	26
Totals	75	100	108	100

To obtain data for a spreadsheet, a survey may be conducted.

For the spreadsheet in Figure 12-1, a research company questioned shoppers in a mall about their fruit flavor preferences. The company then completed the sheet showing the results.

In examining the spreadsheet in Figure 12-1, note that each row shows the results for a particular flavor of fruit. The NO.YOUTH column is a count of the number of young people choosing a particular flavor as their favorite. The NO.ADULTS column is a count of the number of adults choosing a flavor as their favorite. The %YOUTH and %ADULT columns are computed values showing what percent of youth and adults, respectively, chose each flavor. The 32 percent of youth preferring apple, for example, was computed by dividing the 24 youth who selected the flavor by the 75 total youth who participated in the survey. The resulting decimal number was then converted to a percent by rounding and multiplying by 100.

THE PURPOSE OF SPREADSHEET SOFTWARE

Note that in the previous spreadsheet, the data represents a report of existing conditions. That is, the results of a survey are presented. Examples of other existing conditions for which spreadsheets may be prepared are accounting records of a business, sports statistics, and grades from a teacher's grade book.

Spreadsheets may also be used to make projections or predictions of data. For example, a user might compute the predicted population of various cities, assuming that their growth rate continues at the present rate. Or, if you want to have savings in 1995 of $20,000 for a down payment on a house, you can compute how much you will need to invest each month at an assumed rate of return to obtain the desired amount.

While any of these spreadsheet applications can be done by hand, the use of computer software makes the job easier and more accurate. The job is made easier because the spreadsheet software already knows how to make many kinds of computations by the use of built-in formulas. The job is made more accurate because the computer will not make computational errors as a person might. It is good to keep in mind, however, that the computer software does what its user tells it to do. Therefore, if the user instructs the software to use the wrong formula, for example, the results will be inaccurate.

THE ORGANIZATION OF A SPREADSHEET

A spreadsheet is a row and column arrangement of data, as shown in Figure 12-1. Different names or descriptions are applied to various parts of a spreadsheet. Any single horizontal area extending across a spreadsheet is a **row.** This is illustrated by the highlighted area in Figure 12-2. Note the row number at the beginning of each row; it is supplied automatically by the spreadsheet software and is used to identify the row.

```
          A              B            C          D            E
 1: Lyle Marketing Research
 2: FRUIT FLAVOR PREFERENCES
 3: Westland Mall, July 18, 19--
 4:
 5: FLAVOR          NO.YOUTH      %YOUTH NO.ADULTS       %ADULT
 6:
 7: Apple                 24          32         31          29
 8: Banana                13          17         23          21
 9: Peach                 17          23         22          20
10: Strawberry             7           9          4           4
11: Other                 14          19         28          26
12:
13: Totals                75         100        108         100
14:
15:
```

Figure 12-2
A single horizontal area extending across a spreadsheet is known as a row.

A single vertical area running through a spreadsheet is known as a **column.** In Figure 12-3, note the highlighted area illustrating a column. Note also that the spreadsheet software supplies column labels or numbers, again for referring to designated locations. The first column in the example is **A,** the second column is **B,** and so forth. When the alphabet is exhausted with Column **Z,** labeling starts with **AA, BB,** etc. While there are variations in row and column numbering from one brand of software to another, they serve the same purpose.

Figure 12-3
A single vertical area running through a spreadsheet is known as a column.

	A	B	C	D	E
1:	Lyle Marketing Research				
2:	FRUIT FLAVOR PREFERENCES				
3:	Westland Mall, July 18, 19--				
4:					
5:	FLAVOR	NO.YOUTH	%YOUTH	NO.ADULTS	%ADULT
6:					
7:	Apple	24	32	31	29
8:	Banana	13	17	23	21
9:	Peach	17	23	22	20
10:	Strawberry	7	9	4	4
11:	Other	14	19	28	26
12:					
13:	Totals	75	100	108	100
14:					
15:					

While rows and columns refer to more than one value on a spreadsheet, the term **cell** is used to refer to the space on the spreadsheet used for any *one* value, number, character string label, or formula. This is illustrated in Figure 12-4, in which the number 13 is highlighted. The highlighted cell is cell number B8. This is because it is in the column labeled at the top with a B and is in the row labeled at the left with an 8. Any cell is named by the label and number of the column and row intersection.

Figure 12-4
The space on the spreadsheet used for any one value, number, character string label, or formula is known as a cell.

	A	B	C	D	E
1:	Lyle Marketing Research				
2:	FRUIT FLAVOR PREFERENCES				
3:	Westland Mall, July 18, 19--				
4:					
5:	FLAVOR	NO.YOUTH	%YOUTH	NO.ADULTS	%ADULT
6:					
7:	Apple	24	32	31	29
8:	Banana	13	17	23	21
9:	Peach	17	23	22	20
10:	Strawberry	7	9	4	4
11:	Other	14	19	28	26
12:					
13:	Totals	75	100	108	100
14:					
15:					

While the terms row and column refer strictly to defined types of cell arrangements, the term **range** is very flexible. It refers to any contiguous group of cells. In other words, any group of cells next to each other may be known as a range. The range that is highlighted in Figure 12-5 is made of Columns B and C in Rows 8, 9, and 10. It is just one of many possible ranges in the spreadsheet. A range may include only numbers, alphabetic items, special symbols, formulas, or a combination of these. Ranges are useful for specifying cells that are to be deleted, moved, copied, or otherwise manipulated. With some spreadsheet programs, it is possible to select and work with more than one range at the same time.

```
         A              B              C        D             E
 1: Lyle Marketing Research
 2: FRUIT FLAVOR PREFERENCES
 3: Westland Mall, July 18, 19--
 4:
 5: FLAVOR         NO.YOUTH    %YOUTH NO.ADULTS      %ADULT
 6:
 7: Apple                24        32        31          29
 8: Banana               13        17        23          21
 9: Peach                17        23        22          20
10: Strawberry            7         9         4           4
11: Other                14        19        28          26
12:
13: Totals               75       100       108         100
14:
15:
```

Figure 12-5
A range refers to any contiguous group of cells.

In addition to categorizing parts of a spreadsheet by their physical arrangement, as has been done to this point, each cell may also be classified by whether its contents are alphanumeric (any character) or numeric. Alphabetic cells are usually called **labels,** while numeric cells containing numbers that are entered are referred to as **values.** Figure 12-6 highlights all the items in the example spreadsheet that may be known as labels.

```
         A              B              C        D             E
 1: Lyle Marketing Research
 2: FRUIT FLAVOR PREFERENCES
 3: Westland Mall, July 18, 19--
 4:
 5: FLAVOR         NO.YOUTH    %YOUTH NO.ADULTS      %ADULT
 6:
 7: Apple                24        32        31          29
 8: Banana               13        17        23          21
 9: Peach                17        23        22          20
10: Strawberry            7         9         4           4
11: Other                14        19        28          26
12:
13: Totals               75       100       108         100
14:
15:
```

Figure 12-6
Alphabetic cells are usually called labels.

Figure 12-7 shows those numbers that are entered from the keyboard and that are known as values. The numbers not highlighted in Figure 12-7 are computed through the means of **formulas** rather than entered. A formula is a mathematical equation used to compute spreadsheet values.

Figure 12-7
Numeric cells contain numbers that are entered, known as values.

	A	B	C	D	E
1:	Lyle Marketing Research				
2:	FRUIT FLAVOR PREFERENCES				
3:	Westland Mall, July 18, 19--				
4:					
5:	FLAVOR	NO.YOUTH	%YOUTH	NO.ADULTS	%ADULT
6:					
7:	Apple	24	32	31	29
8:	Banana	13	17	23	21
9:	Peach	17	23	22	20
10:	Strawberry	7	9	4	4
11:	Other	14	19	28	26
12:					
13:	Totals	75	100	108	100
14:					
15:					

ENTERING DATA INTO THE SPREADSHEET

Usually data is entered into a spreadsheet by keying it on the keyboard. At times, however, data may be entered into a spreadsheet by importing it from another computer program. For example, data from a database program may be manipulated by use of a spreadsheet. The data entered into a spreadsheet may be in the form of character data, numeric data, or formulas.

Data is usually entered into a spreadsheet by keying it on a keyboard.

Entering Character Data

Character (alphanumeric) data entered into a spreadsheet is not used for computation. However, it can be used to label rows or columns and to locate data by finding the appropriate value. For example, a spreadsheet may be used to compute state income tax withholding based on the state in which the employee lives. The software can look up the labels indicating the state name to determine the proper rate.

To enter character data, the cursor (sometimes known as the **cell pointer**) must be moved to the desired cell. This movement is made either with the arrow keys on the keyboard or with a mouse (if the program supports a mouse). Once the cursor is in the desired cell, the data must be keyed in.

The location on the screen at which the characters appear as they are keyed varies depending on the software being used. With some software, the characters appear in the cell, while with other software, the characters are shown on a data entry line before they are moved to the cell. Figure 12-8 shows a partially entered spreadsheet with the cell pointer at the cell in which a label is to be entered. The label is being keyed at the data entry point above the cells and will appear in the cell when the ***Enter/Return*** key is struck or the mouse is clicked. (The data entry point may appear either above or below the cells depending on the spreadsheet software being used.) Some spreadsheet programs require a certain character (such as "A" for alpha) to be entered before the character data is entered. Others recognize the fact that a non-numeric character has been keyed and automatically enter the data as character (alphanumeric) data.

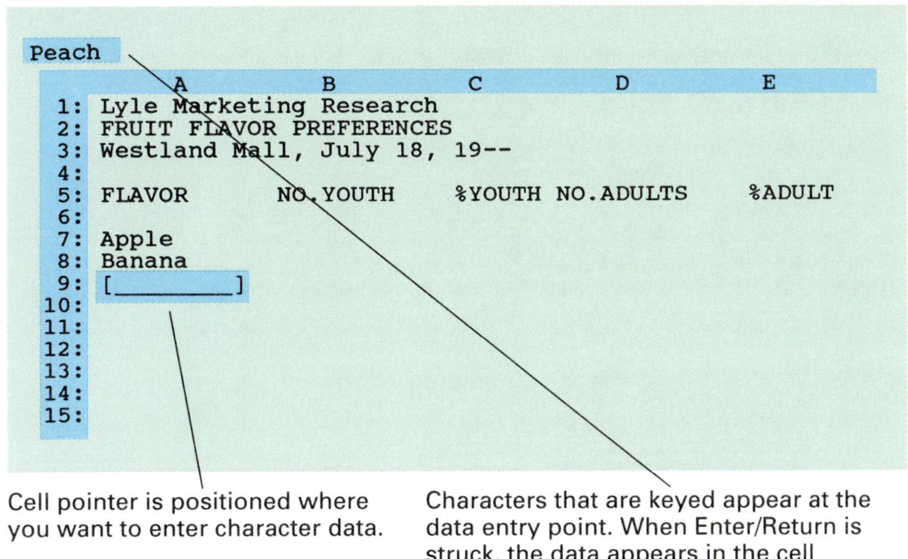

Figure 12-8
To enter character data, the cell pointer must be moved to the proper cell.

Entering Numeric Data

Numeric data is entered in the same fashion as character data. The cell pointer is moved to the desired cell and the data is keyed in. Figure 12-9 shows this procedure.

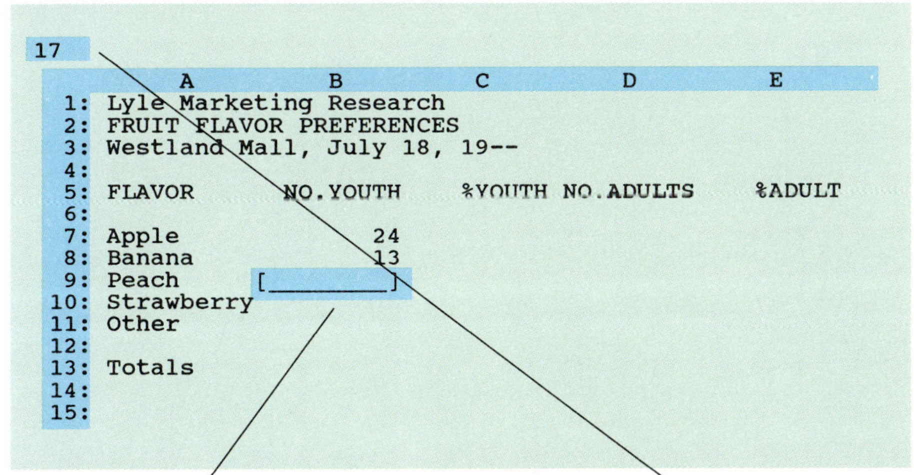

Figure 12-9
To enter numeric data, the cell pointer is moved to the desired cell.

Character and numeric data in a spreadsheet may be entered in any order desired. After entry of data, the sample spreadsheet appears as shown in Figure 12-10. In studying this figure, note that no computed values yet appear, though formulas could have been entered during the process of entering character (labels) and numeric (values) data.

Figure 12-10
After character and numeric data is entered, a spreadsheet may look like the one shown here.

```
             A            B             C          D            E
  1: Lyle Marketing Research
  2: FRUIT FLAVOR PREFERENCES
  3: Westland Mall, July 18, 19--
  4:
  5: FLAVOR        NO.YOUTH      %YOUTH NO.ADULTS       %ADULT
  6:
  7: Apple               24                  31
  8: Banana              13                  23
  9: Peach               17                  22
 10: Strawberry           7                   4
 11: Other               14                  28
 12:
 13: Totals
 14:
 15:
```

Entering Formulas

The computed values in a spreadsheet are calculated by means of formulas. In the example, the total number of youth is computed by adding, or summing, the five values of 24, 13, 17, 7, and 14. These values are in Cells B7, B8, B9, B10, and B11. Therefore, these cells are added to obtain the total. In order to enter this computation, the cell pointer must be moved to B13 (the point at which the total should appear) and the formula must be entered. Figure 12-11 shows how this is done, with the formula appearing at the data entry point.

Figure 12-11
Formulas are often entered to make necessary calculations.

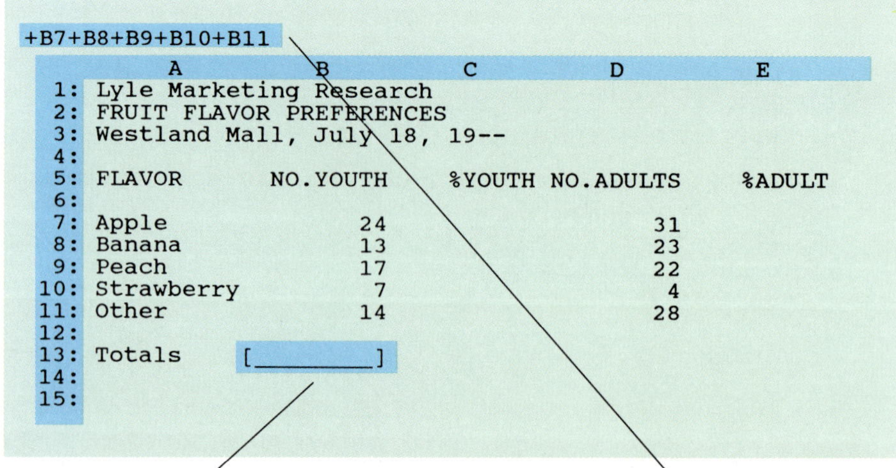

Cell pointer is moved to column in which total should appear.

Formula is entered at data entry point. When formula is finished, the result (75) appears in the cell. The + (= with some software) simply indicates that a formula is beginning; otherwise, the program might think B7 begins a label.

While this method of summing the column works fine, it is somewhat inconvenient, especially when the number of values is large. Therefore, a shorter, easier method may be used. To do this a **function** is used. A function is simply an entry representing something that the spreadsheet software knows how to do, such as sum. Some spreadsheets require that a special symbol, such as the @ symbol, precede the function. Therefore, to sum the column, the @SUM function is entered, followed by the range of cells to be summed indicated inside parentheses. (With some spreadsheets, the range is entered by moving the cursor over the cells rather than by keying the cell numbers.)

After this process has been completed, but before completion of the formula has been indicated by means of the ***Enter/Return*** key or the mouse, the entry line might appear as shown in Figure 12-12. Note that the cells are indicated as @SUM(B7..B11). This means that the sum is to include Cells B7, B8, B9, B10, and B11. While the exact syntax of stating this varies depending on the software, the result will be the same. Also, some spreadsheet software lets you take a short cut in selecting an entire row or column as a range by positioning the cursor on the number of the row or column and clicking the mouse or striking a key combination. Note that while the answer or solution is what appears in the cell, the formula is still considered the actual contents of the cell.

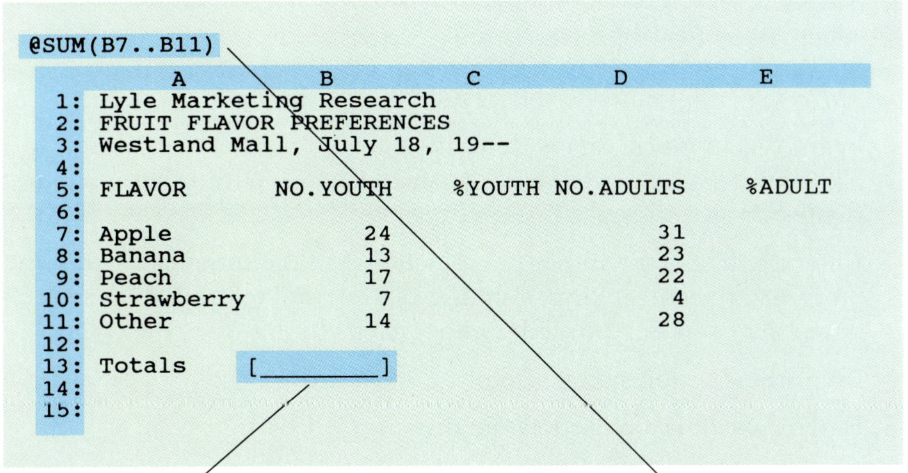

Figure 12-12
Formulas can often be stated in more than one way by using a function.

Functions to perform various actions are included with spreadsheet software. A brief sampling of typical functions includes those which average numbers, round numbers, count data, and perform logarithmic functions.

When entering formulas, there are two methods of indicating cells. In one of them, cells are referred to as **absolute** locations. This means that these cells are not changed when changes are made to the spreadsheet. Absolute cell references usually have a special character such as a dollar sign (B4, for example) to indicate that they are unchanging. The other method refers to cells by their location in relation to the location of the cell containing a formula. This is known as **relative** cell referencing and may appear as a range, such as B1..B6, with no special characters. The advantage of relative cell referencing is that rows or columns can be inserted or deleted in a range covered by a formula, and the range will automatically expand or contract to include the correct rows or columns. Note that absolute and relative cells are indicated differently by different software. Some programs use the row and column notation (such as B4 or B5) for relative locations and use a symbol (such as $B5 or B$5) to indicate absolute locations.

Now that you know how to sum a column of data, look at the method used to compute the percent of youth respondents favoring each of the flavors of fruit. To compute the percent of youths favoring apple, for example, the number of youths preferring apple (24) is first divided by the total number of youths responding (75), yielding a quotient of .32. This is then converted to a percentage by multiplying by 100 to get an answer of 32. To accomplish this calculation with a spreadsheet, the cell pointer would first be moved to the desired location for the answer, then the formula would be entered. Follow the following steps for Figure 12-13 on the next page; numbers in parentheses indicate where the steps take place on the spreadsheet.

1. Move the cell pointer to the desired answer location.
2. Begin the formula; this is done in some spreadsheets by entering a plus sign (+) or parenthesis, as shown here. With others, another symbol (= or −) is used.
3. Enter the first cell number to be included in the formula. With some programs, the cursor keys or mouse can be used to "point" to the cell rather than entering the cell number itself. In this case, the cell is B7.
4. Enter the division sign (/) from the keyboard.
5. Enter the cell to be used as the divisor, Cell B13.
6. From the keyboard, enter the multiplication symbol (*) and the multiplier (100). Strike ***Enter/Return*** or click the mouse to indicate completion of the formula. The answer of 32 will appear in the answer cell.

When using a spreadsheet, all the labels, values, and formulas are entered in a manner similar to that described in this chapter. If you later change any value that is used in a formula, remember that the formula will recalculate using the new value and place the updated result in the formula's cell.

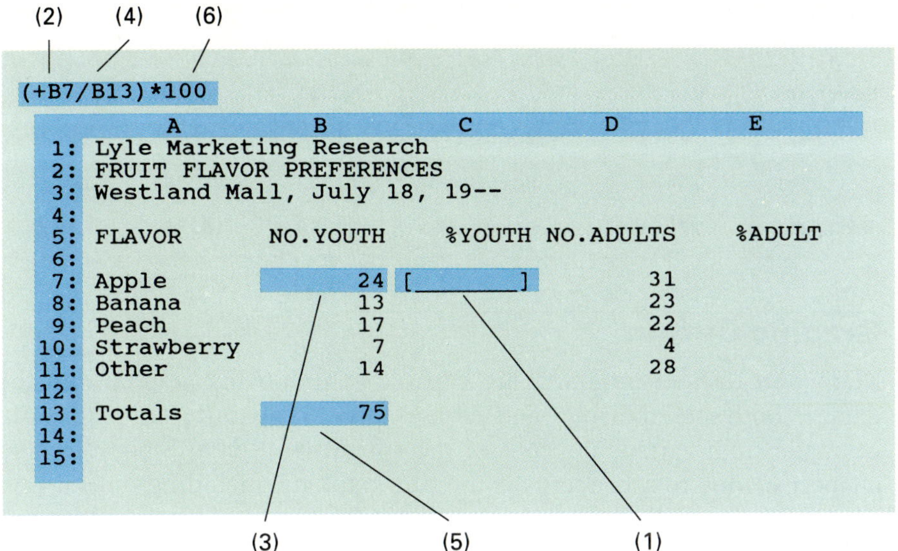

Figure 12-13
Certain steps must be followed when entering formulas.

OBTAINING OUTPUT FROM A SPREADSHEET

The data as generated on the screen is one form of output from a spreadsheet and is a very commonly used one. However, there are two other frequently used methods of output—printed reports and graphs.

Printed Reports

Any of the data stored in a spreadsheet may be printed to produce reports. The user is free to define the items to be printed. Frequently the entire spreadsheet will be printed for reference and filing. However, selected portions often produce more meaningful reports.

When more than one page is required to print a spreadsheet, either of two methods may be chosen. In the first, the entire spreadsheet is printed (using as many pages as necessary) in such fashion that it may be taped together to form one large printout. In the second method, the row and column headings may be repeated on each of several pages, so that the spreadsheet consists of several pages that will not be attached to each other. Figure 12-14 shows a "pasted up" spreadsheet, while Figure 12-15 shows a report with repeated headings.

Figure 12-14
Several pages of a spreadsheet may be taped together to form one large printout.

	January	February	March	April	May	June	July
Yogurt	3543	3417	4321	5234	9832	15323	18480
Hot Dogs	16323	18983	15434	14323	13234	14987	12893
Beverages	15432	14323	15329	14382	16382	16983	18732

	January	February	March
Yogurt	3543	3417	4321
Hot Dogs	16323	18983	15434
Beverages	15432	14323	15329

	April	May	June
Yogurt	5234	9832	15323
Hot Dogs	14323	13234	14987
Beverages	14382	16382	16983

Figure 12-15
When there are several pages of a spreadsheet, the row headings may be repeated on each page.

Graphic Output

Many spreadsheet programs are capable of producing graphs from the data, in both screen display and printed form. Many different graphs can be made from various portions of the spreadsheet data. Since the next chapter of this text concerns computer graphics, including output produced by spreadsheet programs, the details of this process will be discussed in that chapter.

Graphs produced from spreadsheet data can be displayed or printed.

OTHER SPREADSHEET OPERATIONS

While it is possible to get quite a bit of use from spreadsheet software just by using the techniques you have learned to this point, there are several additional operational features that increase the effectiveness and efficiency of spreadsheet use. These features include insertion and deletion, copying, the use of macros, and the use of templates.

Insertion and Deletion

When developing a spreadsheet, it is often desirable to add additional rows or columns that may have been overlooked during the initial entry of data. Also, it may be necessary to remove rows or columns that are no longer needed. To perform these functions, spreadsheet software includes the ability to insert one or more blank rows or columns into which new labels, values, and formulas may be entered. There are also functions for removing one or more rows or columns that are no longer needed.

Insertion and deletion are done by selecting the operations through keyboard commands or use of the mouse.

Columns or rows of data can easily be inserted or deleted when using spreadsheet software.

It is with the use of insertion and deletion that the advantage of using relative cell addressing in formulas becomes obvious. For example, assume that you have entered a formula in Cell C10 to add the values in Cells C7, C8, and C9. Later, if you need to insert another row whose value you would like to have added into the total, your formula will not include it. The only solution is to change the formula. If you use relative cell addressing, however, and sum the cells in Column C, a new row added within that range will automatically be included in the formula since the range of cells will automatically be expanded by the software. Therefore, changing formulas is unnecessary when insertions are made. The same is true for deletions, as the software will contract the range of the formula when a row or column is deleted.

Copying

Many times the same data or formulas are needed in multiple locations in a spreadsheet. In the sample spreadsheet, for example, the formula for computing the percent of respondents preferring each type of fruit flavor is the same for all categories. That is, the number preferring each fruit flavor is divided by the total number of respondents. In a case such as this, spreadsheet software provides the ability to copy from one cell or range of cells to another cell or range of cells. Look at Figure 12-16, which shows where the same formula can be used. Note that the formula from Cell C7 can be copied to Cells C8, C9, C10, and C11. In copying this formula, the dividend on all rows will be the value in the column immediately to the left of the answer cell's column. However, note in the example that the divisor (B13) is specified as being six rows below the dividend in the spreadsheet. If this relationship is copied down to additional rows, this will result in formulas that attempt to find data for the divisor in Rows 14, 15, 16, and 17. To prevent this, the divisor needs to be specified in absolute terms as always being in Row 13. The exact method of doing this will vary depending on the software.

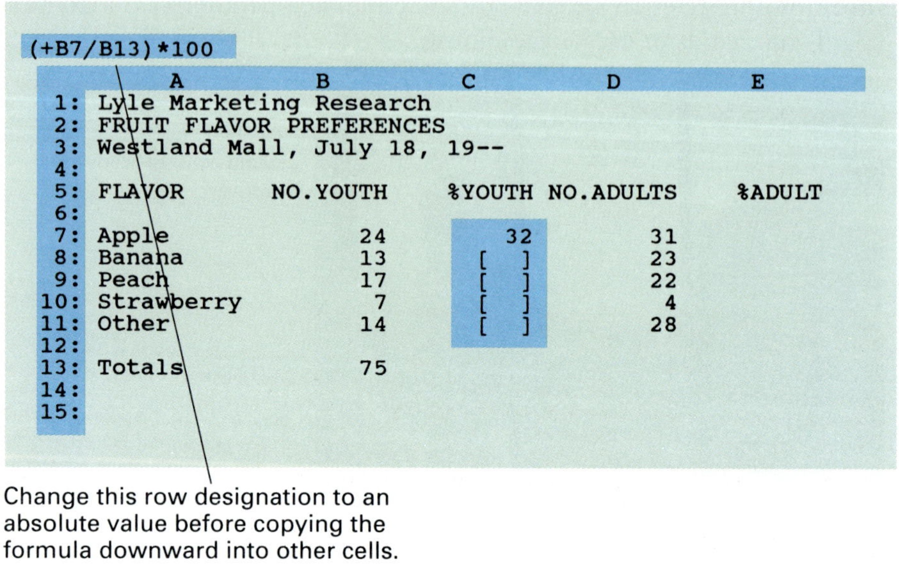

Figure 12-16
A formula may be copied from one cell to another cell or several cells.

```
(+B7/B13)*100
              A            B            C          D          E
 1:  Lyle Marketing Research
 2:  FRUIT FLAVOR PREFERENCES
 3:  Westland Mall, July 18, 19--
 4:
 5:  FLAVOR        NO.YOUTH     %YOUTH NO.ADULTS     %ADULT
 6:
 7:  Apple               24         32        31
 8:  Banana              13        [  ]       23
 9:  Peach               17        [  ]       22
10:  Strawberry           7        [  ]        4
11:  Other               14        [  ]       28
12:
13:  Totals              75
14:
15:
```

Change this row designation to an absolute value before copying the formula downward into other cells.

Using Macros

The term **macro,** as used with computer software, refers to a series of keystrokes or program instructions that is remembered by the software so that the sequence may be executed quickly whenever desired. For example, all the keystrokes necessary to copy a formula from one cell to the cell below it might be recorded by the program. Then, when the user wants to copy a formula, only one or two keystrokes are needed to cause the series of stored commands to be carried out. Some macros may already be stored when spreadsheet software is purchased. Others may be recorded at the option of the user.

Using Templates

A **template** is a "skeleton" spreadsheet that includes labels, formulas, and perhaps macros, but has incomplete or no data. The data is then entered by the user and the computations are made. Templates are often sold by software vendors, or they may be created by users.

As an example of how a template is used, assume that a person who invests in stocks wants to use a spreadsheet to keep records of transactions. The investor also wants to predict what the value of the stock investments might be under various market conditions, along with the tax consequences of various investment decisions. As an alternative to entering all the data and all the formulas from scratch, the investor might purchase a stock investment template. This template would already include all the formulas and would include labels indicating where to key-in the price paid for a stock, the tax rate, etc. Additionally, it might include data related to tax laws and the buying and selling of stock. Upon keying in data, all the pre-defined computations take place with no further effort on the part of the user.

USING A SPREADSHEET

As you learned earlier in this chapter, spreadsheets can be used to record data that already exists or to predict what might happen in the future. In this section, you will learn more details about the use of spreadsheets.

Spreadsheet software can be used to determine how much money is left for clothing each month.

Using the Spreadsheet as a Planning Tool

One of the most common uses of spreadsheets is as a planning tool. A plan is a way of deciding what you want to do. As an example, assume you are a student and want to plan your budget for the year. The budget will show your anticipated income and expenses, making it possible for you to develop a plan under which expenditures can be kept within income. Figure 12-17 shows how such a spreadsheet might be arranged. Once the anticipated income and expenditures are entered, you can then determine if you like the effect on your cash balance. You may want to plan more expenditures or cut expenditures. On the other hand, you may want to try to add more income.

	A	B	C	D	E	F	G	H
1:	Month	Salary	Savings	Clothing	Entertain.	Car	Insurance	Balance
2:	Begin							500
3:	Jan	250	50	40	50	90		520
4:	Feb	250	50	40	50	90		540
5:	Mar	250	50	40	50	90	200	360
6:	Apr	250	50	40	50	90		380
7:	May	250	50	40	50	90		400
8:	Jun	330	50	40	50	90	150	350
9:	Jul	390	75	50	60	90		465
10:	Aug	390	75	50	60	90		580
11:	Sep	250	50	40	50	90	200	400
12:	Oct	250	50	40	50	90		420
13:	Nov	250	50	40	50	90	150	290
14:	Dec	290	50	40	50	90		350
15:								
16:	Total	3400	650	500	620	1080	700	

Figure 12-17
A spreadsheet can be used as a planning tool for preparing a budget.

Using the Spreadsheet for Modeling

Modeling is a term used to describe the process of mathematically mimicking something that happens in the world. If the mathematical mimicking becomes good enough, the model can be used to predict future action with at least some degree of confidence in the prediction. For example, economists use models to try to track the performance of the economy and predict when depressions, recessions, and good times will happen. Similar modeling is done by other persons to try to predict when the stock market will go up or down and by approximately how much.

Most of the models such as these involve many variables and complex formulas. However, spreadsheet software can provide the means to record the variables and compute the desired prediction outcomes.

Many economists use spreadsheet models to track the performance of the economy.

Using the Spreadsheet as a Database Manager

Because of the spreadsheet's ability to record data in its cells, some spreadsheet programs can be used as flat file database managers. When used in this manner, data entry is usually made by keying data into the cells—custom data entry forms are generally not available. Also, the query and report writing capabilities are usually no match for those of a database management system. For many persons who need only simple database capabilities, however, a spreadsheet program can serve those needs adequately.

Linking Spreadsheets

Some spreadsheet programs have the ability to link several spreadsheets together to provide for consolidated reporting. Assume, for example, that you operate three restaurants. The manager of each restaurant fills in financial data using a spreadsheet template that you provide. You then retrieve those spreadsheets from the managers and link them together to form one spreadsheet that automatically sums all the data from the three underlying spreadsheets. In this way, you can examine the financial position of your entire restaurant group and use the consolidated data as a company-wide decision-making tool.

Integrating the Spreadsheet with Other Programs

While much spreadsheet use involves nothing beyond the spreadsheet software, the number of applications that involve additional software is increasing. For example, some spreadsheet programs can be used with database software. Data from the database may be loaded into the spreadsheet for display and analysis. If data is changed in the spreadsheet, the update can then automatically be made in the database. In addition, data from most spreadsheet programs can be easily transferred to many word processing programs for presentation in documents. Depending on the word processing program being used, it may be possible to access the data directly from the word processor. With others, it will be necessary to produce "printed" output from the spreadsheet on disk to be read by the word processor.

Data from spreadsheet programs can often be transferred to word processing programs for use in documents.

STORAGE OF DATA

Data entered and computed in a spreadsheet usually needs to be stored for future use. All spreadsheet programs contain the capability to store spreadsheets on disk and then retrieve them for further editing and processing. Any graphs created from the data in a spreadsheet are typically stored in files separate from the spreadsheet itself.

Some spreadsheets store data in a format that is compatible with other spreadsheets and programs, while some use formats that are somewhat unique. If various persons in a business use different spreadsheet software but need to share worksheets, compatibility of the data becomes more important.

HARDWARE REQUIREMENTS

The same hardware guidelines that apply to most other application software apply for spreadsheet software as well. Some type of spreadsheet software is available for almost all computers. Each new program that is introduced, however, seems to have greater capability and requires more memory and disk space than the program it replaces or competes with. In general, the greater the capability of a spreadsheet program, the greater the memory and disk space required. As the size of a spreadsheet grows, execution speed of the hardware becomes more important. In a small spreadsheet, all the formulas can be recalculated almost instantaneously. Newer spreadsheet programs recompute only formulas whose underlying cells have changed. Even with that computational advantage, however, the increased speed of a faster computer is desirable for large, complex spreadsheets.

FARMING'S NOT WHAT IT USED TO BE

While a dwindling number of farmers still do things the old-fashioned way, most farms are making a home for the computer. Many of the uses of the computer are the same on the farm as in the downtown office, since farming is a business. There is accounting work to do, as well as word processing, and these two functions are carried out using the usual kinds of computer software.

The farmer must do a tremendous amount of planning and forecasting. Spreadsheet software might be used to compute possible income under different sets of circumstances. For example, what if there is a drought resulting in a low yield, but the price of the product goes up because of the low yield? Or, what if there is an excellent growing season, but the price goes down because every farmer has harvested a bumper crop? What happens if the government changes its farm regulations or policies?

With the advent of futures trading on commodity exchanges, the practice of "betting" on crop or herd outcomes is an everyday occurrence. A farmer who wants to guarantee his or her return can sell the rights to the crop at a sure price sometime before the crop is mature. The person who buys the rights to the crop or herd is betting that profit can be made from buying the crop or herd at the agreed upon price and selling it to a processor or distributor at whatever the market price may be at the time of harvest.

The rights may be sold and bought many times in the marketplace between the time a farmer originally sells the rights and the time the goods are actually delivered, with the prices going up or down depending on the buyer's and seller's prediction of yield and price. The price at which a sale commitment can be made by the farmer varies tremendously depending on conditions, and it changes daily. Computers can help farmers track these daily changes, along with their own predictions and actual expenses involved, and can help farmers make more rational decisions as to whether an early sale of the rights should be made.

The truly unique applications of computers on the farm, however, make the computer an integral part of the production process. A prime example of this occurs on a real dairy farm where the cows have been deprived of their privacy, so to speak. Each cow has been equipped with a transponder—a small radio transmitter that the cow wears around her neck.

Various cows come to the feeding barn to eat. The catch is, some cows ought to eat more and some ought to eat less, based on how much milk they are producing. With old, traditional dairy farming, each cow ate until she was full or until the feed trough was empty. Now the computer calculates how much each cow should have and lets the cow eat only that much, making a significant reduction in the farmer's feed bill. When the cow enters a feed station, the transponder radios the computer indicating which cow it is. The computer then quickly looks up how much food that cow should get and slowly dispenses it, delivering the food no faster than the cow can eat it. This way, if the cow gets tired of eating and leaves the feed area, the transponder tells the computer of the exit, and the computer stops releasing food. Therefore, no food is left in the trough for some other cow to eat.

Computers are earning their keep down on the farm.

The computer can also aid the farmer in working with crops. With the increasing use of irrigation equipment—and the great expense of using irrigation—the computer can keep up with exactly what crops are growing in the fields, the precise pattern and amount of water they need, and the dates and amounts of natural rain. With this information, the computer can make an analysis and tell the farmer when and how much water should be applied with irrigation, thereby using the least possible water to keep the crop healthy.

As you can see, farming will never be the same now that computers are becoming commonplace. The use of computers helps improve the efficiency of farming and, thereby, keeps the cost of food from going up as much as would otherwise be the case.

CHAPTER SUMMARY

- A spreadsheet is a row and column arrangement of data.
- Spreadsheets may be computed by hand or by computer.
- Spreadsheets may represent either reports of existing conditions or be used to help make plans or projections for the future.
- A single horizontal area extending across a spreadsheet is a row.

- A single vertical area running down a spreadsheet is known as a column.
- Rows and columns are designated with letters and/or numbers; for example, Columns A, B, C, etc., and Rows 1, 2, 3, etc.
- One space on a spreadsheet—the intersection of a row and a column—is known as a cell and may be designated by its column and row numbers, such as C3.
- Any contiguous group of cells is known as a range.
- Alphabetic cells are referred to as labels.
- Numeric cells are referred to as values.
- Computed values are derived through the use of formulas entered into cells.
- The cursor that indicates where data is to be entered is known as the cell pointer.
- When data is entered, it appears on a data entry line or directly in the cell, depending on the software.
- Formulas entered into cells designate what operations are to be performed and the values to be used in performing the operations.
- Cells in formulas are referred to by the names of their columns and rows.
- Absolute cell references refer to particular row and column intersections on the spreadsheet which do not change.
- Relative cell references refer to cells by relating their positions to other cells. Thus, if the spreadsheet is expanded or contracted, cell references change accordingly.
- The use of pre-defined mathematical functions simplifies the entry of formulas.
- Printed reports can include either all or part of a spreadsheet.
- Reports too large for one page can be printed either as multiple pages that repeat the headings or as pages to be taped or pasted together to form one large printout.
- Some spreadsheet software can present data in the form of graphs.
- Insertion capability allows for the entry of new rows or columns of data between existing rows or columns.
- Much labor can be saved by copying formulas and values from one cell to other cells as appropriate.
- Macros are "recordings" of sequences of keystrokes for later "replay" during spreadsheet use; they simplify spreadsheet use by making it possible to take complex actions with only one or two keystrokes.
- Templates consist of spreadsheets that already have labels and formulas in them, but no or incomplete data. They are available for many common applications and, upon entry of the values by the user, provide all the computed data.
- Spreadsheets are useful in providing data for planning.
- Modeling of real-world events can help predict future events.
- Spreadsheet data becomes more useful when it can be used with other applications.

- Compatibility of spreadsheet data is important for integrating applications.
- The more capable the spreadsheet software and the larger and more complex the spreadsheets to be entered by the user, the more capable the computer hardware must be.

KEY TERMS

The following key terms were introduced or redefined in this chapter:

absolute reference
cell
cell pointer
column
formula
function
label
macro
modeling
range
relative reference
row
spreadsheet
template
value

REVIEW QUESTIONS

1. What is a spreadsheet? (Obj. 1)
2. How were spreadsheets prepared before computer software was available? (Obj. 1)
3. Spreadsheets are used primarily for two types of work. What are they and how are they alike and different? (Obj. 2)
4. Name and define the terms used to describe different parts of a spreadsheet. (Obj. 3)
5. How are the rows and columns of a spreadsheet identified? (Obj. 3)
6. What is the difference between a label and a value? (Obj. 3)
7. How is entering a formula into a cell different from entering a label or a value? (Obj. 4)
8. What is the general procedure for entering a label or a value in a spreadsheet cell? (Obj. 4)
9. What is the purpose of functions? (Obj. 4)
10. What part do ranges play in entering formulas? (Obj. 4)
11. What is an absolute cell reference? What is a relative cell reference? (Obj. 4)
12. What is the advantage of relative cell references? (Obj. 4)
13. When a printed report is desired, what portion of a spreadsheet is printed? (Obj. 5)
14. How can a spreadsheet that is larger than one page be output in printed form? (Obj. 5)
15. What happens to formulas when a row or column is inserted or deleted? Is this always the case? Explain. (Obj. 6)
16. What kind of cell contents can be copied to other cells? (Obj. 6)

17. Define a macro. What is its purpose? (Obj. 6)
18. What is the purpose of a template? (Obj. 6)
19. Define planning and modeling. What is the difference between the two? (Obj. 7)
20. How can a spreadsheet program serve as a database program? (Obj. 7)
21. What is the purpose of linking spreadsheets? (Obj. 7)
22. Do all spreadsheet programs store data in the same format? Why can this be important? (Obj. 8)
23. What can be said of the relationship between spreadsheet software ability and computer hardware requirements? (Obj. 9)
24. How have newer spreadsheets improved speed performance regardless of the hardware on which they are operating? (Obj. 9)

CHALLENGE ACTIVITIES

1. In most cases, relative references are preferred to absolute references. Name at least one example you can think of in which an absolute reference is needed. (Obj. 4)
2. If you have spreadsheet software available, enter the spreadsheet for fruit flavor preferences that was used beginning in Figure 12-1. Be sure to use formulas to calculate the computed values. Save your spreadsheet, then print a hard copy report. (Objs. 3,4,5)
3. If you have spreadsheet software available, prepare a template for the spreadsheet shown in Figure 12-1. Remember that the template should contain all the labels and formulas, but no values (numbers). Conduct your own preference survey, then enter the numbers in the template and watch the spreadsheet compute the percentages. (Obj. 6)
4. If your spreadsheet program has macro capability, research the reference manual and find out how to "record" and "play back" a macro. Record one macro that will insert a column in front of a selected column and another one that will delete a column in front of a selected column. Use the macros to insert and delete a column in your spreadsheet from Exercise 2. (Obj. 6)

CHAPTER 13

COMPUTER GRAPHICS

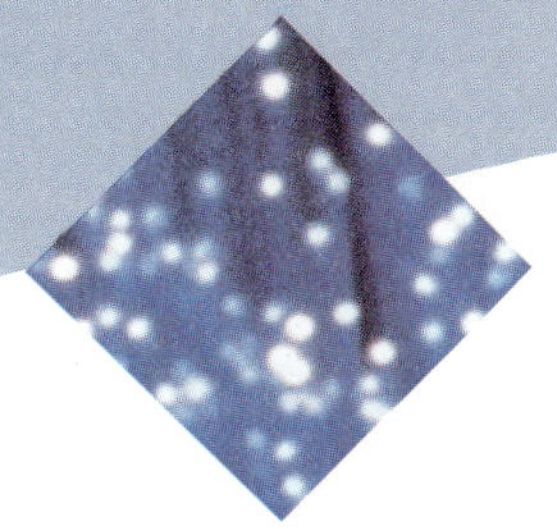

LEARNING OBJECTIVES

After studying this chapter, you will be able to:

1. **Define and give examples of the use of computer graphics.**
2. **Define and describe the use of paint programs.**
3. **Define and describe the use of computer-aided design and drafting programs.**
4. **Define and describe the use of graphing programs.**

INTRODUCTION

In this chapter you will learn about the application software that enables the production of graphics. **Computer graphics** refers to any pictorial representation that can be produced by the computer, either on the display, printer, plotter, or other output device. In many cases, the use of graphics makes communication much clearer than the use of words alone. In general, computer graphics take the form of charts, diagrams, or pictures. The complexity of the graphics is dependent on both the hardware and software in use. While simple graphics can be done with just about any computer, the production of extremely high-quality color graphics (especially with animation) requires very powerful microcomputer equipment with huge amounts of memory and disk space. Some software requires the use of minicomputers or mainframe computers.

Graphics software is a term generally applied to any program that produces "pictures" or "art." **Paint programs** are graphics programs that allow a person to do "art" on the screen and print it out. **CAD programs** are used for computer-aided drafting and used to assist the designer of products in drawing plans. **Graphing programs** produce graphs or charts from data. Paint programs, CAD programs, and graphing programs, therefore, are three kinds of graphics software.

The next section describes some of the common applications of graphics software. It is followed by sections that describe the use of paint programs, CAD programs, and graphing programs.

USES OF GRAPHICS SOFTWARE

Graphics software is used for many purposes. Among them are computer art, computer-aided instruction, computer-aided design and drafting, scientific study, television and movies, and presentation graphics. While all these areas have common roots in computer graphics, each is unique in its purpose and implementation.

Computer Art

The computer has replaced the palette and brush for a growing number of artists. The wide range of available colors, the ability to easily repeat patterns, and the ease of performing special effects, added to the much higher resolution now available with many computers, have led to the growth of computer art.

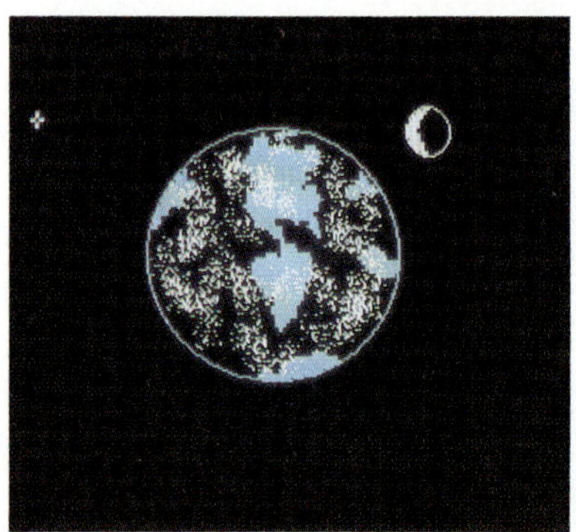

Computers are now used to create many kinds of art.

Computer-Aided Instruction

While artists use the computer for aesthetic reasons, growing numbers of students (both children and adults) are learning from computer-aided instruction. The use of graphics in these lessons makes the material more interesting and easier to learn. The level of sophistication of the graphics varies widely from one vendor's instructional software to another.

The use of graphics makes these lessons more interesting and easier to learn.

Computer-Aided Design and Drafting (CAD)

The number of blueprints (designs) being drafted by hand is decreasing rapidly. This is because of the increased accuracy and efficiency made possible by computer-aided drafting and design software. This software provides many automatic functions, such as dimensioning (providing measurements for the object being drawn), with little effort on the part of the operator. Objects being designed by use of the computer range from automobiles to houses to bottle caps to spacecraft. A tremendous advantage to using the computer is the ability to produce three-dimensional drawings. That is, an object can be drawn and then viewed (even in motion) from any angle with the computational and display abilities of the computer software.

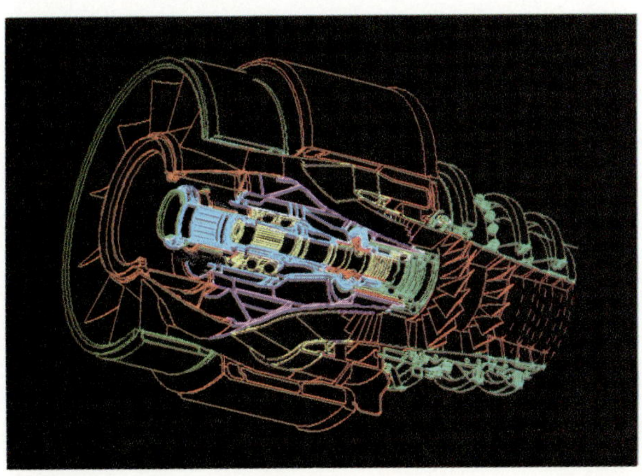

Computers can be used to produce three-dimensional drawings.

Scientific Study

In scientific study graphics are used extensively in many areas. From fields as diverse as medical imaging to modeling the behavior of weather, the computer is proving to be an invaluable tool.

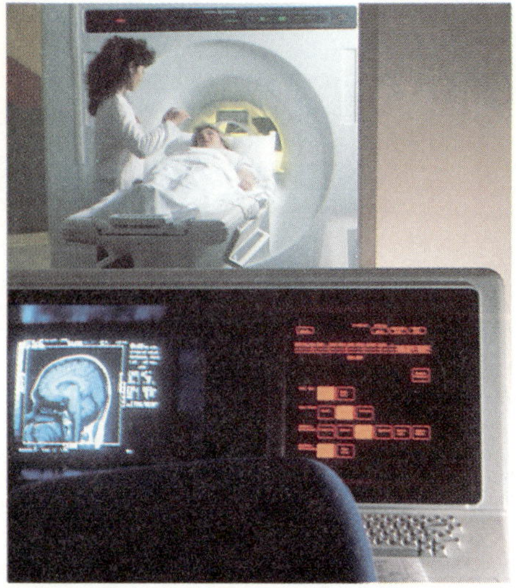

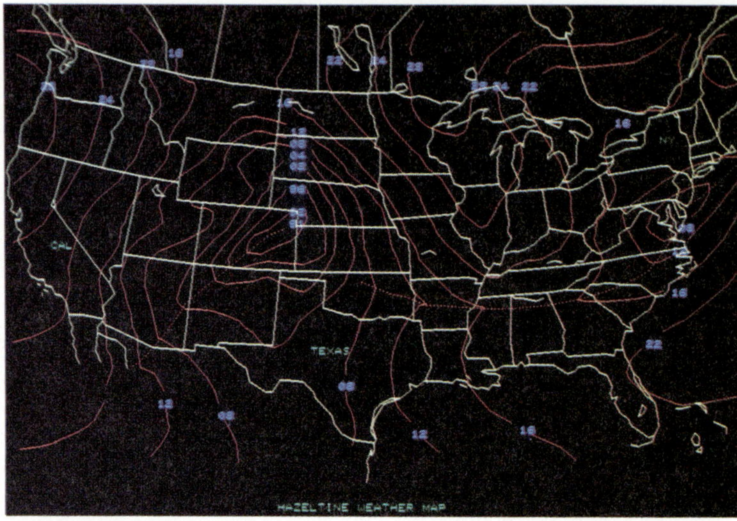

Computers are used for medical imaging and weather modeling.

Television and Movies

Virtually every television show and movie now produced uses computer graphics in some way. Whether just for titles and special effects, or for the total production as in the case of computer-generated cartoons, computers help make the production more interesting and more economical.

Presentation Graphics

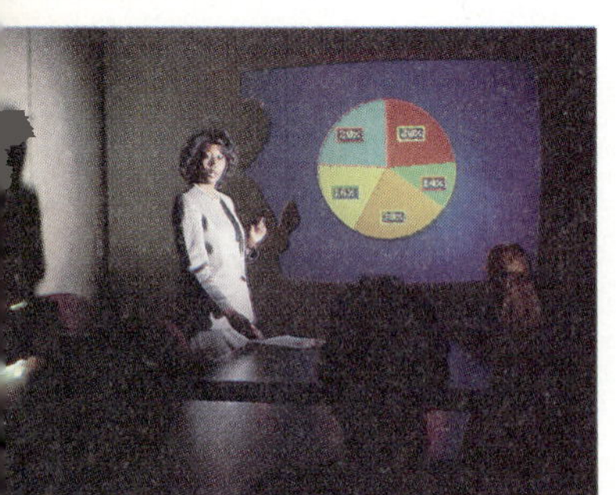

A computer can be used to prepare graphs for slide show presentations.

Presentation graphics are produced by the computer for use as visual aids. These visual aids may be used for everything from sales presentations to classroom instruction to special effects at concerts. Computers are assisting tremendously in the production of visual presentations such as slide shows. Images can be created on the computer and quickly converted to slides by exposing film with a specially fitted camera. As an alternative to making slides, a series of images may be produced with computer software, stored on disk, and "played back" with special software on the computer display or a large projector whenever desired. Any of the kinds of programs described in this chapter can be used to prepare images for presentation graphics.

MICROCOMPUTER GRAPHICS SOFTWARE

In the following sections paint software, CAD software, and graphing software will be discussed. These are three of the most commonly used types of programs on microcomputers. There are also versions of these programs available for mainframes and minicomputers. If you have access to appropriate software, you will want to try out many of the things you learn. The sections obviously address the software in generic terms since there are many different programs available, each of which has its own user interface. You may find it advantageous, therefore, to refer to the user's manual for the software you have available as you study these sections.

Using Paint Software

Paint programs are frequently used with microcomputers and accessed with a mouse. These programs enable a designer to create art, logos, or just about any kind of graphic desired. Paint programs use the computer screen as a canvas and allow the "painter" to paint with computerized tools that give the same general effect as brushes, paint rollers, and paint sprayers. However, many other effects are possible. These include mirror images of part of the screen, flipping part of the screen, or smearing the image across the screen, to name a few.

The Paint Working Environment

The initial screen of most paint programs will look something like that shown in Figure 13-1. While this example screen is similar to that of many programs, remember that other graphics programs may be different in both the arrangement and the exact items shown on the screen.

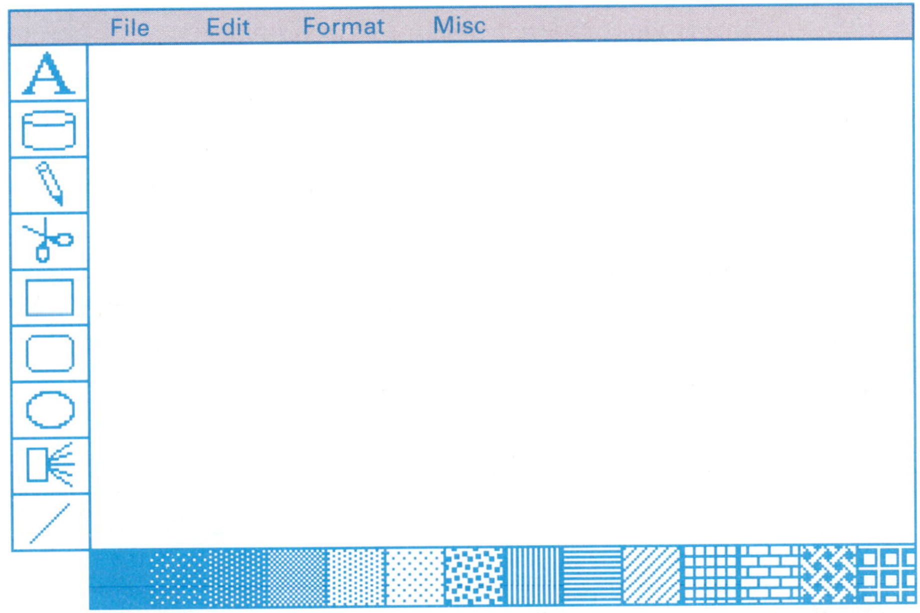

Figure 13-1
A typical screen in a paint program may be arranged like the one shown here.

Note that across the top of the example paint screen are some menu choices; File, Edit, Format, and Miscellaneous. Listed down the left side are kinds of tools that may be used. **Tools** refer to the "computerized implements," such as pencils and erasers, that are used for drawings. The tools are selected by moving the mouse pointer to the desired one and clicking the mouse. From top to bottom they represent the following:

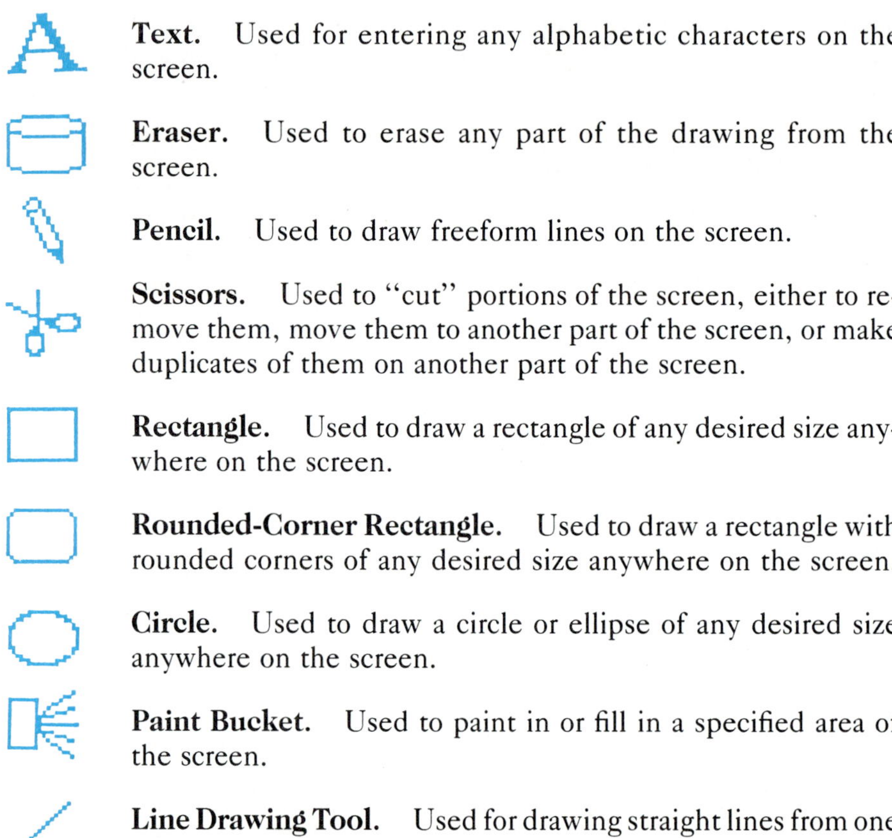

Text. Used for entering any alphabetic characters on the screen.

Eraser. Used to erase any part of the drawing from the screen.

Pencil. Used to draw freeform lines on the screen.

Scissors. Used to "cut" portions of the screen, either to remove them, move them to another part of the screen, or make duplicates of them on another part of the screen.

Rectangle. Used to draw a rectangle of any desired size anywhere on the screen.

Rounded-Corner Rectangle. Used to draw a rectangle with rounded corners of any desired size anywhere on the screen.

Circle. Used to draw a circle or ellipse of any desired size anywhere on the screen.

Paint Bucket. Used to paint in or fill in a specified area of the screen.

Line Drawing Tool. Used for drawing straight lines from one point to another.

Across the bottom of the screen are different patterns or colors of "paint" (known as a palette) that may be used with the drawing tools and the paint bucket. As with other items, these are chosen by pointing at them with the mouse pointer and clicking the mouse button.

Making a Freehand Painting

Look at Figure 13-2 to see how a simple freehand drawing might be accomplished. First, the mouse pointer is moved to the icon (symbol or picture) representing the pencil. Upon clicking the mouse, the pointer icon is replaced with a pencil icon. The pencil is then moved to the desired position, and the mouse button is held down while drawing the line. By holding down the mouse button to "use the pencil" and releasing the mouse button to "lift the pencil," you may continue to draw for as long as you wish.

Figure 13-2
Freehand drawing is possible with most paint programs.

Saving a Painting

Once a drawing has been completed, it should probably be saved. This can be done by pointing to the word **File** in the top line menu and clicking the mouse on the word. A pull-down menu will then appear as shown in Figure 13-3. This menu contains the words **Load, Save,** and **Quit.** The mouse should be moved down until the word **Save** is highlighted. After the mouse button is released with the word **Save** highlighted, a dialogue box will appear similar to the one shown. This box provides a place for entering the file name under which the drawing should be saved. After

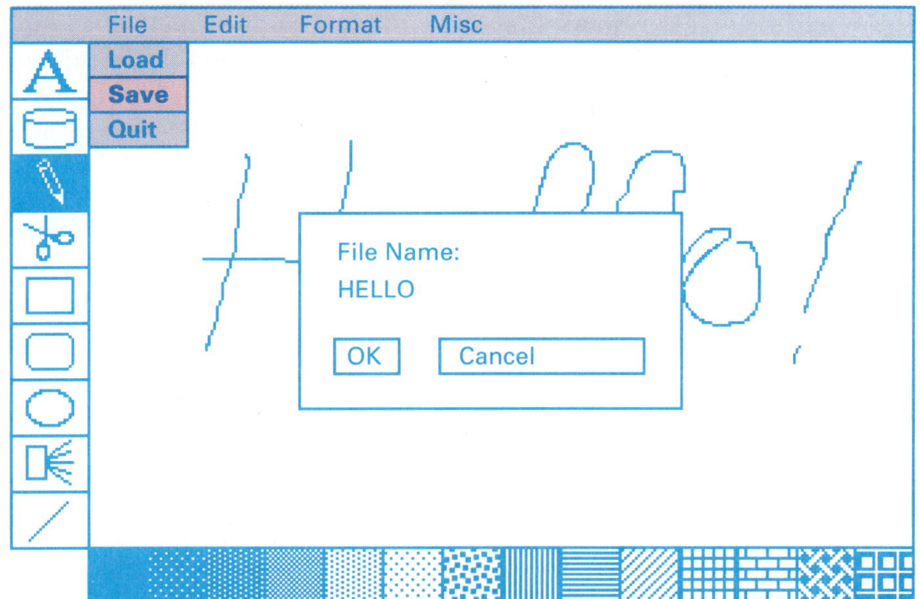

Figure 13-3
Paint programs often make use of pull-down menus and dialogue boxes.

keying the name, it is necessary to press ***Enter*** or click the mouse on the **OK** button. The save may be canceled by clicking the mouse on the **Cancel** button.

Using Geometric Tools

While freeform drawing is valuable, the power of the paint program is not restricted to that mode. Look at Figure 13-4 to see how the built-in tools for drawing geometric shapes may be used. Note in this illustration that the circle icon has been selected with the mouse. To draw the first circle, the pointer is placed at the center of the circle. The mouse button is then held down until the pointer is at a selected point on the circumference of the circle. When the mouse button is released, the circle is drawn. To get a second circle, there are two possibilities. One is to simply use the circle tool to draw another one. The other is to use the scissors tool to "mark" the first circle, and then use the Edit choice from the menu to copy the first circle to the second position.

Figure 13-4
A circle is one of many geometric shapes that can be produced by using the geometric tools in a paint program.

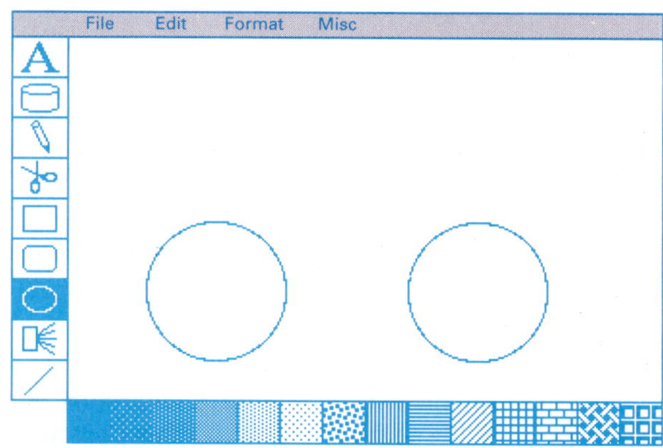

To complete a picture of a bicycle, for example, the pencil tool may be used for freeform drawing as shown in the first segment of Figure 13-5. Alternately, combinations of the geometric tools and the line drawing tool could be used as shown in the second segment of Figure 13-5. Notice that using the geometric tools results in smoother curves and straighter lines.

Figure 13-5
Freeform drawings may be produced by using the pencil tool or the geometric and line drawing tools.

Adding Text to a Painting

Any desired text is added to a painting by using the text tool as shown in Figure 13-6. After clicking on the text icon, a text cursor appears on the screen. The cursor is moved to the desired point for the text, the mouse is clicked to mark the place, and the text is typed. Variations in text style and size may be made by selecting options from the Format menu.

Figure 13-6
Text can easily be added to any design by using the text tool available in the paint program.

Using Special Effects

In addition to the uses of the tools introduced here, many special effects can be performed. For example, once a shape is drawn, it can be duplicated as many times as desired. You can flip the image, rotate it, tilt it, or perform other desired operations. For example, in Figure 13-7, the original image was copied, the copy was flipped, and the two were joined to make the image of two people.

Figure 13-7
Many special effects can be performed with paint programs.

What the Paint Program is Doing

While working on an image with a paint program, the software is turning pixels on and off. **Pixel** is short for picture element. Each pixel represents the smallest area that can be manipulated. That is, if the drawing is black and white, each pixel will be either black or white. If the drawing is in color, each pixel may be any one of the available colors. While the number of pixels on a given computer's screen is limited, a painting may logically be larger than the screen, with the screen serving as a "window" into the total drawing.

The first frame of Figure 13-8 shows how a picture made with a paint program might appear to a person observing from a distance. Upon looking closer, the person might see the picture as it appears in the second frame. Upon zooming in even closer, as in the third frame, a person would see the individual pixels. These pixels are of a small area of the kisser's right eye.

Figure 13-8
An image produced by a paint program is made up of pixels.

Working from External Input

In the painting examples created in this chapter, a clean screen was used upon which a drawing was made. In many cases, however, initial input can come from some other source, with touch-up work being done on the computer. For example, a scanner can be used to input any printed material. The images shown in Figure 13-8 were input into the computer by use of a scanner; they were originally done by an artist using paper and inks. In similar fashion, a video camera may be used to input images, persons, or other three-dimensional objects.

A scanner can be used to input printed material into the computer.

In using a scanner to input materials to the computer, keep in mind that the original creator has a legal right to the work. Copyright law that protects the creator's rights should not be violated when selecting materials to scan.

Using Image Libraries

Image libraries are computer files that contain pre-drawn art for use with paint and publishing programs. Typically, these files are available in collections of related work, such as images for holidays, seasons, business promotions, and so on. The images can be loaded from the disk into the paint program and manipulated as desired, including merging them with other images and performing special effects.

The use of image libraries can make the work of the designer or artist much easier. Again, however, keep in mind that the images are copyrighted by their creator or publisher. The ways in which the images can be used are strictly limited. Therefore, be sure to read the documentation that comes with a given library to determine how the images can be legally used. Many times, for example, the publisher will give permission to use the image in such items as newsletters and flyers but will place restrictions on selling the image in any form to other persons.

Producing Output

Once a painting is finished, it can be printed by selecting the Print command from the Miscellaneous menu. Generally, the size of the printout can be controlled at this point.

Some paint programs work only in black and white, while others can work with up to several thousand colors on the screen. If you have a color printer, the output of color paint programs can also be in color.

Using CAD Software

Computer-aided design or drafting software (CAD) is a category of graphics software designed to assist in the preparation of plans (traditionally called blueprints) for a variety of projects to be constructed. These projects might range from a golf course to a house to an airplane to a highway.

The Geometric Foundation of CAD

CAD software can be contrasted to paint software in the way its images are handled. As stated in the previous section, paint software allows the computer display to be used as an artist's palette, "painting" on it with various tools. Although CAD software allows total freedom of what is placed on the screen, it works with objects that are mathematically defined. A circle, for example, is mathematically defined for a drawing as having a defined center point (which determines its placement in the drawing) and a defined radius (which determines its size).

Because of the mathematical definition of all the shapes, there are some inherent capabilities of CAD software that cannot exist in painting software. For example, the definition of an object can be changed. Suppose a plan for a house includes the same round lavatory (named SINK) in all bathrooms, and the designer wants to change all of them to ovals. By simply redefining SINK to be an oval, all lavatories in the plan are automatically redrawn using the new shape. Or, suppose the designer wants to change all 3-foot by 6-foot windows to 4-foot by 7-foot windows. The size change can be made automatically in all windows on the plan. Additionally, objects can be moved easily from one place to another, even when they overlap other objects on the screen or have other objects drawn on top of them.

Everything in a CAD drawing is made of geometric shapes of some kind, such as straight lines, circles, etc. Figure 13-9 shows some of the typical shapes that can be used.

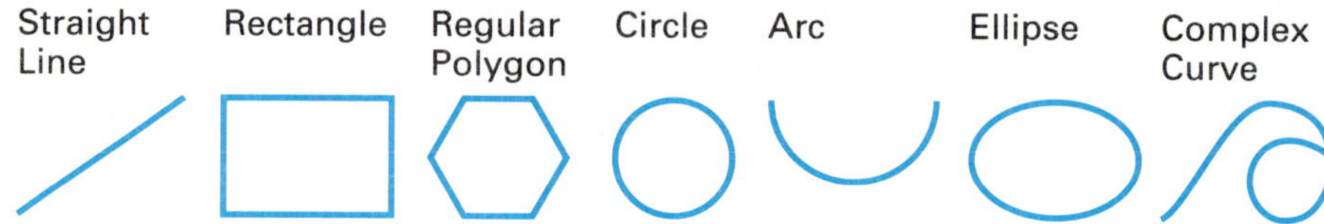

Figure 13-9
The drawings produced by CAD software are made of geometric shapes.

CAD's User Interface

The user interface varies significantly from one CAD program to another. One of the possible ways of interacting is to enter brief commands on the keyboard. For example, the command LI might draw a line from one designated point to another, or the command RP might draw a regular polygon at the designated point and in the designated size. Another possibility is to make choices from a menu, most likely by means of using a mouse or a digitizer pad. To designate points on the screen for the placement and sizing of objects, either the cursor keys, a mouse, or a light pen might commonly be used.

Drawings are made on a blank screen using the geometric shapes that can be handled by the CAD program. The program will automatically supply measurements printed on the display to show how large an object is. Incidentally, a CAD program works in full-size dimensions. That is, when drawing a house plan with a room that will be 15 by 20 feet when the house is built, the measurement readouts on the display will also be in feet, showing the 15 by 20 feet. In other words, plans are not drawn to scale on the screen with a fourth of an inch representing a foot, for example.

To help keep the drawing accurate, points on objects can automatically snap to a grid of defined size. To understand the concept of "snapping" to a point, imagine a drawing on a piece of graph paper. Every line on the drawing must start and stop at an intersection on the grid. Using the computer, the grid is similar to drawing on computerized graph paper. As the designer draws, the drawing point "jumps" (or snaps) from one grid intersection to another; that is, no point of a drawing can be defined as being anywhere other than on the intersection of a horizontal and vertical rule. For example, when a straight line is drawn, the ends of the line will automatically go to the nearest intersection on the grid. For a house plan, the grid may be defined as a 1-inch or 6-inch grid. Having objects snap to the grid ensures that lines that should meet on the drawing do indeed meet. The snap can be turned off temporarily when an object needs to be placed away from a grid point. Figure 13-10 shows how such points might look as an object is drawn.

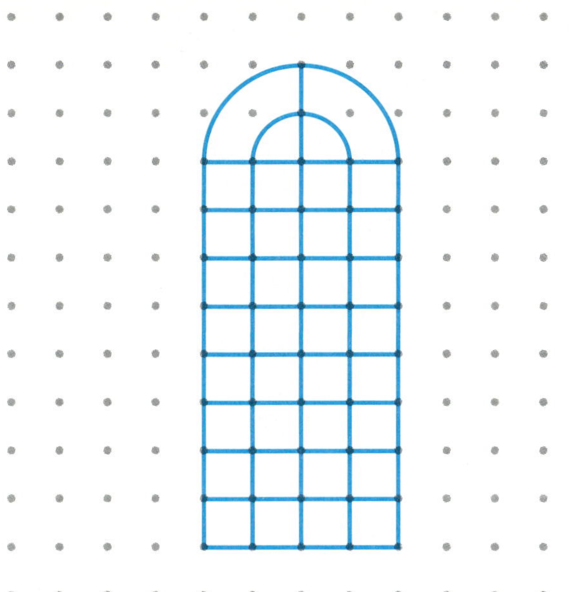

Figure 13-10
With CAD software, objects being drawn can be "snapped" to a computerized grid to help make the drawing more accurate.

Using Components

While just about anything can be drawn from scratch using the geometric shapes, the use of components can make the work much easier and faster. A **component** is an object that has been drawn and given a name. Look at Figure 13-11 which shows a rather ornate window that might appear in the front wall of a house. The window is made of a series of straight lines with two arcs at the top. While this window could be drawn repeatedly, it is much easier to draw it once, label it as a component, and then quickly place the window in all the locations in which it is desired. Components are typically named to refer to their description. With this in mind, the example in Figure 13-11 might be named PAL10X4 meaning a palladian window that is 10 feet high and 4 feet wide.

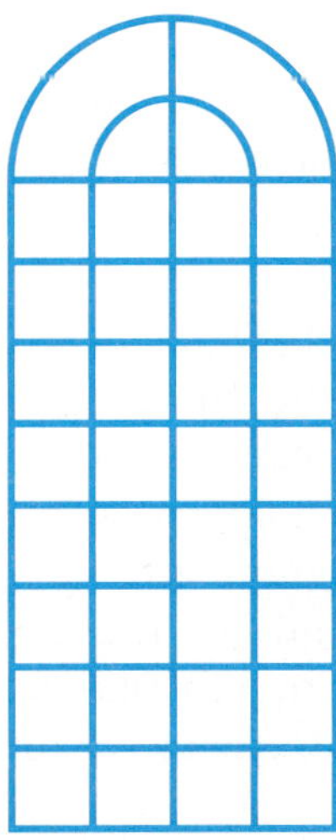

Figure 13-11
An object such as a window may be drawn and labeled as a component so that it may be used whenever desired.

Components may be drawn and named by the user of the CAD program. For many common applications, however, component libraries are included with the CAD program or available from its publisher. Such common applications include architectural design, landscaping, and engineering. The capabilities of CAD software allow for components to be resized, rotated on their axes, or modified for final use in the drawing.

Editing

Editing simply means making changes in something. In the case of CAD, it means making changes or modifications to objects that are in the process of being used in a drawing. Keeping in mind that each object drawn is represented in the computer as a mathematical formula—not as a pattern of pixels that are turned to particular colors—will make the concepts of editing easier to understand. Just a few of the possible editing moves are listed in the following paragraphs.

Moving reference points. Each object drawn has **reference points**, which are points indicating the parameters (boundaries) of the object. For example, a straight line has a reference point on each end. A circle has a reference point in the center and one on the circumference. An ellipse has four reference points—one on each end and one on each side. Any of these reference points may be moved, and when that is done, the size, shape, or position of the object will change accordingly. For example, a straight line can be moved from a vertical position to a horizontal position by moving the reference point for one of the ends.

Moving and copying objects. Entire objects or groups of objects can be moved from one place on the screen to another. One object can be moved by pointing to one of its reference points and then pointing to a new location. One or more objects can be moved by putting a "window" around them and then moving the window. In similar fashion, objects already on the screen can be copied to other locations on the screen.

Mirroring objects. Objects already on the screen can be mirrored; that is, they can be reproduced in other places on the screen as if they were reflected from a mirror. This is true whether the object is a basic geometric shape, a screen area marked with a window, or a named component. This capability is extremely useful when symmetrical objects are being drawn. In this case, half of the object can be drawn and then mirrored to create the other half automatically. Mirroring can be done vertically, horizontally, or at an angle. The mirrored object can be touching the original or placed any desired distance away. While mirroring is somewhat similar to flipping a defined area when using a paint program, it generally offers more powerful alternatives than the flip operation.

Figure 13-12 shows an example of mirroring. In designing a broken pediment (a decorative affair that goes over a door or window), the left half might first be drawn as shown in the first frame of the illustration. This half was drawn with four straight lines and one arc. Upon completion of the left half of the object, mirroring can be used to automatically draw in the right half as shown in the second frame.

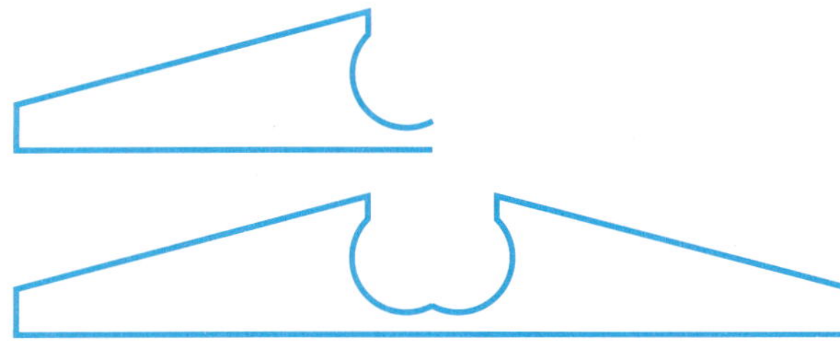

Figure 13-12
Mirroring allows objects to be reproduced on another part of the screen as if they were reflected from a mirror.

Adding Text

Text can be added wherever desired in a drawing by pointing at the location, giving the text entry command, and typing the text. Letters of text are essentially the same as pre-defined components on the drawing. Each letter is made up of geometric shapes. For example, a capital A is made of three straight lines with defined beginning and ending points; a lower-case e is made of a defined arc and a defined straight line. Since letters are made of these mathematically defined components, they can be manipulated the same as any other objects once they are in place; that is, they can be resized, moved, or rotated.

Using Layers

CAD programs typically provide the ability to work in layers on a given drawing. This makes it possible to isolate different kinds of components to make working on them easier. In the design of a house, for example, one layer might contain the layout of the walls, another the fixtures, another the electrical plan, and another the heating and air conditioning plan. By selecting options, the designer can have any number of layers visible at the same time, while drawing and editing are done on one selected layer. In other words, while the designer is working on the fixtures for a house on one layer, the walls on another layer are entirely unaffected by anything that is done, even though they are visible on the screen at the same time.

When plotting or printing finished drawings, selections can again be made by layers. For example, the designer could plot just the wall layer and electrical layer for the electrician or just the walls and the heating and air conditioning for the contractor.

Automatic Dimensioning

Virtually all blueprints contain dimensions. For example, in the plan for a house, the sizes of all the rooms are given. While dimensions can be placed on a drawing manually, much labor is saved by the ability of CAD programs to automatically compute and print all of the desired dimensions on the drawing. The operator simply indicates the points at which dimensions should be given, and the program does the rest.

Using Graphing Software

In contrast to paint programs which work from artistic input and CAD programs that create and place mathematically defined objects, graphing programs do their work from existing data. The data is converted by the software into graphic images that represent the data.

The user interface varies tremendously from one graphing program to another. Many popular spreadsheet and database programs contain modules for making graphs of their data. Additionally, many stand-alone programs are available.

Graphs are also frequently known as charts. Among the frequently used types of graphs are bar graphs, pie charts, line graphs, and area charts. These are discussed in the following sections. With each graph is an example of the data used to create it. The data is shown in the format in which it would appear on a spreadsheet.

Bar Graphs

Bar graphs represent data quantities by the lengths of the bars that are drawn. These graphs are good for showing differences between items. Each item is represented by one bar whose length indicates the value of the item. The bars may be either vertical or horizontal. Some programs use the terms "bar chart" when referring to graphs with horizontal bars and "column chart" when referring to graphs with vertical bars.

Look at Figure 13-13. This illustration shows the data from the spreadsheet that was developed in Chapter 12 as it can be represented in a bar chart (column chart in the vocabulary of some programs, since the bars are vertical). Generally the title to a graph is supplied by the operator of the software.

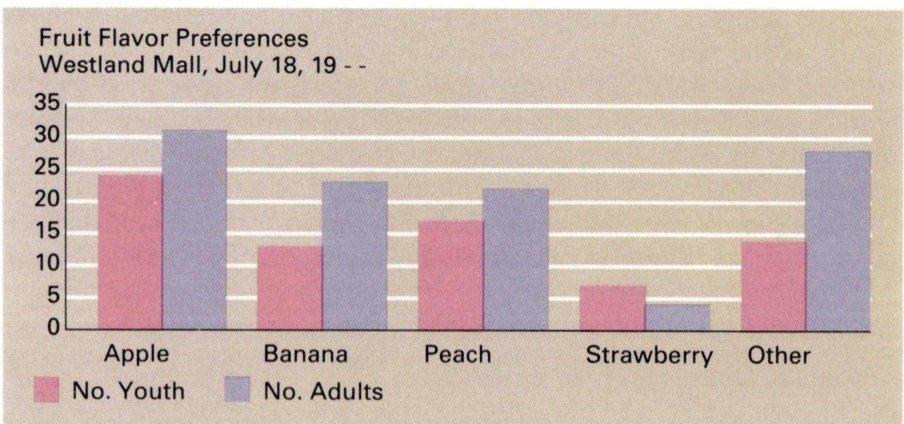

Figure 13-13
A bar graph represents data quantities by the lengths of the bars that are drawn.

FLAVOR PREFERENCES

FLAVOR	NO. YOUTH	NO. ADULTS
Apple	24	31
Banana	13	23
Peach	17	22
Strawberry	7	4
Other	14	28

In preparing bar graphs, the entire length of the bars should be shown. That is, the bars should begin at zero on the scale and extend as far as necessary. For example, if the smallest quantity being graphed is a test score of 80 and the largest is a score of 100, the temptation might exist to cut off the portions of the bars representing scores from 0 to 70. This would result in a graph with bars starting at 70 and extending to 100. This would then have the effect of amplifying or exaggerating the differences; under these circumstances, for example, the bar of a person who scored 90 would be twice as long as that of a person who scored 80, making it appear that the better score was twice as high. Obviously that is not the case, as showing all of the bars would quickly indicate.

Pie Charts

A **pie chart,** as its name implies, divides a total entity into its component parts. In other words, it slices a pie into various-sized pieces to represent the different percentages of each component. To illustrate the concept, look at Figure 13-14. It combines the flavor choices for youth and adults that were used in Figure 13-13. Note in Figure 13-14 that the spreadsheet has added a third column that represents the total number of youths and adults. This new column is used to produce the graph. The graphing program automatically computes the percentages from the values in this column.

FLAVOR PREFERENCES

FLAVOR	NO. YOUTH	NO. ADULTS	TOTAL
Apple	24	31	55
Banana	13	23	36
Peach	17	22	39
Strawberry	7	4	11
Other	14	28	42

Figure 13-14
A pie chart divides a total entity into its component parts.

Line Graphs

While bar graphs are generally used to show comparisons and pie charts are used to represent a division of a whole into its parts, **line graphs** are used to show changes in the same data series over a period of time. For example, to chart the sales of a business over a period of months, a line graph would be appropriate. Refer to Figure 13-15 for such an example. Shirlann's Snack Shack, located in a local shopping mall, sells three lines of merchandise—frozen yogurt, hot dogs, and beverages. The sales for each of these lines of merchandise are plotted for each month, and the plotting points are connected. This results in a line for each item. The line moves up and down as the volume moves up and down from month to month.

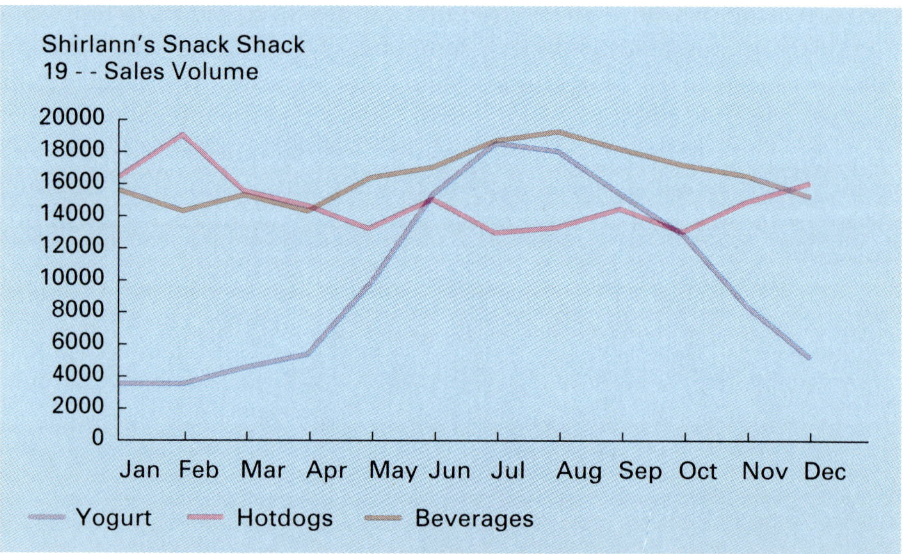

Figure 13-15
A line graph is used to show changes in a data series over a period of time.

	JAN	FEB	MAR	APR	MAY	JUN	JUL	AUG	SEP	OCT	NOV	DEC
Yogurt	3543	3417	4321	5234	9832	15323	18480	17983	15323	12983	8329	5323
Hotdogs	16323	18983	15434	14323	13234	14987	12893	13312	14323	12983	14832	15921
Beverages	15432	14323	15329	14382	16382	16983	18732	19387	18323	17398	16432	15233

Area Charts

The line graphs in the previous section show change over time for each of the three items being sold. It would be advantageous to Shirlann, however, to see the total sales of the shop as well as the sales of the individual items. To do this, she may use an **area chart.** Such a chart adds the total sales figures for each month and shows the total as well as the size of the individual components. This is illustrated in Figure 13-16, which shows two graphs. The first is based on a bar graph, while the second is based on a line graph. The data for these charts is the same as that in Figure 13-15.

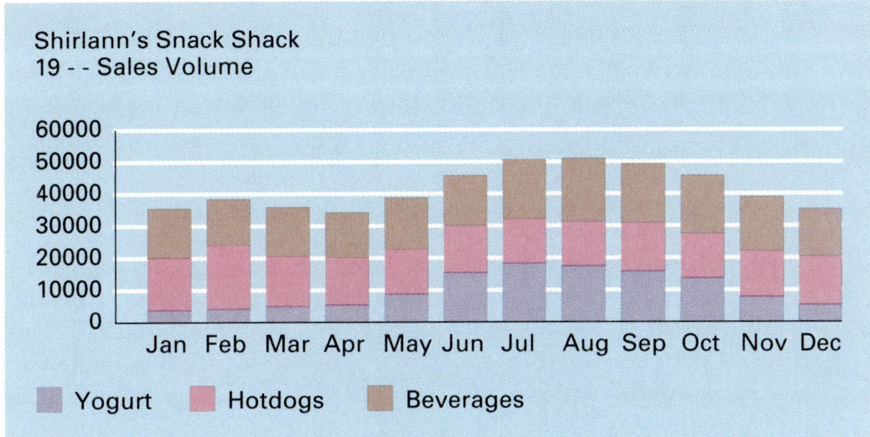

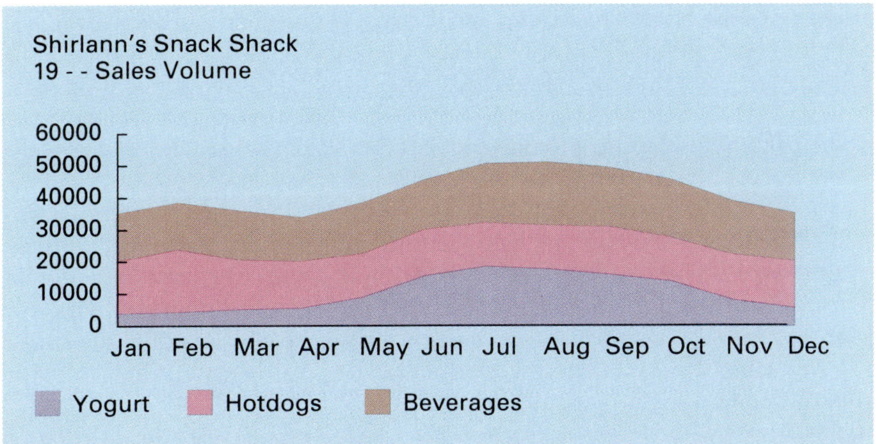

Figure 13-16
Area charts, which show both the total and the size of the individual components, can be represented by different types of graphs.

Here is an example of how to read the graphs. In January, Shirlann's sold $3,543 of yogurt, $16,323 of hot dogs, and $15,432 of beverages. The total of these three figures, $35,298, is shown on the graphs. Note that the total for the month is divided into three parts on the graphs—one part for each of the three products sold.

THE NEW YOU—THROUGH COMPUTER POWER

Are you one of those people who is never happy with clothing you find in the store because the manufacturer never quite manages to size the clothing to perfectly fit your perfect figure? Are you never happy with the hair style cut by your favorite stylist because the hair stylist never makes you look like the pictures in the portfolio?

Of course there is a solution to the clothing problem. Just go to an expensive custom tailor who will measure you, make a garment, then fiddle with it here and there until all is well. Besides being very time consuming, such custom clothing is very expensive—far beyond the means of most folks.

Don't despair, however, for help is on the way via computer and some strategic applications software. Systems that are just now coming into use should soon be widespread. In such a system, you will still go to the store, select the desired design, and be measured. Your new garment will still be ready in a few days for you to try. Instead of being measured by a tailor, however, you are measured by a computer. In addition to the traditional measurements it also takes into account your posture. If you want to see how you would look in the finished garment, there's no reason a new generation of sophisticated graphics software will not be able to provide the preview—scaled exactly to your body size and shape and appearing in the proper color and pattern.

After you are measured by the computer, it sizes the selected pattern to be a perfect match to your physique, and the seamers go to work. With such a perfect pattern, the finished garment is almost certain to fit as well as please.

While under present software you still select fabric for a garment in the traditional way—from swatches—another new development will eventually make it possible for you to have fabric custom designed if you don't like any of the available patterns. Under this new technique, developed at the Georgia Institute of Technology, a pattern is designed on the computer using standard graphic design software. Then the pattern is printed onto fabric using a color copying machine.

Computers are being used more and more frequently and creatively in the clothing industry.

While all along you have been able to try on clothes and have them tailored to fit before appearing in public, the solution to the hair problem hasn't been quite so elegant. The choices were to either try on a wig of the style you're considering or take your chances; once the hair is cut, it's too late to bring it back. Now, the computer can help solve that problem, too.

Salons are beginning to use a computer system which stores the images of a large number of hair styles such as would be seen in a printed portfolio. The same style might even be stored in several variations to take into account differences in head shape.

Upon your entry into the salon, your face is framed by a television camera that feeds its output directly into the computer for storage. Then, with the image of your face and all the hair styles stored in the computer system, the consultant can instantly call up your image onto the screen with any hair style you may be considering. To see the effects of different color treatments, simple commands will make the desired adjustments in the image.

At last, thanks to the imagery of the computer, you can have no-risk clothing and no-risk hair.

CHAPTER SUMMARY

- Graphics refers to any pictorial representation that can be produced by the computer.
- Graphics software is any software that can produce "pictures" or "art."
- Paint programs allow a person to do "art" on the computer screen.
- CAD programs are used for computer-aided design and drafting.
- Graphics programs can produce graphs or charts from data.
- Among other things, computer graphics are used for art, computer-aided instruction, computer-aided design and drafting, scientific study, television and movies, and presentation graphics.
- Paint programs give the user access to computer versions of commonly used tools such as pencils, brushes, paint rollers, and paint sprayers, as well as erasers and special effects tools.
- Freehand drawings may be made with paint programs.
- Text may be entered into the images made with paint programs.
- Paint program images are made from individual picture elements (pixels) that are set to the appropriate color.
- Paint programs can use image libraries to assist in the development of pictures.
- CAD programs base their images on objects made from mathematical formulas.

- Among the shapes that can be drawn with CAD programs are straight lines, rectangles, polygons, circles, arcs, ellipses, and complex curves.
- Any object drawn using the geometric shapes of a CAD program can be named and used as a component in the drawing.
- Component libraries are available for CAD programs.
- Since CAD objects are mathematical they can easily be moved, reshaped, resized, copied, or mirrored.
- Text may be added as desired to CAD images; the text is also represented as mathematical formulas.
- CAD programs allow the use of different layers for different purposes in the drawing.
- Dimensions can automatically be computed and placed by CAD programs.
- Graphing programs produce their output from inputs of existing data.
- Bar graphs are good for comparing different data items, with the length of each bar representing the data value.
- A pie chart shows the divisions of a "whole" into its component "slices"; it is excellent for showing any situation where a total is made up of several lesser amounts.
- Line graphs show changes in one or more series of data over a period of time.
- Area charts show the sum of the parts, usually over a period of time.

KEY TERMS

The following key terms were introduced or redefined in this chapter:

area chart
bar graph
CAD program
component
computer graphics
graphics software
graphing program
image library
line graph
paint program
pie chart
pixel
presentation graphics
reference points
tools

REVIEW QUESTIONS

1. What is meant by computer graphics? (Obj. 1)
2. List the three common types of graphics software. (Obj. 1)
3. Name and describe six uses for computer graphics. (Obj. 1)
4. What characteristics define a paint program? (Obj. 2)
5. Describe the general method of using a paint program. (Obj. 2)
6. What is the purpose of image libraries? (Obj. 2)
7. What characteristics define a CAD program? (Obj. 3)

8. Describe the general method of using a CAD program. (Obj. 3)
9. What are components and what is their purpose? (Obj. 3)
10. What characteristics define graphing software? (Obj. 4)
11. Describe four common types of graphs and briefly describe the kinds of data they are best at graphing. (Obj. 4)

CHALLENGE ACTIVITIES

1. If you have software available, learn how to use a paint program. You may want to start by drawing the examples shown in this chapter. (Obj. 2)
2. If you have software available, learn how to use a CAD program. Draw the layout of your classroom or your home. (Obj. 3)
3. If you have software available, learn how to use a graphing program. Graph the data from the examples in this chapter. (Obj. 4)
4. Visit an architectural firm or engineering firm to observe how computer-aided design and drafting software is used there. (Obj. 3)
5. Visit a television station to observe how graphics software is used there. (Obj. 1)
6. Prepare a research report on how the movie and television industry uses graphics. (Obj. 1)

CHAPTER 14

COMMUNICATION

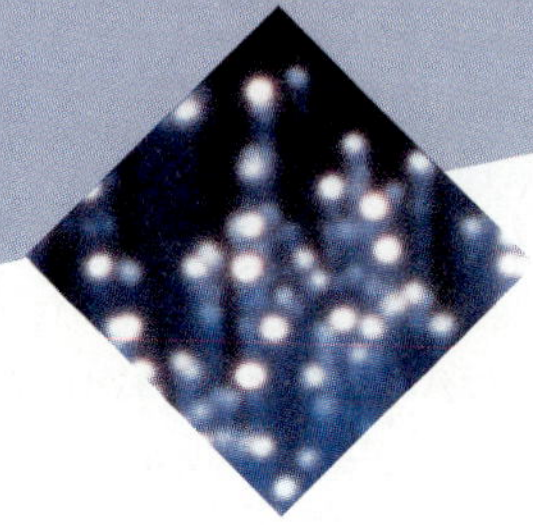

LEARNING OBJECTIVES

After studying this chapter, you will be able to:

1. **Identify the advantages and disadvantages of data communication.**
2. **Identify popular uses of communication hardware and software.**
3. **Identify the components used when communicating with multi-user systems.**
4. **Describe the characteristics of communication devices which are directly connected.**
5. **Describe the characteristics of communication devices which are indirectly connected.**
6. **Identify and describe the common modes of transmitting data.**
7. **Describe bandwidth transmission characteristics.**
8. **Recognize and describe common communication architectures.**
9. **Compare the capabilities and differences among common transmission carriers.**

INTRODUCTION

Some computer systems are stand-alone systems; that is, one processor serves one user. The user may be performing word processing, accounting, or any number of different applications. Other systems, however, must be able to serve more than one user at the same time. An airline reservation system, for example, must be able to send (transmit) and receive reservation requests from thousands of remote locations. This process of transmitting and receiving information from one source (or location) to another is called **communication.** In the computer industry, communication of data from one location to another is known as **data communication.** Data communication is accomplished by using communication hardware, software, and transmission carriers. Computers that are connected to communicate with each other are referred to as being **networked.** In this chapter you will learn how communication hardware and software enable computers and terminals to communicate with each other. In addition, you will learn how several of the common transmission carriers (i.e. telephone lines, satellites, coaxial cable) facilitate this communication and review several common environments in which data communication is used.

ASPECTS OF DATA COMMUNICATION

The ability of computers to communicate with each other or with many terminals has many advantages as well as disadvantages. Some of the advantages of data communication include, but are not limited to, the following issues:

1. More individuals can be users of the hardware and software which is available.
2. Expensive equipment can be shared among several users (as opposed to each person who needs specific capabilities having an individual system), thereby reducing the cost to each user.
3. Data can be shared among the users.
4. The use of a single processor forces standardization in the procedures which must be performed in order to achieve a task.
5. The computer hardware is used more effectively and kept busy via the utilization of more users.
6. Many tasks can be completed more conveniently and efficiently than would have been possible without communication hardware and software.

Communication hardware and software enable brokers to access the data services of the London Stock Exchange.

The use of communication hardware and software is not without its negative aspects. Some of the disadvantages of data communication include the following:

1. If the mainframe computer goes down (is inoperable due to a breakdown and/or repair) the users are unable to use the system.

Consider what would happen in an airline reservation system if the mainframe went down. The hundreds and even thousands of terminals connected to it would be inoperative. It might even bring the entire airline to a standstill. Obviously, this cannot be allowed to happen. Such critical systems usually have two mainframe computers. When one is down the other can be used until the first one is again operative. Also, battery-powered backup (or other alternate power sources) is available in the event of electrical outages.

2. Costs for backup systems and maintenance of backup systems can be very high.
3. Cost for transmission carriers can be high.

Consider how expensive it would be to make a twenty-four hour, long-distance telephone call each day of the week, each week of the month, and each month of the year. Now multiply this by the number of remote locations which must be connected to the computer. (Later in this chapter different methods of transmission and ways in which this cost can be reduced will be discussed.)

4. Because of the sophisticated hardware and software required in a communication environment, highly trained and experienced individuals must be employed to program and maintain the data communication system.

5. Because communication hardware and software must be an integral part of a computer's hardware and operating system, potential incompatibility and conflicts exist at many levels.

Incompatibility can occur because some communication adapters (used to convert parallel transmission into serial transmission and vice versa) will not interface with certain video devices, and some communication software will not work with certain RAM-resident programs. Also, some application uses will cause the entire network to grind to a halt under a heavy processing load.

Although computer networking has become easier and more productive through better hardware and software, it is still not a simple solution to all problems. Most often the decision of whether or not to use data communication is a matter of weighing the advantages against the disadvantages or the cost against the benefits derived. However, in some environments, data communication is used because it is the only way to get the job done. In either case, the goal is to develop efficient ways to keep the system operative when it is most needed and to minimize the costs of transmission, additional hardware, software, and system maintenance.

USES OF COMMUNICATION HARDWARE AND SOFTWARE

It is estimated that by the early 1990s, ten percent of all small computers will be connected to some type of communication network. Based upon the projected sales of computers, this implies a growth rate of a million computers a year that will be utilized in a communication network environment. The primary reason for this growth in communication applications is the availability of new communication software which can take advantage of new communication hardware capabilities. Such capabilities include sharing of hard disks and files, sharing of expensive printers, and the ability to communicate with mainframes while maintaining the computer's local processing power.

Communication network users come in all sizes, from the small, local user to the large corporation with thousands of remote terminals. The applications for which communication is used are also varied. Some examples of communication usage in this rapidly expanding area include: bulletin board systems, information services, bibliographic services, stock exchange services, and electronic banking and transfer of funds.

Bulletin Board Systems

A BBS (bulletin board system) may range from a sophisticated, nationally developed mainframe or small computer system to a simple information exchange system used by a few individuals. Typical users of a BBS include salespersons with offices far removed from their company's main office. They are sent general, company-related messages and announcements as well as personal messages relating specifically to their jobs. Several computer manufacturers have established a BBS to keep their software developers informed of changes and new announcements in their product lines. New software enhancements can be downloaded to their developers' computers, saving much time and expense. (**Download** refers to the transferring of data from a file stored on the **host**—the computer that controls data communication—computer's disk to other computers' disks. **Upload** refers to the transferring of data from files stored on other computers' disks to the host computer's disk.) Individual computer users and computer user groups use bulletin board systems for exchanging information, ideas, and software which are of common interest. Many high schools, colleges, and universities use a BBS for communicating with other students and faculty, for sharing and exchanging ideas and information, and for research.

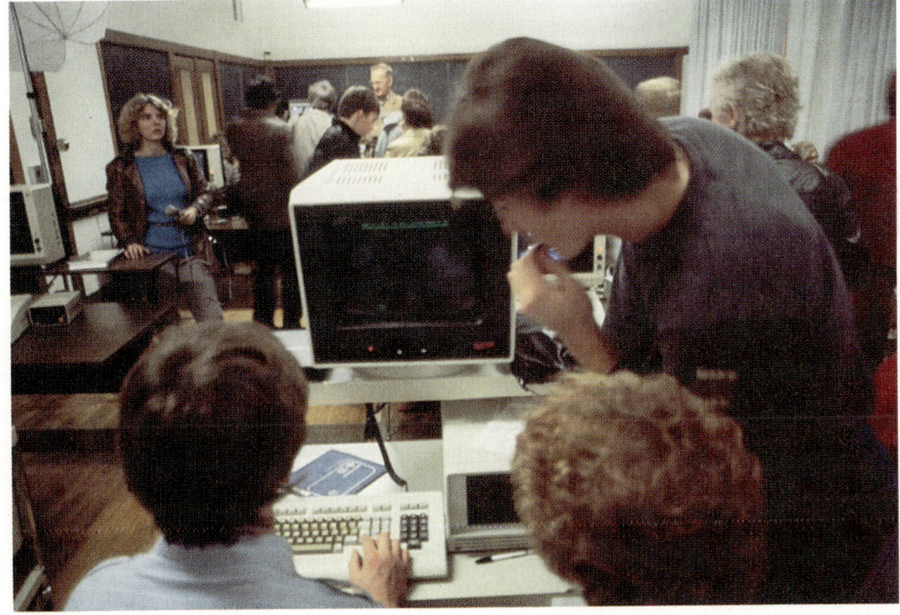

A school can use a bulletin board system to communicate with other schools.

A BBS typically consists of three different services: (1) electronic mail, (2) general messages and announcements, and (3) a file library that can be downloaded to the user's computer. The communication software which drives a BBS can range from a simple program that permits one computer to communicate with another to sophisticated networking software servicing thousands of users over a vast geographic area. Typically, the more sophisticated the software, the greater the number of different devices that can access the service and the greater the number of applications that are available to its users.

Electronic Mail

Electronic Mail is a term given to software that permits users with valid passwords to **log on** (establish connection by dialing the telephone number and keying in the valid password) to a BBS for the purpose of sending and receiving messages to/from each other. All valid users have their own "mailbox" on the disk of the host computer. Messages can be directed to another user's mailbox as shown in Figure 14-1. When that user accesses the mailbox, the message(s) it contains is sent to the proper terminal for display or printout.

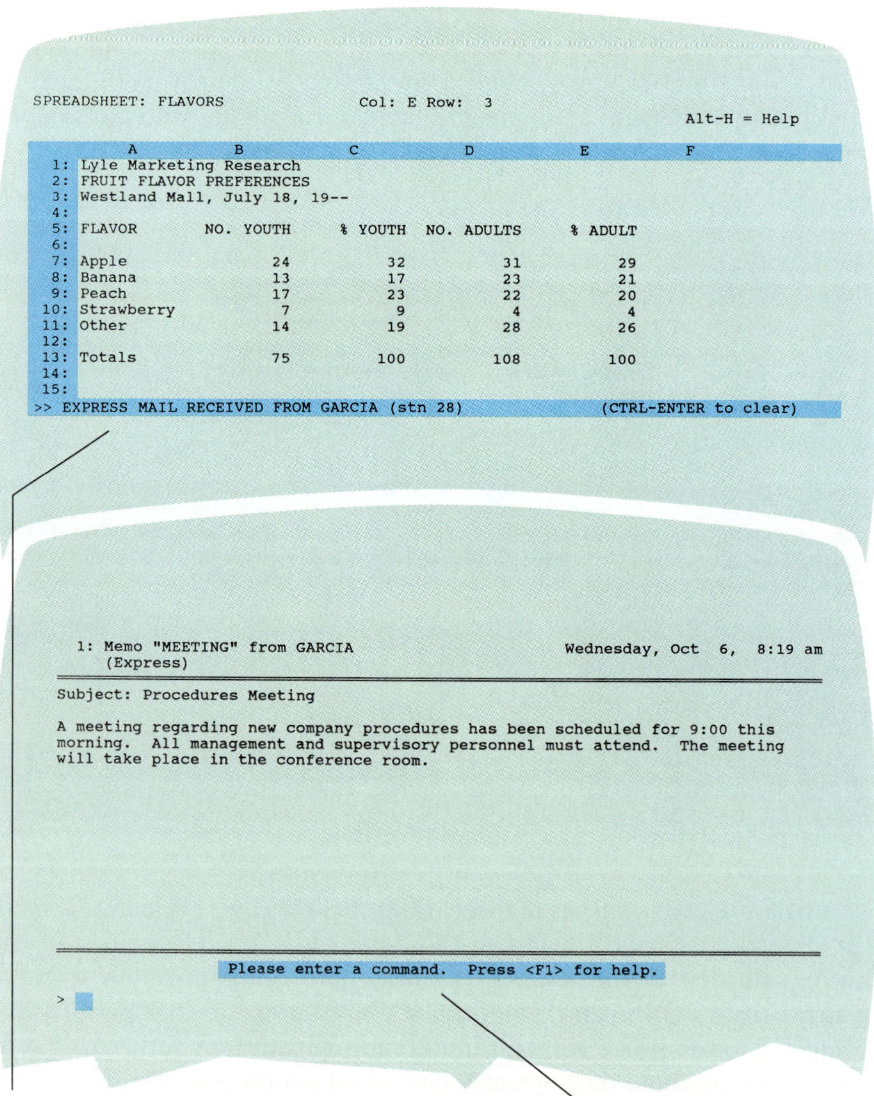

Figure 14-1
Electronic mail permits users to electronically send and receive messages.

General Messages and Announcements

The public message service performs a function similar to the bulletin board in your school. Messages and announcements are placed in a special mailbox for all valid users. The user can then access this special mailbox to receive all the messages and announcements it contains.

File Library

The file library service enables users of a BBS to store programs for sharing with others or to receive software programs already stored in the library. The library of a BBS is stored on the host computer's disk. A list and brief description of each software program stored in the library may be accessed. From the list, a software program can be selected and downloaded to a valid user's computer for subsequent execution or storage.

Information Services

An information network typically consists of sophisticated software running on a large mainframe host computer with large databases capable of providing a wide variety of services to thousands of users all across the country. These systems provide services related to local and national news, weather, sporting events, travel, recipes, shopping, tax advice, computer games, theater listings, and home record keeping, to name a few. Commercial users (businesses and industries) as well as individuals subscribe to the service. A subscriber is given a valid password and telephone number which permits access to the information service's host computer's databases. The user may contract for all or any of the services available, and, once logged on, can access any of the contracted services. The subscriber is usually billed for the amount of **connect time** (time spent communicating with the host computer over a communication channel).

Some information services provide recipes that can be downloaded to a computer in the cook's kitchen.

The popularity of these networks has led to an increased number of users and, in turn, an increase in the revenue generated. This increase in income has been reinvested in additional hardware, software, and databases capable of serving even more users. This has created a "snowball-rolling-down-the-hill" effect. That is, as the utilization of these systems grows, the revenue they generate increases. This in turn enables the money to be reinvested to expand the services in an effort to interest even more users in using the network.

Bibliographic Services

Bibliographic service communication networks have been established to provide retrieval of bibliographic citations. This type of information is necessary since many references needed by students and researchers are not available in their school and public libraries. This type of communication service is structured similarly to the information services discussed previously. Sophisticated software running on a mainframe computer with large databases allows that computer to act as the host computer for information inquiries. These inquiries from individual users, businesses, librarians, etc., may require access to a variety of different host computers and databases. For example, databases which contain information on sources such as popular magazines, newspapers, encyclopedias, international symposiums, corporate directories, and university research papers may be accessed.

In order to access this type of service, the user must obtain a valid password and telephone number of the desired bibliographic service. The user is then billed based on the amount of connect time. The user of a bibliographic service logs on to the system and responds to a series of questions related to the topic at hand. After all questions have been answered, the host computer quickly searches through its database(s) to find all the literature which it contains that meet the user's criteria. When the search is completed, the host computer sends the list of the literature (as well as where it can be found) to the user.

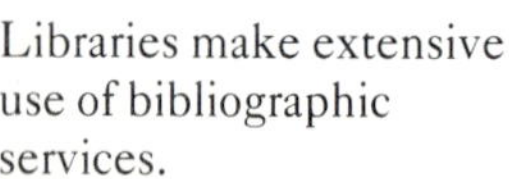
Libraries make extensive use of bibliographic services.

Stock Exchange Services

One of the largest and most popular communication applications is the stock exchange service used by many of the brokerage houses across the country. These brokerage houses provide the computer software, hardware, and communication channels which enable their remotely located offices to work with individual investors. A typical stock exchange communication network is capable of providing a wide range of services which include:

1. Comprehensive company profiles for interested investors, including earnings forecasts, price/volume charts, and financial history.
2. Up-to-date stock prices and quotes.
3. Market news and analyst opinions minutes after they are written.
4. The ability to buy and sell directly over the communication link.
5. Individual customer portfolio management.
6. Alerting the customer to critical situations and times (i.e. when stock prices reach a certain limit established by the customer, when stock options are about to expire, when bonds are about to mature).
7. Individual reporting capabilities which include all investment activities, gains/losses, and year-to-date summaries.
8. Tracking of individual securities or selected stocks.

Software is available that allows stockbrokers to obtain information directly from the stock exchange.

In addition to these services which are available through brokerage houses, communication services are available which permit the independent investor many of these same capabilities. To utilize these services, independent investors must use modems (devices which enable computers to transmit data over telephone lines) and communication software that is compatible with their computers as well as the investment brokerage house's system. They must also obtain a password (or an account number) and the appropriate telephone number. Once logged on to this type of service, independent-minded investors can make decisions, buy and sell, and manage portfolios from their own offices and homes.

Electronic Banking and Transfer of Funds

Another of the largest and most popular users of communication systems is the banking industry. Large banks rely heavily on communication hardware and software to link remotely located offices to their central computer systems.

These communication links permit each remotely located office to serve their customers' needs with all the services the entire bank system is capable of providing. Bank customers can deposit their paychecks into their savings and checking accounts, write checks, withdraw funds, obtain loans, make loan payments, and even pay their utility bills from any of the bank's offices. Electronic teller machines, located in shopping malls and other public access areas, can also be used to make deposits and obtain cash from checking accounts.

Banks rely heavily on communication hardware and software to better serve their customers.

In addition to serving the needs of the individual banking customer, banks rely on communication hardware and software to electronically transfer data (including funds) from one bank to another. For example, the money which is paid an employee in the form of a paycheck may be written on another bank of which the employer is a customer. These funds are electronically transferred from the employer's bank to the employee's bank to cover the amount of the paycheck.

COMMUNICATING WITH MULTI-USER SYSTEMS

Now that some of the uses and capabilities of communication software have been introduced, the way in which communication systems work can be discussed. In addition, this section will discuss how various hardware devices can be connected to enable them to communicate with each other and be utilized by more than one user.

A **multi-user system** can be defined as any computer system which is used by more than one person. As indicated previously, in a multi-user environment, one computer—called the host computer—controls all the communication activities of the terminals connected to it. (Note: The term **terminal** as used in this chapter refers to any device, including a computer, capable of sending and receiving information in a communication environment.) Multi-user systems may range from a large mainframe host computer which controls thousands of terminals or other computers to a personal host computer with only one other terminal or personal computer connected. The applications of these systems range from large information services systems to small businesses in which two personal computers are connected to each other for the purpose of word processing file sharing.

All communication which takes place between computers is under control of communication software running in the host computer. This software must be written in such a way as to follow formal, established rules governing the format and signaling of message exchanges between two or more communicating devices. These formal rules of communication exchange are called **protocols.** Protocols have been developed to permit hardware from different manufacturers to communicate with each other. These protocols are discussed later in this chapter.

Regardless of the size or power of the computer, the number of terminals, the sophistication of the software, or the complexity of the application, all data communication systems must have a passageway by which data can flow to and from the computer. This passageway is called the **communication channel.** It serves as the carrier of data that is transmitted between the computer and its terminals. Communication channels are used to transmit and receive data whether the terminals are **local terminals** (near the computer) or **remote terminals** (sometimes thousands of miles away). There are two types of communication channels: those that handle local terminals (called direct connections) and those that handle remote terminals (called indirect connections).

Direct Connections

A **direct connection** can be defined as a local host computer and one or more local terminals physically connected by coaxial cable and under the control of communication software. A **coaxial cable** is a high-quality communication channel that serves as the carrier of data transmitted between the host computer and its terminals. This is the same cable commonly used to connect the antenna of a TV cable system to a television set.

A coaxial cable (bottom) serves as a carrier of data transmitted between a host computer and its terminals.

In addition to a coaxial cable, two other components are required before a direct connection can be established: (1) a communication software package which will run on the host computer, and (2) hardware in both the host and terminal(s) which enables communication to take place.

The communication software that controls the communication system of the host computer differs from the operating systems software. Unlike the host computer's operating system software which allows the computer to execute programs and access input/output devices, communication software performs a variety of tasks related specifically to data communication. For example, it must establish initial contact with the terminal(s) with which it will be communicating (called a **handshake**). Once the handshake is completed, the software must direct transmission of data to and from the host computer, handle errors, and deal with interrupt conditions (such as operator intervention).

The software also can be used to control the security of the network. That is, different users can be allowed different kinds of access (read-only or modify) to data on various terminals. **Read-only access** allows a user to look at data, print data, or make computations with it, but not to change it. **Modify access** gives a user the power to change data. This security is controlled by passwords.

There are many different communication software packages available. Some are designed and written to handle large mainframe systems while others control small computer systems. They range from very sophisticated software which permits large volumes of data to be accessed and transmitted to packages which permit a simple transfer of data from one source to another. Because there are so many packages to choose from, the user of a communication system must carefully evaluate needs before selecting the software which best meets those needs.

A second component which must be available before communication can take place is hardware. The host computer and each terminal that is connected to it must contain communication hardware as illustrated in Figure 14-2.

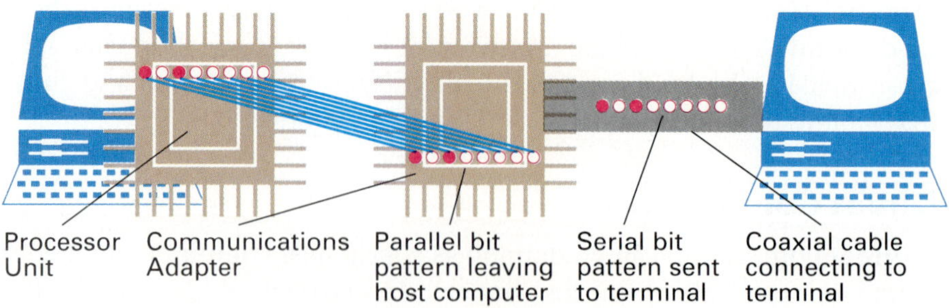

Figure 14-2
Communication hardware must be available before communication between computers can take place.

The communication hardware for a mainframe computer is called a communication controller, and the hardware for a small computer is called a communication adapter. A **communication controller** is often a separate unit which is directly connected to the CPU of the mainframe computer. A **communication adapter** is a circuit board which fits inside a small computer. Both are used to convert parallel transmission into serial transmission and vice versa. That is, when data is received by the host, it enters the coaxial cable through serial transmission (one bit at a time). The communication adapter or controller groups the bits into parallel transmission (one byte at a time) before sending them to the host's memory for processing. Conversely, when data is sent from the host to a terminal, it enters the adapter or controller as parallel transmission (one byte at a time). The communication adapter or controller breaks the byte apart into its appropriate bit pattern and sends each bit through the coaxial cable as serial transmission to the terminal. When these bits are received by the terminal they are again grouped back into parallel transmission for display or processing.

In a communication system, several CRTs can be directly connected to a large mainframe host computer. In this system, each terminal (CRT) can be connected to the host's communication controller via its own coaxial cable.

Small computers can also be directly connected to one another. This type of direct connection can be used to download (transfer data from a file stored on the host computer's disk) to the other computer's disk. The communication software running in the host could also be used to upload (transfer data from a file stored on the computer's disk) to the host computer's disk. Note that although each computer is produced by a different manufacturer, both are able to download and upload files with each other through a communication environment.

Indirect Connections

An **indirect connection** can be defined as two or more remote terminals connected to a host computer via a long-distance transmission carrier and which are under the control of communication software. This type of communication is frequently referred to as telecommunication. The term **telecommunication,** as used in this text, refers to the technique and technology of communication by electrical or electronic means. Long-distance transmission carriers which facilitate telecommunication include telephone lines, satellites, microwaves, and fiber optics cables. These forms of transmission carriers serve as the communication channels over which data can be transmitted between communicating devices.

The components which are required for indirect connection are the same as those required for direct connection; however, in addition, a modem is required. A **modem** (modem is a term derived from the terms **mod**ulation and **dem**odulation) is a device which converts digital data consisting of bits into an analog signal (called **modulation**) that can be transmitted over telephone lines. At the receiving site, another modem must convert the analog signal back into digital data (called **demodulation**) before it can enter the receiving terminal. Data must be converted back and forth between digital data and analog sound because the telephone lines were designed to carry voice (sound or analog) data, not computer data (digital). Therefore, in order to use a transmission carrier which is an analog carrier of data, a modem is needed to convert the computer's digital data (serial transmission) into analog sounds which are then sent over the telephone lines.

Data can be transmitted over various communication channels at various speeds. The speed at which data can be transmitted is measured in baud rates. A **baud rate** can be defined as the number of signal events per second. Since data is transmitted a bit at a time, and each bit represents a signal, baud rates are commonly measured as the number of bits per second that can be transmitted over a particular communication channel. This rate is determined by both the capability of the modem and the type of transmission carrier. For example, common baud rates when using telephone lines as the transmission carrier for bulletin board systems are 300, 1,200, or 2,400 baud. Transmission at a rate of 300 baud is approximately 30 characters per second. Because standard phone lines are designed to carry voice communication (voice transmission is equivalent to approximately 2,000 baud), speeds faster than 2,400 baud may create problems of lost or distorted data. Later in this chapter you will learn how higher quality transmission carriers (i.e. satellites, microwaves, direct telephone lines) are capable of accurately transmitting data at rates of, and exceeding, 9,600 baud.

A salesperson can use a portable computer and communication hardware and software to transmit information to the company's host computer.

There are three basic types of modems used for indirect connection: (1) an acoustic coupler, (2) an internal modem, and (3) an external modem. An **acoustic coupler** is a modem that connects to the computer or terminal by a cable. (In some models the acoustic coupler is built directly into the computer or terminal's casing.) It contains two rubber cups that permit a standard telephone headset to be inserted. The remote user of an acoustic coupler simply dials the telephone number of the host computer. When connection is made, the host computer's software sends a high-pitched tone indicating that it is ready to establish communication. The user then inserts the telephone headset into the acoustic coupler, a handshake is established, and data communication begins. As an example, a salesperson can use a portable computer to transmit sales information to the company's host computer. Once this information is received by the host computer, the data can be used to record the sale, prepare an invoice, calculate the salesperson's commission, and initiate the shipment of the merchandise to the customer.

Acoustic coupler modems are most commonly used with slow-speed terminals and small, portable computers. They typically transmit data at rates of 300 or 1,200 baud over standard telephone lines.

An **internal modem** is a circuit board that is built in or plugged directly into the computer or terminal. It has a standard telephone cord that is plugged directly into a standard telephone outlet. Most internal modems have automatic dial-up capabilities. The user of an internal modem simply executes the communication software and tells it (via keyboard commands) to dial the telephone number of the terminal to which communication must be established. The software dials the number, the terminal answers, a handshake is established, and data communication begins. A diskette accompanying the internal modem contains the communication software that interacts with the internal modem.

Like acoustic couplers, internal modems used with small computers most often use the standard telephone line as their transmission carrier. As a result, transmission speeds are commonly 300 or 1,200 baud.

Large mainframe computers often have internal modem circuitry built directly in the communication controller device. A mainframe system which uses standard telephone lines as its transmission carrier typically transmits at 1,200 or 2,400 baud. However, the internal modem circuitry built in the communication controller is capable of much higher rates of transmission (up to 120,000 baud). These higher rates of transmission are achieved by using a variety of high-tech transmission carriers which will be discussed later in this chapter.

An **external modem** is a modem contained in a small housing which is attached to the computer by a cable and plugged into a standard telephone outlet by a telephone cord. It functions similarly to the internal modem. The major difference is that it is attached to the computer externally.

An external modem must be connected to the computer by a cable.

External modems are commonly used by both small and large computers. Transmission rates are typically 300, 1,200, or 2,400 baud when using standard telephone lines.

Regardless of the type of modem used (acoustic coupler, internal, or external), both the host computer and the terminal with which it communicates must have an identical or a compatible modem. For example, the transmission speeds of both the sending and receiving modems must be the same, and the protocol used by both must be the same. Specifications regarding baud rate, type of transmission carrier, and protocol (to name a few) are often keyed in as information to the communication software. Once this information is known by the communication software, it can interact with the communication hardware to allow communication to take place.

A new form of telephone service, called an Integrated Services Digital Network (ISDN), operates digitally and does not require the use of a modem. Such service is gradually becoming available in more areas.

TRANSMISSION MODES

There are three modes in which data can be transmitted over a communication channel: (1) simplex mode, (2) half-duplex mode, and (3) full-duplex mode. In the **simplex mode** of transmission, data flows in one direction only. Figure 14-3 illustrates a simplex mode of transmission between a mainframe computer and a personal computer.

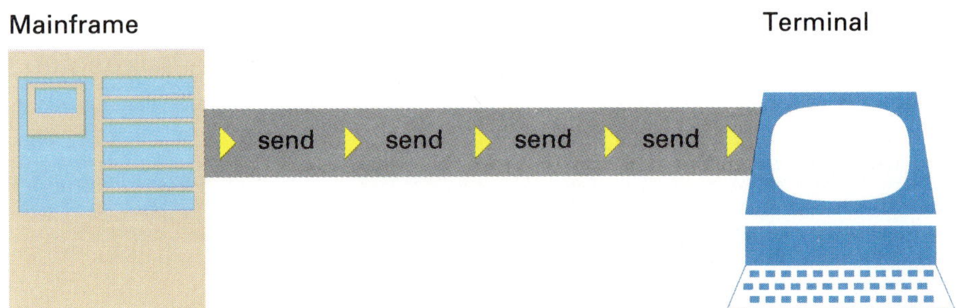

Figure 14-3
Data flows in only one direction in the simplex mode of data transmission.

Notice that the arrow in Figure 14-3 indicates that data is flowing one way (from the mainframe computer to the personal computer). In this environment the host computer could never receive data from the personal computer. Conversely, the personal computer could be used to send data to the mainframe just as long as its data flow is in that one direction. The simplex mode was one of the first modes of data transmission. It used slow-speed, low-quality telegraph lines that have given way to more modern transmission carriers. As a result, it is seldom used in today's modern communication systems.

In a **half-duplex mode** of transmission, data can be transmitted to and from each of the communicating devices but in only one direction at a time. Figure 14-4 illustrates a mainframe and a personal computer using a half-duplex mode of communication.

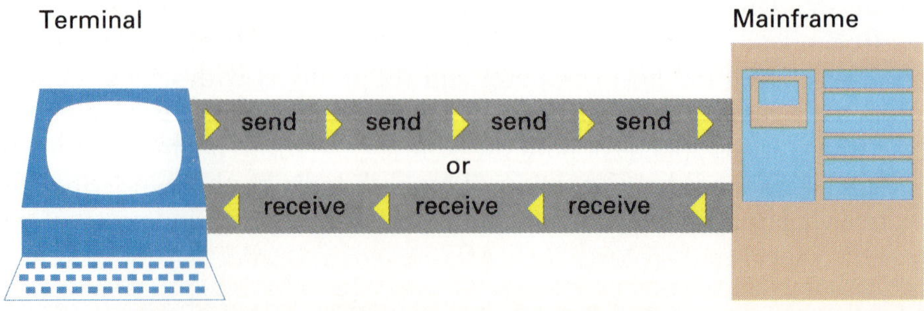

Figure 14-4
Data is transmitted to and from each communicating device, but in only one direction at a time, in a half-duplex mode of transmission.

A half-duplex mode is used when data must be sent in two directions. For example, data can be sent in one direction over a communication channel by a terminal to a host computer. When the data is received by the host, it must send a response back in the opposite direction to the terminal to let it know that the data was received and that it is ready to accept more. The time it takes the host to acknowledge receipt of data and indicate it is ready to accept more is called **turnaround time.** In this type of communication there is no need for data to flow both ways at the same time.

In a **full-duplex mode** of transmission, data can be transmitted in both directions at the same time. The same mainframe and personal computers are illustrated in Figure 14-5, but this time a full-duplex mode is used.

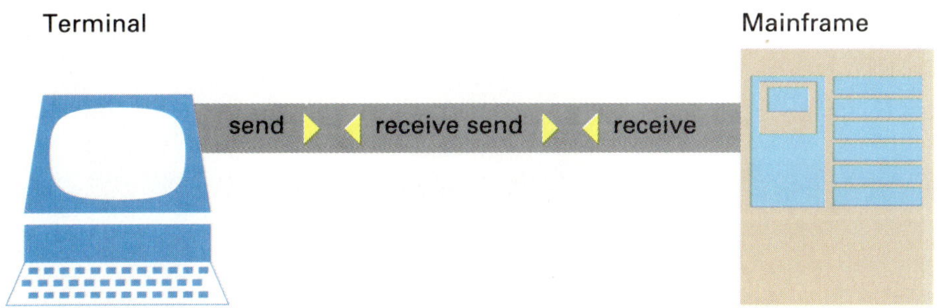

Figure 14-5
Data can be transmitted in both directions at the same time with a full-duplex mode of transmission.

A full-duplex mode is most commonly used for high-speed communication. Because transmission of data can flow in two directions at the same time, turnaround time is eliminated. The elimination of turnaround time alone yields nearly a 25 percent increase in the amount of data that can be transmitted in the same amount of time using a full-duplex mode instead of a half-duplex mode. In addition, high-quality transmission carriers capable of handling speeds up to 120,000 baud (error free) are frequently used for this mode's communication channel.

TRANSMISSION CHARACTERISTICS

Earlier you learned that the speed by which data can be transmitted over the communication channel is dependent on both the communication hardware and the transmission carrier. In this section you will learn more about how communication technology can increase transmission rates, optimize expensive communication channels, and form communication networks. In data communication, the speed by which data can be transmitted over a given communication channel is determined by the **grade,** or **bandwidth,** of that channel. There are three commonly used bandwidth communication channel categories: baseband, voice-grade, and broadband channels. **Baseband** channels transmit data one signal at a time similar to how a standard serial port sends one bit at a time to a printer. This type of channel transmits signals at very high speeds to direct-connected devices using inexpensive twisted-pair wiring, such as that used for telephones, or coaxial cable. The half-duplex mode of transmission is used in this type of channel. **Voice-grade bandwidth** channels are the most popular bandwidth used for telecommunication. This type of channel transmits data utilizing the half-duplex mode of transmission. Telephone lines are used as the transmission carrier for voice-grade bandwidth. **Broadband bandwidth** channels are also used for telecommunication. This type of channel commonly uses the full-duplex mode of transmission; therefore, high volumes of data can be transmitted at high rates of speed. Coaxial cables, microwaves, satellites, and fiber optics are used as the transmission carriers for this type of communication.

Fiber optics can be used to transmit high volumes of data at high rates of speed.

COMMUNICATION ARCHITECTURE

Another factor in determining the rate of transmission as well as reducing cost is to optimize the utilization of the communication channel. For example, a host computer supporting hundreds of remote terminals more than likely would not have a separate communication channel for each terminal. This would be very costly and inefficient since it is highly unlikely that all the terminals would need to communicate with the host at the same time.

In this type of environment, multiplexers and/or concentrators are used to enable more than one terminal to use the same communication channel. A **multiplexer** is a communication hardware device which combines the flow of data from several terminals into a single flow of data that can then be sent over a single channel to the host computer (see Figure 14-6). After the data from several terminals is received, the host sends an acknowledgment back to the multiplexer which then routes acknowledgment signals back to each of the appropriate terminals. In this way a single communication channel can be more efficiently utilized and is also able to handle many terminals, thereby reducing cost.

A **concentrator** is a communication hardware device similar to a multiplexer except that it permits data from only one terminal at a time to be transmitted over a communication channel (see Figure 14-6). The concentrator polls each terminal (looks at each) one at a time to see if they have anything to transmit. When a terminal sends data to the concentrator, it checks to see if the communication channel is busy. If it is not busy, it sends the transmission on to the host. If it is busy, the terminal must wait a short time until it is free, then the concentrator sends its transmission to the host. In short, a concentrator acts like a traffic cop directing traffic from several lanes of a highway into a single lane.

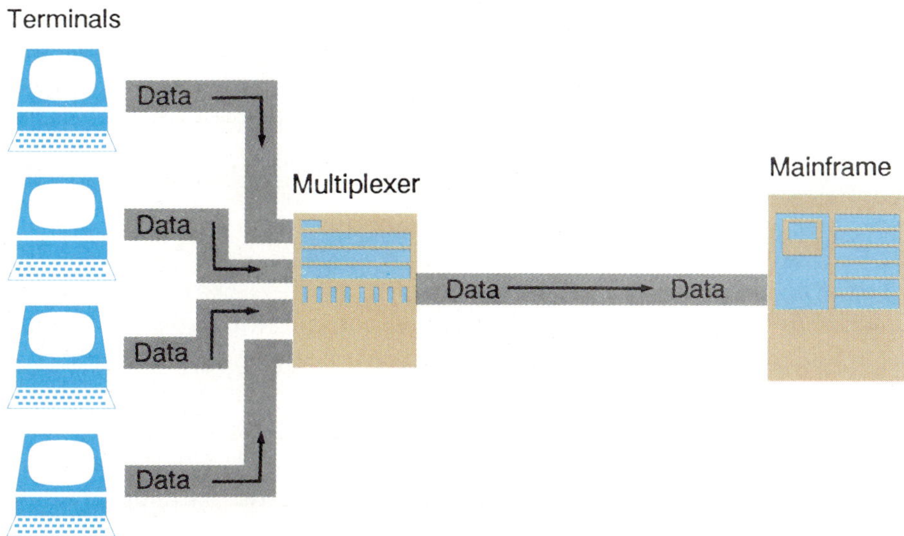

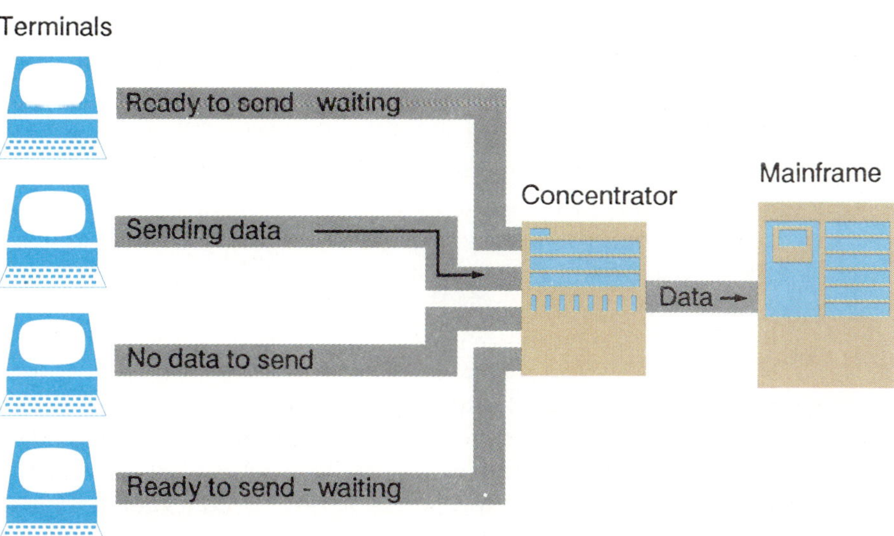

Figure 14-6
Multiplexers and/or concentrators allow more than one terminal to use the same communication channel.

An additional advantage of using either a multiplexer or a concentrator is that less expensive, voice-grade bandwidth channels can be used to connect the terminals to the multiplexer or concentrator. Only one high-speed, broadband channel is needed as the communication channel to carry transmission data to and from the host. Large communication systems, such as airline reservation systems which must support thousands of terminals, use many multiplexers and concentrators to optimize the use of their communication channels and to help reduce transmission carrier cost.

Network Architecture

A **communication network** is a configuration of local and/or remote computers, and other types of terminals, connected together by means of one or more communication channels. Each terminal in a communication network is referred to as a **node.** Each connection, or communication channel, is referred to as a **link.** Nodes and links can be arranged in a variety of different network architectures including: (1) star configuration, (2) ring configuration, (3) bus configuration, and (4) distributed configuration.

Star Configuration

A **star configuration,** as illustrated in Figure 14-7, is arranged so that each of its nodes is linked to a central host computer. Because each node is linked to the host, all communication must first pass to the central host computer before it can be processed or transmitted to another node on the network. This type of configuration is advantageous in some environments which need to have central control over all data in the network. In this network, individual nodes can be inoperative without affecting the others; however, if the central host computer becomes inoperative the entire system is disabled.

Ring Configuration

In a **ring configuration,** one or more computers may act as host systems. As illustrated in Figure 14-7, all the computers and other terminal devices are attached to each other through a ring configuration. This means that data transmitted from any computer or terminal device on the network may be received by any other device. Data simply travels around the ring until it comes to the communicating device for which it is intended (addressed). A device on the ring network can easily be bypassed without disrupting the rest of the network.

Bus Configuration

In a **bus configuration,** each computer or terminal device is linked into a single communication channel by a "drop" line (see Figure 14-7). Data which is transmitted by any device on the bus network is sent to the communication channel to which it is attached. The data then passes in either direction to the appropriate device to which it is addressed. Similar to the ring network, a computer or other terminal device which becomes inoperative may be bypassed or unattached without affecting the other devices on the network. Bus configurations are used primarily with local, direct-connected, small computers.

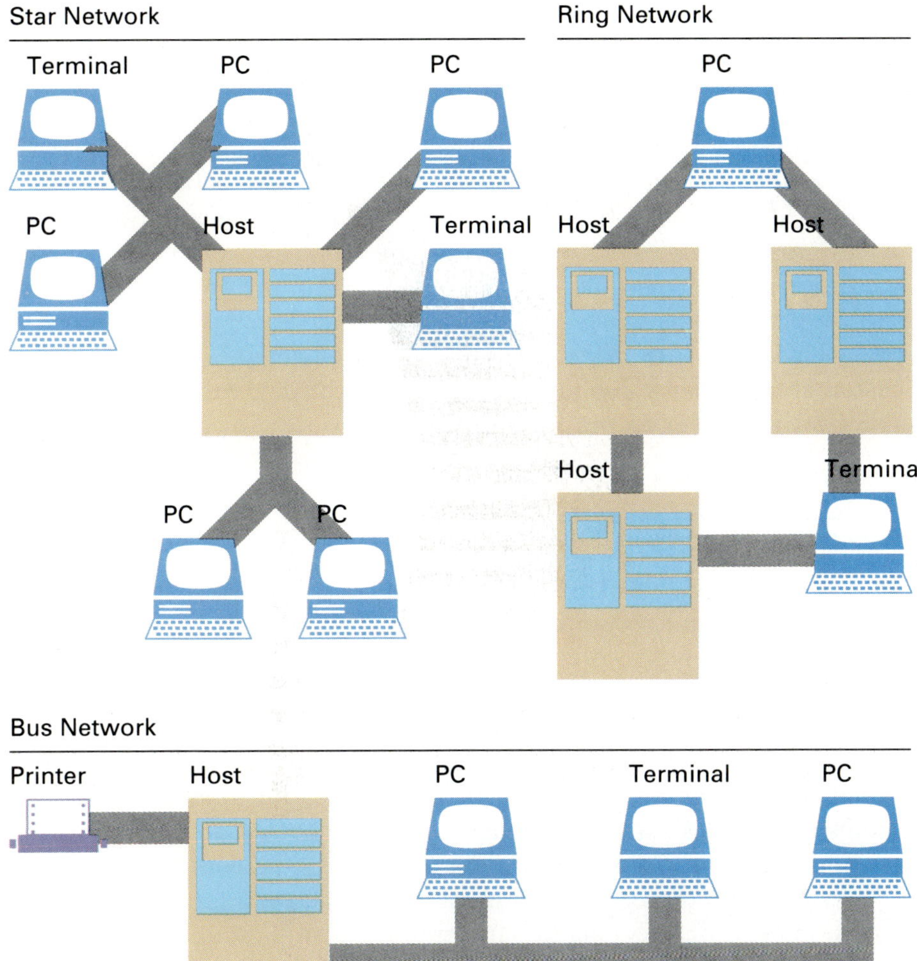

Figure 14-7
Three common network architectures include the star network, the ring network, and the bus network.

Distributed Configuration

In a **distributed configuration,** each node can communicate with every other node through a single link as illustrated in Figure 14-8. What makes a distributed system unique from those already discussed is that each node is a computer system which has its own processing capabilities. This enables the users of each system to be independent of a centrally controlled host computer and to access data and processing capabilities of other systems on the network. A distributed system may be configured in a star, ring, bus, or other network architecture.

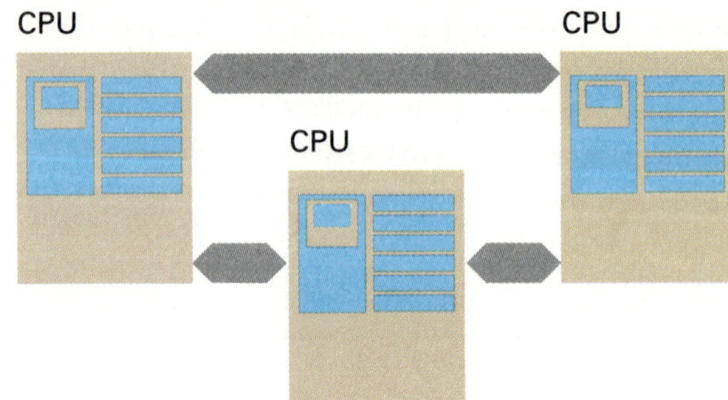

Figure 14-8
In a distributed configuration, each node can communicate with every other node through a single link.

In Figure 14-8, each computer has a communication channel to each of the other computers on the network. This system is being used as a distributed system for a company with offices and warehouses spread across great distances. During the normal work day, each site handles the processing and shipments of its own sales. If any one of the remote site's warehouses is out-of-stock of a particular item, its computer can contact another site on the network and arrange for shipment to the customer from that warehouse. At the end of the day, each sends its total sales activity data to the home office computer for record keeping purposes.

Access Protocols

As you have already learned, access protocols are the operating rules followed by the microcomputers in transmitting on the network. They are necessary in order to control the flow of traffic on the network. If every computer on the network were allowed to transmit data whenever it wanted to with no regard to other nodes, the resulting rush of data on the network cabling would result in garbled codes, and the network would fail to operate. The protocols, therefore, are something like the "rules of the road" to keep signals flowing smoothly. In general, there are three methods used: polling, token passing, and contention.

In a network that uses **polling,** the hub computer asks each of the nodes, in turn, if it has data to transfer or request. Through this method, each node puts data on the network only when requested to do so. Therefore, there is no mixing of data.

Token passing may be used on either a ring or a bus network. In such a system, a packet of data, called the token, controls access to the network. For example, assume that Node 1 has the token and wants to send some data to Node 4. Node 1 will put Node 4's address into the packet of token information, along with the data and its own address as sender. Once it has put the necessary information in the token, Node 1 passes the token onto the network.

The token first comes to Node 2, where the card attaching the computer to the network takes a quick look at the token's address. Not finding its own address, Node 2 simply passes the token along to the next node. The same thing happens in Node 3.

When the token gets to Node 4, Node 4 finds that it is the intended receiver of the token. Therefore, it takes the data, puts a "received" message in the token, and releases the token back onto the ring. The token continues to travel around the ring until it comes back to Node 1, which intercepts it and examines the return message from Node 4. Finding that its network access was successful, Node 1 puts a new "available to anyone" token on the network. This token then proceeds to repeatedly circle the ring until the next node wanting to use the network takes control of it.

In short, token passing controls the traffic on the network by requiring that a node have possession of the token (that is, its address is in the packet of data) before it can use the network. The time required for a node to examine the token for its address and let the token continue its journey may typically be in the range of 1/30,000th of a second. Therefore, as long as the network has a reasonable number of nodes and the work being performed by the computers on the network is not extremely time critical, token passing operates at a good speed. For heavy volumes of traffic on the network, token passing is superior to the contention protocol discussed in the following paragraphs.

On bus networks that operate a **contention** protocol, also known as carrier-sensing multiple access with collision detection (CSMA/CD), any node wishing to use the network first "listens" to see if it can hear a signal on the network indicating that another node is using it. If it does not hear the signal, known as a carrier signal, it transmits a packet of data onto the network. It then listens for the echo signal from the "transmitter" to see if its data remains uninterrupted by any other node's data. If it senses a disruption to the data, it sends a "blocking" signal that cues all nodes to disregard the transmissions that are being mixed. When the transmission is interrupted, the node must wait for a period of time and then retry. The length of the delay before retry is different for each node so that the same two will not try again at exactly the same time.

As long as the quantity of data being transmitted on the network is reasonable, the contention protocol operates nicely. As the volume of data increases, however, the number of collisions increases, and the operating speed slows down. Therefore, the contention protocol is most appropriately used in light-to-medium volume situations. In light load settings, its performance can surpass that of a token-passing protocol.

Local Area Networks

Local, small computers (minis, micros, personal computers) that are linked together in a network architecture for the purpose of communication are referred to as a **local area network** or **LAN.** The small computers on the network (whether host or node) are usually located within 1000 feet of each other. This local, geographic placement of computers to one another is called **topology.** Topologies, which describe the physical shape (configuration) of the network and the placement of each computer on the network, include the star topology, ring topology, and bus topology (see Figure 14-9). Notice, these topologies are identical to the network configurations already discussed. The only difference is that a LAN network links only multiple, small computers, and all links are local, direct connections.

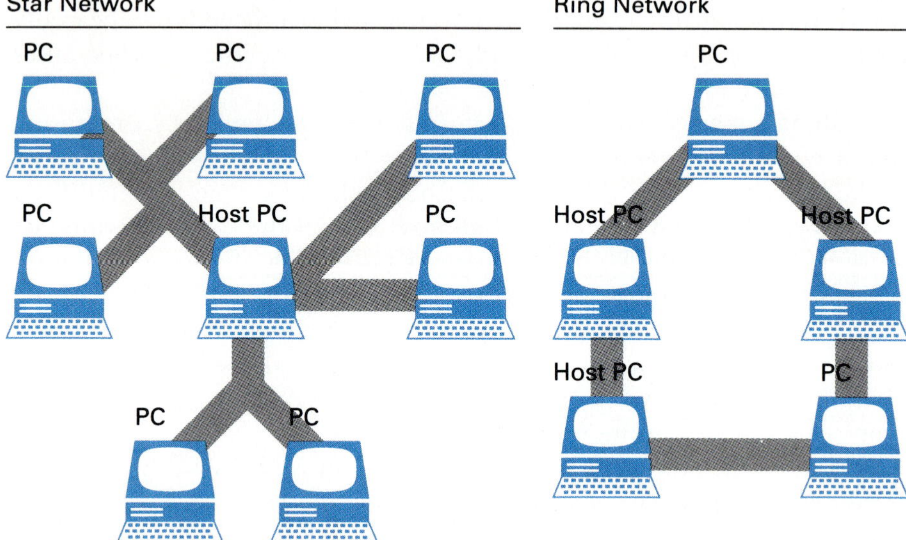

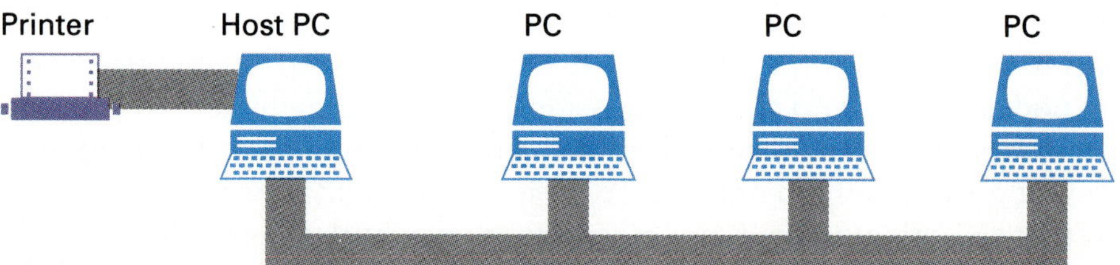

Figure 14-9
Local area networks are often arranged as star, ring, or bus topologies.

The popularity of LANs is growing rapidly. As more and more small computers are used for more and more applications, users are finding LANs a convenient way to share hardware, software, and data and reduce cost.

There are two microcomputer-based methods used for connecting networks—bridges and gateways. **Bridges** are used for connecting similar networks. For example, two ring topology networks might be connected by using a microcomputer that is set up to function as the bridge between the two. For connecting a network to a dissimilar network (a ring topology network to a bus topology network, for example) or to larger computers, a processor functioning as a **gateway** is used.

TRANSMISSION CARRIERS

You have already seen that the communication channels that link network systems together use a variety of transmission carriers. In this section, the most commonly used transmission carriers will be discussed. These include the twisted-pair wire and coaxial cable used for direct connections and the telephone system used for indirect connections.

Twisted-Pair Wire

The **twisted-pair wire** is the name which refers to a standard telephone cord. Twisted-pair wires are inexpensive carriers which can easily connect one device to another. They are used to link LAN devices within short distances of each other (within 250 feet). These copper wires are vulnerable to outside interference. For example, wires which are too close to high voltage electrical lines, air conditioner fans, photocopiers, etc., can cause the data bits they are transmitting to become distorted or lost. The longer the distance, the more chance of outside interference; therefore, users of this type of carrier try to keep the length of twisted-pair wires under 250 feet.

Coaxial Cable

Earlier you learned that a coaxial cable is a high-quality communication channel that serves as the carrier of data transmitted between the host computer and its terminals. The coaxial cable is the most common carrier for local area networks. There are many types of coaxial cable that are used as communication channels.

Coaxial cables are more expensive than twisted-pair wires. However, because of their heavy shielding (a metallic wrapping around the conductor wire), they are much less vulnerable to outside interference. In addition, many coaxial cables contain several wires. Each of these wires can be used as a separate channel similar to how several different channels can be input into a television set. They are also able to carry data over longer distances (usually up to 1000 feet) before the strength of the signal denoting data bits diminishes.

Telephone System

Data which is transmitted over long distances may use a variety of different transmission carriers. Perhaps the most familiar, and most used, long-distance carrier is the standard **telephone line.** Within the community in which you live, telephone wires (either above ground or buried underground) carry the analog signals that allow you to talk to your friends and classmates. These same lines are used as the communication channels that enable data communication to take place. A new transmission carrier called fiber optics may soon replace the conventional telephone lines and coaxial cables used for the LANs described previously.

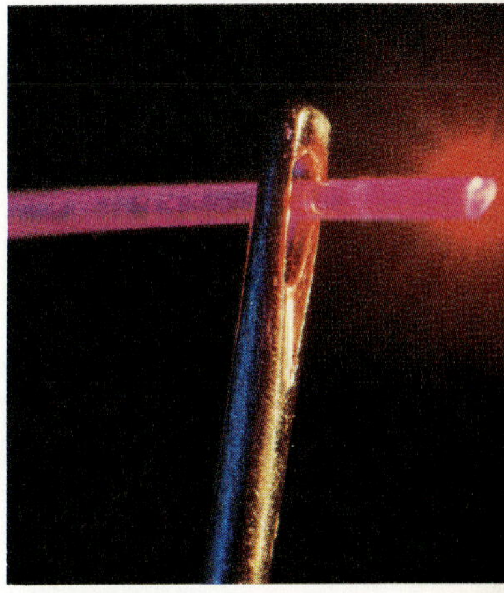

Hair-thin strands of material make up a fiber optics cable.

A **fiber optics** cable consists of one or more hair-thin strands of material capable of conducting light images. These light images can transmit more data over more channels at higher speeds than wire cables.

When long-distance communication is required, the telephone line or fiber optics cable carrying analog signal transmission may connect to and utilize a microwave carrier. **Microwave** carriers transmit data on a straight path from one microwave station to another. Each microwave station must be in a direct line with another station in order to pass the transmission along. Microwave stations vary in the distances they are apart from each other depending upon the location, height, and obstructions between the dishes. Microwave dishes are frequently mounted on water towers or other types of high antenna towers to maximize the distance between stations.

Microwave dishes are frequently mounted on buildings or tall towers.

After a transmission enters a microwave carrier it is directed from one microwave station to another. When it reaches an area closest to its destination, it once again enters a telephone line to complete its journey to the receiving communicating device.

When long-distance communication is required, the telephone line or fiber optics cable carrying analog signal transmission may also connect to and utilize a satellite carrier. A communication **satellite** maintains a stationary position by orbiting 22,000 miles above the earth at a speed which correlates to the earth's rotation.

Many earth stations, strategically located across a large geographical area, direct their large dish antennas at the satellite. Transmission signals can be sent to the satellite by any earth station. Once the satellite receives the transmission signals, it reflects them back to the appropriate receiving station.

A satellite carrier can be used for long-distance communication.

VOICE MESSAGING

Technological advances in the telecommunications industry over the past few decades have been truly remarkable. This technology has given us the ability to communicate with others anywhere in the world in a matter of seconds. Yet, despite all the revolutionary developments in this industry, our businesses are suffering from a lack of efficiency and productivity due to failure to communicate. Many times this failure to communicate is centered around the telephone. Among the common contributors to miscommunication are receiving busy signals, trying to contact sales personnel who are traveling, leaving memos to return calls, and dealing with unanswered phones. Another big factor is the never-ending game of telephone tag (one person attempts to phone another only to find that he/she is not in, then leaves a message; when the call is returned, the original caller is not available). These situations occur much too frequently in a business' day-to-day operation.

A possible solution to this problem is voice messaging (also referred to as voice mail) technology. Voice messaging hardware, software, and services are now available from several sources. The hardware, software, and

Voice messaging will help eliminate the problem of telephone tag.

services may differ from company to company, but in general, voice messaging accomplishes the same result—more effective communication. This technology enables messages to be sent to a computer. If the individual who is being called is not available, the computer digitally records the message onto its disk where it is filed and can be retrieved when needed. The caller's message can be any length and can be immediately channeled to hundreds of individuals who are legitimate users of the network. The caller's message may be placed in a single user's mailbox under strict confidentiality or routed to the company's bulletin board for all employees to see.

Voice messaging systems utilize existing telephone lines. The system is capable of sorting, grouping, routing, and processing a large number of messages, similar to the tasks performed by a switchboard receptionist. The only hardware required is a voice messaging system located at the receiving site. The caller uses a standard touch-tone phone to access the system. Unlike other communication systems, there is no need for modems, keyboards, or terminal hardware on the caller's end. This means that the cost for the installation and use of these systems can be minimized. As a result, smaller companies who were unable to afford the earlier, more expensive voice messaging systems are now flocking to become users. Today's voice messaging systems range from as little as $10,000 to as much as $28,000, depending on the number of messages that must be handled and the features required by the users.

Messages are stored in the originator's voice and can be channeled to the appropriate person for replay at any time—thus eliminating the frustration of telephone tag. The ability to store messages at any time is particularly useful when different time zones are crossed or when messages must be left during abnormal working hours. Perhaps the feature that is most appealing to voice message users is the broadcast feature. One message can be channeled to hundreds of users. For example, management of a company may choose to change the price of one of its major products and then immediately alert the sales staff of the change. Not only has the company saved the cost of mailing this information to its sales staff, but it has been able to communicate important information in an effective and timely manner.

Voice messaging is an effective and efficient way to increase productivity through improving the way a business communicates. Although this technology is still relatively new, it has already proven itself to many companies. Sales of voice messaging systems have mushroomed during the past few years as further evidence of its growing popularity.

CHAPTER SUMMARY

- In the computer industry, communication of data from one location to another is known as data communication. Data communication is accomplished by using communication hardware, software, and transmission carriers.

- Some of the advantages of using communication hardware and software include: (1) more individuals can be users of the hardware and software which is available; (2) expensive equipment can be shared among several users, thereby reducing the cost to each user; (3) data can be shared among the users; (4) the use of a single processor forces standardization of procedures; (5) computer hardware is utilized more effectively and kept busy via the utilization of more users; and (6) many tasks can be completed more conveniently and efficiently than would have been possible without communication hardware and software.
- Some of the disadvantages of using communication hardware and software include: (1) if the mainframe computer goes down, the users are unable to use the system; (2) cost for backup systems can be very high; (3) cost for transmission carriers can be high; (4) highly trained and experienced individuals must often be employed to program and maintain the data communication system; and (5) potential incompatibility and conflicts exist.
- Common uses of communication hardware and software include bulletin board systems, information services, bibliographic services, the stock exchange, and electronic banking and electronic transfer of funds.
- The communication software which drives a communication system can range from a simple program that permits one computer to communicate with another to sophisticated networking software servicing thousands of users over a vast geographic area.
- A multi-user system can be defined as any computer system which is used by more than one user. One computer, called the host computer, controls all the communication activities of the terminals connected to it.
- All communication which takes place between computer hardware is under the control of communication software running in the host computer.
- Protocols are the formal rules of communication exchange between two or more communicating devices.
- A communication channel is a passageway by which data can flow to and from the computer.
- Local terminals are terminals which are geographically located near each other.
- Remote terminals are terminals which are often geographically located hundreds or thousands of miles apart.
- There are two types of communication channels: those that handle local terminals (called direct connections) and those that handle remote terminals (called indirect connections).
- A coaxial cable is a high-quality communication channel that serves as the carrier of data transmitted between the host computer and its terminals.

- Initial contact between two communicating devices is called a handshake.
- The communication hardware for a mainframe computer is called a communication controller, and the hardware for a small computer is called a communication adapter. Both are used to convert parallel transmission into serial transmission and vice versa.
- Download is the term used to describe the process of transferring data from a file stored on the host computer's disk to a communicating computer's disk.
- Upload is the term used to describe the process of transferring data from a file stored on a communicating computer's disk to the host computer's disk.
- The term "telecommunication" refers to the technique and technology of communication by electrical or electronic means.
- A modem (term derived from the terms modulation and demodulation) is a device which converts digital data consisting of bits into an analog signal that can be transmitted over telephone lines.
- A baud rate is the unit of measurement by which data can be transmitted over various communication channels.
- An acoustic coupler is a modem that connects to the computer or terminal by a cable.
- An internal modem is a circuit board that is built in or plugged directly into the computer or terminal.
- An external modem is a modem contained in a small housing which is attached to the computer by a cable and plugged into a standard telephone outlet by a telephone cord.
- In a simplex mode of transmission, data flows in one direction only.
- In a half-duplex mode of transmission, data can be transmitted to and from each of the communicating devices but in only one direction at a time.
- In a full-duplex mode of transmission, data can be transmitted in both directions at the same time.
- The speed by which data can be transmitted over a given communication channel is determined by the grade, or bandwidth, of that channel.
- Baseband channels are used to transmit data between direct-connect devices at very high rates of speed.
- Voice-grade bandwidth channels are the most popular bandwidths used for telecommunication.
- Broadband bandwidth channels are also used for telecommunication. This type of channel utilizes the full-duplex mode of transmission.
- A multiplexer is a communication hardware device which combines the flow of data from several terminals into a single flow of data that can then be sent over a single channel to the host computer.
- A concentrator is a communication hardware device similar to a multiplexer except that it permits data from only one terminal at a time to be transmitted over a communication channel.

- A communication network is a configuration of local and/or remote computers, and other types of terminals, connected together by means of one or more communication channels.
- Each terminal in a communication network is referred to as a node.
- Each connection, or communication channel, is referred to as a link.
- A star configuration is arranged so that each of its nodes is linked to a central host computer.
- In a ring configuration, one or more computers may act as host systems. All the computers and other terminal devices are attached to each other through a ring configuration.
- In a bus configuration, each computer or terminal device is linked into a single communication channel by a "drop" line.
- In a distributed configuration, each node can communicate with every other node through a single link.
- Access by individual microcomputers to a network may be determined by polling, token passing, or contention.
- Local, small computers that are linked together in a network architecture for the purpose of communication are referred to as a local area network or LAN.
- Topology is a term used to describe the physical shape of a network and the placement of each computer on the network.
- Bridges are used for connecting similar networks together, and gateways are used for connecting dissimilar networks together.
- A twisted-pair wire is the name which refers to a standard telephone cord. It is a popular, inexpensive transmission carrier which can easily connect one device to another.
- The coaxial cable is the most common transmission carrier for local area networks.
- The most familiar, and most used, long-distance transmission carrier is the standard telephone line.
- A fiber optics cable consists of one or more hair-thin strands of material capable of conducting light images. These light images can transmit more data over more channels at higher speeds than wire cables.
- Microwave transmission is over a straight path from one microwave station to another.
- Satellite transmission is accomplished via a communication satellite reflecting transmission signals to and from earth stations strategically located across a large geographical area.

KEY TERMS

The following key terms were introduced or redefined in this chapter:

acoustic coupler
baseband
baud rate
bridge
broadband bandwidth
bus configuration
coaxial cable
communication

communication channel
communication adapter
communication controller
communication network
concentrator
connect time
contention
data communication
demodulation
direct connection
distributed configuration
download
electronic mail
external modem
fiber optics
full-duplex mode
gateway
grade/bandwidth
half-duplex mode
handshake
host
indirect connection
internal modem
link
local area network (LAN)
local terminal
log on
microwave
modem
modify access
modulation
multiplexer
multi-user system
networked
node
polling
protocol
read-only access
remote terminal
ring configuration
satellite
simplex mode
star configuration
telecommunication
telephone line
terminal
token passing
topology
turnaround time
twisted-pair wire
upload
voice-grade bandwidth

REVIEW QUESTIONS

1. Identify four advantages and four disadvantages of the use of communication hardware and software. (Obj. 1)
2. What is meant by log on? What is connect time? (Obj. 2)
3. What is a multi-user system? What is a host computer? (Obj. 3)
4. Define protocol. (Obj. 3)
5. What is a communication channel? (Obj.3)
6. Explain the difference between local terminals and remote terminals. (Obj. 3)
7. What is a direct connection? (Obj. 4)
8. What is a coaxial cable? (Obj. 4)
9. What is the term used to describe initial contact between two communicating devices? (Obj. 4)
10. Describe the purpose of a communication adapter. (Obj. 4)
11. Describe the difference between download and upload. (Obj. 4)
12. What is an indirect connection? (Obj. 5)
13. Define telecommunication. (Obj. 5)

14. What is a modem and what does it do? (Obj. 5)
15. Explain what is meant by a transmission rate of 300 baud. (Obj. 5)
16. Briefly describe the differences between an acoustic coupler, an internal modem, and an external modem. (Obj. 5)
17. Briefly describe the differences between simplex mode, half-duplex mode, and full-duplex mode of transmission. (Obj. 6)
18. Briefly describe the differences between baseband, voice-grade, and broadband bandwidth channels. (Obj. 7)
19. What is the difference between a multiplexer and a concentrator? (Obj. 8)
20. Sketch a star network configuration, a ring network configuration, and a bus network configuration. (Obj. 8)
21. What is a distributed configuration? (Obj. 8)
22. Contrast the three network protocols of polling, token passing, and contention. (Obj. 8)
23. What is a LAN? (Obj. 8)
24. There are two microcomputer-based methods used for connecting networks—bridges and gateways. What is the difference between them? (Obj. 8)
25. What are the two most commonly used transmission carriers for direct connections? What are the most commonly used long-distance (indirect connection) transmission carriers? (Obj. 9)

CHALLENGE ACTIVITIES

1. Consult a computer magazine, your local newspaper, a computer store, your school library, or other sources for information about the use of a mainframe computer in a communication environment. Prepare a report describing the application and the hardware, software, and type of transmission carrier(s) used. (Objs. 1,2,3,4,5,6,9)
2. Consult a personal computer magazine, your local newspaper, a computer store, your school library, or other sources for information about the use of a micro- or personal computer in a communication environment. Prepare a report describing the application and the hardware, software, and type of transmission carrier(s) used. (Objs. 1,2,3,4,5,6,9)
3. Visit a local user of communication hardware and software. Find out what information must be provided to the communication software before communication can take place. Observe the operating procedures required to log on (establish a communication link) and how the computer confirmed that the handshake (initial contact) was completed successfully. Write a brief report or prepare an oral report of what you observed to share with your classmates. As an alternative, and if your school uses local or remote communication, prepare a similar report based on your school's system. (Objs. 2,3,4,5,6,7,8,9)

CHAPTER 15

ADDITIONAL APPLICATION SOFTWARE

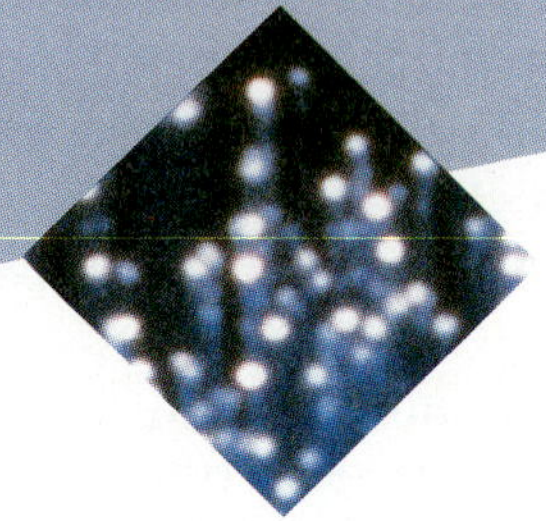

LEARNING OBJECTIVES

After studying this chapter, you will be able to:

1. **List and explain advantages and disadvantages of integrated software.**
2. **Define and describe some of the functions of desktop tools software.**
3. **Define and describe some of the functions of accounting software.**
4. **State the purpose of financial analysis software.**
5. **State the purpose of project management software.**
6. **Define and describe the relationships in CAD/CAM/CIM.**
7. **State the purpose of expert systems.**
8. **Name some of the ways software is used in transportation.**
9. **Name some of the ways software is used in medicine.**

INTRODUCTION

In previous chapters, several types of application software were discussed. These programs included word processing software, database software, spreadsheet software, graphics software, and communications software. These programs represent the bulk of software that is used on microcomputers today.

There are, however, combinations of these types of software, as well as many other types of application software. In fact, there is software available for almost any type of application imaginable. This chapter, however, will introduce some of the more commonly used combinations and additional applications in the areas of integrated packages, desktop tools (also referred to as desktop accessories), accounting, project management, financial analysis, CAD/CAM/CIM, expert systems, transportation and medicine.

INTEGRATED PACKAGES

Integrated software combines the functions of two or more kinds of software. For example, it is very common to find spreadsheet functions, database functions, and graphing functions combined in the same package. Another example is found in packages that contain most or all of what can be considered the "big five" of personal productivity software packages—word processing, spreadsheet, database, graphing, and communication software.

There are two primary advantages of integrated packages. First, the user interface tends to be fairly consistent across all the applications in the package, though this is not always the case. This makes the package easier to use than several different packages with different user interfaces. Secondly, data can usually be transferred easily from one portion of the package to another. For example, a spreadsheet or graph might be combined with text in a word processing document.

Just as there are two main advantages, there are also two primary disadvantages to integrated software. One is that the components sometimes represent compromises. That is, the process of merging the pieces into one product results in the individual components being less powerful or more difficult to use than equivalent stand-alone software packages. The second disadvantage is that integrated packages tend to require more computer memory to run than stand-alone packages of the same capability.

DESKTOP TOOLS

Desktop tools is a name applied to a classification of computer software designed to make day-to-day work and personal activities a little easier in a practical way. It performs such functions as keeping up with a calendar, dialing the phone from numbers stored in its directory, providing a notepad for keeping track of miscellaneous information, and providing a calculator for quick computations.

A characteristic of desktop tools (accessory) programs is that they are ready to be used at a moment's notice. The exact method by which this is accomplished is dependent upon the kind of computer system on which they are to run. Only a couple of keystrokes are usually required, however, to make the programs active, regardless of what other program may be running. When use of the desktop accessory is completed, the other program is once again available for use, just as it was left.

For growing numbers of computer models, desktop tools software is included with the system. For others, the software is available from a variety of vendors. The following paragraphs discuss some of the common accessories.

Calendar

The basic function of calendar software is to computerize the functions of a paper desk calendar. As can be seen in Figure 15-1, the calendar can hold entries of appointments and activities to be accomplished at specified times each day. Additionally, most calendar software can be set to alert the user when it is time for certain events. For example, if a user is working intently on a project but has a three o'clock meeting, the computer can sound an alarm shortly before three to signal the approaching time. A calendar program running on one computer can handle the calendars of several different persons.

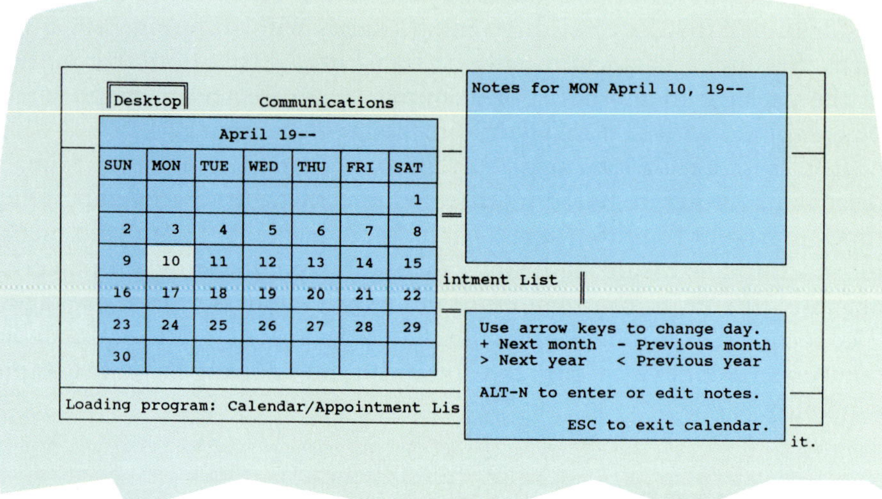

Figure 15-1
Calendar software computerizes the functions of a paper desk calendar.

In network or time-share settings, where various computer workstations are connected, calendar software can become even more useful. In such circumstances, the software can help dramatically in the scheduling of meetings. For example, suppose an executive wishes to meet with four other employees sometime next week. By entering the names of the people who should attend the meeting, along with the desired time frame for the meeting, the computer can examine the calendars of all the proposed participants and tell the executive the times when all are available. Electronic mail messages can then automatically be sent to those individuals inviting them to the meeting. Obviously, this works nicely only if all persons in the organization faithfully use their computer calendars to keep up with their appointments.

Calendaring software works well when computers are networked.

Phone Directory/Dialer

Just as the calendar accessory can take the place of a paper calendar, the phone directory/dialer can take the place of a personal paper phone directory. Names, phone numbers, and any other desired information about each person are entered into the program. When the program is called up, as shown in Figure 15-2, the directory appears, and the desired person is located. Then a keystroke tells the computer to dial the number. To use the dialing portion of a phone directory/dialer, it is necessary that the computer contain communication hardware and be connected through a modem to the phone system. In the absence of a modem, however, the directory portion can still be used to look up phone numbers that can then be dialed manually.

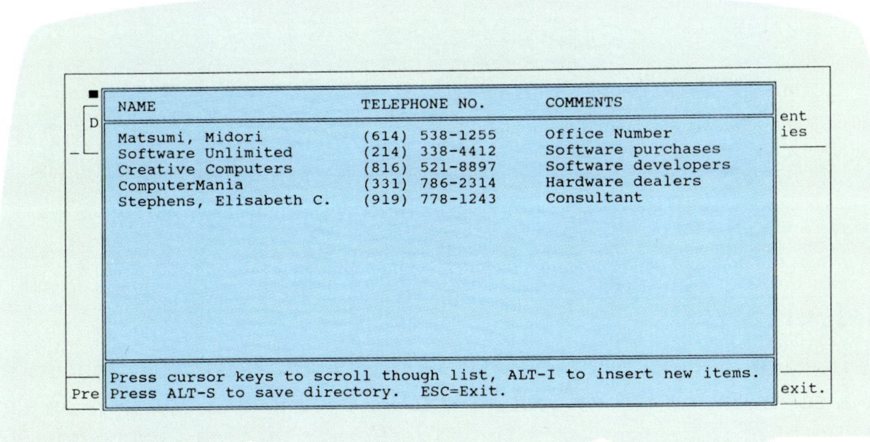

Figure 15-2
The phone directory/dialer accessory takes the place of a personal paper phone directory.

In a computer network or time-share system, it is possible for the phone directory portion to contain some numbers from a central directory that is accessible to all users. Additional personal numbers can then be added by each user.

Notepad

The notepad capabilities of desktop accessory programs vary tremendously. The simplest programs are the equivalent of a stack of blank note cards upon which anything desired can be written. Usually, the cards can be arranged and located by using a few designated keywords. More sophisticated software allows cards to be "linked" to other cards simply by pointing at the linkage point. For example, a main note card may contain the name and address for a customer, Helen Ayres. Other cards may contain notes related to her, such as the contents of phone conversations regarding her future purchase needs or her preferences of brand names of products. These related cards could be easily accessed from the main card. The most advanced software allows graphic images or sounds as well as text to be stored on the cards.

While sophisticated notepad capabilities come with some computers, they are available for virtually all computers through vendors. Figure 15-3 shows the use of a notepad accessory.

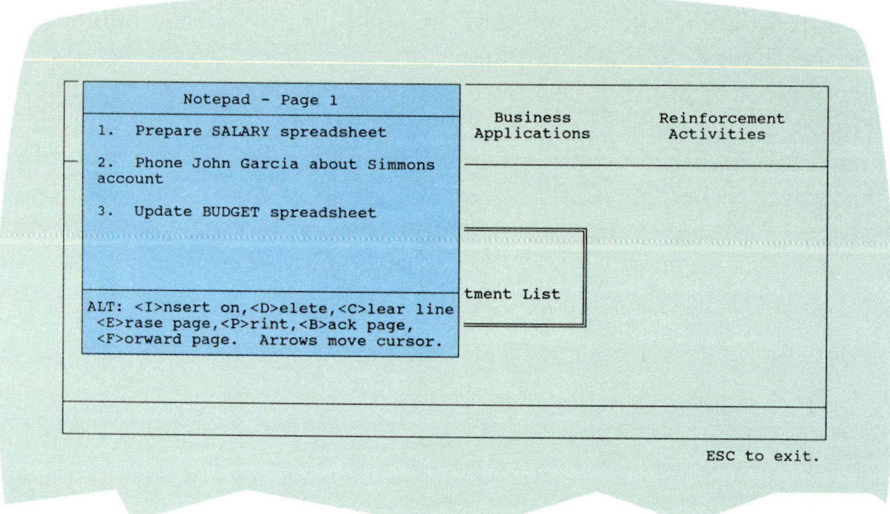

Figure 15-3
A computerized notepad is the equivalent of a stack of blank note cards upon which notes or any other information may be entered.

Calculator

As its name indicates, the calculator accessory displays what appears to be a calculator on the computer's screen. By entering numbers on the keyboard of the computer as shown in Figure 15-4, this calculator can serve the same purpose as a desk calculator. With some programs, the calculator can input numbers from the underlying program being used and send the results back to the underlying program. Calculator programs are very useful for computations that are needed while another program is in use.

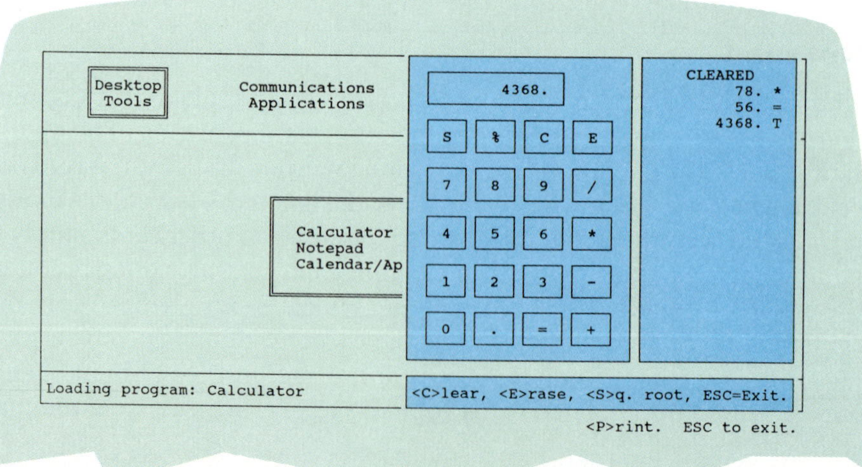

Figure 15-4
The calculator accessory serves the same purpose as a desk calculator.

ACCOUNTING

Many businesses first began using computers to automate their accounting systems. **Accounting systems** are used to maintain the financial records of a business. For sending bills to customers and keeping records of what they owe, computers can save a tremendous amount of money and make the operation much more efficient.

Many other applications have also become extremely important, and virtually all accounting in businesses of any size is done on the computer. Simple accounting systems can run on even the smallest microcomputer. Accounting systems for large businesses generally run on mainframe computers. Accounting systems can be purchased as an entire package, or they can be purchased as modules to meet the needs of the business. The most popular modules are described in the following paragraphs.

General Ledger

The heart of any accounting system is the **general ledger.** In the days when accounting was done by hand, a ledger simply meant a book in which financial transactions were recorded. Now, the ledger may refer to the electronic records of the accounting system. The "general" in the name means that the ledger contains the records of a general or all-encompassing nature rather than the specialized records maintained by the modules. The records in the general ledger may be entered from the keyboard by an operator, or they may be automatically generated by the operation of one of the other modules. Figure 15-5 displays the main menu in a typical general ledger system.

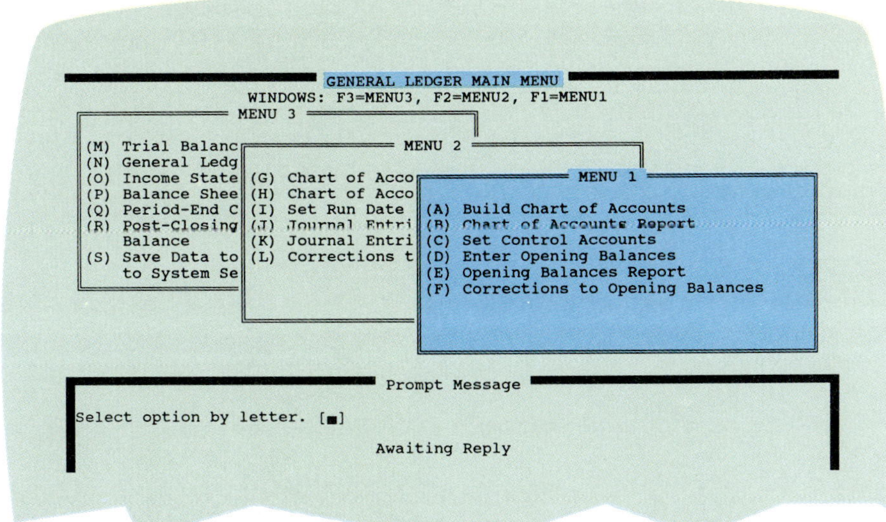

Figure 15-5
The general ledger contains the electronic records of an automated accounting system.

The general ledger records of a business bring together the summaries of all the activities and the status of the business. From the records kept in the general ledger, two common financial statements are prepared.

They are the income statement and balance sheet. The **income statement,** a sample of which is shown in Figure 15-6, shows the revenue or income of the business along with its costs and expenses. The difference in these two figures indicates how much money the business made or lost.

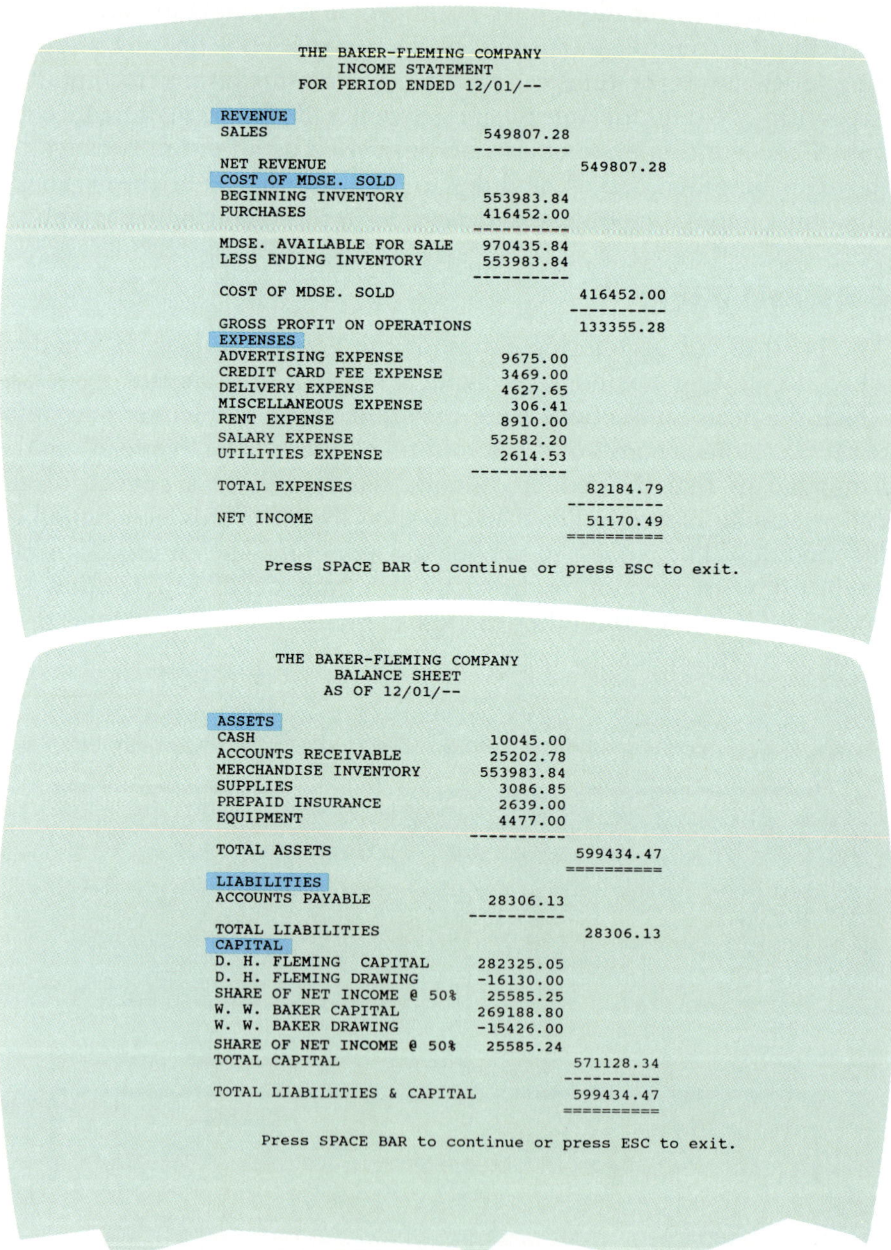

THE BAKER-FLEMING COMPANY
INCOME STATEMENT
FOR PERIOD ENDED 12/01/--

REVENUE		
SALES	549807.28	

NET REVENUE		549807.28
COST OF MDSE. SOLD		
BEGINNING INVENTORY	553983.84	
PURCHASES	416452.00	

MDSE. AVAILABLE FOR SALE	970435.84	
LESS ENDING INVENTORY	553983.84	

COST OF MDSE. SOLD		416452.00

GROSS PROFIT ON OPERATIONS		133355.28
EXPENSES		
ADVERTISING EXPENSE	9675.00	
CREDIT CARD FEE EXPENSE	3469.00	
DELIVERY EXPENSE	4627.65	
MISCELLANEOUS EXPENSE	306.41	
RENT EXPENSE	8910.00	
SALARY EXPENSE	52582.20	
UTILITIES EXPENSE	2614.53	

TOTAL EXPENSES		82184.79

NET INCOME		51170.49
		==========

Press SPACE BAR to continue or press ESC to exit.

THE BAKER-FLEMING COMPANY
BALANCE SHEET
AS OF 12/01/--

ASSETS		
CASH	10045.00	
ACCOUNTS RECEIVABLE	25202.78	
MERCHANDISE INVENTORY	553983.84	
SUPPLIES	3086.85	
PREPAID INSURANCE	2639.00	
EQUIPMENT	4477.00	

TOTAL ASSETS		599434.47
		==========
LIABILITIES		
ACCOUNTS PAYABLE	28306.13	

TOTAL LIABILITIES		28306.13
CAPITAL		
D. H. FLEMING CAPITAL	282325.05	
D. H. FLEMING DRAWING	-16130.00	
SHARE OF NET INCOME @ 50%	25585.25	
W. W. BAKER CAPITAL	269188.80	
W. W. BAKER DRAWING	-15426.00	
SHARE OF NET INCOME @ 50%	25585.24	
TOTAL CAPITAL		571128.34

TOTAL LIABILITIES & CAPITAL		599434.47
		==========

Press SPACE BAR to continue or press ESC to exit.

Figure 15-6
The status of a business can be summarized in two financial statements—the income statement and the balance sheet.

The first thing the **balance sheet** (also in Figure 15-6) shows is the value of everything the business owns (assets). Secondly, it shows the amount the business owes (liabilities). Lastly, it shows the difference in these two amounts. This difference, referred to generally as capital or owner's equity, is the theoretical amount the business is worth.

It is possible to enter all the financial transactions of a business—every sale or purchase, weekly payrolls, etc.—in the general ledger program. Most businesses, however, use one or more of the following modules to keep detailed records in some areas.

Accounts Receivable

Amounts owed to a business by its customers are known as **accounts receivable.** The record of each customer is called an account. For example, the amounts owed by customers to a credit card company are that company's accounts receivable.

Most businesses use a computer to record the transactions that create accounts receivable. At the time each sale is made, a form known as an invoice is printed and given to the customer as a record of the sale. The amount of the invoice, as well as the date and other pertinent information, is recorded on a computer. When a customer pays on account, the amount of payment is recorded on the computer.

Many businesses use the computer to print a monthly statement for each customer. The monthly statement tells the amount that was owed at the beginning of the month, the amount of new charges for the month, the amount paid during the month, and the balance owed at the end of the month.

Invoices and statements are usually printed on special forms. Traditionally, the forms have been preprinted with the business logo, address, and rulings. Now, however, it is common for a laser printer to print everything on blank paper, including the logo, business name, and rulings as shown in Figure 15-7.

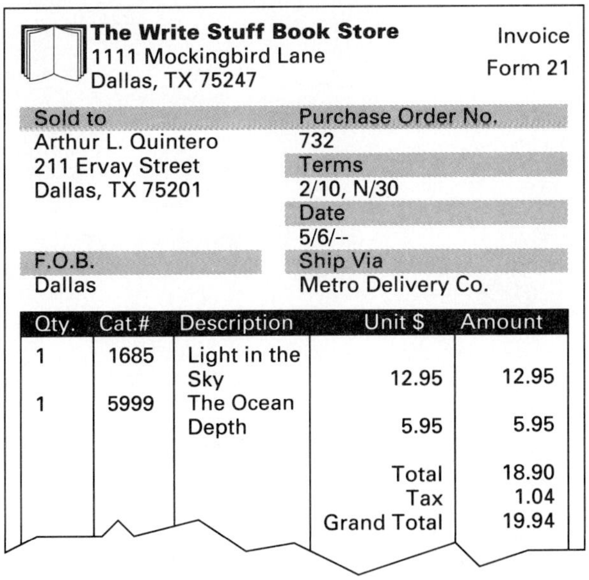

The Write Stuff Book Store
1111 Mockingbird Lane
Dallas, TX 75247

Invoice
Form 21

Sold to
Arthur L. Quintero
211 Ervay Street
Dallas, TX 75201

Purchase Order No.
732
Terms
2/10, N/30
Date
5/6/--

F.O.B.
Dallas

Ship Via
Metro Delivery Co.

Qty.	Cat.#	Description	Unit $	Amount
1	1685	Light in the Sky	12.95	12.95
1	5999	The Ocean Depth	5.95	5.95
			Total	18.90
			Tax	1.04
			Grand Total	19.94

Figure 15-7
Invoices, which are now often printed by laser printers, are commonly used to record sales transactions.

Recall from the previous section that the general ledger keeps a record of everything the business owns. One of the things it owns is its accounts receivable. Usually the accounts receivable module will automatically tell the general ledger module how much money is owed by customers so that this total amount may appear on the balance sheet as an asset.

Accounts Payable

Accounts payable are exactly the opposite of accounts receivable. **Accounts payable** are the amounts that a business owes to someone else. Many of these amounts are owed to suppliers for purchases. Others may be owed for rent on buildings or leases on vehicles.

Typically, when a business wishes to purchase something, it generates a special form called a purchase order. This form specifies the name of the vendor, the merchandise to be purchased, and the amount of the purchase. These purchase orders are frequently printed by computer. In any case, if an accounts payable module is being used, the data on the purchase order goes into the computer.

When it is time to pay the bill, the computer can automatically determine the amount of the payment, or the amount can be entered manually into the computer. In either case, the computer prints checks to pay the bills. The use of an accounts payable module helps a business keep track of when certain amounts of money are due, enabling it to make plans to have enough money on hand to pay the bills.

Some accounts payable software can automatically print checks to pay bills.

Since accounts payable represent amounts owed, their total appears on the balance sheet as a liability. Most accounts payable software automatically transmits this amount to the general ledger module so that it will be up to date.

Inventory

Inventory is made up of the materials a business owns. Materials refers to physical, tangible items as opposed to amounts of money that may be owned. Such things as buildings, trucks, and manufacturing equipment are all inventory. In a wholesale or retail business, the merchandise in stock for sale, either on the sales floor or in a warehouse, is inventory.

Inventory software monitors the quantity of each item in inventory.

The inventory module of an accounting system keeps track of how many of each item are in inventory. When new items come in, they are added to the count, and when items are sold or otherwise disposed of, they are taken from the count.

Inventory modules are usually tied electronically to (integrated with) the accounts payable and accounts receivable modules. By doing this, items being purchased are automatically added to the inventory records, while items being sold are automatically subtracted from the inventory records. Most inventory modules have the capability of automatically producing purchase orders for items that are getting low in stock. There is a growing trend for these purchase orders to be transmitted electronically to suppliers rather than to prepare paper purchase orders.

The total of all inventory on hand is an asset owned by the business. Most inventory modules electronically transmit the total value of inventory back to the general ledger module for summarizing.

Payroll

The last of the common accounting modules, the **payroll module,** maintains the employee pay records of a business. It is probably the one employees are most familiar with since it is the one that prepares their paychecks. All employee earnings records are maintained by the payroll module, and all required federal and state tax forms are prepared by the system.

Before paychecks are printed at the end of each pay period, the necessary data is entered into the payroll module. This includes hours worked, absences, vacation time taken, special payroll deductions, etc. For hourly employees, some payroll modules take the hours worked data directly from time clocks that are connected to the computer system. This results in far less manual labor to enter data for the payroll. Since the cost of paying employees is one of the costs reflected in the business's income statement, the payroll module automatically transmits information back to the general ledger module for inclusion in the income statement.

Time clocks can be directly connected to the computer system for use by payroll software.

FINANCIAL ANALYSIS

Financial analysis software is used by both businesses and individuals. It helps make plans for investments, helps track the performance of investments, and helps analyze the long-term outcome of investments. Such software varies widely in capability from one package to another. The least capable packages do little more than record the numbers from an individual's checkbook and maintain the balance—a job that is easier done in the checkbook with a pocket calculator.

More sophisticated packages can calculate the return on investment for a person's or business's portfolio of investments and can project cash flow and future returns. An analysis of cash flow lets the investor know how much cash is needed each week or month and how much should be available if the projections are accurate.

Some sophisticated programs on properly equipped computers can even receive stock market data that is transmitted over FM radio or transmitted directly from the stock exchange. This data can then be used to do immediate analyses of the value of stocks owned and the amount of return that would be gained if the stocks were immediately sold. Many more stock traders are now relying on computers to help them track their investments and decide when to buy or sell.

Financial analysis software can be used to track investments.

PROJECT MANAGEMENT

Project management software helps plan and track the sequence of activities necessary to complete a complex project. The management of such projects has always been a challenge. A good example of this can be found in the construction of a building. When construction is started, the foundation must be completed before work on the walls can begin. However, once the foundation is complete and walls are roughed in, electrical and plumbing work can commence at the same time. But the finish wall cannot be put up until both the electrical and plumbing work are complete. The coordination of all these activities is difficult, and often many persons have waited around with no work until necessary prior steps were completed. In other cases, time was wasted after the completion of certain steps because workers were not available to begin the next step. Frequently, the estimated time necessary for completing a project would go by and the project would not be finished because the estimates were just not accurate.

Project management software can help schedule the various activities that must go into the completion of a project. The software certainly does not make the job foolproof or relieve the human of the burden of good judgment. It can, however, assist greatly by making the work of preparing complex charts that map activities and keep up with their progress much easier and more accurate.

Project management software can be used to coordinate the activities involved in completing a construction project.

CAD/CAM/CIM

In a previous chapter you learned about computer-aided design and drafting, which is the CAD of CAD/CAM/CIM. CAM, which stands for **computer-aided manufacturing**, goes a step beyond CAD and automates the manufacturing process based on the input of the designer using a CAD system.

As an example, consider the process of replacing a human hip joint with an artificial joint. Previously, artificial joints came in several standard sizes, with the surgeon selecting the size closest to the needs of the patient. With the use of CAD/CAM, the process has changed. Now a designer working with CAD designs a joint tailored exactly to the needs of the patient—exactly the right size with exactly the right direction and range of movement. Then automated machines in the computer-aided manufacturing phase take over, using the output of the CAD program to produce the joint exactly to the designer's dimensions.

CAD software is used to design items to be manufactured.

Computer-integrated manufacturing, or CIM, refers to the process of integrating computers throughout a manufacturing plant. Much pioneering work in this area has resulted in the development of a standard called the Manufacturing Automation Protocol (MAP) that links all the computers together so they can communicate with each other. A factory may have many integrated computers being controlled by MAP communications.

MAP can be used to control the communication between computers in a manufacturing plant.

EXPERT SYSTEMS

Expert systems are software packages that enable the computer to make recommendations about courses of action to be taken. In some cases, the actions are taken automatically by the computer system. In other cases, the computer makes recommendations that humans can decide whether or not to follow.

Many persons use the terms expert systems and artificial intelligence interchangeably. The term **artificial intelligence**, for the most part, seems to give computers more credit than they presently deserve. It implies that computers can think. That is not the case, even though expert systems are the closest anyone has yet come to making computers think.

Rather than making computers think, however, expert systems software allows the computer to analyze complex conditions. That is, under certain combinations of conditions, one course of action will be recommended, while under other combinations of conditions other courses of action will be recommended. This process is designed to accept numerous inputs of data and to produce the most logical recommendation as output. To prepare expert systems, developers glean everything they can from acknowledged experts in the field for which the system is being developed. The program then becomes an automated version of the experts' knowledge. Specialized programming languages have been designed to help in the development of expert systems.

Expert systems have been developed for a wide range of applications. Among one of the earliest was a medical diagnosis program that suggested possible diseases after analyzing the patient's symptoms. Among many other systems are ones that suggest the most likely places to drill for oil, the kind of packaging to use for a new product, and the likely cause of problems in a computer system.

Expert systems can help diagnose mechanical problems.

TRANSPORTATION

Companies in the transportation industry use many of the same types of application software as other industries. For example, they use accounting software and financial analysis software. In addition, they use many specialized programs such as the examples discussed in the following sections.

Air Passenger Transport

Airlines use many special-purpose computers, such as on-board systems on aircraft and flight simulator systems for pilot training. However, they also have many applications that run on general-purpose computers. Among the most visible of those are reservations systems and crew scheduling systems.

Airlines make extensive use of general-purpose computers when making flight reservations.

Reservations systems receive input from hundreds of terminals in the airlines' own reservation centers, plus additional input from thousands of terminals and personal computers at airline ticket counters and in travel agencies. These systems function as huge databases, storing the information on every passenger who has made a reservation on every flight. From this data, the airline is able to prepare for each flight as it nears.

A recent development is the use of special computer software that works with a reservations system to help travelers make their plans. Being installed in growing numbers of travel agencies, the system uses computer-controlled laser disks. The system not only helps travelers with their schedules, but it also shows them color pictures of the exterior and interiors of prospective hotels and tourist attractions at their destinations.

The same reservations system that handles their airline ticketing can then be used to make hotel and rental car reservations.

Freight

While airlines use computers to keep track of their passengers, many freight companies use computers to keep track of their freight. Whether freight is shipped by truck, railroad, air, or a combination of modes, its movement can be tracked. This allows shippers and receivers to have a better idea of when to expect delivery, which makes it easier to locate lost shipments. Software that tracks the movement frequently makes use of bar scanners to enter data into the system.

Many freight companies use computers to keep track of their freight.

MEDICINE

The field of medicine also makes use of both special-purpose and general-purpose computers. In the area of diagnosis and treatment, many special-purpose computers are used in various scanners, imagers, and treatment machines such as those that administer radiation therapy. General-purpose computers are also used in many applications. As stated previously in this chapter, expert systems exist that can assist in diagnosis or treatment planning. Software is also used to keep up with patient bills as well as other aspects of accounting.

Patient information systems are the most visible software in the medical industry. These systems, used in both doctors' offices and hospitals, maintain the complete medical history of a patient, including all diagnoses and treatments. Since they are usually on-line, real-time systems, doctors use them to enter treatment instructions for patients in hospitals. The system then prompts nurses and other caretakers when each treatment step is to be administered. For example, administration of drugs on the assigned schedule, or the administration of physical therapy, would be prompted by the system. The person who administers the instructions can then enter information concerning the completion of the assigned action into the computer.

The health care industry uses computers not only to diagnose illnesses, but also to keep up with patient bills.

ARE WE RELYING TOO MUCH ON COMPUTERS?

As you have learned throughout this text, computers can be used to improve the quality of life, to make business more efficient, to help people make better decisions, to control transportation systems, and to make medical treatment more effective. But as the computer's role increases in all these areas, are we as humans becoming complacent in our interaction with it? Many people seem to accept that whatever a computer does is correct. If the computer says something is so, then it must be so. But how accurate is that assumption? Are we even putting our lives in danger by over-reliance on the computer?

You have probably heard horror stories about computer record keeping systems gone awry. Such simple things as trying to get billing errors on charge accounts corrected or trying to get a magazine to fulfill your subscription are common occurrences. Stories exist of bank teller machines that spit out money because of programming errors, of persons repeatedly getting bills for $0.00 owed, and similar events.

An error on a computer-generated bill can be a shocking experience.

At least one factory worker has been killed by a robot gone astray. Several brands of automobiles have been accused of sudden and unexpected acceleration; could this be caused by program bugs in the computerized systems that control the engine? And what about airplanes that essentially fly themselves? Even if nothing goes wrong with the program, there is great concern that pilots with little to do for hours at a time but watch the computer will go to sleep.

In the medical field computer program failure in radiation therapy machines has resulted in at least two known deaths, with the manufacturer of the machines now putting mechanical safeguards in the equipment. How likely is it that patients have received too little or too much medication because of data entry errors in a medical records system, without the nurse questioning the output of the computer?

While computers undoubtedly have been very beneficial in many areas, the wise person will not place unwarranted faith in the reliability or infallibility of systems. Remember that humans by nature make mistakes occasionally and that computer hardware and software are created from the minds of humans.

CHAPTER SUMMARY

- Integrated software that combines common program functions makes learning and using the software easier.
- Desktop tools (accessories) refers to software designed to make day-to-day work and personal activities easier in a practical way.
- Common desktop accessory software includes calendars, phone directory/dialers, notepads, and calculators.

- Accounting software keeps the financial records of a business.
- The general ledger module keeps the all-encompassing or summarizing financial records.
- The accounts receivable module keeps up with the money owed to the business and handles billing and collections.
- The accounts payable module keeps up with money owed by the business and handles the payment of obligations.
- The inventory module keeps up with the assets owned by a business, whether they be merchandise for sale or items for use in the business.
- The payroll module keeps up with the pay records of employees.
- Financial analysis software helps persons or businesses plan investments and then track the performance of those investments.
- Project management software helps plan the steps in a complex project and then track the completion of those steps according to the designated time schedule.
- While CAD aids in the design or drafting of an object, computer-aided manufacturing (CAM) uses CAD's output to actually produce the product that was designed.
- Computer-integrated manufacturing (CIM) integrates computers into the manufacturing process.
- The manufacturing automation protocol (MAP) is an increasingly popular way for computers in manufacturing applications to communicate with one another.
- Expert systems synthesize the knowledge from known experts in a field to apply that knowledge to computer solution of problems.
- Computer applications in the transportation field include airline reservations and crew scheduling systems, as well as freight tracking systems involving all modes of transportation.
- Medical applications of computers include diagnosis, treatment, and medical record keeping.

KEY TERMS

accounting system
accounts payable
accounts receivable
artificial intelligence
computer-aided manufacturing
computer-integrated manufacturing
desktop tools
expert systems
financial analysis software
general ledger
income statement
integrated software
inventory
payroll module
project management software

REVIEW QUESTIONS

1. List and explain the advantages and disadvantages of integrated software. (Obj. 1)

2. What is desktop tools (accessory) software? (Obj. 2)
3. What functions are commonly performed by desktop accessory software? (Obj. 2)
4. What advantage does calendaring software offer on a networked or time-shared system? (Obj. 2)
5. What does phone directory/dialer software do? (Obj. 2)
6. What piece of hardware is required in order to make full utilization of a directory/dialer program? (Obj. 2)
7. What is the general purpose of notepad software? (Obj. 2)
8. What differences in capability exist between simple notepad software and the most advanced notepad software? (Obj. 2)
9. What is an accounting system? (Obj. 3)
10. Of what modules do most accounting systems consist? (Obj. 3)
11. What two financial statements does the general ledger module produce? (Obj. 3)
12. What is the purpose of the general ledger module? (Obj. 3)
13. What are accounts receivable? (Obj. 3)
14. What kind of information does the accounts receivable module integrate with the general ledger module? (Obj. 3)
15. What are accounts payable? (Obj. 3)
16. What kind of information does the accounts payable module integrate with the general ledger module? (Obj. 3)
17. What is inventory? (Obj. 3)
18. What kind of information does the inventory module integrate with the general ledger module? (Obj. 3)
19. What does the payroll module do? (Obj. 3)
20. What kind of information does the payroll module integrate with the general ledger module? (Obj. 3)
21. What is the purpose of financial analysis software? (Obj. 4)
22. Name three functions of sophisticated financial analysis software. (Obj. 4)
23. What is the purpose of project management software? (Obj. 5)
24. What is the relationship between CAD and CAM? (Obj. 6)
25. What is the difference between CAM and CIM? (Obj. 6)
26. What is the purpose of an expert system? (Obj. 7)
27. Name three purposes for which expert systems have been written. (Obj. 7)
28. Name two applications that airlines run on general-purpose computers. (Obj. 8)
29. Name a way in which computers are used in the freight business. (Obj. 8)
30. Name three applications of special-purpose computers in the field of medicine. (Obj. 9)
31. Describe a medical application that runs on general-purpose computers. (Obj. 9)

CHALLENGE ACTIVITIES

1. Try out some desktop tools software. Make sure you try all the capabilities of the package available to you. Discuss with classmates how the capabilities can make work easier and more productive. (Obj. 2)
2. Talk with a businessperson about the accounting system he or she uses. Find out which module he or she thinks is the most indispensable and why. Find out how many additional employees would be necessary to do manual accounting and how much longer it might take to keep the records. (Obj. 3)
3. If a store that sells computer software is nearby, examine the financial analysis and project management software that are available for sale. Report on the differing capabilities of the different packages. (Objs. 4,5)
4. Research information about how computers are being integrated into the manufacturing environment. (Obj. 6)
5. Research information about areas in which expert systems are being used. (Obj. 7)
6. Research information about how computer software is being used in transportation or medicine. (Objs. 8,9)

SYSTEM DESIGN AND PROGRAMMING

CHAPTER 16

SYSTEM DEVELOPMENT

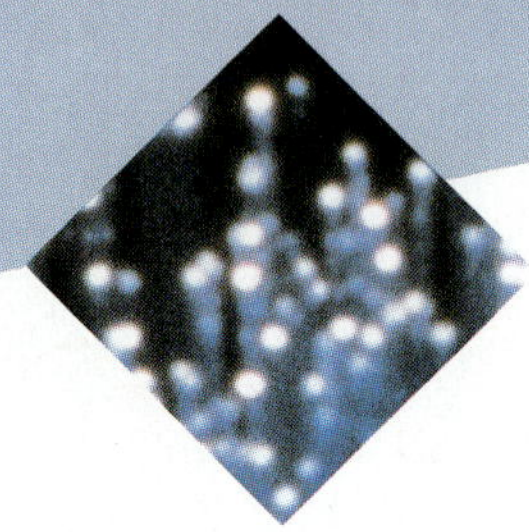

LEARNING OBJECTIVES

After studying this chapter, you will be able to:

1. **Understand why systems must change in order to keep pace with our rapidly changing environment.**
2. **Describe a computer system's life cycle.**
3. **Explain and describe the tasks associated with systems analysis.**
4. **Explain and describe the tasks associated with systems design.**
5. **Explain and describe the tasks associated with software acquisition and testing.**
6. **Explain and describe the tasks associated with implementation.**
7. **Explain the purpose of evaluation and maintenance.**
8. **Identify the factors that cause systems to require updating or become obsolete.**

INTRODUCTION

It is said that the human race's knowledge is doubling every five to ten years and that this rate of knowledge accumulation is accelerating. Increased research and development, coupled with a growing need for more sophistication, has contributed to this rate of knowledge expansion and has fueled an accelerated pace of technological improvement. One only needs to look around the environment (home, town or city, school) to see the many changes brought about by technology over the past few years. Rapid advances in technology have also affected how our country's businesses and industries function, causing them to become more complex and dependent upon more information to be competitive.

This chapter will discuss procedures and techniques that can help develop computer systems which address the changes in our environment, businesses, and industries. How computer systems are developed and how these systems must change in order to keep pace with their surroundings will also be examined.

WHY SYSTEMS MUST CHANGE

The term **system**, as used in this chapter, can be defined as related devices and/or procedures that function together in order to achieve a common goal or objective. For example, the picture tube, tuners, antenna, and electronic components of a TV all functioning together compose a system called a television set. The workers, machines, buildings, and materials of a factory which work together in order to produce goods which can be sold is a system. The procedures that an accountant performs when working with journals, ledgers, computers, and other people to produce financial reports for a company can be called an accounting system.

Systems encompass such diverse areas as accounting and manufacturing.

The television set has undergone many changes during the past four decades. It is a system which is constantly being perfected and changed to reflect technological advances in the electronic industry. A factory may hire new employees, other employees may retire, newer, more sophisticated machines may be brought in to replace older machines, new buildings may be built or old ones renovated, and the materials which were once used to produce a product may be changed. All or any of these changes affect the way in which the factory must go about meeting its goal of producing a product. The procedures an accountant performs can also change drastically if the company for which he/she is working grows, acquires additional businesses, or takes on additional services. External factors, such as changes in tax laws, may affect accounting rules, methods, and procedures.

In a world of accelerated accumulation of human knowledge, technological improvement, and the human race's thrust to improve its work and personal environment, there is only one constant: change. No one can accurately predict what inventions will make our world and life better, but one can be assured that change will continue at an accelerated pace. Improved systems and procedures will be required in order to cope with these changes.

The computer is a device which can be used to help keep pace with the rapidly changing environment. As discussed in the previous chapters, there have been several advances in computer technology which enable the computer to handle more sophisticated applications and store more data than possible in the past. However, despite recent advances in hardware and software, there is still a lack of "brainware." That is, today's computers are capable of doing much more than humans have been able to program them to do. It is estimated that the capabilities of today's computers are five years ahead of our abilities to utilize them to their potential. Nonetheless, the computer is considered to be one of the most powerful tools of this century.

THE SYSTEM LIFE CYCLE

Just as changes must be made to help humans keep pace with their environment, so must changes be made to computer systems in order for them to keep up with technological advances. Once a computer program is written, it does not automatically change in accordance with the tasks it is expected to perform. Unless it is given new instructions, a computer will process its data and produce reports in the same way year after year. As businesses' or industries' needs change, or as technological improvements are made, so must the software be changed in order to keep pace and keep from becoming obsolete. Therefore, computer systems have what is referred to as a system life cycle. A computer's **system life cycle** can be defined as the period of time in which a given computer system's usefulness to perform a given task is measured.

Most computer systems are developed with the recognition that change is constantly occurring and must be dealt with within the system life cycle in order to produce information which is current and useful. In order to accomplish this, a systematic, step-by-step procedure for system development can be established. This procedure can be broken into five different tasks or stages of development: analysis, design, acquisition and testing, implementation, and evaluation and maintenance. After all the stages in the development process are complete and the system is up and running, the system must be updated as necessary to prolong its life cycle of usefulness. Figure 16-1 illustrates each of the stages of system development and changes which require the system to be updated during its system life cycle.

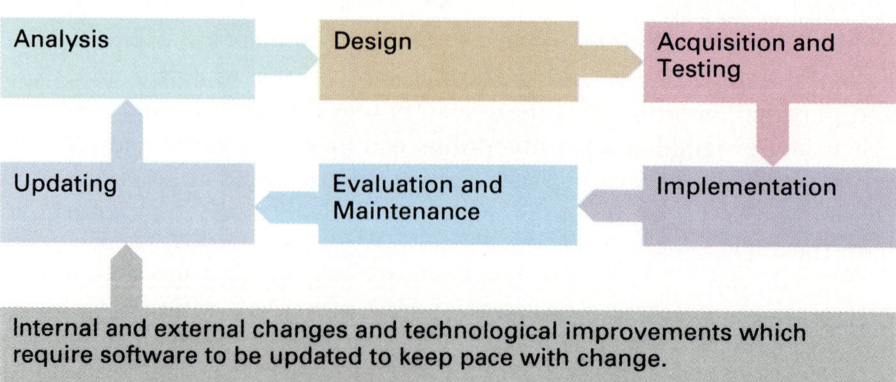

Figure 16-1
The system life cycle can be broken into various stages of development.

In the remainder of this chapter it will become evident how each stage of system development (analysis, design, acquisition and testing, implementation, and evaluation and maintenance) is performed and leads to a comprehensive computer system. Next, you will learn how a system, once developed, is periodically updated to increase its life cycle and remain an effective information resource for its users.

STAGES OF SYSTEM DEVELOPMENT

The five stages of analysis, design, acquisition and testing, implementation, and evaluation and maintenance comprise a model that can be used as a systematic approach to the development of computer systems. Because the operation of many organizations is so complex, the task of developing a new computer system must involve a carefully thought-out plan or approach. The five stages of the system development model can be used to break down such a task into meaningful and effective information flows. These effective information flows can in turn be used by management, decision makers, and production personnel to more efficiently meet their company's objectives and goals. The individual responsible for the overall system development is called a systems analyst. The **systems analyst** acts as a link between the users of the system and the technical personnel who actually develop and install the system. The systems analyst often has expertise in the area being considered for development as well as a technical knowledge of the computer industry.

The systems analyst acts as a link between the users of the system and the technical personnel who actually develop and install the system.

Stage 1 – Analysis

The first stage of system development is the systems analysis stage. In this stage of development, the systems analyst must perform four separate tasks. First, a definitive and precise statement of the problem or reason for the development must be stated. Second, measurable objectives of what the system is to accomplish must be stated. Third, the sources of information and the actual information that is needed to meet the system's objectives must be identified. Finally, an analysis report must be prepared which states the findings of this analysis stage to management.

Statement of the Problem

Often the reason for developing a new computer system is to meet a specific need of the organization. For example, a business may have grown to a size at which it is no longer efficient to produce its employees' payroll checks and records manually. At the same time, and since personnel records contain similar information about each employee, the personnel files could be integrated with the payroll files. The statement of the problem in this example could be as follows: "The purpose of the systems analysis study is to determine the feasibility of developing an integrated payroll/personnel information system."

Another reason for developing a new computer system occurs when an organization's existing computer system becomes obsolete due to the availability of newer, faster, less costly computer hardware. Management may decide to explore the possibility of replacing the old computer system with the newer system. Because the new system is not compatible with the existing system, the existing software must be rewritten. Therefore, the newly rewritten software should be developed to take advantage of the new system's capabilities while at the same time addressing additional user needs the new hardware is capable of meeting. The statement of this problem could be expressed as follows: "The purpose of the systems analysis study is to determine the feasibility of upgrading the organization's existing hardware and information system software."

Measurable Objectives

Whether the system being developed is a new system or a replacement of an obsolete system, its objectives should be stated in measurable terms. The reason for doing this at this stage is to help more precisely define what the system is to do and how efficiently it is to perform its tasks. Later, during the review stage, these initial objectives will be compared to actual system performance. Based upon the results, the new system may be accepted for meeting the stated objectives, fine-tuned, or rejected for failure to perform as expected.

An example of measurable objectives for the company seeking an integrated payroll/personnel information system may include the following:

1. The integrated payroll/personnel information system must be able to produce and maintain internal and external government reporting information with at least a 97 percent accuracy rate.
2. The integrated payroll/personnel information system must be able to produce paychecks and complete payroll processing for 500 employees within 1 hour after all pay period data has been entered into the system.

3. The integrated payroll/personnel information system must accurately maintain personnel and employee data on a random-access device capable of accessing any employee's record within 1-3 seconds.
4. The integrated payroll/personnel information system must be capable of producing personnel and payroll reports in various sequences based upon the categories of employee name/number, department, classification, date, and pay history for 500 employees within 5 minutes of program execution.

Sources and Information Identification

The individuals who will supply the data and use the informational output of the system being analyzed must be identified. It is from these individuals that existing data and new data needed in the system will be obtained. Interviews should be conducted with individuals within the organization as well as outside the organization (i.e. government agencies, suppliers, customers) to find out what their informational requirements are. In addition, existing reports and data files should be examined to make sure that the new system will meet existing information requirements.

A Data Element Identification form similar to the one shown in Figure 16-2 can be used to record the data fields (called data elements). This document acts as a form of control to insure that all data elements required to meet the system's objectives have been identified. Also, it helps insure that no data elements are listed twice. Notice the two columns to the right side of the document (Maximum Size and Frequency). These two columns indicate the maximum size of the element and the frequency of use (times per week). The purpose of the maximum size of element column is to assist in estimating the size of the record which must be stored for each employee and, in turn, the total storage capacity required of the system. The purpose of the frequency of use column is to assist in arranging the data items which are referenced the most frequently first. This consideration in the arrangement of the data elements within the data file can significantly reduce the time (access time) it takes the computer to locate any given data element in a database system.

DATA ELEMENT IDENTIFICATION CONTROL FORM

Data Element Name	Maximum Size	Frequency Per Week
Employee Number	6	60
Employee Name	25	32
Employee Classification (Exempt or Nonexempt)	1	15

Figure 16-2
A Data Element Identification form helps to insure that all data elements required to meet the system's objectives have been identified.

Analysis Report

After stating the problem, stating the measurable objectives, and identifying the sources and data elements required to meet the objectives and produce the desired information, the system analyst prepares the **analysis report.** It should contain each of the items mentioned above plus an explanation of the present system (whether automated or manual), the procedures used, and any problems which must be overcome in a new system. In addition, an estimate of the resources (in terms of equipment, personnel, money, and time) required to develop the new system should be specified.

After the analysis report is prepared, it is presented to management by the systems analyst. If management decides to proceed after reviewing the analysis report, Stage 2 of the system development procedure—design—can begin. If, however, management determines that the cost of the new system is too great for the benefits derived, or for some reason the system is no longer feasible, the system development project is stopped. Management's decision to continue or stop the process after the analysis stage is critical. If it is determined to continue, hundreds of thousands of dollars may be committed to the development of the new system.

Stage 2—Design

The second stage of systems development is the detailed design stage. In this stage, the systems analyst has four major tasks which must be performed. First, a systems design flowchart must be prepared. This flowchart shows each of the major components which comprise the system and how these components interact with each other. Second, several viable alternative designs that meet the stated objectives should be developed within the organizational constraints. Third, a feasibility analysis study weighing the costs-to-benefits derived, time, effort, etc., must be performed for each of the viable alternatives. Finally, the systems design report must be prepared which, among other things, recommends the best alternative.

During the design stage, the systems design flowchart must be prepared.

Systems Design Flowchart

One of the most useful tools of the systems analyst is a flowchart template. Symbols on the flowchart template represent various input/output devices and processing operations. The analyst uses the symbols on this tool to draw a diagram which depicts what components are involved in the system and how each of these components interact with each other. For example, the system flowchart for the integrated payroll/personnel system discussed previously may be depicted as shown in Figure 16-3. A description and explanation of the symbols used in a flowchart template are provided in Figure 16-4.

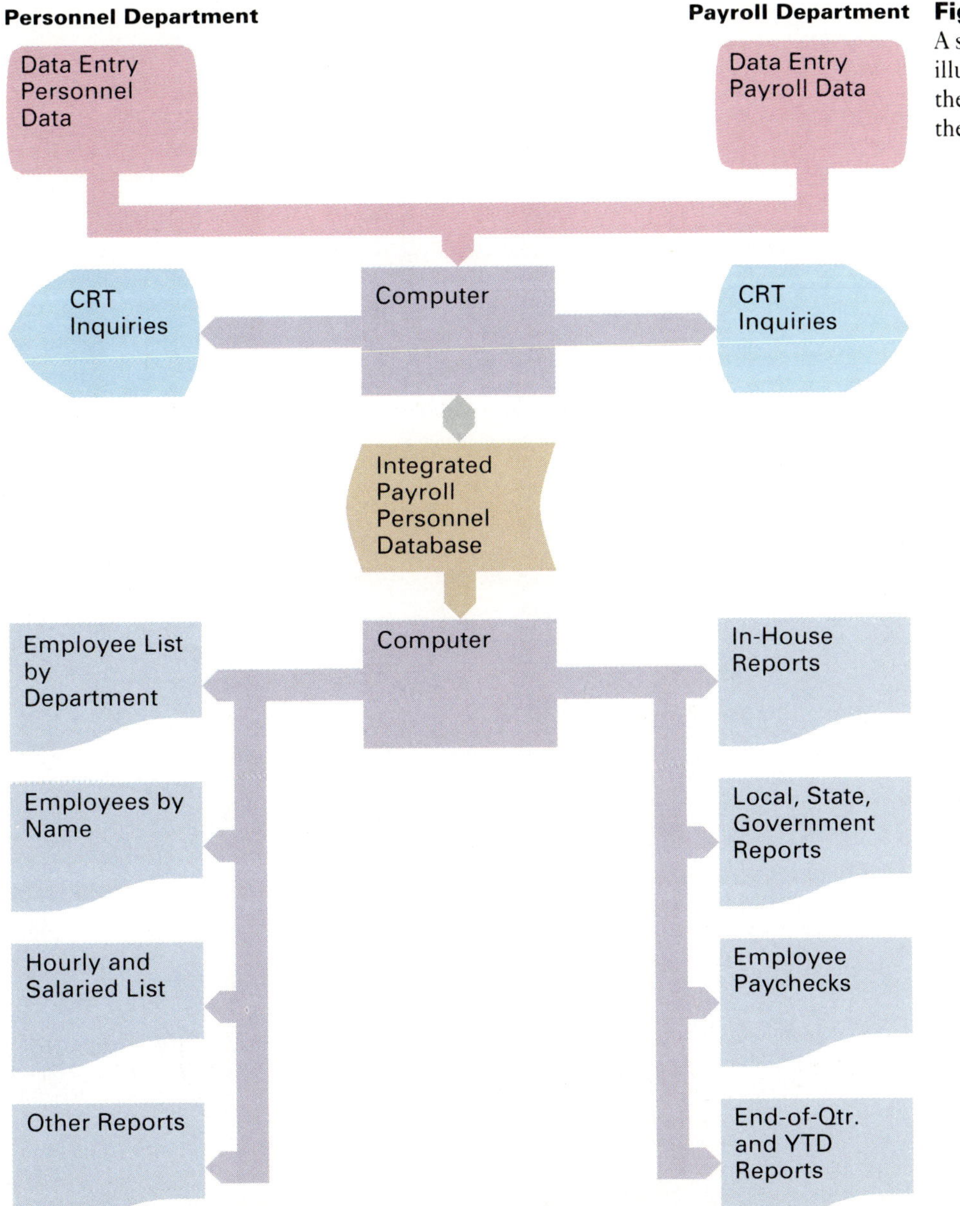

Figure 16-3
A system flowchart illustrates the interaction of the components involved in the system.

Figure 16-4
A flowchart template contains symbols that represent various input/output and processing operations.

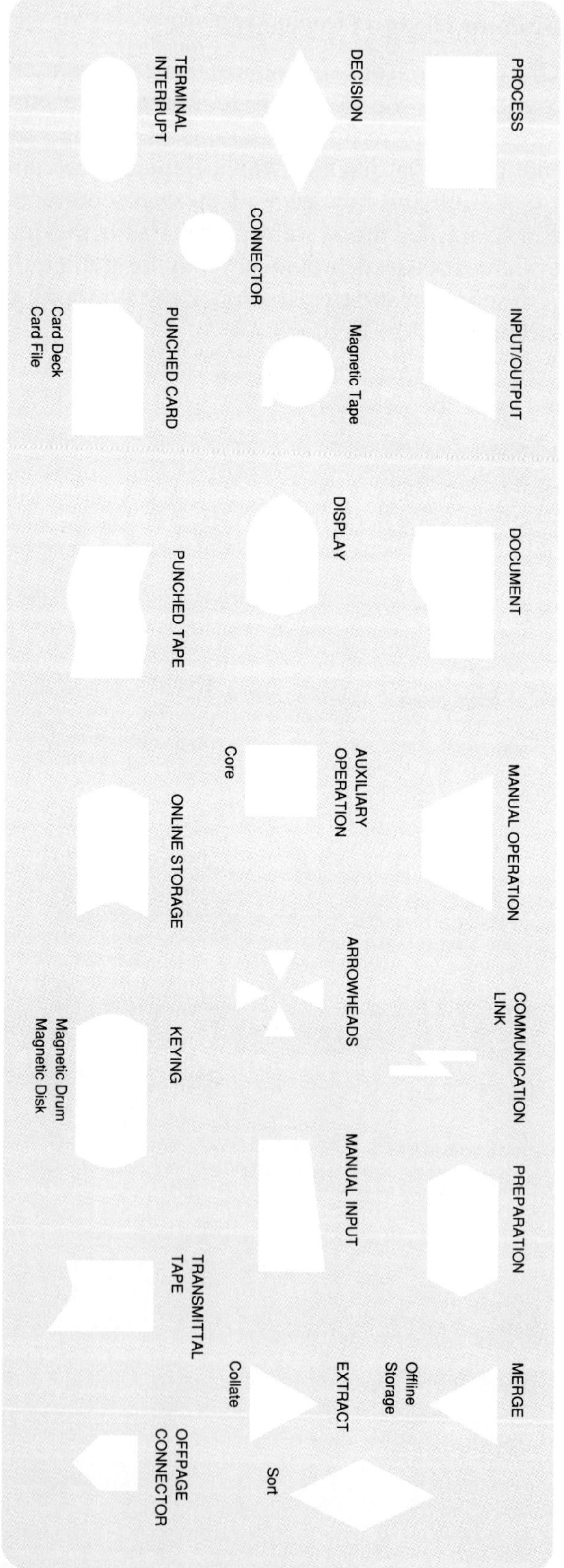

FLOWCHARTING TEMPLATE

Symbols are in three groups: (1) BASIC symbols; (2) processing and sequencing symbols related to programming; (3) input/output, communication link, and processing symbols related to systems.

BASIC Symbols

PROCESS — Any processing function; defined operation(s) causing change in value, form, or location of information.

Comment, Annotation — Additional descriptive clarification, comment. (Dotted line extends to symbols as appropriate.)

INPUT/ OUTPUT — General i/o function; information available for processing (input), or recording of processed information (output).

CONNECTOR: Exit to, or entry from, another part of chart.

Special OFFPAGE CONNECTOR for entry to or exit from a page.

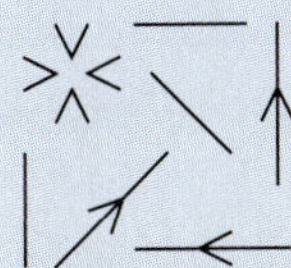

Arrowheads and Flowlines: These show the order of operations and direction of data flow. Arrowheads required if path of any flowline is not left-to-right or top-to-bottom.

Symbols Related to PROGRAMMING

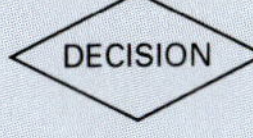

A decision operation that determines which of a number of alternative paths to follow.

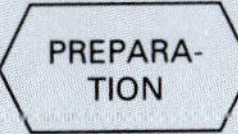

Instruction modification to change program—set a switch, modify an index register, initialize a routine.

Pre-defined Process — One or more named operations or program steps specified in a subroutine or another set of flowcharts.

TERMINAL INTERRUPT — A terminal point in a flowchart—start, stop, halt, delay, or interrupt; may show exit from a closed subroutine.

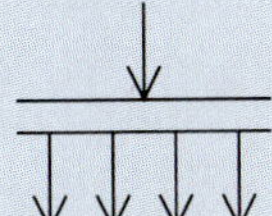

Parallel Mode: Beginning or end of two or more simultaneous operations.

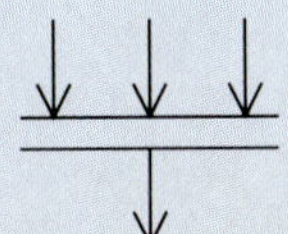

Symbols Related to SYSTEMS

PUNCHED CARD — Input/output function in card medium (all varieties):

A collection of punched cards.

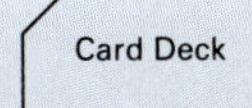

Card File — A collection of related punched-card records.

Other specific media:

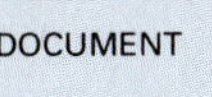

Magnetic Tape

PUNCHED TAPE

TRANSMITTAL TAPE: Proof- or adding machine tape or other batch-control info.

ONLINE STORAGE — Input/output using any kind of online storage—magnetic tape, drum, disk.

KEYING — An operation using a key-driven device—such as punching, verifying, typing.

Other specific media for input/output functions:

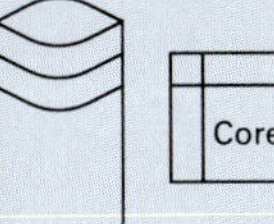

Magnetic Disk

Core

Magnetic Drum

MERGE: Combining two or more sets of items into one set.

EXTRACT: Removal of one or more specific sets of items from a set.

Collate: Merging with extracting; forming two or more sets of items from two or more other sets.

Sort: Arranging a set of items into sequence.

Offline Storage: Storing offline, regardless of recorded medium.

DISPLAY — Information display by online indicators, video devices, console printers, plotters, etc.

MANUAL INPUT — Information input by online keyboards, switch settings, pushbuttons.

MANUAL OPERA-TION — Any offline process (at "human speed") without mechanical aid.

AUXILIARY OPERATION: Offline performance on equipment not under direct control of central processing unit.

COMMUNICATION LINK: Function of transmitting information by a telecommunication link. (Vertical, horizontal, or diagonal, with arrowheads for clarity; bidirectional flow shown by two opposing arrowheads.

Notice that both the personnel and payroll departments are the primary users of the system shown in Figure 16-3. Each department submits data to the computer which, in turn, accesses and updates a database containing the payroll and personnel data stored on disk. From the data submitted and the data stored in the computer's database, each department can perform inquiries as needed to obtain valuable information about any employee in the organization. Also, each department can obtain the various reports it requires. The analyst has used the appropriate symbols of the flowchart template to denote each component involved in the system and the directional flow of data and information.

After the **systems design flowchart** is complete, it becomes the model by which the analyst will develop the various ways, or alternatives, of achieving what is depicted. The general design of the entire system must be reflected in this model. The individuals (or departments) which are responsible for keeping the data up to date and the information which the system must generate should be shown. The analyst must be careful not to overlook others (i.e. management and co-workers in other departments) who could also benefit from the system.

Alternative Designs

The way in which an organization is structured has a great influence on how the system is designed. For example, if all the component parts (individuals, users, equipment, etc.) are located within the same building, the design will be different than if the component parts were spread across great distances. Also, the way in which the company is managed, the education and expertise of its employees, the type of business or products that are produced, and the technology of the computer equipment available all contribute to the system design. In most organizations, management will impose constraints which also affect the design. These constraints may include a fixed budget to which the new system must adhere, the number of personnel that can work on its development, or a time frame by which the new system must be operational.

There are often several ways to design a system to meet given objectives within established constraints. The analyst must use her/his creativity and knowledge to develop these alternative designs. In putting together each design, the analyst must consider many different variables. These variables include considerations such as:

1. Interactions of the personnel who will be the users of the system
2. Capabilities and capacities of the computer hardware
3. New technological improvements in equipment
4. Communications (if any) to be used
5. Number of terminals
6. Speed and types of input/output devices
7. Capabilities and capacities of a database

8. Method of collecting and inputting data into the system
9. Method of processing
10. Potential expansion of the system
11. Ease of programming or availability of software

From the alternatives designed, management will choose the one best suited for the good of the organization. Therefore, each alternative must be able to meet the objectives established during the analysis stage. In order to determine if a design is worthy of being presented to management, however, the systems analyst must perform a feasibility analysis on each alternative.

From the alternative designs presented, management must choose the system that will most benefit the organization.

Feasibility Analysis

A **feasibility analysis** study can be defined as an analysis that is performed on each design alternative to determine whether or not the alternative meets the given objectives while remaining within the constraints of the organization. Often cost/benefit considerations are at the heart of the feasibility analysis study. The costs of the development, installation, and ongoing operation of each design must be weighed against the benefits that it could bring to the organization. The costs should include such things as additional personnel which may be required to set up, run, and maintain the system; new hardware; writing or purchasing of new software; and educational expenses.

The benefits of each design must also be identified. Benefits, however, are not always as easy to measure as the costs are. Benefits can be measurable (called *tangible*) as well as unmeasurable. Measurable benefits may include the reduction of salaries if fewer workers are needed, the reduction of equipment cost if the newer hardware is less expensive, or the reduction of maintenance cost if an obsolete system is replaced. Benefits which are considered unmeasurable include the availability of better information, improved customer service, or more efficient utilization of employees' time.

In addition to cost/benefit considerations, the feasibility analysis must determine if each design is within the constraints the organization has established. Recall, these constraints may be a budget within which the new system must operate, the number of new employees that can be hired, or the time it will take to get the new system operational.

Systems Design Report

After the feasibility analysis has been completed and the various alternative designs have been identified as worthy to present to management, the **systems design report** must be prepared. This report brings together the information which has been created from each of the tasks described previously. The systems design report should include the following information.

I. Introduction
   A. Review of the statement of the problem
   B. Review of the objectives
II. Identification of the components involved
   A. The users
   B. The computer hardware and software
III. Systems Design Summary for each of the design alternatives
   A. Flowchart and written documentation of the proposed design
   B. Employees affected, hired, and/or reassigned
   C. Educational requirements
   D. Time schedule for implementation
   E. Cost/benefit considerations
   F. Other constraint considerations
   G. Conclusions
IV. Recommendations of the first, second, and third best alternative

It is from this information that management will make its decision to continue or stop the system development project. If the decision is to proceed, management will select the alternative it believes best meets the needs of the organization within the established constraints. Often the systems analyst's recommendation is chosen. This is because the analyst has become so familiar with the project, management realizes he/she is in the best position to recognize the alternative with the most potential.

Stage 3—Acquisition and Testing

After management has chosen the new system design, the new hardware (if needed) and software must be acquired. Software may be acquired by in-house programming, custom programming, off-the-shelf programs, or a combination of all three. Once the software is obtained (regardless of the method of acquisition) it must be tested to make sure it is working properly and producing accurate output. Finally, the software must be documented for its operational use and for those responsible for its future maintenance and updating.

New software must be tested for accuracy.

Software Acquisition

Organizations large enough to have their own programming staff often write their own software. Typically, in this environment, the design is unique to the organization's needs. Therefore, the software must be created specifically to meet the needs of the systems design management has chosen. Often, these in-house programs will be written to interface with database or communications software provided by the manufacturer of the computer being used.

Custom programming is the term used when the design specifications are given to a professional programming resource outside the organization for development. It is called custom programming because the software is written specifically to meet the customer's design specifications. This method of software acquisition is used by organizations with a limited technical staff, or a small staff which can support only the operational and maintenance requirements of the system. Rather than hire additional personnel to write the software for a new system, which is a one-time task, the programming is contracted out of house to a company which specializes in this type of custom work.

Off-the-shelf software may be used by companies whose needs and objectives can be accomplished by software which already exists. The purchase and use of such software can save hundreds of thousands of dollars of personnel costs, time, and testing. However, users of off-the-shelf software must often adjust their requirements to what the software can or cannot do. Seldom will an organization find pre-written software that does everything according to the company's specifications. Some companies, with limited programming staff, will select an off-the-shelf program and modify it in order to more closely meet their needs. Many small companies which utilize small computers can find off-the-shelf programs which enable them to effectively and efficiently do all the processing they require. Due to the popularity of personal computers, an abundance of software packages for many different applications is now available from which to choose.

Some organizations' needs can be met by software purchased from an outside source.

Testing

After the software is written or acquired from an outside source it must be tested. The testing of the software must include checking for error-free execution of the software, the accuracy of the output, and the procedures the users must follow in order to communicate with the system.

After the software is installed in the computer, it must be debugged. (Recall that errors which may cause the program to crash, or operate incorrectly, are called bugs. These bugs must be removed, which is called debugging). In addition, input data must be validated, processing routines which interface with the software must be checked, and output must be checked to make sure files are updated properly and reports appear in the correct format.

Once the software is operational, the output must be checked for accuracy. This can be accomplished by comparing similar output of the old system (whether computerized or manual) to that created by the new system. Manual calculations should also be performed and compared to that generated by the new software. Remember that a computer can generate incorrect output just as easily as it can generate correct output. It is essential that the new system reports correct and accurate information in which management, decision makers, and production workers can have confidence.

The testing process must also consider how the entire system interacts and interfaces with its users. These processes include clerical tasks involving data collection and input, data storage, file access, backup, security, and operational procedures of both the users of the system and those operating the computer. In order to test the entire system, it may be necessary to run the new system in parallel (at the same time) to the existing system. By running the new system in parallel, programs can be debugged, procedures can be smoothed out, and all aspects of the system can be checked.

Documentation

Before, during, and after software and hardware testing, documentation should be prepared. Two sets of documentation should be prepared, each addressing a different audience: (1) the users of the system, and (2) the programmer who will be responsible for future updating and maintenance of the software. For example, a user may refer to the documentation when entering data into the system while a programmer may use the documentation to determine where a program must be changed to reflect new data.

Users and programmers rely on documentation for different types of information.

Documentation written for the user of the system should contain an overview of the entire system, a flowchart which shows how each of the component parts interact, and a description of how the system functions. In addition, input forms or screen illustrations with an explanation of each data field to be entered should be included. An example of each of the various outputs, with instructions on how to obtain this information, should also be provided.

Documentation written for the programmer who will be responsible for future updating and maintenance of the software should contain program listings, detailed program flowcharts, and key formulas or logic descriptions of each program. Layouts illustrating the data and its location in input, database files, and printed reports should be included. Procedures for keeping the documentation up to date as changes are made over time should also be a part of this documentation.

Stage 4—Implementation

The implementation stage involves two primary tasks: (1) training and educating the personnel who will be the users of the system, and (2) converting from the existing system to the new system. The training and educating of personnel must address two different audiences—the users of the system and the personnel responsible for operating the computer system. Once the personnel are ready to use and operate the system, the conversion from the old to the new system can take place.

Education

The key component in any system is knowledgeable, cooperative employees. Even the best of systems is doomed to failure if the individuals who work with it do not know how to use it correctly. To make sure this does not happen, the training and educating of individuals who will use and operate the system is given a high priority. The systems analyst is usually the person responsible for the training and educating of personnel. The analyst must make sure that users of the system know what their individual responsibilities are and how to use the information the system provides. Likewise, the analyst must make sure the personnel who operate and maintain the system know what their responsibilities are and how to perform their jobs.

Once the system has been installed, the new users of the system must be trained to use it.

Education and training may be provided in-house, out-of-house, or both. For example, if new computer hardware is to be used, the computer programmers and operators may attend special classes at the computer manufacturer's educational center. After certain key personnel have completed these courses, they may, in turn, teach others what they have learned. Users of the system may be given a short, in-house, hands-on course which actually utilizes the new system during the parallel testing period to learn and become familiar with the new system.

Conversion

After the new system has been fully tested and personnel have been trained, the new system is ready to be installed. This process of installing a new system, or replacing an old system with a new one, is called **conversion.** Several different methods may be used to convert to a new system. One method is to do a direct conversion. That is, at a given, convenient point, the old system is replaced with the new system, and the new one is used from that time on. A second method is to run the new system in parallel with the old system in much the same way that testing is performed. Some organizations prefer to simply extend the test period until it is deemed time to discontinue the old system. A third method is to phase-in the new system. For example, one branch office may be converted to the new system as a trial project prior to converting the rest of the branch offices. Another example of the phase-in method would be to convert one of several of the major components of the system at a time. In the example of the integrated payroll/personnel system, the payroll system could be implemented first, then the personnel system could follow at a later date.

Regardless of the conversion methods used, careful thought and planning must be given to this task. The personnel affected, how they are affected, and the best time to convert must be considered by the systems analyst in order to minimize effort and work disruption. A smooth conversion can contribute greatly to the users' future cooperation and confidence in the system.

Stage 5 – Evaluation and Maintenance

After the implementation stage is completed and the new system is operational, an evaluation of the system should be conducted. The purpose of the evaluation is to determine whether or not the system has met the stated objectives. The evaluation will also act as a summary of the system development project. An evaluation document to be presented to management should evaluate the following:

1. Whether the new system has adequately addressed the statement of the problem.
2. How the implemented system meets each of the organization's stated objectives.
3. Whether the system has stayed within its given constraints.
4. Whether the cost/benefits have been realized.
5. How personnel have adapted to the new system.
6. How new information is utilized.
7. Whether the new system has been accepted by its users.

As a result of this evaluation, minor alterations or modifications may be made to improve the system.

When the evaluation document has been prepared, it should be presented to management to recap the systems development project and to receive management's stamp of approval. Seldom at this stage would management decide to toss aside all the resources that the organization had invested in the system, especially with all the checkpoints along the way. However, if for some reason the system turned out to be a total failure, it would be better to discontinue the system and acknowledge the losses than to continue investing in a bad system.

The evaluation document must be presented to management for final approval.

Finally, system updating, necessitated by change, should be an integral part of system design. A system must be designed to recognize change in the form of feedback. **Feedback** can be defined as a continuous monitoring of the system in order to ensure that its purpose and objectives are being met. Feedback from both within and outside the organization can help ensure the system's effectiveness over a long period of time. Systems, therefore, should be designed in such a way that programming changes can be made with minimum effort. Flexible database software, for example, should permit data to be changed, added, and deleted from the system as required without adversely affecting the users of the system.

Changes which require a system to be updated occur both inside and outside of the organization. The number of changes and the extent of these changes contribute to the length of a system's life cycle. Figure 16-5 illustrates several internal and external factors which require systems to be updated.

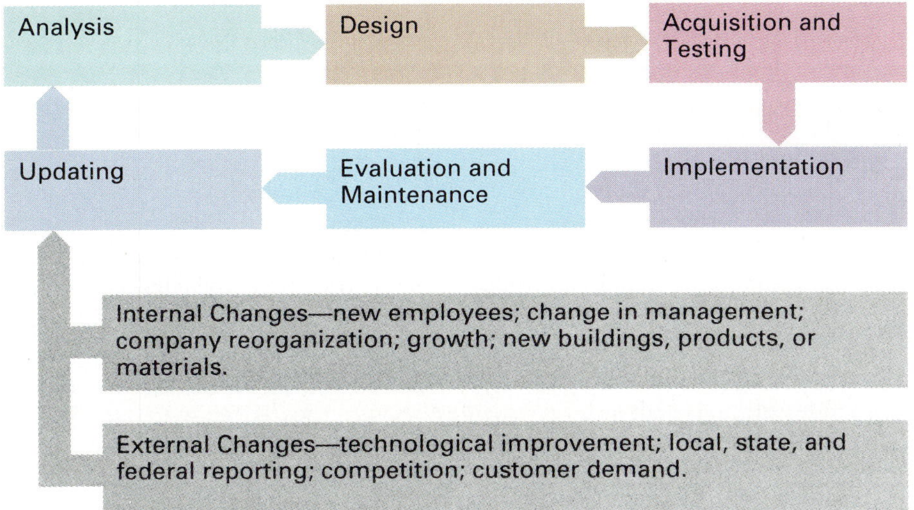

Figure 16-5
Both internal and external factors influence a system's life cycle

Over time, systems become obsolete and too costly to maintain for the benefits they provide. Eventually, a new system will need to be developed to take advantage of technological improvements and to facilitate new requirements of the organization. The entire system development procedure of analysis, design, acquisition and testing, implementation, and evaluation and maintenance will again be used to develop the new replacement system. Once implemented, this system will also require updating during its life cycle to remain effective as long as possible; and so the cycle continues.

MAIL ORDER HARDWARE AND SOFTWARE

Shopping for computer hardware and software through mail order sources can be a way to find exactly what you need, avoid crowds, eliminate travel, and save money. Today, in addition to the computer retail stores commonly found in shopping malls and discount outlets located in most major cities, there are literally thousands of mail order companies competing for customer dollars. They promote their products through catalogs mailed to hundreds of thousands of individuals and companies and through advertising in popular computer magazines.

Most mail order companies operate on the premise of minimizing the number of individuals involved between the manufacturer and customer. By keeping the number of those involved to a minimum, the mail order

Mail order provides a convenient way for users who live in remote locations to purchase hardware and software.

company can obtain a reasonable profit, yet provide savings for its customers. Legitimate mail order companies that are capable of offering quality products, quick service, good prices, technical support, maintenance/repair, attractive warranties, and convenient shopping have met the needs of many buyers.

There are a few helpful hints that, if followed, will help insure customer satisfaction when buying from a mail order company. The first task the customer must perform is to collect and analyze as much information as possible about the item to be ordered. This information is usually acquired during the analysis and design stages of system development. If the item is a closed-architecture computer, this task is very easy. Such closed-architecture systems (i.e. specialized, lap-top, and home computers) are easy to order through mail order companies because they're ready to use right out of the box. However, when purchasing an open-architecture computer with many options, the process can be more involved.

Although the time and effort to secure and analyze the information may be great, the savings are usually good enough to justify the effort. Computer magazines can be a good source for finding information about hardware and software. Often these magazines will print detailed technical articles, offer comparisons of similar products, and rate products based upon cost and performance.

Another good way to obtain information and advice is to join a local computer user group. Members of the user group may share their experiences, offer classes, or give advice to other members considering a purchase. Some user groups may even get involved in assisting their members in purchasing hardware and software.

Perhaps the most effective (but least used) method of obtaining information and advice is to phone several mail order companies' order and technical support lines. Competent sales and technical personnel should be able to answer questions and, thereby, help the buyer make his/her purchasing decision. It is always good to phone several mail order companies and compare their responses before placing an order. While talking to each mail order company representative, the customer should find out how long they have been in business. The more stable the company, the better the customer's chance of satisfaction. Knowing that the company will be there to ship the merchandise, provide technical support, and back up their warranty is more important than buying from the company with the cheapest price. Additional information concerning the stability and customer satisfaction rate of a particular mail order company can be obtained from the Better Business Bureau located in its area.

Finally, the mail order company's written policies should be read and understood. Most advertisements provide all the detailed information a buyer requires to place an order. Items such as guarantees (30-day, money-back guarantee with a one-year warranty on parts and labor); payment methods (COD—Collect On Delivery); and credit card policies, shipping procedures, and insurance charges should be clearly stated.

Many mail order firms spend a lot of money on advertising to get customers to place an order. Once the orders are placed, the legitimate firms will use their resources to try to keep their customers satisfied.

CHAPTER SUMMARY

- Increased research and development, coupled with a growing need for more sophistication, has contributed to the doubling of the human race's knowledge every five to ten years.
- The term system can be defined as related devices and/or procedures that function together in order to achieve a common goal or objective.
- In a world of fast-paced technological invention and the human race's thrust for better and more sophisticated tools there is only one constant: change.
- Despite recent advances in hardware and software, there is still a lack of "brainware." That is, today's computers are capable of doing more than humans have been able to program them to do.
- Just as changes must be made to help us keep pace with our environment, so must changes be made to computer systems in order for them to keep up with technological advances.
- Computer systems have a life cycle. A life cycle can be defined as the period of time in which a given computer system's usefulness to perform a given task is measured.
- The five stages of systems development are (1) analysis, (2) design, (3) acquisition and testing, (4) implementation, and (5) evaluation and maintenance. In addition, once the new system is operational, it must be updated as necessary to prolong its life cycle of usefulness.
- Stage 1—Analysis—has four tasks which must be performed:
  1. A definitive and precise statement of the problem or reason for the development must be stated.
  2. Measurable objectives of what the system is to accomplish must be stated.
  3. The sources of information and the actual information that is needed to meet the system's objectives must be identified.
  4. The analysis report must be prepared.
- Stage 2—Design—has four major tasks which must be performed:
  1. A systems design flowchart must be prepared.
  2. Several viable alternative designs that meet the stated objectives should be developed within the organizational constraints.
  3. A feasibility analysis study weighing the costs-to-benefits derived, time, effort, etc., must be performed for each of the viable alternatives.
  4. The detailed systems design report must be prepared.
- Stage 3—Acquisition and Testing—has three tasks which must be performed:

1. Software must be acquired through in-house programming, custom programming, off-the-shelf programs, or a combination of all three.
2. Once the software is obtained, it must be tested to make sure it is working properly and producing accurate output.
3. The software must be documented for the users of the system as well as for those responsible for its future maintenance and updating.

- Stage 4—Implementation—involves two primary tasks:

1. Personnel who will be the users of the system must be trained and educated.
2. The old system must be converted to the new system.

- Stage 5—Evaluation and Maintenance—is conducted after the implementation stage is completed and the new system is operational. The purpose of the evaluation is to determine whether or not the system has met the stated objectives and to act as a summary of the systems development project.
- System updating necessitated by future change should be an integral part of system design. A system can be designed to recognize change in the form of feedback.
- Feedback can be defined as a continuous monitoring of the system in order to ensure that its purpose and objectives are being met.
- Feedback from both inside and outside the organization can help ensure the system's effectiveness over a long period of time.

KEY TERMS

The following key terms were introduced or redefined in this chapter:

analysis report
conversion
feasibility analysis
feedback
system
system life cycle
systems analyst
systems design flowchart
systems design report

REVIEW QUESTIONS

1. What factors have fueled an accelerated pace of technological improvement? (Obj. 1)
2. Identify two changes which technology has brought about in your home, town, or city within the past five years. (Obj. 1)
3. What is a system? Give examples of three different systems. (Obj. 1)

4. Why must computer systems be changed periodically? (Obj. 1)
5. Describe a computer system's life cycle. (Obj. 2)
6. What are the five stages of systems development? (Obj. 2)
7. Identify the four tasks which must be performed during the analysis stage of systems development. (Obj. 3)
8. Identify the four tasks which must be performed during the design stage of systems development. (Obj. 4)
9. What are the three tasks which are performed during the acquisition and testing stage of systems development? (Obj. 5)
10. Identify the two tasks involved in the implementation stage. (Obj. 6)
11. What is the purpose of the evaluation and maintenance stage of the systems development project? (Obj. 7)
12. What is feedback? (Obj. 8)
13. Why should systems be developed for ease of future updating? (Obj. 8)
14. Identify at least three internal factors which can require an existing system to be updated or become obsolete. (Obj. 8)
15. Identify at least three external factors which can require an existing system to be updated or become obsolete. (Obj. 8)

CHALLENGE ACTIVITIES

1. Consult a computer magazine, your local newspaper, a computer store, your library, or other sources to obtain information about a new use of the computer which has occurred due to technological change over the past five years. Prepare a report describing the application. (Obj. 1)
2. Visit a local police department, business, hospital, industry, or other computer user. Find out how that organization is currently utilizing its computer and what changes have occurred recently that have necessitated an update to the existing system. Prepare a report describing how the computer is utilized and what changes have prompted the update. (Obj. 8)
3. Visit with a systems analyst, or invite him/her to your class. Ask the analyst to describe the procedures he/she follows when developing a new computer system. Find out what considerations are given during system development to anticipate changes. Prepare a report summarizing what you learned. (Objs. 1,2,3,4,5,6,7,8)

CHAPTER 17

PROGRAMMING CONCEPTS

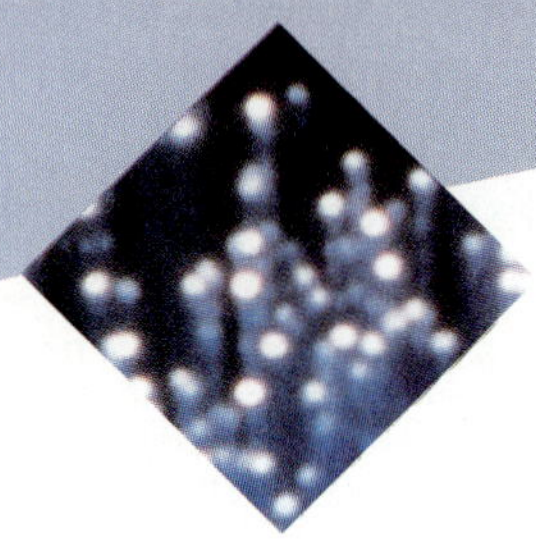

LEARNING OBJECTIVES

After studying this chapter, you will be able to:

1. **Describe the differences between low-level and high-level programming languages.**
2. **Identify the characteristics of commonly used programming languages.**
3. **Describe the procedures and methods used for program development.**

INTRODUCTION

Without software a computer is absolutely useless. Software is the means by which the computer is directed to perform its given tasks. Software can be purchased, or it can be written by the user. In this chapter, you will learn the two general classifications of languages, take a look at the most commonly used programming languages, and find out how programs are developed.

CLASSIFICATION OF LANGUAGES

All computer programs, whether they are manufacturer-supplied, off-the-shelf, custom, or user-written are written in some language the computer can understand. There are more than 150 different programming languages that are available for a wide variety of computers.

Some of these languages are general-purpose and have been designed to be used for a wide variety of applications. Other languages have been designed to be used for specific purposes, such as mathematics and engineering. Regardless of which language is chosen by the programmer or required by the application, it can be classified as either a low-level or a high-level language.

Low-Level Languages

Programs written in the computer's native language, or in a language similar to the computer's native language, are said to be written in **low-level languages.** Originally, computers were programmed in **machine language,** in which the instructions were written in the numeric code directly understood by the processor of the target machine. Each different type of processor has its own unique machine language. For example, because the processor in an IBM personal computer is different than the processor in an Apple microcomputer, the machine language of each computer is also different.

As you already know, all data is represented inside the computer as binary numbers. The instructions that are understood by the computer's processor are also expressed as binary numbers. Therefore, computer instructions written in machine language are written as a string of binary numbers which are unique to that processor. For example, the instructions to tell the IBM PC processor to add 2 plus 2 can be represented as shown in Figure 17-1.

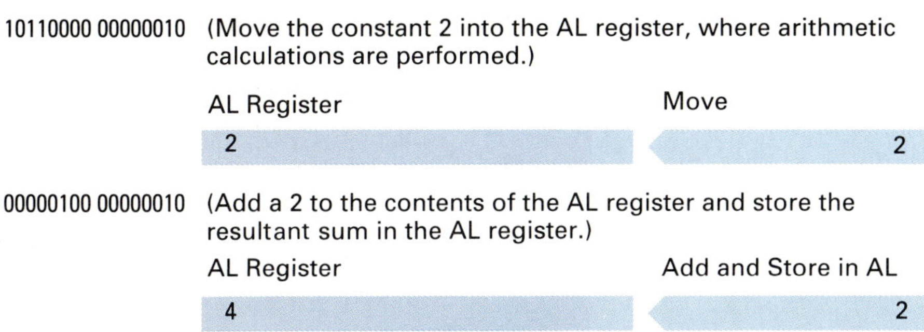

Figure 17-1
Computer instructions are expressed in binary numbers.

Programming in machine language is very technical and time-consuming. Not only must the instructions be in numbers, the programmer must keep track of the exact memory locations where the data items are to be stored. All programs must be translated (interpreted) into the machine language that the computer can understand regardless of what programming language is used. Therefore, each programming language provides a means by which programs written in its language are translated into machine language code prior to execution.

High-Level Languages

Machine language programs require that the programmer think in terms of the particular processor being used and the instructions the processor requires. That is, machine languages are unique to the processor. **High-level languages,** on the other hand, are similar for all kinds of different processors. This allows the programmer to think in terms of solving the problem rather than how to use the processor to its fullest potential. The programmer is able to write instructions to the computer using English and English-like terms.

Because it is easier to use, a high-level language is used to write most application programs. Programs written in a high-level language must first be entered into the computer using a word processor or text editor and then translated into machine language before they can be understood by the processor. The translation is done by either an **interpreter program** or a **compiler program.** The interpreter or compiler is supplied by the computer manufacturer or another vendor.

The operation of an interpreter can be compared to an English-speaking person talking to a Spanish-speaking person through an interpreter. The English-speaking person says a sentence, then the interpreter repeats the sentence in Spanish. This process is repeated as long as the English-speaking person talks. In a similar fashion, an interpreter program for a computer looks at one instruction written in a high-level language, translates the instruction into machine language, and relays it to the processor. The processor immediately carries out the instruction. Then the interpreter looks at the next instruction and translates it. The process is repeated until all instructions are carried out. Using an interpreter causes a program to operate more slowly because each instruction must first be translated into machine language before it can be executed. The use of an interpreter makes it easy for a programmer to **debug** (find and correct the errors) a program.

An interpreter program works very much like a human interpreter.

Compilers also translate high-level languages into machine language. A compiler operation is similar to that of a person who translates a book from English to French. After the entire book is translated and written in French, a person literate in French can read it. A compiler program similarly translates the entire high-level language program into machine language and stores the machine language version in RAM or on an auxiliary storage device. Once the compiled program is loaded in the CPU's RAM, the processor executes the instructions it provides. Programs that have been compiled operate faster than those translated with an interpreter because all the instructions have been converted into machine language before the program is executed. Debugging compiled programs, however, is more difficult and time consuming than debugging interpreted programs because it is often more difficult to isolate problems. Also, each time the program is changed, it must be re-compiled before it can again be executed.

CHARACTERISTICS OF COMMONLY USED PROGRAMMING LANGUAGES

You have already learned that programming languages are either general-purpose or designed to be used for specific applications. In addition, there may be several versions of the same language, each with different capabilities and slightly different instructions. For example, the BASIC programming languages used on a mainframe computer, an IBM personal computer, and an Apple microcomputer use different instructions to read and write data to/from disk. Therefore, a program written in the BASIC language for one machine will not necessarily run on another machine.

Programming languages also differ in structure. That is, their makeup, design, and degree of organization may vary greatly. Some are very structured and require the programmer to follow strict rules of organization. Other languages are free-form and give the programmer a great deal of flexibility. Programming languages also vary greatly in the ease in which they are learned. Some languages are very easy to learn while others can be very difficult.

In the following sections several of the commonly used programming languages will be examined. The purpose of briefly discussing these languages is to provide a brief outline of low- and high-level languages, their use for general-purpose or specific applications, their varying structures, and their ease of learning and use.

Assembly Language

Assembly language is similar to machine language but is considered to be a step above machine language. An assembly language program is a program that works intimately with the machine's hardware. It is a language for those programmers that want to communicate at the lowest level with the inner-workings of their computer. Also, assembly languages enable the programmer to interface with a computer's operating system.

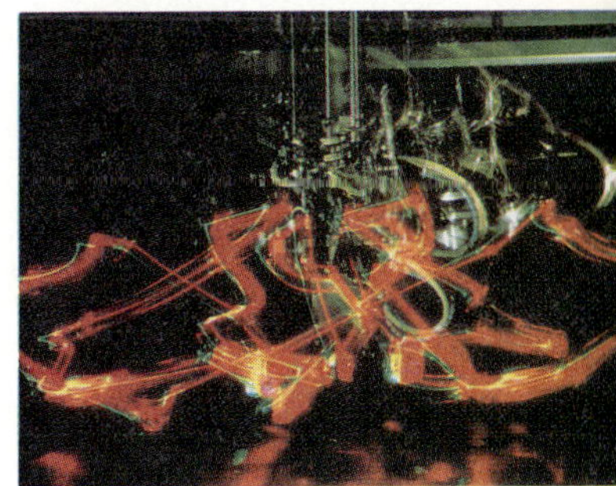

Assembly language can be used when it is necessary to work intimately with the machine's hardware, as is the case with the language used to program this robot.

When using high-level languages, compilers and interpreters read in a given language's commands and must convert them into machine language before the program can be executed. To do this, these compilers and interpreters must churn out a sequence of machine language instructions that: (1) enable the computer to perform the given task, (2) handle a wide variety of error conditions, and (3) include code which may not be used or needed. This means that there is often a large amount of overhead required for even a small program. For example, a compiled

BASIC program will take at least 25K of RAM and disk storage to display one character on the screen. However, an assembly program that does the same thing can be written that uses fewer than 25 bytes. Because the computer does not have to execute all the unnecessary instructions, it can execute the assembly language program much faster.

While assembly language programs are often faster and more efficient than compiled and interpreted programs, their greatest disadvantage is that *everything* must be coded by the user. For example, programs written in assembly languages make no provisions to permit the user to rekey incorrect data unless they have been specifically designed and coded to do so. Also, the user must provide instructions to make sure a given disk drive is available and ready, with the heads positioned at the proper location, when attempting to write or read data from/to disk.

Before programs written in assembly language can be understood by the computer, they must be translated into machine language. The translation is done by a program called an **assembler.** The assembler is supplied by the computer manufacturer or another vendor. The assembler program simply reads the programmer's assembly language program, translates each instruction into its machine language equivalent, and creates a second executable version of the original.

Figure 17-2 contains a segment of an assembly language program that simply counts backward from 5 to 1 and outputs the contents of the counter each time through the loop. A loop is a break in the normal processing sequence so that previous instructions can be re-executed. Line numbers have been placed in front of each program line in order to make reference to the program easier. However, line numbers are not used when entering assembly language programs.

Figure 17-2
Assembly languages are considered to be a step above machine languages.

```
Line:  Program Code:

 1              .
 .              .
 .              .
21              MOV   AL,5     ;set up the loop counter
22     LOOP:
23              OUT   123,AL   ;send the contents of AL to port 123
24              DEC   AL       ;subtract 1 from the contents of AL
25              JNZ   LOOP     ;loop back unless AL has become 0
 .              .
 .              .
 .              .

        The following output will be sent to port 123:

        5
        4
        3
        2
        1
```

Line 21 moves the constant value 5 into AL in order to establish the loop counter AL. Line 22 identifies the following instructions as those belonging to the routine LOOP. Line 23 sends the content of what is stored in AL to port 123 (output device). Line 24 deducts (subtracts) 1 from the contents of AL. Line 25 (Jump Not Zero) causes control to jump back to line 22 and the following instructions to be repeated until the contents of AL are equal to 0.

FORTRAN

FORTRAN was the first problem-oriented computer language. FORTRAN is an acronym which stands for **FOR**mula **TRAN**slation. As its name implies, it was specifically designed for mathematical and scientific applications. FORTRAN statements resemble algebraic expressions which use a combination of variables, constants, and operators. One of its greatest advantages is the extensive collection of scientific and mathematical subroutines that are available. Since these subroutines are a part of the FORTRAN language, complex calculations can automatically be performed without the need to code the formulas each time they are needed. Another of its advantages is that it is a relatively easy-to-learn, problem-oriented language. That is, it does not require a programmer familiar with the internal operation of the computer to use it. Instead, a mathematician, scientist, or engineer that understands mathematics could use FORTRAN most effectively. Thus, the programming effort can focus on the solution of the problem rather than the hardware characteristics of the computer.

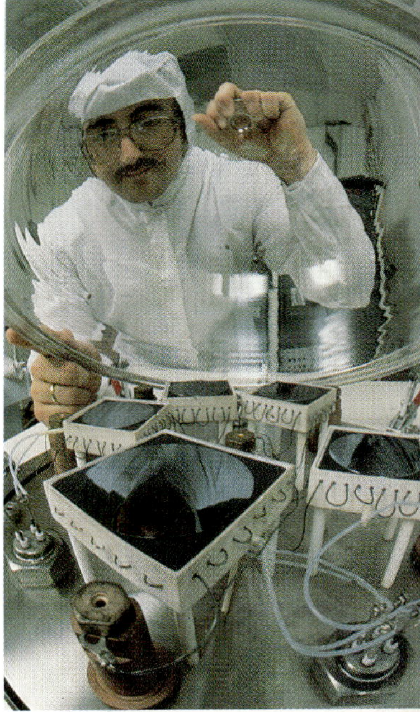

FORTRAN is often the language of choice for scientists.

The major disadvantage of the FORTRAN language is in its limited ability to handle character data and input/output operations. Because it was designed to be a mathematical language used to solve problems that are numeric in nature, it does not lend itself for use in business applications.

The FORTRAN program in Figure 17-3 calculates and then prints the area of a triangle, given the base and height. Refer to this program as you study the comments in the following paragraph about how the program works.

```
Stmnt: Program Code:

 10     READ (5,20) BASE,HEIGHT
 20     FORMAT (F5.2,F5.2)
        IF (BASE.LE.0) GOTO 100
           AREA = 0.5 * BASE * HEIGHT
           WRITE (6,30) BASE,HEIGHT,AREA
 30        FORMAT (F6.2,3X,F6.2,3X,F7.3)
           GOTO 10
100     STOP
        END

        Execution of the Program:

          7.50     10.00      37.5
         (BASE)   (HEIGHT)   (AREA)
```

Figure 17-3
FORTRAN programs are often used to solve mathematical problems.

The statement numbers under the column labeled Stmnt (statement) are used as references to instructions contained within other instructions in the program code. For example, the first statement in the program contains a statement number 10. Notice the third line from the end of the program contains a GOTO instruction that references this first program statement. The READ command instructs the computer to read input data and store this data into the variables BASE and HEIGHT according to the parameters specified within parentheses. The first number within the parentheses (5) identifies the input device from which the data will be read. The second number (20) references the following FORMAT statement which specifies the format of the input data. In this program both input data fields can contain a maximum of five numeric digits, two of which are decimal digits.

The IF statement compares the contents of the variable BASE to 0. If the BASE is less than or equal (LE) to 0, program execution will jump to (GOTO) statement 100 where the program will stop its execution and end. If the BASE is greater than 0, the next instruction will be performed. Notice how the FORTRAN language permits the programmer to write the formula to find the area of a triangle in a format which closely resembles an algebraic expression. In this instruction, 0.5 will be multiplied by the contents of the variable BASE. The product of 0.5 times BASE will then be multiplied by the contents of the variable HEIGHT, and the result will be stored in the variable AREA.

The WRITE statement which follows has a format similar to the READ statement. The contents of BASE, HEIGHT, and AREA will be written to an output device according to the parameters specified within parentheses. The first number within the parentheses (6) identifies the output device to which the data will be written (display screen, printer, disk drive, etc.,). The second number (30) references the following FORMAT statement which specifies the format of the output data. In this program, BASE will be output as a six-digit numeric field with two of the digits being decimal. The 3X instructs the computer to leave three spaces before outputting the second variable (HEIGHT) which also contains six numeric digits, two of which are decimals. Another three spaces are left before outputting the content of the AREA variable containing seven digits, two of which are decimal digits.

The GOTO 10 statement sends control back to statement number 10, and the entire process is repeated for a new set of input BASE and HEIGHT data. This process continues until a BASE data field containing a 0 or negative value is read.

BASIC

BASIC is the acronym for **B**eginner's **A**ll-Purpose **S**ymbolic **I**nstruction **C**ode. The BASIC language was designed to be a high-level, interactive programming language. It is usually translated by an interpreter, which makes the identification and correction of program bugs easier than with most other languages. BASIC has always been considered an easy-to-learn language, partly because of its free-form structure and its English-like instructions. Recent versions of the language have enhanced its capabilities and made it suitable for writing application programs in virtually any area.

BASIC is often used as a student's introduction to programming.

Like all high-level languages, BASIC translates English-like instructions into machine language for execution by the processor. Unlike most others, however, BASIC also includes the necessary software for entering a program into the computer's memory, editing the program, and saving it on an auxiliary storage device. The use of a separate word processor or text editor is not required.

The BASIC program in Figure 17-4 calculates and then prints the area of a circle, given the radius. Refer to this program as you study the comments in the following paragraph about how the program works.

```
10 REM  CALCULATE THE AREA OF A CIRCLE
20 INPUT "ENTER THE RADIUS OF A CIRCLE: ";RADIUS
30 AREA = 3.14 * RADIUS^2
40 PRINT "THE AREA OF THE CIRCLE EQUALS ";AREA
50 END

   Execution of the program:

   ENTER THE RADIUS OF A CIRCLE: 5
   THE AREA OF THE CIRCLE EQUALS 78.5
```

Figure 17-4
BASIC programs make use of English-like instructions.

Each numbered line of a BASIC program is known as a **BASIC statement.** In this program, statements have been assigned numbers beginning with 10 and incremented by 10. This type of numbering scheme allows additional statements to be added between existing BASIC statements if required. Statement 10 is a Remark (REM) statement that is used to tell the reader what this program does. Remark statements are optional and are used for documentation purposes only. Statement 20 prints the prompt message enclosed within quotes to the screen and waits for the user to enter a numeric value representing the radius of a circle from the keyboard. Once the radius is entered, statement 30 calculates the area of the circle by multiplying Pi (3.14) times the radius squared. The result is stored in the variable named AREA. Statement 40 prints the message contained within quotes followed by the contents of AREA (the computed area of the circle) to the display screen. Finally, statement 50 ends the program.

Appendix C, "BASIC Programming," has been provided to cover this language in more detail and enable you to learn how to write simple BASIC programs.

Pascal

The Pascal language was named in honor of the mathematician Blaise Pascal, who lived in the seventeenth century. It was designed to be a high-level, general-purpose language useful for writing programs for nearly every application. Like all high-level languages, Pascal must be translated into machine language for execution by the computer. A Pascal program must first be entered into the computer with a word processor or text editor and stored on an auxiliary storage device. The program keyed into the computer is known as a **source program** since it is the source from which the translation is to be made.

Many businesses, such as this flower shop, use Pascal to calculate sales commissions.

After the source program is keyed into the computer and stored, the Pascal compiler is used to translate the program into an **object program,** the result or object of the translation. Depending on the implementation of Pascal, the translation may be directly into machine code or into an intermediate type of code. If the translation is into machine code, the translated program can be executed directly and will run at a high speed. If the translation is into intermediate code, the source program is translated into "pseudo commands" (made-up processor commands that do not necessarily match the machine code commands of any processor). A special interpreter program, called a **run-time program,** translates these commands to machine code at the time the program is executed. The advantage of this procedure is that the same translated Pascal code can be used regardless of the processor on which the program is to run. It is only necessary to provide a different run-time interpreter program for each different model of processor. The disadvantages are slower program execution and the requirement that the run-time interpreter program always be available on the disk.

One of the primary advantages of the Pascal language is that it encourages the use of good programming techniques through an established structure which must be followed. For example, each program must be named, all variables must be specified before use, and all processing must be performed between the Begin and End statements. In addition, the code resembles English-like sentences, which makes learning the language and modifying the program easier than with most other languages.

As stated previously, a variable is a named storage location in the computer's memory. As a program is executed, various data may be stored in this location. One of Pascal's strong points is the many different types of data that may be stored in variables. In addition to the data types provided by the language, the programmer may define other types. For example, if a program is to be used by a bakery, a data type known as PIES could be defined. The programmer could then specify that this data type could have only the values CHOCOLATE, COCONUT, LEMON, and PECAN. The program could contain a statement that says, in effect, "print sales figures for all the chocolate, coconut, lemon, and pecan pie sales."

The three most commonly used data types are character data, integer numbers, and real numbers. Character data consists of alphabetic, numeric, and special symbols (i.e. street address—952 Creek Drive). An integer is a whole number (i.e. 10), while a real number is a number with a decimal point (i.e. 85.5). The variables which are used to store these various data types are given names known as **identifiers.**

The Pascal program shown in Figure 17-5 calculates the amount of commission to pay a salesperson. If a salesperson sells less than $5,000 worth of merchandise for the week, the commission will be computed at a rate of 7 percent. If the sales for the week are $5,000 or greater, the commission will be computed at a rate of 9 percent. Refer to this program as you study the comments in the following paragraphs about how the program works. Note, line numbers have been placed in front of the statements in order to make reference to the program easier. However, line numbers are not used when entering Pascal programs.

Line 1 names the program PAY and indicates that the program will do both input and output operations. Lines 2 and 3 contain comments indicated by braces, { }, which are ignored by Pascal when the program is compiled. The comments are optional and are for the benefit of those reading the program. In line 4 the variables which are used in the program are declared. This program is using only real variables. The program instructions begin with line 5. Line 6 prints a prompt message, followed on line 7 by the READLN procedure to get a sales amount from the keyboard and place it in the variable SALES.

Figure 17-5
Pascal programs can be written for nearly any application.

```
Line:   Program code:

 1      PROGRAM PAY (INPUT,OUTPUT);
 2         {Written by Harmon Perez, 11/10/--}
 3         {This program calculates commissions}
 4      VAR SALES, COMMISSION, RATE: REAL;
 5      BEGIN
 6         WRITE('Enter the amount of sales: ');
 7         READLN(SALES);
 8         WRITELN;
 9         IF SALES<5000 THEN RATE:=0.07
                         ELSE RATE:=0.09;
10         COMMISSION:=SALES*RATE;
11         WRITELN('Rate:   ',RATE:3:2,'   Commission:   ',COMMISSION:7:2);
12      END.

        Execution of the program with less than $5,000:

        Enter the amount of sales: 4750.18

        Rate:   0.07   Commission:   332.51

        Execution of the program with sales greater than $5,000:

        Enter the amount of sales: 7432.98

        Rate:   0.09   Commission:   668.97
```

Once the input is received from the keyboard, line 8 prints a blank line. Next, a decision must be made on whether the commission rate to be used should be 7 percent or 9 percent. This is done in line 9 by using the IF...THEN...ELSE statement. Here, one of two alternative actions may be taken. As stated, if the amount stored in SALES is less than (<) 5,000, store 0.07 in the variable named RATE, else store 0.09 in RATE. Line 10 multiplies this rate times the sales amount and places the product into the variable that holds the amount of commission. On line 11, the WRITELN procedure is then used to print the result. Finally, line 12 ends the program.

COBOL

COBOL was the first high-level language written for use in business applications. Its name is an acronym derived from **CO**mmon **B**usiness **O**riented **L**anguage. It was developed through the efforts of the Department of Defense working in conjunction with representatives from the computer industry, government, and computer user groups. By 1960 the first commercial versions of COBOL were made available. Several revisions of the COBOL language have occurred since then. COBOL is still a commonly used language for business applications, especially with minicomputers and mainframes. Its strong point is the handling of large amounts of data stored on auxiliary storage devices. It is also one of the wordiest languages and a language which uses a great deal of RAM. While some programmers object to the large number of words required and/or the amount of memory it consumes, its English-like sentences make COBOL programs easier to understand than those written in some other languages. Therefore, they are also easy to modify and maintain. COBOL is most often translated by a compiler; however, interpreted versions are also available on mainframe computers.

COBOL is still commonly used in business environments.

COBOL is generally considered a standard language. A COBOL compiler must contain certain standard capabilities. With some exceptions (the reference manual for the version of COBOL being used will point out variations from the standard), the COBOL program that runs on one computer can be easily changed to run on another computer. For this reason, COBOL is said to be a machine-independent language.

All COBOL programs are written in four parts, known as **divisions.** These divisions and their titles must appear in every program in the following order:

1. **IDENTIFICATION DIVISION.** This division is used to identify the name of the program, the author, and the date the program was written.
2. **ENVIRONMENT DIVISION.** This division specifies the type of computer on which the program is to run. It also names the input and output files and may specify the input and output devices to be used.
3. **DATA DIVISION.** This division describes the data files and data structures to be used by the program.
4. **PROCEDURE DIVISION.** This division specifies the actual steps the computer is to follow in processing the data to solve a problem. This part of a COBOL program is the part most like a BASIC program.

Each of these four divisions can be sub-divided into several **sections.** These sections are used to categorize related information and define files, data, or processing steps.

The English-like words used in writing a COBOL program are of two types: those on a reserved word list and those supplied by the programmer. A **reserved word** is a word that has a specific meaning to a COBOL compiler. The compiler reserves such words for given purposes, such as ADD, SUBTRACT, MOVE, and WRITE. **Programmer-supplied words** are any nonreserved words used in a program. These words must be defined in the Data Division of the program.

The COBOL program shown in Figure 17-6 has been written to record student data in a student scores file on disk. A record containing the name, class code, and three test scores are recorded to disk for each student keyed into the computer. Lines 1, 5, 12, and 26 identify the four divisions of the program.

Figure 17-6
COBOL programs are written in four parts, known as divisions.

```
Line:   Program Code:

 1      IDENTIFICATION DIVISION.
 2      PROGRAM-ID.      STSCORE.
 3      AUTHOR.          J. SAMUELSON.
 4      DATE-WRITTEN.    SEPTEMBER 15, 19--.
 5      ENVIRONMENT DIVISION.
 6      CONFIGURATION SECTION.
 7      SOURCE-COMPUTER.     IBM-PC.
 8      OBJECT-COMPUTER.     IBM-PC.
 9      INPUT-OUTPUT SECTION.
10      FILE-CONTROL.
11          SELECT SCORES-FILE, ASSIGN TO DISK.
12      DATA DIVISION.
13      FILE SECTION.
14      FD  SCORES-FILE
15          LABEL RECORDS STANDARD
16          VALUE OF FILE-ID IS "A:SCORES".
17      01  STUDENT.
18          05  STUDENT-NAME      PIC A(20).
19          05  CLASS-CODE        PIC 9.
20          05  SCORE-1           PIC 999.
21          05  SCORE-2           PIC 999.
22          05  SCORE-3           PIC 999.
23      WORKING-STORAGE SECTION.
24      77  CONTINUE-OPTION       PIC X.
25          88 FINISHED VALUE IS 'N'.
26      PROCEDURE DIVISION.
27      MAIN-MODULE.
28          OPEN OUTPUT SCORES-FILE.
29          PERFORM DETAIL-PROCESSING-MODULE UNTIL FINISHED.
30          CLOSE SCORES-FILE.
31          STOP RUN.
32      DETAIL-PROCESSING-MODULE.
33          DISPLAY 'ENTER STUDENT NAME:'.
34          ACCEPT STUDENT-NAME.
35          DISPLAY 'ENTER CLASS CODE (1,2,3, OR 4):'.
36          ACCEPT CLASS-CODE.
37          DISPLAY 'ENTER THE FIRST SCORE:'.
38          ACCEPT SCORE-1.
39          DISPLAY 'ENTER THE SECOND SCORE:'.
40          ACCEPT SCORE-2.
41          DISPLAY 'ENTER THE THIRD SCORE:'.
42          ACCEPT SCORE-3.
43          WRITE STUDENT.
44          DISPLAY 'ANY MORE SCORES (Y/N)?'.
45          ACCEPT CONTINUE-OPTION.
```

Notice how lines 2-4 of the Identification Division are used to identify the name of the program (STSCORE), the name of the author (J. SAMUELSON), and the date the program was written (SEPTEMBER 15, 19--).

Lines 6-11 of the Environment Division contain two sections: Line 6 identifies the Configuration Section, and Line 9 identifies the Input-Output Section. The Source-Computer (line 7) identifies the computer that the COBOL program will be compiled on, while the Object-Computer (line 8) identifies the computer that will execute the compiled program. In this case, both the source and object computers are the same (IBM-PC). Lines 9-11 of the Input-Output Section identify the file called SCORES-FILE as the file which will be written to disk.

Lines 13-25 of the Data Division are used to describe the file and data fields used in the program. Two sections are also contained in this division: the File-Section (line 13) and the Working-Storage Section (line 23).

Lines 27-45 make up the Procedure Division. Notice that this division is broken into two modules: a main module, which controls the processing, and a sub-module, which does the detailed processing.

PL/1

PL/1 (**P**rogramming **L**anguage/**1**) was designed to be a general-purpose language which combined the business processing features of COBOL with the mathematical and scientific features of FORTRAN. The language can be easily learned because it can be written in a free-form format or structured format, uses English-like sentences, and is self-documenting. Like FORTRAN, it contains many features that permit solutions to complex mathematical problems. Like COBOL, it contains many features that permit a high level of input/output operations and efficient handling of large amounts of both character and numeric data. PL/1 has not enjoyed the popularity of many of the languages already discussed. This is primarily because users of the FORTRAN and COBOL languages have such a large investment in the development of their software that they have been reluctant to change. As a result, the potential of PL/1 has appealed to users who are relatively new computer users or to those companies who do not have heavy investments in a particular language.

RPG

The RPG (**R**eport **P**rogram **G**enerator) language was initially designed for users of small computer systems as a general-purpose, business-oriented language for generating reports. Since its initial development, it has undergone two major enhancements which has made it second to COBOL as the most popular business programming language. The first enhancements identified the language as RPG II and the second as RPG III. Each enhanced version of the language included extensive data management and database capabilities.

RPG is a very structured, high-level language with built-in logic. All programming is built around its pre-defined, built-in logic structure which facilitates quick and easy report generation from various databases. It requires the programmer to code onto special coding forms (see Figure 17-7) that specify unique processing requirements. For example, the Input Specifications form describes the particular input device(s) to be used, the format of the record(s) to be read, the fields that make up each record, and the characteristics of each field within the record(s) (i.e. numeric, alphabetic, etc.). Conversely, the Output Specifications form is used to describe the same types of information about the output to be created by the program. A Calculations Specifications form is used to identify the mathematical calculations and data fields used. Once the required coding forms are complete, the program can be keyed into the computer, compiled, and executed without a great deal of concern about the program logic.

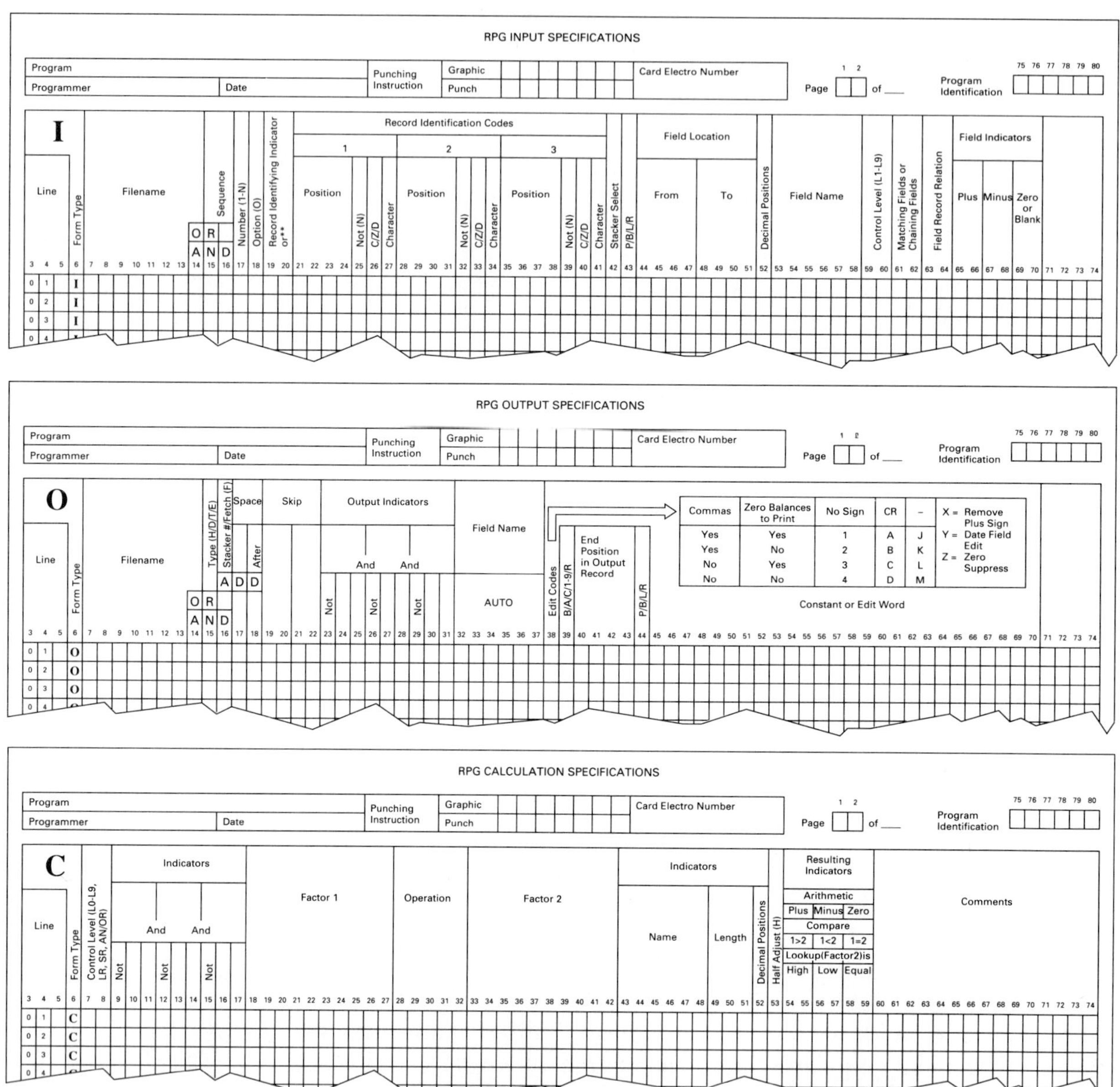
RPG INPUT SPECIFICATIONS

Program | Programmer | Date | Punching Instruction | Graphic | Punch | Card Electro Number | Page 1 2 of ___ | Program Identification 75 76 77 78 79 80

I

Line | Form Type | Filename | Sequence | OR / AND | Number (1-N) | Option (O) | Record Identifying Indicator or** | Record Identification Codes: 1 (Position, Not (N), C/Z/D, Character), 2 (Position, Not (N), C/Z/D, Character), 3 (Position, Not (N), C/Z/D, Character) | Stacker Select | P/B/L/R | Field Location (From, To) | Decimal Positions | Field Name | Control Level (L1-L9) | Matching Fields or Chaining Fields | Field Record Relation | Field Indicators (Plus, Minus, Zero or Blank)

3 4 5 6 7 8 9 10 11 12 13 14 15 16 17 18 19 20 21 22 23 24 25 26 27 28 29 30 31 32 33 34 35 36 37 38 39 40 41 42 43 44 45 46 47 48 49 50 51 52 53 54 55 56 57 58 59 60 61 62 63 64 65 66 67 68 69 70 71 72 73 74

0 1 I
0 2 I
0 3 I
0 4 I

RPG OUTPUT SPECIFICATIONS

Program | Programmer | Date | Punching Instruction | Graphic | Punch | Card Electro Number | Page 1 2 of ___ | Program Identification 75 76 77 78 79 80

O

Line | Form Type | Filename | OR / AND | Type (H/D/T/E) | Stacker #/Fetch (F) | Space (A D D) | After | Skip | Output Indicators (Not, And Not, And Not) | Field Name | AUTO | Edit Codes | B/A/C/1-9/R | End Position in Output Record | P/B/L/R | Constant or Edit Word

Commas	Zero Balances to Print	No Sign	CR	–
Yes	Yes	1	A	J
Yes	No	2	B	K
No	Yes	3	C	L
No	No	4	D	M

X = Remove Plus Sign
Y = Date Field Edit
Z = Zero Suppress

3 4 5 6 7 8 9 10 11 12 13 14 15 16 17 18 19 20 21 22 23 24 25 26 27 28 29 30 31 32 33 34 35 36 37 38 39 40 41 42 43 44 45 46 47 48 49 50 51 52 53 54 55 56 57 58 59 60 61 62 63 64 65 66 67 68 69 70 71 72 73 74

0 1 O
0 2 O
0 3 O
0 4 O

RPG CALCULATION SPECIFICATIONS

Program | Programmer | Date | Punching Instruction | Graphic | Punch | Card Electro Number | Page 1 2 of ___ | Program Identification 75 76 77 78 79 80

C

Line | Form Type | Control Level (L0-L9, LR, SR, AN/OR) | Indicators (Not, And Not, And Not) | Factor 1 | Operation | Factor 2 | Indicators (Name, Length) | Decimal Positions | Half Adjust (H) | Resulting Indicators: Arithmetic (Plus, Minus, Zero); Compare (1>2, 1<2, 1=2); Lookup(Factor2)is (High, Low, Equal) | Comments

3 4 5 6 7 8 9 10 11 12 13 14 15 16 17 18 19 20 21 22 23 24 25 26 27 28 29 30 31 32 33 34 35 36 37 38 39 40 41 42 43 44 45 46 47 48 49 50 51 52 53 54 55 56 57 58 59 60 61 62 63 64 65 66 67 68 69 70 71 72 73 74

0 1 C
0 2 C
0 3 C
0 4 C

Figure 17-7
Special coding forms can be used when developing an RPG program.

C Programming Language

The C language was developed in the early 1970s by Dennis Ritchie at Bell Laboratories for the purpose of rewriting the company's Unix operating system. Today, after several revisions, it is considered to be a general-purpose programming language. The C programming language enables programmers to code their programs using a high-level type symbolic code, yet it offers low-level control over the hardware. C is considered a low-level language that makes extensive use of pre-written routines (called library routines) that can be used in different programs for a variety of applications. Its greatest use is by programmers who need (or like) to work at machine level in order to get the best possible performance from their computers. C is also considered to be a very transportable language. That is, it can execute on a wide variety of different computers with minor modification. For these reasons, C is becoming a popular language among programmers writing software for personal computers.

Fourth-Generation Languages

Fourth-generation languages (i.e. FOCUS, RAMIS, NOMAD) are the highest level of high-level programming languages. Several fourth-generation languages have been developed as a result of the recent advancements in computer technology. New high-speed computers with vast amounts of storage and sophisticated auxiliary storage devices have been developed because of a demand for additional processing capabilities. More users of computers have also contributed to this rapid growth of technology and the applications for which the computer is utilized. As a result, new languages have been developed to take advantage of this technology and to improve the applications services to the users.

Fourth-generation languages have been designed to be general-purpose in nature and to be used by both programmers and computer users. They can be learned with a minimum amount of training. Most of these languages require the user to respond to a series of questions that request information about the tasks to be performed. After all the needed information is supplied, a program is automatically generated by the language itself. Once the program is generated, it can be compiled and executed. This procedure can be completed in a fraction of the time it would take a programmer to write a program in any of the languages previously discussed.

The speed with which programs can be written and the ease with which fourth-generation languages can be used hold great potential for permitting users who are not computer programmers to satisfy their own information needs. These languages remove the technical concerns of using the computer and direct the emphasis on the applications which are to be performed.

PROGRAM DEVELOPMENT

Structured programming is a method used to write programs from logically organized, detailed plans which define the steps that must be performed. Some persons separate the process into **structured design** (the planning of the program) and **structured programming** (the actual writing of the program). In the remainder of this section, the methods used in structured programming will be discussed. These steps can be used regardless of which high-level language is used. Writing structured programs is easier in some languages, however, than in others.

Top-Down Design/Hierarchy Charts

Top-down design of a program begins by defining what the program is to do and then gradually increases the level of detail in the plan. This begins with a hierarchy chart. A **hierarchy chart** looks like an organizational chart for a business which shows the boss at the top and the workers below. The following example will help clarify this concept.

The example program to be developed will be a mailing labels program. It must be able to perform four functions: (1) add names and addresses, (2) make corrections in names and addresses, (3) delete names and addresses, and (4) print mailing labels. The illustration in Figure 17-8 depicts the completed hierarchy chart for the mailing labels program.

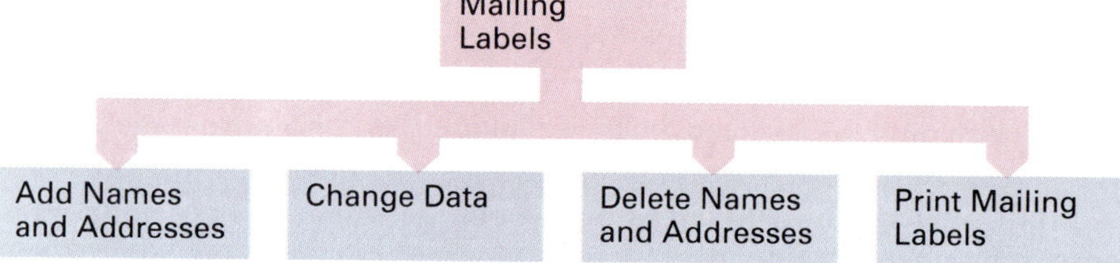

Figure 17-8
Top-down design of a program begins with the development of a hierarchy chart.

Think of each box as being a functional component of a computer program. The top box (labeled Mailing Labels) is the boss part of the program. Under the boss there are four workers; each of the workers knows how to perform one of the four functions of the program. Each of the workers performs its duty when instructed to do so by the boss.

Output Design

The output to be produced by the program must also be designed. In this example, the output is mailing labels. A **report spacing chart,** as shown in Figure 17-9, is used to illustrate what the output should look

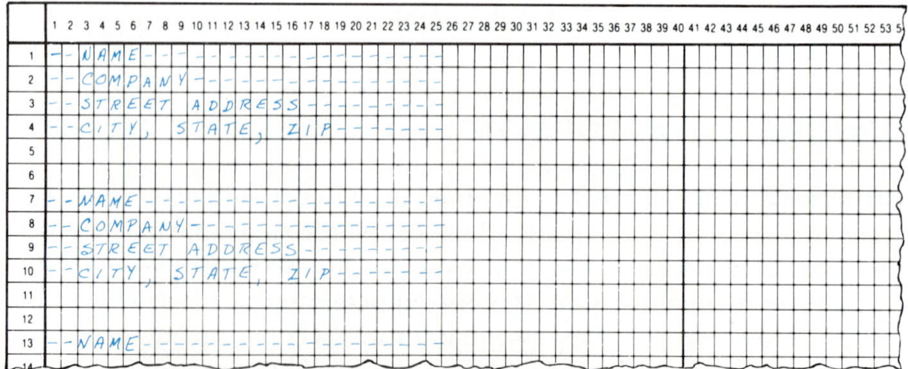

Figure 17-9
Program output is designed on a report spacing chart.

like. Note that the report spacing chart is a form arranged in rows and columns with space for each position in which a character can be printed. When completed, it shows the length of each data item that is to appear on the output as well as its location. The spacing for this example shows two labels to indicate that the layout is repeated down a page of labels.

Program Design

One of the main concepts of structured programming is that any program can be written using only four kinds of instructions. These four kinds of instructions are described below:

1. **Sequential instructions** are simply steps that are performed one after another. For example:

   Clear the display screen.
   List the four functions on the screen.
   Obtain the user's choice of functions.

2. **Case instructions** provide a way for executing one set of instructions out of numerous possibilities included in the program. For example:

   Depending on the user's choice, perform one of the four functions.

3. **Loop control instructions** are those that are used to make the computer repeat certain instructions. Instructions may be repeated until some condition becomes true, or they may be repeated as long as some condition remains true. For example:

   While the user wants to add more people:
   Get name from keyboard.
   Check to see if name is already stored.

4. **IF...THEN...ELSE instructions** instruct the computer to perform one task if a statement is true or another task if the statement is false. For example:

   IF name is already stored, THEN inform the user
   ELSE get street address, city, state, and ZIP code
   data from the keyboard and store it on disk.

With these kinds of instructions in mind, a program design is written on a Module Documentation form for each of the boxes from the hierarchy chart shown in Figure 17-8. Each box, which represents a function or task the program must perform, is known as a **module.** A **program design** (also known as **pseudocode**) consists of the detailed steps that must be performed by each module within a program. The program design is written in ordinary English. By consolidating the steps given in the example above and adding a few more instructions, the program design for the **main module** (the top box) is created. The program designs for the main module and the names and addresses module are shown in Figure 17-10. Note that what is written in Figure 17-10 is really a detailed outline of the instructions that the computer must perform in order to accomplish its tasks. In addition, and in a similar fashion, program designs must be written onto Module Documentation forms for each of the remaining three modules.

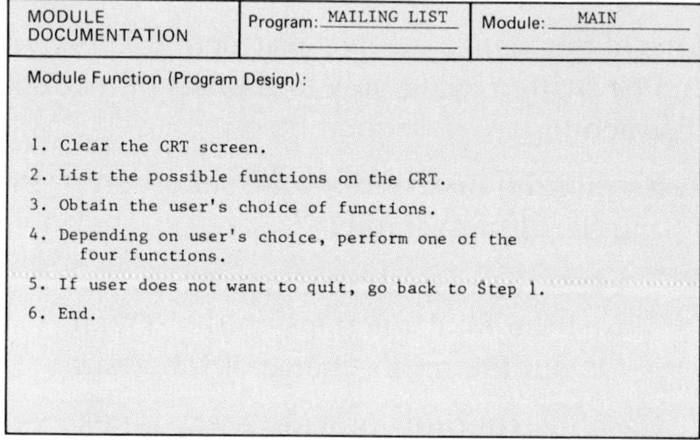

MODULE DOCUMENTATION | Program: MAILING LIST | Module: MAIN

Module Function (Program Design):

1. Clear the CRT screen.
2. List the possible functions on the CRT.
3. Obtain the user's choice of functions.
4. Depending on user's choice, perform one of the four functions.
5. If user does not want to quit, go back to Step 1.
6. End.

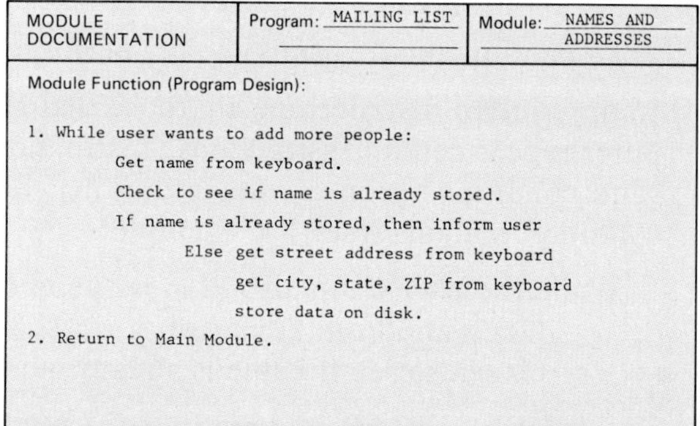

MODULE DOCUMENTATION | Program: MAILING LIST | Module: NAMES AND ADDRESSES

Module Function (Program Design):

```
1. While user wants to add more people:
        Get name from keyboard.
        Check to see if name is already stored.
        If name is already stored, then inform user
              Else get street address from keyboard
                   get city, state, ZIP from keyboard
                   store data on disk.
2. Return to Main Module.
```

Figure 17-10
Program design consists of listing the program steps in English.

Some programmers prefer to draw a flowchart to identify the detailed steps that must be performed rather than use pseudocode and module documentation forms. A **flowchart** is a method of using graphic representations to illustrate the detailed steps of a hierarchy chart. In order to illustrate the design of a program in flowchart form, each detailed step of the program is placed inside a symbol that indicates what kind of action is taking place at each step. Arrows, called **flowlines,** are used to connect the different steps and show the direction of data flow. The flowline usually proceeds from top-to-bottom and left-to-right, although there can be exceptions.

A template (the same, or similar, to the one used in Chapter 16 to illustrate the component parts of a system) is used to draw the flowchart. There are many symbols that can be used in flowcharting. However, the logic of most programs can adequately be illustrated by using only the symbols shown in Figure 17-11.

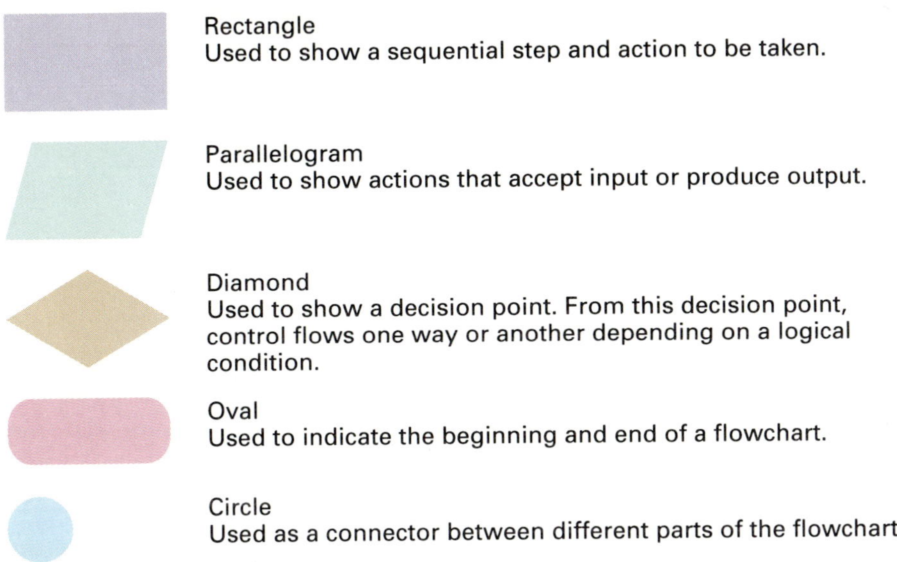

Figure 17-11
Most programs can be depicted using these flowchart symbols.

Figure 17-12 on the following page illustrates how our example Mailing Labels program could be flowcharted from the hierarchy chart shown in Figure 17-8. Notice the flowlines and how each of the commonly used flowchart symbols have been used to illustrate the detailed logic of the program.

Coding and Testing

Writing the instructions of a computer program in a computer language is known as **coding** the program. Up to this point in the program development process, the language in which the program is to ultimately be coded has not been considered. This is because the program design (pseudocode) or flowchart that was developed can be converted to assembly language, FORTRAN, BASIC, Pascal, COBOL, or virtually any other programming language. For each of the statements in the program design or for each step in the flowchart, one or more statements are written in the chosen programming language.

When using structured design, the main module is coded and tested first, then all the other modules are coded and tested. In order to illustrate the process, Figure 17-13 on page 385 shows the main module of the Mailing Labels program coded in a version of BASIC used by the IBM PC and many other popular microcomputers. Remark statements are included to help explain the program.

After the program has been coded, it must be tested. Recall that errors in a program are called "bugs." Programs with errors either will not execute properly or will produce incorrect results. In order to determine if bugs exist, the newly coded program must be tested. **Testing** is the process of finding and correcting errors and is commonly known as "debugging." The process typically involves inputting data similar to the

Figure 17-12

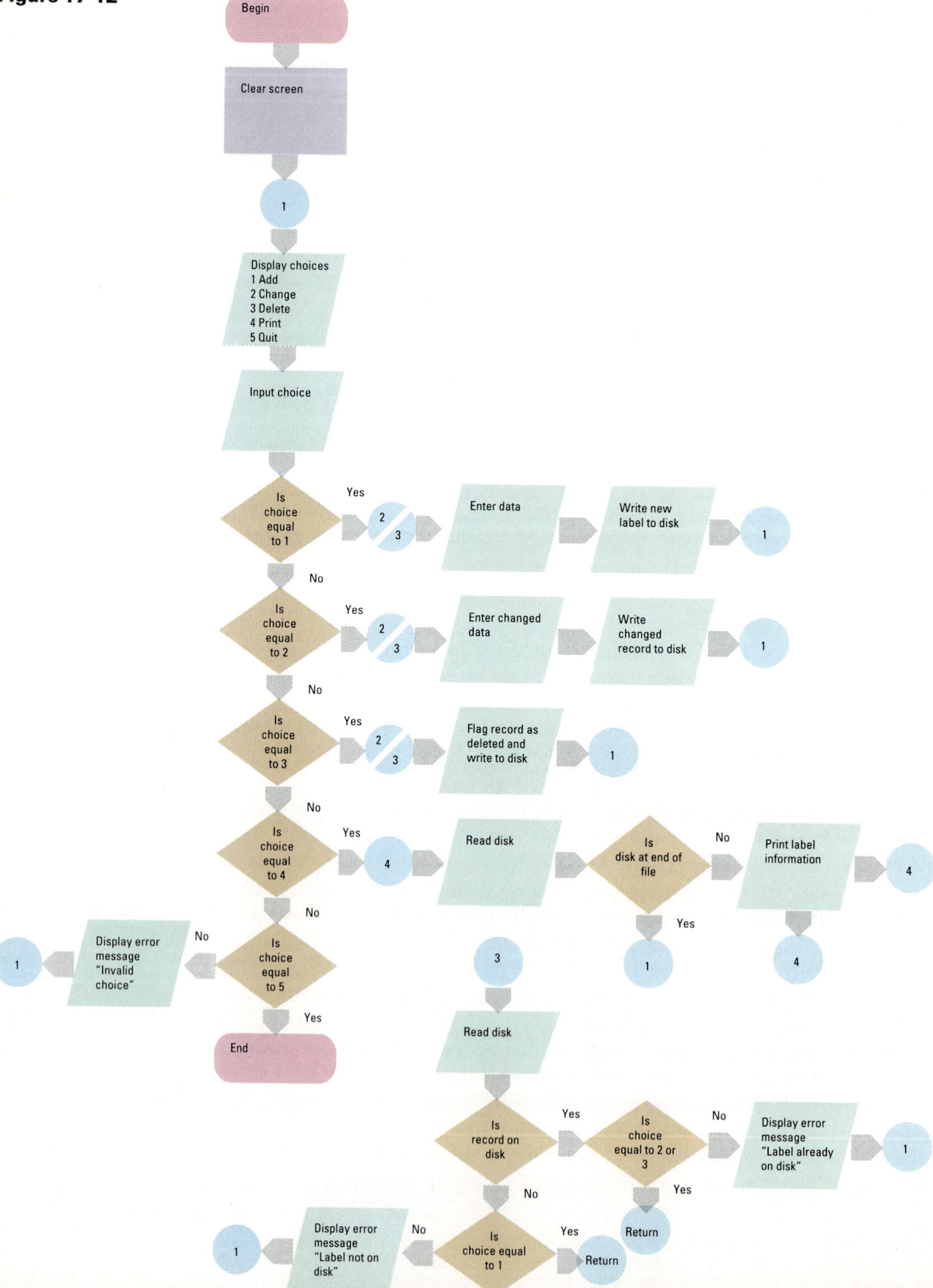
Begin
Clear screen
1
Display choices
1 Add
2 Change
3 Delete
4 Print
5 Quit
Input choice
Is choice equal to 1
Yes
2
3
Enter data
Write new label to disk
1
No
Is choice equal to 2
Yes
2
3
Enter changed data
Write changed record to disk
1
No
Is choice equal to 3
Yes
2
3
Flag record as deleted and write to disk
1
No
Is choice equal to 4
Yes
4
Read disk
Is disk at end of file
No
Print label information
4
Yes
1
4
No
Is choice equal to 5
No
Display error message "Invalid choice"
1
Yes
End
3
Read disk
Is record on disk
Yes
Is choice equal to 2 or 3
No
Display error message "Label already on disk"
1
Yes
Return
No
Is choice equal to 1
Yes
Return
No
Display error message "Label not on disk"
1

```
10 REM MAILING LABELS PROGRAM
20 REM WRITTEN BY SARA WILKINS, 9/15--
30 REM THIS PROGRAM MAINTAINS MAILING LABELS
40 CLS: REM CLEAR THE DISPLAY SCREEN
50 PRINT "1. ADD NAMES AND ADDRESSES"
60 PRINT "2. CHANGE DATA"
70 PRINT "3. DELETE NAMES AND ADDRESSES"
80 PRINT "4. PRINT LABELS"
90 PRINT "5. QUIT"
100 PRINT
110 INPUT "ENTER THE NUMBER OF THE DESIRED ACTION: ",C
120 ON C GOSUB 1000,2000,3000,4000
130 IF C <> 5 THEN GOTO 40
140 END
```

Figure 17-13
The instructions of a computer program must be coded in a computer language, such as BASIC.

actual input the program has been designed to process and then checking the output produced against expected results. The testing process also involves inputting a wide assortment of data (including data with errors) to make sure the program can adequately deal with a variety of situations.

Two different types of bugs are checked for during the testing process—syntax bugs and logic bugs. Syntax bugs are those errors that occur when the rules of the language the program is coded in are violated. These types of bugs often cause the program to stop execution when they are encountered. Logic bugs are those that occur when poor decisions, incorrect formulas, or incorrect conclusions have been coded in the program. These bugs are the most difficult to find since they do not cause program execution to stop, and they are often the most serious since they frequently cause incorrect output to be generated.

In this chapter you have learned that programming languages vary greatly in structure, purpose, and usage. Languages are tools that, when used properly, help the programmer accomplish his/her job. Similar to choosing the right tool to do a given job, the proper programming language must be chosen to complete a given task. Each language has unique features that must be considered during the selection process. These considerations include the type of problem to be solved, the personnel that will be using the language, the ease of use, and the type of computer system that will be used.

Each programming language is unique in its syntax, function, and capabilities. Because of these differences, there is little if any compatibility among them. The greatest compatibility exists in data file sharing; that is, files created by a program written in one programming language can usually be read by a program written in another language. There are commercial software programs available that claim to be able to convert a program written in one language to another. However, additional manual conversion efforts are often required.

COMPUTER VIRUS

A computer virus is similar to a human virus. Like a human virus, a computer virus can not only disrupt its system, but can also be spread from one computer to another. A computer virus is a small program (usually no more than 1-20 lines of code) that is intentionally designed to do some type of damage. It may delete data, garbage files, or even destroy hardware.

The virus program buries itself deep within the computer's operating system program. Since the operating system program is run each time the computer is used, the virus can execute itself and issue commands to make room for a copy of itself on every data diskette or every program stored to diskette. Every time a new diskette is used, the virus attaches itself. Then, when an infected diskette is used on another computer system, the virus goes along and spreads to that operating system. Thus, the virus spreads, just like a common cold or flu.

A computer virus can be spread from one computer to another.

Often, virus programs are designed to activate themselves based upon a certain event, time, or date. As a result, they are likely to inflict their damage and spread among several other programs and users before they are detected.

With today's trend toward connecting computers and sharing information over electronic bulletin boards, virus programs can become more contagious. Corporations are also threatened due to the trend of their employees to take work home—where diskettes could be infected.

The planting of a computer virus is a form of software sabotage. This type of sabotage is unique in that it has the ability to propagate. It makes no distinction among its victims and has the potential of infecting school, business, industry, government, and military computers.

Many companies are trying to control the spread of computer viruses by requiring employees to use only specific software monitored by the company. Software is also being developed and marketed to detect a virus. This type of software is known as inoculation or anti-virus software. One type of inoculation software (called a vaccine) has been developed that, when run, warns the computer user if a self-executing file attempts to attach itself into the system. It then blocks the file so the suspect file cannot attach itself. Another method being used to control the spread of viruses is to download or copy only original source code programs, examine the code, and then compile the program. Thus, a new, executable object program is created. Other security measures and policies are being implemented by many computer users to test for and avoid the threat of viruses.

CHAPTER SUMMARY

- Without software a computer is useless.
- All computer programs, whether they are manufacturer-supplied, utilities, off-the-shelf, custom, or user-written are written in some language the computer can understand.
- Some languages are general-purpose and have been designed to be used for a wide variety of applications. Other languages have been designed to be used for a specific purpose—such as mathematics or engineering.
- Low-level languages use the numeric code that is directly understood by the processor of the target machine and are known as machine language programs.
- High-level languages allow the programmer to think in terms of solving the problem rather than how to utilize the processor to its fullest potential.
- High-level languages are translated into machine language by either an interpreter program or a compiler program.
- An interpreter program looks at one instruction written in a high-level language, translates the instruction into machine language, and relays it to the processor for execution.
- A compiler translates the entire high-level language program into machine language and stores the machine language version in RAM or on an auxiliary storage device ready for execution.
- Assembly language is a low-level programming language used by programmers who want to communicate at the lowest level with the interworkings of their computer. Assembly language programs usually consume less RAM and execute faster than high-level languages.
- An assembler is a program that translates assembly language programs into machine language.
- FORTRAN (**FOR**mula **TRAN**slation) was the first problem-oriented compiler language. It was specifically designed for mathematical and scientific applications. One of its greatest advantages is the extensive collection of scientific and mathematical subroutines that are available.

- BASIC is the acronym for **B**eginner's **A**ll-**P**urpose **S**ymbolic **I**nstruction **C**ode. The BASIC language was designed to be a high-level, interactive programming language. BASIC is an easy-to-learn language, partly because of its free-form structure and its English-like instructions.
- The Pascal language was designed to be a high-level, general-purpose language useful for writing programs for nearly every application. It can be compiled and executed directly or translated into intermediate code and executed with a run-time program. The advantage to the run-time method is that the same translated Pascal code can be run on many different computers.
- COBOL (**CO**mmon **B**usiness **O**riented **L**anguage) was the first high-level language written for use in business applications. Its strong point is the handling of large amounts of data stored on auxiliary storage devices. It is also one of the wordiest languages and a language which uses a great deal of RAM. COBOL is written in English-like sentences that make its programs easier to understand than those written in some other languages.
- PL/1 (**P**rogramming **L**anguage/**1**) was designed to be a general-purpose language which combined the business processing features of COBOL with the mathematical and scientific features of FORTRAN. The language can be easily learned because it can be written in a free-form format or structured format, uses English-like sentences, and is self-documenting.
- The RPG (**R**eport **P**rogram **G**enerator) language was initially designed for users of small computer systems as a general-purpose, business-oriented language for generating reports. Since its initial development, it has undergone two major enhancements which has made it second to COBOL as the most popular business programming language. RPG is a very structured, high-level language with built-in logic.
- The C programming language is considered a low-level programming language that enables the programmer to code programs using a high-level type of symbolic code, yet it offers low-level control over the hardware.
- Fourth-generation languages are the highest level of high-level programming languages. Most fourth-generation languages require the user to respond to a series of questions that request information about the tasks to be performed. After all the needed information is supplied, a program is automatically generated by the language itself. Once the program is generated, it can be compiled and executed.
- Structured programming is a method used to write programs from organized, detailed plans which define the steps that must be performed.
- Top-down design of a program begins by defining what the program is to do and then gradually increases the level of detail in the plan.
- A hierarchy chart is similar to an organizational chart and is used to graphically illustrate the top-down design.

- Before a program can be coded, the output to be produced must be designed. The report spacing chart is a form arranged in rows and columns with space for each position in which a character can be printed. When completed, it shows the length of each data item that is to appear on the output as well as its location.
- One of the main concepts of structured programming is that any program can be written using only four kinds of instructions: (1) sequential, (2) case, (3) loop control, and (4) IF . . . THEN . . . ELSE instructions.
- Each function or task the program must perform is known as a module.
- A program design (also known as pseudocode) consists of the detailed steps that must be performed by each module within a program.
- A flowchart is a method of using graphic representations to illustrate the detailed steps of a hierarchy chart.
- Arrows, called flowlines, are used in a flowchart to connect the different steps and show the direction of data flow.
- For each of the statements in the program design or flowchart, one or more statements are written in the chosen programming language. When using structured design, the main module is coded and tested first; then all the other modules are coded and tested.
- The testing process involves inputting a wide assortment of data (including data with errors) to make sure the program can adequately deal with a variety of situations and yield the correct output. Two different types of bugs are checked for during the testing process—syntax bugs and logic bugs.
- There is little compatibility among the various programming languages.

KEY TERMS

The following key terms were introduced or redefined in this chapter:

assembler
assembly language
BASIC
BASIC statement
C programming language
case instruction
COBOL
coding
compiler program
debug
division
flowchart
flowline
FORTRAN
fourth-generation language
hierarchy chart
high-level language
identifier
IF...THEN...ELSE instruction
interpreter program
loop control instruction
low-level language
machine language
main module
module
object program
Pascal

PL/1
program design
programmer-supplied word
pseudocode
report spacing chart
reserved word
RPG
run-time program
sections
sequential instruction
source program
structured design
structured programming
testing
top-down design

REVIEW QUESTIONS

1. Why is a computer useless unless it has software? (Obj. 1)
2. What is a low-level programming language? (Obj. 1)
3. What is a high-level programming language? Name three high-level programming languages. (Obj. 1)
4. What is the difference between an interpreter program and a compiler program? (Obj. 1)
5. Identify two characteristics of an assembly language. (Obj. 2)
6. What is an assembler? (Obj. 2)
7. Identify two characteristics of the FORTRAN language. (Obj. 2)
8. Identify at least two characteristics of the BASIC language. (Obj. 2)
9. Identify at least two characteristics of the Pascal language. (Obj. 2)
10. What is the advantage and what are the disadvantages of using a run-time program when using the Pascal language? (Obj. 2)
11. Identify at least two characteristics of the COBOL language. (Obj. 2)
12. What is the difference between a reserved word and a programmer-supplied word? (Obj. 2)
13. Identify at least two characteristics of the PL/1 language. (Obj. 2)
14. For what purpose was the RPG language initially designed? (Obj. 2)
15. Why is the C programming language becoming so popular among programmers writing software for personal computers? (Obj. 2)
16. Briefly describe how most fourth-generation languages work. (Obj. 2)
17. What is structured programming? (Obj. 3)
18. What is meant by top-down design? (Obj. 3)
19. What is a hierarchy chart? (Obj. 3)
20. For what purpose is a report spacing chart used? (Obj. 3)
21. Identify the four general kinds of instructions used when writing any program. (Obj. 3)
22. What is pseudocode? (Obj. 3)
23. What is a main module? (Obj. 3)
24. What is a flowchart? (Obj. 3)
25. What are flowlines? (Obj. 3)
26. What does it mean to code and test a program? (Obj. 3)

CHALLENGE ACTIVITIES

1. Consult the help wanted section of a computer magazine or your local newspaper for employment advertisements for computer programmers. Prepare a brief report showing the number of programming positions advertised. For each programming position, list the type of application, the kind of computer, and the programming language used. (Objs. 1,2)
2. Visit a local business, industry, governmental agency, your school's administration computer center, or other computer user. Find out what programming language is being used, why that language was chosen, and how new programs are developed. Prepare a report summarizing what you learned. (Objs. 1,2,3)
3. Choose one of the languages discussed in this chapter and prepare a report explaining the applications for which it is most commonly used. In addition, show an example program and briefly explain how the code is written. (Obj. 2)

PART 6

CAREERS

CHAPTER 18

CAREERS IN THE COMPUTER INDUSTRY

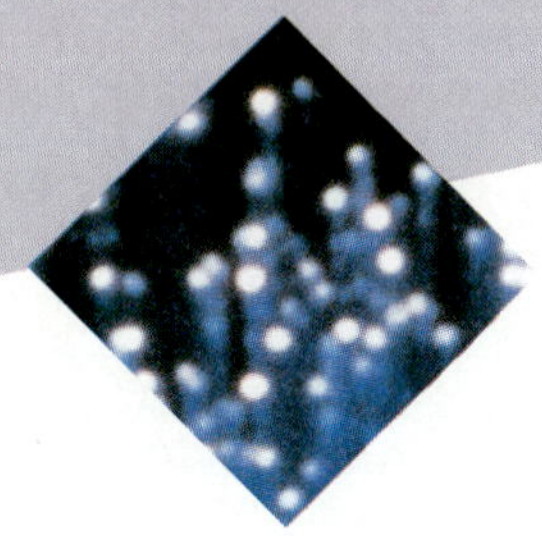

LEARNING OBJECTIVES

After studying this chapter, you will be able to:

1. **Name the two main categories of careers in the computer industry.**
2. **Name five areas in which careers are available in the computer hardware industry.**
3. **Name five areas in which careers are available in the computer software industry.**
4. **Describe some of the opportunities available in the computer industry for trainers or teachers.**
5. **Describe the role performed by those who plan and manage computer use.**
6. **Name and describe five areas in which computer industry careers involving development, programming, and technical skills are available.**
7. **Name and describe the most common job related to computer operations.**
8. **Name and describe the most common job related to data entry.**
9. **Describe the skills and education usually required for each of the common job categories in information processing.**
10. **Describe the career ladders for the common information processing careers.**
11. **Describe the relationships among salaries for various jobs in the information processing field.**

INTRODUCTION

Careers related to computers are not limited to persons who work in the information systems department of a business. There are also entrepreneurs, scientists, salespeople, promoters, assemblers, retailers, trainers, and a multitude of users. The secretary using a word processor is using a computer. The retail salesperson may be using a cash register that is a computer. The inventory clerk may enter stock quantities into a computer or into a terminal connected to a larger computer. A personal computer may be on the company president's desk to aid in financial analysis. This chapter will discuss the opportunities that are available in many of these areas.

TYPES OF CAREERS IN THE COMPUTER INDUSTRY

Careers in the computer industry might be visualized as a universe, as shown in Figure 18-1. Careers in information processing may be thought of as being the center of the universe. Persons working in the hardware, software, teaching, and service and supply industries as well as persons who are dependent upon the computer in the performance of their job duties support this central area.

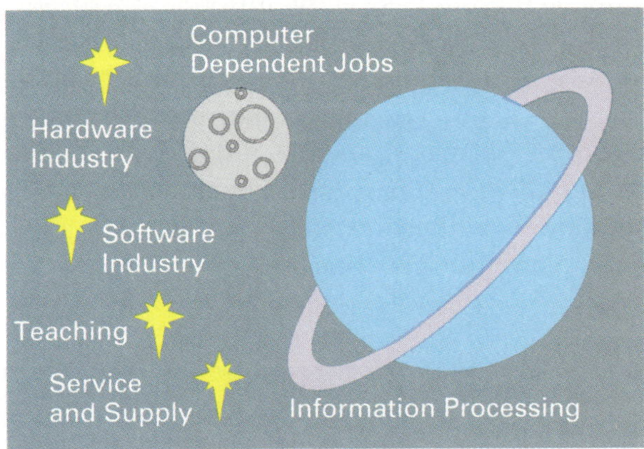

Figure 18-1
Careers in the computer industry can be pictured as a universe.

Careers in this universe of a supported information processing industry generally fall into one of two main categories: the users who get benefit in their personal or business life and the persons who provide the hardware, software, and support for those users. The user area makes up most of the central information processing segment. The design, training, and support area includes many jobs in the hardware, software, teaching, and service and supply industries. Those in the support group provide the necessary environment in which the users in the other group function.

Everyone from veterinarians, who monitor feeding programs, to inventory clerks can benefit from the use of computers in their work life.

Careers in the Hardware Industry

Perhaps it is safe to say that the very first computer careers were in the hardware industry involving the design of the first computer. The research and design of computer hardware continues to be a career area of great importance and great challenge. Recent developments, for example, include basic research on superconductivity, the creation of parallel processing computers for tremendously increased speed, the introduction of multiplexing busses for microcomputers, and the introduction of color printers.

Persons working in computer design may be involved with basic research, with the development of a new computer hardware system, or with the development of component parts, such as a processor chip or communications circuits. Generally, those persons involved in the design of computers and their components will use existing computers as a tool in their work. For example, a computer may be used to help design the layout of a new processor chip.

An existing computer can help design a chip to be used in a new generation of computers.

While persons with little or no college education have designed important computer products, that is the exception. Persons doing basic research most likely have advanced degrees in the area of their study. Those working on the application of research findings in new computer designs likely have engineering or computer science degrees.

The designers of new computer hardware are not the only ones involved in the hardware side of the computer industry, however. New designs must be documented, calling for the skills of technical writers. Production of the product must be planned, calling for manufacturing experience. The product must be produced and sold, requiring the expertise of production and marketing personnel. If the product breaks new ground, it may even be necessary to make use of lobbyists and other resources in an effort to change the laws or regulations relating to the product.

Careers in the Software Industry

In many respects, careers in the software industry parallel those in the hardware industry. There are those who work on basic research, those who apply the research to the development of specific software such as database or word processing programs, and those who market the software.

As the hardware market has progressed, software has been developed to keep up with the improvements. For example, a computer using a new type of processor is useless without appropriate software to make it function. In many ways, the development of the software may be more difficult than the development of the hardware and calls for the application of algorithms (problem-solving steps) that must be developed from scratch.

The developers of systems software tend to be persons with computer science degrees. Some developers of applications software have a computer background, while others have a background in the area for which the program is being written. For example, accounting software may be at least partially developed by persons whose background is in accounting. Most major pieces of software are developed by teams, though significant programs may still be developed by only one or two individuals.

A person with a background in accounting may be called upon to assist in the development of accounting software.

In addition to jobs related to the creation of software for large computers, the rapidly increasing use of microcomputers within businesses, schools, and homes has created an increased need for qualified people to create pre-written software for these machines. Many job opportunities exist for persons who can program business applications for microcomputers. Many students still working on their education have started their careers by learning to program on the microcomputers available in their schools or homes.

As with hardware, new software must be documented and users manuals prepared. This need calls for technical writing skills. While the manufacture (duplication) of software is a very simple job in comparison to the manufacture of hardware, the full range of marketing efforts is still required for software, thus providing career opportunities for many persons.

Once software is created and marketed, it must be supported. For most software companies, this means a staff of telephone support specialists who can respond to every user's call for help. For simple software, the support specialist may orally question the user about the symptoms of the problem. For more complex software, the user may be outfitted with a modem hookup so that the vendor's support specialists can query the user's computer system directly in an effort to isolate the difficulty and solve the problem.

Careers in Teaching

The introduction of every new hardware product and every new software product helps ensure that those involved in teaching about computers and the use of software will continue to be employed. While the computer itself is being used to deliver training, the human instructor remains an essential element in most cases. Employment opportunities for teachers or trainers run the gamut from public schools, universities and private training firms, to hardware and software manufacturers, computer retailers, and companies that use particular hardware and software.

As might be suspected, trainers working for vendors tend to concentrate on training persons in using that one product. Educators working for public schools or colleges, on the other hand, are usually expected to be knowledgeable in a broader area.

Persons involved in teaching about computers and software are often in demand.

Careers in Information Processing

The largest number of computer-related jobs is in the area generally known as information processing. This includes the group of people who use computers for the daily processing of information in just about every business regardless of size and type.

Two features may be helpful in identifying certain jobs as information processing jobs. The first feature is the amount of work time actually spent using computers. The second feature is the job qualifications required of persons who hold the positions. A major portion of the work in information processing jobs involves computer usage. Furthermore, special computer training is generally necessary for information processing occupations.

Four generally distinct types of jobs exist in information processing:

1. Jobs involving the planning or managing of computer use within a company.
2. Jobs requiring computer development, programming, and technical skills.
3. Jobs requiring computer operating skills.
4. Jobs requiring the input of data into computers.

One common position in the information processing field involves entering data into the computer.

These four types of jobs are described in the following sections. The major tasks and personal qualifications to perform these tasks will be explained. A different amount of formal education is required for each position. Descriptions of the positions will also clarify the basic functions needed to plan, develop, and operate an information processing system.

Jobs Involving Planning or Managing Computer Use

The top information processing jobs in a business are those related to management. The title of the chief information officer **(CIO)** of a business will vary. This person may be called the Vice President for Management Information Systems, the Director of Management Information Systems, or various other titles. Obviously, the total number of information management personnel working under the CIO in a business will vary depending on the size and organization of the business. The duties of the chief information officer include working with other executives to develop strategic plans for the management information function of the company, making detailed plans for the execution of the strategy, and overseeing the daily operations of the department.

Growing numbers of businesses are recognizing the strategic importance of information management and are making the chief information officer an integral part of the top management team of the business. While most CIOs are experienced persons with college training in information systems, some of them come from backgrounds in other areas of business, such as finance, and acquire the necessary information processing skills.

The chief information officer is an important part of the top management team of a business.

Jobs Requiring Computer Development, Programming, and Technical Skills

Jobs in this category represent the technical heart of the information processing department of a business. While titles and responsibilities can vary greatly from one business to another, the following descriptions are typical of many installations.

Consultants. Consultants may be "in-house" persons or independent persons who work for a fee. Consultants have computer expertise in particular areas and work with others who have need of this expertise. Consultants are found in every area of computer usage, from database management, to systems development, to computer maintenance, to selection and use of software.

As the use of microcomputers has proliferated, many businesses have added a consultant frequently known as a **data center manager** or **information center manager.** This person is available to work with individuals in the company, to select appropriate microcomputer hardware and software, and to obtain training in the use of the systems. The data center manager also is the resource for getting questions answered and problems resolved as the system is used.

Computer consultants work with other persons who have need of their expertise.

The education and experience required for a consultant vary depending on the area of expertise in which the consulting is to be done. The more technically demanding an area is, the more education and experience the consultant will generally have. Before becoming a consultant, that person usually will have gained experience by working in the same general skill area for another employer.

Database Administrators. Database administrators (or managers) have become much more common as businesses have begun using database software to maintain the corporate data that is strategic to the successful operation of the business. The database administrator is responsible for developing and maintaining the integrity (correctness) of the database used by the business.

It is the database administrator's duty to plan the design of the data elements in the database and to define their relationships to one another. After the initial planning, the database must continually be upgraded. That is, new data elements may be added, relationships between different data elements may be redefined, and some data elements may be dropped because they have outlived their usefulness. The database manager's duties are not performed in a vacuum, but in close consultation with the users of the database.

The database administrator works closely with users to help define the data to be included in the database.

It is the database administrator's responsibility to coordinate the data needs of many different persons in the business. Their needs must be met while at the same time undesirable replication of data from one application to another must be avoided.

The database administrator is usually an experienced person with a bachelor's degree in information systems. Persons working in this position usually have experience in planning information systems and programs. As businesses move away from stand-alone computer applications to applications based on one underlying database structure, the database administrator's job becomes more critical to the success of the business.

Systems Analysts. The starting point for using a computer in information processing is planning the procedures to be used for solving a problem. This is the systems analyst's job. The systems analyst usually works under the supervision of the manager of the information processing center or a project leader. The primary role of the systems analyst is the design and creation of an information processing system.

In order to perform successfully as a systems analyst, a person needs a strong background in business as well as in the technical aspects of computer systems and programming. A bachelor's degree is usually required. This degree may be in information systems or in a related academic program that emphasizes a broad business management background. The systems analyst should know at least one programming language. As businesses move toward integrated database systems, it is becoming more imperative that the systems analyst be an expert in the application of database technology.

A keen interest in solving problems and an ability to think logically are mandatory for the systems analyst. Furthermore, a creative mind is a must in order to see new ways of doing things. The ability to compare the costs of several different ways of solving problems with and without the computer is necessary. The systems analyst must also be able to communicate well with users in order to plan a successful system. Once the system is planned, more communication is needed as the users become familiar with the system. The systems analyst's verbal and written communication skills should be well developed, and he or she should be able to communicate with others without using computer jargon. For persons wanting to advance into management positions within the company, a solid foundation in business administration is necessary, as is a broad general knowledge of the operation of the company.

A systems analyst works closely with employees to determine the input and output needed from the system.

Programmers. Programmers generally work under the supervision of a systems analyst. There may also be supervisors with other titles, such as lead programmer or project leader. Depending on the complexity of a programming assignment, a programmer may work alone or as part of a team. Experienced programmers may be promoted to systems analyst positions.

The exact duties of a programmer depend on the business for which the programmer is working. In a larger business, the programmer may receive complete details about a program from the systems analyst. In this case, the programmer simply writes the steps required by the program in computer language and completes the necessary documentation. In other instances, the programmer may be required to complete detailed plans for a program before beginning the coding process. In some cases, the entire planning process is done by the programmer before beginning to code a program. In smaller businesses, the programmer may also operate a minicomputer or small mainframe. For security reasons, however, the jobs of programmer and computer operator should be separated whenever possible.

Programmers must write the computer programs as well as the necessary documentation.

Most programming jobs require education beyond the high school level, although there are some beginning jobs available to high school graduates. Depending on the company, either a technical school diploma or a bachelor's degree is usually required.

A programmer must know at least one programming language. Because it is not always possible to predict the language a programmer will need when employed, the training of programmers often includes several high-level languages. Many courses of instruction also include work with program generators and other fourth-generation tools, which are of growing importance as methods to improve programmer productivity.

There is a growing trend for programmers to enter or modify their programs directly on keyboards, rather than first writing them on paper. Programmers are also sometimes called upon to write user documentation for programs they develop. Because of this, it is important for programmers to have keyboarding and word processing skills.

Successful programmers think logically and like working with precise details. They can concentrate on a programming problem until it is solved. In the past, it was thought that programmers should have well-honed mathematical knowledge and skills. However, logical thinking seems to be the essential trait, with advanced math skills mandated only if the subject area of the program requires advanced mathematical computations.

Telecommunications Specialists. As computer networking has become more common, the need for telecommunications specialists has increased. Telecommunications specialists have the responsibility of planning, overseeing the operation of, and troubleshooting the connections that tie the various computers, terminals, and other devices of a computer network together. This is true whether the network is made up of microcomputers or a mix of various-sized computers. Persons in these jobs must have an in-depth knowledge of both the hardware and software involved in operation of the network. They are not so much concerned about the actual programs being executed on the system but are more involved in providing and maintaining the communication pathways over which the programs and data must flow. Telecommunications specialists usually have bachelor's degrees.

Telecommunications specialists have responsibility for overseeing the computer network.

Jobs Requiring Computer Operating Skills

While the jobs described in the preceding section relate to preparing computer programs and systems for operation, the **computer operator** actually operates the computer using the programs that have been developed and implemented. Companies using mainframe computers have one or more computer operators. The computer operator usually works under the supervision of a lead operator or the manager of the information processing center. In some installations, the operator may have other duties, such as filing media or entering data.

The computer operator is responsible for sequencing computer jobs and running them in order of priority. On a large computer system, some programs may be running continually, while others are executed only occasionally.

The computer operator sequences computer jobs and runs them in the order of their importance.

The computer operator must follow instructions closely. The computer may send messages to the operator while a program is running. The operator must then make correct responses to these messages and enter commands to carry out the desired actions. If errors or problems occur during the running of a program, the operator must know how to handle them.

In addition to actually running the computer, the operator is responsible for making sure that the correct disks or tapes are mounted on auxiliary storage devices. It is also the operator's responsibility to make sure that the printer has the correct paper and that the output of a job is complete. In larger installations, **tape or disk librarians** may be employed to catalog, store, and retrieve the storage media as needed, while in smaller installations the operator generally performs these functions.

Technical training in equipment operation and an introduction to computer programming can often be acquired at a two-year technical school or community college. Some employers will hire operators with only a high school education and provide them with on-the-job training for the computer being used. Many computer operators continue their education to obtain the skills necessary to move to supervisory positions in the operations area or to work as programmers.

Jobs Involving Inputting Data Into Computers

At one time, almost all programs and data were keyed in by **data entry operators.** Now, however, more and more entry is being done by other persons. For example, programs may be entered by programmers, and accounting data may be entered by accountants. Additionally, much data that previously had to be keyed in is being transmitted electronically from one computer to another. These developments have reduced tremendously the number of persons carrying the job title of data entry operator. However, there continue to be opportunities in this area for those who are interested.

The data entry operator enters programs or other data into the computer system. In doing so, the operator works with different source documents, such as handwritten forms, typed forms, or specially marked sheets of paper. The data on these source documents is entered by using a keyboard. The operator must understand the layout of the records and know how to enter the data from the source documents. Understanding the equipment and following directions carefully are also important.

In companies using data entry operators, the high volume of data often makes data entry a 24-hour activity. For this reason, data entry operators may have a choice of day or night working hours.

The main requirement for the data entry operator is the ability to type or key data rapidly and accurately. Persons in this position should enjoy working with modern data entry equipment and doing the same kind of work for long periods of time. They should be able to gain satisfaction from producing a large volume of high-quality work. Data entry operators must be able to follow detailed instructions carefully and work under time pressure when needed. Also, as technology advances and changes in equipment take place, operators must be able to adjust to these changes.

Persons wishing to begin work as data entry operators can learn to use data entry equipment in high school or technical school. Some businesses provide on-the-job training. If an individual has good keyboarding skills, on-the-job data entry training may take only three to six weeks.

There may be lead or supervisory positions within the data entry department to which data entry operators may be promoted. For those desiring to move into other positions in information processing, however, additional training is almost always necessary.

CAREER ENTRY AND ADVANCEMENT

The job level at which a person may enter the field of information processing primarily depends on the amount of education completed. In this section, the kinds of jobs which may be available with various amounts of education will be presented.

Secondary Education

Computer-related high school courses can help students decide if they are interested in information processing careers, as well as prepare them for some entry-level jobs. Some appropriate courses are those involving an introduction to information processing, programming, keyboarding, and word processing. Other courses, such as accounting and an introduction to business, are also helpful.

Courses taken in high school can help familiarize you with computers and prepare you for some computer-related jobs.

Generally the jobs available to high school graduates who have the necessary skills are in word processing, data entry, and computer support. Computer support jobs are those jobs that are related to the computer in some way but which require no special computer skills. They include such responsibilities as filing computer media, accepting and logging in source documents, and distributing printouts. Some jobs as computer operators and programmers are available to high school graduates who have completed appropriate course work while in high school. Part-time jobs in these areas are frequently available to persons who are continuing their education at technical schools or colleges.

Community College or Technical School Education

By obtaining more education at a community college or technical school, individuals can usually enter the information processing field at a higher level or at a higher starting salary than would be possible with a high school education alone. Two years or less of specialized training should allow students to determine whether information processing really interests them. With information processing training beyond high school, many more opportunities are available in the areas of computer operation and programming. Also, many businesses prefer that their word processing operators have education beyond the high school level.

College or University Education

Job opportunities in information processing are more extensive for those who obtain a four-year bachelor's degree in a computer-related field.

Job opportunities in information processing will be more extensive upon earning a four-year bachelor's degree in a major field related to computers and business information management. Data processing, information systems, management information systems, computer science, and office systems management are such majors.

Many businesses require bachelor's degrees for positions in programming and systems analysis, as well as for promotions to supervisory and management positions. However, many top-level positions require extensive on-the-job experience in addition to a bachelor's degree.

Figure 18-2 reviews some of the different job titles in the information processing field and shows the approximate amount of education needed. Once people enter a certain field, they may advance to higher-level positions. Advancement may depend upon their interests, education, experience, and willingness to learn on the job. The amount of preparation may vary, depending on the size of the information processing installation. The figure gives only a general idea of the education needed.

The number of entry-level jobs that are available requiring little or no training beyond high school is decreasing. Almost all positions beyond the entry level require specialized training and/or experience. Note in Figure 18-2 that most entry-level positions are in the area of operations. In many cases, there is an opportunity for a worker to continue an academic program while working. Many employees in information processing departments are also part-time students.

The jobs shown at the bottom of Figure 18-2 are entry-level jobs that may be available with a high school education. The next division shows the positions available with a postsecondary, technical, or community college education. The third section shows the jobs that can be obtained with on-the-job training or with additional education toward a bachelor's degree. The top section shows the jobs that require at least a bachelor's degree. The managerial jobs are available only to persons with experience as well as a degree.

For the positions in the top two sections of Figure 18-2, persons who have had on-the-job training while working toward a degree are more likely to be hired than are those who have had academic training only. Also, individuals with on-the-job experience may advance to other positions within the companies that employed them while they were going to school. Other companies are also interested in persons who have experience using the same types of computers that they have. On-the-job programming experience with specific language and development tools is also important to an employer.

Figure 18-2

Bachelor's Degree Required
Senior Analyst
Database Manager
Systems Manager
M.I.S. Manager
Data Communications Manager
Programming Manager
Systems Analyst
Programmer Analyst
Senior Programmer
Word Processing Manager
Operations Manager
Bachelor's Degree Preferred (Experienced persons can sometimes hold these positions.)
Systems Analyst Trainee
Applications Programmer
Software Programmer
Word Processing Manager
Data Communications Specialist
Data Entry Supervisor
Word Processing Supervisor
Lead Data Entry Operator
Operations Supervisor
Entry Level—Postsecondary Technical School
Lead Computer Operator
Lead Word Processing Operator
Programmer Trainee
Data Entry Operator
Computer Operator
Word Processing Operator
Data Clerk
Media Librarian
Data Processing Secretary
Entry Level—High School or Vocational-Technical High School
Word Processing Operator Trainee
Clerk Typist
Data Entry Trainee
Media Librarian
Control Clerk
Computer Operator Trainee

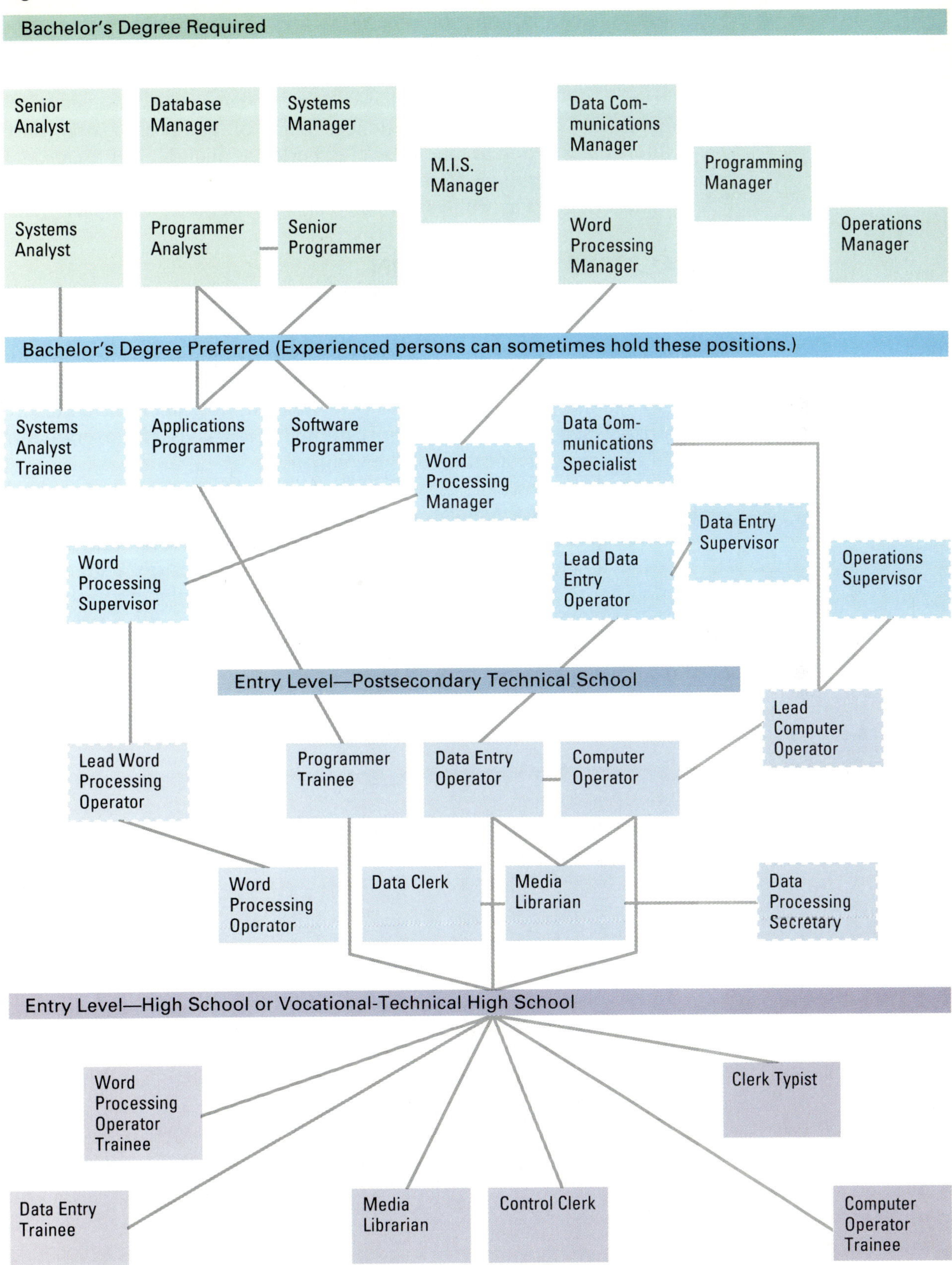

In any given information processing area, such as operations or programming, there are persons with varying levels of education and experience. In general, the junior positions require the appropriate education and very little experience. Intermediate positions usually require at least two years of experience. Senior or lead positions typically require at least three to four years of experience, including at least some supervisory experience. Persons in managerial positions frequently have advanced degrees as well as several years of experience in supervision.

SALARIES AVAILABLE IN INFORMATION PROCESSING CAREERS

The salaries available to persons in the information processing field vary considerably. Some of the factors affecting salaries are (1) amount of job experience; (2) size of the company; (3) industry of which the company is a part, such as manufacturing, banking, retail sales, or government; and (4) geographic location of the company.

Figure 18-3 shows the general relationships of typical salaries received by information processing employees. The salary of the top information manager in a company is shown as 100 percent. Each job area is then shown as a percent of that largest salary. In each career area column, the bottom figure shows the average for professional employees in the area while the top figure shows the average for managerial persons in the area. Keep in mind that, as with any average, some people are paid less than the average and some are paid more.

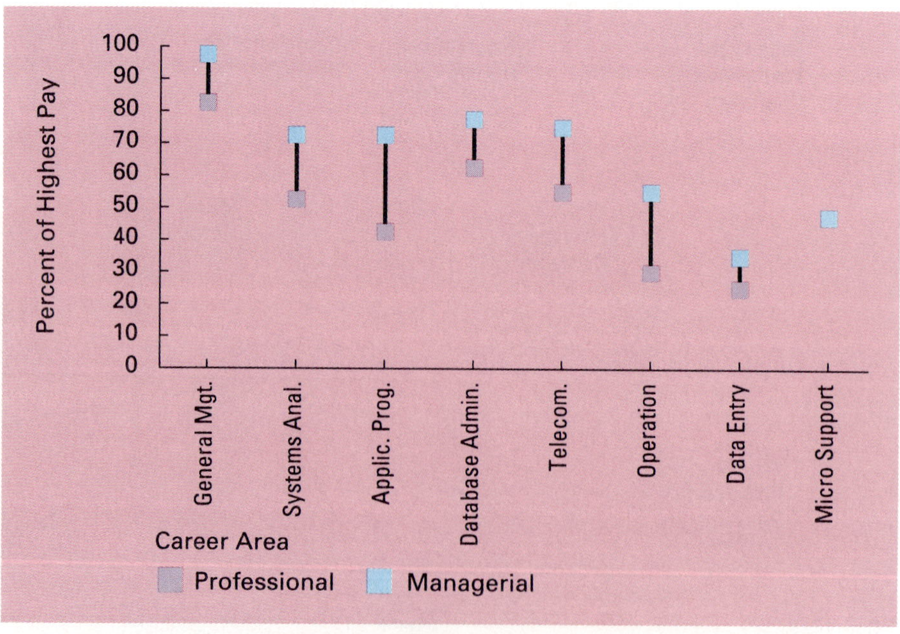

Figure 18-3
There is a wide range in the salaries available in the information processing field.

COMPUTERS PUT THE MAGIC IN YOUR MOTORING

Come back with us to the dark days of the 1970s. The price of gasoline is becoming stratospheric, causing automobile manufacturers to drop most of their large engines and go to smaller cars and smaller engines. In an effort to reduce atmospheric pollution and make the earth a safer place to live, automobile manufacturers have been required to put all manner of anti-pollution devices on the engines of their cars. While the levels of pollutants are being reduced, the price being paid by motorists is severe: in place of the previous power they have known in automobiles, owners are having to become accustomed to real anemic laggards in the performance arena. Other difficulties encountered are that engines are difficult to start and run very raggedly, especially when idling at stop lights; engines have a severe run-on problem, causing them at times to go through all manner of coughing and convulsing when the owner tries to switch them off; and even with the switch to smaller engines, miles per gallon figures are atrocious, dragged down by the effects of the anti-pollution equipment.

Into this dilemma came the first computers to be used in automobiles. These first computers were engine control computers. Using various sensors, they measured the contents of the engine exhaust and made adjustments as necessary to the ignition and fuel systems to keep pollutants within the necessary range. While these early computer systems were notorious for malfunctioning and creating difficult-to-repair dilemmas, they started a trend that has led to today's sophisticated computer controls.

Using the expertise of people involved in a variety of different computer-related careers, engine control computers from all manufacturers have now gone through several generations of development and improvement. The performance of these computers is now so good that engines usually run flawlessly, and rubber-burning acceleration and great fuel economy are able to peacefully coexist.

Engineers didn't stop, however, with engine control computers, as necessary as they now are. Computers were next used to control suspension systems and steering systems, making near-instantaneous corrections as needed. The luxury car that used to float over slight road imperfections but bottom out on the big bumps and handle in the corners as if it had sponge rubber springs can now have a dual personality. It can still perform as its smooth former self over small road imperfections, yielding a perfect boulevard ride, but it can also switch to sports car handling within a fraction of a second when it meets with a sudden turn or a vicious bump. Using similar computer technology, power steering can exert a lot of assistance in slow-speed parking situations, but back off and let the road feel through at highway speeds. With the smooth control provided by the computer, the driver is never conscious of the steering changing its character; he or she just knows that the car drives well.

Just coming into use are collision avoidance systems and computer controlled mapping. While the use of radar to detect objects ahead of the car and apply a vehicle's brakes has long been possible, the first such systems were prone to many "false alarms," as they thought that guard rails on curves, trees by a curve in the road, bridge guard rails, and many other objects the vehicle was not in danger of hitting were cause to apply the brakes. With the use of sophisticated computer programming, newer collision avoidance systems do an excellent job of separating real dangers from the false alarms. And, while a collision avoidance system can help keep you from hitting things you don't want to hit, a mapping system can help you get to places you want to get to. These systems keep up with the location of your vehicle and display its position on a moving map on the car's instrument panel.

Computerized maps are showing up on the dashboards of many automobiles.

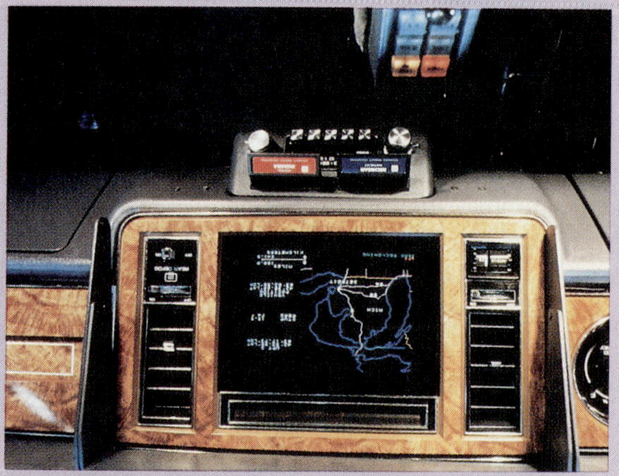

Within 15 years, computers have almost revolutionized the behavior of the everyday automobile, with most cars getting assistance from multiple processors. Perhaps within the next 15 years computer technology will help cars drive themselves to their destination with little assistance from the driver. As technology continues to advance in industries such as automobile design and manufacturing, computer-savvy employees will become more and more valuable to their employers.

CHAPTER SUMMARY

- Careers related to computers are available in many areas of a business.
- Careers in the computer industry may be divided into those related to design, training, and support and those related to the use of computers.
- In the hardware industry, careers may be related to the actual design of the hardware, or to documentation, production, marketing, or government relations.

- Careers in the software industry may be related to the actual design and coding of the software, or to documentation, production (manufacture), marketing, training, and support.
- The proliferation of computer use has opened many positions related to teaching and training.
- Information processing jobs involving the planning or managing of computer use include those of the chief information officer (CIO), who may go by any of several titles.
- The chief information officer of a company is charged with the strategic planning and management of the business' information systems.
- Jobs related to the development, programming, and technical aspects of computers include consultants, database administrators, systems analysts, programmers, and telecommunications specialists, among others.
- Jobs in computer operations involve the daily implementation of plans and programs prepared by others.
- Jobs in data entry involve inputting data into the computer system.
- Consultants are found in every area of expertise and work with other persons who need access to their expertise.
- Database administrators are charged with developing and maintaining the integrity of a business' database.
- The systems analyst works with computer users to develop the procedures and program plans to be used to solve a problem.
- Programmers write computer software to solve particular problems.
- While information processing jobs available to high school graduates are usually entry level or data entry positions, such positions can help one determine whether he or she has an interest in the area.
- Persons with community college or technical school education frequently find information systems jobs in computer operations or programming.
- Positions in systems analysis, as well as promotions into database administration and management, are usually available only to those with a four-year college degree.
- The number of entry-level jobs requiring relatively little education is decreasing, especially in the data entry field.
- Salaries are dependent upon many factors, including experience, size of the company, industry of which the company is a part, and the geographic location of the company.

KEY TERMS

The following terms were introduced or redefined in this chapter:

CIO
computer operator
consultant
data center manager/information center manager
data entry operator

database administrator
programmer
systems analyst
tape/disk librarian
telecommunication specialists

REVIEW QUESTIONS

1. Into what two main areas may careers in the computer industry be divided? (Obj. 1)
2. Name some of the careers in the computer hardware industry. (Obj. 2)
3. In what ways do careers in the computer software industry parallel those in the hardware industry? (Obj. 3)
4. Name several employment opportunities related to the computer industry for persons interested in a teaching career. (Obj. 4)
5. What information processing jobs involve the planning or managing of computer use in a company? (Obj. 5)
6. What information processing jobs require computer development, programming, and technical skills? (Obj. 6)
7. What information processing jobs require computer operating skills? (Obj. 7)
8. What information processing jobs involve inputting data into computers? (Obj. 8)
9. Describe the duties of a systems analyst. (Obj. 6)
10. What kinds of skills and education are usually necessary for employment as a systems analyst? (Obj. 9)
11. Describe the duties of a programmer. (Obj. 6)
12. What kinds of skills and education are usually necessary for employment as a programmer? (Obj. 9)
13. Describe the duties of a computer operator. (Obj. 7)
14. What kinds of skills and education are usually required for employment as a computer operator? (Obj. 9)
15. Describe the duties of a data entry operator. (Obj. 8)
16. What kinds of skills and education are usually necessary for employment as a data entry operator? (Obj. 9)
17. What kinds of information processing jobs are available to persons with a high school education? (Obj. 9)
18. What kinds of information processing jobs are available to persons with a technical school or community college education? (Obj. 9)
19. What kinds of information processing jobs are available to persons holding bachelor's degrees? (Obj. 9)
20. Describe the typical promotion path that might be taken to get to a position in database administration or information systems management. (Obj. 10)
21. What would a likely promotion be for a programmer trainee? For a computer operator? (Obj. 10)

22. Referring to Figure 18-3, compare the salary levels for different jobs in information processing. Which jobs are among the lower paying ones? Which jobs are among the higher paying ones? (Obj. 11)

CHALLENGE ACTIVITIES

1. Select a computer industry career in which you might be interested. Research several technical schools or colleges that provide training for that career. (Obj. 9)
2. Talk with a local employer who hires people for computer-related jobs. Find out what kinds of jobs are available and what kinds of education are required. (Objs. 1,2,3,4,5,6,7,8,9)
3. If your school provides access to career and/or educational counseling computer software, use the software and evaluate its results. (Such software may help you complete Question 1.) (Objs. 1,2,3,4,5, 6,7,8,9,10,11)
4. Do research on current employment trends and projections in various computer industry jobs, including number of jobs to be available, changes in job requirements, and salaries paid. (Objs. 9,10,11)

APPENDIX A

COMPUTING HISTORY AND TRENDS: FROM FINGER COUNTING TO ELECTRONIC COMPUTERS

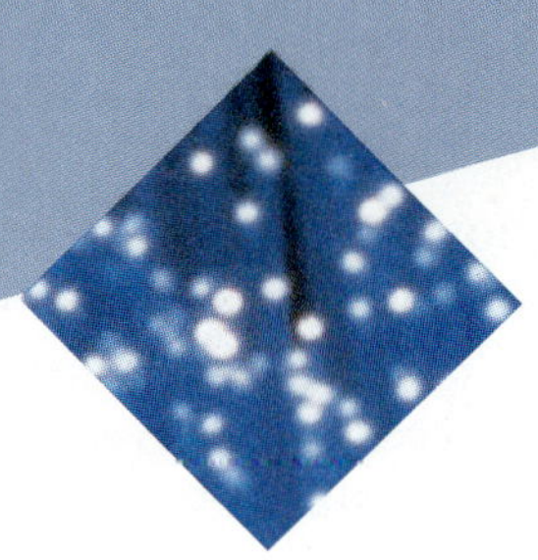

LEARNING OBJECTIVES

After studying this chapter, you will be able to:

1. **Name and describe early calculating devices.**
2. **Name and describe the machines in the electromechanical era of data processing.**
3. **Name and describe the earliest computers.**
4. **Name and give the characteristics of each of the generations of computers.**
5. **Trace the progress of the microprocessor era.**
6. **Trace the improvements in data entry.**
7. **Trace improvements in the development of software.**
8. **List two emerging trends in computer technology.**

INTRODUCTION

The extensive use of computers to make business procedures easier and more efficient is a fairly recent phenomenon. The first digital computer used in business was installed in 1954. Although slow compared to today's computers, it made computations automatically and rapidly. Individuals who are accustomed to the ease and speed of performing calculations on modern computers might well wonder what people did before that date to speed up calculations and make them less tiresome.

THE EARLY BEGINNING

Primitive people relied on whatever materials were available to perform almost any kind of action. As time went on and people became more civilized, they were able to develop the tools needed to perform tasks, including such activities as counting and calculating, more quickly and efficiently.

Finger Counting

Before the nineteenth century, most calculations were made in a person's brain. The first computations usually involved simple counting, and no doubt the person used all ten fingers to help. The early Roman schools actually taught finger counting and devised a method of multiplying and dividing using the fingers. From the use of fingers, people moved to aids such as pebbles, sticks, and beads for computations.

The Abacus

More than three thousand years ago the **abacus**, the first counting machine, was invented. It consists of a frame in which rods strung with beads are set. The beads represent digits and the rods represent places: units, tens, hundreds, and higher multiples of ten. In the abacus illustrated in Figure A-1, each bead in the top compartment has an assigned value of five; each bead in the bottom compartment, a value of one. The beads in both compartments have a counting value when they are pushed toward the board that separates the two compartments. In the illustration, the beads represent a total of 249.

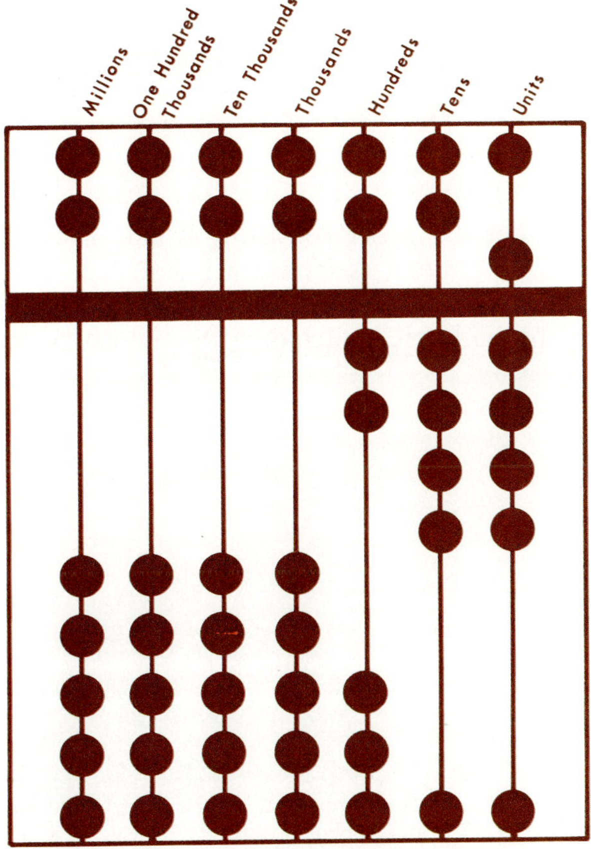

Figure A-1
The abacus was first used more than three thousand years ago.

The origin of the abacus is uncertain. Some say it is a product of the ancient Hindu civilization. Others say it came from Babylon or Egypt. Some believe that the Chinese invented it. The Chinese modified and adopted it early in their history; it has, therefore, generally become known as a Chinese invention.

The Japanese also modified and adopted the abacus. The Japanese model (Figure A-2) is known as a soraban. It differs from the abacus in that it has only one bead on each rod in the upper compartment and five beads on each rod in the lower compartment. Note in Figure A-1 that the abacus has two beads on each rod in the upper compartment and five beads on each rod in the lower compartment. The abacus and the soraban are still used in some countries. In skilled hands, they are amazingly rapid and efficient in making computations.

Figure A-2
The soraban was the Japanese version of the abacus.

Napier's Bones

In the 1600s, John Napier invented a device consisting of rods or strips of bone on which numbers were printed, as shown in Figure A-3. The device became known as **"Napier's bones."** By means of these rods or bones, computations could be performed, including the extraction of square and cube roots.

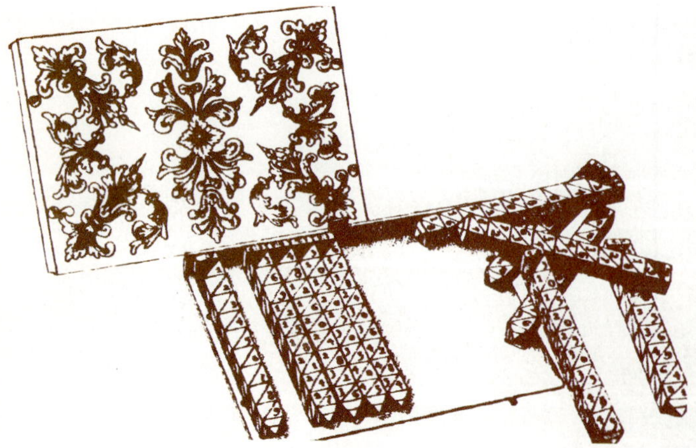

Figure A-3
John Napier invented "Napier's bones" for use in computations.

The Slide Rule

The **slide rule**, conceived by William Oughtred in 1622, consists of an outer rule and a central sliding rule. Both rules are divided into scales. The rules are moved either backward or forward until a selected number on one scale lines up with a selected number on the other scale. The desired result is then read from a third scale. The slide rule, shown in Figure A-4, was widely used by engineers and scientists as recently as the 1970s. The electronic calculator put the slide rule out of business.

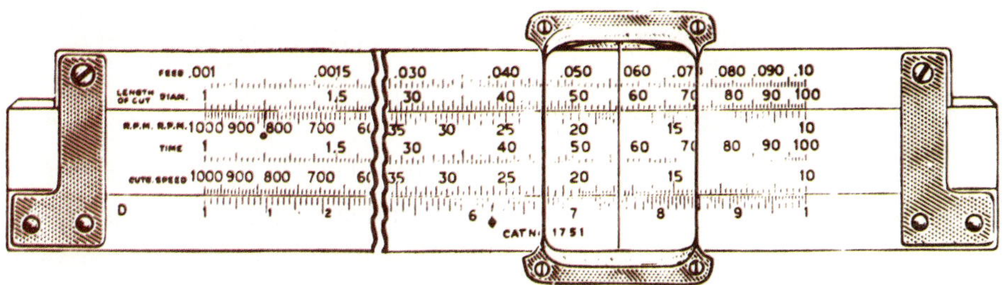

Figure A-4
The slide rule consists of rules that move backward or forward to yield the desired result.

INVENTORS OF EARLY CALCULATORS

The development of mechanically operated adding machines and calculators began in the 1600s. Some of the early developers are discussed in the following paragraphs.

Blaise Pascal

In 1642, Blaise Pascal invented the first mechanical adding machine, shown in Figure A-5. It was capable of carrying tens automatically. His machine consisted of wheels with cogs or teeth on which the numbers

Figure A-5
The first mechanical adding machine was invented by Blaise Pascal.

0-9 were engraved. The first wheel on the right represented units; the second, tens; the third, hundreds; and so on. As the wheels were turned, the numbers appeared in a window at the top of the machine. When the units wheel was turned beyond Digit 9, the tens wheel at the left would reflect the carry. For example, to add 7 and 4, the 7 was stored on the first wheel by turning the wheel until the 7 appeared in the window. Then the wheel was turned again through four places. This procedure resulted in a carry, which was accomplished by a series of gears arranged in such a way that they turned the next wheel. As a result, 1's appeared in the windows above the tens and units wheels. The contemporary computer language known as Pascal was named for Blaise Pascal.

Gottfried von Leibnitz

In 1671, Gottfried von Leibnitz drew the plans for a calculator that could multiply and divide as well as count, add, and subtract. A drawing of the machine is shown in Figure A-6. In 1694, a machine was actually built using his plans, but it did not work very well. The plans were correct, but the technology capable of making precision parts had not yet been developed.

Figure A-6
Plans for this calculator were developed as early as 1671.

Charles Xavier Thomas

For the next two hundred years, many attempts were made to improve on the Pascal and von Leibnitz inventions. Progress was made, although it was slow and sometimes painful. Gradually, calculators became faster, smaller, more reliable, and at least partially automatic. In the 1820s, Charles Xavier Thomas invented a calculator that was the first to add, subtract, divide, and multiply accurately. It was widely copied by other inventors and was thus considered to be the ancestor of the mechanical calculators that preceded today's electronic calculators. Figure A-7 shows a typical 1880 machine; it was capable of performing the four principal arithmetic operations.

Figure A-7
A typical 1880 calculator would have looked like the one shown here.

Early American Inventors

All early calculator inventors were Europeans. In 1872, Frank S. Baldwin developed the first calculator to be invented in the United States. The invention of this machine, shown in Figure A-8, marked the beginning of a rapidly growing calculator industry in this country. The first practical adding machines which listed amounts and sums on paper were invented in the late 1800s by Dorr Eugene Felt and William S. Burroughs.

Figure A-8
The first U.S. calculator was invented by Frank Baldwin in 1872.

Oscar and David Sundstrand invented the 10-key adding-listing machine in 1914. This machine introduced the keyboard arrangement that became the standard for calculators used in business offices. The same basic keyboard arrangement is used on most of today's electronic calculators.

ELECTROMECHANICAL MACHINES

While development was proceeding on calculating machines, a new idea in processing data was being introduced in the late 1800s. It was the punched card, which was processed electromechanically.

Punched-Card Machines

Herman Hollerith developed the punched card system of processing data.

Using **punched cards** to record factual information, Herman Hollerith developed an entirely new system of processing data. Punched paper tape and punched cards had been used as early as 1728 to control weaving machines. The punched-card principle for weaving patterns in rugs on the first automatic loom was perfected in 1801 by Joseph Jacquard. The principles of these early applications were adapted by Hollerith for use by the U.S. Census Bureau.

Hollerith was an independent inventor who was contracted by the Bureau in 1880 to help speed up the sorting and tabulating of census data. (It had become apparent that it would take over ten years to tabulate the next census figures.) By 1887, he had worked out a code of representing census information through a system of punched holes in paper strips. He later changed to a standard-sized card because the paper strips did not work very well. Thus, Hollerith developed the first machine capable of processing statistical information from punched cards. The system included the cards, a card punch, a sorting box, and a tabulator equipped with electromagnetic counters. With this equipment, cards could be sorted at the rate of about 80 cards per minute. Data appearing in the cards could be tabulated and counted at the rate of 50 to 75 cards per minute. Figure A-9 shows Hollerith's punched-card machine.

Figure A-9
The punched-card machine was the first machine capable of processing statistical information from punched cards.

The Hollerith system was used to process the 1890 census. As a result, the 1890 census was completed in one fourth the time needed to compile the 1880 census. Hollerith then organized a company to manufacture and market his system. This company later became known as the International Business Machines Corporation (IBM).

The Punched-Card Era

Over the years many improvements were made on the original punched-card machines. The machines for punching holes in the cards were improved and equipped with a number of automatic devices. A calculator that could read the punched cards and multiply or divide the data was developed. Various models of machines were developed for sorting the cards and printing reports from data contained in them. From the 1920s through the mid-1970s, punched-card equipment was widely used for business data processing. Cards were punched on a **card-punch machine** (also known as a keypunch) with a keyboard similar to that found on a present-day computer or terminal. A later model card-punch machine is shown in Figure A-10.

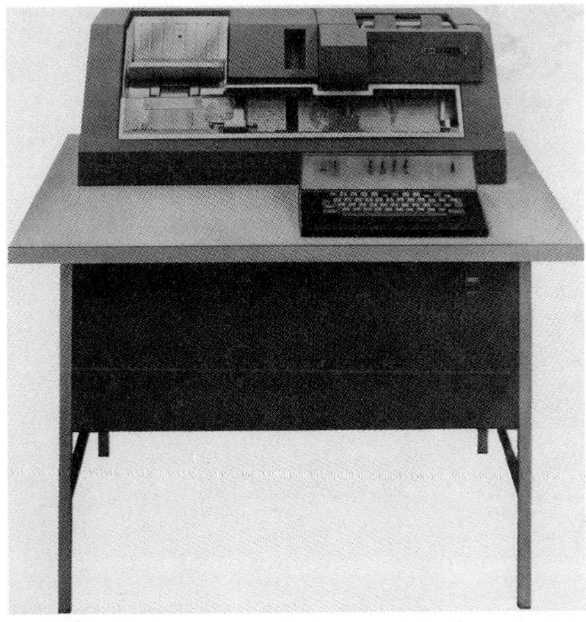

Figure A-10
Card-punch machines (keypunches) were used to punch holes in cards.

Cards to be punched were placed in the card hopper and passed through the machine one card at a time as the operator entered the data on the keyboard. Each character was punched according to a predetermined code. The most commonly used code was known as the Hollerith code and is shown on the card in Figure A-11. The standard card was divided into 80 columns, and one character was punched in each column. Note that a digit was recorded by punching one hole in a column, while an alphabet letter was recorded by punching two holes.

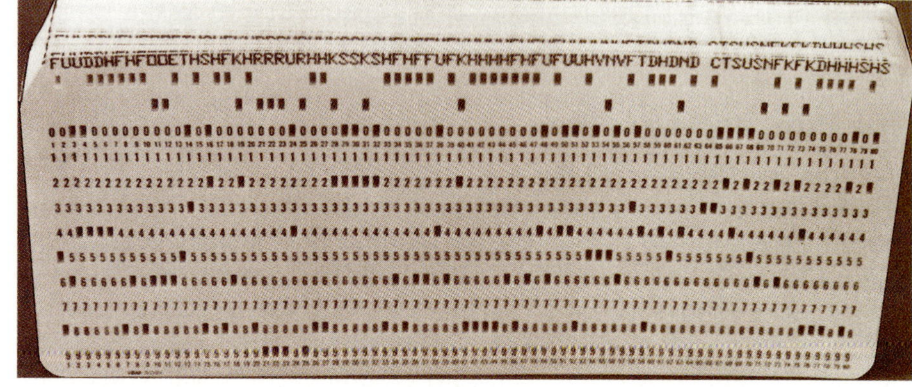

Figure A-11
The Hollerith code was most often used to record data on punched cards.

The different items of information in a punched card were divided into fields in the same manner that a record from a disk file is divided into fields. A card field was a vertical column or group of consecutive columns set aside to record a single fact. A field could contain a name, an amount, or a code, for example. Once the cards were punched, they were arranged or sorted with a **sorter** such as the one shown in Figure A-12. A **tabulator** (Figure A-13) was then used to print reports from the data.

Figure A-12
Punched cards were sorted with a sorter.

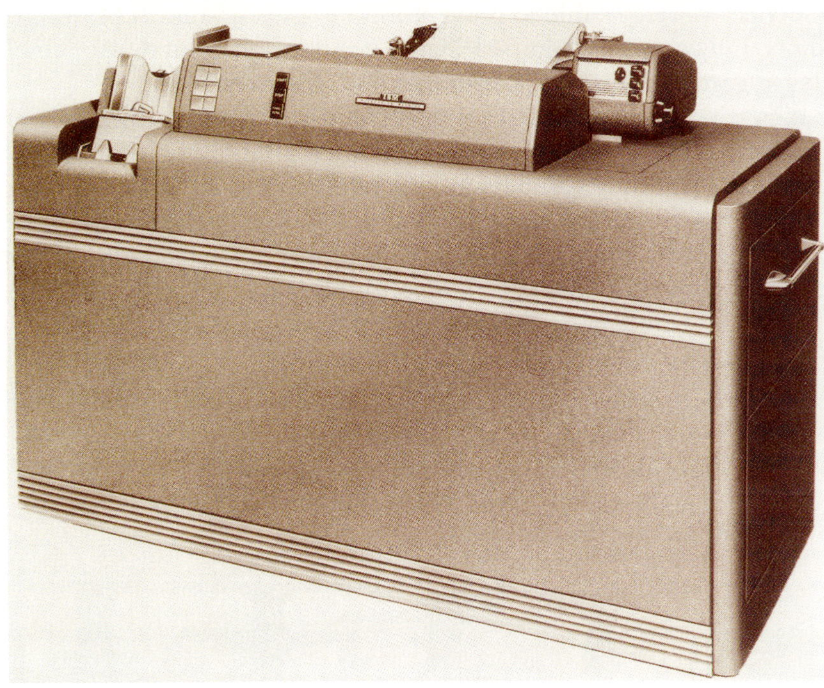

Figure A-13
A tabulator was used to produce printed reports from the data on the cards.

EARLY COMPUTERS

It is important to remember that, although the machines cited previously could do arithmetic and print reports, they were not computers. They contained many mechanical parts and did not make use of stored programs to control their operation. The following paragraphs will look at some of the developments leading up to the stored-program computer as it exists today.

The Analytical Engine

Turn your clock back briefly about one hundred and fifty years to the middle 1800s and meet another inventor, Charles Babbage. Babbage had some entirely new and advanced ideas on designing a computer. Babbage wrote that he was going to construct a machine that would incorporate a memory unit system, an external memory unit, and conditional transfer. He was going to call this device an **analytical engine.** What Babbage described with startling accuracy is the computer.

Babbage was a mathematician of good reputation who spent his life and his fortune, as well as large sums of money from the British government, on the design of an automatic computer. The machine designed by Babbage was to have four basic parts. One part, consisting of the memory, was to be used to store the numeric data used in calculations. A second part, consisting of gears and cog wheels on which digits were engraved, was to be used for computing. A third part, consisting of gears and levers, was to be able to move numbers back and forth between the memory and computing units. Finally, Babbage planned to use punched cards for getting information into and out of his machine.

Babbage believed he could use cards to program his machine to handle computations automatically. He also seemed able to envision the possibility of programming his machine to change from one series of steps to another when certain conditions were encountered. This, of course, is one of the most valuable abilities of a computer. Babbage did not complete his machine, a drawing of which is shown in Figure A-14, but he did leave for a new generation of inventors a great many details of his plan. Due to the technological conditions existing then, the various parts of his machine simply could not be made to the exact specifications required. He was ahead of his time. Had he been successful, his machine would have been the first true computer. As it was, his work was largely forgotten until the 1940s, when new attempts were made to design and build a rapid automatic computer.

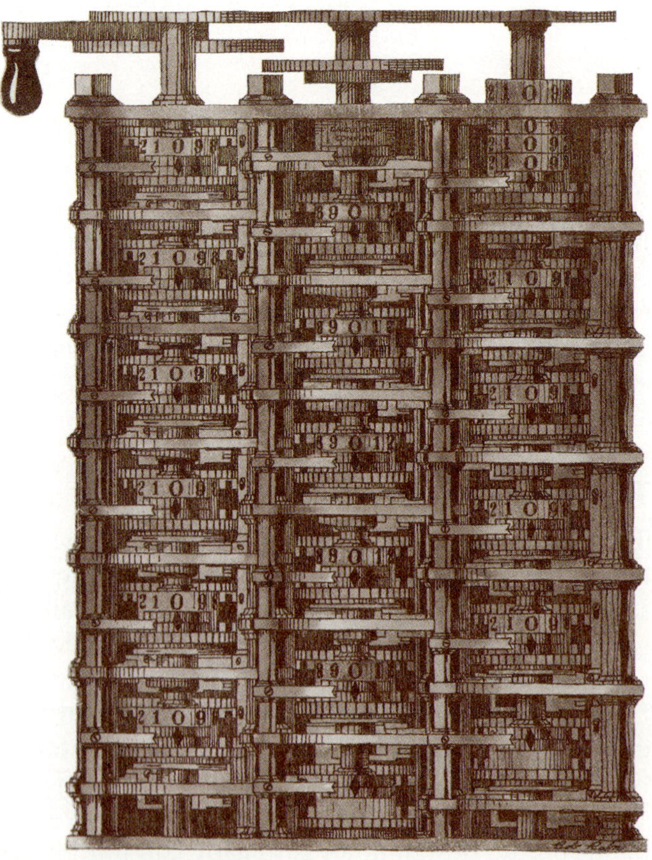

Figure A-14
Charles Babbage seemed to envision the coming of the computer when he designed the analytical engine.

The Mark I

In 1944, Howard Aiken developed a calculator called the **Mark I.** The Mark I obtained data from punched cards, made calculations with the aid of mechanical devices, and punched the results into a new set of cards. The most unusual aspect of the new machine, however, was that it was controlled automatically by instructions punched into paper tape attached to the machine. Thus, it was the first machine to use a stored program to control its actions. The Mark I, although it can be regarded as the first successful computer, was not an electronic computer. It was mechanically operated.

The ENIAC

Another early pioneer working on computers was Dr. John V. Atanasoff, who can be given credit for developing the ideas on which the first electronic computers were based. Many of these ideas were used in **ENIAC**, developed by Dr. John W. Mauchly and J. Presper Eckert, under a contract from the U.S. Army. The first electronic computer to go into operation, ENIAC (the Electronic Numerical Integrator and Calculator) contained thousands and thousands of vacuum tubes. To program ENIAC required changes in thousands of wires and switches. In other words, its program was hard-wired to memory instead of being read into memory as with today's computers. ENIAC, shown in Figure A-15, was completed in 1946 and was used for several years.

Figure A-15
The ENIAC was the first electronic computer to go into operation.

EDSAC and EDVAC

The first electronic computers to utilize the stored-program concept were the **EDSAC** (Electronic Delay Storage Automatic Calculator) and **EDVAC** (Electronic Discrete Variable Automatic Computer). Though the

EDVAC (Figure A-16), developed by Dr. John von Neumann, was conceived first, the EDSAC was completed first in 1949.

Figure A-16
The EDVAC was one of the first computers designed to use a stored program.

FIRST-GENERATION COMPUTERS

ENIAC, EDSAC, and EDVAC were largely experimental or military machines. The first computer available for data processing use was the **UNIVAC I,** a machine developed by Eckert and Mauchly after ENIAC was finished. Remington Rand bought Eckert and Mauchly's company and the UNIVAC I. Remington Rand thus became the first company in the business of selling computers. The first commercially used UNIVAC I was installed at the U.S. Census Bureau in 1951. In 1954, General Electric became the first business to use a computer when it purchased a UNIVAC I. The UNIVAC I is illustrated in Figure A-17 on the next page.

IBM, which for years had dominated the market for electromechanical data processing machines for business use, announced its first commercially available computer in 1953. It shortly overtook Remington Rand in sales. Since then, IBM has continued to be the leading company in the computer business.

All the early computers are known as **first-generation computers.** They used vacuum tubes in their circuitry. For this reason, the machines were very large in size, were very slow by today's standards, and required almost constant maintenance. Typical components of a vacuum tube computer system are shown as part of Figure A-18.

Figure A-17
UNIVAC I was the first commercially available computer.

Figure A-18
Large vacuum tubes made up the circuitry of first-generation computers. Transistors were used in second-generation computers, and integrated circuits were developed for the third generation.

The large number of vacuum tubes in these early computers created many problems because of the amount of heat generated by the tubes. This heat problem made it necessary to install heavy-duty air conditioning units. The first-generation computers were mostly computational machines. Their input/output capabilities were usually limited to keyboard and/or punched-card input and printer and/or punched-card output, although some used magnetic tape. First-generation computers could make over 100,000 calculations per second, which is a speed far surpassed by microcomputers of today.

SECOND-GENERATION COMPUTERS

Second-generation computers, first available in the late 1950s, used transistors instead of vacuum tubes. This change brought many improvements. The cost of computers decreased, and more businesses could afford them. The amount of heat put out by the machines was much less, thus reducing air conditioning requirements. The use of transistors also made it possible to reduce the size of the equipment. This change further increased the computer's computational speed. Also, the transistors proved to be much more reliable than vacuum tubes. Figure A-18 shows the transistors of a second-generation computer.

A typical second-generation computer was the IBM 1401, shown in Figure A-19. Introduced in 1959, it was designed for business use. This machine used transistor circuitry.

Figure A-19
The IBM 1401 was a typical second-generation computer.

Removable disk storage units and magnetic tape input/output units were developed for use on second-generation computers. The speed of the line printers was increased from three hundred lines per minute, which was fairly common on first-generation computers, to one thousand lines per minute. The speed of card readers and card punches was also increased, although not as dramatically as that of the printers. These changes in the computer made it more useful as a tool in business because of the large volume of data to be processed and the lengthy printed reports required.

THIRD-GENERATION COMPUTERS

Third-generation computers introduced the use of very small electronic circuits, called integrated circuits, rather than transistors. This change further decreased the size, the heat output, and the maintenance complexity of the computer, while increasing its speed. The third generation was typified by the IBM 360 series, one of which is shown in Figure A-20.

Figure A-20
The IBM 360 is an example of a third-generation computer.

The speed of the first-generation computers was described in milliseconds (1/1,000 of a second). The speed of the second-generation computers was described in microseconds (1/1,000,000 of a second). The speed of the third-generation computers was described in nanoseconds (1/1,000,000,000 of a second). The speed of line printers on many third-generation computers was increased to two thousand lines per minute, while one printer could print over twenty thousand lines per minute.

FOURTH-GENERATION COMPUTERS

Fourth-generation computers use what is known as **VLSI** circuitry. The abbreviation VLSI refers to **very large scale integration.** This means that extremely large numbers of electronic components are crammed into each integrated circuit chip. This allows still faster speeds while decreasing the need for special power or air conditioning, and at the same time increases the reliability of the equipment.

The types of technology employed in the four generations of computers outlined in the preceding paragraphs were applied to specialized as well as general-purpose computers. In the first generation days, special-purpose computers were used for military purposes such as aiming guns. In the fourth generation, special-purpose computers are used for everything from auto ignitions to the operation of satellites.

THE MICROPROCESSOR ERA

Figure A-21
One chip can contain the circuitry required for the microprocessor of a microcomputer.

The microprocessor era was made possible by the invention of VLSI circuitry. With such techniques, it is possible to place all the components required for the central processing unit of a computer on one chip. Figure A-21 shows a chip containing all the circuitry required for the microprocessor engine of a microcomputer.

The microprocessor era started in the mid-1970s with the introduction of processor chips that could handle four bits of data at a time. These were quickly followed by chips that could handle eight bits of data at a time. The ability to handle eight bits at a time allowed the processor to handle an entire ASCII character at once or a number with more significant digits.

Among the earlier microcomputers to come on the market were offerings from Altair, Imsai, Heathkit, and Apple. The earliest machines generally came in kit form, and the happy new owner had to assemble the unit before it could be used. Figure A-22 shows the parts the user had to assemble from one of these early kits, which typically contained four or eight kilobytes of main memory.

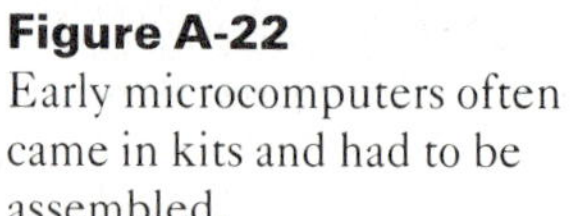

Figure A-22
Early microcomputers often came in kits and had to be assembled.

The 8-bit microprocessors were quickly supplanted for the most part by 16-bit processors. By the late 1980s, 32-bit processors had taken over much of the market. Each of these upgrades was much faster and handled much more memory. While 64 kilobytes of memory was common with many late generation 8-bit machines, 640 kilobytes became the norm for

16-bit machines, and it is common for 32-bit machines to be equipped with several megabytes of main memory.

IMPROVEMENTS IN DATA ENTRY

At the same time the computers themselves were undergoing tremendously fast development, the methods of getting data into the computers were also changing. As indicated earlier, most of the first-generation computers used keypunch machines and punched cards to input data.

For years, the keypunch was the mainstay of data entry. A keypunch machine punched data into cards as punched holes and printed the meanings of the punched holes at the tops of the cards. Usually data was keyed twice: once for the original input, and again to verify its accuracy.

The first data entry improvement over punched cards was the **key-to-tape machine,** shown in Figure A-23. This machine records data on magnetic tape instead of punched cards. The machine has a typewriter-like keyboard. Data is keyed as digits, letters of the alphabet, and special characters. Data is recorded on the tape as magnetized spots in a form of binary code. Some key-to-tape machines have cathode-ray tube displays. The transaction appears on the screen as it is being entered and is transferred to tape once it is complete.

Figure A-23
The key-to-tape machine records data on magnetic tape.

Following the key-to-tape machine was the **key-to-disk machine.** The general principles remained the same. Instead of recording on tape, however, the key-to-disk machine recorded its data on magnetic disks.

The present trend in data entry is toward using input devices connected directly to the computer. Much data is still entered into a terminal or microcomputer. However, more and more data is being automatically generated as a by-product of some process, bypassing the need for manual entry of data.

THE PROGRESSION OF SOFTWARE DEVELOPMENT

While chapters in the text have covered in detail various types of computer languages and software, it is appropriate to review the progression of software development in a historical perspective. Programmers told the earliest computers what to do by manually setting a large number of switches to on or off positions. By setting these switches to on or off positions, binary instructions were being sent to the machine.

From the manual setting of switches, computers progressed to the entry of programs written in the pure binary language of the computer. Needless to say, these programs required meticulous attention to detail in their development, and it was extremely time-consuming to develop programs that ran error free.

The use of symbolic languages was the next step. In these languages, mnemonic abbreviations were used instead of the binary representations of instructions. A translator program could then translate the abbreviations into the binary code needed by the computer.

The development of what became known as high-level languages allowed the development of computer applications to proceed much more efficiently than ever before. These languages allowed the programmer to concentrate on the procedure to be followed by the computer rather than on the infinite details of the internal machine instructions of the computer. The instructions written in the high-level languages were then translated into binary codes through the use of a supplied program known as a compiler. Two of the earliest high-level languages were COBOL and FORTRAN, which in revised versions remain in use today. Other high-level languages in use include BASIC and Pascal, among many others.

High-level languages are giving way to what may be known as application generators or fourth-generation tools. While the user of a high-level language writes code that describes the procedure or process to be used by the computer, the user of application generators concentrates on defining what is to be done rather than on defining how it is to be done.

TECHNOLOGY TRENDS

While it is always dangerous to attempt to predict the future in relation to computers, two trends in technology bear mentioning. They are reduced instruction set computing and parallel processing.

Reduced instruction set computing (popularly known as RISC) has been in existence for several years and is gaining in popularity. Under this technology the number of different machine-level instructions built into the processor is reduced. This allows the processor to run much faster for most operations. When the "missing" instructions are needed in an operation, they are carried out by program steps rather than as a hard-wired function.

Since the conception of the EDVAC by Dr. von Neumann, computers have traditionally carried out instructions sequentially—one after another. This has limited the speed with which computers can operate. Now, the concept of **parallel processing** has broken that speed block. In parallel processing, a computer has more than one processor. The problem to be solved is broken into various parts, with each processor solving one part. The results are then reconstructed back into one whole. As you might suspect, development of the software to break problems into parts and put them back together again is a formidable task. However, tests have indicated that some kinds of problems can be solved thousands of times faster by the use of parallel processing. Thus, the fifth-generation computers currently under development should offer dramatic increases in processing speed and power over the computers being used today.

APPENDIX SUMMARY

- Development of computational machines has been going on for over three thousand years, beginning with the abacus.
- The first machine capable of adding, subtracting, multiplying, and dividing was developed in the 1820s.
- Another giant step forward occurred in the 1880s when Herman Hollerith invented a punched-card method of processing data.
- Punched cards were the mainstay of business data processing through the middle part of the twentieth century.
- The first electronic computer was developed in the late 1940s. From that point, development has been incredibly rapid.
- Each major improvement in technology has led to the development of a new "generation" of computers.
- Since the first commercial use of the computer in the early 1950s, four different generations of computers have been developed.
- The fifth generation of computers is currently under development and may become available at any time.
- With each generation, computers have become much faster, much more capable, easier to use, and smaller in physical size.
- Substantial price reductions have accompanied each advance in technology.
- The computer has truly become a universal machine.

KEY TERMS

The following terms were introduced or redefined in this appendix:

abacus
analytical engine
card-punch machine
EDSAC
EDVAC
ENIAC
first-generation computer
fourth-generation computer
key-to-disk machine
key-to-tape machine
Mark I
Napier's bones
parallel processing
punched cards
reduced instruction set computing
second-generation computer
slide rule
sorter
tabulator
third-generation computer
UNIVAC I
VLSI

REVIEW QUESTIONS

1. Name and describe three early computational devices that preceded the development of calculators. (Obj. 1)
2. Describe the calculators devised by Pascal, von Leibnitz, Thomas, Baldwin, Felt, Burroughs, and Oscar and David Sundstrand. (Obj. 1)
3. Describe the processing of data using the equipment developed by Herman Hollerith. (Obj. 2)
4. What parts were to be contained in Babbage's analytical engine that he conceived in the mid-1800s? (Obj. 3)
5. Why did Babbage never succeed in making the analytical engine work? (Obj. 3)
6. What were the characteristics of Howard Aiken's Mark I calculator? (Obj. 3)
7. What three persons can generally be given credit for the ideas and creation of the first working computer, the ENIAC? (Obj. 3)
8. What was the distinguishing characteristic of the EDSAC and the EDVAC? (Obj. 3)
9. What was the first commercially used computer and when was it first installed? (Obj. 4)
10. What were the characteristics of first-generation computers? (Obj. 4)
11. What were the characteristics of second-generation computers? (Obj.4)
12. What were the characteristics of third-generation computers? (Obj. 4)
13. What are the characteristics of fourth-generation computers? (Obj. 4)
14. Briefly describe the developments in the microprocessor era. (Obj. 5)

15. What were the steps in the progression of data entry, beginning with the use of punched-card equipment and continuing to the present? (Obj. 6)
16. Briefly describe the progress in the development of software. (Obj. 7)
17. Describe two trends in the development of computer technology. (Obj. 8)

CHALLENGE ACTIVITIES

1. Prepare a report or have a class discussion on what you think life today would be like if the computer had never been invented. Consider what each of the following areas would be like: (Objs. 5,6,7)
   a. Manufacturing
   b. Workplace
   c. Communications, including telephone and television (remember, these were invented before computers)
   d. Transportation, including air, sea, and ground
   e. Government
   f. The general economy of the United States and the world
2. Prepare a report or have a class discussion on what you think may happen in computer development during the next 20 years and describe the effect on society. (Obj. 8)

APPENDIX B

INTERNAL REPRESENTATION OF DATA

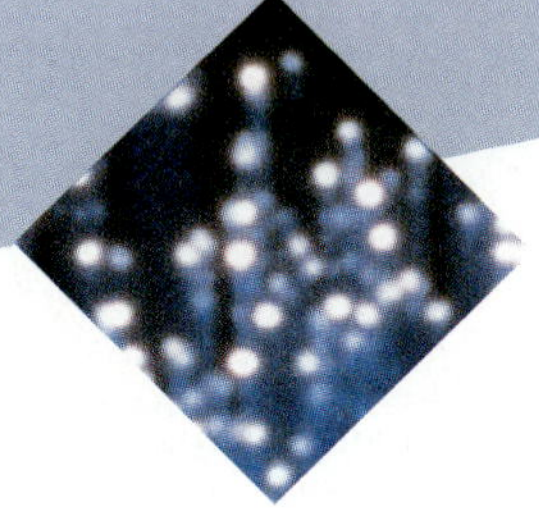

LEARNING OBJECTIVES

After studying this appendix, you will be able to:

1. **Explain why each character is represented inside the computer as a number.**
2. **Identify the ASCII and EBCDIC codes for letters, numbers, special symbols, and control characters.**
3. **Explain how a number is represented in binary in computer memory.**
4. **Explain how an alphabetic character is represented in binary.**
5. **Describe how a numeric value can be stored in pure binary.**
6. **Explain how a numeric value can be represented in the hexadecimal number system.**
7. **Explain how ASCII and EBCDIC characters are represented in hexadecimal.**
8. **Describe what is meant by even and odd parity.**

INTRODUCTION

Each character is represented inside the computer by a coding scheme made up of a series of 0's or 1's which represent "off" or "on." Recall that a computer can only understand the state of an electric circuit as being on or off. Therefore, the data that humans understand as numbers, letters of the alphabet, and special symbols must be converted into numeric codes which the computer can convert to 0's or 1's (or off/on states of electricity). In other words, inside the computer, the letter A is not stored as an A; it may be coded by the computer as the number 65 and represented internally as 1000001.

Two different codes are commonly used for representing data inside the computer—the ASCII and EBCDIC codes. In each of the codes, a number is assigned to each character, digit, and symbol. Each time a key on a keyboard is struck, the code number for that key is generated and input into the computer's memory. When output is to be produced, the code number of each character is sent to the output device, such as a printer. In addition to code numbers for all the numeric, alphabetic, and special symbols, there are also code numbers for various control functions, such as tabulating, backspacing, and positioning the cursor.

ASCII CODE

Most small computers use a code known as **ASCII.** ASCII, which stands for American Standard Code for Information Interchange, uses the numbers 0-127, for a total of 128 possible characters. Figure B-1 (the ASCII code chart) shows the standard 128-character ASCII code. Many manufacturers have expanded the code to the numbers 0-255, for a total of 256 possible characters. Different manufacturers assign different characters, such as graphics, to the extra numbers. In standard ASCII, code numbers 0-31 are nonprinting characters known as **control characters** and are not defined in the chart. Control characters are designed to control the communication between a computer and another device, such as a terminal or printer. Therefore, when sent to an output device, the control

ASCII CHARACTER CODES

Figure B-1
The ASCII Code has a total of 128 possible characters.

Code	Character	Code	Character	Code	Character
0-31	Control Characters	64	@	97	a
32	(space)	65	A	98	b
33	!	66	B	99	c
34	"	67	C	100	d
35	#	68	D	101	e
36	$	69	E	102	f
37	%	70	F	103	g
38	&	71	G	104	h
39	'	72	H	105	i
40	(	73	I	106	j
41	)	74	J	107	k
42	*	75	K	108	l
43	+	76	L	109	m
44	,	77	M	110	n
45	- (hyphen)	78	N	111	o
46	.	79	O	112	p
47	/	80	P	113	q
48	0	81	Q	114	r
49	1	82	R	115	s
50	2	83	S	116	t
51	3	84	T	117	u
52	4	85	U	118	v
53	5	86	V	119	w
54	6	87	W	120	x
55	7	88	X	121	y
56	8	89	Y	122	z
57	9	90	Z	123	{
58	:	91	[	124	|
59	;	92	\	125	}
60	<	93	]	126	~
61	=	94	^	127	(delete)
62	>	95	_(underscore)		
63	?	96	`		

character code numbers normally do not produce a display that can be seen. Some manufacturers, however, have chosen to use various control character code numbers for shapes that can be displayed.

ASCII is used internally by most small computers. ASCII is also widely used in **data communications**, which is the process of sending data from one computer system or device to another.

EBCDIC CODE

EBCDIC stands for **E**xtended **B**inary **C**oded **D**ecimal **I**nterchange **C**ode. It is used by many larger computers. EBCDIC uses code numbers 0-255, for a total of 256 possible characters. The code number representing each character is different than those in ASCII, but the idea is the same. Even though some computers and devices use the ASCII code and some use the EBCDIC code, communication can easily be made between devices using different codes; it just takes a simple translation step by one of the systems to communicate between the two codes. An EBCDIC character code table for special symbols and alphabetic and numeric characters is shown in Figure B-2 on the next page. (Note that dashes represent missing numbers.)

INTERNAL REPRESENTATION OF CODED INFORMATION

The circuits which make up a computer's memory can be thought of as many electronic switches that are either turned on or off. Since on and off represent only two conditions, it is impossible to directly store code numbers such as 65 and 117; that is, the ASCII or EBCDIC codes cannot be stored directly inside the computer. Instead, they are converted into a series of *on's* and *off's*. In effect, imagine eight on/off switches grouped inside the computer. These eight switches can store only one ASCII or EBCDIC character code. By turning various switches on and off, there are 256 different combinations possible. These combinations represent the 256 different characters of the ASCII or EBCDIC codes.

Binary Number System

To get the proper combination for each character, the code is converted to a binary number. **Binary** means two, so a binary number is made using only two digits, 0 and 1. There can be as many 0's and 1's as required within the eight switches to represent a particular number. Each 0 can be thought of as representing a switch that is turned off, while each 1 represents a switch that is turned on. Each 0 or 1 is known as a binary digit, usually referred to as a **bit** (BInary digiT).

Before the representation of numbers in the binary number system is explained, the decimal number system used everyday will be reviewed. In the decimal system, a digit's value becomes ten times larger each time

EBCDIC CHARACTER CODES

Figure B-2
The EBCDIC Code has a total of 256 possible characters.

Code	Character	Code	Character	Code	Character
0		131	c	200	H
_		132	d	201	I
_		133	e	_	
_		134	f	_	
75	.	135	g	_	
76	<	136	h	209	J
77	(	137	i	210	K
78	+	_		211	L
79	'	_		212	M
80	&	_		213	N
_		145	j	214	O
_		146	k	215	P
_		147	l	216	Q
90	!	148	m	217	R
91	$	149	n	_	
92	*	150	o	_	
93	)	151	p	_	
94	;	152	q	226	S
_		153	r	227	T
_		_		228	U
97	/	_		229	V
_		_		230	W
_		162	s	231	X
_		163	t	232	Y
108	%	164	u	233	Z
109	- (hyphen)	165	v	_	
110	>	166	w	_	
111	?	167	x	_	
_		168	y	240	0
_		169	z	241	1
_		_		242	2
122	:	_		243	3
123	#	_		244	4
124	@	193	A	245	5
125	`	194	B	246	6
126	=	195	C	247	7
127	"	196	D	248	8
128		197	E	249	9
129	a	198	F	_	
130	b	199	G	_	

it is moved left. There are ten digits, 0-9. Since each column represents a value ten times as large as the one to the right of it, it can be said that the number system has a base of 10. The **base** is the number you multiply a digit by when you move it one column to the left. For example, the digit 1 has a value of 1 when placed in the right-hand column. When the 1 is moved to the left, with a zero taking its place in the right-hand column, its value becomes 10. With another move to the left, the digit 1 takes on a value of 100.

$10^2 =$ 100	$10^1 =$ 10	$10^0 =$ 1	◀ **Column Values**
		1	In the right-hand column, 1 has a value of 1.
	1	0	Move the digit one column to the left, and its value becomes 10 times as large.
1	0	0	Move the digit one more column to the left, and its value again becomes 10 times as large; that is, 100 times as large as the digit in the right-hand column.
100 +	10 +	1 =	111 Add the values in the columns to get a total of 111.

When there are digits in more than one column, just add their column values. For example, the number 521 can be represented as shown in the following table.

$10^2 =$ 100	$10^1 =$ 10	$10^0 =$ 1	◀ **Column Values**
		1	In the right-hand column, 1 has a value of 1.
	2	0	The 2 in the second column is worth 10 times 2, or 20.
5	0	0	The 5 in the third column is worth 100 times 5, or 500.
500 +	20 +	1 =	521 Add the values in the columns to get a total of 521.

Representing Numeric Values in Binary

The same concept used in the decimal numbering system can be applied to the binary system. Each column has a value twice as large (rather than 10 times as large) as the previous column, so the binary system has a base of 2. As you know, there are only two digits, 0 and 1, as shown in the following table.

$2^2 =$ 4	$2^1 =$ 2	$2^0 =$ 1	◀ **Column Values Given as Decimal Numbers**
		1	In the right-hand column, 1 has a value of 1.
	1	0	Move the digit one column to the left, and its value becomes twice as large (2).
1	0	0	Move the digit one more column to the left, and its value again becomes twice as large; that is, four times as large as the digit in the right-hand column.
4 +	2 +	1 =	7 Add the values in the columns to get a total of 7.

Again, with digits in more than one column, just add their column values. For example, the binary value 101 is equal to 5 as shown in the following table.

$2^2 =$ **4**	$2^1 =$ **2**	$2^0 =$ **1**	◀ **Column Values Given as Decimal Numbers**
		1	In the right-hand column, 1 has a value of 1.
1			The 1 in the third column is worth 4 times 1, or 4.
1	0	1	Add the values in the columns to get a total of 101 in binary. To convert to decimal, add the decimal column values (4+1), for a total of 5. In other words, 101 in binary and 5 in decimal are the same value.
4+	0+	1=	5 Add the values in the columns to get a total of 5.

Each code number used to represent characters inside the computer consumes eight columns consisting of 1's and 0's. The eight 1's and 0's make up a unit known as a **byte**. A byte is the smallest unit which can be referenced at one time in memory. Since each 1 or 0 is known as a bit, it can be said that eight bits make a byte. Since each column is twice as large as the column to the right of it, 1's in the various positions within the byte have the values as shown in the following table.

$2^7 =$ **128**	$2^6 =$ **64**	$2^5 =$ **32**	$2^4 =$ **16**	$2^3 =$ **8**	$2^2 =$ **4**	$2^1 =$ **2**	$2^0 =$ **1**	◀ **Column Values**
1	1	1	1	1	1	1	1	
128	64	32	16	8	4	2	1	◀ Values of each position in a byte

When numbers are to be used for mathematical computations, they are frequently stored in what is called **pure binary**. Pure binary is a method in which a number is stored directly in binary, rather than being coded first in some other manner such as ASCII or EBCDIC. This means that a number is represented as in the above example by simply placing 1's in the columns whose values add up to that number. For example, the value 14 is represented in just one byte by placing 1's in the columns with values of 8, 4, and 2.

$2^7 =$ **128**	$2^6 =$ **64**	$2^5 =$ **32**	$2^4 =$ **16**	$2^3 =$ **8**	$2^2 =$ **4**	$2^1 =$ **2**	$2^0 =$ **1**	◀ **Column Values**
0	0	0	0	1	1	1	0	◀ The value 14 stored in pure binary
				8+	4+	2+	0=	14

If necessary, an adjacent byte can be used if the value to be represented is too large for one byte. Storing the number 521, for example, requires 10 bits. Since a byte (which consists of eight bits) is the smallest unit that can be addressed, this value will require two bytes of memory.

2nd Byte

2^{15}	2^{14}	2^{13}	2^{12}	2^{11}	2^{10}	$2^9 =$	$2^8 =$
						512	256
S	0	0	0	0	0	1	0
▲ **Sign (plus or minus)**						512+	

1st Byte

$2^7 =$	$2^6 =$	$2^5 =$	$2^4 =$	$2^3 =$	$2^2 =$	$2^1 =$	$2^0 =$	
128	64	32	16	8	4	2	1	
0	0	0	0	1	0	0	1	
				8+			1=	521

Notice that the left-most bit contains a sign. The sign is used to indicate whether the value represented is positive or negative.

Representing ASCII Characters in Binary

Now look at how several characters may be stored in binary. The letter *A* has an ASCII code of 65 (see Figure B-1). Therefore, it is stored in binary by placing a 1 in the column worth 64 and a 1 in the column worth 1, for a total of 65.

$2^7 =$ 128	$2^6 =$ 64	$2^5 =$ 32	$2^4 =$ 16	$2^3 =$ 8	$2^2 =$ 4	$2^1 =$ 2	$2^0 =$ 1	◀ **Column Values**
0	1	0	0	0	0	0	1	
	64+						1=	65 (the ASCII code for *A*)

The underscore character (__) has an ASCII code of 95 (see Figure B-1). To store it in binary, place 1's in the columns with values of 64, 16, 8, 4, 2, and 1 (decimal 95 is equal to binary 1011111). Note that these column values added together make 95, which is the appropriate ASCII code number for the underscore character.

$2^7 =$ 128	$2^6 =$ 64	$2^5 =$ 32	$2^4 =$ 16	$2^3 =$ 8	$2^2 =$ 4	$2^1 =$ 2	$2^0 =$ 1	◀ **Column Values**
0	1	0	1	1	1	1	1	The underscore (__)
	64+		16+	8+	4+	2+	1=	95 (the ASCII code for the underscore character)

Digits may also be stored in character form. For example, the ASCII code for the digit 4 is 52 (see Figure B-1). Therefore, the digit 4 can be represented in character form by the value 52. Note that a software program contains specific instructions so it knows whether the contents of a given byte of data represent a numeric value to be used in computations or an ASCII (or EBCDIC) character (as in this example).

2^7 = 128	2^6 = 64	2^5 = 32	2^4 = 16	2^3 = 8	2^2 = 4	2^1 = 2	2^0 = 1	◀ **Column Values**
0	0	1	1	0	1	0	0	
		32+	16+		4=			52 (the ASCII code for the character 4)

Hexadecimal Number System

The **hexadecimal number system** is frequently used when referring to data stored in the computer or data being transmitted from one unit to another. The hexadecimal system has a base of 16. That is, each column's value is 16 times as large as the column to the right (versus 10 times for the decimal system or 2 times for the binary system).

A number system has the same number of digits as its base. Therefore, the decimal system has 10 digits, and the binary system has 2 digits. Likewise, the hexadecimal system has 16 digits. The digits are 0-9 plus A, B, C, D, E, and F. The digit *A* is equivalent to the decimal number 10, *B* is equivalent to 11, *C* is equivalent to 12, *D* is equivalent to 13, *E* is equivalent to 14, and the largest digit, *F*, is equivalent to 15.

Representing Numeric Values in Hexadecimal

Hexadecimal numbers cannot be used inside the computer; only binary numbers work there. Hexadecimal numbers, however, form a convenient "shorthand" notation for referring to the contents of a byte.

The following table illustrates how the decimal value 35 is represented as hexadecimal 23.

16^3 4096	16^2 256	16^1 16	16^0 1	◀ **Hexadecimal Column Values**
		2	3	The number 23 in hexadecimal converts to 35 in decimal: the 2 in the second column is worth 2 times 16, or 32; adding the 3 in the first column gives 35.
		32+ (16 x 2)	3=	35

Representing ASCII Characters in Hexadecimal

Now take a look at how alphabetic and special characters are represented in hexadecimal. The letter *N*, which has an ASCII code of 78 (see Figure B-1) is stored in a byte as shown in the following table.

$2^3 =$ 8	$2^2 =$ 4	$2^1 =$ 2	$2^0 =$ 1	$2^3 =$ 8	$2^2 =$ 4	$2^1 =$ 2	$2^0 =$ 1	◀ **Column Values**
0	1	0	0	1	1	1	0	◀ ASCII code 78
	4			8+	4+	2=		14 (equivalent to *E* in hexadecimal)

With the byte divided into two units, each half may be referred to as a **nibble.** Here is the way hexadecimal may be used. First, look at the left-hand nibble, 0100. Add the values of the columns containing 1's. In this case there is just one in the 4 column. This gives a total of 4. Now look at the right-hand nibble. Add together the column values where there are 1's. That is, add 8, 4, and 2 to get a total of 14. A total of 4 from the first four bits and a total of 14 from the last four bits produce the number 4E in hexadecimal terms. (Remember that the value 14 is known as the digit *E* in hexadecimal.)

Shown below is proof that ASCII code 78 (stated in decimal) is exactly the same thing as ASCII code 4E (stated in hexadecimal).

16^3 4096	16^2 256	16^1 16	16^0 1	◀ **Hexadecimal Column Values**
		4	E	The E in the right-hand column is the same as decimal 14. Now remember that the second column in hexadecimal is worth 16 times as much as the first column. Therefore, the 4 in the second column is really worth 4 times 16, or 64. Add the 64 to the 14 from the first column, and you get 78.
		64+ (16 x 4)	14=	78

Representing EBCDIC Characters in Hexadecimal

EBCDIC characters are represented in hexadecimal using the same process as the one used to represent ASCII characters in hexadecimal. For example, the EBCDIC code for the letter *N* is 213. This translates to 11010101 in binary or D5 in hexadecimal.

Parity Checking

When data is being transmitted from one device to another, especially over long distances, it is possible for various kinds of interference to cause errors in the character codes. That is, the code received may have a 1 where a 0 was transmitted or a 0 where a 1 was transmitted. By counting the number of 1's in each code received, many errors can be caught. For example, if all code numbers should contain an even number of 1's, a code with an odd number of 1's would be in error. This would work well, except that some correct character codes contain an even number of 1's while others contain an odd number. To overcome this problem, an extra bit, known as a **parity bit,** is added. Therefore, with eight bits used to represent a character, the parity bit becomes the ninth bit. Parity means equality; therefore, the parity bit may be recorded by the transmitting device as either a 1 or a 0, whichever is required to equal an odd or even number of 1's.

Counting the number of 1's in each character code to make sure they are all even or all odd is known as a **parity check.** The use of odd numbers is known as odd parity. The use of even numbers is known as even parity. Look at the example shown using even parity. The letter *A*, as stored in binary, contains two 1's (an even number of 1's). Therefore, if using even parity, a 0 would be recorded as the parity bit. That is because there is already an even number of 1's.

	$2^7 =$ 128	$2^6 =$ 64	$2^5 =$ 32	$2^4 =$ 16	$2^3 =$ 8	$2^2 =$ 4	$2^1 =$ 2	$2^0 =$ 1	◀ **Column Values**
0	0	1	0	0	0	0	0	1	◀ The letter *A* (ASCII code 65) stored in binary

▲ With even parity, a 0 is recorded as the parity bit since the letter *A* already contains an even number of 1's.

The letter *X* (ASCII code 88), as stored in binary, contains three 1's (an odd number). Therefore, if using even parity, a 1 is recorded as the parity bit to make a total of four 1's (an even number).

	$2^7 =$ 128	$2^6 =$ 64	$2^5 =$ 32	$2^4 =$ 16	$2^3 =$ 8	$2^2 =$ 4	$2^1 =$ 2	$2^0 =$ 1	◀ **Column Values**
1	0	1	0	1	1	0	0	0	◀ The letter *X* (ASCII code 88) stored in binary

▲ With even parity, a 1 is recorded to make an even number of 1's.

Any time data is stored, retrieved, transmitted, or received, the number of 1's in each character ("on" bits in each byte) can be counted. If the quantity is not properly even or odd, it is obvious that either a 1 accidentally changed to a 0 or a 0 accidentally changed to a 1 during the operation. The response of the system to a parity error depends on how it has been programmed. It may ignore the error, retransmit the data, or just stop.

All the work of handling a parity check is normally done by software supplied with the computer. The user or programmer is usually not concerned with adding parity bits, checking parity bits, or handling parity errors. Frequently, however, the user setting up a system for data communications will be required to specify whether parity is to be checked and whether it should be odd or even.

To review, even parity is the state of parity in which a 1 is added in the parity bit position as necessary to maintain an even number of 1's for each character. Odd parity, on the other hand, is the reverse of even parity; a 1 is placed in the parity bit position as necessary to maintain an odd number of 1's for each character. The parity bit does not change the character that is coded. The bit is automatically added as a check on the accuracy of the computer equipment. Note that a parity check does not check for mistakes in the actual data.

APPENDIX SUMMARY

- Each character is represented inside the computer by a number.
- Two different codes are commonly used for representing data inside the computer—ASCII and EBCDIC codes. Each time a key on the keyboard is struck, the code number for that key is generated and input into the computer's memory.
- ASCII stands for American Standard Code for Information Interchange.
- EBCDIC stands for Extended Binary Coded Decimal Interchange Code.
- The circuits which make up a computer's memory can be thought of as many electronic switches that are either turned on or off. In order to represent the ASCII or EBCDIC codes, these on and off switches are grouped together in groups of eight.
- In order to get the proper combination for each character, the code is converted to a binary number. Binary means two, so a binary number is composed of only two digits (0 and 1).
- Each 1 or 0 is known as a binary digit, usually referred to as a bit (BInary digiT).
- The base of a number is the number a digit is multiplied by when it is moved one column to the left.
- The decimal number system commonly used each day uses the numbers 0-9 and has a base of 10. The binary number system uses the numbers 0 and 1 and has a base of 2.
- Each code number used to represent characters inside the computer consumes eight columns consisting of 1's and 0's. The eight 1's and 0's make up a unit known as a byte. A byte is the smallest unit which can be addressed (referenced) in the computer's memory.
- Since each 1 or 0 is known as a bit, it can be said that eight bits make a byte.
- Pure binary is a method in which a number is stored directly in binary, rather than being coded first in some other manner such as ASCII or EBCDIC.
- The hexadecimal number system is frequently used when referring to data stored in the computer or data being transmitted from one unit to another.

- The hexadecimal number system uses the numbers 0, 1, 2, 3, 4, 5, 6, 7, 8, 9, A, B, C, D, E, and F and has a base of 16.
- One half of a byte (or four bits) may be referred to as a nibble.
- Parity checking is the means by which a computer verifies that data transmitted from one device to another, especially over long distances, is free of errors in the character codes. An extra bit, known as a parity bit, is added to each byte to facilitate this checking.
- The checking for odd numbers is known as odd parity. The checking of even numbers is known as even parity.

KEY TERMS

The following key terms were introduced or redefined in this appendix:

ASCII
base
binary
bit
byte
control characters
data communications
EBCDIC
hexadecimal number system
nibble
parity bit
parity check
pure binary

REVIEW QUESTIONS

1. Why is each character represented inside the computer as a number? (Obj. 1)
2. What are the two different codes commonly used for representing data inside the computer? (Obj. 2)
3. What does the acronym ASCII stand for? (Obj. 2)
4. What does the acronym EBCDIC stand for? (Obj. 2)
5. How many different characters can be represented in either the EBCDIC or the expanded ASCII code? (Obj. 2)
6. What is the purpose of control characters? (Obj. 2)
7. What does binary mean? (Obj. 3)
8. What is a bit? (Obj. 3)
9. What is a number base? (Objs. 3,4,6,7)
10. What is a byte? (Obj. 3)
11. Represent the numbers 4, 7, and 8 in binary. (Obj. 3)
12. Represent the ASCII letters *B*, *I*, and *Z* in binary. (Obj. 4)
13. Represent the EBCDIC letters *B*, *I*, and *Z* in binary. (Obj. 4)
14. Represent the values 42, 64, and 139 in pure binary. (Obj. 5)
15. What are the equivalent hexadecimal values for 38, 65, and 586? (Obj. 6)
16. What are the hexadecimal equivalents of the ASCII letters *A*, *J*, and *Y*?) (Obj. 7)

17. What are the hexadecimal equivalents of the EBCDIC letters *A*, *J*, and *Y*?) (Obj. 7)
18. What is a parity bit? (Obj. 8)
19. What is the difference between odd and even parity? (Obj. 8)

CHALLENGE ACTIVITIES

1. Represent the word *COMPUTER* in ASCII and binary code. (Objs. 2,3,4)
2. Represent the word *COMPUTER* in EBCDIC and binary code. (Objs. 2,3,4)
3. Each computer manufacturer has allocated areas of its computer's memory (called a memory map) that are designated for specific code or tasks that must be performed. For example, a range of memory addresses may be set aside for the Disk Operating System code, and another range of addresses may be reserved for graphic characters. Research a memory map for a popular microcomputer. Prepare a report explaining how the computer's memory is mapped. *Hint:* Consult a programming language manual or a manufacturer's technical specifications manual for your research. (Objs. 1,2,3,4,5,6,7)

APPENDIX C

BASIC PROGRAMMING

LEARNING OBJECTIVES

After studying this appendix, you will be able to:

1. **List the advantages and disadvantages of BASIC.**
2. **Distinguish between immediate and deferred execution modes.**
3. **Describe data types with which BASIC operates.**
4. **Identify and explain the use of common BASIC keywords and terms.**
5. **Write several software programs using the BASIC programming language.**

INTRODUCTION

BASIC has always been considered an easy-to-learn language, partly because of its English-like code. More recent versions of the language have enhanced its capabilities so that it is now suitable for writing application programs in virtually any area. **BASIC** is the acronym for **B**eginner's **A**ll-Purpose **S**ymbolic **I**nstruction **C**ode. In this appendix, you will learn about this language, a language which is "standard" on millions of microcomputers. The discussion of the BASIC language which follows is only a brief, working overview of how to program a computer using the BASIC programming language. It is not intended as a comprehensive treatment of the BASIC language.

ADVANTAGES AND DISADVANTAGES OF BASIC

BASIC has many advantages as a programming language. Among them are the following:

1. The BASIC language is especially well-suited for interactive programming. **Interactive programming** refers to the process of keying a program into the computer and immediately executing (running) the program. This type of programming is possible only with an interpreted language that has its own built-in editing program (a program capable

of text revision). The built-in editing program allows the programmer to enter the program into the computer's memory, then enter a command to execute the program. An interpreter translates the program statements into machine language one at a time as the program executes.

2. Because of the interactive nature of BASIC, many programs are much easier to write. Also, finding and fixing **bugs** (programming errors) are easier with BASIC than with many other languages.
3. A program can be compiled with a BASIC compiler to speed up its operation and make it impossible for others to see (it is very difficult to read binary machine code). A **compiled program** is one that has been converted into machine-readable code that the computer can execute directly. A BASIC interpreter can be used to enter and **debug** (correct program errors) the program before compiling it.
4. BASIC is available for most small computers. This means that many individuals and companies have written programs in the BASIC language, thus leading to an increased availability of software. As software has become more plentiful, it has also become less expensive, thereby enabling more individuals and small businesses to utilize the computer.
5. Many present versions of BASIC are very powerful, making programming of complex problems quite easy and efficient.
6. BASIC is a free-form language; that is, there is no particular order in which programming instructions must be stated when the program is written. The sequence of instructions is determined totally by the required order of instructions for solving the problem and the desires of the programmer.
7. Many versions of BASIC have commands that enable the creation of sound and graphics.
8. BASIC is useful for doing business computations and for solving complex mathematical formulas.

BASIC also has some disadvantages, although with many applications, the advantages far outweigh the disadvantages. Listed below are some of the disadvantages:

1. Interpreted languages, including interpreted BASIC, make the computer appear to run slower than those programmed with compiled languages. This disadvantage may be overcome, however, by using a BASIC compiler.
2. Some programming managers see BASIC's free-form nature as a disadvantage. Because the programmer can write statements in any order desired, poor programming habits can be acquired. BASIC's free-form nature also leads to what is called "spaghetti code," which means that the program continuously jumps from one location to another. Needless to say, such programs are difficult to follow when one programmer

is trying to find a bug or make a modification to another programmer's program. Good programming technique can avoid this problem.

3. There are many different versions of BASIC from many software developers and computer manufacturers. Frequently there are differences in the instructions used to accomplish the same task. Therefore, a program written for one version of BASIC probably will not run under another version. Also, a program written for one manufacturer's computer may not run on another manufacturer's computer. A person who knows one version of BASIC, however, finds it quite easy to adapt to other versions.
4. Depending on the version of BASIC being used, the handling of complex data files may be difficult and somewhat inefficient.
5. With older versions of BASIC, the formatting of printed output is minimally supported. Newer versions, however, provide additional formatting capabilities which improve the appearance, understanding, and readability of the output.

AN OVERVIEW OF BASIC

Understanding more about how BASIC works will make learning the language easier. Since the BASIC language is most frequently used in an interpreter environment, the discussion in the remainder of this appendix will limit itself to the use of a BASIC interpreter.

Like all high-level languages, BASIC translates English-like instructions into machine language for execution by the processor. Unlike most others, however, BASIC also includes the necessary software for entering a program directly into the computer's memory and saving it on an auxiliary storage device. The use of a separate word processor or a text editor to input the BASIC instructions is not required.

Program Modes

The fact that BASIC allows a program to be directly entered into the computer's memory and that BASIC is an interpreted language make two modes (ways of operating) possible. These modes are the immediate execution mode and the deferred execution mode. The **immediate execution mode** is in effect when an instruction is entered and immediately executed by the computer. The **deferred execution mode** is in effect when the instruction is part of a program and is executed when the entire program is run.

Immediate Execution Mode

By using the immediate execution mode, many arithmetic problems can be performed without writing a program. Look at some examples of the things that can be done by using BASIC in immediate execution mode. In the examples, **keywords** are words that BASIC understands. The keyword **PRINT**, which the computer understands, is used to display words and numbers on the display screen as shown in the following examples:

```
Example 1:  PRINT 10 + 2 - 4
            8

Example 2:  PRINT "THE AVERAGE SCORE IS ";(100 + 90 + 80) / 3
            THE AVERAGE SCORE IS 90
```

To repeat an instruction used in immediate execution mode, the instruction must be reentered.

Deferred Execution Mode

In deferred execution mode, each instruction is preceded by a line number. This gives BASIC the clue that the instruction is part of a program and is not to be performed until it is commanded to do so. Before entering a program in deferred mode, the NEW command should be entered. The **NEW** keyword erases the previously entered instructions and data from the computer's memory. It should always be used before a new BASIC program is entered. **RUN** is the keyword that tells BASIC to execute the instructions that have been entered in the form of a program. Look at an example of using BASIC in deferred execution mode. The input is as follows:

```
NEW

50 PRINT "PRINT THESE NUMBERS:"
60 PRINT 45,50.78,125.55,67.5
70 PRINT 3879,18.624,7,943.2

RUN

PRINT THESE NUMBERS:
45              50.78             125.55            67.5
3879     18.624           7               943.2
```

The program above has only three program statements. They are identified as line numbers 50, 60, and 70. When the program is RUN, the program statement with the lowest line number is executed first (line number 50 in this example). Next, the program statement with the second lowest line number will be executed (line number 60), and so on until the entire program has been run.

Note that a literal (words enclosed in quotation marks) is printed by line 50, while constants (numbers) are printed by lines 60 and 70. (These are further defined under the section "Constants and Literals.") The constants are separated by commas. The commas cause BASIC to move to a new print zone before beginning each number. A **print zone** is an area into which each print line is divided. For example, an 80-column print line might be divided into 5 print zones of 16 characters each. The width of each print zone may vary depending on the computer and version of BASIC being used. If items after the keyword PRINT are separated by semicolons rather than commas, the items are printed next to each other rather than in different print zones. Many computers, however, leave one space before each number for a sign (a blank if positive, or a minus sign if negative), even when separation is with semicolons.

Variables

The location of data stored in the computer's memory is identified by a numeric address. The numeric address which identifies a specific value or a related group of alphanumeric characters is given a name called a **variable.** For example, suppose "THE AVERAGE IS" and 90 are to be stored in memory. The location where this data is to be stored may be labeled in a program by variable names such as AV$ and A1 respectively. In this example, the literal "THE AVERAGE IS" is stored in a memory location identified as AV$ (which the programmer has chosen to stand for Average), and 90 is stored in a memory location identified as A1 (which the programmer has chosen to stand for the first average score). In BASIC there are two kinds of variables: numeric variables and character variables.

Numeric Variables

A **numeric variable** is a storage place for a numeric value that is not known in advance; that is, a value that will be created or changed while the program is carrying out instructions. Examples of numeric values are student numbers, test scores, total test points for the term, and student averages. Some versions of BASIC make a distinction between variables that hold **integers** (whole numbers) and those that hold **real numbers** (numbers with a decimal point, also known as **floating-point numbers**). In these versions, a numeric variable is set up to hold real numbers unless the programmer specifies otherwise.

Character Variables

A **character variable** is also referred to as a **string variable.** Character variables are used to store any data that contains numeric, alphabetic, and/or special symbol characters. For example, such data as a student name or the student's street address (which may also contain numeric characters) is stored in character variables.

A variable whose name ends with a dollar sign ($) is a character variable. To help remember this, imagine the dollar sign as resembling the letter *S* (the first letter in String). A variable *without* a dollar sign at the end of its name is a numeric variable. An error will occur if the programmer attempts to assign character data to a numeric variable or numeric data to a character variable.

Names of Variables

Each variable stored in the computer's memory is identified by a variable name. Variable names must begin with a letter of the alphabet. Other characters in the name can be either alphabetic letters or digits. When naming variables, it is desirable to name them to describe the kind of data they are to store. For example, if the variable to be stored is the name of a city, it makes sense to call the variable CITY$. However, several versions of BASIC restrict the programmer to the use of shorter variable names; typically, a letter of the alphabet and one digit. This gives variable names such as A, C1$, X3, or M$. In this case, about the best option for naming a city variable is to call it C$, using the first letter of *city*.

Most versions of BASIC allow at least a two character variable name: an alphabetic letter followed by another letter or numeric digit. Newer BASIC versions, such as those used by the IBM PC and similar or compatible computers, allow use of longer names for variables, sometimes as many as 40 characters. With one of these versions, the following variable names would be acceptable:

> PHONE$, STORE1832, WORKPHONE, ADDRESS$,
> DISCOUNT3, PRICE, TAXRATE

Constants and Literals

In addition to storing data in variables as discussed above, BASIC also has provisions for storing an item of data that does not change. Such data is known as either a constant or literal. A **constant** is a number that does not change as the program executes. For example, pi (3.14) and a sales tax rate (.05) are considered constant numbers. A **literal** is any combination of alphanumeric characters which is entered between quotation marks, such as a student's address (962 Creek Side Dr.). As with a constant, a literal does not change during execution of the program.

DEVELOPING EXAMPLE PROGRAMS

One of the easiest and quickest ways to become familiar with the BASIC language is to look at some example programs. The remainder of this appendix is composed of five logically organized parts, each containing example programs that will help you learn how to write simple programs using the BASIC language. The example programs are followed by two programming exercises to make sure you comprehend the material before proceeding to the next part. Do not enter the example programs until you are instructed to do so in the programming exercises.

Part 1 - Getting Input from the Keyboard

One of the most common routines used in programming involves getting input from the keyboard. Assume that one student in a course has three grades that will be keyed in and averaged. The steps to the solution of the problem are as follows:

1. Input the three grades from the keyboard and store them in numeric variables.
2. Print the average found by summing the grades and dividing the sum by 3.

Translating these steps into BASIC gives the program shown in Figure C-1. Refer to the program while studying the following comments about how it works.

Figure C-1

```
NEW

10 REM PROGRAM NAME = GRADEAVG
20 REM GRADE AVERAGING PROGRAM
30 REM WRITTEN BY JUDITH WILLIAMS, 10/15/--
40 REM <--- Replace with HOME for Apple or CLS if IBM or
            Tandy 1000 user.
50 INPUT "ENTER 3 NUMBER GRADES SEPARATED BY COMMAS: ";G1,G2,G3
60 PRINT "THE AVERAGE IS ";(G1+G2+G3)/3
70 END
```

Recall that the NEW command is issued to clear memory of all previous instructions and data. Statements 10, 20, and 30 contain remarks, or comments about the program. The abbreviation **REM** stands for remark. They have no effect on the program and are not required by the BASIC language. It is a good practice to use them, however, as part of good program documentation.

Line 40 clears the screen. **HOME** is the keyword used on the Apple II microcomputers to clear the display screen. If an Apple II microcomputer is being used, the keyword REM in line 40 should be replaced with HOME. The IBM PC, Tandy 1000, and many other computers require the use of the keyword **CLS,** which stands for "clear screen," to clear the screen. If an IBM or Tandy 1000 is being used, the REM in line 40 should be replaced with CLS.

On line 50, the keyword **INPUT** causes the computer to stop and wait for the user to enter data from the keyboard. (Enter, as used in this appendix, means key the data *then* press the ***Enter*** or ***Return*** key.) Since there is a literal following the keyword INPUT, the computer will print the literal before waiting for the user's response. Such a literal is known as a **prompt** and tells the user what kind of input is required. Once the user enters the required data, the data is stored in the variables named at the end of the statement. In response to line 50, the user must enter three numeric grades, separating them with commas. The first grade will be stored in variable G1, the second grade will be stored in variable G2, and the third grade will be stored in variable G3.

Line 60 causes the computer to calculate and print the average of the three grades. First, the grades are added together, as indicated by the plus signs between the names of the variables. Note that the parentheses cause the addition to take place before the division. If the parentheses were not used, grade G3 would be divided by 3 and then added to the other two grades, yielding an incorrect result. This is because BASIC and most other languages follow the normal math rule stating that multiplication and division should be done before addition and subtraction. As soon as the answer is calculated, it is printed on the screen along with the literal.

Line 70, the **END** statement, causes the program to stop executing. In most versions of BASIC, the END statement is optional. The program will stop even if there is no END statement.

Note that only one keyword, INPUT, was required to tell BASIC to get data from the keyboard. Note, too, that only one keyword, PRINT, was required to display an answer on the display screen. This simplicity of setting up the flow of data from the computer to the operator, as well as from the operator to the computer, is one of the primary advantages of the BASIC language. It was designed specifically for such two-way communication between the computer and the user.

Suppose that a student has grades of 80, 90, and 88. After the program is keyed into the computer, the RUN command may be entered as shown below to execute the program. Study the interaction that takes place between the computer and the user.

```
RUN

ENTER 3 NUMBER GRADES SEPARATED BY COMMAS: 80,90,88
THE AVERAGE IS 86
```

Note: If an IBM or Tandy 1000 computer is being used, a question mark (?) will appear after the INPUT statement prompt message is displayed to indicate that data input is required.

The **LIST** command will display the entire program in the computer's memory on the display screen. If the program is too long and sections have to be displayed one at a time, LIST may be followed by the range of line numbers to be displayed. For example, LIST 10-50 would display lines 10 through 50; LIST 30 would display only line 30.

BASIC TIPS

A program can also be listed to an attached printer to obtain a printed copy (called a hardcopy). If you are using an IBM or Tandy 1000 computer, the LLIST command will direct your program listing to the printer. If you are using an Apple, enter PR#1 (to direct output to the printer), then enter the LIST command. Enter PR#0 when you are finished to direct the output back to the display screen.

Programming Exercise

1. Enter, list, and run the program illustrated in Figure C-1. When entering the program, use your name and the current date in statement 30. Enter grades of 75, 88, and 98 from the keyboard to test your program. Save your program as GRADEAVG. For information on BASIC Start-up, SAVE, and LOAD procedures, see the BASIC TIPS that follow.
2. Write a BASIC program that will calculate and display a salesperson's average dollar sales for a five-day work week. Use $1,500.00, $1,350.00, $1,280.00, $1,475.00, and $1,900.00 to test your program. *Note:* Do not enter the dollar sign ($) or the comma (,) as part of the sales amounts. Save your program as DOLLARS.

BASIC TIPS

Apple BASIC Start-up Procedures:

1. Turn on the monitor.
2. Open the door to Disk Drive 1 and carefully insert your ProDOS diskette.
3. Close the door to the disk drive.
4. Turn on the power switch.
5. When a menu appears, select the Applesoft BASIC option or the option to Exit System Utilities and strike the ***Return*** key.
6. You are now in Applesoft BASIC and ready to key-in the example programs and programming exercises in this appendix.

IBM and Tandy 1000 BASIC Start-up Procedures:

1. Open the door to Disk Drive A and carefully insert your copy of the IBM PC DOS or Tandy 1000 DOS diskette.
2. Close the door to the disk drive.

3. If the computer is off, turn on all power switches. If the computer is already on, hold down the ***Ctrl*** (Control), ***Alt*** (Alternate), and ***Del*** (Delete) keys at the same time. This will boot the system master diskette, and the computer will be ready for use.
4. The computer will prompt you to enter the date and time. You may either enter the date (in the MM/DD/YY format) and time (in the HH:MM:SS format), or simply press the ***Enter*** key to bypass these entries. The next line on the screen will then display "A>."
5. Key the word BASIC and press the ***Enter*** key. The disk drive will run for a short time, and the screen will then display a message ending with "OK."
6. You are now in BASIC and ready to key-in the example programs and programming exercises in this appendix.

Saving and Loading BASIC programs:

The **SAVE** command is used to store a program on disk for future reference, and the **LOAD** command is used to retrieve it back into memory for execution or modification. The procedure to save a program onto disk is to key-in SAVE followed by the name of the program (enclosed in quotation marks if an IBM or Tandy 1000 computer is being used). For example, to save the program in Figure C-1 on disk with the name GRADEAVG on the Apple, SAVE GRADEAVG would be keyed (SAVE GRADEAVG,D2 would save to the diskette in drive 2). To save it on an IBM or Tandy 1000 computer, SAVE"GRADEAVG" would be keyed (SAVE"B:GRADEAVG" would save to the diskette in drive B).

The procedure to load a previously saved program from disk into memory is to key-in LOAD followed by the name of the program (enclosed in quotation marks if an IBM or Tandy 1000 computer is being used). For example, to load the program saved above on the Apple, LOAD GRADEAVG would be keyed (LOAD GRADEAVG,D2 would load from the diskette in drive 2). To load it on an IBM or Tandy 1000 computer, LOAD"GRADEAVG" would be keyed (LOAD"B:GRADEAVG" would load from the diskette in drive B). The program can then be executed with the RUN command or displayed with LIST.

Part 2 - Making Decisions

One advantage to using BASIC is its decision-making power; that is, the power of BASIC to take different actions depending on various circumstances. This ability can be shown in this program, which will calculate the amount of commission to pay a salesperson. As you know, a commission is calculated by multiplying the total amount of sales by a rate (expressed as a decimal number). For example, if a salesperson sells less than $5,000 worth of merchandise for the week, the commission will be calculated at a rate of 7 percent (.07 in decimal). If the sales for the week are $5,000 or greater, the commission will be calculated at a rate of 8 percent (.08 in decimal). The steps to the solution of this problem are:

1. Input the sales amount for the week for one salesperson and store the amount in a variable.
2. If the sales are less than $5000, then calculate the commission at 7 percent.
3. If the sales are equal to or greater than $5000, then calculate the commission at 8 percent.
4. Print the amount of commission.

The program, written from the above steps, is shown in Figure C-2. Refer to it as you study the comments in the following paragraphs about how it works.

Figure C-2

```
NEW

10 REM CALC1
20 REM THIS PROGRAM CALCULATES COMMISSIONS
30 REM WRITTEN BY JERRY HICKS, 10/15/--
40 REM <--- Replace with HOME for Apple or CLS if IBM or
         Tandy 1000 user.
50 INPUT "ENTER THE SALES AMOUNT: ";S
60 IF S < 5000 THEN LET C = S * .07
70 IF S => 5000 THEN LET C = S * .08
80 PRINT "THE COMMISSION IS $";C
90 END
```

As in Figure C-1, the first three statements are remarks used for documentation purposes. Also, as in Figure C-1, the computer's screen is cleared in line 40 before starting. Recall that if an IBM or similar version of BASIC is being used, change the keyword in statement 40 to CLS. If Applesoft BASIC is being used, change the keyword in statement 40 to HOME.

Line 50 causes the computer to print the prompt "ENTER THE SALES AMOUNT" on the display screen and then wait for user input. Whatever value the user enters will be stored in the numeric variable S. The computation in line 60 is computed only if the statement is true. The keyword pair IF ... THEN makes the decision. If the sales are less than 5000, the amount stored in S is multiplied by .07 (the asterisk indicates multiplication), and the result is stored in the variable C. Conversely, if the result of the IF ... THEN comparison is not true, the computation in line 60 will *not* be performed, and the computer will continue on to execute statement 70. In statement 70, if the sales are equal to or greater than 5000, the amount stored in S will be multiplied by .08, and this result will be stored in the variable C.

In either case (via statement 60 or 70), the result of the computation is stored in the variable C. The keyword **LET** is used in these two statements to assign the result to the variable on the left side of the equal sign. (In most versions of BASIC, the LET keyword may be omitted; the statement still works properly.) In other words, the commission computed via the formula on the right side of the equal sign is stored in the variable immediately to the left of the equal sign. Line 80 then prints the literal and computed value stored in variable C.

In this program, you have seen the use of relational operators. **Relational operators** are the symbols used for determining the relationship of one value to another. Figure C-3 illustrates the relational operators used in BASIC.

Figure C-3

SYMBOL	MEANING
=	equal to
<	less than
<=	less than or equal to
>	greater than
>=	greater than or equal to
<>	less than or greater than (not equal to)

It is unlikely that only one salesperson's commission must be calculated. Therefore, it would be beneficial if the commission program would continue operating to allow the commissions for several different salespersons to be calculated. For this to happen, two changes in the program plan must be made. These changes are shown in bold print below:

1. Input the sales amount for the week for one salesperson and store the amount in a variable.
2. **If the sales are less than 0, then end program execution.**
3. If the sales are less than $5000, then calculate commission at 7 percent.
4. If the sales are equal to or greater than $5000, then calculate commission at 8 percent.
5. Print the amount of commission.
6. **Go back to Step 1 for the next salesperson.**

Modifying the program as indicated gives the results shown in Figure C-4. Note that line 10 has been changed, and lines 55 and 85 have been added to the program. These changes were made by rekeying line 10 and entering lines 55 and 85. The BASIC interpreter automatically replaced the old line 10 with the new one and inserted lines 55 and 85 in their proper line number order. To delete a line, enter that line number (with nothing following it), and the BASIC interpreter will remove it. The same procedure should be followed to add, delete, and modify program statements that have been detected by BASIC to be in error. Errors detected by BASIC are called syntax errors and must be corrected before a program will execute.

Figure C-4

```
10 REM CALC2
20 REM THIS PROGRAM CALCULATES COMMISSIONS
30 REM WRITTEN BY JERRY HICKS, 10/15/--
40 REM <--- Replace with HOME for Apple or CLS if IBM or
            Tandy 1000 user.
50 INPUT "ENTER THE AMOUNT OF THE SALES ";S
55 IF S < 0 THEN END
60 IF S < 5000 THEN LET C = S * .07
70 IF S => 5000 THEN LET C = S * .08
80 PRINT "COMMISSION IS $";C
85 GOTO 50
90 END
```

In the program in Figure C-4, NEW *is not* entered because the program in the computer's memory should not be erased. Line 85 introduces the **GOTO** statement, which transfers control to a specified line number (program statement), in this case, line 50. Once all the data has been input and the program's processing has repeated for each salesperson, the user enters a value less than 0 (i.e. -1) to terminate the program.

Programming Exercise

1. Enter and run the program illustrated in Figure C-4. When entering the program, use your name and the current date in statement 30. Change the commission percentages and sales amount to: 8 percent if less than $6,000.00 and 10 percent if equal to or greater than $6,000.00. Enter sales of $5,000.00, $6,000.00, and $8,000.00 to test your program. Save your program as CALC2.
2. Write a BASIC program that will calculate the sales commissions for any number of salespersons based on the following amounts and percentages: A 5 percent commission is to be paid on sales less than $10,000.00; 7 percent commission for sales of $10,000.00 to $50,000.00; and 10 percent commission for sales equal to and greater than $50,000.00. Enter sales of $9,000.00, $20,000.00, $50,000.00, and $60,000.00 to test your program. Save your program as CALC3.

Part 3 - Reading Data

Just as BASIC can get input from the keyboard, it can also get it from within the program itself. An example of this would be a computerized telephone directory. The names and numbers in the program can be put on lines such as those shown in Figure C-5.

Figure C-5

```
500 DATA SUSAN,783-9873,HENRY,313-9871,RALPH,129-9873,HUBERT,987-3748
510 DATA AARON,348-3382,MARION,338-9938,HELEN,333-3312,IRIS,339-5554
520 DATA EOD,EOD
```

Each of these lines begins with the keyword **DATA,** which is BASIC's way of identifying input data. Data lines do not contain instructions. They hold data so that other lines of the program can read it. Data lines may be placed anywhere within the program; however, it is best to place them at the end to keep them all together and provide additional line numbers for additional data.

In Figure C-5, each of the data lines consists of a name followed by a phone number, then another name and phone number, and so on. Commas are used to separate the items. On the last data line, EOD has been entered twice where the name and phone number should be placed. EOD is an abbreviation for "End Of Data." The programmer can use either EOD or other fictitious data that can be checked by the program to tell it when it has finished reading all the needed data. The fictitious data items are known as **terminators** since they are located at the end of the data and serve to terminate the program.

To use the computerized phone directory, the user enters the name of the person whose phone number needs to be found. The computer will then look up the name in the data and print the person's telephone number. The plan for this program is as follows:

1. From the keyboard, input the name to be found in the directory.
2. Read the next name and phone number from the data lines.
3. If the name just read is equal to the name entered from the keyboard, print the phone number and end the program.
4. If the name just read is the data terminator, print "not found" and end the program. (This will occur if the name entered does not match any names in the data statements.)
5. If neither Step 3 nor 4 is true, return to Step 2 to continue checking for a name match.

By coding the above plan in BASIC and including the DATA lines from Figure C-5, a new program is developed as listed in Figure C-6. Refer to the program as you study the description of how it works.

Figure C-6

```
NEW

10 REM PHONEDIR
20 REM WRITTEN BY T. BROOKS, 11/10/--
30 REM THIS PROGRAM LOOKS UP PHONE NUMBERS
40 REM <--- Replace with HOME for Apple or CLS if IBM or
         Tandy 1000 user.
50 INPUT "ENTER THE NAME TO LOOK UP (IN CAPS): ";PR$
60 READ NM$,NO$
70 IF NM$ = PR$ THEN PRINT NO$:END
80 IF NM$ = "EOD" THEN PRINT "NOT FOUND":END
90 GOTO 60
500 DATA SUSAN,783-9873,HENRY,313-9871,RALPH,129-9873,HUBERT,987-3748
510 DATA AARON,348-3382,MARION,338-9938,HELEN,333-3312,IRIS,339-5554
520 DATA EOD,EOD
530 END
```

Line 50 uses the keyword INPUT to get a person's name from the keyboard and store it in the variable called PR$. Line 60 uses the keyword **READ** to read two items from the data statements (the presence of two variables following READ means to read two items). The first item read is placed in variable NM$, and the second item is placed in variable NO$. Note that because the phone number contains a hyphen, it must be placed in a character string variable; the hyphen is a non-numeric character.

Line 70 uses a relational operator to check if the name that was read (variable NM$) is equal to the name entered from the keyboard (variable PR$). If this relationship is true, the phone number (variable NO$) which accompanies the matched name in the directory will be printed, and the program will end. Notice the END statement is preceded by a colon. A colon indicates to BASIC that another BASIC keyword follows. In this case, the program will end if statement 70 is true and after the phone number is printed.

Line 80 is executed by the program if statement 70 is not true. This statement also uses a relational operator to check if the name that was read is equal to the literal "EOD." If this condition is true, the entire directory has been read without a match, and a "NOT FOUND" message will be printed to end the program.

If lines 70 and 80 did not end program execution, then neither a match has been found nor the "EOD" terminator has been reached; therefore, the search must continue. Execution should be directed back to the READ statement to check the next name.

Programming Exercise

1. Enter and run the program illustrated in Figure C-6. When entering the program, use your name and the current date in statement 20. Change the names and phone numbers in the data statements to include at least eight additional names and phone numbers of your classmates and friends, or use fictitious names and numbers. *Hint:* Add the additional data statement(s) before line number 500 or between line numbers 510 and 520. Save your program as PHONEDIR.

2. Write a BASIC program that will input a number from 1 through 10 from the keyboard, then multiply that number by each number in the data statement(s) within your program and print the product. Enter the number 2 and use 5, 10, 8, 1, 15, 4, 2, 7, 3, 9, 6, 12, and 11 in your data statement(s) to test your program. Save your program as NUMBER.

Part 4 - Program Looping

You have already seen how a BASIC program can alter its sequential execution of a program via relational operators and the GOTO instruction. Next, you will learn how the BASIC language takes advantage of a computer's ability to do repetitive tasks quickly and efficiently. The controlled repetition of program instructions is called **program looping.** In the BASIC language, the **FOR...NEXT** keywords (also referred to as a statement pair) are often used to control program looping. Take a look at a program which uses the FOR...NEXT statement pair in a program loop. This program will count from one number (entered via the keyboard) to another number (entered via the keyboard) by 1's. The program plan for this program is as follows:

1. Input the beginning number from the keyboard.
2. Input the ending number from the keyboard.
3. Check for valid numbers (check that the ending number is not equal to or less than the beginning number).
4. Print the loop counter variable (a variable which keeps a count) each time through the established loop.
5. Repeat program execution if the user wishes. If not, end the program.

The result of coding and executing (running) the program developed is shown in Figure C-7.

Figure C-7

```
NEW

10 REM COUNT
20 REM THIS PROGRAM COUNTS FROM N1...Nn
30 REM WRITTEN BY JOYCE SIMS, 10/15/--
40 REM <--- Replace with HOME for Apple or CLS if IBM or
            Tandy 1000 user.
50 INPUT "ENTER THE BEGINNING NUMBER: ";BN
60 INPUT "ENTER THE ENDING NUMBER: ";EN
70 IF EN =< BN THEN PRINT "ENDING NUMBER TOO SMALL":GOTO 50
80 FOR LP = BN TO EN
90 PRINT LP
100 NEXT LP
110 INPUT "DO YOU WANT ANOTHER COUNT (Y=YES, N=NO): ";YN$
120 IF YN$ = "Y" THEN GOTO 40
130 IF YN$ <> "N" THEN PRINT "INVALID RESPONSE - REENTER":GOTO 110
140 END

RUN

ENTER THE BEGINNING NUMBER: 1
ENTER THE ENDING NUMBER: 10
1
2
3
4
5
6
7
8
9
10
DO YOU WANT ANOTHER COUNT (Y=YES, N=NO):
```

Statements 50 and 60 ask the user to enter a beginning (BN) and ending (EN) number from the keyboard. These numbers will be used to control the range of the program loop. Statement 70 checks to see if the ending number entered from the keyboard is equal to or less than the beginning number. If it is equal to or less than the beginning number, an error message is printed, and execution is directed back to statement 50, where the user must input new beginning and ending numbers. It is always a good idea to check the accuracy of the input data whenever possible. (Remember, garbage in - garbage out.) If an error is detected, an error message should briefly describe the error, and the program should allow corrective action. If the ending number is greater than the beginning number, processing proceeds to statement 80.

Statements 80 through 100 contain the program loop controlled by the FOR...NEXT statement pair. In statement 80, the FOR keyword tells the computer a FOR...NEXT loop follows and that all statements between these two keywords are to be executed each time the loop is repeated. Immediately following the FOR keyword is a counter variable. In this example, the counter variable is named LP (for LooP). When the FOR instruction is executed the first time, the value of the variable containing the beginning of the loop (BN) is placed in the variable LP (each time the loop is repeated, the value in LP is increased). The TO tells the computer to repeat the program loop the number of times specified by the value stored in EN (in this example, 10 was entered and stored in EN). In statement 90, the value stored in LP is printed. Statement 100 contains the NEXT keyword. It is followed by the same counter variable (LP) as used in the matching FOR statement. The NEXT statement tells the computer to increment the counter variable, then check to see if the counter variable is equal to or greater than the value provided in the FOR statement. If the counter variable is less than the ending number (EN), the loop is repeated. If it is equal to, or greater than the TO value (stored in EN), execution continues with the statement immediately following the NEXT statement.

Statement 110 contains a prompt which enables the user to run the program again or discontinue program execution. Two key points should be made here: (1) the prompt should contain a descriptive message which clearly defines the valid input permissible, and (2) the user's response should be checked for accuracy. In statement 120, if the response stored in YN$ is "Y," then the program execution is repeated by returning control to statement 40. In statement 130, if the response is less than or greater (anything other) than "N," an invalid response message is printed, and the program returns execution to statement 110 to obtain valid input. Finally, statement 140 ends program execution with an "N" response.

Programming Exercise

1. Enter and run the program illustrated in Figure C-7. When entering the program, use your name and the current date in statement 30. Insert an additional check (with appropriate error message) in the program to make sure the beginning and ending numbers entered are no more than 100 apart before entering the FOR...NEXT program loop.

This check will prevent long program loops. Enter a 10 to 25 range to check for proper execution of your program and a 1 to 200 range to check for an invalid range. Save your program as COUNT.

2. Write a BASIC program that will input a number between 1 and 100 from the keyboard. In a FOR...NEXT loop, multiply that number by 1 through 10 and print the products on one line. For example, if 5 were entered from the keyboard, the products of 5 from 1 through 10 would appear as: 5 10 15 20 25 30 35 40 45 50. Verify all input for accuracy and permit the user to repeat execution as many times as desired. *Hint:* Use a semicolon, a blank literal, and another semicolon after the calculated product variable in the print statement to force printing on one line (i.e. PRINT P;" ";). Save your program as NUMBER2.

Part 5 - Tables and Structured Programming

To date, when storing data in variables, a separate variable has been used for each item of data. This meant that if hundreds of student names and grades had to be entered into the computer for processing, coding and keeping track of each variable would be very cumbersome. BASIC, however, provides a means by which related data may be stored in tables. A **table** is a variable that can store more than one data item at a time. (A table is also commonly referred to as an **array**.) Tables are used in programs in which large volumes of related data must be stored. Tables are simple lists of data items as shown in the two examples in Figure C-8.

Figure C-8

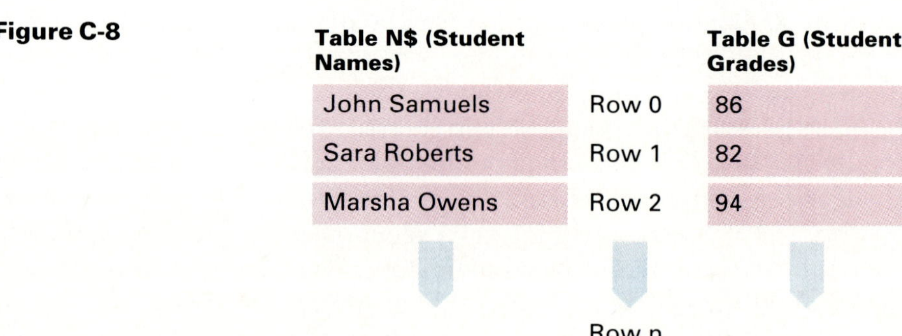

Note that each data item is stored in one row of each of the tables. For example, JOHN SAMUELS is stored in table N$ in row 0; MARSHA OWENS is also stored in table N$, but in row 2. Table G has a student grade of 86 stored in row 0, a grade of 82 in row 1, and a grade of 94 in row 2. Each individual data item stored in a table is referred to as an **element.** Therefore, the data stored in row 1 of table N$ is referred to as element 1. The row number which references each element in a table is called a **subscript.** Subscripts are written in parentheses. For example, a reference to element 1 in table N$ (containing the name SARA ROBERTS) is written as N$(1).

In the example in Figure C-8, hundreds of student names could be stored in table N$. Similarly, hundreds of student grades could be stored in table G, thus greatly reducing the number of separate variable names required to store all this data in a program.

When referencing elements within a table, the BASIC keywords such as LET, INPUT, READ, and PRINT may be used. The only difference is that the variable name (table name in this case) must also include a subscript in parentheses. This tells the computer which element in the table to READ, PRINT, etc.

A method of planning and coding a program so that logically organized modules of code can be easily written and maintained is called **structured programming.** A **module** is simply a part of something else. Therefore, a structured program is made up of small parts or sections known as modules, each performing a particular task. Structured programs consist of two types of modules: a main module and one or more submodules. The main module controls the sequence of the execution of each of the submodules. The submodules perform specific, logically related tasks such as inputting the data, performing calculations, and outputting the results. An example of a structured program illustrating how the main module and submodules are coded is shown in Figure C-9.

Figure C-9

```
NEW

10 REM SALES
20 REM THIS PROGRAM PRODUCES A SALES COMMISSION REPORT
30 REM WRITTEN BY DAVID JARARD, 11/01/--
40 DIM S(5)
50 REM <--- Replace with HOME for Apple or CLS if
          IBM or Tandy 1000 user.
60 REM ****** MAIN MODULE ******
70 GOSUB 1000
80 GOSUB 2000
90 GOSUB 3000
100 END
1000 REM ****** INPUT SUBMODULE ******
1005 REM <--- Replace with HOME for Apple or CLS if IBM
              or Tandy 1000 user.
1010 INPUT "ENTER THE SALESPERSON'S NAME: ";SP$
1020 FOR LP = 1 TO 5
1030 PRINT "ENTER SALES FOR DAY ";LP;
1040 INPUT S(LP)
1050 NEXT LP
1060 RETURN
2000 REM ****** OUTPUT SUBMODULE ******
2010 REM <--- Replace with HOME for Apple or CLS if IBM
              or Tandy 1000 user.
2020 PRINT "SALESPERSON: ";SP$
2030 PRINT
2040 PRINT "DAY","SALES"
2050 FOR LP = 1 TO 5
2060 PRINT LP,S(LP)
2070 TS = TS + S(LP)
2080 NEXT LP
2090 PRINT
2100 PRINT "TOTAL SALES = ";TS
2110 IF TS < 2000.00 THEN C = TS * .05
2120 IF TS => 2000.00 THEN C = TS * .07
2130 IF TS > 3999.99 THEN C = TS * .10
2140 PRINT "COMMISSION = ";C
2150 RETURN
3000 REM ****** REPEAT DECISION SUBMODULE ******
3010 INPUT "ANOTHER SALESPERSON (Y=YES, N=NO): ";YN$
3020 IF YN$ = "Y" THEN TS = 0:GOTO 60
3030 IF YN$ <> "N" THEN PRINT "INVALID RESPONSE - REENTER"
     :GOTO 3010
3040 RETURN
```


continued

```
RUN

(screen is cleared)

ENTER THE SALESPERSON'S NAME: LINDA TROXELL
ENTER SALES FOR DAY 1
?500
ENTER SALES FOR DAY 2
?200
ENTER SALES FOR DAY 3
?300
ENTER SALES FOR DAY 4
?400
ENTER SALES FOR DAY 5
?600

(screen is cleared)

SALESPERSON: LINDA TROXELL

DAY          SALES
1            500
2            200
3            300
4            400
5            600

TOTAL SALES = 2000
COMMISSION = 140
ANOTHER SALESPERSON (Y=YES, N=NO)? N
```

The keyword **GOSUB** is used by the main module to send control of the computer to the first program statement in a submodule. GOSUB is an abbreviation of GO to SUBroutine. The keyword **RETURN** is used at the end of each submodule to return to the main module. Each GOSUB must have a corresponding RETURN statement.

The sample program shown in Figure C-9 illustrates how a program is coded to utilize tables in the structured programming method. The salesperson's name is entered and the amount of his/her sales during each day of a five-day work week are entered into a table. After all sales information for the week has been keyed into a table, a sales report is produced which shows the salesperson's name, sales, and commission for the week. The commission is calculated as 5 percent of sales less than $2,000.00; 7 percent of sales $2,000.00 - $3,999.99; and 10 percent of sales equal to or greater than $4,000.00. The structured program plan for this program is as follows:

1. Set up a sales table containing room to store five elements and clear the display screen.
2. Main Module:
   a. Input Submodule - Input the salesperson's name and the program loop to store the amount of the salesperson's sales for each day of a five-day work week in a table.
   b. Output Submodule - Program loop to print a report from data stored in the table showing salesperson's name and sales for each work day. Accumulate total sales as the report is printed, print total sales, then calculate and print the commission amount earned.

c. Repeat Decision Submodule - Provide the user the option to repeat processing for another salesperson or end the program.

3. End Program.

The result of coding and executing the structured program from the given plan is shown in Figure C-9. Note that the steps from the program plan identify the BASIC code which accomplishes each of the tasks identified in the plan.

Statement 40 defines a numeric table containing 5 elements. It is a numeric table because the table name, S, is a numeric variable (character tables are defined with a dollar sign at the end of the table name). Defining a table is also known as **dimensioning** a table. The keyword **DIM** (short for dimension) is used by BASIC to establish a table. The number in parentheses tells the computer the largest number of elements that may be stored in the table. In this example, the table contains 6 elements (0 through 5); however, only elements 1 through 5 will be used—one for each day of the five-day work week.

Statement 60 is a remark statement that identifies program statements 70, 80, 90, and 100 as those of the main module. First, the submodule beginning at line number 1000 is executed, next the submodule beginning at line number 2000 is executed, then the submodule beginning at line number 3000 is executed. Finally, depending upon whether another salesperson's sales are to entered or not, the program ends.

When the GOSUB in statement 70 is executed, control transfers to the input subroutine beginning on line number 1000. An input statement in line 1010 prompts the user to enter the salesperson's name. Statements 1020 through 1050 comprise the program loop which inputs and stores the sales figures into the table. In statement 1020, a FOR keyword specifies that the variable LP will be initialized by 1 (the beginning value) and will execute the loop 5 times (TO the ending value). Statement 1030 prints a prompt message telling the user to enter the sales for a specific day of the week. This day of the week is printed as part of the prompt message from the value stored in the variable counter LP. The variable LP corresponds to the number of times through the loop as well as the day of the week for which the data is to be entered. Statement 1040 accepts the sales data from the keyboard and stores the value in the element in Table S specified by the value in LP. For example, the first time through the FOR...NEXT loop, the value entered from the keyboard will be stored in S(1). The second time through the program loop the value entered will be stored in S(2), and so on until all five work day sales are entered and stored. After all sales are entered, the RETURN statement in Statement 1060 returns control to line number 80 in the main module.

When the GOSUB statement in line 80 is executed, control transfers to the output submodule beginning with line number 2000. Statement 2010 clears the display screen. Statement 2020 prints the literal "SALESPERSON:" followed by the name entered at the beginning of the run.

The next statement, 2030, prints a blank line (nothing following the keyword PRINT) to separate the salesperson's name from the body of the report. Statement 2040 prints the DAY and SALES report column headings.

Once the report heading information has been printed, the FOR... NEXT loop in statements 2050 through 2080 is executed. As specified in statement 2050 the statements which follow are to be executed five times (once for each day of the work week). Statement 2060 prints the value in LP, which corresponds to the day of the week, and the sales stored in table S for that day of the week. Statement 2070 accumulates the sales in a variable named TS. The variable TS has not been used previously in the program; therefore, the first time through the loop it contains zero. The sales value stored in S(1) is added to TS, and the result is stored back in TS. The second time through the loop the value stored in S(2) is added to TS, and the sum is again placed back in TS. Each time through the loop the next day's sales are added to TS.

After the program loop which prints the body of the report is completed, a blank line (statement 2090) and the total sales, TS (statement 2100), are printed. Statements 2110 through 2130 use relational operators to compare and calculate the amount of commission based upon the total sales for the week. The result is stored in variable C, and statement 2140 prints the calculated commission amount. Finally, statement 2150 returns control back to line number 90 of the main module.

When the GOSUB statement in line 90 is executed, control transfers to the repeat decision submodule beginning with line number 3000. Line numbers 3010 through 3030 contain the coding to repeat processing for another salesperson or end the program. Note that statement 3020 resets the sales accumulator TS back to zero if processing is to be repeated. This is done to prevent the next salesperson's sales from being added to the previous salesperson's. Also note that if an "N" (for No) response is entered from the keyboard, the RETURN statement (3040) is executed, and control returns to line number 100 of the main module where program execution ends. Examine the output of the program and the appearance of the generated report.

Programming Exercise

1. Enter and run the program illustrated in Figure C-9. When entering the program, use your name and the current date in statement 30. Change the program to process sales over a seven-day work week. Also, change the sales and commission rate as follows: 6 percent on sales less than $4,000.00; 8 percent on sales from $4,000.00 through $9,999.99; and 12 percent on sales equal to and greater than $10,000.00. Enter sales for Donald Grimms of $1,000.00, $1,150.00, $1,050.00, $1,200.00, $1,300.00, $900.00, and $950.00 to test your program. Save your program as SALES.

2. Write a structured BASIC program that will input and store the name of a store's department and the sales for each day of a six-day work week into a table. Produce a report showing the department name, sales by day, and total sales for the week. Also calculate the sales tax by multiplying the total sales for the week by 6 percent. Permit the user of this program to repeat processing in order to produce a similar report for each department within the store. Check all input to verify its accuracy. Enter the following weekly sales for the Automotive Department to test your program: $2,450.00, $1,800.00, $1,790.00, $2,100.00, $2,040.00, and $2,825.00. Save your program as AUTO.

APPENDIX SUMMARY

- BASIC is an acronym for Beginner's All-purpose Symbolic Instruction Code.
- The advantages of the BASIC language far outweigh the disadvantages.
- Interactive programming refers to the process of keying a program into the computer and immediately executing the program.
- A compiled program is one that has been converted into machine-readable code that the computer can execute directly.
- BASIC is considered a high-level language because it is written in English-like instructions.
- BASIC operates in two modes: immediate and deferred execution modes. Immediate execution mode is in effect when an instruction is entered and immediately executed by the computer. Deferred execution mode is in effect when the instruction is part of a program and is carried out when the entire program is run.
- Keywords are words that BASIC understands. For example, INPUT and PRINT are keywords that enable BASIC to input and output data.
- The NEW keyword causes the previously entered instructions and data to be erased from the memory of the computer.
- The RUN keyword tells BASIC to execute the instructions that have been entered in the form of a program.
- A print zone is an area into which each print line is divided.
- There are two kinds of variables: numeric and character (string) variables. A numeric variable is a storage place for a numeric value that is not known in advance; that is, a value that will be created or changed while the program is carrying out instructions. A character (or string) variable is used to store alphanumeric characters. Character variables are distinguished from numeric values by a dollar sign ($) following the variable name.
- A constant is a number that does not change as the program is executed.

- ♦ A literal is any combination of alphanumeric characters which is entered between quotation marks.
- ♦ The REM keyword is an abbreviation for remark. Remark statements contain information which help document what the program does, who wrote it, and the date it was written.
- ♦ The HOME (CLS for the IBM and compatibles) statement is the keyword which causes BASIC to clear the display screen.
- ♦ The INPUT keyword causes the computer to stop execution and wait for the user to enter data from the keyboard. The INPUT keyword may also cause a prompt message to be displayed which tells the user what kind of input is required.
- ♦ The END statement causes the program to stop execution.
- ♦ The LIST command will display the entire program in the computer's memory on the display screen.
- ♦ The LET keyword is used to assign the result into the variable on the left side of the equal sign. (In most versions of BASIC, the LET keyword can be omitted.)
- ♦ Relational operators are the symbols used for determining the relationship of one value to another.
- ♦ The GOTO keyword causes BASIC to transfer control to a specified statement.
- ♦ DATA statements are used to hold data so that a corresponding READ statement may read the data into variables for processing.
- ♦ A terminator is any entered character which can be checked (with a relational operator) to indicate that all data has been input or read.
- ♦ The controlled repetition of program instructions is called program looping.
- ♦ The FOR...NEXT statement pair controls program looping. All statements between these two keywords are executed each time the loop is repeated.
- ♦ A table (also commonly referred to as an array) is a variable that can store more than one data item at a time.
- ♦ Each individual data item stored in a table is referred to as an element.
- ♦ The row number which contains the element being referenced is called a subscript. Subscripts are written in parentheses.
- ♦ A method of planning and coding a program so that logically organized modules of code can be easily written and maintained is called structured programming.
- ♦ A module, which is simply a part of something else, performs a particular task.
- ♦ The keyword GOSUB is used by the main module to send control of the computer to the first program statement in a submodule.
- ♦ The keyword RETURN is used at the end of each submodule to return to the main module.
- ♦ The keyword DIM (short for dimension) is used by BASIC to establish a table. The number in parentheses tells the computer the largest number of elements that may be stored in the table.

KEY TERMS

The following key terms and BASIC keywords were introduced or redefined in this appendix:

BASIC
bugs
character (string) variable
compiled program
constant
DATA
debug
deferred execution mode
DIM
dimensioning
element
END
FOR...NEXT
GOSUB
GOTO
HOME (CLS)
immediate execution mode
INPUT
integers
interactive programming
keywords
LET
LIST
literal
LOAD
module
NEW
numeric variable
PRINT
print zone
program looping
prompt
READ
real (floating point) numbers
relational operators
REM
RETURN
RUN
SAVE
structured programming
subscript
table (array)
terminators
variable

REVIEW QUESTIONS

1. Identify five advantages of the BASIC language. (Obj. 1)
2. Identify three disadvantages of the BASIC language. (Obj.1)
3. Explain the difference between immediate and deferred execution mode. (Obj. 2)
4. What is a variable? (Obj. 3)
5. Explain the difference between a numeric and a character (string) variable. How does BASIC distinguish between the two? (Obj. 3)
6. Describe the rules for naming variables. (Obj. 3)
7. What is a constant? (Obj. 3)
8. What is a literal? (Obj. 3)
9. What keyword is used to document a BASIC program? (Obj. 4)
10. What keyword is used by the computer you are using to clear the display screen? (Obj. 4)
11. Explain the purpose of the INPUT keyword. (Obj. 4)
12. What is a prompt message? (Obj.4)
13. What happens when the END keyword is executed? (Obj. 4)

14. What command is used to display an entire program on the display screen? (Obj. 4)
15. Explain the purpose of the GOTO keyword. (Obj. 4)
16. Describe how the READ...DATA keywords are used in a BASIC program. (Obj. 4)
17. What is a data terminator? (Obj. 4)
18. Define program looping. (Obj. 4)
19. Describe how the FOR...NEXT keywords are used to control program looping. (Obj. 4)
20. Explain what a table is in the BASIC language. (Obj. 4)
21. What is an element in a table? How are elements referenced? (Obj. 4)
22. What is structured programming? What is a module? (Obj. 4)
23. Describe how the GOSUB and RETURN keywords are used by the main module to control program execution. (Obj. 4)
24. What is meant by dimensioning a table? (Obj. 4)
25. What does it mean if your "program has a bug"? What does it mean to "debug a program"? (Obj. 4)

CHALLENGE ACTIVITIES

1. Write a BASIC program that will (1) input a student name and four test scores; (2) calculate the average test score; (3) clear the screen and print the student name, the four test scores, and the average; and (4) repeat the processing (if desired) for another student. Enter the following test scores for Karen Bradley to test your program: 90, 88, 92, 78. The computer-generated output should be in the following format: (Obj. 5)

   STUDENT NAME: KAREN BRADLEY

   TEST SCORE 1 = 90
   TEST SCORE 2 = 88
   TEST SCORE 3 = 92
   TEST SCORE 4 = 78

   AVERAGE TEST SCORE = 87

   DO YOU WANT TO CONTINUE (Y=YES, N=NO)?

2. Modify the program above to input five students with their corresponding grades using READ...DATA statements within the program. Instead of giving the user the chance to enter scores for another student, display a prompt that asks if the next student should be displayed. Use the following data to test your program: (Obj. 5)

   KAREN BRADLEY,90,88,92,78
   RICHARD HOMES,85,80,90,75
   JANICE HANSEN,88,70,83,72
   TODD LAMB,84,68,78,84
   TI NUYGEN,98,86,80,80

3. Write a BASIC program to calculate compound interest on any amount for 1 to n years (where n is any number from 2 through 20) with an interest rate of x percent (where x is a rate from 5 through 12 percent). Calculate and print the interest earned and the new principal that will be used in next year's calculation for each of the n years. The formula for compound interest is P = P + (P * R) for each of the n years. Use a beginning principal of $2,000.00, an interest rate of 10 percent, and a 10-year period to test your program. The computer-generated report should be in the following format: (Obj. 5)

```
BEGINNING PRINCIPAL: $ 2000.00
INTEREST RATE: .10
 YEAR      PRINCIPAL
   1         2200.00
   2         2420.00
   |            |
   |            |
   |            |
```

4. Write a BASIC program that will check a given license plate number entered via the keyboard against license plates of stolen vehicles stored in a table. If a match is found, the program is to notify the user that the vehicle has been reported stolen. If no match is found, a message should be displayed informing the user that the vehicle in question has not been reported stolen. The program should be written so that additional inquiries can be made without the program ending. Store the following list of stolen vehicle license plate numbers into a table using READ...DATA statements. (Obj 5.)

   FRH-211, CHC-411, JHN-788, JNH-901, HM-473, 951-CE, 2V-568, ULL-7D4, 540-HPC, IPV-661, 77K-DHK, WAA-117

   To test your program enter the following license plate numbers: ABC-123, 77K-DHK, RTR-879, JWQ-887, ULL-7D4, and YYL-443

GLOSSARY

abacus: an ancient calculating device consisting of a frame in which rods strung with beads are set; by sliding the beads, computations can be performed

absolute reference: a cell reference which does not change even after changes are made to the spreadsheet

access time: the time it takes the computer to load a desired record from an auxiliary storage device into memory

accounting system: software used to maintain the financial records of a business

accounts payable: amounts owed by a business

accounts receivable: amounts owed to a business by its customers

acoustic coupler: a modem that connects to the computer or terminal by a cable which contains two rubber cups that permit a telephone headset to be inserted

analysis report: a document that states the need for and proposed cost of a new computer system

analytical engine: a machine that was designed, but never built, by Charles Babbage; had the machine been built, it would have been the first true computer

appending: the process of entering (adding) data into a database (also referred to as loading)

application generator: a program included with database software that generates menus and underlying commands simply by having the operator answer a series of questions

application program: a program that instructs the computer to perform a specific, user-defined task

application software: software designed to meet a particular computing need of the user

area chart: a chart which shows a total as well as the size of individual components

array: a variable that can store more than one data item at a time (also referred to as a table)

artificial intelligence: the concept that computers have the ability to think (sometimes used interchangeably with expert system)

ASCII: American Standard Code for Information Interchange; a code used to represent data in a computer

assembler: a program that converts assembly language programs into machine code

assembly language: a language a step above machine language in which the instructions to the processor may be represented in alphabetic terms.

auxiliary storage: storage that is not part of memory but is available to and under control of the processor

background task: in a time slicing environment, the task to which the processor devotes time only during pauses in the foreground activity

backing up: the process of copying data to another medium so that a duplicate is available for use should the original copy be destroyed or become unusable

balance sheet: a financial statement on which the assets, liabilities, and owner's equity in a business are recorded

band printer: an impact printer that contains characters on a rotating band or belt

bandwidth: a method of determining the speed by which data can be transmitted over a given communication channel (also referred to as grade)

bar-code scanner: an input device that can read bars (lines) printed on a product

bar graph: a type of graph in which data quantities are represented by the lengths of the bars that are drawn

base: the number by which a digit is multiplied when it is moved a column to the left

baseband channel: a communication channel that transmits data one signal at a time

BASIC: Beginner's All-Purpose Symbolic Instruction Code; an easy-to-learn, general-purpose, high-level language

BASIC statement: each numbered line of a BASIC program

baud rate: the rate of transmission at which the binary digits that make up a character are transmitted over the same conductor (also referred to as bits per second)

Bernoulli disk: a flexible disk drive in which the disk spins at a very high speed and is aerodynamically stabilized so that the head remains a fraction of an inch above the disk surface

binary: a number system having a base of 2 and using the digits 0 and 1

bit: a binary digit (either 1 or 0)

bit-mapped display: a method of moving output from the computer to a monitor in which a group of locations in main memory is dedicated to holding information for the display (also referred to as memory-mapped display)

bits per second (bps): the rate of transmission at which the binary digits that make up a character are transmitted over the same conductor (also referred to as baud rate)

boilerplate text: standard paragraphs used in word processing applications that are pre-stored on an auxiliary storage device

boot record: the first record loaded into the computer that then controls the loading of the remainder of the system

bridge: a microcomputer-based method for connecting similar networks

broadband bandwidth channel: a communication channel that transmits data using the full-duplex mode of transmission

bubble memory: memory that is made up of small magnetic bubbles arranged to represent data on a thin film of semiconductor material

bug: programming error

bus configuration/topology: a computer network in which each computer or terminal is linked into a single communication channel by a "drop" line

business software: software used to facilitate the management or record keeping functions of a business

byte: the amount of space required to store one character or one value in memory; eight bits make up one byte

C: a general-purpose programming language that enables programmers to code their programs using a high-level type symbolic code, yet offers low-level control over the hardware

CAD/CAM: computer-assisted (or aided) drafting (design)/computer-aided manufacturing

caps lock key: the key used to lock the keyboard in either upper- or lowercase

card-punch machine: a machine used to punch holes in a punched card (also referred to as a keypunch machine)

case instruction: an instruction that provides a way for executing one set of instructions out of numerous possibilities included in the program

cathode-ray tube (CRT): a television-like display device used for computer output

CD-I: Compact Disk/Interactive

CD-ROM: Compact Disk/Read Only Medium

cell: a space on a spreadsheet used for any one number, character string label, or formula

cell pointer: another name for the cursor that is used with spreadsheets

central processing unit (CPU): a hardware device that stores data and programs, executes program instructions, and performs arithmetic and logic operations

chain printer: an impact printer that contains characters on a rotating chain

channel: a recording path along magnetic tape

character-oriented display: a method of moving output from the computer to a monitor in which character codes are transmitted one after another from the processor to the display

character variable: a variable that stores alphanumeric data (also referred to as a string variable)

Chief Information Officer (CIO): the top information processing job in a business

CIM: Computer-Integrated Manufacturing

closed architecture: a method of assembling the components of a microcomputer in such a manner that expansion of the system is not easily accomplished

CLS: the BASIC keyword used on the IBM and Tandy 1000 computers to clear the screen

coaxial cable: a high-quality communication channel that serves as the carrier of data transmitted between the host computer and its terminals

COBOL: COmmon Business Oriented Language; a high-level language designed for use in business applications

coding: writing the instructions of a computer program in a computer language

column: a single vertical area running through a spreadsheet

communication: the process of transmitting information from one source (or location) to another

communication adapter: a circuit board which fits inside a small computer and is used to convert parallel transmission into serial transmission and vice versa

communication channel: the passageway by which data can flow to and from the computer

communication controller: the communications hardware which is directly connected to the CPU of the mainframe computer and which is used to convert parallel transmission

communication network: a configuration of local and/or remote computers, and other types of terminals, connected together by means of one or more communication channels

Compact Disk/Interactive (CD-I): a technology that will enable optical disks to be utilized by flexible, general-purpose devices

Compact Disk/Read-Only Medium (CD-ROM): laser disks with large storage capacities

compiled program: one that has been converted into machine-readable code that the computer can execute directly

compiler program: a program that translates an entire high-level language program into machine code at once

component: an object that has been drawn with a CAD program and given a name

composite video monitor: a color monitor that uses a single electronic signal to turn on the phosphorescent material within each pixel
computer: an electronic device that does computations and makes logical comparisons according to instructions that have been given to it
computer-aided design (CAD): the process of using graphic computer programs to assist in the design of the program
computer-aided manufacturing (CAM): the process of using a computer to operate tools used to manufacture a product
computer graphics: any pictorial representation that can be produced by the computer
computer-integrated manufacturing (CIM): the process of using networked computers to control the operations of a manufacturing plant
computer operator: a person who is responsible for sequencing computer jobs and running them in order of priority
computer output microfilm: an output method in which data is placed on microfilm rather than on paper
computer system: a combination of related elements (hardware and software) working together as a whole to achieve a common goal
concentrator: a communication hardware device that permits data from only one terminal at a time to be transmitted over a communication channel
condition: a situation that involves a comparison of two values
configuring: the process of making the desired match between logical and physical computer devices
connect time: the time spent communicating with the host computer over a communication channel
constant: a number that does not change
consultant: an "in-house" or independent person who shares his or her computer expertise for a fee
contention: a method of network protocol in which any node wishing to use the network first "listens" to see if it can hear a signal on the network indicating that another node is using it (also referred to as CSMA/CD)
control break: an indication that a new page or report is to be started when a named data item changes
control character: a nonprinting character designed to control the communication between a computer and another device, such as a terminal or printer
conversion: the process of installing a new system, or replacing an old system with a new one
CPU: central processing unit
CRT: cathode-ray tube
CSMA/CD: carrier-sensing multiple access with collision detection (also referred to as contention)
cursor: a marker on a video display, often depicted as a flashing square

custom application software: software that is written specifically to meet the needs of an organization or individual
cut and paste: the process of marking and moving text to a new location
cylinder: all the tracks of the same number on different disk surfaces

daisy wheel printer: an impact printer that uses a raised-character print wheel that resembles a flower
data: facts in the form of numbers, alphabetic characters, special symbols, or words
DATA: a BASIC keyword used to store data on a program line
database: an organized collection of related data
database administrator: the person responsible for developing and maintaining the integrity of the database used by the business
database management system (DBMS): software that is used to maintain the data of a business or individual
database software: a program which groups related facts into an organized and usable data collection
data bit: each bit of a seven- or eight-bit code
data communication: communication of data from one location to another
data elements: individual items, or pieces of data, stored on auxiliary storage device media (also referred to as data fields)
data entry operator: a person who keys data and programs into a computer
data fields: individual items,or pieces of data, stored on auxiliary storage device media (also referred to as data elements)
data/information center manager: an employee who works with company individuals to select appropriate microcomputer hardware and software and to obtain training in the use of the systems
data processing: the process of manipulating data into a form that humans can use, or learn new knowledge from (also referred to as information processing)
data set: another name for a file
data transfer rate: the time required to transfer the data from the auxiliary storage device into primary memory
debit card: a small plastic card that enables the amounts of purchases to be immediately deducted from the user's checking account
debug: to find and correct errors in a program
decryption: the decoding of data
deferred execution mode: a method of running a program whereby an instruction is executed when the entire program is run
demodulation: the process of converting an analog signal back into digital data
desktop publishing: the use of the computer to produce an original layout for newsletters, catalogs, brochures, books, and other materials that contain different types of print

desktop tools (accessories): a classification of software designed to make day-to-day work and personal activities a little easier
device driver: a piece of software that makes the connection between a logical device and a physical device
digital audio tape: cassette tape used in the home or automobile
digitizer: an input device that converts shapes into numbers for storage by computers
DIM: the BASIC keyword used to establish (dimension) a table
dimensioning: the process of defining a table
direct access: another name for random access
direct connection: a local host computer and one or more local terminals under the control of a communications software
directional keys: those keys on the keyboard that enable the user to work with various areas on the display screen
disk pack: a group of disks on a spindle in a hard disk drive
diskette: a small, pliable magnetic disk (also referred to as a flexible disk or floppy disk)
distributed configuration: a computer network in which each node can communicate with every other node through a single link and in which each node has its own processing capabilities
distributed relational database: a database with data stored in different locations and visible to all users
division: one of four parts of a COBOL program
document construction: the act of combining various pre-saved paragraphs or sentences to produce a finished document
dot matrix: a row and column arrangement of dots
dot-matrix printer: an impact printer that produces a character by forming it from rows and columns of dots
download: the transfer of data from a file stored on the host computer's disk to the other computer's disk
dumb terminal: a terminal that does not have memory and which is totally dependent upon the stored program in the CPU to which it is connected

EBCDIC: Extended Binary Coded Decimal Interchange Code; a code used to represent data in many large computers
EDSAC: Electronic Delay Storage Automatic Calculator; the first stored-program computer to be completed
EDVAC: Electronic Discrete Variable Automatic Computer; the first stored-program computer to be designed
electronic mail: software that enables users to electronically send and receive messages
element: an individual data item stored in a table
encryption: the coding of data
END: The BASIC keyword that causes the program to stop executing

ENIAC: Electronic Numerical Integrator and Calculator; the first electronic computer

enter key: the key on the keyboard that is used to tell the computer to accept data as it appears on the display screen for processing or storage

executive: the portion of the operating system that acts as the manager of all other operating system functions

expert system: software designed to assist in the application of a known body of knowledge and that enables the computer to make recommendations about courses of action to be taken (sometimes used interchangeably with artificial intelligence)

external modem: a modem contained in a small housing which is externally attached to the computer by a cable and plugged into a standard telephone outlet

feasibility analysis: an analysis that is performed on each design alternative to determine whether or not the alternative meets the given objectives while remaining within the constraints of the organization

feedback: the continuous monitoring of a system in order to ensure that its purpose and objectives are being met

fiber optics cable: a cable which consists of one or more hair-thin strands of material capable of conducting light images

file: a collection of related records

file server: the main computer to which others are connected and which serves as the main data storage computer

filter: a DOS command (instruction) that reads data from a standard input device, manipulates it in some way, and writes it to a standard output device

financial analysis software: software used by individuals and businesses to plan, track, and analyze investments

first-generation computer: an early computer that used vacuum tubes in its circuitry

flat file database: the simplest form of a database in which data can be visualized as being in one table

flexible disk: a small, pliable magnetic disk (also referred to as a diskette or floppy disk)

floating-point number: a number with a decimal point (also referred to as a real number)

floppy disk: a small, pliable magnetic disk (also referred to as a flexible disk or diskette)

flowchart: a graphic representation that illustrates the design of a program

flowlines: arrows used to connect the different steps and show the direction of data flow in a flowchart

foreground task: in a time slicing environment, the task to which the processor devotes most of its time

formats: pre-stored settings that may be called upon when starting a new document (also referred to as style sheets or templates)

formatting: the process of preparing the disk surface for storing data
formula: a mathematical equation used to compute spreadsheet values
FOR...NEXT: BASIC keywords often used to control program looping
FORTRAN: FORmula TRANslation; a problem-oriented, high-level language that was designed for mathematical and scientific applications
fourth-generation computer: a computer which uses VLSI circuitry
fourth-generation language: the highest level of high-level programming languages
full-duplex mode: a mode of data transmission in which data can be transmitted in both directions at the same time
function: an entry representing something that the spreadsheet software knows how to do
function key: a special key on a keyboard designed to work in conjunction with the instructions in a stored program

gas-plasma display screen: a monochrome display screen producing orange-colored images that is used with portable computers
gateway: a microcomputer-based method for connecting dissimilar networks
general ledger: the records of a business that bring together the summaries of all the activities and the status of the business
general-purpose computer: computer that can be used for almost any type of application
generic software: software created by a developer for sale to various users
GOSUB: a BASIC keyword that transfers control of the program to the first program statement in a specified submodule
GOTO: a BASIC keyword that transfers program control to a specified line number (program statement)
grade: a method of determining the speed by which data can be transmitted over a given communication channel (also referred to as bandwidth)
grammar/style program: a program that can do various types of technical checking of a document
graphics software: software that can produce either presentation graphics or art
graphics tablet: a flat drawing surface, connected to the computer, upon which the user can draw graphic figures
graphing program: a program used to produce graphs or charts from data

half-duplex mode: a mode of data transmission in which data can be transmitted to and from each of the communicating devices but in only one direction at a time
handshake: the initial contact made between the communication software and the terminal(s) it will be communicating with
hard copy: output produced on paper
hard disk: a disk made from rigid material which does not bend

hardware: the tangible, physical equipment in a computer system

hexadecimal number system: a number system having a base of 16 and the digits 0-9 and A-F

hierarchical database: a database that assumes data exists in some predefined rational order and in which the data is organized according to a parent/child relationship

hierarchical directory structure: a directory which maintains a record of where individual files are located on disk by dividing the storage space on disk into directories and subdirectories (also referred to as tree structure directory)

hierarchy chart: a chart similar to an organization chart, showing the functions to be performed by a computer program

high-level language: a language in which instructions are expressed in English-like terms

high-resolution graphics: very detailed graphics

hologram: an image which appears to the human eye as a three-dimensional image

HOME: the BASIC keyword used on the APPLE II computer to clear the display screen

home computer: a microcomputer which is small enough to fit on a desk and powerful enough to satisfy the entertainment and informational processing needs of the household

host: the computer that controls all the communication activities of the terminals connected to it

identifiers: variables used in Pascal to store various types of data

IF...THEN...ELSE: an instruction that instructs the computer to perform one task if a statement is true or another task if the statement is false

image library: a computer file that contains pre-drawn art for use with paint and publishing programs

immediate execution mode: a method of running a program whereby an instruction is entered and immediately executed by the computer

impact printer: a printer that strikes the paper to form images

income statement: a financial statement which shows the revenue or income of the business along with its costs and expenses

indirect connection: a communication channel that handles remote terminals

information: knowledge that is given or received of some fact or circumstance

information processing: the process of manipulating data into a form which humans can use or learn new knowledge from (also referred to as data processing)

information system: a computer system used to process data for the purpose of generating information from that data

information utility: business that uses one or more computers to store large amounts of information available for personal use

ink-jet printer: a non-impact printer that forms characters by spraying ink onto the paper

input: data that enters a computer system

INPUT: the BASIC keyword that causes the computer to stop and wait for the user to enter data from the keyboard

input device: a hardware device which enables the computer to accept data

input/output redirection: the capability of a device to accept input from or direct output to various sources

integer: a whole number

integrated software: software that combines the functions of two or more kinds of software

interactive programming: the process of keying a program into the computer and immediately executing the program

internal modem: a circuit board that is built in or plugged directly into the computer or terminal

interpreter program: a program that translates a high-level language into machine code one statement at a time, then relays it to the processor, which immediately executes each statement as it is received

inventory: the materials owned by a business

joystick: an input device which sends coordinates of an x and y (horizontal and vertical) direction to the computer

keyboard: a commonly-used input device that sends data to the computer each time a key is pressed

keypunch machine: a machine used to punch holes in a punched card (also referred to as a card-punch machine)

key-to-disk machine: a data entry machine with which data is recorded on magnetic disks for later input to a computer

key-to-tape machine: a data entry machine with which data is recorded on magnetic tape for later input to a computer

keyword: a word that the BASIC interpreter or compiler understands

kilo (k): one thousand. "k" is often used as an abbreviation for "kilobyte," which refers to the number of memory locations in a computer system; one k of memory is equal to 1,024 memory locations

kilobyte: 1,024 memory locations

label: an alphabetic cell on a spreadsheet

lap-top computer: a lightweight, transportable microcomputer designed for easy carrying and/or use on a person's lap

laser printer: a nonimpact printer that uses a laser beam to create characters on a light-sensitive drum that then transfers the characters to paper

latency: the time it takes the record containing the desired data to pass under the reading mechanism of an auxiliary device while it is being read

LCD: liquid crystal display

LET: the BASIC keyword used to assign values to variables

light pen: an input device used to point out locations on a display screen

line graph: a chart used to show changes in the same data series over a period of time

link: each connection or communication channel in a communication network

liquid crystal display (LCD): a display screen composed of an electrokinetic fluid positioned between two layers of glass

LIST: the BASIC keyword that will display the entire program in the computer's memory or the display screen

literal: any combination of unchanging alphanumeric characters which is entered between quotation marks

LOAD: the BASIC keyword used to retrieve a stored program into memory

loading: the process of entering (adding) data into a database (also referred to as appending)

local area network (LAN): small, networked computers that are in the same general location and connected through a single set of cables for the purpose of communication

local terminal: a device (usually a display screen and keyboard) located near the computer and directly cabled into the computer's CPU

logical device: a generic reference to a device (for example, a printer may be referred to as PRN)

logical view: a method of viewing data in a database in which connections are made between two or more tables

log on: establish connection

loop control instruction: an instruction used to make the computer repeat certain instructions

low-level language: the computer's native language, or a language similar to the computer's native language

machine language: a language in which the instructions are written in the numeric code that is directly understood by the processor

macro: a series of keystrokes or program instructions that is remembered by the software so that the sequence may be executed quickly whenever desired

magnetic disk: an input, output, and storage medium coated on both sides with microscopic bars using a substance that can be magnetized

magnetic ink character recognition reader (MICR): an input device that is used to process data printed in magnetic ink with specially designed numbers and symbols

magnetic scanner: an input device that reads magnetically encoded data from a short strip of magnetic tape such as that used on the back of credit cards

magnetic tape: a long strip of flexible plastic coated with microscopic bars of a material that can be magnetized

mail merge: a function that allows the software to insert varying values into documents as they are being printed
main module: the top box of a modular program
main storage: storage locations for the instructions that the computer follows (also referred to as memory or primary storage)
mainframe: a computer that is large in size and capable of processing very large volumes of data quickly
Mark I: the first programmable calculator
math co-processor: a computer chip that speeds up the computation of complex mathematical operations
megabyte: one million bytes
megahertz one million cycles per second
membrane keyboard: a touch sensitive, keyless keyboard covered with a seamless material for protection
memory: storage locations for the instructions that the computer follows (also referred to as main storage or primary storage)
memory-mapped display: a method of moving output from the computer to a monitor in which a group of locations in main memory is dedicated to holding information for the display (also referred to as bit-mapped display)
memory protection: the process in which the operating system assigns a section of memory to a program and then keeps close watch over the program to make sure it does not attempt to use another memory location
microcomputer: a computer that is smaller and less powerful than a minicomputer
microfiche: small rectangular sheets of microfilm
micro-miniaturization: the technological process which enables an entire microprocessor to occupy the space of a tiny chip
microprocessor: a processor whose processing circuits are all on one integrated chip
microsecond: one millionth of a second (1/1,000,000)
microwave carrier: a carrier that transmits data on a straight path from one microwave station to another
millisecond: one thousandth of a second (1/1,000)
minicomputer: a computer that is smaller and less powerful than a mainframe, but which is capable of processing and storing large volumes of data
modeling: the process of mathematically mimicking something that happens in the world
modem: a device that allows the computer to communicate over a telephone line with a computer at another location by converting digital signals to analog and vice versa
modify access: access which gives a user the power to change data
modulation: the process of converting digital data into an analog signal
module: a small part of a computer program

monitor: a video display screen that displays information processed by the computer
monochrome screen: a one-color (green, amber, or white) display
mother board: the main electronic circuit board of a computer (also referred to as a system board)
mouse: a pointing device that is moved across a surface; as it is moved, the cursor on the display screen moves in the same direction
multiplexer: a communication hardware device which combines the flow of data from several terminals into a single flow of data that can then be sent over a single channel to the host computer
multiprocessing: an operating system's ability to handle more than one user at a time
multiprogramming: an operating system's ability to run more than one application program at a time
multitasking: an operating system's ability to handle more than one action at a time
multi-user system: any computer system which is used by more than one person
music synthesizer: an output device which can blend sound waves to create music or brand-new sounds

nanosecond: one billionth of a second (1/1,000,000,000)
Napier's bones: a calculating device invented by John Napier in the 1600s; it consisted of rods or strips of bones
network card: a card that provides the method for attaching a microcomputer to other computers for the sharing of data and programs
network database: a database that sets up alternative paths through the data to make access of data more flexible
networked: a term used to describe computers that are connected to communicate with each other
NEW: the BASIC keyword that erases previously entered instructions and data from the computer's memory
nibble: four bits, or one half of a byte
node: a microcomputer or terminal on a communication network
nonimpact printer: a printer that forms characters without actually striking the paper
nonvolatile memory: memory that does not lose its data when the power is turned off (also referred to as read-only memory)
numeric address: the numeric label applied to a location in memory
numeric pad: the section of the keyboard used to key numeric data into the computer quickly
numeric variable: a variable that stores numbers

object program: the resulting program obtained from a compiler translation

open architecture: a method of assembling the components of a microcomputer in such a manner that expansion of the system is easily accomplished
operating system: the software that controls the operation of the computer and enables communication between components to take place
optical character reader (OCR): an input device that recognizes written letters, numbers, and symbols
optical mark reader: an input device that can sense the presence or absence of marks made by regular pencil or pen on specially designed forms
original data: data that is fed into the computer for processing
output: useful information which leaves a computer system
output device: a device which reports information processed by the computer in a useful form

paint program: a graphics program that allows the user to do "art" on the screen and print it out
parallel port: a port that allows all eight bits representing a character to be transmitted at the same time over eight different conductors
parallel processing: a process in which a problem is broken into various parts, with each part being solved concurrently by a different processor housed in the same computer
parity bit: a bit that is added to each character that acts as an error detection mechanism
parity check: the process of counting the number of 1's in each character code to make sure they are all even or odd
Pascal: a high-level, general-purpose language useful for writing programs for nearly every application
payroll module: the component of an accounting system that maintains the employee pay records of a business
peripheral: a piece of equipment that is connected to a computer to perform tasks which a computer cannot do itself
personal computer: a microcomputer designed for, and used primarily in, small and large businesses
physical device: the actual brand and model of a particular device
picosecond: one trillionth of a second (1/1,000,000,000,000)
pie chart: a chart in which a total entity is divided into its component parts
pipe: the method of taking the output of one DOS command and using it as input for another one
pixel: a small dot or light that is lit when electrons hit the phosphorescent material on a screen
PL/1: Programming Language/1; a high-level language which combines the business processing features of COBOL with the mathematical and scientific features of FORTRAN

plotter: an output device that draws output by using one or more pens controlled by instructions from the processor

polling: a method of network protocol in which the hub computer asks each node if it has data to transfer or request

port: a connection on a microcomputer into which peripherals may be plugged

portable computer: a lightweight, transportable microcomputer designed for easy carrying and/or use on a person's lap.

presentation graphics: graphics produced by the computer for use as visual aids

primary storage: storage locations for the instructions that the computer follows (also referred to as memory or main storage)

PRINT: the BASIC keyword that causes output to be displayed on the screen or printer

printhead: the mechanism of a dot-matrix printer that actually does the printing

print zone: an area into which each print line is divided

process control software: software designed to control a sequence of events

processing: activities performed on data to produce information. These activities include performing mathematical calculations, making comparisons, and arranging data into a desired order

processor: a hardware device that carries out the detailed instructions of a software program to manipulate data into meaningful information

program: a series of detailed, step-by-step instructions that tell the computer precisely what actions to perform

program design: the steps to be performed by a computer program, written in English instead of a particular computer language (also referred to as pseudocode)

program looping: the controlled repetition of program instructions

programmer: a person who designs and writes the code for computer programs

programmer-supplied word: any nonreserved word used in a program

project management software: software that helps plan and track the sequence of activities necessary to complete a complex project

prompt: a message that tells the user of a program what type of input is necessary

protocols: the formal rules of communication exchange

pseudocode: the steps to be performed by a computer program, written in English instead of a particular computer language (also referred to as program design)

punched card: a card in which data can be represented by punching holes

pure binary: a method in which a number is stored directly in binary, rather than coding it first in some other manner

query language: a language that specifies the required syntax of statements that may be keyed in for the database to provide a response

RAM: random-access memory
random access: a method by which a device can go directly to the location of specific data without having to read through all the data preceding it
random-access memory (RAM): memory in which the processor can jump directly from one location to another in random order as data is stored and retrieved and which loses its data when the power is turned off (also referred to as volatile memory)
range: any contiguous group of cells in a spreadsheet
raw data: data that is fed into the computer for processing (also referred to as original data)
READ: the BASIC keyboard used to read data from a DATA line and assign it to variables
read-only access: access that allows a user to look at data, print data, or make computations with it, but not to change it
read-only memory (ROM): memory which can be read but not written to and which does not lose its data when the power is off (also referred to as nonvolatile memory
real number: a number with a decimal point (also referred to as a floating-point number)
real-time controller: an output device that converts computer output to some kind of action that controls a process
real-time sensor: an input device that constantly monitors a process or event and transmits its findings to the processor without the need of human assistance
record: a collection of related data fields
redundant data: data that exists in more than one place
reference point: points indicating the parameters of an object drawn with a CAD program
relational database: a database that presents its data in the form of tables that may be "connected" or "related"
relational operator: a symbol used to determine the relationship of one value to another
relative reference: a cell reference which is updated as changes are made to the spreadsheet
remote terminal: a device (usually a display screen and keyboard) located at some remote geographical site and connected to the computer by telephone line
report spacing chart: a row and column arrangement showing what the output of a particular computer program should look like
report writer: a feature of database software used to design reports
reserved word: a word that has a specific meaning to a COBOL compiler
restoring: the process of copying data from the backup media to a hard disk after a failure has been rectified
RETURN: the BASIC keyword used at the end of each submodule to return to the main module

RGB monitor: a color monitor that uses three different electronic signals (one each for red, green and blue) to turn on the phosphorescent material within each pixel

RISC: reduced instruction set computing; a technology under which the number of different machine-level instructions built into the processor is reduced

ring configuration/topology: a computer network in which all computers and terminals are attached to each other and in which one or more computers may act as host computers

robotics: research exploring additional utilization of robots

ROM: read-only memory

row: any single horizontal area extending across a spreadsheet

RPG: Report Program Generator; a high-level, business-oriented language designed for users of small computer systems for generating reports

RUN: the keyword that tells BASIC to execute the instructions that have been entered in the form of a program

run-time program: a special interpreter program that translates intermediate Pascal code to machine code at the time the program is run

satellite: a long-distance communication device that maintains a stationary position 22,000 miles above the earth at a speed which correlates to the earth's rotation

SAVE: the BASIC keyword used to store a program on disk

search time: the amount of time it takes to position the access mechanism of an auxiliary storage device over the desired data (also referred to as seek time)

secondary storage device: any storage medium capable of storing computer data and information for future reference

second-generation computer: a computer available in the late 1950s that used transistors instead of vacuum tubes

section: a part of a COBOL program used to categorize related information and define files, data, or processing steps

sector: one segment of a floppy disk

seek time: the amount of time it takes to position the access mechanism of an auxiliary storage device over the desired data (also referred to as search time)

semantic database: a database that has some relationships between data built in when the database is created

sequential access: a method by which a device records and reads back data in a one-after-the-other sequence

sequential instructions: steps that are performed one after another

serial port: a port that transmits binary digits representing a character over a conductor one after the other

simplex mode: a mode of data transmission in which data flows in one direction only

slide rule: a computing tool consisting of an outer rule and a control sliding rule
slot: a connector into which additional boards may be plugged
smart terminal: a terminal that has memory and that can perform tasks ranging from simple text editing to sophisticated data processing
software: the intangible instructions that tell the computer what to do
soraban: a Japanese version of the abacus
source documents: forms on which raw data may be written
source program: a program keyed into the computer from which the translation to machine language is to be made
special-purpose computer: a computer designed to perform specific, specialized tasks.
speech recognition device: an input device that recognizes human speech, allowing voice command or voice response
speech synthesizer: an output device which projects an imitation of the human voice
spelling checker: a program or feature of word processing software that looks up words of text in its dictionaries and calls attention to not-found words
spindle: a vertical shaft in a hard disk drive upon which several disks are stacked
spreadsheet: a row and column arrangement of data
star configuration/topology: a computer network that is arranged so that each of its nodes is linked to a central host computer
start bit: a bit indicating that a character immediately follows
stop bit: a bit indicating the end of a character
storage device: a hardware device which permits storage of data
streaming: the process used by high-speed cartridge-tape drives to move tape continuously, without starting or stopping
string variable: a variable that stores alphanumeric data (also referred to as a character variable)
structured design: the planning of a structured program
structured programming: a method of planning and coding a program so that logically organized modules of code can easily be written and maintained
style sheets: pre-stored settings that may be called upon when starting a new document (also referred to as formats or templates)
subscript: the raw number which references each element in a table
supercomputer: a computer with lightning speed and tremendous power
synthesizer: a device which can combine parts or elements of different sounds into a complex whole
system: related devices and/or procedures that function together in order to achieve a common goal or objective
system architecture: the method by which the components of a computer are assembled

system board: the main electronic circuit board of the computer (also referred to as a mother board)
system life cycle: the period of time in which a given computer system's usefulness to perform a given task is measured
system program: a program that controls the computer's circuitry and hardware devices
systems analyst: the employee responsible for the design and creation of an information processing system; this person serves as a link between the users of the system and the technical personnel who actually develop and install the system
systems design flowchart: a diagram that depicts the components that are involved in a given system and how each of the components interact with each other
systems design report: a report that brings together the information which has been created from each of the tasks completed during the design stage of system development

table: a variable that can store more than one data item at a time (also referred to as an array)
tape: a long strip of flexible plastic wound on a reel
tape cartridge: a device used primarily on personal computers to provide backup for hard disks
tape/disk librarian: a person who catalogs, stores, and retrieves storage media
tape reel: a device containing 1/2-inch-wide magnetic tape used primarily by mainframe computers for processing sequential applications and/or backup
telecommunication: the technique and technology of communication by electrical or electronic means
telecommunications specialist: a person who has the responsibility for planning, overseeing the operation of, and troubleshooting a network
telephone line: the most familiar, and most used, long-distance carrier
template: a "skeleton" spreadsheet that includes labels, formulas, and perhaps macros, but has incomplete or no data; with word processing software, a template is a pre-stored setting that may be called upon when starting a new document (also referred to as format or style sheet)
terminal: any device which inputs or outputs data to or from a computer system; common usage refers to equipment which consists of a display screen, a keyboard, and a communications channel
terminator: a fictitious piece of data used to indicate the end of data items
testing: the process of finding and correcting errors in a computer program
thermal printer: a nonimpact printer that produces images on special heat-sensitive paper by using heated rods to burn the desired image onto the paper

thesaurus program: a program or feature of word processing software that looks up words in a thesaurus stored on disk and suggests alternative words

third-generation computer: a computer which used integrated circuits instead of transistors

time sharing: the process of having multiple terminals attached to a single processor which handles all operations for all the terminals

time slicing: the process of dividing the processor's time between two or more tasks

token passing: a method of network protocol in which a packet of data, called a token, controls access to the network

tools: computerized implements that are used for drawings

top-down design: a method of program planning whereby the programmer defines what the program is to do and then gradually places more and more detail into the plan

topology: the local, geographic placement of computers to one another

touch display screen: a display screen that allows users to use their fingers as pointing devices

track: a path on which data is recorded, usually on a magnetic medium

trackball: an input device that can be thought of as a stationary mouse

transients: functions or commands of the operating system that reside on disk until needed

tree structure directory: a directory which maintains a record of where individual files are located on disk by dividing the storage space on the disk into directories and subdirectories (also referred to as hierarchical directory structure)

turnaround time: the time it takes the host to acknowledge receipt of data and indicate it is ready to accept more data

twisted pair wire: a standard telephone cord used as a transmission carrier

typewriter keyboard: the section of a computer keyboard that is similar to the key arrangement of a typewriter

UNIVAC I: the first commercially available computer

universal product code (UPC): a series of vertical bars of varying widths printed on a product

upload: the transfer of data from a file stored on one computer's disk to the host computer's disk

user group: an organization of persons who use a particular kind of computer and/or software and are interested in mutual support in the use of that hardware and/or software

user interface: the way commands are given by the user to the operating system

utility programs: the instructions loaded from disk when needed to carry out DOS functions

value: a cell on a spreadsheet that contains numeric data that is entered

variable: a named storage location in the computer's memory

VCR tape: tape used in home video cassette recorders that can also be used as computer auxiliary storage media

videodisk: a disk device that records both the video impulses (pictures) and audio impulses (sound) of a TV signal

video display screen: a commonly used output device that produces images that can be seen on a screen

virtual memory: the method under which some of the data that needs to be in main memory is temporarily stored on disk while its application is not executing

VLSI: very large scale integration; extremely large numbers of electronic components are crammed into each integrated circuit chip

voice-grade bandwidth channel: a communication channel that transmits data across telephone lines utilizing the half-duplex mode of transmission

volatile memory: memory that loses its data when the power is turned off (also referred to as random-access memory)

word processing software: software specially designed to assist in the document preparation needs of an individual or business

WORM: (Write Once/Read Many times) an optical disk storage device which uses laser beam and precision optics technology

WYSIWYG: "What You See Is What You Get"; the capability of word processing software to display a document on the screen the same way it will look when it is printed

INDEX

A

B

C

D

E

F

J

K

L

M

N

O

Q

R

T

U

V

W